Guide to
Operating Systems,
Enhanced Edition

Michael Palmer and
Michael Walters

COURSE TECHNOLOGY
CENGAGE Learning

Australia • Brazil • Japan • Korea • Mexico • Singapore • Spain • United Kingdom • United States

COURSE TECHNOLOGY
CENGAGE Learning

Guide to Operating Systems, Enhanced Edition
Michael Palmer and Michael Walters

Managing Editor: William Pitkin III

Production Editor: GEX Publishing Services

Manufacturing Coordinator: Susan Carroll

Product Manager: Amy M. Lyon

Quality Assurance Coordinator:
    Christian Kunciw

Editorial Assistant: Allison Murphy

Text Design: GEX Publishing Services

Developmental Editor: Deb Kaufmann

Senior Channel Marketing Manager:
    Dennis Williams

Cover Design: Abby Scholz

Compositor: GEX Publishing Services

© 2007 Course Technology, Cengage Learning

For product information and technology assistance, contact us at
Cengage Learning Customer & Sales Support, 1-800-354-9706

For permission to use material from this text or product,
submit all requests online at **cengage.com/permissions**
Further permission questions can be emailed to
permissionrequest@cengage.com

ISBN-13: 978-1-4188-3719-8
ISBN-10: 1-4188-3719-9

Course Technology
25 Thomson Place
Boston, Massachusetts, 02210
USA

Cengage Learning is a leading provider of customized learning solutions with office locations around the globe, including Singapore, the United Kingdom, Australia, Mexico, Brazil, and Japan. Locate your local office at: **international.cengage.com/region**

Cengage Learning products are represented in Canada by Nelson Education, Ltd.

For your lifelong learning solutions, visit **course.cengage.com**

Purchase any of our products at your local college store or at our preferred online store **www.ichapters.com**

Printed in the United States of America
4 5 6 7 CS 12 11 10 09

Contents

BRIEF

TABLE OF
Contents

CHAPTER SIX
Using and Configuring Storage Devices

Introduction

If you use a computer, you also use a computer operating system to tap into the computer's power. The more you know about a computer's operating system, the more you are able to enjoy the full versatility of your computer. This book opens the door to understanding your computer's operating system. Also, the book enables you to understand many types of operating systems so you can compare the advantages of each for your personal and professional use.

In this book, you learn about the most popular operating systems in use today:

- Windows 2000

- Windows XP

- Windows Vista

- Windows Server 2003 and Windows Server 2003 R2

- UNIX/Linux, including Red Hat, Fedora, and SUSE Linux

- NetWare 6.0/6.5

- Mac OS X Panther and Tiger

For this revision, the newest operating systems—Windows Vista, Mac OS X Tiger, SUSE Linux 10.0, and Windows Server 2003 R2—are presented in appendices that explain new features and enable you to perform Hands-On Projects to experience the features.

You can use the book to learn about one, two, or all of the operating systems. The book starts at a basic level and builds with each chapter to put you on track to become an accomplished user for each operating system.

You learn the operating systems in clear language through a hands-on, practical approach. An advantage of studying several operating systems is that you can compare the functions of each side-by-side as you learn. If you are taking an introductory operating systems course or an operating systems survey course, this book offers a strong foundation for mastering operating systems. Also, if you are preparing for one or more computer certifications, such as for hardware systems, networking, programming, or security, you'll find this book provides a vital background for your preparations. If you are relatively new to computers, the book starts with the basics to build your confidence. If you are more experienced in computers, you'll find lots of useful information to further build your repertoire of knowledge and experience.

The Intended Audience

Guide to Operating Systems, Enhanced Edition is written in straightforward language for anyone who uses a computer and wants to learn more. No prior computer experience is required, although some previous basic experience with a computer is helpful. The Hands-On Projects in this book use a variety of operating systems. You can learn the concepts if you have access to one or a combination of the operating systems presented. The more operating systems that are available to you, the better the opportunity to compare their features. For the most part, the projects can be performed in a classroom, computer lab, or at home.

Chapter Descriptions

The chapter coverage is balanced to give you a full range of information about each topic. The following is a summary of what you will learn in each chapter. Besides the instruction provided through the chapter text, you can build on your knowledge and review your progress in each chapter using the extensive Hands-On Projects, Case Projects, Key Terms, and Review Questions at the end of each chapter. Also in this revision, Appendices C through F have Hands-On Projects to enable you to learn about the newest operating systems.

- *Chapter 1: Operating System Theory* gives you a basic introduction to operating systems, including the types of operating systems and how they work. You also learn about the history of operating systems.

- *Chapter 2: PC Operating System Hardware* describes operating system hardware components, including the popular processors, buses, hard drives, and other components. You also learn the characteristics of popular operating systems and how hardware and operating system software interact.

- *Chapter 3: File Systems* explains the functions common to all file systems and then describes the specific file systems used by different operating systems, from FAT to NTFS to ufs/ext to NSS, to HFS+.

- *Chapter 4: Installing and Upgrading Operating Systems* shows you how to prepare for installing operating systems and then shows you how to install each operating system discussed in this book. You learn about installing operating systems from scratch and how to upgrade operating systems.

- *Chapter 5: Configuring Input and Output Devices* explains how devices such as monitors, keyboards, mice, disk drives, network cards, and other devices interface with operating systems. You learn about the latest input and output technologies for modern operating systems and computers.

- *Chapter 6: Using and Configuring Storage Devices* describes popular storage devices including hard drives, RAID, CD technologies, network storage, USB devices, and others. Storage device configuration is covered for the operating systems.

- *Chapter 7: Modems and Other Communications Devices* prepares you for communicating with the outside world through wide-area network technologies. You learn about relatively low-speed modem communications to high-speed communications through cable TV, DSL, satellite, and other means. You also learn to configure operating systems for communications over the Internet.

- *Chapter 8: Network Connectivity* provides an introduction to how networks function, including network topologies and protocols. You learn how to configure protocols in each operating system.

- *Chapter 9: Resource Sharing Over a Network* shows you all types of ways to share resources through a network, such as sharing disks, folders, and printers. Besides covering how to share resources, the chapter also discusses how to secure them through accounts, groups, and access privileges.

- *Chapter 10: Standard Operating and Maintenance Procedures* presents many techniques for maintaining systems, such as cleaning up unused files, defragmenting disks, and addressing problems. The chapter also describes how to perform system backups and how to tune systems for top performance.

- *Appendix A: Operating System Command-Line Commands* shows you how to access the command line in each operating system and presents tables that summarize general and network commands. This appendix provides in one place the ability to quickly find or review the operating system commands.

- *Appendix B: Using Fedora With This Book* discusses the Fedora version of Linux that is provided on the CDs accompanying this book and shows you how to install Fedora.

- *Appendix C: Microsoft Windows Vista* presents the new look and features of Windows Vista such a virtual folders, the Startup Repair Tool, recovery features, security, and management options. You learn about the hardware requirements and how to upgrade to Windows Vista.

- *Appendix D: Mac OS X Tiger* explains new features in this latest version of Mac OS X which comes with lots of new software. You learn to use Dashboard, Spotlight, and other new features. Instructions are provided for upgrading to Mac OS X Tiger.

- *Appendix E: SUSE Linux* covers the latest SUSE Linux version, which is 10.0. You learn about SUSE Linux and how it is integrated into the Novell environment. Installation instructions are provided in case you go to Novell's Web site or the openSUSE.org Web site to download and use your own desktop copy of SUSE

Linux. You also learn about applications that come with SUSE Linux, such as the OpenOffice.org office software.

- *Appendix F: Windows Server 2003 R2* discusses new features in this update to Windows Server 2003, such as new clustering capabilities, the Print Management Console, and the Dynamic Systems Initiative. You learn why the update may be right for your situation and how to upgrade to the R2 version.

Features

To aid you in fully understanding operating system concepts, there are many features in this book designed to improve its pedagogical value.

- **Chapter Objectives.** Each chapter in this book begins with a detailed list of the concepts to be mastered within that chapter. This list provides you with a quick reference to the contents of that chapter, as well as a useful study aid.

- **Illustrations and Tables.** Numerous illustrations of operating system screens and components aid you in the visualization of common setup steps, theories, and concepts. In addition, many tables provide details and comparisons of both practical and theoretical information.

- *From the Trenches* **Stories and Examples.** Each chapter contains boxed text with examples from the authors' extensive experience to add color through real-life situations.

- **Chapter Summaries.** Each chapter's text is followed by a summary of the concepts it has introduced. These summaries provide a helpful way to recap and revisit the ideas covered in each chapter.

- **Key Terms.** A listing of the terms that were introduced throughout the chapter, along with definitions, is presented at the end of each chapter.

- **Review Questions.** End-of-chapter assessment begins with a set of review questions that reinforce the ideas introduced in each chapter.

- **Hands-On Projects.** The goal of this book is to provide you with the practical knowledge and skills to troubleshoot desktop operating systems in use in business today. To this end, along with theoretical explanations, each chapter provides numerous Hands-On Projects aimed at providing you with real-world implementation experience. There are also new Hands-On Projects in Appendices C through F to give you experience with the new operating systems introduced in these appendices.

- **Case Projects.** Located at the end of each chapter is a multipart case project. These extensive case examples allow you to implement the skills and knowledge gained in the chapter through real-world operating system support and administration scenarios.

CDs Included with this Book

A copy of the Fedora Linux operating system is provided on the CDs that accompany this book. Fedora is a free version of Linux offered by the Fedora Project, which is sponsored by Red Hat. In relation to the UNIX/Linux topics, the book discusses both Fedora and Red Hat Enterprise Linux as prime examples. Appendix E presents SUSE Linux 10.0 with Hands-On Projects. Further, the UNIX/Linux Hands-On Projects in Chapters 1 through 10 can be used with either Fedora or Red Hat Enterprise Linux, and those projects using the terminal window can also be used with SUSE Linux 10.0. The desktops have a somewhat different appearance, but in the case of the Hands-On Projects in this book, the keystrokes are the same or very similar and the commands in the terminal windows are identical. A majority of the UNIX/Linux Hands-On Projects use the terminal window, which helps train students across many versions of UNIX/Linux.

Note that if you choose to use SUSE Linux 10.0 for the Hands-On Projects in Chapters 1 through 10, you can access the terminal window by clicking Applications, pointing to System, pointing to Terminal, and clicking Gnome terminal. (Or, you can right-click an open area on the desktop and click Open Terminal.)

Text and Graphic Conventions

Wherever appropriate, additional information and activities have been added to this book to help you better understand what is being discussed in the chapter. Icons throughout the text alert you to additional materials. The icons used in this textbook are as follows:

NOTE

The Note icon is used to present additional helpful material related to the subject being described.

TIP

Tips are included from the author's experience to provide extra information about how to configure a network, apply a concept, or solve a problem.

CAUTION

Cautions are provided to help you anticipate potential problems or mistakes so that you can prevent them from happening.

Each Hands-On Project in this book is preceded by the Hands-On Projects icon and a description of the exercise that follows.

Case Project icons mark each case project. Case Projects are more involved, scenario-based assignments. In each extensive case example, you are asked to implement what you have learned.

Instructor's Materials

The following supplemental materials are available when this book is used in a classroom setting. All of the supplements available with this book are provided to the instructor on a single CD-ROM.

Electronic Instructor's Manual. The Instructor's Manual that accompanies this textbook includes:

- Additional instructional material to assist in class preparation, including suggestions for classroom activities, discussion topics, quizzes, and additional exercises.
- Solutions to the Hands-On Projects, including some suggestions for supplementing activities with in-class discussions. (Solution files for Appendixes C through F Hands-On Projects can be found on the Thomson Course Technology Web site, www.course.com.)
- Solutions to all end-of-chapter materials, including the Review Questions and Case Projects.

ExamView®. This textbook is accompanied by ExamView, a powerful testing software package that allows instructors to create and administer printed, computer (LAN-based), and Internet exams. ExamView includes hundreds of questions that correspond to the topics covered in this text, enabling students to generate detailed study guides that include page references for further review. The computer-based and Internet testing components allow students to take exams at their computers and save the instructor time by grading each exam automatically.

PowerPoint presentations. This book comes with Microsoft PowerPoint slides for each chapter. These are included as a teaching aid for classroom presentation, to make available to students on the network for chapter review, or to be printed for classroom distribution. Instructors, please feel at liberty to add your own slides for additional topics you introduce to the class.

Figure files. All of the figures and tables in the book are reproduced on the Instructor's Resource CD, in bitmap format. Similar to the PowerPoint presentations, these are included as a teaching aid for classroom presentation, to make available to students for review, or to be printed for classroom distribution.

Electronic glossary. An electronic glossary of the key terms used in this book is available at www.course.com for instructors to provide to their students. The glossary contains hyperlinks for fast lookup. Instructors can obtain this glossary by going to the Course Technology website, *www.course.com*, and going to the specific web page for this book.

LAB REQUIREMENTS

You can study the operating system concepts in this book without any hardware. Screen shots and other illustrations help support the discussions presented here. However, to get the most of this material you should step through the Hands-On Projects. For this, you'll need access to at least one computer and operating system. To pursue a complete, broad-based study of operating systems as presented in this book, you will need several computers and operating systems, or a computer with one or more hard drives that you can partition and load with multiple operating systems.

Here are suggestions for each of the operating systems covered in this book:

Windows 2000

Windows 2000 is a significant upgrade to Windows NT and as such, you will want to run it on a more powerful computer than for Windows NT. We recommend a Pentium-class 500 MHz or faster processor, with 256 MB of RAM, 4 GB hard drive, floppy disk, and CD-ROM drive. Depending on the use of this Windows 2000 computer, you may want to replace the CD-ROM drive with a CD/DVD drive.

Windows XP

Windows XP is a substantial upgrade to the Windows 98/Me operating systems. The Home version is for recreational users whereas the Professional version is intended for office and networked environments. We recommend a Pentium-class 500 MHz or faster processor, with 256 MB of RAM, 10 GB hard drive, and a CD/DVD drive for the Home version. For the Professional version, we suggest a Pentium-class 900 MHz or faster processor, with 512 MB of RAM.

Windows Vista

Windows Vista (discussed in Appendix C) is an important upgrade from Windows XP, particularly for the video capabilities. We recommend a Pentium-class 4 CPU or faster, 512 MB to 1 GB of RAM, a 10 GB hard drive or larger, a CD/DVD drive, and a graphics processor compatible with the Windows Vista Display Driver Model.

Windows Server 2003 and Windows Server 2003 R2

For these server operating systems we recommend at least a Pentium-class 550 MHz processor, but you'll have better response if you use a faster processor, such as a Pentium-class 900 MHz or faster. We also recommend at least 512 MB of RAM, a 10 GB or larger hard drive, and a CD/DVD drive.

Mac OS X Panther and Tiger

As with Windows, Mac OS X has many versions. Earlier versions can get by with basic hardware, but the Mac OS X Panther and Tiger versions need a machine comparable to one for Windows XP. These versions will run on a PowerPC G3, G4, or G5. For Panther you can use 128 MB or more of RAM. For Tiger (in Appendix D) you need 256 MB or more of RAM. You'll also need a CD/DVD drive for both operating systems

UNIX/Linux

You can use virtually any high-end Pentium-class computer for Red Hat Enterprise Linux, Fedora, or SUSE Linux. Plan to use a Pentium-class 900 MHz or faster processor (although you can use one that is slower). For the Red Hat Enterprise and Fedora versions discussed in this book, use 256 MB or more of RAM and at least 3 GB of disk space (to install X Window interfaces and applications). For SUSE Linux 10.0 (in Appendix E) you'll need 512 MB or more of RAM and 2 GB or more of disk space. For all systems include a CD or CD/DVD drive.

ACKNOWLEDGMENTS

Writing is a wonderful opportunity to work with interesting ideas in a community of fine people. We are very grateful for the opportunity to write and revise this book while working with dedicated people through Course Technology. First, we thank Managing Editor Will Pitkin for making this project possible and for his continuing support. Our thanks also go to our product manager for the Enhanced Edition, Amy Lyon for her steadfast work and encouragement; and to Manya Chylinski the product manager for the previous edition for all of her fine work on the project. We are also gifted to have Deb Kaufmann as the developmental editor, who has carefully guided our ideas and language into clear and reachable text.

The production editor, Gina Dishman, has helped ensure the text and figures are ready for the press. Further, our technical editor Randy Weaver has helped at every step to verify technical content as have our reviewers Gerlinde Brady, Pamela Silvers, and Terrance (Ed) Walsh. Also, the quality assurance and validation team of Christian Kunciw, Danielle Shaw, Peter Stefanis, and Serge Palladino have been invaluable in helping to assure the accuracy of the text, review questions, and projects. And we thank you, the reader, for purchasing this book and for your interest in the operating systems we have described.

DEDICATIONS

Michael Palmer —I dedicate this book to Deb Kaufmann, who has given tremendous support and encouragement on many rewarding book projects.

Michael Walters —I dedicate this book to my wife, Donna. Your support and encouragement is invaluable. I would also like to dedicate this to my mother, Betty Walters, who while making sacrifices was also able to teach the values of following your dreams, working hard, and persevering.

1

OPERATING SYSTEM THEORY

After reading this chapter and completing the exercises, you will be able to:

♦ Understand how an operating system works

♦ Describe the types of operating systems

♦ Understand the history of operating system development

♦ Discuss single-tasking versus multitasking

♦ Differentiate between single-user and multiuser operating systems

♦ List and briefly describe current operating systems

Anyone who owns a computer relies on an operating system to enable them to do work on that computer. An operating system is the software that starts the basic functions of a computer, displays text on the computer's monitor, accesses the Internet, and runs applications—it transforms the computer from a helpless box of electronic parts to a powerful tool for work and play. There are many kinds of operating systems, but only a few have really captured a wide audience. Some popular operating systems are used on computers that fit on your desktop. Others are used on more powerful computers called servers that are accessed by multiple users through a computer network. Some, like UNIX/Linux, are used on both desktop and server computers.

This book is your guide to the most popular operating systems. In the beginning chapters, you take an in-depth look at popular desktop operating systems: Windows 2000 Professional, Windows XP, UNIX (focusing on the Linux version), and Mac OS X. Later in the book, you examine popular server operating systems: Windows 2000 Server, Windows Server 2003, UNIX/Linux, and NetWare 6.x. This chapter sets the foundation for understanding desktop and server operating systems by introducing you to theory and concepts that apply to all operating systems. With this theory under your belt, you will have a solid frame of reference to understand operating system specifics as they are discussed in later chapters.

UNDERSTANDING OPERATING SYSTEMS

An **operating system (OS)** is a set of basic programming instructions to computer hardware, forming a layer of programming code on which most other functions of the computer are built. Computer **hardware** consists of physical devices on the inside or outside of the computer, such as the central processing unit (CPU), circuit boards, the monitor and keyboard, and disk drives. **Code** is a general term that refers to instructions written in a computer programming language.

The two types of operating systems that are the focus of this book are desktop and server operating systems. A **desktop operating system** typically is one installed on a personal computer (PC) type of computer that is used by one person at a time, and that may or may not be connected to a network. A **server operating system** is usually installed on a more powerful computer that is connected to a network, and can act in many roles to enable multiple users to access information, such as electronic mail, files, and software. Another important term that applies to operating systems is **network operating system (NOS)**. A NOS—a desktop or server operating system, for example—is an operating system that enables a computer to communicate with other computers through network cable or wireless transmissions. A NOS enables coordination of network communications, from sharing files and printers to sending e-mail.

One of the most basic tasks of an operating system is to take care of what are known as **input/output (I/O)** functions, which let other programs communicate with the computer hardware. The I/O functions take requests from the software the user runs (the application software), and translate them into low-level requests that the hardware can understand and carry out. In general, an operating system serves as an interface between application software and hardware, as shown in Figure 1-1. Operating systems perform the following I/O tasks:

- Handle input from the keyboard, mouse, and other input devices
- Handle output to the monitor and printer
- Handle communications using a modem
- Manage network communications, such as for a local network and the Internet
- Control input/output for devices such as a network interface card
- Control information storage and retrieval using various types of disk and CD-ROM drives
- Enable multimedia use for voice and video composition or reproduction, such as recording video from a camera or playing music through speakers

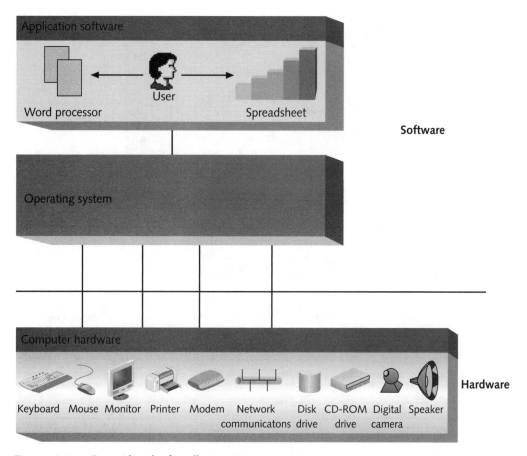

Figure 1-1   General tasks for all operating systems

The operating system communicates directly with all of these devices. Some operating system programs exchange information with specific hardware (chips) inside the computer. The code (instructions) for this information exchange is typically referred to as a device driver. A **device driver** translates computer code to display text on a screen, or translates movements of a mouse into action, for example. A separate device driver is usually present for each I/O device, as shown in Figure 1-2. In general, operating systems have a standardized way of communicating with a certain type of device driver. The device driver contains the actual code (instructions) to communicate with the chips on the device. This way, if another piece of hardware is introduced into the computer, the operating system code does not have to change. All that needs to be done to enable the computer to communicate with the new device is to load a new device driver onto the operating system.

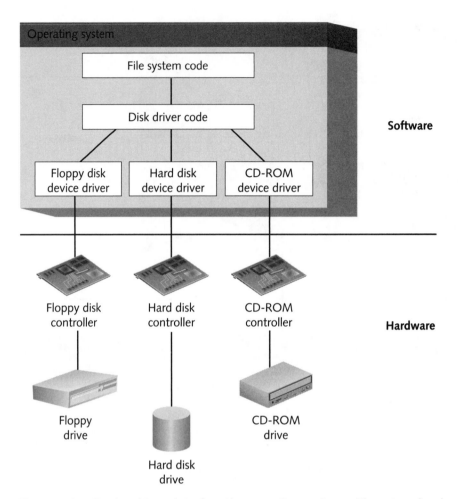

Figure 1-2   Device drivers interface the operating system with various hardware devices

TIP   If a particular device is not working, one way to troubleshoot the problem is to obtain and install the latest device driver for that device, which usually can be downloaded from the manufacturer's Web site.

For example, compact disc read-only memory (CD-ROM) drives for computers were introduced a long time after many operating systems were written. Thus, earlier versions of operating systems did not natively support CD-ROM drives. However, because CD-ROM drives are similar to other types of disk drives, early versions of operating systems could be adapted to use CD-ROM drives by loading a few simple drivers for the operating system. You may encounter device drivers that interface with your operating system for other devices, including:

- Floppy and hard disk drives
- Computer monitors
- Keyboards
- Mouse and trackball devices
- Modems
- Printers and scanners
- Tape drives, Zip drives, flash drives, and other removable media
- Digital cameras and video hardware
- MP3 players or other audio hardware
- DVD drives
- CD-ROM/R/RW drives
- Gaming interfaces
- PDA interfaces
- Wired and wireless network interfaces
- PCMCIA interfaces

In addition to communicating with computer hardware, the operating system communicates with the application software running on the computer, as shown in Figure 1-3. **Application software** is a fairly vague term; it can mean a word processor, spreadsheet, database, computer game, or many types of other applications. Basically, it means any program a user may choose to run on the computer. If an application program accesses a piece of hardware, it sends a request to the operating system to execute the job. For example, the application program may have to access the keyboard to see if a user has pressed a key, or the monitor to show the user a message. This makes the application programmer's job easier because she does not have to know exactly how to manipulate the chips in the computer to communicate with the keyboard, monitor, or printer. She only has to know how to communicate with the operating system.

In its most basic form, an operating system manages the communication among the application programs, the user, and the computer. This level of management allows application programmers to concentrate on applications that will run on any hardware, as long as the operating system can control them. In other words, an application program can submit a general request to the operating system, such as "write this information to disk," and the operating system handles the details. The application programmer doesn't have to worry about how to queue data, update the disk directory, or physically copy the data from memory to the disk drive.

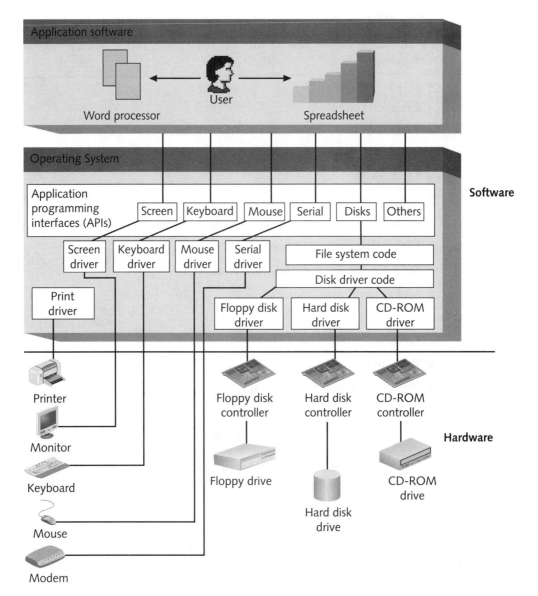

Figure 1-3   Application programs communicate with hardware through the operating system

Of course, there are some applications—particularly those that are designed for DOS or UNIX (both early operating systems)—that directly access hardware devices. At one time, many programmers designed code to directly access hardware to improve overall application performance. This practice can make hardware response fast, but there are serious drawbacks. A significant drawback is that memory is often required for directly managing the hardware. If a memory block is programmed for use that conflicts with the same (or a part of) the memory block used by other hardware or that is used by the operating system, the hardware devices involved may become unstable or the operating system may crash. Another drawback is incompatibility with other software that also needs to use the hardware or that uses the same memory block, which can cause the software applications to hang or "crash."

NOTE

Some operating systems, such as Windows 2000, Windows XP, and Windows Server 2003 do not allow the programmer to directly access hardware. Instead, the programmer must call on an intermediary process that decides how to handle the request. This design means that it is harder for an application program to crash a computer, such as when two application programs access the same memory location at the same time. This was a significant problem in earlier versions of Windows, such as Windows 3.x, Windows 95, and even Windows 98.

An essential step in starting a computer is to load the **basic input/output system**, or **BIOS**. The BIOS is low-level program code that:

- Initiates and enables communications with hardware devices

- Performs tests at startup

- Conducts basic hardware and software communications inside the computer

- Starts a full-fledged operating system that interfaces with the user

Some consider the BIOS a rudimentary operating system and others consider it to simply be a set of important program code routines between the hardware and the main operating system.

Every PC has a BIOS, which is stored in **read–only memory**, or **ROM**. Figure 1-4 shows a sample BIOS setup screen on a computer. ROM is a special kind of memory that does not lose its contents when the power is removed from the computer. Whenever you turn on your PC, the machine wakes up and jumps to a startup program inside the BIOS. This program initializes the screen and keyboard, tests some central computer hardware, such as the central processing unit (CPU) and memory, initializes the floppy drive and other disk drives, and then loads the main operating system—Windows XP or UNIX, for example—that provides more advanced functionality for application programs.

TIP

If a computer is turned on, but cannot access a device, such as the main disk drive or display monitor, check the BIOS settings to make sure that the BIOS knows about and is correctly configured for that disk drive or monitor. Also, on many computers you can set up a password in the BIOS to control who can start the operating system or who can access a particular drive at startup. You can access the BIOS settings when the computer first starts by pressing a designated key (on many computers the key is F1, F2, or ESC—check onscreen when the computer first boots, or consult your computer's documentation). You learn more about configuring BIOS settings in Hands-on Project 4-1 in Chapter 4.

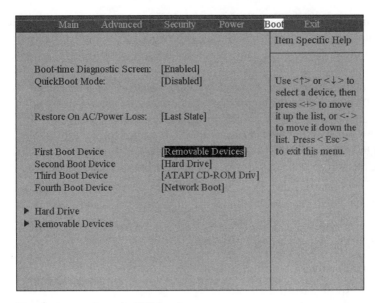

Figure 1-4   Sample BIOS setup screen

Figure 1-5 shows a general conceptual drawing of various main operating system components, including the relationship of an operating system to the BIOS. The elements in Figure 1-5 include the following, from the application down:

- *Application software*, such as a spreadsheet or a word processor.

- *Application programming interface*. An **application programming interface (API)** is software designed to communicate with the application software and the user. The API is program code that is like a specialized "hook" into the operating system. It translates requests from an application into code that the operating system kernel can understand and pass on to the hardware device drivers, and translates data from the kernel and device drivers so the application can use it. The API also provides an interface to the BIOS. This is the part of the operating system most visible to users. For example, a word-processing application may request to create a specific display of characters on the monitor, and the API translates the request from the application to the kernel. Another example is the use of messaging APIs, enabling an e-mail program to send a message through the operating system to a computer network or the Internet.

- *BIOS*, which provides the basic input/output functions to communicate with system devices, such as the monitor, the keyboard, and disks. BIOS resides in ROM, so it is always present in the computer. It usually loads other operating system components on startup.

- *Operating system kernel*. The **kernel** is the core of the operating system that coordinates operating system functions, such as control of memory and storage.

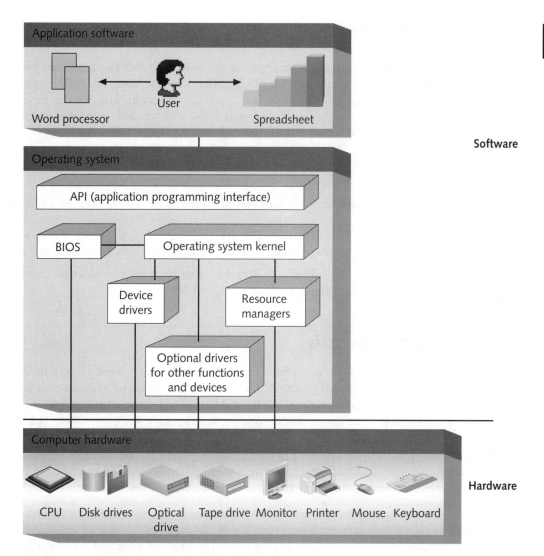

Figure 1-5 General operating system design

The kernel communicates with the BIOS, device drivers, and the API to perform these functions. It also interfaces with the resource managers.

- *Device drivers*, programs that take requests from the API via the kernel and translate them into commands to manipulate specific hardware devices, such as disks, tape drives, keyboards, monitors, modems, and printers.

- *Resource managers*. **Resource managers** are programs that manage computer memory and central processor use.

- *Optional drivers*, for other functions and devices, such as sound.

- *Computer hardware*, such as disks, storage, CPU, mouse, keyboard, monitor, printer, and so on.

Although all operating systems incorporate the basic I/O functions, the operating systems you are accustomed to, such as Mac OS X, Microsoft Windows, or UNIX/Linux, include many additional functions. Examples are the logic to handle files, set the time and date, manage memory, and other more advanced features to deal with the various devices connected to the system. Some elements that most operating systems have in common are:

- Provide an interface between the computer hardware and application programs

- Act as an intermediary between the user and applications

- Provide a user interface into computer hardware and application programs

- Manage memory and central processor use

- Manage peripheral devices, such as printers, monitors, keyboards, and modems

Hands-on Projects 1-1, 1-2, and 1-3 enable you to view the interfaces (desktops) of Windows XP, Red Hat Enterprise Linux 3.0, and Mac OS X.

TYPES OF OPERATING SYSTEMS

There are many types of computer operating systems, which work in very different ways, intended for very different purposes. The functions a computer requires to a large extent dictate what the operating system will do and how it will do it. As an example, the computer in a microwave oven needs device drivers for the light-emitting diode (LED) display, numeric keypad, and door close switches, whereas the computer in a television needs drivers to monitor the remote control and tell the tuner to change the channel. The same goes for various types of small and large computers; a computer designed to handle a high volume of numerical operations for many users needs different functions than the PC used to run a word processor.

In general, operating systems are organized by the size, type, and purpose of the computer on which they run. For example, PC-class computers are designed for individual users to perform tasks, such as word processing, database and spreadsheet management, and networking with other computers. Over the years, PCs have become faster, more complex, and more powerful, offering the user more features. As a result, many PCs now can handle complex operations that go beyond simply running a user's application software. This has resulted in advanced, elaborate operating systems that are designed to deal with more hardware and provide advanced functions. The lines of division by size, type, and purpose are therefore getting more vague every day. Hardware is becoming more compact, but capable of doing more, and operating systems are getting larger and more complex.

One example of how PC operating systems have become more complex is the comparison of lines of code in Windows 95 to Windows XP. Windows 95 has only a couple million lines of code; Windows XP has over 50 million.

For instance, in the seventies, corporate computing was confined to mainframe- and minicomputer-class devices. These were refrigerator-sized or larger computers that required a full staff to manage them, and large, expensive air-conditioned rooms to hold them. The operating systems for these machines were quite complex and often included such intrinsic functions as text editing (not quite "word processing" by today's standards), database management, networking, and communications. There were few PC-class devices at the time. Those that were available were capable of minimal functionality, and used what could only be described as rudimentary operating systems. Many of those early devices didn't support any storage hardware (disk drives), or if they did, it was frequently serial, low-density tape. In this comparison, it should be easy to see that "in the old days," operating systems for large machines were very different from operating systems used for small ones.

From the Trenches...

In the early 1990s, one of the authors managed the installation of a new IBM 9000-class mainframe. Installing the hardware and operating system, plus porting (relocating) programs and data from the previous mainframe, was such a complex process that it took several months to plan and many more months to test and execute. The computer equipment was so large that it was delivered by a moving van. Compare this to setting up a new PC-based server and operating system, which requires very little space and can take as little as a few hours to a few days to complete.

At the same time, applications for these early large machines were written with efficient code so they could maximize all of the resources on the computer. As a result, appearance, programming, and management were very terse and basic.

To a lesser extent, this is still true today. There are still "big" machines and "small" machines, except that none of today's computer equipment is physically large. The days of room-sized, or even refrigerator-sized computers are about gone. A "big" machine today simply has more processing power, more memory, more storage (disk drive capacity), and better network connectivity. To operate these more powerful computers, more powerful and more capable operating systems are employed. For example, a company that sells computer time to thousands of other users—an Internet service provider (ISP), for instance—requires computers capable of performing multiple tasks for many users at the same time.

Although the computers used for such large installations don't look much different from the PC or Macintosh designed for a single user, they are quite different inside. They use a network operating system (such as a version of UNIX/Linux, Windows 2000 Server, or Windows Server 2003) or another multitasking, multiuser operating system. Also, they may include multiple CPUs and have more powerful I/O capabilities. The differences are significant, but also subtle. For example, Linux is a popular desktop operating system (used by a single person) based on UNIX, and it is also applied as a network operating system to power Web servers, mail servers, and other Internet-related multiuser applications. Again, the hardware used for an individual Linux computer is likely much different from the design of these Linux Internet service computers, even though the operating system is the same. On the other hand, even with the enhanced hardware, an Internet service provider (ISP) wouldn't likely replace Linux or any other server operating system, such as Windows Server 2003 or NetWare, with a system intended for the desktop, such as Windows XP Professional or Home Edition.

So-called "high-end" workstations are used by engineers for graphical design, or by editors for film design and animation. Again, these machines may look much like a school or home PC, but inside they include extremely fast hard disk controllers, 3D graphics interfaces, lots of memory, and, often, support for multiple CPUs. The needs of these workstations are very different from the multitasking, multiuser needs of an Internet server, but they too have special requirements that can't be met by some operating systems. Although some graphics applications use Linux or UNIX, the Windows 2000, Windows XP, and Mac OS X operating systems are more popular foundations for these applications, and can be used for powerful business applications as well.

So there must be other factors that differentiate high-end from low-end computers. The main factor is the application software used with the computers. Again, the differentiation among computers is getting more vague. You have seen some of these factors, but the confusing concept is that even high-end applications often can run on what are considered low-end machines, on the same operating system. When this is the case, the main differentiating factor is the hardware: speed of the disk controller, size and speed of the hard disk, amount of memory and memory capacity, size of the data pathways in the computer (such as 32 bit, 64 bit, or larger), or speed and number of CPUs.

One way to look at computer and operating systems is to consider them in terms of one or more of the following characteristics:

- Time sharing
- Real time
- Multiuser

Time Sharing

A **time-sharing system** is a central computer system that is used by multiple users and applications simultaneously. Mainframe computers typically fall into this category. These computers are used to conduct massive calculations or manipulate huge amounts of data. Mainframe computers are common at scientific institutions, banks, and insurance companies. They are built to quickly perform tasks, such as keeping track of thousands of checking account balances. Most of their work is done in batches or **batch processes**—clearing two million checks and updating their associated bank accounts—instead of single, sequential repetitive tasks. When the batch process is finished—all checks have been posted, for example—the statements can be printed. Contrast this approach to that of smaller computers, such as PCs, that are interactive and use **sequential processing**, where each process request is completed, and the data returned before the next process is started.

 Big batch processing jobs, or multiple batch jobs that must occur in a specific order on large computers, are often scheduled to run after work hours because they require so many machine resources. This makes batch processing less **NOTE** convenient than the instant response you get with a sequential process.

Besides batch processing, there often are many clerks, customer representatives, and ATM machines that use a mainframe to do daily transactions. They all share the resources, or processor time, of the large machine, which is why these machines are called time-sharing systems.

From the Trenches...

A downside of batch processing is that if the order of processing is inadvertently changed, the result may be a disaster to the data. A bank experienced this when performing its fiscal year-end closing. Some preliminary financial calculations and database updates were scheduled after all files were formally closed for the fiscal year. To restore the files to their year-end condition, it was necessary to restrict access to the mainframe the next day, and the batch processes were rescheduled. No new business could be done on the mainframe for a day until the data was restored and corrected. The bank's auditors were very critical of the error and the bank's business suffered.

Real-time Systems

A **real-time system** is an operating system that interacts directly with the user and responds in real time (immediately or almost immediately) with required information. For example, when a scientist calculates the size of an iceberg or the distance to the eye of a hurricane, the computer program immediately performs the calculation and returns the answer—using sequential processing instead of batch processing.

Real-time systems are what most of us are familiar with today. Windows XP and Mac OS X are examples of these systems that interact directly with the user—even multiple users (on shared drives)—and respond in real time with the required information.

Multiuser Systems

A **multiuser system** is one that supports multiple users who are accessing the computer's and operating system's hardware and software facilities. Both time-sharing and real-time systems can be multiuser systems. For example, originally a time-sharing mainframe was accessed by running cables from terminals to a specialized communications box connected to the mainframe, creating a multiuser system, as shown in Figure 1-6. Today, multiple users typically access mainframes through a computer network. Also, servers running operating systems such as NetWare or Windows Server 2003, can provide real-time access to multiple users over a network, as shown in Figure 1-7. In this environment, multiple users can do many different things on the multiuser computer at the same time.

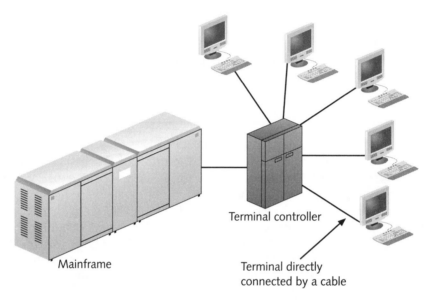

Mainframe

Terminal controller

Terminal directly
connected by a cable

Figure 1-6   Time-sharing mainframe with terminals

In another example, there may be a multiuser environment in which multiple users are accessing one or a group of computers. For example, customer service representatives taking clothing orders over the telephone all may use one server to start and process orders and another server to store the actual data associated with the orders.

In a departure from mainframes and time sharing, one of the newer approaches to multiuser operations is the use of **client/server systems**. On a multiuser mainframe, all of the work is typically done on the big machine, such as running programs, storing data, and accessing data. In the client/server model, only a small part of the work is done on the central computer or computers. In a client/server system, the central multiuser computer (or computers) may hold all the data and files, and may even perform some of the database functions or calculations required, but much of the work, such as running programs, is performed on the client side—on the computer at the user's desk. If you have used PC-class computers in a networked environment, chances are you have used the client/server model, at least to some degree. A minimally configured Windows XP computer or one running Mac OS X connected to a network that includes a Windows 2000 or 2003 server, for

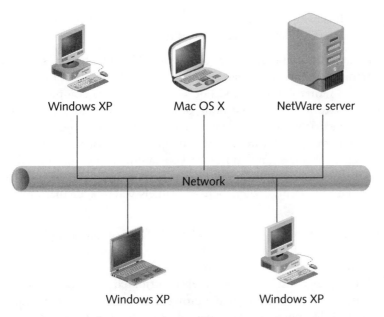

Figure 1-7   Using a network to access a real-time NetWare server

example, is well suited for client/server operations. Notice, again, the importance of the combination of operating system and application. Operating system differences are beginning to narrow, but the applications that run on them help differentiate how the computer is used and classified. Client/server computing was not possible until the PC was introduced. After all, it requires a computer at the user's desk, a facility that was not available until the introduction of the PC.

A SHORT HISTORY OF OPERATING SYSTEMS

The history of operating systems is a very elaborate subject. As a matter of fact, there are many books on this subject. This short history is not meant to be comprehensive; it merely presents enough background information to show how some of the features in modern PCs and PC operating systems developed.

Initially, computers were used as large automated calculators to solve all sorts of mathematical and statistical problems. Computers were extremely large, often taking up entire rooms. Although you can legitimately trace the history of today's digital computers back 100 years or more, there were no practical designs used by significant numbers of people until the late 1950s. Scientists programmed these computers to perform precise tasks, the exact tasks for which they were built. The operating systems were rudimentary, often not able to do more than read punch cards or tape, and write output to Teletype machines (machines resembling typewriters). A tape or deck of cards was loaded, a button was pushed on the machine to indicate the input was ready, and the machine started to read the tape and perform the operations requested. If all went well, the work was done and the output was generated. This output would be sent to the Teletype, and that was that.

Yes, there was computer history before this point, but it did not involve any sort of operating system. Any program that the computer ran had to include all logic to control the computer. Because this logic was rather complex, and not all scientists were computer scientists, the operating system was a tool that allowed non-computer scientists to use computers. That reduced programming work and increased efficiency. Obviously, there was not all that much to "operate" on, mainly the punch card and punch tape readers for input, and the Teletype printer for output. There also was not that much to operate with; memory capacity was very limited and the processing speed of the computer was slow by our standards (but fast for that time). The art in operating systems design, therefore, largely was to keep them very small and efficient.

It did not take long (in terms of world history, at least) before computer applications evolved to actually do something useful for a broader audience. Although computers of the late sixties and early seventies were crude by today's standards, they were quite capable and handled extremely complex tasks. These computers contributed to the development of space travel, submarine-based ballistic missiles, and a growing global financial community (all on much less than 1 MB of memory). This period also saw the beginning of a global, computer-based communications system called the Internet. Applications became logically more complex, requiring larger programs and large amounts of data. With more useful applications being developed, the wait to "run" programs became longer.

From the Trenches...

Less than 15 years ago, student registration, accounting, student aid, and all other administrative functions in a state's community college system were performed on one large computer at each community college—that had only 4 MB of RAM. The computer system administrators of those computers considered these machines to have more than enough memory to run all administrative functions for a single college. Today, those functions are performed at each location on two or more servers, each much smaller in physical size, and each using 512 MB to 1 GB of RAM.

As always, necessity was the mother of invention. Input and output devices were created, and computer memory capacity and speed increased. With more devices to manage, operating systems became more complex and extensive, but the rule of thumb, small and fast, was still extremely important. This round of evolution, which really began to take off in the mid seventies, included the display terminal, a Teletype machine with a keyboard that did not print on paper, but projected letters on a screen. The initial "glass Teletype" was later followed by a terminal (a keyboard and monitor without a CPU) that could also show simple graphics. The magnetic tape drive, used to store and retrieve data and programs on tape, could store more, and was less operator intensive than paper tape. It was quickly followed by numerous incarnations of magnetic disks.

The next evolution was the ability to share computer resources among various programs. If a computer was very fast and could quickly switch among various programs, you could do several tasks seemingly all at once, and serve many people simultaneously. Some of the operating systems that evolved in this era are long lost to all but those who worked directly with them. But there are some notable players that were responsible for setting the stage for the full-featured functionality we take for granted today. Digital Equipment Corporation's (DEC's) PDP series computers, for example, ran the DEC operating system, simply known as OS, in one version or another. A popular one was OS/8, which came in various versions, such as Release 3Q, and was released in 1968. PDP-8 computers were general-purpose machines that at one time were the top-selling computers across the world. The PDP series could also run Multics, which was the basis for the development of the first version of UNIX, a multiuser, multitasking operating system. (Multics is widely considered to be the first multiuser, multitasking operating system. You'll learn about multitasking later in the chapter.)

TIP To find out more about the once popular PDP-8 computers, visit *www.pdp8.net* or *www.cs.uiowa.edu/~jones/pdp8*. For information on the PDP-9 (and to view a photo), visit www.osfn.org/ricm/c-pdp9.html.

The original UNIX was developed at AT&T Bell Labs in 1969 by Kenneth Thompson and Dennis Ritchie as an improvement on Multics. Later, DEC VAX computers used VMS, a powerful, multitasking, multiuser operating system that was strong on networking. IBM mainframes made a series of operating systems popular, including GM-NAA I/O in the early sixties, an operating system that effectively enabled the machine to perform batch processing jobs. The letters "GM" indicate the company for which this OS was originally developed. Many others would follow, including CICS, which is still in use today.

Programming computers at this time was still a very complicated process best left to scientists. In the mid sixties, right after the first interactive computer game was invented at the Massachusetts Institute of Technology (MIT), a simple programming language was developed, aimed at the nonprogrammer. It was dubbed **BASIC**, or **Beginner's All-purpose Symbolic Instruction Code**. A few years later, in 1975, Bill Gates discovered BASIC, and became interested enough to write a compiler (software that turns computer code written by people into code that is understood by computers) for it, which he sold to a company called Micro Instrumentation Telemetry Systems (MITS). MITS was the first company to produce a desktop computer that was widely accepted, and could conduct useful work at the hands of any knowledgeable programmer. That same year, Gates dropped out of Harvard to dedicate his time to writing software. Other programming languages introduced at about this time included Pascal, C, and other versions of BASIC supplied by various computer manufacturers. Only a couple of years later, Gates' new company Microsoft and others released FORTRAN, COBOL, and other mainframe and minicomputer languages for desktop computers. There were also highly proprietary languages that gained some popularity—languages primarily designed for database programming, for example—but they neither lasted, nor are they significant to our discussion in this book.

The introduction of the microcomputer in the mid seventies was probably the most exciting thing to happen to operating systems. These machines typically had many of the old restrictions, including slow speed and little memory. Many microcomputers came with a small operating system and ROM that did no more than provide an elementary screen, keyboard, printer, and disk input and output. Bill Gates saw an opportunity and put together a team at Microsoft, consisting of Paul Allen, Bob O'Rear, and himself, to adapt a fledging version of a new microcomputer operating system called 86-DOS to run on a prototype of a new microcomputer being developed by IBM, called the personal computer (PC). 86-DOS, which was originally written by Tim Patterson (from Seattle Computer Products) for the new 8086 microprocessor, evolved in 1980 through a cooperative effort between Patterson and Microsoft, into the **Microsoft Disk Operating System**, or **MS-DOS**. MS-DOS became a runaway success for the five-year-old Microsoft company, and it was the first widely distributed operating system for microcomputers that had to be loaded from disk or tape. There were earlier systems, including Control Program/Monitor (CP/M) that used some of the features and concepts of the existing UNIX operating system designs, but when IBM adopted MS-DOS for its PC (calling it PC DOS), the die was cast.

What did this MS-DOS do? It provided the basic operating system functions described earlier in this chapter, and it was amazingly similar to what was used before on larger computers. It supported basic functions, such as keyboard, disk, and printer I/O—and communications. As time went on, more and more support functions were added, including support for such things as hard disks. Then along came the Apple Macintosh in 1984, with its **graphical user interface (GUI)** and mouse pointing device, which allowed users to interact with the operating system on a colorful graphical screen, using the mouse to point at or click icons or to select items from menus to accomplish tasks. Initially, Microsoft chose to wait on development of a GUI, but after Microsoft saw the successful reception of the interface on Apple computers, it developed one of its own.

When the Macintosh was introduced, it seemed light years ahead of the IBM PC. Its operating system came with a standard GUI at a time when MS-DOS was still based on entering text commands. Also, the Macintosh OS managed computer memory closely for the software, something MS-DOS did not do. And, because Mac OS managed all computer memory for the application programs, you could start several programs sequentially and switch among them. Mac OS was also years ahead in I/O functions such as printer management. In MS-DOS, a program had to provide its own drivers for I/O devices; MS-DOS provided only the most rudimentary interface. On Mac OS, many I/O functions were part of the operating system.

Microsoft, however, did not stay behind for long. In 1990, Microsoft introduced an extension to its DOS operating system, called Microsoft Windows, which provided a GUI and many of the same functions as the Mac OS. The first Windows was really an operating "environment" running on top of MS-DOS, made to look like a single operating system. Today's Windows is no longer based on DOS and is a full-fledged operating system.

NOTE Although Apple was six years ahead of Microsoft in offering a friendly GUI-based OS, Apple ultimately fell well behind Microsoft in sales because it chose not to license the Mac OS to outside hardware vendors.

The incarnations of operating systems since those days have been numerous, maybe 12 versions of Windows and 10 of Mac OS. Today, both Windows and Mac OS are very similar in what they can do and how they can do it; they have a wealth of features and drivers that make the original DOS look elementary. Their principal functions are unchanged, however: to provide an interface between the application programs and hardware, and to provide a user interface for basic functions, such as file and disk management.

Let's review the important pieces of operating system development history. Although pre-1980s computing history is interesting, it doesn't hold much relevance to what we do with computers today. Table 1-1 shows the major milestones in operating system development. Note that we mention 16-, 32-, and 64-bit operating systems in the table. In general, a 64-bit operating system is more powerful and faster than a 32-bit system, which is more powerful and faster than a 16-bit system. You will learn more about the differences in Chapter 2.

Table 1-1   Operating system releases

Operating System	Approximate Date	Bits	Comments
UNIX (Bell/AT&T)	1968	8	First widely used multiuser, multitasking operating system for minicomputers.
CP/M	1975	8	First operating system that allowed serious business work on small personal computers. VisiCalc, released in 1978, was the first business calculation program for CP/M, and to a large extent made CP/M a success.
MS-DOS	1980	16	First operating system for the very successful IBM PC family of computers. Lotus 1-2-3 was to MS-DOS in 1981 what VisiCalc was to CP/M. Also in 1981, Microsoft introduced the first version of Word for the PC.
PC DOS	1981	16	IBM version of Microsoft MS-DOS.
Mac OS	1984	16	The first widely distributed operating system that was totally graphical in its user interface. Also, the Mac OS introduced the use of a mouse to PC-based systems.
Windows 3.0	1990	16	First usable version of a graphical operating system for the PC.

Table 1-1   Operating system releases (continued)

Operating System	Approximate Date	Bits	Comments
Windows for Workgroups (Windows 3.11)	1993	16	First version of Microsoft Windows with peer-to-peer networking support for the PC.
Windows NT (New Technology)	1993	32	Microsoft's first attempt to bring a true 32-bit, preemptive, multitasking operating system with integrated network functionality to the world of personal computing. Windows NT was later offered in a Workstation version and a Server version.
Windows 95	1995	16/32	An upgrade to Windows 3.x, with a much-improved user interface, and increased support for hardware and mostly 32-bit code. Native support to run 32-bit applications, and many networking features. Windows 95 represented a different direction than Windows NT because it was intended to provide backward-compatibility for 16-bit applications, and it continued to allow applications to directly access hardware functions.
Windows 98	1998	32	Implemented many bug fixes to Windows 95, more extended hardware support, and fully 32 bit.
Windows 2000	2000	32	A major revision of the Windows NT operating system, with the notable characteristics that it is much faster and more reliable than Windows NT. The Windows 2000 kernel contains more than 45 million lines of code, compared to 15 million for Windows NT. Windows 2000 comes in several versions, including Professional, Server, Advanced Server, and Datacenter.
Windows Millennium Edition (Me)	2000	32	Microsoft's operating system upgrade of Windows 98, designed specifically for the home user, with improved multimedia capabilities.

Table 1-1 Operating system releases (continued)

Operating System	Approximate Date	Bits	Comments
Windows XP	2001	32/64	The successor to Windows Me and Windows 2000 Professional. It is available in four editions: Home, Professional, Tablet PC, and Media Center. The Home Edition is a 32-bit system that focuses on home use for photos, music, and other multimedia files. The Professional Edition, available in 32-bit and 64-bit versions, is intended for office and professional users who need more computing power and extensive networking capabilities. The Tablet PC Edition is tailored for tablet PCs that use speech and pen capabilities and offer great mobility, such as native wireless communications. Finally, the Media Center Edition is for enhanced digital media use involving television, audio, video, and graphics.
Windows Server 2003	2003	32/64	Available at this writing in Standard Edition, Web Edition, Enterprise Edition, and Datacenter Edition, this operating system is designed as a server platform for Microsoft's .NET initiative, which is integrating all types of devices—PCs, handheld computers, cell phones, and home appliances—for communications over the Internet.

TIP   For a fascinating review of the evolution of Windows NT to Windows Server 2003 (and changes at Microsoft), go to Paul Thurrott's SuperSite for Windows at: *www.winsupersite.com/reviews/winserver2k3_gold1.asp*, *www.winsupersite.com/reviews/winserver2k3_gold2.asp*, and *www.winsupersite.com/reviews/winserver2k3_gold3.asp*.

What have all these PC operating systems done to the dynasty of the big machines? They have changed their roles. Many big machines are now obsolete; others are used for calculation and data storage as back-end functions for the PC. Even in this arena they are threatened today as PC operating systems and hardware extend further and further.

Many older operating systems are no longer around because of hardware changes. In Chapter 2, you look more closely at hardware architecture and what it means for the operating system. A good example of hardware that is no longer a feasible option to run an OS is the Z80 CPU produced by Zilog. Zilog manufactures semiconductors and created the first microprocessor. When the cheaper and more flexible Intel 8088 and 8086 microprocessors were introduced in the IBM PC, the MS-DOS platform was a more attractive choice for most users. The Z80 and its CP/M operating system slowly died out. The same happened to some operating systems that used IBM PC hardware for other reasons. A prime example is IBM's own OS/2 operating system. The OS/2 system required extensive hardware, and it could not run older MS-DOS applications. Many people wished to continue to run MS-DOS applications, so OS/2 was not a big hit. Because new software for OS/2 was slow to come and offered no substantial new features, users were hesitant to use OS/2. Today, you will find OS/2 mainly in environments where it is used to interface to large IBM mainframes with custom-developed applications. For an operating system to be successful, many things must work together: availability of hardware and application programs, the right mix of features, and a little luck. Try Hands-on Project 1-4 to learn more about the history of operating systems.

SINGLE-TASKING VERSUS MULTITASKING

There are a few aspects of operating systems that deserve a closer look. As pointed out, today's PC operating systems go way beyond basic I/O. In practice, almost every resource in the computer, such as the memory and the CPU, is managed by the operating system. This is both good and bad; it results in a lot more consistency and a lot of added functionality. However, application programs can no longer directly access hardware in creative ways, as they could before, particularly under MS-DOS. A good example of this is the chip used to make sound. This chip includes an electronic timer that can be accessed by external programs. Many older MS-DOS programs used this chip as a timer to halt program execution for a specified period of time. This is done by manipulating the internal workings of the chip directly from the application program, without the intervention of MS-DOS. Some earlier versions of Windows, such as Windows 3.x, Windows 95, Windows 98, and Windows Me enable programs to directly access hardware, whereas Windows NT, Windows 2000, and Windows XP do not. A disadvantage of systems such as Windows 95/98 that enable programs to directly access hardware is that these operating systems are more prone to unexpected hangs, system instability, or crashes when a problem occurs in software as it is accessing the hardware.

One of the major reasons for giving the operating system so much control over resources is to facilitate **multitasking**, a technique that allows a computer to run two or more programs at the same time. Because most personal computers have only one CPU chip, which can in general only do one thing at a time, multitasking is typically achieved by splitting processor time between applications, switching so rapidly that the user is not aware of any discontinuity.

There are two general types of multitasking. The first method is known as **cooperative multitasking**. In this method, the operating system hands over control to a program, sits back, and waits for the program to hand control back to the operating system. The assumption here is that the program will do some work, and then give control back to the operating system. If, for some reason, the program does not hand control back to the operating system, this one program will hog the CPU until its operations are complete, while all other programs on the computer are on hold. If the program does not release control, for example, because it is stuck in an endless loop, the operating system may never regain control. As a result, no other programs can run until the computer is reset—an undesirable scenario. This could also be a problem if some of the programs on the computer are time sensitive. If a program must collect data every second, or regularly update a clock, a cooperative multitasking environment may cause trouble. You will find this behavior in older operating systems such as Windows 3.1. If you print a word-processing file and try to play Solitaire at the same time, you will find that you cannot play a card until the print job is finished. Figure 1-8 shows the basic concept of cooperative multitasking.

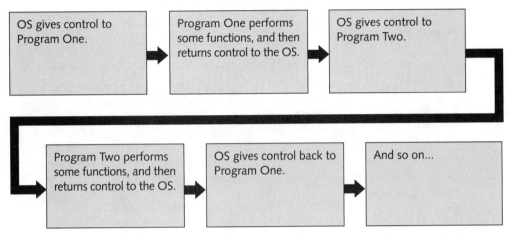

Figure 1-8   Cooperative multitasking basics

A better method is the second alternative, **preemptive multitasking**, illustrated in Figure 1-9. In this scenario, the operating system is in control of the computer at all times. It lets programs execute a little bit of code at a time, but immediately after the code executes, it forces the program to relinquish control of the CPU back to the operating system. It then takes the next program and repeats the same process. Because the operating system is in charge, it has a lot of control over how much of the computer's resources are allocated to each program. As a result, the computer must use more of its processor power and memory to support the operating system, but the behavior of programs and the computer as a whole is a little more predictable. Playing Solitaire while printing a word-processing file in Windows NT, 2000, XP, or Server 2003 is not a problem; preemptive multitasking results in both processes getting some CPU time to do their jobs. Windows 95, 98, and Me all use an enhanced version of cooperative multitasking, so you can format a floppy disk and play Solitaire with less delay than in earlier versions of Windows. One reason is that the program code used to format the floppy disk was rewritten to be more cooperative. If you compare the speed and response of Solitaire in Windows 95, 98, or Me against the speed and response of Solitaire in Windows NT, 2000, XP, or Server 2003 while both are printing a word-processing file, you will see a slight to significant difference in favor of Windows NT, 2000, XP, and Server 2003 (particularly because applications run up to 30 percent faster in Windows 2000/XP/Server 2003).

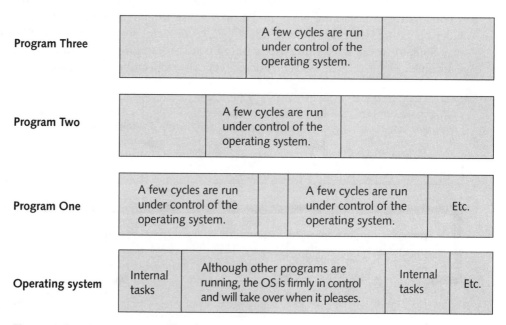

Figure 1-9   Preemptive multitasking basics

There are still some single-tasking operating systems used on some PCs. A **single-tasking** operating system executes one program at a time (see Figure 1-10). To do something else, one program must be stopped, and a new program must be loaded and executed. Because there is normally never a situation in which there are multiple programs trying to use the same resources, single-tasking operating systems are a lot simpler. This is, however, considered older technology, and as new operating systems are released, they are seldom single-tasking. An example of a single-tasking operating system is MS-DOS. New single-tasking operating systems are found only in computers with very limited processor capacity, such as personal digital assistants (PDAs). An exception is Windows CE, which is designed for PDAs, but also can be multitasking.

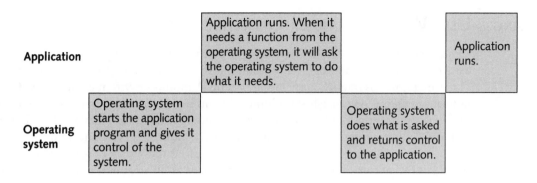

Figure 1-10   Single-tasking operating system

A special note must be made of a hybrid system called a **task–switching** operating system. This system offers many of the device management functions of the multitasking operating system, and it can load multiple application programs at once. It will, though, actively execute only one of these programs. If the user wants to use another application, he can ask the operating system to switch to that task. When the switch is made, the operating system gives control to the newly selected task. Obviously, many of the programs associated with switching among various applications and their use of various devices do not have to be addressed, making this a less complicated type of operating system. This is also considered an older technology that isn't used in any of the new PC operating systems. Many earlier versions of Mac OS are task switching, as are some of the operating systems found on much older PCs made by companies such as the Atari ST series, which focus more on the home computer market. You can see the concept of task switching in Figure 1-11.

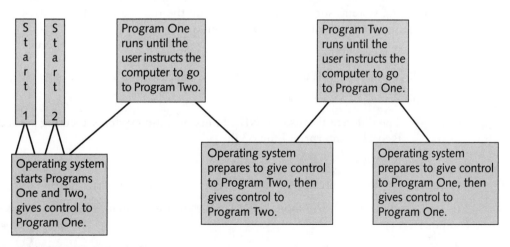

Figure 1-11   Task switching

SINGLE-USER VERSUS MULTIUSER OPERATING SYSTEMS

Some operating systems, in addition to being able to run multiple programs at the same time with multitasking technology, allow multiple users to use an application simultaneously. These are known as multiuser operating systems. A multiuser system is almost, by definition, also a multitasking system. Most multiuser systems use preemptive, multitasking technology. The desktop operating systems covered in this book initially were designed as **single-user systems** (only one user at a time), with the exception of UNIX and Linux, which have always been multiuser operating systems by design. Windows NT Server, Windows 2000 Server, and Windows Server 2003 also are designed as full-featured multiuser systems.

You might think that the operating systems used to run client/server networks would be considered multiuser operating systems; however, this is not always the case. An OS can be multitasking without being multiuser. For example, although one computer on the network may act as a network server, making files or printers available to many other computers, and thereby to many other users, the operating system that performs those tasks may not be a multiuser operating system. In general, to qualify as multiuser, the operating system must allow multiple users to run individual applications simultaneously. For this reason, manyclient/server operating systems are not strictly multiuser. Some experts predict that client/server approaches will eventually make multiuser systems obsolete, but the trend to client/server really enables all types of operating systems to work together seamlessly. A good example of an operating system that is multitasking but not multiuser is Windows 98.

CURRENT OPERATING SYSTEMS

The operating systems surveyed in this book are the most common in today's computing environments, and they fall into several families:

1. Windows 2000 Professional and Server.

2. Windows XP (Home, Professional, Tablet PC, and Media Center).

3. Windows Server 2003.

4. The different flavors of UNIX/Linux operating systems, focusing particularly on Red Hat Enterprise Linux 3.0.

5. NetWare 6.x.

6. Apple Macintosh Mac OS X (version 10.3 or Panther).

In later chapters, you learn about these families in more detail. This section gives a brief summary.

At the time of this writing, there are two popular desktop operating systems used most frequently in corporate America—Windows 2000 Professional and Windows XP Professional. Windows 2000 Professional and Windows XP Professional offer a stable work environment that is appealing for office use. Further, Microsoft continually issues updates for these systems that increase their security and performance. It is also possible to find some corporate users hanging on to older versions of Windows and even MS-DOS, but they are becoming more and more rare. The most popular Microsoft server operating systems are Windows 2000 Server and Windows Server 2003, although a few organizations still use Windows NT Server 4.0.

The multiuser UNIX operating system has been popular among industrial-strength users for many years. It is especially appealing to members of the scientific and research communities for its power to perform complex tasks and maintain large databases. There are many flavors of UNIX, but two main design standards, the Berkeley Software Distribution (BSD) standard and the System V Release 4 (SVR4) standard. This book focuses on SVR4 UNIX. Linux is a UNIX look-alike system that is popular as a server operating system in business, education, and government. Also, the desktop version of Linux is popular among many individual users, and particularly on college campuses.

NetWare's development roots go back to 1982 as the first server operating system created for networks. It remains popular today as a stable server system used in business, education, and government. NetWare version 6.5 is the most recent version at this writing.

The Mac OS X operating system for Apple Macintosh computers is popular in the educational and graphics sectors, particularly for video editing, but typically you will not find it much in the corporate world. It is also popular among home users.

In Chapter 2, you take a much closer look at the individual operating systems mentioned here. In that chapter, you find out more about the hardware required to run each operating system, and which versions you will see in what environment and for what reason. Try Hands-on Projects 1-5 through 1-12 to learn more about the Windows-based, UNIX/ Linux, and Mac OS X operating systems, including how to use tools for obtaining system information, how to view device drivers, and how to see multitasking in operation.

CHAPTER SUMMARY

- An operating system provides the foundation upon which to run the components of a computer and execute applications.

- Two common types of operating systems are desktop and server operating systems. A desktop system may or may not be a network operating system, while a server is always a NOS.

- Device drivers can extend the native functions of an operating system to provide access and control over different types of devices, such as printers and CD-ROM drives.

- The BIOS is low-level program code that operates between the computer hardware and a higher-level operating system to initiate communications with hardware devices, perform hardware tests at startup, and enable the startup of the higher-level operating system.

❑ An operating system may be geared to run a large mainframe or a small PC-type of computer. However, the small PC-type systems now can be very powerful and are used in many places instead of mainframe systems.

❑ Operating systems can be understood in terms of characteristics such as time sharing, real-time operation, and multiuser capabilities.

❑ The history of operating systems and computers represents a progression from physically huge computers to large computers to desktop-sized computers that have powerful processing capabilities and operating systems.

❑ From the standpoint of the user, among the most significant advances in operating systems is the refinement of the GUI, as seen in the development of Windows-based and Mac OS systems.

❑ Early operating systems tended to be single-tasking, but modern systems are largely multitasking.

❑ A true multiuser system is one in which multiple users access and run a single application on a single computer at the same time.

❑ Currently popular operating systems are the topic of this book and include Windows 2000/XP/Server 2003, UNIX/Linux, NetWare 6.x, and Mac OS X. Of the systems listed, the server operating systems are primarily discussed in the last three chapters of the book, along with some networking basics.

KEY TERMS

application programming interface (API) — Functions or programming features in an operating system that programmers can use for network links, links to messaging services, or interfaces to other systems.

application software — A word processor, spreadsheet, database, computer game, or other type of application that a user runs on a computer. Application software consists of computer code that is formatted so that the computer or its operating system can translate that code into a specific task, such as writing a document.

basic input/output system (BIOS) — Low-level program code that conducts basic hardware and software communications inside the computer. A computer's BIOS basically resides between computer hardware and the higher level operating system, such as UNIX or Windows.

batch processing — A computing style frequently employed by large systems. A request for a series of processes is submitted to the computer; information is displayed or printed when the batch is complete. Batches might include processing all of the checks submitted to a bank for a day, or all of the purchases in a wholesale inventory system, for example. Compare to *sequential processing*.

Beginner's All-purpose Symbolic Instruction Code (BASIC) — An English-like computer programming language originally designed as a teaching tool, but which evolved into a useful and relatively powerful development language.

client/server systems — A computer hardware and software design in which different portions of an application execute on different computers, or on different components of a single computer. Typically, client software supports user I/O, and server software conducts database searches, manages printer output, and the like.

code — Instructions written in a computer programming language.

cooperative multitasking — A computer hardware and software design in which the operating system temporarily hands off control to an application and waits for the application to return control to the operating system. Compare to *preemptive multitasking*.

desktop operating system — A computer operating system that typically is installed on a PC type of computer, used by one person at a time, that may or may not be connected to a network.

device driver — Computer software designed to provide the operating system and application software access to specific computer hardware.

graphical user interface (GUI) — An interface between the user and an operating system, which presents information in an intuitive graphical format that employs multiple colors, figures, icons, windows, toolbars, and other features. A GUI is usually deployed with a pointing device, such as a mouse, to make the user more productive.

hardware — The physical devices in a computer that you can touch (if you have the cover off), such as the CPU, circuit boards (cards), disk drives, monitor, and modem.

input/output (I/O) — Input is information taken in by a computer device to handle or process, such as characters typed at a keyboard. Output is information sent out by a computer device after that information is handled or processed, such as displaying the characters typed at the keyboard on the monitor.

kernel — An essential set of programs and computer code built into a computer operating system to control processor, disk, memory, and other functions central to the basic operation of a computer. The kernel communicates with the BIOS, device drivers, and the API to perform these functions. It also interfaces with the resource managers.

Microsoft Disk Operating System (MS-DOS) — The first widely distributed operating system for microcomputers, created by Tim Patterson and a team, including Bill Gates, at Microsoft. This is generic computer code used to control many basic computer hardware and software functions. MS-DOS is sometimes referred to as DOS.

multitasking — A technique that allows a computer to run two or more programs at the same time.

multiuser system — A computer hardware and software system designed to service multiple users who access the computer's hardware and software applications simultaneously.

network operating system (NOS) — An operating system that enables a computer to communicate with other computers through network cable or wireless transmissions. A NOS enables the coordination of network communications, from sharing files and printers to sending e-mail.

operating system (OS) — Computer software code that interfaces with user application software and the computer's BIOS to allow the applications to interact with the computer hardware.

preemptive multitasking — A computer hardware and software design for multitasking of applications in which the operating system retains control of the computer at all times. See *cooperative multitasking* for comparison.

read-only memory (ROM) — Memory that contains information that is not erased when the power is removed from the memory hardware. ROM is used to store computer instructions that must be available at all times, such as the BIOS code.

real-time system — An operating system that interacts directly with the user and responds in real time with required information.

resource managers — Programs that manage computer memory and CPU use.

sequential processing — A computer processing style in which each operation is submitted, acted upon, and the results displayed before the next process is started. Compare to *batch processing*.

server operating system — A computer operating system usually found on more powerful PC-based computers than those used for desktop operating systems, which is connected to a network, and that can act in many roles to enable multiple users to access information, such as electronic mail, files, and software.

single-tasking — A computer hardware and software design that can manage only a single task at a time.

single-user system — A computer hardware and software system that enables only one user to access its resources at a particular time.

task switching — A single-tasking computer hardware and software design that permits the user or application software to switch among multiple single-tasking operations.

time-sharing system — A central computer system, such as a mainframe, that is used by multiple users and applications simultaneously.

REVIEW QUESTIONS

1. Which of the following are tasks performed by an operating system? (Choose all that apply.)

   a. handling output to a monitor

   b. managing network communications

   c. retrieving files from a CD-ROM drive

   d. enabling voice communications with a word processor

2. BIOS is a(n) _____ .

   a. type of disk drive

   b. digital signature process used for securing modem communications

   c. interface speed enhancer primarily employed for network communications

   d. set of low-level program code routines that initiates hardware and software communications and performs startup tests

3. You are a statistics student who accesses an older mainframe to run a statistical analysis program. Other students access the mainframe to run the same program or to run programs for other classes. This is an example of _____ .

    a. time sharing

    b. batching

    c. forward processing

    d. dataplexing

4. When you use an accounting system in your organization, your PC does some of the processing, but you store data and perform database searches on a remote server. This is an example of _____ .

    a. a client/server system

    b. delayed computing

    c. batch processing

    d. data reciprocation

5. _____ was the first widely distributed operating system that was totally graphical from the standpoint of the user.

    a. Windows 2000

    b. UNIX

    c. Mac OS

    d. NetWare

6. You and a colleague are discussing the DEC VAX operating system, VMS. Your colleague notes that VMS was never a multitasking system. What is your response?

    a. Your colleague is right. VMS has never been multitasking.

    b. VMS is multitasking and multiuser.

    c. VMS is not multitasking but represents the first operating system to work on a PC.

    d. VMS is multitasking but does not work on a network, which is its main limitation.

7. Which of the following are desktop operating systems that are also multitasking systems? (Choose all that apply.)

    a. Mac OS X

    b. Windows XP Home

    c. Windows 2000 Professional

    d. CP/M

8. You have purchased a flat-screen monitor that is new to the market. When you attach it to a computer running Windows 2000 Professional, the monitor displays text only in large characters. What might be the problem?

   a. The monitor's battery is overcharged.

   b. You need to obtain a device driver for that monitor and install the driver in the operating system.

   c. You need to access the Device Handler in Windows 2000 and configure the monitor.

   d. You have plugged the monitor into the parallel port by mistake.

   e. There is no problem. Flat-screen monitors only display large characters, which is why you purchased this kind of monitor.

9. The kernel is _____ .

   a. another name for a word-processing application

   b. a famous computer game developed in 1972

   c. the program that displays the Dock in Windows XP Professional for managing the display of application icons

   d. the core code of an operating system

10. Which of the following operating systems do not allow the programmer of applications to directly access the hardware? (Choose all that apply.)

    a. Windows 3.0

    b. Windows 2000

    c. Windows XP

    d. Windows 95

11. Linux is an operating system that closely resembles _____ .

    a. Windows Server 2003

    b. UNIX

    c. Mac OS 8.5

    d. Windows XP Home

12. MS-DOS evolved from _____ .

    a. 86-DOS

    b. PC-DOS

    c. CP/M

    d. VMS

1

13. _____ is Microsoft's first multitasking operating system.

    a. Windows 2000

    b. Windows 3.0

    c. Windows NT

    d. Windows Server 2003

14. _____ is software that communicates with application software and the user.

    a. Resource director

    b. User driver

    c. Device interface

    d. Application programming interface

15. Your class is holding a discussion comparing high-end computers to lower-end computers. Some factors that they should mention that help to differentiate these computers include which of the following? (Choose all that apply.)

    a. number of CPUs

    b. size of the monitor

    c. size of the data pathways in the computer

    d. whether or not a modem is installed

16. Which of the following are types of multitasking? (Choose all that apply.)

    a. active

    b. passive

    c. preemptive

    d. cooperative

17. Linux and UNIX can be _____ or _____ systems.

    a. 140-bit, 280-bit

    b. SVR14, SVR20

    c. desktop, server

    d. ASCII, EBCDIC

18. Initially, MS-DOS supported which of the following? (Choose all that apply.)

    a. printer I/O

    b. CD-ROMs

    c. modems

    d. keyboard

19. You need an operating system that is fast and powerful for very complex mathematical computations. Which of the following is the best candidate?

    a. an 8-bit operating system

    b. a 16-bit operating system

    c. a 32-bit operating system

    d. a 64-bit operating system

20. PCs use sequential processing, while older mainframes typically use
    _____ .

    a. generic processing

    b. batch processing

    c. group processing

    d. RISC processing

HANDS-ON PROJECTS

At the end of each chapter in this book there are Hands-on Projects to give you direct experience in applying what you have learned about the operating systems. As you are completing the Hands-on Projects, keep a lab book, notebook, or computer with a word processor handy so that you can record your findings for later reference.

These projects use Windows 2000 Professional or Server, Windows XP Professional or Home, Windows Server 2003, Red Hat Enterprise Linux 3.0 (or other UNIX/Linux versions as indicated), NetWare 6.5, and Mac OS X version 10.3 (Panther). The projects for Windows XP Professional and Windows Server 2003 use the newer experiential desktop or modified theme (the default installation), and not the classic desktop. Also, unless otherwise specified, the Windows XP Control Panel should be set to use Category View. The Red Hat Enterprise Linux 3.0 projects use the GNOME desktop with the additional KDE menu options installed, but many of the projects are actually performed from the command line in a GNOME terminal window. The Mac OS X projects primarily use the default Mac OS X desktop. Because Mac OS X is built on BSD UNIX, some projects also use the terminal window in Mac OS X for practicing UNIX commands.

HANDS-ON PROJECTS

Project 1-1

A good place to start learning about an operating system is to perform a preliminary exploration of its GUI or desktop. In this project, you explore the **Windows XP** (**Professional** or **Home Edition**) interface and then in the next two projects, you contrast it to the interfaces for Red Hat Enterprise Linux 3.0 and Mac OS X. For this project, ask your instructor for an account from which to log on to Windows XP (unless your systems do not require an account, which is not recommended for network-based computers).

To explore the Windows XP desktop:

1. Press **Ctrl+Alt+Del**.

1

2. Enter your username, password, and domain name (if required), and click **OK**.

3. Notice the taskbar, which is at the bottom of the desktop on most systems.

4. Click the **Start** button to view the available options. Record some of the options. Some options, such as All Programs, Control Panel, and Help and Support are always displayed. Other options, particularly in the left side of the Start menu may change to reflect the last programs you have accessed.

5. Point to **All Programs** to view programs that you can start or program menus, such as Accessories.

6. Move the pointer to the right side of the Start menu to close All Programs.

7. Click **My Computer** on the Start menu to view its options, such as the option to double-click a drive to view its contents.

8. Close My Computer.

HANDS-ON PROJECTS

Project 1-2

In this project, you briefly explore the **Red Hat Enterprise Linux 3.0** desktop. You need a computer set up with the GNOME and Bluecurve desktops. Also, you need an account and password to access the desktop.

To explore the Red Hat Enterprise Linux 3.0 desktop:

1. To log on, type your username and press **Enter**. Next type your password and press **Enter**.

2. Notice the bar at the bottom of the desktop. This is called the Panel (see Figure 1-12). It contains icons you can click, such as icons to start the Main Menu, to access the Internet, and to access e-mail.

3. Move the pointer over the red hat on the Panel to see its label, which is the Main Menu.

4. Click the **Main Menu**.

5. Record some of the options you see on the Main Menu.

6. Point to **Accessories**, and notice there are more menu options. Record some of the options.

7. With the Main Menu still open (or open it if it is now closed), point to other menu options to see what they offer.

8. Click in a blank space on the desktop to close the Main Menu.

Figure 1-12   GNOME desktop with the Panel in Red Hat Enterprise Linux 3.0

**HANDS-ON
PROJECTS**

Project 1-3

This project enables you to briefly explore the **Mac OS X** desktop. Depending on the setup of your Mac OS X system, you may or may not need an account and password to access the operating system.

To learn about the Mac OS X desktop:

1. If you need to provide logon information, enter your Name and Password and click **Log In** (or press **return**).

2. Notice the menu options at the top of the screen and record them.

3. Next, observe the bar at the bottom of the screen (by default on most systems). This is called the Dock.

4. Point to each icon (see Figure 1-13 in which the Grab application is started) in the Dock to see what it does and record some of the icon names (note that the contents of the Dock can be customized, and so different systems may have different icons).

5. Click the **Go** menu at the top of the desktop. How would you access an application from the Go menu?

6. Click an open area of the desktop to close the Go menu.

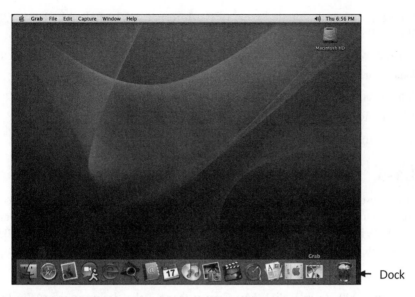

← Dock

Figure 1-13 Mac OS X desktop with the Dock

Project 1-4

The Internet can be a rich source of information about the history of computers. In this project, you use the Internet to review the history of computers, software, and the Internet. You will need a computer that has access to the Internet.

To learn more about the history of computers:

1. Open a Web browser, such as Netscape Navigator or Windows Internet Explorer.

2. Point your browser to *www.computerhistory.org/timeline/index.page*, and press **Enter** (for Intel-type computers) or **return** (for Macintosh).

3. Determine the answers to the following:

   a. Which two PCs were released in 1977?

   b. What was the first non-kit PC developed in 1972?

   c. What important data storage medium was released in 1985?

   d. What does ASCII stand for, and in what year did it come out?

   e. What was the name of the first fully transistorized computer developed in 1955?

   f. What input and output devices were used by the Manchester Mark I computer?

   g. In what year was the World Wide Web born via the development of Hypertext Markup Language (HTML), and who developed HTML?

4. Visit the Hobbes' Internet Timeline v7.0 (Hobbes's Internet Timeline Copyright 1993-2004 by Robert H. Zakon) by accessing the Web site *www. zakon.org/ robert/internet/timeline*, and determine the answers to the following:

a. BITNET, one of the predecessors of the Internet was launched in 1981. What does BITNET stand for?

b. In 1972, who wrote the first e-mail management program, and what did it do?

c. What worm struck the Internet in 2001?

d. What food could you order through the Internet in 1994?

e. What famous person sent an e-mail in 1976?

5. Close your Internet browser.

Project 1-5

The operating systems discussed in this book provide many tools that enable you to find out more about them. In this project, you use tools in **Windows 2000** (**Server** or **Professional**), **Windows XP** (**Professional** or **Home**), or **Windows Server 2003** to find out about the operating system version and devices that are attached to your computer.

To find out more about these Windows-based operating systems:

1. In Windows 2000, double-click **My Computer** on the desktop; or in Windows XP/Server 2003, click **Start** and click **My Computer**.

2. Click the **Help** menu and click **About Windows**, as shown in Figure 1-14.

Figure 1-14   Accessing information about the Windows XP operating system

3. What version of the operating system do you have? Are there any service packs (major operating system updates) installed? Record your observations.

4. Click **OK**, and close the My Computer window.

5. In Windows 2000, right-click **My Computer** on the desktop and click **Manage**. Or in Windows XP/Server 2003, click **Start**, right-click **My Computer**, and click **Manage**.

6. In the tree (see the left pane) under Computer Management and System Tools, click **Device Manager**.

7. What types of devices that can be used with the computer do you see displayed in the right pane? Record some of your observations.

8. Double-click **Keyboards**. What type of keyboard does your computer have?

9. Double-click **Modems**. Does your system show that a modem is attached for telephone line communications?

10. Close the Computer Management window.

HANDS-ON PROJECTS

Project 1-6

In this project, you access tools to find out more about **Red Hat Enterprise Linux 3.0** with the GNOME desktop installed. You also learn some tools that will work from a system prompt on most versions of UNIX/Linux.

To find out more about Red Hat Enterprise Linux 3.0:

1. Right-click the **Panel** in an open spot and click **About GNOME**.

2. What version of the GNOME desktop are you using? How can you find out more about GNOME?

3. Click **OK** to close the About GNOME window.

4. Click **Main Menu** (the red hat) and click **Help**. Notice the help contents you can access.

5. Close the Help Contents – Help Browser window.

6. Click **Main Menu**, point to **System Tools**, and click **Terminal** to access a terminal window so you can enter commands (see Figure 1–15).

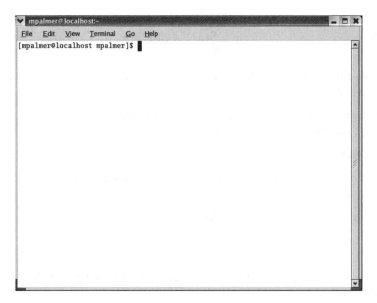

Figure 1-15 Red Hat Enterprise Linux terminal window

7. Type **man ls** and press **Enter** (in some other UNIX versions you would type *help ls*). The resulting screen provides documentation (*man* is the command for manual) about the *ls* command that is used to list files.

8. Press the **space bar** to page through the manual information for the *ls* command. Keep pressing the spacebar until you reach the end of the documentation.

9. Press **q** to exit the manual documentation.

10. Type **ls –la** and press **Enter** to view information about files, and practice using the *ls* command.

11. Type **exit** and press **Enter** to close the terminal window.

HANDS-ON PROJECTS

Project 1-7

In this project, you learn how to access and use the **Mac OS X** help resource and how to open a terminal window in Mac OS X from which to execute UNIX-based commands.

To use the Mac OS X help and terminal window tools:

1. Click **Help** on the menu bar at the top of the desktop.

2. Click **Mac Help**.

3. Type **How do I connect a printer** in the Ask a Question box and press **return**.

4. Notice the range of topics from which to choose.

5. Close the Search Results window.

6. Click the **Go** menu.

7. Click **Utilities**.

8. Double-click **Terminal**.

9. Type **man ls** and press **return** to view documentation about the *ls* command.

10. Press the **space bar** to page through the documentation (you don't need to type q to go back to the main screen). Page through all of the documentation until you are back at a new command prompt.

11. Type **ls –la** and press **return**. What is displayed?

12. Click the **Terminal** menu at the top of the desktop and click **Quit Terminal**.

13. Close the Utilities window.

Project 1-8

This project shows you how to configure the desktop theme in **Windows XP Professional** or **Home** and **Windows Server 2003**. (For Windows XP projects in this book, you should use the Category View in Control Panel.)

To configure the desktop theme:

1. Click **Start** and click **Control Panel**. You should use the default Category View for this and all Windows XP projects in this book. If you are not in Category View, Switch to Category View option in the left pane. "Pick a category" displays in the right pane when you are in Category View.

2. Click **Appearance and Themes**.

3. Click **Display**.

4. Make sure that the **Themes** tab is selected. What Theme selection is currently displayed in the Theme box?

5. Click the down arrow to display all of the selections in the Theme box. What options are available? Record your observations.

6. Close the Display Properties dialog box.

7. Close the Appearance and Themes window.

Project 1-9

Devices connected to a computer, such as the keyboard, are linked into the operating system through device drivers. In this project, you view the keyboard device drivers installed in **Windows 2000/XP/Server 2003**.

To view the keyboard device driver:

1. In Windows 2000, right-click **My Computer** on the desktop and click **Manage**. In Windows XP/Server 2003, click **Start**, right-click **My Computer**, and click **Manage**.

2. Click **Device Manager** under the tree in the left pane.

3. Double-click **Keyboards** in the right pane.

4. Double-click the keyboard description under Keyboards.

5. Click the **Driver** tab. Who is the provider of the keyboard device driver, and is the device driver digitally signed (for security)? Record your observations.

6. Click the **Driver Details** button (see Figure 1-16). How many driver files are displayed and what are they?

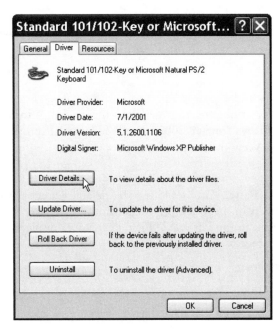

Figure 1-16   Obtaining keyboard device driver information in Windows XP

7. Click **OK**.

8. Click **Cancel**.

9. Close the Computer Management window.

Project 1-10

In this project, you list the contents of a particular driver file in **Red Hat Enterprise Linux 3.0** but the same procedures apply to many versions of UNIX/Linux. UNIX/Linux systems have two types of driver files: block special files and character special files. A block special file enables communication between a device and a device driver using blocks of characters, compared to a character special file in which only one character is sent at a time during communications. In this example, the hda1 (hda and the number one) file contains driver information pertaining to hard drives.

To view the contents of a device file:

1. Click **Main Menu**, point to **System Tools**, and click **Terminal**.

2. Type **ls –l /dev/hda1** and press **Enter**. (Note that this file has different names in different versions of UNIX, such as "ad0h1a" in some versions of BSD UNIX, "disk0" in some BSD UNIX versions, "vg00" in HP-UNIX, and "hd4" in IBM's AIX.) What devices are represented on the screen display? Record your results.

3. Type **exit** and press **Enter** to close the terminal window.

Project 1-11

Multitasking enables a desktop operating system user to perform many activities at once, such as running a text editor, using a calculator, and running an address book program, all at the same time. In this project, you take advantage of multitasking using **Windows 2000 Professional** or **Windows XP Professional** or **Home**.

To explore multitasking in Windows 2000/XP:

1. Click **Start**, point to **Programs** (in Windows 2000) or **All Programs** (in Windows XP), and point to **Accessories**. You may need to point to a down arrow on the Accessories menu to view all of the items.

2. Record some of the menus and programs that are available from the Accessories menu. For example, if you point to Accessibility (notice the right pointing arrow to show it is a menu), you will see an additional menu of Accessibility programs. Items without the arrow, such as Paint, are applications that you can run directly by selecting them.

3. Click **Notepad** (a text editor) on the Accessories menu.

4. Click **Start**, point to **Programs** (in Windows 2000) or **All Programs** (in Windows XP), point to **Accessories**, and click **Calculator**.

5. Click **Start**, point to **Programs** (in Windows 2000) or **All Programs** (in Windows XP), point to **Accessories**, and click **Address Book**. How many applications (and windows) are now running?

6. Notice that there is a button for each application in the taskbar. Click the **Calculator** button to bring it to the front. Windows 2000/XP is now multitasking.

7. Press **Ctrl+Alt+Del**. In Windows XP Home, this action takes you directly to the Windows Task Manager (which is yet another application that is started). In Windows 2000, Windows XP Professional, and Windows Server 2003, the Windows Security dialog box displays when you press **Ctrl+Alt+Del**. Next, in Windows 2000, Windows XP Professional, and Windows Server 2003, click the **Task Manager** button. What information do you see on the Applications tab? Also, notice that the CPU Usage Meter now appears on the right side of the taskbar as one of the icons near the time (see Figure 1-17).

Figure 1-17   CPU Usage Meter on the Windows 2000 taskbar

8. While you still have Task Manager open, click the **Performance** tab. This tab displays information about the system resources in use, such as the CPU (processor) and memory usage. Close one or two applications and observe the effect on the use of resources (observe both the Performance tab and the CPU Usage Meter). Close Task Manager. What happens to the CPU Usage Meter when you close Task Manager?

9. Close the remaining open windows.

Project 1-12

Mac OS X is another example of a multitasking operating system in which you can run several applications at the same time. This project enables you to start three applications in **Mac OS X** to demonstrate multitasking.

To multitask in Mac OS X:

1. Double-click **Macintosh HD** on the desktop.

2. Double-click the **Applications** folder.

3. Double-click **TextEdit**. What happens to the Dock when you start this program?

4. Click the **Applications** window to bring it to the front and double-click **Calculator**. How is the Dock changed? Record your observations.

5. Click the **Applications** window and double-click **Address Book**. (Note that in many cases you can also start Address Book from the Dock because it typically has an Address Book icon in the default setup.)

6. Click the **Applications** window to activate it and to display the Go menu at the top of the screen. Next, click the **Go** menu and click **Utilities**.

7. Double-click **Activity Monitor** in the Utilities window.

8. Make sure that CPU is selected. Notice the changes (or lack of changes) in the CPU activity as you close windows in the following steps.

9. Click the **Utilities** window and close it.

10. Click the **Calculator** on the desktop or its icon in the Dock to bring it to the front. Click the **Calculator** menu at the top of the desktop and click **Quit Calculator**.

11. Click the **Address Book** window (or icon in the Dock). Click the **Address Book** menu at the top of the desktop and click **Quit Address Book**.

12. Click the **TextEdit** window (or icon in the Dock). Click the **TextEdit** menu and click **Quit TextEdit**.

13. Click the **Activity Monitor** window (or icon in the Dock). Click the **Activity Monitor** menu and click **Quit Activity Monitor**. How has the Dock now changed?

CASE PROJECTS

The Wilshire Public Library has received funding from the Wilshire county commissioners to upgrade its desktop computers and servers. Currently, they are using an old Windows NT server to catalog library holdings. Also, there are Windows 98 computers that the librarians use in their offices. Library patrons use Windows 95 and Windows 98 computers within the library to access the catalog of holdings electronically (or they use the old card catalog, which is cards arranged in banks of drawers in the catalog section of the library).

Case Project 1-1: Discussing the Limitations of Early Operating Systems

What are some limitations of the present Windows 95 and 98 computers for use in the context of this library, compared to more modern operating systems? In what ways would library patrons and staff benefit from using more modern operating systems?

Case Project 1-2: Outfitting a Graphics and Audio/Video Facility

The library wants to create a facility so that elementary and secondary-school children can use graphic programs and create and edit audio and video clips for school projects. What systems should the library consider for this facility?

Case Project 1-3: Choosing a New Server

High on the list of needs is to implement a new server. A committee of library employees has been formed to look at their options for a server operating system. What options should they consider, which of these do you recommend, and why?

Case Project 1-4: Choosing New Desktop Systems

What desktop operating systems might be used to replace the Windows 95 and 98 computers? What operating system capabilities should the library look for when replacing these computers?

Case Project 1-5: Uncovering a Problem with a Newly Released Operating System

While the library is researching their computer options, the resource librarian comes across an article in a computer magazine about a newly released operating system that is experiencing frequent memory and CPU problems, such as slow or occasionally no response when accessing disk drives or displaying characters on the monitor. What might be the cause of these problems?

2

PC OPERATING SYSTEM HARDWARE

After reading this chapter and completing the exercises, you will be able to:

♦ Explain operating system hardware components, which will include design type, speed, cache, address bus, data bus, control bus, and CPU scheduling

♦ Describe the basic features and system architecture of popular PC processors

♦ Identify the basic features and characteristics of popular PC operating systems

♦ Understand how hardware components interact with operating systems

Operating systems and hardware work in a unified relationship to make computers useful for business, educational, personal, and network computing applications. The features of an operating system used for a particular application depend on the capabilities of the hardware. In many cases, modern operating systems do not support older hardware. When you upgrade an operating system, you may need to upgrade the hardware to match the new operating system's capabilities.

This chapter gives you a foundation in hardware basics, including the design of CPUs, clock speeds, and types of computer buses. Also, you learn about CPUs and how they are used by particular operating systems. After you learn about the hardware, you examine the features of the most popular operating systems, enabling you to become acquainted with the general characteristics of each operating system, its strengths and weaknesses, and its hardware requirements. With this overview, you understand how to choose the operating system that is best suited for a particular work or home environment, and for specific hardware. You know which operating system to use when new computers are installed, or when existing computers are upgraded. Likewise, you are able to identify situations in which the wrong operating system is used.

UNDERSTANDING CPUs

As you learned in the previous chapter, one of the main functions of the operating system is to provide the interface between the various application programs running on a computer and the hardware inside. Central to understanding the hardware is the system architecture of the computer, which is built around the central processing unit (CPU), or processor. The **system architecture** includes the number and type of CPUs in the hardware, and the communication routes, called **buses**, between the CPUs and other hardware components, such as memory and disk storage.

The CPU is the chip that performs the actual computational and logic work. Most modern PCs have one such chip, and are referred to as **single-processor computers**. In reality, for complete functionality, the CPU requires several support chips, such as chips that help manage communications with devices and device drivers. There are also computers that have multiple CPUs; many have two, some have as many as 64 or more. These computers are generally referred to as **multiprocessor computers**. You will take a closer look at single-processor and multiprocessor computers later in this chapter.

CPUs can be classified by several hardware elements, the most important of which are:

- Design type
- Speed
- Cache
- Address bus
- Data bus
- Control bus
- CPU scheduling

Each of these elements is considered in the following sections.

Design Type

Two general CPU designs are used in today's computers: **Complex Instruction Set Computer (CISC)** and **Reduced Instruction Set Computer (RISC)**. The main difference between the two is the number of different instructions the chip can process. When a program executes on a computer, the CPU reads instruction after instruction from the program to perform the tasks the program wants completed. When the CPU has read such an instruction, it carries out the operations associated with it. In the current generation of PCs, the CPU can process as many as 20 million complex operations per second on the low end, and several billion on the high end. Clock speed and CPU design are the factors that determine how fast operations are executed. Obviously, it is convenient for the programmer to have many instructions available to do many different operations.

2

Let's say, for example, that the programmer wants to multiply two numbers. It would be convenient to give the CPU the two numbers, then tell it to multiply them, and display the result. Because different kinds of numbers (such as integers and real numbers) must be treated differently, it would be nice if there were functions to perform this multiplication on all number types. You can see that as we require the CPU to perform more and more functions, the number of instructions can rapidly increase. The **instruction set**, or the list of commands the CPU can understand and carry out, can get quite complex as programs perform more functions. A processor that works like this is called a CISC CPU. When a CISC CPU gets a command, it assigns specific instructions to different parts of the chip. When a command is finished and the CPU gets the next command, it typically uses the same parts of the chip it used before to carry out this command. Current versions of CISC-based chips typically recognize more than 200 different instructions. The Intel x86 family of computers is based on the CISC CPU.

The CISC CPU offers advantages and disadvantages. A big advantage is that you need only general-purpose hardware to carry out commands versus hardware designed for a specific purpose. If you later want to add new commands to a new revision of your chip, that likely can be done with the same general-purpose hardware. Another big advantage is that the chip is driven mainly by software, which is cheaper to produce than hardware. Major disadvantages to the CISC design include the complexity of hardware needed to perform many functions, and the complexity of on-chip software needed to make the hardware do the right thing. An even bigger disadvantage is, ironically, the need to continually reprogram the on-chip hardware. If you use the same part of the chip to add a number as you use to multiply a number—two functions that are obviously related but slightly different—you must reconfigure the hardware in between the multiplication and addition operations. This reconfiguration, changing the CPU from multiplication to addition, takes a little time, which is one reason a CISC chip can be a little slower than RISC chips.

Also, when you use general-purpose hardware to perform specific functions, the functions won't always be executed in the most efficient way, which can slow the CPU's execution of program code. One solution to this problem is to customize hardware for specific functions. You can add a module that is optimized to do all computational functions (a **math coprocessor**), for example. Such an addition increases CPU performance, but it also increases the price. Fast hardware is expensive.

 Early system architectures have a processor and an optional slot for a math coprocessor. The math coprocessor is used to perform complex math calculations, such as those required for computations in a spreadsheet. CPUs in modern system architectures have built-in math coprocessors.

NOTE

Considering the disadvantages of the design of the CISC CPU, it is easy to understand the idea behind the other major CPU design, the RISC CPU. The complex operations that a CISC CPU carries out slow it down because all sorts of hardware on the chip must be set up to perform specific functions. The RISC CPU design, on the other hand, requires very little setup for specific tasks because it has hardware on the chip that is specially designed and optimized to perform particular functions. As mentioned before, the disadvantage of this approach is that you need a lot of hardware to carry out instructions, which will make the chip more expensive because it is more complex. This is the main reason a RISC CPU has so few instructions; most of the instructions it performs are conducted by hardware on the chip that is dedicated to perform just that function. Because most of the hardware on the RISC CPU is not shared among many instructions, RISC CPUs typically use a technique called **pipelining**, which allows the processor to operate on one instruction at the same time it is fetching one or more subsequent instructions from the operating system or application. Motorola manufactures a RISC chip for the Apple Power Mac computers (PowerPC), for example.

The difference between the RISC approach and the CISC approach is best explained by the example in Figure 2-1, which shows how each design carries out five multiplications.

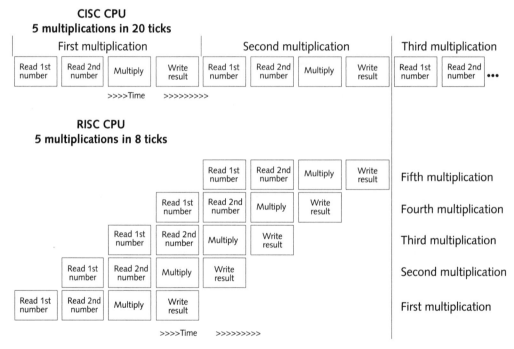

Figure 2-1   CISC versus RISC processing

The general steps required to perform the multiplications are as follows:

1. Read the first number out of memory.

2. Read the second number out of memory.

3. Multiply the two numbers.

2

4. Write the result back to memory.

5. Repeat Steps 1-4 for each of the four remaining multiplications.

On a simple CISC CPU, the CPU is first configured to get (read) the numbers. It then reads the numbers. Next, the CPU is configured to multiply the numbers. Then the numbers are multiplied. Next, the CPU is configured to write the result to memory. Then the numbers are written to memory. If you wish to multiply five sets of numbers in this way, the whole process must be repeated five times.

On a simple RISC CPU, the process looks slightly different. A part of the CPU is dedicated to reading the first number. When this operation is complete, another part of the CPU reads the second number. When that operation is complete, yet another part of the CPU performs the multiplication, and when that is complete, yet another part of the CPU writes the result to memory. If this operation must happen five times in a row, the piece of RISC hardware dedicated to obtaining the first number from memory obtains the first number for the second operation, while the second number for the first operation is obtained. And while the first two numbers are being multiplied, the second number for the second operation is retrieved from memory, while the first number for the third operation is obtained. As the first result is written back to memory, the second multiplication is performed, while the second number for the third operation is read from memory, while the first number for the fourth operation is read from memory, and so on. As you can see, when many operations must be performed, the RISC CPU's pipelining performs a lot more efficiently than a CISC CPU. Intel, Motorola, and AMD are three of the most popular manufacturers of this CPU.

The RISC processor design has evolved into a relatively new concept called **Explicitly Parallel Instruction Computing (EPIC)**, created as a joint project by Intel and Hewlett-Packard (HP). EPIC enables the processor to handle massive numbers of operations simultaneously by implementing large storage areas and executing parallel instruction sets. The EPIC technology enables a single processor to execute as many as 20 operations at a time.

EPIC enables the chip to predict and speculate about which operations are likely in the future. For example, if many mathematical operations have already been requested to obtain and multiply certain data, EPIC makes predictions that additional similar operations will occur in the future. Through prediction and speculation, the chip actually performs some operations before they are requested. For other operations, it sets up rotating registers, or work areas, so that the tools needed for similar operations are already present, and those operations are handled one after the other. EPIC can support up to 256 64-bit registers, far more registers than CISC and traditional RISC processors. By using more registers, EPIC reduces or eliminates bottlenecks at the processor, which enables the processor to work faster.

Another advantage of a RISC-based EPIC processor is that it can build three instructions into one "word." A **word** is like a single communication with the processor, and CISC and traditional RISC processors use one instruction per word. By using three instructions per word, EPIC enables the processor to work much faster. Also, EPIC instructions can be combined into instruction groups, consisting of multiple words, and it attempts to execute all of the instructions in one group at the same time, if possible. The number of instructions in one instruction group is theoretically unlimited.

By performing parallel operations, the EPIC processor can do several things simultaneously. For example, in Figure 2-1 on page 50, the CISC processor takes 20 ticks to perform five multiplications and the RISC processor takes 8 ticks. The RISC-based EPIC processor, such as the Intel Itanium processors, can do five multiplications in 1 tick, and at the same time it predicts additional tasks or completes other tasks for a different software application.

Speed

The speed of a CPU defines how fast it can perform operations. There are many ways to indicate speed, but the most obvious indicator is the **internal clock speed** of the CPU. As you may know, a CPU runs on a very rigid schedule along with the rest of the computer. The clock provides this schedule to make sure that all the chips know what to expect at what time. The internal clock speed tells you how many clock pulses, or ticks, are available per second. Typically, the CPU performs some action on every tick. The more ticks per second, the faster the CPU executes commands, and the harder the electronics on the CPU must work. The clock speed for a CPU can be lower than 1 million ticks per second (1 megahertz or MHz), and higher than 3 billion ticks per second (3 gigahertz or GHz). The faster the clock, the faster the CPU, and the more expensive the hardware. Also, as more components are needed to make a CPU, the chip uses more energy to do its work. Part of this energy is converted to heat, causing faster CPUs to run warmer, and require more fans in the chassis.

From the Trenches...

A business upgraded from 1.8 GHz computers to a model running at 3.06 GHz. The computers were plugged in and ran for about five minutes before the video became scrambled and stopped working. Several calls were made to customer service and after four days of working on the problem, it was determined to be a heating problem. The computers were built at sea level, where they all worked just fine. The business was in a city with an elevation over 5000 feet. Air contains fewer molecules the higher you go. The molecules hitting the surface of the CPU carry away the heat, and at higher elevations, there aren't as many molecules, and thus less air movement to cool the warmer CPUs. These warmer CPUs were overheating the video circuitry and causing the problems. The addition of dual chassis fans to each computer corrected the problem.

NOTE RISC CPU hardware is less complicated than CISC CPU hardware, so a RISC CPU can theoretically operate at higher clock speeds. RISC CPUs operating at clock speeds of 700 MHz have been around for years. Some designs are now available that run at speeds over 3 GHz.

In addition to performing fast operations inside the CPU, the chips also must be able to communicate with the other chips in the computer. This is where the **external clock speed** of the CPU comes in. While a CPU may run internally at a speed of 3 GHz, it typically uses a lower clock speed to communicate with the rest of the computer. The reason for this is again, to a large extent, cost. It would be extremely expensive to make every component in the computer run as fast as the CPU. It is therefore common practice to run the other components in the computer at a reduced clock rate. Usually, the external clock speed is one-half, one-third, one-fourth, or one-eighth the speed of the internal CPU clock.

Cache

If a CPU wants to get a few numbers out of memory, and its internal clock speed is four times faster than its external clock speed, it obviously must wait on the external clock, which could be very inefficient. To avoid this problem, most modern CPUs have **cache memory** built into the chip. This memory is extremely fast—and therefore expensive. It typically runs at the same speed as the processor. If the processor needs a number stored in the cache memory on the CPU, it probably won't have to wait to obtain that number. This memory is referred to as **level 1 (L1) cache**. Some CPUs have one or two more levels of cache memory, which are typically on the same chip. This is called **level 2 (L2) cache**, and it normally runs at the same speed as the external CPU clock. For example, L2 cache is generally accessed faster than other memory in the computer, except for L1 cache.

When both L1 and L2 cache are built into the processor chip, the cache on a separate chip is called **level 3 (L3) cache**. This cache structure is used on some modern chips, particularly those that employ EPIC architectures. The combination of L1, L2, and L3 caching can significantly reduce bottlenecks at the processor.

The amount of L1, L2, and L3 cache, especially for larger CPUs, determines the speed of the CPU. In many cases, up to 90 percent of the data a CPU needs to transfer to and from memory is present in the L1, L2, or L3 cache when the CPU needs it. This is because there is a specialized piece of hardware called the **cache controller** that predicts what data will be needed, and makes that data available in cache before it is needed. Most modern CPUs also can use the cache to write data to memory to ensure that the CPU will not have to wait when it wishes to write results to memory. You can see that intelligent, fast cache controllers and large amounts of L1, L2, and L3 cache are important components for increasing the speed of a CPU.

TIP One way to improve the performance of a Web server that is often slow is to upgrade to a processor that has a large amount of fast L2 cache, or a combination of L1, L2, and L3 cache.

Address Bus

The **address bus** is an internal communications pathway that specifies the source and target addresses for memory reads and writes. It is instrumental in the transfer of data to and from computer memory. The address bus typically runs at the external clock speed of the CPU. The address, like all data in the computer, is in digital form and is conveyed in the form of a series of bits. The width of the address bus is the number of bits that can be used to address memory. A wider bus means the computer can address more memory, and therefore store more data or larger, more complex programs. For example, a 16-bit wide address bus can address 64 kilobytes (KB) (64,000 bytes) of memory. This bus size is no longer found in PCs sold today. Most PCs today use a 32-bit address bus, which allows them to address roughly 4 billion (4,000,000,000) memory addresses, or 4 gigabytes (GB). However, many systems, although they have a 32-bit address bus, cannot actually address that much memory. Newer processors have even wider address buses, some as wide as 64 bits, allowing them to address 16 terabytes (TB) of memory.

Data Bus

The **data bus** allows computer components, such as the CPU, display adapter, and main memory, to share information. The number of bits in the data bus indicates how many bits of data can be transferred from memory to the CPU, or vice versa, in one clock tick. A CPU with an external clock speed of 1 GHz will have 1 billion ticks per second to the external bus. If this CPU has a 16-bit data bus, it could theoretically transfer 2 GB (2,000,000,000 bytes) of data to and from memory every second. (One byte consists of 8 bits, so 1 billion × 16 bits ÷ 8 bits per second = 2 GB per second.) A CPU with an external clock speed of 1 GHz and a 32-bit data bus could transfer as much as 4 GB per second (1 billion × 32 bits ÷ 8 bits per byte). That is twice as much data in the same time period, so in theory, the CPU will work twice as fast.

There are a couple of catches here. First, the software must be able to instruct the CPU to use all of the data bus, and the rest of the computer must be fast enough to keep up with the CPU. Most CPUs work internally with the same number of bits as on the data bus. In other words, a CPU with a 32-bit data bus typically can perform operations on 32 bits of data at a time. Almost all CPUs can also be instructed to work with chunks of data narrower than the data bus width, but in this case the CPU is not as efficient because the same number of clock cycles is required to perform an operation, whether or not all bits are used.

Control Bus

The CPU is kept informed of the status of resources and devices connected to the computer, such as the memory and disk drives, by information that is transported on the **control bus**. The most basic information that is transported across the control bus is whether or not a particular resource is active and can be accessed. If a disk drive becomes active, for example, the disk controller provides this information to the CPU over the control bus. Other information that may be transported over the control bus includes whether a particular function is for input or output. Memory read and write status is transported on this bus, as well as **interrupt requests (IRQs)**. An interrupt request is a request to the processor to "interrupt" whatever it is doing to take care of a process, such as a read from a disk drive, which in turn might be interrupted by another process, such as a write into memory.

CPU Scheduling

CPU scheduling is determining which process to start given the multiple processes waiting to run. During the disk operating system (DOS) days, most operating systems were basically single threaded, meaning they would run just one process until it was completed and then turn to the next process. Beginning with the Windows NT operating system, the use of CPU scheduling algorithms began to evolve to allow **multithreading**, which is the ability to run two or more processes, known as threads, at the same time.

POPULAR PC PROCESSORS

The following sections give an overview of the CPUs found in PCs, and a few more powerful 64-bit processors that are available for higher-end PCs and servers.

Intel

The most popular CPUs in use in PCs today are designed by Intel. The first player in this line of processors was the 8088, the CPU found in the original IBM PC. Early Intel CPUs were identified by model numbers: 8088, 8086, 80286, 386, and 486. The model numbers are sometimes shown without the 80 prefix, or preceded by an "i" as in 80486, 486, or i486. The Pentium family of chips followed the 486 ("penta" means five in Greek). Pentium chips are sometimes identified with just a P and a number, for example P4 for Pentium 4. Table 2-1 shows Intel CPUs. Intel processors that are in current use include the Celeron, Pentium III, and Pentium 4. The Intel Itanium and Itanium2 are newer 64-bit processors for higher-end PCs and servers. Notice in Table 2-1 the trends toward ever-faster internal and external clock speeds, more and larger cache, and increasing capability to handle multimedia and large amounts of data.

NOTE

A very important feature of Intel CPUs is **backward-compatibility**, which means that a significant number of features from an older chip can function on a newer chip. Code written to run on an 8088 processor runs on a newer CPU without change. Because the 8088 code is 16-bit code, it does not use many of the advanced features of the newer CPUs, and it runs slower than code written especially for the CPU. Backward-compatibility is one of the major reasons for the success of the Intel line of CPUs. The Itanium line of Intel CPU chips are not backward-compatible.

Table 2-1 Intel CPUs

CPU	Year Introduced	Data Bus/ Address Bus Bits	Internal Clock (MHz)	External Clock (MHz)	Cache	Comments
8088	1978	8/20	4–8	4–8	No	CPU of the first IBM PC.
8086	1978	16/20	4–16	4–16	No	First Intel CPU to have a 16-bit data path.
80286	1982	16/24	8–40	8–40	No	Beginning of the 80x86 line.
80386SX	1985	16/24	16–40	16–40	No	Less expensive version of 386 chip; supports only 16-bit data bus.
80386DX	1985	32/24	16–40	16–40	No	Introduced 32-bit data bus.
80486SX	1989	16/24	16–80	16–40	Yes	Less expensive version of 486 chip; supports only 16-bit data bus.
80486DX	1989	32/24	16–120	16–40	Yes	First Intel chip to use different internal and external clocks, include a math coprocessor, L1 cache on the chip, and external L2 cache.
Pentium	1993	32/28	16–266	16–66	Yes	More instructions added and L1 cache was made more efficient.
Pentium Pro	1995	64/28	33–200	33–50	Yes	Optimized for running 32-bit instructions. Intel also releases the **Multimedia Extension (MMX),** with new instructions to deal with multimedia.
Pentium II	1997	64/36	66–550	66–100	Yes	Inclusion of L1 cache, running at internal clock speed, as well as L2 cache, running at external or twice external clock speed, built right onto the CPU module.

Table 2-1   Intel CPUs (continued)

CPU	Year Introduced	Data Bus/ Address Bus Bits	Internal Clock (MHz)	External Clock (MHz)	Cache	Comments
Xeon	1998	64/36	500–1700	400	Yes	Offered as a version of the Pentium II and Pentium III. Uses a daughterboard L2 caching technique that is twice as fast as non-Xeon processors. The Xeon MP has a similar architecture to the Pentium 4, with the addition of **execution-based cache**, which is faster than the original Xeon cache. Newer Xeon chips also have a new instruction set that improves video, encryption, and authentication. The Xeon MP also uses hyperthreading and Level 3 cache of 512 KB to 2 MB.
Celeron	1998	64/36	850–2600	66–100	Yes	Low-end processor for PC multimedia and home markets.
Pentium III	1999	64/36	600–1200	100–133	Yes	Introduced **Streaming SIMD Extensions**, designed to provide better multimedia processing.
Pentium 4	2001	64/36	1300–3200	800	Yes	Includes two math coprocessors and execution-based cache. Extreme Edition supports **hyper threading (HT)**, which enables a single processor to appear to the operating system as two separate processors.
Itanium	2001	64/128	733–800	266	Yes	First RISC-based Intel chip, 64-bit with EPIC architecture, designed for high-end PC workstations and servers.
Itanium 2	2003	64/128	1300–1500	400	Yes	Extends the Itanium family optimized for dual processor servers and workstations.

The Intel Itanium and Itanium 2 processors are a significant departure from previous Intel processors in two respects: they are built on the RISC-based EPIC architecture and they are 64-bit chips. The Itanium features the complete EPIC design allotment of 256 64-bit registers that can operate as rotating registers. In order to use the capabilities of the Itanium 64-bit processor, the operating system and applications must be recompiled or rewritten to use 64-bit processing. 64-bit versions of Windows XP, Windows Server 2003 Enterprise Edition, and Windows Server 2003 Data Center Edition are available to run on the Itanium 64-bit processors. Novell has introduced applications such as Novell Internet Caching System, NetWare Management Portal and Java Web server that run on Itanium-based servers.

NOTE   The Intel Itanium processor is intended for very large-scale operations that match powerful mainframes. For this reason, the chip architecture and bus design include the capability to run more than 1000 processors as a group. Of course, currently there are no server operating systems that can run this many processors in one computer, but the Itanium processor design is setting the stage for this possibility.

Try Hands-on Projects 2-1 and 2-2 to practice monitoring Intel-type processor usage in a Windows-based operating system. Also, try Hands-on Project 2-3 to test the processor.

AMD and Cyrix

Advanced Micro Devices, Inc. (AMD) and VIA Technologies (Cyrix) manufacture CPU chips that compete with Intel PC chips. The more recent of these chips are shown in Table 2-2.

Table 2-2   AMD and VIA processors

Processor	Latest Clock Speeds (MHz or GHz)	Compares to Intel Chip	System Bus Speed (MHz)
AMD Processors			
AMD-K6-2	166 to 475 MHz	Pentium II, Celeron	66, 95, 100
AMD-K6-III	350 to 450 MHz	Pentium II	100
Duron	1 GHz to 1.3 GHz	Celeron	200
Athlon	Up to 1.9 GHz	Pentium III	200
Athlon Model 4	Up to 1.4 GHz	Pentium III	266
Athlon MP	1.4 GHz to 2.1 GHz	Pentium III	200 to 400+
Athlon XP	Up to 2.2 GHz	Pentium 4	266, 333, 400
Opteron (64-bit)	1.4 GHz to 2.0 GHz	Itanium	244
VIA (CyRIX) Processors			
Cyrix M II	300, 333, 350	Pentium II, Celeron	66, 75, 83, 95, 100

Table 2-2 AMD and VIA processors (continued)

Processor	Latest Clock Speeds (MHz or GHz)	Compares to Intel Chip	System Bus Speed (MHz)
Cyrix III	433 to 533	Celeron, Pentium III	66, 100, 133
VIA C3	Up to 1 GHz	Celeron	100 or 133

Other Processors

In addition to Intel and its direct competitors, several other manufacturers produce processors for various types of computers. These chips include Motorola, PowerPC, SPARC, and Alpha chips.

Motorola

Motorola chips are typically found in Macintosh computers. Its line of CISC CPUs is used in many older Macintosh computers, as well as in many UNIX computers. The popular models were the 68000, 68020, 68030, and 68040. The development of the features in the chips is roughly similar to the development in the Intel line; the 68020 shows many similarities to the 80286, the 68030 is similar to the 80386, and the 86040 is similar to the 80486. Although there are major differences between the Intel and Motorola chip lines, and they are in no way interchangeable, their development was similar.

PowerPC

Although Motorola continues to develop chips in the 68xxx line, modern Macintosh computers do not use this line of chips. A new non-compatible line of chips—chips that use different instruction sets and a different general architecture than the 68xxx line—was developed jointly by IBM, Motorola, and Apple Computer. These RISC chips are known as the PowerPC line. The initial PowerPC chips, known as models 601, 602, 603, and 603e, were similar in design and functionality. As the model number increased, so did the internal clock speeds, L1 cache size, and the efficiency of the chip designs.

The PowerPC G4 (fourth generation) chip begins the family of 64-bit RISC-based MPC74xx chips. The internal clock speed of the MPC7450 chip is 733 MHz, with an external clock speed of up to 100 MHz. The MPC74xx chips offer a 64-bit data bus, and have both L1 and L2 cache built into the processor. L3 cache is fast and operates via a 64-bit bus between the processor and the separate cache board. The system bus operates at up to 500 MHz, which is five times faster than the previous generation (G3) of the chip. The MPC74xx chips also feature a technology that enables them to use less power than previous chips, and to save additional power by using the doze, nap, and sleep modes—all designed to shut down various parts of the computer while it is idle.

The system bus creates the connection between memory and the CPU. Other names for the system bus include memory bus or local bus.

TIP

The newest chip in the PowerPC line is the G5, developed jointly by IBM and Apple. It has a 64-bit data architecture. The G5 PowerPC runs at up to 2 GHz and can address up to 8 MB of memory.

SPARC

SPARC is a RISC processor designed by Sun Microsystems. SPARC CPUs have gone through many incarnations, and the RISC processor is the most popular on the market today. The UltraSPARC III is the current version of the SPARC processor. It is a 64-bit chip with both 64-bit address and data buses. The internal clock on this chip is currently available at speeds up to 1.28 GHz. The external clock speed is 150 MHz. L1 cache is similar to other chips at 64 KB. The external L2 cache, however, can be relatively large, at up to 8 MB.

Primarily, you'll see various implementations of the UNIX operating system running on these CPUs, performing high-end engineering and networking duties. The most popular operating system using the chip is Sun Microsystems's SunOS UNIX and Solaris (Solaris is the SunOS with a desktop window system). Versions of Linux and BSD UNIX are also available for SPARC architectures.

Alpha

Another CPU of interest is the Alpha CPU, originally designed by Digital Equipment Corporation (DEC), later purchased by Compaq/HP. Today, the Alpha CPU is found in high-end Compaq servers. This CPU has a 64-bit data bus and a 64-bit address bus. The internal clock speed can be as high as 1 GHz. The Alpha uses a traditional 64 KB L1 cache and an external L2 cache that can go up to 8 MB. Similar to the SPARC, Alpha chips are widely used in the UNIX environment. And, like the SPARC, Alpha chips are found in computers conducting heavy networking, engineering, and graphics duties. There are now many proprietary devices, such as file servers, firewall products, and routers, that run custom operating systems based on an Alpha architecture.

In 2001, Intel and Compaq signed an intellectual property rights deal that will allow features of the Alpha chip to live on in Intel's Itanium chip. With the purchase of Compaq, HP has reinforced its support of the Alpha. HP will continue development of the Alpha through 2004, production through 2006, and support through 2011.

NOTE

There are many other CPUs, and there are many details about these chips that are beyond the focus of this book. The CPUs discussed here are those that are most popular in PCs today and most often used by the operating systems covered in this book.

POPULAR PC OPERATING SYSTEMS

There are many operating systems available for today's computers. Chapter 1 gave a brief historical survey of operating systems. This chapter takes a closer look at MS-DOS, Windows 3.x, Windows NT, Windows 95/98, and Windows ME, operating systems that laid the groundwork for current desktop and server operating systems, and then focuses on these more recent operating systems. These include Windows 2000, Windows XP, and Windows Server 2003, as well as UNIX, NetWare, and Mac OS.

NOTE

System hardware requirements for the operating systems discussed in this book are given in Chapter 4.

MS-DOS and PC DOS

Microsoft's original operating system for the IBM PC hardware platform, called MS-DOS or more simply DOS, runs on any of the Intel 8088, 80x86, or Pentium-class CPUs on a PC hardware platform. The version of MS-DOS that runs on early IBM computers is called PC DOS because it was customized and marketed by IBM.

DOS is a 16-bit, single-tasking, single-user operating system. It operates in **real mode**, meaning that only one program or process can run at a time, that there is a 640 KB limit on memory that is accessible to applications, and that applications directly access and control hardware like printers, rather than going through the operating system. Most programs operating under DOS use a simple text-based command-line user interface. Figure 2-2 illustrates a typical DOS screen. Although DOS was widely used in early PCs, its limitations in terms of lack of support for current software applications and graphical user interfaces (GUIs) have all but relegated it to the annals of computer history.

```
C>dir

  Volume in drive C is 123
  Volume Serial Number is 2C1D-19D4
  Directory of C:\

CONFIG   SYS           713  08-06-98   6:27p
COMMAND  COM        93,812  08-24-96  11:11a
AUTOEXEC BAT         4,320  08-06-98   6:27p
WRPLOG   TXT           489  08-06-98   6:11p
BORLAND       <DIR>        08-06-98   6:11p
PROGRAMS      <DIR>        08-06-98   6:11p
DOCUMENT      <DIR>        08-06-98   6:26p
CICOMNDD LOG           450  09-12-98  11:08p
          5 file(s)        99,774 bytes
          3 dir(s)     41,831,680 bytes free

C>mkdir test

C>cd test

C>cd
C:\TEST\

C>
```

Figure 2-2   Typical DOS screen

Windows 3.x

Microsoft released the first version of Windows, implementing a GUI interface to compete with the Apple Macintosh, in 1985. This early version of Windows was quite slow and not well accepted. Windows 3.1 in the early 1990s was the first popular, usable Microsoft GUI, and it paved the way for Windows to become the dominant PC operating system.

With Windows 3.11, Microsoft added significant networking capabilities to Windows, such as the options to have workgroups and set up shared drives. In fact, Windows 3.11 is also referred to as Windows for Workgroups (WFW), and represents Windows' true initiation into networking. WFW is a **peer-to-peer network operating system**, which means each computer on a network can communicate with other computers on the same network. One significant limitation of Windows 3.11 is the lack of security options to protect shared files. This is because when Windows 3.11 was first introduced, security was not recognized as the critical issue it is today.

The Windows 3.x (Windows 3.0, 3.1, and 3.11 versions) operating systems run on top of the MS-DOS or PC DOS operating system on the IBM PC system architecture (from 8088 through 486). These are still 16-bit real mode operating systems running on top of MS-DOS.

Windows 95

As the PC platform became more powerful and the Pentium architecture became more common, Microsoft created a true 32-bit operating system that could use the functionality of the new 32-bit computer architecture. Windows 95 eliminated the 640 KB memory limit and the 16-bit code, and thus can not run on the oldest 16-bit CPUs (8088 and 8086). For backward-compatibility, it is still possible to run old MS-DOS and Windows 3.x programs in Windows 95.

Compared to Windows 3.x, Windows 95 required about twice the memory, twice the hard disk space, and twice the processor speed of Windows 3.x. Using more computer resources, Windows 95 was able to introduce several advanced functions that have now become standard Windows features. These include:

- The Windows desktop
- Plug and Play
- ActiveX and the Component Object Model (COM)
- The registry
- Multitasking
- Enhanced network and Internet capabilities

The Windows Desktop

Windows 95 introduced the GUI now called the desktop (see Figure 2-3), which became the foundation for the GUI used in all later versions of Windows. The Windows 95 GUI introduced the Start button that provides direct access to system utilities and application programs. Other desktop features included the taskbar at the bottom of the screen, which contains icons that represent currently running programs and other information about the operation of the system, and shortcut and program icons to seamlessly run programs, manipulate files, and access network connections from one place.

The directories used in MS-DOS and Windows 3.x are called folders in Windows 95 (a naming convention borrowed from the Apple Mac OS). Folders and files are managed using Windows Explorer—a utility that can also be used to run programs, access control panels, and perform just about anything else on the Windows 95 computer or network to which it is connected.

Plug and Play

Plug and Play is possibly the most exciting hardware feature introduced in Windows 95 and continued in later versions of Windows (except Windows NT). **Plug and Play (PnP)** enables the operating system to automatically detect newly installed hardware. When PnP detects new hardware, it determines vital information, such as what device drivers to use for that hardware, and what computer resources (IRQ and memory) to link with the hardware. Reciprocally, the hardware has some built-in functions that let the operating system dictate how to configure the hardware. PnP is a great time saver because it reduces many of the tedious tasks of configuring hardware and software, previously done manually. Not all hardware was PnP compatible when Windows 95 was introduced, but most hardware for Windows computers is PnP compatible today.

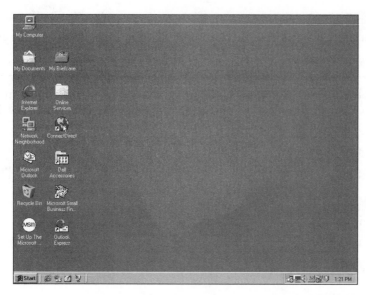

Figure 2-3   Windows 95 desktop shortcuts, Start button, and taskbar

ActiveX and the Component Object Model (COM)

Much of the easy manipulation of the user interface in Windows 95 is made possible by a Microsoft technology called ActiveX. **ActiveX**, along with its parent, the **Component Object Model (COM)**, is a standardized way for objects, such as programs, files, computers, printers, control panels, windows, and icons, to communicate with each other. It is a simple but revolutionary concept. Objects (such as folders, icons, menus, and almost any other object you see on the desktop) consist of a series of properties. To show you a folder full of files, the operating system makes a folder, then places the file objects in the folder. The COM and ActiveX technologies enable an object to "sense" when it is interacting with other objects, such as the mouse pointer, the desktop, the trash can, or the Start menu. The COM and ActiveX technologies allow you to simply drag files from one place to another. The icons you drag, through the use of COM, make it possible for the object onto which they are dragged to know what to do with them. By building this concept into its operating system, Microsoft provided a new level of user interface consistency and program interoperability. The use of COM and ActiveX made Windows 95 easier to use than its predecessors, and once again broadened the functionality provided by the operating system.

The Registry

Windows 95 also introduced a new way of storing and managing operating system information. Up to this point, such information was kept in files in various locations on the hard disk. The new concept was called the **registry**, a database that stores operating system information, information about hardware and software configuration, as well as general information that is shared by parts of the operating system or application programs to make COM and ActiveX work.

The registry is a hierarchical database that provides the following information:

- Operating system configuration
- Service and device driver information and configuration
- Static tuning parameters
- Software and application parameters
- Hardware configuration
- Performance information
- Desktop configuration

It is also possible to share registry data over a network, a function that has turned out to be extremely useful in situations with many users and many computers.

TIP When you back up Windows 95 or later, make sure that you also back up the registry because sometimes information in the registry is corrupted from power failures, or because an application software installation may go bad and change important information in the registry. With a backup, it is easy to restore the operating system without reinstalling it. Backing up the registry is covered in Chapter 4.

Multitasking

Multitasking in Windows 95 is cooperative for 16-bit applications, but preemptive for 32-bit applications. Windows 95 introduced a **task supervisor** that detects tasks that appear stuck, and that presents the option to close hung tasks without having to restart the operating system. The methods used for cooperative multitasking in Windows 95 are more advanced than the methods used in earlier versions of Windows, largely because of the COM technology. In Windows 95 preemptive multitasking, the operating system has complete control of the multitasking environment. This makes it very difficult for a program to gain absolute control of the CPU.

Enhanced Network and Internet Capabilities

The networking functionality in Windows 95 is substantially extended from earlier versions of Windows. Unlike earlier versions of Windows, in Windows 95, the network drivers are part of the Windows operating system. In all but the early versions of Windows 95, all the networking code is written as a 32-bit application. This results in a significant boost in network performance. The networking functions, as in Windows for Workgroups 3.11, consist of two parts, the **client** and the **server**. Unlike Windows 3.11, Windows 95 can communicate over a network with many other operating systems, such as Novell NetWare, a popular server operating system.

Another important feature started in Windows 95 and carried on through future Windows generations is integration with the Internet. When Windows 95 was originally released,

Microsoft did not support Internet connectivity, but by 1997, Microsoft integrated Internet access through its **Web browser**, Internet Explorer, and the ability to share computer resources over the Internet into its operating systems.

 NOTE The United States Department of Justice, a number of states, and Microsoft were involved in litigation over several points, including the integration of the Internet Explorer Web browser into the OS. Almost all of these lawsuits have been settled.

In terms of communications, Windows 95 was a giant leap forward. With the growing demand for access to the Internet and corporate networks over telephone lines, Microsoft included **dial-up networking (DUN)** as part of Windows 95. DUN could be used not only to make connections via telephone and modem to remote networks or computers, but also to set up a Windows 95 computer as a **DUN server**, to answer telephone lines, authenticate the callers, and give them access to shared resources on the computer. Windows 95 also offered built-in fax support.

Windows 98/Me

Windows 98 and its slightly newer sibling, Windows Millennium Edition (Me) are similar to Windows 95 in many ways. They run on similar computers and provide roughly the same capabilities. Windows Me includes all Windows 98 features, but expands multimedia and networking capabilities.

Windows 98

The Windows 98 user interface is slightly different from Windows 95, especially with the Web interface settings intrinsic to Windows 98 (see Figure 2-4).

Some of the changes from Windows 95 to Windows 98 include:

- Expanded PnP support
- Automatic registry checks and repairs
- Advanced power management features
- Support for new hardware standards such as Universal Serial Bus (USB)
- Improved cooperative multitasking for 16-bit applications
- Greater integration of Internet and networking features
- Extended multimedia support

- Expanded support for high-speed networking
- Ability to perform upgrades over the Internet

Figure 2-4   Windows 98 desktop

Windows 98 is a 32-bit operating system, much like Windows 95. PnP support is greatly expanded, and advanced **power management** features are included. These features make it possible to power down parts of the hardware that are not being used to conserve energy. This is especially important for users of battery-operated laptop computers. Windows 98 also supports newer hardware standards, such as **Universal Serial Bus (USB)**, a relatively high-speed input/output port, and updated standards for multimedia, data storage, and networking.

NOTE   USB is a bus standard that enables you to attach all types of devices—keyboards, cameras, pointing devices, telephones, tape drives, and flash memory, for example—to one bus port on a computer. Up to 127 devices can be attached to one port, and it is not necessary to power off the computer when you attach a device. USB was developed to replace the traditional serial and parallel bus technologies on computers.

In Windows 98, it is possible to put shortcuts to Internet objects right on the desktop through the use of ActiveX technology, and these objects can even be made to update automatically. In addition, Windows 98 can be updated over the Internet. The system can automatically check whether updates are available online, and if they are, it can download and install them, either with or without user intervention. Windows 98 includes more support for multimedia applications, ranging from video conferencing to high-end video production.

Windows Millennium Edition (Me)

Windows Millennium Edition (Me) is the last in the 95/98 track of Windows operating systems that uses cooperative multitasking for 16-bit applications, preemptive multitasking for 32-bit applications, and retains substantial capability to run older 16-bit MS-DOS and Windows software. It is also the last in the line of Windows operating systems that gives software applications direct access to hardware, without going through the operating system kernel.

Windows Me was developed for home computer users, not office or professional users, and it implements applications that appeal to home users better than Windows 95 or 98. These applications include playing music, storing family photos, playing games, and accessing the Internet. Windows Me also makes it easier to connect all kinds of new devices to a computer, such as Internet cameras, digital cameras, scanners, read/write CD-ROM drives, TV converters, and specialized printers for color photo reproduction.

TIP   Windows 98/Me is still found on many home PCs, portable computers, and general-purpose office desktop computers. Some small companies still use Windows 98/Me to run their entire operations, including all of the networking functions needed via a peer-to-peer workgroup. The limitation in using Windows 98/Me on a corporate network is that there can be problems in getting it to communicate with a Windows NT, Windows 2000, or Windows Server 2003 domain—so such computers may have to be used as standalone computers that cannot fully communicate with others.

Windows Me enhances support for infrared devices, such as **Infrared Data Association (IrDA)** support, and implements the enhanced PnP standard, called **Universal Plug and Play (UPnP)**. UPnP provides better discovery of new devices, such as TVs and cameras that can be connected to a computer. Also, with UPnP, modern devices can be shown through the My Network Places icon on the Windows desktop, so that the devices can be managed using a Web page type of interface.

Windows Me also comes with better networking capabilities for home use, including the Connection Manager, which is used to manage and create network and dial-up connections, similar to the Connection Manager used in Windows 2000 (discussed later in this chapter).

Windows NT

While Microsoft was developing the Windows line of operating systems to run on the lower end of IBM PC hardware, it also developed a high-end operating system referred to as Windows New Technology, or Windows NT. Over the course of its development, Windows NT has supported the IBM PC architecture, the DEC Alpha architecture, and for a while, the PowerPC architecture as each of these hardware platforms gained its time in the industry spotlight. The idea was to make an operating system that could be used on some very powerful computers, with a choice of RISC or CISC processor architecture. The support for various system architectures has shifted over the years, but support for the high-end IBM PC architecture and the DEC Alpha architecture has been a constant for Windows NT.

Windows NT was initially an extension to IBM's high-end operating system, OS/2, and was intended to support the emerging client/server networking environment. As client/server applications gained popularity, Windows NT development and the successive operating systems in the NT line, Windows 2000, Windows XP, and Windows Server 2003 have experienced wide reception.

Windows NT, as is true of most operating systems, has gone through many iterations. You will find that there are very few installations of Windows NT prior to version 3.51 still in use because these versions were not stable or reliable. Windows NT 4.0 was successful, and today most installations have evolved or are evolving to Windows 2000, Windows XP, or Windows Server 2003.

Windows NT 4.0 looks and feels a lot like Windows 95 or Windows 98. Many of the GUI elements are the same, such as the desktop, Windows Explorer, and the taskbar with the Start menu, as shown in Figure 2-5.

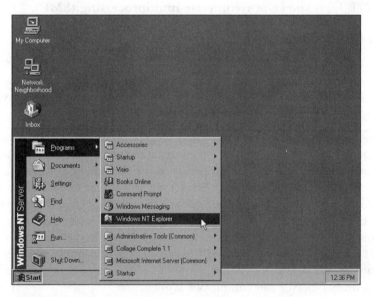

Figure 2-5   Windows NT Server desktop

One very significant difference between Windows 95/98 and Windows NT is that the operating system kernel in Windows NT runs in **privileged mode**, which protects it from problems created by a malfunctioning program or process. Privileged mode gives the operating system an extra level of security from intruders, and prevents system crashes due to out-of-control applications. Privileged mode is a protected area in Windows NT from which the operating system kernel or program code runs. Direct access to the computer's memory or hardware is allowed from this mode. Application program threads that need to access memory and hardware issue a request to an operating system service, rather than to a direct memory or hardware instruction.

Another significant improvement in Windows NT is the way it handles multitasking. Windows NT uses preemptive multitasking rather than cooperative multitasking. The advantage of preemptive multitasking is that the operating system is tightly in control of what the system will do at what time, which results in a much more predictable performance. Because Windows NT was built as a 32-bit operating system from the ground up, and the requirement to run all legacy 16-bit applications was set aside, Windows NT can significantly outperform Windows 95 and 98 running 32-bit applications. Besides preemptive multitasking, Windows NT 4.0 employs multithreading.

The performance comes at a price. Windows NT requires a faster CPU and more memory and disk space to run successfully, but it makes much better use of the resources available. Windows NT 4.0 can also function well with more than one CPU. Because the operating system is in tight control of how the resources in the computer are allocated to various processes, Windows NT Workstation can use up to two CPUs and Windows NT Server can use up to four. The system architecture that is used to perform this form of multiprocessing under Windows NT 4.0 is known as **symmetric multiprocessing (SMP)**.

NT Server and NT Workstation

Windows NT is offered in two versions: Windows NT Workstation and Windows NT Server. Windows NT Workstation is a high-end, stable, and secure workstation/client operating system. Windows NT Server is designed as a multiuser server operating system for access over a network.

In Windows NT Workstation, the kernel is optimized for maximum performance when used to run interactive applications, such as screen updates and fast retrieval and storage of data in memory and on disk. In the NT Server edition, the kernel is optimized to provide maximum network and disk performance. Everything the server kernel does is aimed at serving clients' requests rapidly. This is done at the expense of speed in the user interface and other interactive functions. The kernel of the Windows NT Server version provides a few extra functions that are not available in the NT Workstation kernel. All features of the NT Workstation kernel are included in the NT Server kernel. As a result, you can run any software that runs on Windows NT Workstation on Windows NT Server, but not all software that runs on NT Server can run on NT Workstation.

 One important difference between Windows NT Server and Windows NT Workstation is the number of users who can simultaneously connect to these multiuser systems. With enough processor and system power, up to 15,000 **NOTE** users (theoretically) can connect to Windows NT Server at the same time. Only up to 10 simultaneous users can feasibly connect to Windows NT Workstation.

2

The registry, mentioned earlier in the Windows 95 and Windows 98 sections, plays an equally important role in Windows NT. It is used as the central repository for configuration, hardware, software, and user information.

Networking Support

The networking features in Windows NT are more powerful than in Windows 95 or 98 because Windows NT is designed as a multiuser system. Windows NT supports network connectivity protocols that are compatible with IBM mainframes, UNIX computers, Macintosh computers, all Windows-based computers, Novell NetWare servers, and others. It also supports high-speed networking connectivity and remote access over telephone lines or the Internet.

Security

Security is a significant feature of Windows NT. The operating system requires the user to log on and be authenticated by submitting a username and password to gain access to the computer. This authentication process is stronger than that of Windows 3.x, 95, or 98. In fact, Windows NT 4.0 Server has a C2 top-secret security rating from the United States government. The C2 rating means that the Windows NT Server network operating system provides security at many levels, including the following:

- File and folder protection
- User accounts and passwords
- File, folder, and account auditing
- File server access protection on a network
- File server management controls

If an operating system running Windows 95 or 98, for example, is part of a Windows NT network that uses the domain system, these computers are able to use a similar kind of security to protect their resources. The **domain** is an integral part of the Windows NT security model. In every domain there is one Primary Domain Controller (PDC). The PDC computer is responsible for keeping all usernames and passwords for all users who may want to contact the domain. Any other server that is part of the domain can request password and permission information from this PDC. This is convenient when there are many servers and users that must be tracked. In addition to user and password information, the PDC can also contain system policies, which provide general information on what certain users are and are not allowed to do on certain computers on the network, down to what function and features of the user interface should be enabled. The array of network services a computer running Windows NT can provide, using optional software, extends to central database management and Internet services.

Another networking feature of Windows NT is the **Remote Access Service (RAS)**. Although computers running Windows 95 and 98 can be used as dial-up hosts (computers that can be accessed via dial-up phone lines), security is limited because the client has access to any resources to which that computer has access. Through Windows NT RAS, the user information in a PDC can be used to grant or deny various levels of network access. This is a very powerful tool for allowing limited remote access to the resources available on the network. Remote access is a feature that enables workers to telecommute or work while traveling.

Windows 2000

Built on the Windows NT technology, Windows 2000 is a more robust operating system than Windows 95, 98, or NT. The operating system represented a significant rewrite of the Windows NT kernel, and runs about 30 percent faster than Windows NT. Like Windows 95, 98, and NT, you can use desktop features such as My Computer, and you can run programs from the Start button. Figure 2-6 illustrates the Windows 2000 desktop. Also, like its Windows NT predecessor, Windows 2000 uses preemptive multitasking, multithreading, and the kernel runs in the privileged mode.

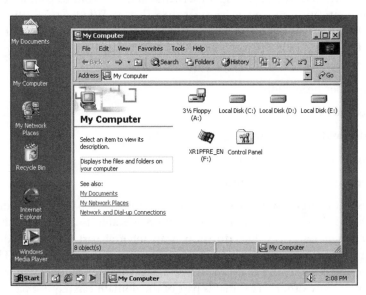

Figure 2-6   Windows 2000 desktop

Windows 2000 has more advanced networking support than Windows NT and it supports new networking technologies, such as **virtual private networks (VPNs)**. A VPN is a private network that is like a tunnel through a larger network—such as the Internet, an enterprise network, or both—that is restricted only to designated member clients.

People who have experience troubleshooting problems with mismatched drivers, or who have overwritten portions of the operating system in previous versions of Windows, will like the built-in protection of the core operating system files and driver-signing features of Windows 2000. Windows 2000 keeps a copy of operating system files in a safe place, so if a critical file is overwritten or deleted, the operating system automatically replaces it. **Driver signing** means that you can set up all drivers so that they cannot be inadvertently overwritten by earlier driver versions, and only certified versions of drivers can be installed.

New features in Windows 2000 include:

- *Active Directory*: **Active Directory** is a database that is used to store information about resources such as user accounts, computers, and printers; and it groups resources at different levels (hierarchies) for local and universal management. These groupings are called containers because they are like storage bins that can hold network resources and other bins at lower levels. Active Directory also provides a centralized means to quickly find a specific resource through indexing. Active Directory is managed by a Windows 2000 server, but its resources are used by both Windows 2000 Server and Professional.

- *Distributed network architecture*: Windows 2000 offers new ways to distribute network and management resources to match the needs of all types of networks. In Windows 2000 Server, multiple servers can be designated as domain controllers, each containing a copy of Active Directory and able to verify a user who wants to log on to the network. This is an important change from Windows NT Server 4.0, in which one server, the PDC, maintains the master copy of account and security information; and one or more servers, called backup domain controllers (BDC), keep copies of this information as a backup.

- *Kerberos security*: **Kerberos** is a security system that enables two parties on an open network to communicate without interception by an intruder. Kerberos works through a special communications protocol that enables a client to initiate contact with a server and request secure communication. The server responds by providing an encryption key that is unique to that communication session, and it does so by using a protected communication called a ticket. Kerberos is supported by Windows 2000 Server and Professional versions.

- *IntelliMirror*: IntelliMirror is a concept built into the combined use of Windows 2000 Server and Windows 2000 Professional. It is intended to enable Windows 2000 Professional clients to access the same desktop settings, applications, and data from wherever they access the network, or even if they are not on the network. IntelliMirror also uses information in Active Directory to ensure that consistent security and group policies apply to the client, and that the client's software is upgraded or removed on the basis of a central management scheme.

- *International language compatibility*: Windows 2000 supports more languages and language capabilities than previous versions of Windows, including Hindi, Chinese, and multiple versions of English. This is an important feature because servers are used all over the world.

Windows 2000 Server and Windows 2000 Professional

Microsoft offers versions of Windows 2000 designed for server and workstation implementations. The basic server version is called Windows 2000 Server, and Windows 2000 Professional is designed for workstations. When it introduced Windows 2000, Microsoft's overall goal was to combine Windows 2000 Server and Windows 2000 Professional on a server-based network to achieve a lower **total cost of ownership (TCO)**. The TCO is the total cost of owning a network, including hardware, software, training, maintenance, and user support costs. Windows 2000 Professional is intended as a reliable, easy-to-configure, workstation operating system to be used in a business or professional environment. Recognizing that professionals are highly mobile, Windows 2000 Professional is designed to work equally well on a desktop computer or a notebook computer. Windows 2000 Server is intended to play a key management role on the network by administering Active Directory and a multitude of network services. Active Directory is also used to manage domains in Windows 2000. By combining Windows 2000 Professional workstations and Windows 2000 Server on the same network, along with Active Directory, it is possible to centralize software updates and workstation configuration via a server.

Windows 2000 Server supports up to four processors, while Windows 2000 Professional supports up to two. Windows 2000 Server also offers more services and user connectivity options that are appropriate for a server instead of a workstation. These services include the following:

- The capability to handle virtually unlimited numbers of users simultaneously (depending on the hardware platform; Windows 2000 Professional is designed optimally for only 10 simultaneous users)
- Active Directory management
- Network management
- Web-based management services
- Network-wide security management
- Network storage management
- Remote network access, network-wide communications services, and high-speed network connectivity
- Application services management
- Network printer management through Active Directory

Windows 2000 Server, Advanced Server, and Datacenter Server

Windows 2000 Server is divided into three different products to match the network application: Windows 2000 Server, Windows 2000 Advanced Server, and Windows 2000 Datacenter Server. Windows 2000 Server provides a comprehensive set of server and Web services for up to 4 processor systems, and supports up to 4 GB of RAM. Windows 2000 Advanced Server is intended for high-end enterprise networks that require up to 8 processor servers, clustered servers, or both. **Clustering** is a technique in which two or more servers are linked to equally share the server processor load, server storage, and other server resources (see Figure 2-7). Windows 2000 Advanced Server also has the ability to handle up to 8 GB of RAM. Windows 2000 Datacenter is targeted for large database and data manipulation services. The Datacenter version supports 64 GB of RAM, clustering, and individual servers with up to 32 processors.

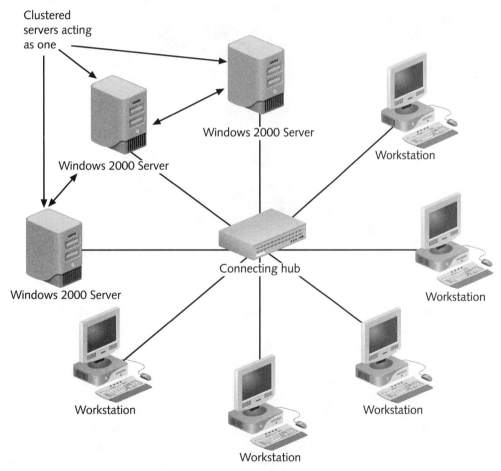

Figure 2-7   Server clustering

Windows XP and Windows Server 2003

Windows 2000 has evolved into two products, both containing the core elements of the Windows 2000 kernel: Windows XP and Windows Server 2003. Windows XP is the desktop version of the new operating system, while Windows Server 2003 is the server version. Both of these operating systems offer a new desktop GUI, as shown in Figure 2-8. Besides having a new GUI, the Windows XP and Windows Server 2003 desktop removes the clutter of icons by incorporating more functions into the Start menu. Try Hands-on Project 2-4 to compare the Windows XP desktop to that of Windows 95/98 to see how the desktop has evolved.

Figure 2-8   Windows XP desktop

Besides the new GUI, Windows XP and Windows Server 2003 offer more capabilities than Windows 2000 for keeping photo albums, playing music, running video and audio files, playing games, and using other multimedia applications. Windows XP and Windows Server 2003 also offer better Internet security through a built-in firewall and the ability to remotely control the computer over an Internet connection via a tool called Remote Desktop. Remote Desktop is designed to be secure so that the computer being controlled must first grant access. Another new feature of the Windows XP operating system is that you must **activate** it after installation by contacting Microsoft for an activation code. The activation code is linked to a particular computer on which the operating system resides. If the operating system is moved to another computer, it is necessary to contact Microsoft to obtain a new activation code for that computer. The activation code is another mechanism, besides the key code, that is entered during installation to help ensure that software is not pirated.

Windows XP Versions

Windows XP comes in several versions. These include Windows XP Home, Windows XP Professional, Windows XP Tablet PC, Windows XP Media Center, and Windows XP 64-Bit.

Windows XP Home and Professional Editions

Windows XP, which stands for "Windows Experience," originally came in two versions: Windows XP Professional and Windows XP Home Edition. Windows XP Professional is the upgrade to Windows 2000 Professional, and is intended for office and professional use. This version of Windows XP has the ability to create accounts for different users who might use the operating system. Also, Windows XP Professional, like Windows 2000 Professional, can be used as a small server for up to 10 users. Windows XP Home Edition is meant as the next upgrade from Windows Me, and is a scaled-down version of Windows XP Professional. For example, user accounts cannot be created in Windows XP Home Edition, nor is it designed to support 10 simultaneous users. Another difference is that Windows XP Professional can run on computers using up to two processors and on 64-bit Itanium computers, whereas Windows XP Home Edition runs only on 32-bit single-processor computers.

One change that is exclusive to Windows XP is a different look and feel for the Control Panel (Figure 2-9). In previous versions of Windows, the Control Panel consisted of icons or applets. In Windows XP, the Control Panel is designed to reflect the user's experience of a particular setting, such as the "appearance and themes" of the desktop, which includes settings such as font, background, screensaver, and so on.

Figure 2-9   Windows XP Professional Control Panel

TIP

Even though there is a new interface, users who are familiar with Windows 2000, and prefer its interface, can simulate it in Windows XP and Windows Server 2003 by selecting the Classic view option. To select Classic view, go to the Control Panel and select Switch to Classic View in the left panel. If your choice is Switch to Category View, you are already using the Classic view. You can switch back and forth between views by clicking these entries.

A much improved feature of Windows XP is the help and support documentation. This documentation includes articles to help you become familiar with the new Windows XP desktop, and there are many "Troubleshooter" articles that can help users solve problems. There are options to help you reach others for assistance, and there is a "Do you know?" section that contains new articles automatically updated daily via the Internet, which provides information about new releases and service packs. Try Hands-on Project 2-5 to practice using Windows XP help and support documentation.

Programs written for Windows 95 and earlier operating systems may not run in Windows XP without using its Program Compatibility Wizard. In the Program Compatibility Wizard, you first select the program that you want to run, and then select the operating system, such as Windows 95, that the program is designed to run under. The operating system options that are available in the Program Compatibility Wizard are shown in Figure 2-10. Hands-on Project 2-6 enables you to practice using the Program Compatibility Wizard.

Figure 2-10   Windows XP Program Compatibility Wizard

Windows XP Tablet PC Edition

Windows XP Tablet PC Edition is an operating system for tablet PCs, small portable computers that use speech and pen capabilities and often wireless communications. This operating system is a superset of Windows XP Professional and thus all of the Windows XP compatible application software will run on the Tablet PC Edition. Additional features used for pen-based personal computing are included.

New features available in the Windows XP Tablet PC Edition include:

- *Customization*: Allows you to set up your Tablet PC for left or right handed use, calibrate the pen, and program the buttons for a specific task.

- *Tablet PC Input Panel*: One can write notes from a class or meeting on the screen and then save these notes in either their own handwriting or change them into text and then save them.

- *Microsoft Windows Journal*: A note-taking utility that lets you capture the notes, drawings, doodles, etc., one would normally write on paper. You can then organize these notes and even search through them to find a reference you are looking for in the handwritten document.

NOTE Windows XP Tablet PC Edition runs on tablet PCs from a variety of manufacturers. Point your browser to *www.microsoft.com/windowsxp/tabletpc/* and search for evaluation and tours to view a tour of vendors that currently manufacture a tablet PC.

Windows XP Media Center Edition

Windows XP Media Center Edition is also a superset of Windows XP Professional and allows the user to control all digital media with a single remote control. These include DVD movies, photos, music, videos, radio, and live television.

A few of the enhancements included with XP Media Center include:

- *Set-top box Learning Mode*: Configure the system to work with your set-top box.

- *Build and play your digital music library*: Copy music from CDs to your PC hard drive.

- *View and share your digital pictures*

- *Internet and FM radio*: Skip forward, pause, and replay.

- *Display Calibration Wizard*: Set up the best picture on monitors, flat panels, plasma displays, and standard cathode-ray tubes (CRTs).

Windows XP 64-Bit Edition

Windows XP 64-Bit Edition runs on the Intel Itanium processors. The target audience is workstation users who need large amounts of memory and superior mathematical calculation capabilities. Hewlett-Packard sells an Itanium 2 workstation with Windows XP 64-Bit

Edition preloaded. This 64–Bit Edition supports 16 GB of RAM and up to 8 TB of virtual memory and will run 32-bit applications unmodified.

Windows Server 2003

Windows Server 2003 comes in four versions, which are similar to the versions that are available for Windows 2000 Server: Standard Edition, Enterprise Edition, Datacenter Edition, and Web Edition. An upgrade from Windows 2000, Windows Server 2003 contains new features that include:

- The GUI interface used with Windows XP.
- Improvements for faster network logon authentication through Active Directory.
- Several hundred new group policies that can be set to manage user workstations via Active Directory.
- New tools for managing server resources.
- Ability to run on 64-bit Itanium processors.
- Remote server management through the Remote Desktop tool.
- Enhanced ability for users to run programs on the server, through Microsoft Terminal Services. (Terminal Services were introduced as a service pack enhancement to Windows NT and perfected in Windows 2000.)
- Runtime code for the Windows .NET development environment to run applications through the Internet on all types of devices.

Microsoft has listened to the demands for tighter security in their operating systems. With Windows Server 2003, they have taken a huge step in this direction. After the initial installation, you must set up the server functions manually, which is a big change from previous versions of the operating system where many functions were set up as the default. In Windows Server 2003 you set up only the functions you want to use. (Operating system installation is covered in Chapter 4.)

Another new feature in Windows Server 2003 is the addition of digital rights management. This is accomplished through Windows **Rights Management Services (RMS)** which allows companies to secure their documents from copying, forwarding, and printing. Microsoft Office 2003 works hand in hand with Windows Server 2003 to accomplish this.

Another feature developed in Windows Server 2003 is called the **common language runtime (CLR)**. This verifies code before it is run and monitors memory to clean up any leakage before it becomes a problem.

Windows Server 2003 also makes configuring the server for various roles much easier, with the Configure Your Server Wizard. This wizard allows the server to be configured to defined roles, such as file server, print server, application server, and mail server. You answer questions and then the role is installed automatically. To access the wizard, go to the Start Menu, click Administrator Tools, and then Configure Your Server Wizard. Figure 2-11 shows the screen where you select the role you want to install.

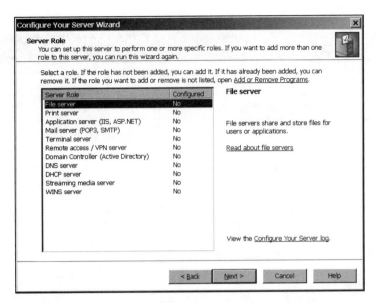

Figure 2-11   Configure Your Server Wizard

UNIX System V Release 4

The UNIX operating system comes in many different formats. Of all the operating systems covered in this book, it is the oldest, most diverse, and most complicated. The reason for this is that one manufacturer does not have the exclusive license for UNIX. After UNIX was developed at AT&T, the company never formally licensed the kernel to prevent others from using it and implementing their own specialized utilities. AT&T used the operating system within the company and made the source code available outside the company. The end result is that there are many UNIX versions with many diverse utilities.

Versions of UNIX today adhere to one of the two main design standards, the **Berkeley Software Distribution (BSD)** standard or the **System V Release 4 (SVR4)** standard. Examples of BSD-style UNIX include the freely available NetBSD and FreeBSD operating systems, as well as the commercially available BSDi UNIX. SVR4 versions include freely available versions of Linux, and commercial versions such as Sun Microsystems Solaris and SCO UNIX. All UNIX systems include security features. Table 2-3 lists several versions of UNIX along with the manufacturer and origin. It also includes Web addresses to check for additional information.

This book uses Linux for its UNIX examples; Linux is a version of UNIX that is available free of charge, but some enhanced versions of Linux must be purchased. Linux is considered to be "UNIX-like" because the kernel is new code based on standards that were developed after UNIX originally came out. Linux runs on Intel-based and PowerPC computers.

Table 2-3   UNIX versions

Version	Manufacturer/Source	Origin	Web Addresses
AIX	IBM	A combination of SVR4 and BSD	*www.ibm.org* or *www-1.ibm.com/servers/aix*
Digital Equipment UNIX (previously called Ultrix)	HP/Compaq/Digital	**BSD**	*www.hp.com,* *www.compaq.com,* or *www.tru64unix.compaq.com*
FreeBSD	The FreeBSD Project	BSD	*www.freebsd.org*
Hewlett-Packard UNIX (HP-UX)	Hewlett-Packard	SVR4	*www.hp.com*
HURD	GNU	BSD	*www.gnu.org/software/hurd/hurd.html*
IRIX	Silicon Graphics	SVR4	*www.sgi.com*
Linux	There are several sources, but Red Hat is one popular commercial source	SVR4	*www.linux.org* or *www.redhat.com*
Mac OS X	Apple Computers	BSD	*www.apple.com*
NetBSD	The NetBSD Project	BSD	*www.netbsd.org*
OpenBSD	The OpenBSD Project	BSD	*www.openbsd.org*
Red Hat Enterprise Linux 3.0	Red Hat	SVR4	*www.redhat.com*
SINUX	Siemens Nixdorf	BSD	*www.siemens.com*
Solaris	Sun Microsystems	BSD	*www.sun.com*
SunOS	Sun Microsystems	BSD-prior to 5.x SVR4-ver. 5.x	*www.sun.com*
SuSE Linux	SuSE has been acquired by Novell	SVR4	*www.suse.com*
Turbolinux	Turbolinux, Inc.	SVR4	*www.turbolinux.com*
Tru64	HP/Compaq/Digital	BSD	*www.tru64unix.compaq.com*
UnixWare	Caldera International	SVR4	*www.caldera.com*

There are a number of Linux versions available worldwide. Red Hat Linux is probably the most well known in the United States, but is also popular worldwide. SuSE Linux is another popular product, especially in Europe. Their product comes in both a professional and

2

personal version. Turbolinux is the leading Linux distributor in the Asian-Pacific region. They provide workstation, desktop, and server versions of their product.

Because UNIX comes in such a wide variety of implementations, it runs on almost any hardware. There are UNIX versions available for all hardware mentioned up to this point. For this reason, it is hard to define exactly what specifications a platform should meet to run UNIX.

UNIX is a true multitasking, multiuser operating system. This means, as explained before, that it has the ability to fully serve all the computing needs of multiple users running multiple applications at the same time. Depending on the hardware, a single UNIX computer can support from 1 to more than 1000 users.

After startup, UNIX typically presents you with a request for a logon, or username, followed by a request for a password. The username and password you provide determine what privileges you will be granted on the system. When your identity has been verified, you are presented with a shell, that is, the user interface. This is another point where UNIX is substantially different from most other operating systems: by default, most UNIX versions come with several different shells, and it is up to the user to pick the shell they wish to use. Different shells provide you with different levels of functionality, but all of the shells function much like the shell in MS-DOS, with a series of built-in commands and the ability to call **external commands** (operating system commands that are stored in a separate program file on disk) and application programs by simply typing commands at the command line.

The most popular UNIX shells are the Bourne shell (sh) and its cousin the Bourne Again shell (bash), and a version of the Bourne shell in which some of the commands are formatted to be similar to the C programming language, called the C shell (csh). Overall, these shells function in the same way: you get a prompt, you type a command, and they do what you ask. When you are done with the shell, you can exit from it by using the *exit* command. Typically, this returns you to the logon prompt. Try Hands-on Project 2-7 to determine the UNIX shell you are using.

Many versions of UNIX can also provide you with a GUI. The most popular interface is the X11 Window System, known commonly as X Window. **X Window** is similar to other windowed interfaces. A unique feature of X Window is that it is network enabled. Using an X terminal, it is possible to run X Window and all the application programs on a remote UNIX computer, and remotely interact with your applications. One UNIX system can support many X terminals and users. X Window is, however, an optional part of many UNIX versions. Just as there are many different UNIX versions, there are also many different versions of X Window. Linux generally uses a version called Xfree that can be obtained for free. X Window, by default, does not include programs like Windows Explorer for managing files, or the Windows-based Start menu for starting programs, but many utilities are available to provide file and application management.

Red Hat Enterprise Linux 3.0, for example, offers an X Window type GUI interface called GNOME (see Figure 2-12), which can be installed or omitted. Even when GNOME is installed, you can still execute regular Linux commands by starting the terminal emulation program window shown in Figure 2-13. To start the terminal emulation program in Red Hat Enterprise Linux 3.0 for instance, click the icon on the taskbar at the bottom of the GNOME interface that resembles a computer monitor. Hands–on Project 2-8 enables you to learn more about the Red Hat Enterprise Linux 3.0 GNOME interface.

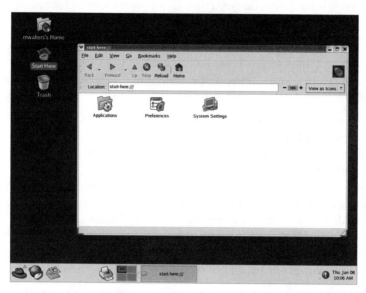

Figure 2-12   Linux GUI desktop

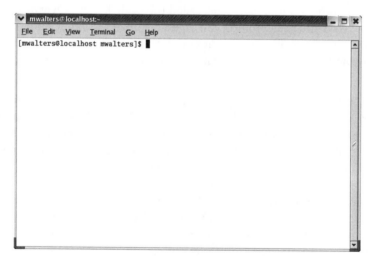

Figure 2-13   Linux terminal emulation window

2

All networking functions in UNIX are based on the BSD networking model, which provides support for the Transmission Control Protocol/Internet Protocol (TCP/IP). This is the standard protocol in use on the Internet, and as such, UNIX computers are qualified to provide numerous Internet services (network protocols are discussed later in this book). The standard UNIX operating system does not provide many network functions. Most of these functions are provided by add-ons. The standard functions include login services, allowing a user to connect to the UNIX computer from another remote computer on the network; file transfers through the File Transfer Protocol (FTP); and some form of e-mail service, usually the Simple Mail Transfer Protocol (SMTP). Other services can be standard as well. In Linux, additional standard services include the Network File System (NFS), and support for other network systems such as those used by Microsoft, Apple, and Novell. It is also possible to add modules to UNIX to provide other services, such as World Wide Web (WWW) service.

The security model in the UNIX operating system made it an early system of choice for providing many Internet functions, such as Internet server and firewall. It is possible to turn services on and off at the user's desire, and it is also possible to run services in ways that do not result in security issues for other services on the computer. Windows 2000 Server and Windows Server 2003 also use TCP/IP by default and have implemented many of the security features found in UNIX. This makes them competitive with UNIX as Internet and Web servers.

In addition to their roles as Internet server and firewalls, UNIX computers are often used as database or application servers that many users can access at the same time. You will also find UNIX computers used for technical design and industrial control applications.

Most versions of UNIX come with a line editor, a text editor, or both. A **line editor** is an editor that is used to create text a line at a time. Line editors are often used to create scripts, programs in which each line executes a specific command. A text editor enables you to edit text in a full-screen mode.

One reason that UNIX is so popular is that it is compatible with an extensive range of programming tools, particularly program compilers and interpreters, which means that you can create nearly any kind of software application. UNIX is also compatible with many popular databases, such as Oracle and Informix. With the combined power of programming languages and databases, UNIX systems are frequently used for administrative computing, such as accounting systems, and for all kinds of scientific applications.

Mac OS

Apple Computer has always had a unique approach to operating systems. Its Macintosh line of personal computers revolutionized the world of operating systems with its all-graphical user interface and an all-graphical shell. Although there are subtle differences in the way Mac OS functions, you will see many similarities between it and Microsoft Windows, which many would say was designed to mimic the look and feel of the Mac OS. Mac OS X is a significant update of the Mac OS as it is now based on UNIX. The Mac OS X desktop is shown in Figure 2-14. In the figure, you see a folder for Mac OS 9. This folder contains applications that require Mac OS 9 to run. Mac OS 9 comes bundled with Mac OS X.

Figure 2-14 Max OS X desktop

The hardware architecture of the Mac OS is substantially different from the architecture used on most other platforms, especially because many of the graphical functions are included in the basic input/output system (BIOS) functions, located in the read-only memory (ROM) of the hardware. (Apple calls this "firmware.") Beginning with System 7.1, Apple began using system enabler files that allowed the previous version of the operating system to support new hardware. When the next version of the operating system was released, support for the most recent Macs was included so the enabler file was no longer needed for that model. The hardware architecture needed to run Mac OS is very dependent on the version of the operating system. If you run version 7.0, you could be using any Macintosh hardware architecture, except for the PowerPC platform, which is supported as of version 7.5. If you are running the newest generation of hardware (G5), you will want to run Mac OS X. Apple has always made the hardware and software closely interconnected, which results in strict requirements when it comes to operating system/ hardware coordination.

NOTE

One significant difference between the Mac OS and other operating systems covered in this chapter is that only one company makes hardware capable of running Mac OS, and that company is Apple. A few years back, Apple licensed Power Computing, Motorola, and other companies to make Mac OS-compatible hardware, but that is no longer the case.

Versions of Mac OS prior to 8.0 were not multitasking; they were essentially task switching with the aid of MultiFinder. In Mac OS version 8.0 and newer, multitasking is a standard feature of the operating system that is available to all applications. When more than one application is active, the CPU resources are shared among them.

The network functions in Mac OS are fairly evolved. Peer-to-peer networking has been a standard feature of the Mac OS since its inception. The protocol used is called AppleTalk, which originated in the Macintosh world. The nice thing about AppleTalk is that it has remained compatible as new Mac OS versions arrived, and any Mac can be networked to any other Mac by simply plugging in a few cables and configuring some software. Apple implemented LocalTalk networking hardware with every Macintosh printer port, which provides a combination networking and serial solution in one inexpensive interface. This is, to our knowledge, the only hardware architecture and operating system combination that has consistently had these features. Through the use of optional clients, or through servers that can provide AppleTalk-compatible services, many Macintoshes can also be networked easily to other networks.

 Not all Macintosh hardware is equipped with standard network hardware. Many older computers only have LocalTalk, a proprietary Apple hardware standard. For these computers to be able to network with other systems, additional hardware is needed.

NOTE

Mac OS was always meant to be a desktop operating system, and there are no extended security features to keep users from getting access to files on the local computers. For networking, Mac OS allows the user to generate user profiles. A user can be given a username and a password. Based on this combination, a user may access some of the resources made available on the network. The Mac OS can use its networking features to share printer and disk resources. In version 8.x and later, there are extensions that will let the Macintosh share resources using protocols other than AppleTalk, including TCP/IP, the standard Internet protocol, enabling greater flexibility in how Macs can be networked.

Throughout its history, the Mac OS has been known for its support of graphics, video, and sound capabilities. In this respect, Mac OS has been ahead of the industry. Because Apple has had tight control over both the Macintosh hardware architecture and operating system, and it chose to actively enhance the audiovisual functions of both hardware and software, you will find that the Mac and the Mac OS are favored by people in the graphics, sound, and video fields. Macintosh computers are used in many different environments, especially those that deal with the creative process. The Mac font management and ColorSync color matching technologies have endeared it to graphic arts and prepress professionals, while QuickTime has made the Mac popular for multimedia sound and video production. You will also find many Macs in the educational environment. The home computer market has a small but substantial share of computers running Mac OS. Apple PowerBook notebook computers continue to be popular, even in organizations that have settled primarily on the Windows-Intel platform.

Mac OS 9.x introduces features for better hardware and Internet access. For example, version 9.1 introduces a Printer Sharing panel to manage and share a USB printer on a network (try Hands-on Project 2-9). There is a capability to connect to another computer over the Internet by using the Point-to-Point Protocol (PPP), a network communications protocol designed for remote communications (you will learn more about protocols later in this book). Mac OS also has Personal Web Sharing for creating a Web page that others can access over the Internet, or through a private network. Also, Mac OS 9.x includes a runtime execution tool for running Java applets from the Finder tool. For users who are connected to a network, there is the Network Assist Client tool that is used by network administrators to control the computer.

Mac OS X

Mac OS X, where X means version 10, is a significant update of the Mac OS because it sports the "Aqua" interface (try Hands-on Project 2-10). One of the main changes for users of Mac OS 9.x and earlier is that some programs and utilities were replaced. The Apple menu can no longer be customized as in the past. New menu features include System Preferences, which is similar to the Control Panel on Windows systems. System Preferences enables you to set functions such as the time and date, display settings, startup functions, energy saving functions, and network functions. The Dock function can now be customized through the System Preferences tool for the applications you wish to include. Through Dock, you can start multiple applications, and switch between them in a multitasking environment.

Out of the box, Mac OS X is configured so that different users can access the operating system in their own workspaces, without affecting other users. If one user wants to log out so that another user can access Mac OS X, the first user can now select the new Log Out option from the Apple menu, instead of turning off the computer and then rebooting.

Many windows in Mac OS X now can be customized so that their contents appear in columns, similar to Windows-based systems. Also, the title bar in a window displays buttons to close, minimize, or maximize (zone) that window. Throughout each window, the icons have a modern look. Further, some windows have "drawers" that slide out like file cabinet drawers to offer information.

Internet connectivity is enhanced in Mac OS X through the Internet Connect tool, which performs functions that users of previous Mac OS versions associated with the Remote Access tool. Internet Connect enables you to set up an Internet connection and monitor the status of a connection. Internet applications include the Mail application, from Apple, used for e-mail; and the Internet Explorer application, a Web browser from Microsoft.

Mac OS X Version 10.3 Panther

Mac OS X version 10.3 Panther is the next evolution of the Mac OS X operating system. It includes a completely new Finder, new mail application, and faster user switching to name just a few features. A neat feature for the home user is iChat AV, which provides personal video conferencing where one can have video conversations with another Mac user in full screen video. It also supports voice calls over a 56k modem.

NetWare

NetWare is a network operating system that has evolved steadily since the days in the late 1970s when it was a typical time-sharing system to NetWare 6.5, the full-service server operating system released in 2003.

From the Trenches...

When Novell NetWare was first becoming a popular network operating system (NOS), two system engineers set up Novell servers for seven branch offices. The system engineers wanted to provide each of the seven sites with detailed instructions on how to reload the NetWare 2.12 operating system in case they experienced problems. One engineer carefully wrote down the steps, checking against detailed notes on the installations. Then the second engineer went through them to make sure they were correct. It was discovered that steps were missing and some were out of order. Again, the first engineer went through the steps to verify them with the corrections. Again, the steps were not completely accurate. After doing this five times, the engineers realized that their NetWare installations varied depending on circumstances that were not always definable. Windows NT also had similar installation oddities.

Today when you install an operating system, whether on Novell NetWare or Windows Server 2003, it works the same every time you perform the process. Operating system installations have matured over the years.

Novell chose to develop a file server rather than a disk server. A disk server is one that provides a way to split up a large hard drive into a smaller partition for each user. In contrast, a file server is a large hard drive that users attach to over the network and access files in a shared space. Novell was one of the first vendors to develop a client/server operating system, with the NetWare operating system installed on the server, and Novell client software installed on workstations. This Novell client software allows the desktop operating system you have on your computer to communicate with the Novell NetWare server.

Novell developed partnerships with a number of hardware vendors, with each running the NetWare operating system. This was a strategic move that paid off well. As the hardware vendors competed for a sale, Novell was secure in the knowledge that whoever won the contract; they were locked in as the operating system vendor.

Today, most NetWare shops run NetWare 5.x or NetWare 6.x. Novell allows downloads of the latest version of NetWare for a 90-day evaluation period. Check this out by visiting *www.novell.com*. Figure 2-15 shows the download screen for NetWare 6.5.

TIP

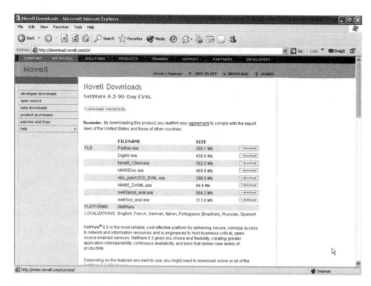

Figure 2-15   Download screen for NetWare 6.5

The following sections briefly describe the latest two versions of NetWare.

NetWare 6.0

In late 2001, Novell released NetWare 6.0; their vision of "one Net" had come of age. One Net provides any device, wired or wireless, the ability to access the corporate network. The days of each workstation having a Novell client are gone. Any workstation that can access the Internet can access a NetWare 6.0 server.

A NetWare 6.0 server can be added relatively easily to a network that contains Microsoft, UNIX, and other NetWare servers. It is also very scalable to allow for expansion as the organization grows.

NetWare 6.5

NetWare 6.5 shipped in mid 2003 and contained major **open-source** enhancements including such applications as Apache Web server, MySQL, Tomcat, and support for Perl. The exciting aspect of these features is that an organization can install the same software on Windows, NetWare, or Linux servers. Novell's Virtual Office is another enhancement in NetWare 6.5. It allows users to have the same desktop configuration by using a Web browser.

The NetWare Administrator console is shown in Figure 2-16. It is used to perform many of the tasks necessary to maintain NetWare 6.5 server.

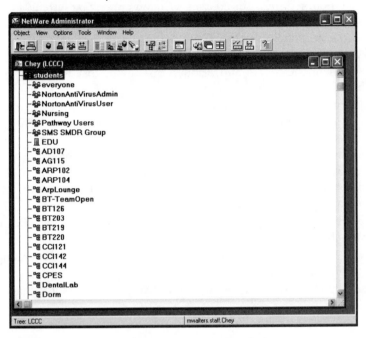

Figure 2-16   NetWare Administrator console

CHAPTER SUMMARY

◻ Hardware and operating systems are interrelated because in many ways they grew up together. We've seen a steady march of hardware from the early 8088 chip to the modern 64-bit Itanium processor. Processors are much faster and more efficient, and operating systems paralleled this change to take advantage of the capabilities of new processors at each stage of development.

◻ The early computer operating systems, such as MS-DOS, were well suited to the early processors, which included the 8088, 8086, and 80286. As processors became faster and more advanced, so did operating systems such as the early Windows and Macintosh operating systems. UNIX operating systems, too, have grown to take advantage of improvements in 32-bit and 64-bit processors.

◻ Today, 32-bit processors, such as the Pentium 4, provide a foundation for operating systems like Windows XP to take advantage of high-speed networking and multimedia capabilities. Also, new 64-bit processors have emerged, such as the PowerPC G5 generation of processors, and new operating systems, such as the Mac OS X Panther, are available to take advantage of the new features of these processors.

Key Terms

activate— A procedure to register your copy of Windows operating systems starting with the Windows XP version. Without this activation, you will not be able to run your operating system for more than a small amount of time.

Active Directory — A Windows 2000 database of computers, users, shared printers, shared folders, and other network resources and resource groupings that is used to manage a network and enable users to quickly find a particular resource.

ActiveX — An internal programming standard that allows various software that runs under the Windows operating system to communicate with the operating system and other programs.

address bus — An internal communications pathway inside a computer that specifies the source and target address for memory reads and writes. The address bus is measured by the number of bits of information it can carry. The wider the address bus (the more bits it moves at a time), the more memory available to the computer that uses it.

backward-compatibility — A significant number of features from an older chip can function on a newer chip.

Berkeley Software Distribution (BSD) — A variant of the UNIX operating system upon which a large proportion of today's UNIX software is based.

bus — A path or channel between a computer's CPU and the devices it manages, such as memory and disk storage.

cache controller — Internal computer hardware that manages the data going into and loaded from the computer's cache memory.

cache memory — Special computer memory that temporarily stores data used by the CPU. Cache memory is physically close to the CPU, and is faster than standard system memory, enabling faster retrieval and processing time.

client — In a networking environment, a computer that handles certain user-side software operations. For example, a network client may run software that captures user data input and presents output to the user from a network server.

clustering — The ability to share the computing load and resources by linking two or more discrete computer systems (servers) to function as though they are one.

common language runtime (CLR) — Verifies code before it is run and monitors memory to clean up any leakage before it becomes a problem.

Complex Instruction Set Computer (CISC) — A computer CPU architecture in which processor components are reconfigured to conduct different operations as required. Such computer designs require many instructions and more complex instructions than other designs.

Component Object Model (COM) — Standards that enable a software object, such as a graphic, to be linked from one software component into another one. COM is the foundation that makes object linking and embedding (OLE) possible.

control bus — An internal communications pathway that keeps the CPU informed of the status of particular computer resources and devices, such as memory and disk drives.

2

data bus — An internal communications pathway that allows computer components, such as the CPU, display adapter, and main memory, to share information. Early personal computers used an 8-bit data bus. More modern computers use 32- or 64-bit data buses.

dial-up networking (DUN) — A utility built into Windows 95 and later versions to permit operation of a hardware modem to dial a telephone number for the purpose of logging on to a remote computer system via standard telephone lines.

domain — A logical grouping of computers and computer resources that helps manage these resources and user access to them.

driver signing — Setting up all drivers so that they cannot be inadvertently overwritten by earlier driver versions, and only certified versions of drivers can be installed.

DUN server — In Windows 95 and later versions, a software utility that permits a desktop computer to answer incoming calls, log on a user, and, with other software, permits the user access to the computer's resources.

execution-based cache — First-level cache in a Xeon CPU that stores decoded instructions and delivers them to the processor at high speed.

Explicitly Parallel Instruction Computing (EPIC) — A computer CPU architecture that grew out of the RISC-based architecture, and enables the processor to work faster by performing several operations at once, predicting and speculating about operations that will come next (so that they are even completed before requested). EPIC uses larger and more work area registers than CISC or traditional RISC-based CPU architectures.

external clock speed — The speed at which the processor communicates with the memory and other devices in the computer; usually one-fourth to one-half the internal clock speed.

external commands — Operating system commands that are stored in separate program files on disk. When these commands are required, they must be loaded from disk storage into memory before they are executed.

hyper-threading (HT) — An Intel multithreading technology that enables a single processor to appear to the operating system as two separate processors, in which multiple threads of software applications are run simultaneously on one processor.

Infrared Data Association (IrDA) — A group of peripheral manufacturers that developed a set of standards for transmitting data using infrared light. Printers were some of the first devices to support the IrDA specifications.

instruction set — In a computer CPU, the group of commands (instructions) the processor recognizes. These instructions are used to conduct the operations required of the CPU by the operating system and application software.

internal clock speed — The speed at which the CPU executes internal commands, measured in megahertz (millions of clock ticks per second) or gigahertz (billions of clock ticks per second). Internal clock speeds can be as low as 1 MHz and as high as more than 2 GHz.

interrupt request (IRQ) — A request to the processor so that a currently operating process, such as a read from a disk drive, can be interrupted by another process, such as a write into memory.

Kerberos — A security system developed by the Massachusetts Institute of Technology to enable two parties on an open network to communicate without interception by an intruder, creating a unique encryption key per each communication session.

level 1 (L1) cache — Cache memory that is part of the CPU hardware. See *cache memory*.

level 2 (L2) cache — Cache memory that, in most computer CPU designs, is located on hardware separate from, but close to, the CPU.

level 3 (L3) cache — Cache memory that is located on a chip or daughterboard, which is separate from, but close to the CPU, when L1 and L2 cache are both already built into the CPU.

line editor — An editor that is used to create text a line at a time.

math coprocessor — A module optimized to perform complex math calculations. Early system architectures have a processor and an optional slot for a math coprocessor. Modern system architectures have a CPU with one or more built-in math coprocessors.

Multimedia Extension (MMX) — A CPU design that permits the processor to manage certain multimedia operations—graphics, for example—faster and more directly. MMX technology improves computer performance when running software that requires multimedia operations.

multiprocessor computer — A computer that uses more than one CPU.

multithreading — Running several program processes or parts (threads) at the same time.

open-source — Source code for software that is available to the general public free of charge.

peer-to-peer network operating system — A network operating system through which any computer can communicate with other networked computers on an equal or peer-like basis without going through an intermediary, such as a server or network host computer. Windows 3.11 (Windows for Workgroups) is a peer-to-peer network operating system.

pipelining — A CPU design that permits the processor to operate on one instruction at the same time it is fetching one or more subsequent instructions from the operating system or application.

Plug and Play (PnP) — Software utilities that operate with compatible hardware to facilitate automatic hardware configuration. Windows versions starting with 95 recognize PnP hardware when it is installed, and, in many cases, can configure the hardware and install required software without significant user intervention.

power management — A hardware facility in modern computers that permits certain hardware to shut down automatically after a specified period of inactivity. Proper use of power management facilities reduces hardware wear and tear, as well as energy usage.

privileged mode — The opposite of real mode and where you only use segment registers rather that real mode addressing.

real mode — A limited, 16-bit operating mode in PCs running early versions of Windows.

Reduced Instruction Set Computer (RISC) — A computer CPU design that dedicates processor hardware components to certain functions. This design reduces the number and complexity of required instructions and, in many cases, results in faster performance than CISC CPUs.

2

registry — A Windows database that stores information about a computer's hardware and software configuration.

Remote Access Service (RAS) — A computer operating system subsystem that manages user access to a computer from a remote location, including security access.

Rights Management Services (RMS) — Allows you to secure documents from copying, forwarding, and printing.

server — A computer on a network that performs a function such as a file server that serves files to clients, or a print server that prints information for clients, or a database server that passes data from the server to the client.

single-processor computer — A computer capable of supporting only a single CPU.

symmetric multiprocessing (SMP) — A computer design that supports multiple, internal CPUs that can be configured to work simultaneously on the same set of instructions.

system architecture — The computer hardware design that includes the processor (CPU), and communication routes between the CPU and the hardware it manages, such as memory and disk storage.

System V Release 4 (SVR4) — A variation of the UNIX operating system. It is very popular today along with the Berkeley Software Distribution (BSD).

task supervisor — A process in the operating system that keeps track of the applications that are running on the computer and the resources they use.

total cost of ownership (TCO) — The cost of installing and maintaining computers and equipment on a network, which includes hardware, software, maintenance, and support costs.

Universal Plug and Play (UPnP) — An initiative of more than 80 companies to develop products that can be quickly added to a computer or network. These include intelligent appliances for the home. More information can be found at the Web site, *www.upnp.org*.

Universal Serial Bus (USB) — A relatively recent serial bus designed to support up to 127 discrete devices with data transfer speeds up to 12 Mbps (megabits per second). USB 2.0 is out with a transfer speed of 480 Mbps. It is fully compatible with the original USB specifications. USB 2.0 is also referred to as Hi-Speed USB.

virtual private network (VPN) — A private network that is like a tunnel through a larger network—such as the Internet, an enterprise network, or both—and restricted to designated member clients.

Web browser — Software to facilitate individual computer access to graphical data presented over the Internet on the World Wide Web, or over a local area network in a compatible format.

word — Used to hold data or programming code in a computer. The size of a word varies among computers. 16-bit computers have a word of 16 bits and a 64-bit computer has a word of 64 bits.

X Window — A windowed user interface for UNIX and other operating systems.

REVIEW QUESTIONS

1. An EPIC CPU design _____ .

   a. evolved from the CISC processor

   b. was created in a joint project between Apple and IBM

   c. allows a single processor to execute 20 or more operations at a time

   d. uses a companion chip with a built-in compiler

2. Instruction pipelining is a processing technique that allows the processor to operate on one instruction at a time with the pipeline keeping the instructions in order. True or False?

3. A specialized piece of hardware called the _____ predicts what data will be needed and makes it available in cache before it is needed.

4. The most recent graphical Microsoft Windows family of server operating systems is the _____ family.

5. The _____ bus is used to keep the CPU informed of the status of resources and devices connected to the computer.

6. Hyper-threading (HT) technology enables two separate processors to appear to the operating system as a single processor. True or False?

7. The first widely used personal computer CPU was manufactured by Intel, and its model number was _____ .

   a. 68040

   b. 80286

   c. 8086

   d. 8088

8. In Windows 95, Microsoft introduced a way to add hardware to a computer in a much easier way than had been available before. This feature is called .

9. A virtual private network (VPN) is _____ .

   a. a standalone virtual network

   b. a virtual network residing within one computer

   c. a private network that is like a tunnel through a larger network

   d. a network that can only be observed from the outside on rare occasions

10. Kerberos security was introduced in Windows _____ .

11. The five versions of Windows XP are: _____ , _____ , _____ , _____ and _____ .

12. Windows 2000 resolved some of the security problems in Windows NT by not turning on any of the services by default. True or False?

2

13. UNIX versions adhere to one of the two main design standards which are the
_____ or the _____ .

14. The X Window type GUI interface in Red Hat Enterprise Linux 3.0
is called _____ .

15. Novell's NetWare 6.5 shipped with major open-source enhancements. True or False?

16. One benchmark of the speed of a CPU is the number of instructions it can perform
with each clock cycle. How many clock cycles does a 3.06 GHz computer have?

17. What version of the Mac OS provides personal video conferencing where one can
have video conversations with another Mac in full screen video?

18. What relatively high-speed input/output port was first supported in Windows 98?
    a. Firewire
    b. USB
    c. parallel
    d. Ethernet

19. In which operating system(s) might you find the utility Microsoft Windows Journal?

20. The latest generation of the PowerPC processor is called the _____ .

21. The Intel Itanium processor family is built on what architecture?

HANDS-ON PROJECTS

As you are completing the Hands-on Projects, remember to keep a lab book, notebook, or
computer word processor handy so that you can record your findings for later reference.

**HANDS-ON
PROJECTS**

Project 2-1

In this project, you use the System Monitor tool in **Windows 95** or **Windows 98** to
monitor the processor response to system and network demands. The System Monitor can
help you determine if the processor is meeting the usage demands, or if it needs to be
upgraded. For example, a processor that is frequently at 80 to 100 percent usage may need
to be upgraded.

To use the System Monitor:

1. Click **Start**, point to **Programs**, point to **Accessories**, point to **System Tools**, and
   click **System Monitor**. What information is displayed and in what format?

2. Watch the monitor for several minutes and determine how the information changes.

3. Close the System Monitor.

Project 2-2

In **Windows 2000**, **Windows XP**, and **Windows Server 2003**, you can monitor the processor usage through the Task Manager.

To monitor processor usage:

1. Right-click the **Task Bar** and click **Task Manager** on the shortcut menu.

2. Click the **Performance** tab.

3. Watch the CPU Usage and the CPU Usage History graphs. How do the graphs change as you are watching? Does the CPU ever go over 80 percent usage and stay at this level for a long time?

4. What other information can you monitor on the Performance tab? How can you determine the amount of RAM or physical memory in the computer? How much memory is used by the kernel?

5. Close the Task Manager.

Do not leave the Task Manager running in the background when you are not using it. The Task Manager uses CPU and memory resources and could slow down the computer.

Project 2-3

Most Windows-based systems have the ability to show you if the processor (or any other hardware device) is working properly. This project shows you how to test the processor, first in **Windows 9x**, then in **Windows 2000/XP/Server 2003**.

To test the processor in Windows 95/98:

1. Click **Start**, point to **Settings**, and click **Control Panel**.

2. Double-click the **System** icon.

3. Click the **Device Manager** tab.

4. Double-click **System devices** if the entities under it are not displayed. What is displayed under System devices?

5. Find the processor in the list and double-click it (or click the processor's connection to a controller or bridge, such as the PCI bridge). Look for the device status box in the resulting dialog box. What is the device status? Close the dialog box for the processor.

6. Look at the list of devices under System devices. Is there an option to check the numeric or math coprocessor? Is there an option to check the Plug and Play BIOS?

7. Close the System Properties dialog box, and then close the Control Panel.

To test the processor in Windows 2000/XP/Server 2003:

1. In Windows 2000, right-click the **My Computer** icon on the desktop, and click **Manage**. Or, in Windows XP and Windows Server 2003, click **Start**, right-click **My Computer**, and click **Manage**.

2. Double-click **System Tools** in the left pane, if necessary, to display the objects under it.

3. Click **Device Manager**.

4. For Windows XP and Windows Server 2003, double-click **Processors** in the right pane. How many processors are displayed? Double-click a processor in the list (if there are more than one). In Windows 2000, double-click **System Devices** and notice the devices that are displayed. Double-click a processor in the list (or click the processor's connection to a controller or bridge, such as the PCI bridge).

5. Make sure that the General tab is shown, and if not, click it. What is the status of the processor? Also, notice that there is a Troubleshoot button to help you diagnose a problem with the processor.

6. Close the Processor Properties dialog box, and then close the Computer Management Window.

Project 2-4

In this project, you compare the desktop of **Windows 95/98** to **Windows XP** Home Edition or Professional.

To compare the desktops:

1. Log on to Windows 95 or Windows 98. What icons are displayed on the desktop?

2. Click the **Start** button. What options do you see?

3. Log off Windows 95 or 98, and then log on to Windows XP or Windows Server 2003. What icons are displayed on the desktop?

4. Compare the similarities and differences of the Windows 95/98 desktop to that of Windows XP or Windows Server 2003.

5. Click the **Start** button. How is the Windows XP or Windows Server 2003 Start button menu different from that of Windows 95/98?

6. Log off Windows XP or Windows Server 2003 when you are finished examining the similarities and differences of the desktop to Windows 95/98.

Project 2-5

Windows XP has some of the most extensive help and support information available for an operating system. In this project, you have an opportunity to view the **Windows XP** Help and Support Center.

To view the Windows XP help and support information:

1. Click **Start**, and then click **Help and Support**. What information categories are available?

2. Click **Windows basics**. How might this information help you learn more about Windows XP?

3. Click the **Back** arrow on the menu bar.

4. Click **Fixing a problem**. Which option provides help with hardware problems? Which option offers help for software problems?

5. Click **Troubleshooting problems**.

6. Scroll the right pane and click **List of troubleshooters** under the Overviews, Articles, and Tutorials section. What are some of the Troubleshooters that you can access? Select one of the Troubleshooters to see how it can provide help for a problem.

7. Close the Help and Support Center tool.

Project 2-6

Windows XP has a Program Compatibility Wizard from which to run programs adapted to earlier operating systems, such as Windows 95. This project gives you the opportunity to use the Program Compatibility Wizard. You'll need to obtain from your instructor a program originally designed for Windows 95, such as Word 95.

To use the Windows XP Program Compatibility Wizard:

1. Click **Start**, point to **All Programs**, point to **Accessories**, and click **Program Compatibility Wizard**.

2. Click **Next** after the wizard starts. What options do you see for selecting programs?

3. Select the option **I want to locate the program manually**, and then click **Next**.

4. Enter the path to the program that you want to start, or click the Browse button to find and select the program.

5. Click **Next**. What compatibility modes are available?

6. Select **Microsoft Windows 95**, and then click **Next**.

7. Select the appropriate display settings, such as 640 X 480 screen resolution (ask your instructor if you are unsure about what to select). Click **Next**.

8. Review the program, path, and compatibility settings. Click **Next**. What happens?

9. Test the program and then close it.

10. If the program ran successfully, click the option **Yes, this program worked correctly**, and click **Next**. If it did not run successfully, click **No, try different compatibility settings**, and repeat Steps 7 through 10, trying different settings.

11. Click **Finish**.

HANDS-ON PROJECTS

Project 2-7

In this project, you learn how to determine what shell you are using while in the **Linux** operating system.

To determine the shell that you are using:

1. Access the command prompt, such as by opening a terminal window in the Red Hat Enterprise Linux 3.0 GNOME desktop. To open a terminal window, click **Main Menu**, click **System Tools**, then click **Terminal**.

2. Start by looking at the command prompt. The $ prompt means that you are in either the Bourne, Bourne Again, or Korn shell.

3. Enter **echo $SHELL**, making sure that the word "SHELL" is all capital letters and press **Enter**. What response do you see? If /bin/sh appears, you are in the Bourne shell. A response of /bin/bash means you are using the Bourne Again shell. And /bin/ksh signifies the Korn shell.

4. If you get an error message in Step 3, enter **echo $shell** (making sure that the word "shell" is all lowercase letters). Now you should see the response /bin/csh, which means that you are in the C shell.

5. Type **exit** and press **Enter**, or click the **x** in the upper right corner of the window to close the terminal window.

Project 2-8

In Windows-based systems, you can start a program by beginning from the Start button and Programs option, for example. In **Red Hat Enterprise Linux 3.0**, the X Window GNOME interface has a similar structure. For instance, you can click the Main Menu and select the Programs option to access many programs and utilities. In this project, you have an opportunity to briefly become acquainted with the GNOME interface.

To become more acquainted with the GNOME interface:

1. Log on to Red Hat Enterprise Linux 3.0, either using the root account or another account provided by your instructor. What icons do you see already on the desktop? The bottom of the screen contains the Panel, which is similar to the taskbar in Windows-based systems. Notice the icons on the Panel. The red hat icon is the Main Menu. The icon that looks like a globe with a mouse opens Mozilla, which is a Web browser, and the icon that resembles an envelope and stamp accesses Ximian Evolution for e-mail communications. There's also a clock display on the right side of the Panel that shows the day of the week, the date, and the time.

2. Click the **red hat** icon to open the Main Menu. What options do you see?

3. Point to **Accessories**. What options are on the Accessories menu?

4. Point to **Office**. What applications are available from this menu?

5. Move your pointer away from the menus and click in open space so that you close the menus.

Project 2-9

In this project, you download an evaluation copy of **NetWare 6.5** from the Novell Web site.

To download NetWare 6.5:

1. Start your Web browser and enter the URL **www.novell.com**.

2. Click **MY NOVELL**.

3. If you have a username and password, click **login** and enter your username and password. Then click **login** again.

4. If you do not have a username and password, click **create account** and follow the steps to create an account.

5. Click the **DOWNLOAD** button.

6. Select the **Product** option, if necessary.

7. Next, select **NetWare** from the choose a product drop-down box.

8. Then select **NetWare** from the choose a platform drop-down box.

9. Click **submit search**.

10. From the resulting selections, click **download** on the *6.5 90-Day EVAL on NetWare* line.

11. Click **download instructions** and study them.

12. Next download the files necessary to create the two CDs for NetWare 6.5.

13. Once you have downloaded the files, follow the instructions and create the CDs.

Project 2-10

In this project, you examine the **Mac OS X** desktop.

To view the Mac OS X desktop:

1. Start Mac OS X and observe the desktop. What features are on the desktop?

2. Click each of the menus at the top. What are some examples of options that you see? What are some examples of applications in the Applications window? How would you run an application?

CASE PROJECTS

Darts is a sporting goods company with outlets in most of the western states. This company has a network of 278 computers consisting of the following hardware:

- ❑ Eight Windows NT 4.0 servers
- ❑ Two Linux servers running Red Hat Enterprise Linux 3.0
- ❑ 20 computers running Mac OS 8.1
- ❑ 32 computers running Windows 95
- ❑ 216 computers running Windows 98

Darts realizes that with the projected growth of their company, they need to upgrade the computers and servers on their network.

Case Project 2-1: Accounting Department Upgrade

The Accounting Department has all of the Windows 95 computers that are running on 90 MHz Pentium hardware. The accounting director wants to upgrade to Windows XP. What are the advantages of upgrading for this department in terms of the enhanced operating system functions that are available in Windows XP? What are some possible disadvantages?

Case Project 2-2: Legacy Billing System

If the Accounting Department does upgrade to Windows XP, will it have to upgrade the processors, and if so, to what? Also, will the department be able to run a legacy 16-bit billing program that was designed for Windows 95?

Case Project 2-3: New Computer for the Marketing Department

The Marketing Department uses the Mac OS 8.1 computers, which are G3 computers. Because they plan to purchase new computers, what is the newest Mac operating system to which they can upgrade, and what new processor can they upgrade to? What would be the advantage of this upgrade for their department?

Case Project 2-4: President's Problem

The president of Darts is convinced that the processor on his Windows 98 system is overloaded. How can you help him determine if there is a problem with the processor?

Case Project 2-5: Chief Financial Officer's Concerns

The new chief financial officer believes that all of the Windows 98 computers should be upgraded to Windows Me because Windows XP Professional is too new. What are the advantages and disadvantages of upgrading to Windows Me compared to Windows XP Professional or Windows 2000 Professional?

Case Project 2-6: Server Upgrades

What would be the advantage of upgrading the Windows NT servers, and if you recommend upgrading them, what operating system do you recommend? Why?

3

FILE SYSTEMS

After reading this chapter and completing the exercises, you will be able to:

♦ Understand the basic functions common to all file systems

♦ Explain the file systems used by Windows 2000, Windows XP, and Windows Server 2003 (FAT16, FAT32, and NTFS)

♦ Describe the file systems used by UNIX and Linux systems, including ufs and ext

♦ Discuss the NetWare file system and NSS

♦ Explain the Mac OS X Extended (HFS+) file system including new features added in Mac OS X version 10.3

In this chapter, you learn the general characteristics and functions of file systems, including their organization and specific features. Next, you explore the file systems used by Microsoft, UNIX/Linux, Novell, and Macintosh operating systems. You also learn about the tools available for the file systems, such as tools for locating files and tools for fixing damaged files.

UNDERSTANDING FILE SYSTEM FUNCTIONS

An operating system exists to enable you to store and access information on a computer—which might be letters, a report, spreadsheet files, your favorite music, or pictures of your family. All of this vital information is managed, stored, and retrieved through a **file system**. In one sense, a file system is like your personal assistant, properly saving and keeping track of the location of your important data. The file system allocates locations on a disk for storage and it keeps a record of where specific information is kept. When you need the information, the file system consults its records to determine the location and then retrieves the information. Some file systems also implement recovery procedures when a disk area is damaged or when the operating system unexpectedly goes down, such as during a power failure.

To fulfill all these functions, the file systems used by computer operating systems perform the following general tasks:

- Partition and format disks to store and retrieve information
- Enable files to be organized through directories and folders
- Establish file-naming conventions
- Provide utilities to maintain and manage the file system and storage media
- Provide for file and data integrity
- Enable error recovery or prevention
- Secure the information in files

The overall purpose of a file system is to create a structure for filing data. The image that is typically used for a file system is that of file cabinets, file drawers, and file folders. For example, the computer could be considered the file cabinet and the disk drives the drawers. Within each drawer (drive), information is organized into hanging folders (directories), manila folders (subdirectories), and individual documents (files), as shown in Figure 3-1.

A file is a set of data that is grouped in some logical manner, assigned a name, and stored on the disk. As the file is stored, the file system records where the file is located on the disk so that it has a way to later retrieve that file. Whenever the file is needed, the operating system is given the filename, and it retrieves the data in the file from the disk.

The data contained in files can be text, images, music and sounds, video, or Web pages for the Internet. But no matter what kind of data is stored in the file system, it must be converted into digital format—a series of 1s and 0s—that the computer understands. The operating system, along with the applications you use for word processing, graphics, and so on, performs this function of converting data into digital format for the computer, and back into the end user format as text or pictures, for example.

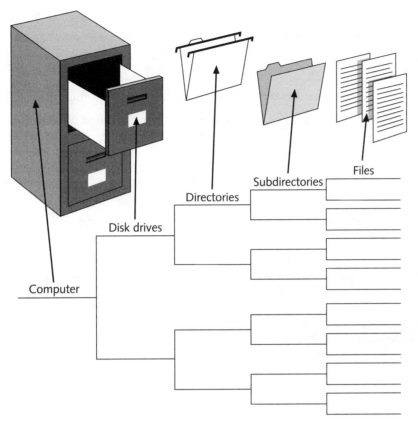

Figure 3-1   A file system

Moreover, there must be a way to write digital information onto disk, track it, update it when necessary, and call it back when the user, or a program under the user's control, wants it. To achieve all this, the operating system typically groups disk sectors in some logical way, creates a record of this structure, and builds a directory or folder to track the type of data stored in each file. A **directory** or **folder** is an organizational structure that contains files and may additionally contain subdirectories (or folders) under it. The directory connects names to the files that are stored on the disk, which makes it easy for users and programs to obtain the right data at the right time.

NOTE   The term directory can have two meanings: the internal database maintained by the operating system to track file locations, sizes, and attributes; and the actual list of this information displayed and accessed by the user through the UNIX/Linux *ls* command or Windows Explorer, for example.

In addition to the names of files and where to find them on the disk, directories (and individual files) also store the following information:

- Date and time the directory or file was created (a timestamp for that directory or file)

- Date and time the directory or file was last modified (another form of timestamp)

- Date and time when the directory or file was last accessed (recorded by some file systems)

- Directory or file size

- Directory or file attributes, such as security information, or if the directory or file was backed up

- If the information in a directory or file is compressed or encrypted (recorded by some file systems)

Figure 3-2 illustrates some of the information that is stored for a file in Windows XP, which can be displayed using Windows Explorer or My Computer. As you learn later in this chapter, the way in which this information is stored depends on the design of the file system.

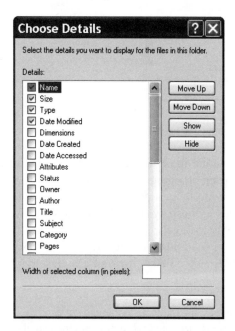

Figure 3-2   Information stored about Windows XP files

Hands-on Project 3-1 enables you to view folder and file information in My Computer. Also, Hands-on Projects 3-2 and 3-3 give you experience viewing folders and files using the Nautilus tool in Red Hat Enterprise Linux 3.0 and the Macintosh HD icon in Mac OS X.

Designing a Directory Structure

For users, one of the most important features of a file system is the ability to store information according to a pattern of organization that is enabled by the use of directories. In the early Windows and UNIX/Linux systems, files are organized by directories, while in later Windows versions and the Mac OS, these are called folders. For example, in Windows 2000 (all versions), the default folder in which the system files are organized is called \Winnt, while in Windows XP and Windows Server 2003 the system files are organized in the \WINDOWS folder. In UNIX/Linux, many system files are located in the /etc directory, while in Mac OS X, the folder called System contains the Mac OS X critical system files. Mac OS X also has a folder called the System Folder, which contains files for the Mac OS version 9 files with programs for the classic (prior to Mac OS X) desktop.

NOTE   When Windows Server 2003 is upgraded from Windows 2000 Server, the system files remain in the \Winnt folder. If Windows Server 2003 is installed from scratch, then it uses the \Windows folder.

Directories and folders can be organized in a hierarchy that is similar to a tree structure. For example, in Windows XP, the \WINDOWS folder contains subfolders such as \WINDOWS\addins, \WINDOWS\Config, \WINDOWS\Help, \WINDOWS\Media, \WINDOWS\system, and \WINDOWS\system32. Many of these subfolders contain subfolders under them, such as the Restore and SPOOL subfolders under the System32 subfolder—giving the folder system a tree-like structure. In Red Hat Enterprise Linux (and other Linux versions), the /etc directory has many subdirectories— /etc/firmware, /etc/ httpd, /etc/mail, /etc/security, and /etc/sysconfig, to name a few. Building a hierarchy of folders and subfolders enables you to fine tune the organization of files and folders in a methodical way so that information is easy to find and use.

Without a well-designed directory or folder structure, it is common for a hard disk to become cluttered and disorganized with different versions of files and application software. Some personal computer users keep most of their files in the computer's primary level or **root directory**, or they load all application software into a single directory. As a partial solution, some application software programs use an automated setup that suggests folders for new programs, such as creating new subfolders under the Program Files folder in many Windows systems—but some users still have difficulty organizing files. A chaotic file structure makes it difficult to run or remove programs or determine the most current versions. It also makes users spend unproductive time looking for specific files.

To avoid confusion, carefully design the file and folder structure from the start, particularly on servers that are accessed by many users. Plan to design a folder structure that comple-ments the one already set up by the operating system. The default operating system structure, along with the structure that you add might consist of folders for the following:

- Operating system files (typically set up by the operating system)

- Software applications (often set up by both the operating system, the software applications that you install, and decisions you make about how to install those applications)

- Work files, such as word-processing, graphics, spreadsheet, and database files (set up by you and by applications such as Microsoft Word)

- Public files that you share over the network (set up by you)

- Utilities files (set up by the operating system, the utilities applications, and your decisions about how to install specific utilities)

- Temporary files (set up by the operating system, applications that use temporary files, and your decisions about where to store temporary files)

In deciding how to allocate folders for specific types of files, consider following some general practices. For instance, the root folder should not be cluttered with files or too many directories or folders. Each software application should have its own folder or subfolder, so updates and software removal are easy to administer. For easy access control, similar information should be grouped, such as accounting systems or office productivity software. Operating system files should be kept separate and protected so important files are not accidentally deleted by a user. Directories and folders should have names that clearly reflect their purposes. For example, consider a law office administrator who uses legal time accounting software, legal forms software, Microsoft Office, confidential and shared spreadsheets, and Word documents—all on a computer running Windows XP Professional. The same office administrator also maintains specialized Web pages for the law firm's Web site. The folder structure from the root might be as follows:

- *Windows* for the system files (the default set up by the operating system)

- *Program Files* for general software and utilities (the default set up by the operating system)

- *Documents and Settings* for work files such as spreadsheets and Word documents (the default set up by the operating system)

- *Shared* for spreadsheets that are shared over the network (a sample folder the user could set up, or the user could employ the default Shared Documents folder set up by the operating system as noted below)

- *Forms* for specific types of forms used by the legal forms software (a sample folder the user might set up)

- *Inetpub* for Web pages (a sample folder the user might set up in conjunction with the installation of Web design software)

NOTE

By default, Windows XP creates a \Documents and Settings\All Users\Shared Documents folder when sharing is turned on. Some users choose to use this folder for sharing files over a network. However, make sure that you know what security is set on shared folders so you don't host unwelcome guests. You learn about security later in this chapter.

Each major folder has subfolders to keep grouped files or application software separate. For example, the Program Files folder contains subfolders for each different software package, such as \Program Files\Microsoft Office for the Microsoft Office software, and \Program Files\Time Accounting for the legal time accounting software folder. The Documents and Settings folder would have subfolders for confidential spreadsheets and Word documents, while shared spreadsheets would be in the Shared folder. Figure 3-3 illustrates this folder structure.

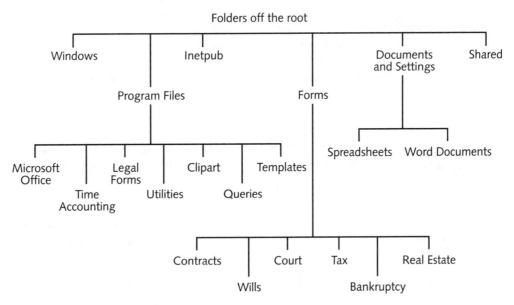

Figure 3-3   Sample folder structure for a Windows-based system

For UNIX and Linux systems, such as Red Hat Enterprise Linux, a typical directory (or folder) structure that is already provided by the operation system is as follows:

- *bin* for user programs and utilities (binary files)
- *lib* for runtime library files needed by programs, stored in the /bin and /sbin directories
- *usr* for user files and programs
- *var* for files in which content often varies or that are used only temporarily
- *tmp* for files used only temporarily
- *dev* for devices
- *mnt* for floppy drives, CD-ROM drives, and other removable media that can be mounted
- *etc* for system and configuration files

- *sbin* for user programs and utilities (system binary files)

- *root* for files used by the root account

- *home* for users' home directories (or folders) and typically stored in subfolders named for each user

- *proc* for system resource tracking

NOTE Red Hat Enterprise Linux now uses the term "folders" instead of "directories," as it had in early versions. When you view folders using the GNOME-based Nautilus tool, you see folder icons similar to those in the Windows-based My Computer tool. Also, note that the term root folder or root directory is used in two ways. One way is to refer to the root or main level from which all folders are created. All of the folders in the previous list are in the root, which is designated as /. Also, the root account stores files in the root folder (/root) that is one of the folders within the main root level.

NOTE Windows operating systems use backslashes to designate a folder, but UNIX and Linux use a forward slash. For example, the main level root is / and the bin folder is denoted as /bin.

You can view folders in Red Hat Enterprise Linux 3.0 from the command line—for example by using a terminal window—and from the Nautilus tool as demonstrated in Hands-on Project 3-2.

In Mac OS X, the default folder structure created by the operating system from the root level includes:

- *Applications* for Mac OS X software applications

- *Applications (Mac OS 9)* for applications used with the earlier Mac OS 9

- *System Folder* for Mac OS 9 system files

- *System* for Mac OS X system files

- *Library* for library files (such as fonts)

- *Users* for user accounts, with subfolders for each user account to store files

- *Documents* for documents

Try Hands-on Projects 3-4, 3-5, and 3-6 to practice making folders in different operating systems. You learn about the default Netware directory structure in Chapter 9 as part of resource sharing on a network.

Disk Storage Basics

When a hard disk is delivered from the manufacturer, it is low-level formatted. A **low-level format** is a software process that marks the location of disk tracks and sectors. Every disk is divided into **tracks**, which are like several circles around a disk. The number of tracks on a hard disk depends on the disk size and manufacturer. Each track is divided into sections of equal size called **sectors**. Figure 3-4 illustrates a hard disk divided into tracks and sectors.

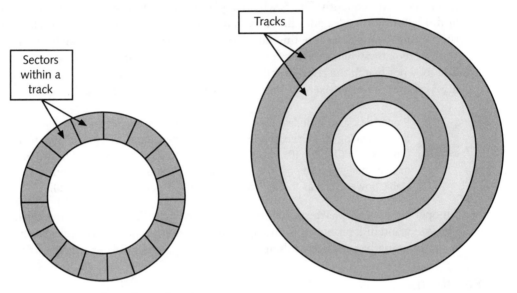

Figure 3-4   Disk tracks and sectors

Block Allocation

The operating systems discussed in this book use a method called **block allocation** to keep track of where specific files are stored on the disk. Rather than storing absolute track, sector, and head information for every sector on a disk, block allocation divides the disk into logical blocks (Windows-based systems are called **clusters**), which in turn correlate to sectors, heads, and tracks on the disk. Each hard disk platter has two sides, with a read/write head on each side. Tracks that line up on each platter from top to bottom are called **cylinders** and are all read at the same time.

When the operating system needs to allocate some disk space, it does so based on a block address. Lower-level drivers translate block numbers into real disk addresses. The reference to a file in the directory and in the file allocation data is based on block numbers.

The data regarding block allocation is stored on the disk itself using two techniques. One technique uses a fixed portion of the disk to store this data, such as the **file allocation table (FAT)** file system initially implemented in MS-DOS and supported by all versions of Windows (although some Windows versions, such as Windows 2000/XP/Server 2003, also support other file systems). The other technique uses various locations on the disk to store a special type of file that is used for directory and file allocation information, such as the **New Technology File System (NTFS)** and the UNIX/Linux file systems. As you can imagine, the areas of the disk in which allocation information and directory information are stored are very important; without this data, it would not be possible to access any of the files on the system (without using specialized disk repair tools).

If a system uses a specific area or set of areas on the disk to store this data, obviously that disk area is accessed frequently. This is why many problems in accessing disk files arise as problems in disk allocation tables and directory information (you learn about disk allocation tables later in this chapter). Because this data also is stored in a location separate from the actual file, you can see how when there is a problem with the disk, some of the directory or allocation data may not match the data actually stored on the disk. These occurrences are common, so it is very important to exercise proper care of disks to minimize such problems.

TIP Proper disk care includes, for example, regularly maintaining a disk through defragmenting (discussed later in this chapter), periodically deleting unused files (discussed in Chapter 10), maintaining good security (discussed in Chapter 9), implementing protection from viruses and malicious software, and providing stable power (such as through an uninterruptible power supply or UPS).

All operating systems have special tools that let you check, and sometimes repair, common file system and disk problems. Some operating systems can perform checks on the file system on an ongoing basis. These tools are discussed in more detail later in this chapter.

Partitions

Before a file system can be placed on a hard disk, the disk must be partitioned and formatted. **Partitioning** is the process of blocking a group of tracks and sectors to be used by a particular file system, such as FAT or NTFS. After a disk is partitioned, it must be **high-level formatted** (or simply formatted) so that the partition contains the disk divisions and patterns needed by a particular operating system to store files. With today's technology creating disks with more capacity, and as disks are used in more diverse applications, sometimes it is desirable to have more than one file system on a single disk, which is accomplished by having a partition for each file system. You might need multiple file systems to allow the installation of Windows 2000 alongside Windows XP, or to install Red Hat Enterprise Linux and Windows XP on the same computer, for example. Multiple operating systems may be required on a single system to accommodate various applications.

When you want to have multiple file systems on one disk, you can partition the disk so that different file systems can be installed on different disk partitions. You can also create partitions in one operating system to segment a single **physical drive** into multiple logical volumes to which you can assign distinct drive letters. This technique of dividing a hard disk into **logical drives** is very useful for organizing file storage, and was necessary with older operating systems, such as MS-DOS and Windows 3.1, which didn't recognize very large hard drives. Figure 3-5 illustrates a Windows 2000 system that has multiple partitions (FAT, NTFS, and **CD-ROM File System** or **CDFS**) used for segmenting data on two hard disks and a CD-ROM drive.

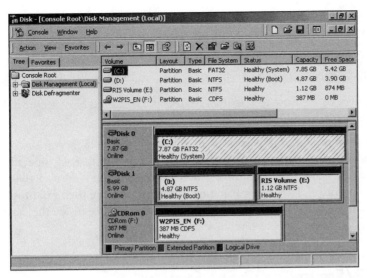

Figure 3-5   Multiple partitions used in one Windows 2000 system

NOTE

Partitioning can typically be done only on hard disks or large removable disks. Floppy disks and other low-capacity media do not support partitioning because there simply isn't enough room on these low-capacity disks to make partitioning practical. Also, some large-capacity media, such as CD-ROMs, CD-Rs, CD-RWs, DVDs, Zip drives, and tapes are not partitioned by the user.

The logical programming that creates disk partitions resides at an even lower level than the actual file system, and it lets you divide the disk into "slices." The slices are done at the low-level format portion of the disk, and are stored in special sections of the hard drive itself, separate from the operating system. Obviously, the partitioning scheme must be communicated to the operating system and file system. On most disks, there is a separate area that stores the partition information. This area has room to hold information about a set number of partitions. Whenever you create a partition, information about that partition is stored in this special area of the disk. On systems in the IBM/Intel PC hardware architecture, for example, typically there is room to store information for up to four partitions on each disk. This area is known as the **partition table** in MS-DOS, Mac OS, and Windows, and the **disk label** in UNIX/Linux. In addition to the disk label and partition table, there is another piece of disk reserved, known as the **boot block** in UNIX/Linux and Mac OS X, or the **Master Boot Record (MBR)** in MS-DOS and Windows. In Windows-based systems, the MBR can be up to 512 bytes long and consists of four elements:

- The *boot program*, which examines the partition table to determine the partition from which to boot (the **active partition**) and enables the program code in the active partition's start area to execute and then point to the code that starts the operating system.

- The *disk signature*, which stores information about the disk and is used by management software in some operating systems, such as the Windows registry.

- The *partition table* for the active partition.

- The *end-of-MBR marker*, which signifies where the MBR contents end on the disk.

Try Hands-on Project to see how to repair an MBR or a damaged boot sector in Windows 2000, Windows XP, or Windows Server 2003.

Not all operating systems support partitions in the same way, which you discover in the following sections on file systems for individual operating systems. Each operating system also uses specific utilities to create partitions. When a disk partition is created, the file system is stored inside the partition. The folder and directory structures are then built inside the file system. When files are stored on the disks, they are given some space inside the partition, and data about the files is written in the directory area.

WINDOWS 2000/XP/SERVER 2003 FILE SYSTEMS

Windows 2000, XP, and Server 2003 support three file systems: extended FAT16, FAT32, and NTFS version 5. These operating systems also support file systems for CD-ROM drives.

NOTE

These operating systems also support the very early FAT12 on volumes under 16 MB, but the use of volumes this small is not very likely on today's systems.

Extended FAT16

The extended FAT16 file system under Windows 2000/XP/Server 2003 evolved from the FAT16 system used in early versions of MS-DOS and Windows (3.x/95/98/Me). FAT uses a file allocation table to store directory information about files, such as filenames, file attributes, and file location. The "16" in FAT16 means that this file system uses 16-bit entries in the file allocation table and uses 2^{16} clusters. Remember that clusters are blocks of space containing one or more sectors into which the disk is divided.

When FAT16 is used with Windows 2000/XP/Server 2003, there are actually two FAT tables (one is a duplicate copy in case the main table is unusable) that follow the MBR at the beginning of the active partition, and the root folder follows the FAT tables. This table structure must be searched in sequential fashion, one entry at a time, whenever users access folders or files. FAT disks contain a series of clusters (called allocation units in later Windows versions) that form a partition. A cluster or allocation unit can consist of two, four, or eight sectors on a disk.

3

In extended FAT16, the maximum size of a volume is 4 GB, and the maximum size of a file is 2 GB. One advantage to using the extended FAT16 file system is that it has been around for a long time, and even non-Windows operating systems, such as UNIX/Linux can read disks written in FAT16 format. Further, because the file system is simple, there is relatively little that can go wrong, which makes this a stable file system.

Originally, FAT16 used **"8.3" filenames**, which can be up to eight characters long, followed by a period and an **extension** of three characters, such as Filename.ext. This convention led to the proliferation of many common three-letter file extensions such as .txt for text files, .doc for word-processing files, .xls for Excel spreadsheets, and so on. The limitations of this naming convention contributed to the development of **long filenames(LFNs)** in extended FAT16. An LFN:

- Can contain as many as 255 characters

- Is not case sensitive

- Cannot include characters such as " / \ [ ] : ; = , (this applies to both 8.3 filenames and LFNs)

NOTE Compatibility with the 8.3 naming convention of earlier FAT16 versions used by MS-DOS, Windows 3.x, and Release 1 of Windows 95 is maintained. This is done through a clever trick with directory entries, which allows them to be converted into 8.3 equivalents. The first of the directory entries looks just like an MS-DOS directory entry, except in place of the filename, there is an abbreviated filename. This filename is obtained by taking the first six characters of the old filename, adding a tilde (~), and a number or letter behind it, such as the 8.3 name CIRC09~1.TXT for the LFN circ09Copyright.txt. This means someone using MS-DOS or Windows 3.11 to access a folder in a later version of Windows can still view the contents of a folder with these modifications to the view of file names in that folder.

Because LFN characters are stored in **Unicode,** a coding system that allows for representation of any character in any language, it is possible to use any legitimate character in Windows in a filename. The advantage of LFNs and Unicode is that LFNs can be read by Mac OS and UNIX/Linux systems (such as on a Windows Server 2003 server that has file services installed for Mac OS and UNIX/Linux clients).

Normally, letters and digits are represented by ASCII (American Standard Code for Information Interchange, pronounced "as-key") values. The problem with this standard is that it uses an entire byte to represent each character, which limits the number of characters that can be represented to 255. This is not enough to handle all the characters needed to represent world languages, including several different alphabets (Greek, Russian, Japanese, and Hindi, for example). ASCII deals with this problem by employing many different character sets, depending on the characters you're trying to represent. The Unicode Consortium, a not-for-profit organization, represents an alternative in which there is a single, unique code for each possible character in any language. Unicode is a 16-bit code that allots two bytes for each character, which allows 65,536 characters to be defined. It includes distinct character codes for all modern languages. To the user who communicates primarily in English, Unicode will not make a big difference, but in this age of worldwide communication, it is a necessity.

CAUTION   Long filenames should be used and manipulated only with utilities that support LFN. MS-DOS and early Windows operating system utilities that support only 8.3 filenames can truncate long filenames, leaving only the 8.3 equivalents. This also happens if you move files with an older MS-DOS utility, such as an archiving utility. Only the short filenames will appear in the archive. This is one of the common problems with files on disks that are swapped between machines that run Windows 3.x and machines that run later versions of Windows.

Partitioning

The original FAT16 file system supports two partitions per hard drive, a primary partition and a secondary partition. The secondary partition may then be divided further into a maximum of three logical drives (see Figure 3-6). Each of these four possible logical drives can hold an individual FAT16 file system. Under control of the operating system, up to 26 logical drives (pointers to separate file systems), each with its own file system can be active at one time. A floppy disk does not support multiple file systems because each floppy drive is allocated as one removable file system. Under MS-DOS, Windows, UNIX/Linux, and Mac OS X, a CD-ROM is always treated as one file system.

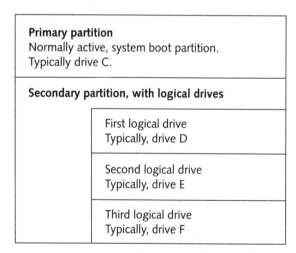

Figure 3-6   Sample partition table structure

NOTE

Although 26 drive definitions are technically possible, Windows-based systems by default reserve drives A and B for floppy drives, practically limiting the number of hard drives (including logical drives) to 24.

3

Each drive and its associated file system is assigned a letter followed by a colon: A:, B:, C:, and so on through Z:. This design lets you easily address the individual file systems by specifying a drive letter. Letters A: and B: are reserved for two removable file systems on floppy disk drives. Typically, C: is reserved for the first hard disk or removable disk file system (and is normally the system that contains the bootable partition). All other file systems located on fixed disks that are controlled by the hard disk drivers in the operating system follow in sequential order. So, a machine with two hard disks with two partitions each will have the drive letters C: for the first partition on the first disk, D: for the second partition on the first disk, E: for the first partition on the second disk, and F: for the second partition on the second disk. Disks that require special drivers, such as CD-ROM drives or removable disks, can be assigned any unused drive letter. By default, they will be assigned the next letter after the drive letter used by the last hard disk. In the previous example, a CD-ROM would be drive G.

In earlier versions of Windows, it was common to use the *fdisk* utility to partition hard disks. However, in Windows 2000/XP/Server 2003 you typically partition disks during the installation of the operating system and can add or reconfigure partitions after the operating system is installed. During the installation, it is necessary to partition at least the area on which the operating system is loaded. After the operating system is loaded, you can use the Disk Management tool to partition additional free space and disks. Refer to Figure 3-5 for an example of the Disk Management tool in Windows 2000. A quick way to access the Disk Management tool is to right-click My Computer on the Windows 2000 desktop or click Start and then right-click My Computer in Windows XP or Server 2003. Next, click Manage and then click Disk Management in the tree. In Windows 2000 Server and Windows Server 2003, you can also access Disk Management from one of many server management tools, such as the Microsoft Management Console (MMC). You learn more about managing disks with this tool in Chapter 6.

Formatting

After you partition a disk, it is time to place the file system on the partition in the process called formatting. When you first install a Windows-based operating system, you format the partition you created for a file system so that the installation process can write files to the disk, such as the system files needed for the operating system. After the operating system is installed, you can use the Disk Management tool to partition and format additional free space. Another option for formatting a floppy or hard disk is to use the *format* command from the Command Prompt window. This command writes all of the file system structure to the disk. In the case of a floppy disk, it uses the first sector of the disk as the boot block. This block contains some information about the disk, such as the number of tracks and the number of sectors per track, in coded form. As with many system-level commands, *format* includes several additional switches that modify precise program operation. You can view a list of these switches by typing *format /?* in the Command Prompt window. See Table 3-1 for a list of *format* command switches.

NOTE

Commands frequently use **switches** (extra codes) to change the way a particular command operates. In many operating systems, these extra commands follow a forward slash and take the form of a letter, or combination of letters, such as the *dir* command in Windows-based systems, which shows the contents of one or more directories and can take several switches or arguments, including /p (pause when the screen is full) and /s (include subdirectories). In UNIX/Linux systems the command switches frequently begin with one (-) or two (--) dashes.

Table 3-1   *format* command switches

Switch	Function
/v[:*label*]	Specifies the volume label
/q	Uses a quick format technique that does not check the disk for damaged clusters or bad spots
/f:*size*	Specifies the size of the floppy disk to format (such as 160, 180, 320, 360, 720, 1.2, 1.44, 2.88 where the file sizes are in MB or GB)
/fs:*filesystem*	Specifies whether to format for FAT16, FAT32, or NTFS
/t:*tracks*	Designates the number of tracks on a side (disks can be formatted on both sides)
/n:*sectors*	Designates how many sectors are in a track
/1	Formats a single side of a floppy disk
/4	Formats a 5.25-inch 360 K floppy disk in a high-density drive
/8	Formats eight sectors per track
/c	In FAT, tests clusters that are currently marked "bad"; in NTFS, this causes all files to be compressed

TIP

It is possible to run Windows operating systems and UNIX/Linux systems on the same machine. For example, if you only format a portion of a partitioned hard disk for Windows, you can format another portion (if you save the room required by the operating system) for UNIX/Linux—but it is advised that you use the appropriate disk formatting utility for your UNIX/Linux operating system or let the UNIX/Linux installation program do the formatting.

The boot block is placed in the first sector on the disk, which also contains the root folder (the highest level folder). The root folder is also where the system stores file information, such as name, start cluster, file size, file modification date and time, and **file attributes** (file characteristics such as Hidden, Read-only, Archive, and so on). The root folder on every partition is a fixed size that can contain a maximum of 512 entries in FAT16 (and unlimited entries in FAT32). The FAT on a floppy disk consists of several 12-bit entries. Each entry corresponds with a cluster address on the disk. When the file system performs its format operation, it divides the disk into clusters that are sequentially numbered. In the case of a floppy disk, each cluster corresponds to a sector on the disk. Each of the two copies of the FAT has exactly one entry for each cluster.

When a file is stored to disk, its data is written in the clusters on the disk. The filename is stored in the folder, along with the number of the first cluster in which the data is stored. When the operating system fills the first cluster, data is written to the next free cluster on the disk. The FAT entry corresponding with the first cluster is filled with the number of the second cluster in the file. When the second cluster is full, the operating system continues to write in the next free cluster. The FAT entry for the second cluster is set to point to the cluster number for the third cluster, and so on. When a file is completely written to the disk, the FAT entry for the final cluster is filled with all 1s, which means end of file. At this time, the directory entry for the file is updated with the total file size. This is commonly referred to as the **linked-list** method.

Clusters are of a fixed length, and if a file does not exactly match the space available in the clusters it uses, you can end up with some unused space at the end of a cluster. This is a little wasteful, and it also explains why a file's directory entry must include the exact file size. The operating system sets all FAT entries to 0s when it formats the disk, indicating that none of the clusters is being used. When you write a file to disk, the operating system finds free space on the disk by simply looking for the next FAT entry that contains all 0s. In most cases, the *format* command reads every address on the disk to make sure they are usable. Unusable spots are marked in the FAT as **bad clusters**, and these areas are never used for file storage. It then writes a new root directory and file allocation table, and the disk is ready for use.

Formatting a disk removes all data that was on the disk. On disks that have never been formatted, the *format* command writes new sector and track markers on the disk. On disks used previously, you can use the */q* (Quick Format) option. This tells *format* to dispense with the disk check, and simply write a new root directory and FAT table. Using the */q* switch makes the format operation a lot faster, but it also skips the detailed checking of the disk, which can cause trouble later if an application tries to write information to a bad disk location.

The format process on a hard disk is the same as on a floppy disk, with two exceptions. The first is related to the size of each entry in the FAT16 table, which is 16 bits long on any disk larger than 16 MB. The second difference is in the cluster size. On a floppy disk, there are very few sectors, and there are enough FAT entries to use a cluster size of one sector per cluster. On a hard disk, several sectors are combined into a cluster. Exactly how many sectors per cluster depends on the size of the hard disk.

Recall that the largest possible partition in a FAT16 file system is 4 GB. Keep in mind that the smallest allocation unit is one cluster. If you store a file that is 300 bytes long on a file system that has clusters of 64 KB, you will waste a lot of space. It is for this reason that smaller cluster sizes are generally considered desirable. As a result, Windows systems using FAT with large hard disks frequently have many hard disk partitions.

Each partition stores an extra copy of the FAT table in case the first copy gets damaged. However, there is only one copy of the root directory on each partition. This concept is shown in Figure 3-7.

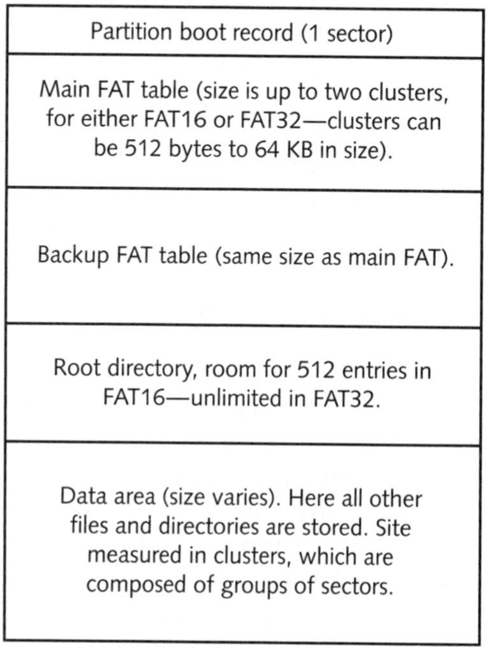

Partition boot record (1 sector)
Main FAT table (size is up to two clusters, for either FAT16 or FAT32—clusters can be 512 bytes to 64 KB in size).
Backup FAT table (same size as main FAT).
Root directory, room for 512 entries in FAT16—unlimited in FAT32.
Data area (size varies). Here all other files and directories are stored. Site measured in clusters, which are composed of groups of sectors.

Figure 3-7   Typical FAT directory structure

The FAT tables and root directory are found at the beginning of each partition, and they are always at the same location. This makes it possible for the boot program to easily find the files needed to start the operating system. Other directories in the file system are specialized files. They are identical to any other file in the operating system, with the exception of having the directory attribute set in their own directory entry. There can be a virtually unlimited number of directories, with a virtually unlimited number of files in each (limited only by the amount of storage space on the disk).

The FAT directory structure is simple. In each directory entry, information about the file is stored, including the filename, the file change date and time, the file size, and the file attributes. As mentioned earlier, the filename consists of two parts: the name and the extension, which contains up to three characters. Extensions can have a special meaning. Files with a .sys extension are generally device drivers; files with .com or .exe extensions are program files the operating system can execute; and files with the .bat extension are batch files of commands that can be executed as if they were typed on the keyboard. The filename and extension are separated by a period.

Apart from the filename, each directory entry also contains some **status bits** that identify the type of filename contained in each entry. The status bits in use are Volume, Directory,

System, Hidden, Read-only, and Archive. The Volume bit indicates a file system **volume label**, or a nickname for the file system. The volume name can be set with the /v option of the *format* command, or by using the *volume* command. The volume name appears at the top of folder listings (using the *dir* command). The Directory bit is used to signify that a file contains folder data and should be treated as a folder by the file system. Folders may in turn contain subfolders, as long as the names of all subfolders in a path do not exceed 80 characters. You will see a folder marked with a <DIR> label when you use the *dir* command in the Command Prompt window or designated with a file folder icon in My Computer or Windows Explorer. The four remaining attributes indicate additional information about a file. Files that are part of the operating system and should not be touched by programs or users are marked with a System or S flag. Files that should not be visible to the user are known as Hidden files and are marked with the H bit. Files that should not be written to are known as Read-only files and are marked with the R flag. Lastly, files that should be backed up the next time a backup is made are said to have the Archive, or A flag, set.

All in all, there are four optional flags—H, S, R, and A. The *attrib* Command Prompt window command can be used to look at or set these attributes. Typing *attrib* followed by a folder name shows all of the attribute settings for all the files, whereas typing *attrib* followed by a filename shows only attributes specific to that file. The *attrib* command can also be used to set file attributes. To do this, the *attrib* command is followed by the attribute letter, the + sign to set, or the − sign to unset an attribute, and the filename in question. To make a file named test.txt hidden, for example, you would type *attrib +h test.txt*. If you then typed *dir*, you would not see the test.txt file, but if you typed *attrib test.txt*, you would once again see test.txt, with the letter H in front of it, letting you know it is a Hidden file. A file with the S attribute set also does not show in *dir* listings, but you can view it with the *attrib* command, and you can remove the System attribute with *attrib* as well. Table 3-2 shows the various arguments and switches you can use with the *attrib* command.

Table 3-2   Attribute command (*attrib*) arguments and switches

Argument/Switch	Description
r	Read-only file attribute
a	Archive file attribute
s	System file attribute
h	Hidden file attribute
/s	Processes files in all folders in the specified path
/d	Configures folders as well as files

FAT32

Windows 2000, XP, and Server 2003 all support FAT32, which is the same file system available in Windows 95 Release 2, Windows 98, and Windows Me. FAT32 is designed to accommodate larger capacity disks than FAT16 and avoid the problem of cluster size limitations. A file allocation table entry in FAT32 is 32 bits in length and FAT32 supports up to 2^{28} clusters (this figure is not to the 32nd power because some extra space is reserved for the operating system). In FAT32, the root folder does not have to be at the beginning of a volume, it can be located anywhere. Also, FAT32 can use disk space more efficiently than FAT16 because it can use smaller cluster sizes. FAT32 partitions have a theoretical size of 2 terabytes (TB); however, the largest volume that can be formatted is 32 GB (still much larger than FAT16). The maximum file size in FAT32 is raised to 4 GB.

FAT32 shares characteristics of extended FAT16 such as the double FAT structure at the beginning of a partition for fault tolerance and the use of LFNs and Unicode.

In Windows 2000/XP/Server 2003, sometimes users choose to employ FAT16 or FAT32 because they are familiar with these file systems or they have dual-boot systems, such as a system with Windows XP and the older Windows 98. Another reason for using FAT16 or FAT32 is that these file systems offer fast response on small 1 or 2 GB partitions.

From the Trenches...

Sometimes Windows NT/2000/XP users create two partitions, one for FAT and one for NTFS. The FAT partition is relatively small, between 2 and 4 GB, and contains the system directory, \Winnt or \Windows. Program and data files are kept on the larger NTFS partition. In this way, the FAT partition enables fast response for the system files, and the NTFS partition affords reliability and security for the application and data files. However, with today's fast computers and disk drives, creating two partitions is less and less common. Also, keeping your system files on a FAT partition does not afford much security, particularly for a server. And, if you run an Internet browser from the FAT partition, it doesn't take long for the limited disk space on that partition to fill up with temporary Internet files.

Any Windows 2000, XP, or Server 2003 system can be converted from FAT16 or FAT32 to NTFS, either during installation or at a later date. If you convert at a later date, use the *convert* command at the Command Prompt window. However, you cannot convert from NTFS to FAT16 or FAT32, except by reformatting to use FAT16 or FAT32 and then performing a full file restore. A file restore is performed from media that was used to backup files in advance, such as a tape. You can use the Windows Backup tool to perform a backup or a restore from a previously made backup. The Backup tool is opened by clicking Start, pointing to Programs (in Windows 2000) or All Programs (in Windows XP/Server 2003), pointing to Accessories, pointing to System Tools, and clicking Backup.

CAUTION Converting from FAT16 or FAT32 to NTFS can take many hours on a volume that is over 1 GB, and the conversion process may appear hung, even though it is not. Thus, give any conversion a day or more to complete, and do not interrupt it by powering off the computer in the middle of the process.

TIP

If a partition is set up for FAT and is 2 GB or smaller, Windows 2000, XP, and Server 2003 will format it as FAT16 during installation (if the option to use FAT is selected). Partitions that are over 2 GB are formatted as FAT32.

NTFS

New Technology File System (NTFS) is the native Windows 2000/XP/Server 2003 file system, a modern system designed for the needs of a networked environment. Windows 2000, XP, and Server 2003 use NTFS version 5 (NTFS 5), which evolved from NTFS 4 used in Windows NT 4.0 The Windows NT Service Pack 4 update for Windows NT 4.0 also provides an add-on that enables that operating system to read partitions that are formatted for NTFS 5. The basic features initially incorporated into NTFS 4 include:

- Long filenames
- Built-in security features
- Better file compression than FAT
- Ability to use larger disks and files than FAT
- File activity tracking for better recovery and stability than FAT
- POSIX support
- Volume striping and volume extensions
- Less disk fragmentation than FAT

NTFS enables the use of LFNs that are compatible with LFN FAT filenames. If an LFN is used in NTFS, that file can be copied to a FAT16 or FAT32 volume, and the filename remains intact (although the NTFS security permissions not supported in FAT16 or FAT32 are not carried over).

As a full-featured network file system, NTFS is equipped with security features that meet the U.S. government's C2 security specifications. C2 security refers to high-level, "top-secret" standards for data protection, system auditing, and system access, which are required by some government agencies. One security feature is the ability to establish the type of access allowed for users of folders and files within folders. The file and folder access can be tailored to the particular requirements of an organization. For example, the system files on a server can be protected so only the server administrator has access. A folder of databases can be protected with read access, but no access to change data; and a public folder can give users in a designated group access to read and update files, but not to delete files.

File compression is a process that significantly reduces the size of a file by removing unused space within a file or using compression algorithms. Some files can be compressed by more than 40 percent, saving important disk space for other storage needs. This is particularly useful for files that are accessed infrequently. NTFS provides the ability to compress files as needed. Try Hands-on Project 3-8 to compress files in Windows 2000, Windows XP, or Windows Server 2003.

NTFS can be scaled to accommodate very large files, particularly for database applications. A Microsoft SQL Server database file might be 20 GB or larger, for example. This means an organization can store pictures, scanned images, and sound clips in a single database. The NTFS system can support files up to 2^{64} bytes (in theory).

Another NTFS feature is **journaling**, the ability to keep a log or journal of file system activity. This is a critical process should there be a power outage or hard disk failure. Important information can be retrieved and restored in these situations. FAT does not offer this capability.

NTFS supports **Portable Operating System Interface (POSIX)** standards to enable portability of applications from one computer system to another. POSIX was initially developed as a UNIX standard designed to ensure portability of applications among various versions of UNIX, but now POSIX is used by other file and operating systems as well. NTFS 5 follows the POSIX 1 standard, which includes case-sensitive filenames and use of multiple filenames (called hard links, a concept discussed later in this chapter). For example, the files Myfile.doc and MYFile.doc are considered different files (except when using Windows Explorer or the Command Prompt window).

NOTE

For complete compatibility, POSIX must be supported via the file system and the operating system. Windows XP is not technically fully compatible with POSIX, because it implements a proprietary Microsoft environment called Interix, which is intended to be similar to POSIX, but with more functionality. However, Windows 2000 and Windows Server 2003 are compatible with POSIX.

An important volume-handling feature of NTFS is the ability to create extensions on an existing volume, such as when new disk storage is added. Another feature is volume striping, which is a process that equally divides the contents of each file across two or more volumes to extend disk life, enable fault tolerance features, and balance the disk load for better performance.

Last, NTFS is less prone to file corruption than FAT in part because it has a **hot fix** capability, which means that if a bad disk area is detected, NTFS automatically copies the information from the bad area to another disk area that is not damaged.

In addition to the NTFS 4 features already described, NTFS 5 adds several new features:

- Ability to encrypt files.
- No system reboot required after creating an extended volume.
- Ability to reduce drive designations.
- Indexing for fast access.

3

- Ability to retain shortcuts and other file information when files and folders are placed on other volumes. (In Windows systems, a shortcut is a link or icon that can start software in the same or in a different location through a simple mouse click or double-click.)

- Ability to establish disk quotas.

With NTFS 5, files can be encrypted so that their contents are available only to those granted access. Also, volume extensions can be set up without the need to reboot the system. (In NTFS 4 you must reboot after adding an extension onto an existing volume.) Volume mount points can be created as a way to reduce the number of drive designations for multiple volumes, instead of designating a new drive for each new volume. In Windows, a mount point appears to the user as a folder, but this is really a link to a hard drive, CD-ROM, or other storage medium. NTFS 5 incorporates fast indexing in conjunction with Active Directory to make file searching and retrieval faster than in NTFS 4. A new technique called **Distributed Link Tracking** is available in NTFS 5 so that shortcuts you have created are not lost when you move files to another volume. Finally, NTFS 5 enables you to set up **disk quotas** to control how much disk space users can occupy. Disk quotas are a vital tool for disk capacity planning to ensure that there is enough disk space for all server operations and critical files.

NTFS 4 in Windows NT Server 4.0 does not have built-in disk quota capabilities, but third-party software is available to set up disk quotas.

TIP

The way NTFS keeps track of files and clusters is a little different from the FAT file systems. Rather than using a structure of FAT tables and directories, NTFS uses a **Master File Table (MFT)**. Like the FAT tables and directories, this table is located at the beginning of the partition. The boot sector is located ahead of the MFT. Following the MFT, there are several system files that the file system uses to make all the features of NTFS work. Note that the MFT in itself is nothing more than a file on the file system, as are all other system files. The second file on the disk is a copy of the first three records of the MFT. This ensures that if the MFT is damaged, it can be re-created. File number five, known as $, contains the entries in the root directory, whereas file number six, known as $Bitmap, contains data about what clusters on the disk are in use. Normally, the MFT and related files take up about 1 MB of disk space when the disk is initially formatted. As you can see, this would make it impractical to use NTFS on floppy disks. It is therefore not possible to format floppy disks in NTFS format.

When a file is created in NTFS, a record for that file is added to the MFT. This record contains all standard information, such as filename, size, dates, and timestamps. It also contains additional attributes, such as security settings, ownership, and permissions. If there is not enough room in an MFT record to store security settings, the settings that don't fit are put on another cluster somewhere on the disk, and the MFT record points to this information. If a file is very small, there is sometimes enough room in the MFT record to store the file data. If there is not enough room, the system allocates clusters elsewhere on the disk. The MFT record reflects the sequence of clusters that a file uses. The attributes can generally be repeated; it is possible to have a whole series of different security attributes for different users. It also is possible to have multiple filenames that refer to the same file, a technique known as **hard linking**. This is a feature, also available in UNIX/Linux file systems, sometimes used to make the same file appear in multiple directories without having to allocate disk space for the file more than once. Table 3-3 compares FAT16, FAT32, and NTFS.

Table 3-3   FAT16, FAT32, and NTFS compared

Feature	FAT16	FAT32	NTFS
Total volume size	4 GB	2 GB to 2 TB	2 TB
Maximum file size	2 GB	4 GB	Theoretical limit of 2^{64} bytes
Compatible with floppy disks	Yes	Yes	No
Security	Limited security based on attributes and shares	Limited security based on attributes and shares	Extensive security and auditing options
File compression	Supported with extra utilities	Supported with extra utilities	Supported as part of NTFS
File activity tracking	None	None	Tracking via a log
POSIX support	None	Limited	POSIX 1 support
Hot fix	Limited	Limited	Supports hot fix
Large database support	Limited	Yes	Yes
Multiple disk drives in one volume	No	No	Yes

CAUTION

When you copy a file from an NTFS system to a FAT16 or FAT32 system, the security permissions of the file that are not supported in FAT16 or FAT32 are lost. This may not sound like a big deal, but if you consider that all security settings to a confidential payroll spreadsheet can be lost by copying it to a temporary file on another partition (or on a floppy disk), and then back to the NTFS partition, you may change your mind.

Basic and Dynamic Disks

When you upgrade a Windows NT Server 4.0 to Windows 2000 Server or Windows Server 2003, the current NTFS disk partitions are automatically converted to basic disks, with a limited number of volumes on one disk. Also, basic disks use traditional disk management techniques, such as partitioning. Windows 2000 Server introduces the use of dynamic disks, which do not use traditional partitioning techniques. Dynamic disks make it

3

possible to set up a large number of volumes on one disk and provide the ability to extend volumes onto additional physical disks. You can convert basic disks to dynamic disks by using the Disk Management tool.

NTFS File System and Disk Utilities

Sometimes disk performance is affected by corrupted files, or when the file allocation table loses pointers to certain files. You can correct these problems and maintain the integrity of the data by periodically running the "Checkdisk" utility, called *chkdsk*. Windows 2000, Windows XP, and Windows Server 2003 all come with *chkdsk*, which is run from the Command Prompt window or by clicking Start, clicking Run, entering *chkdsk*, and pressing OK. The *chkdsk* utility can detect and fix an extensive set of file system problems in FAT and NTFS systems. Table 3-4 presents a list of the switches that are available for this utility and Figure 3-8 illustrates the *chkdsk* results for a computer running Windows XP Professional.

Table 3-4   *chkdsk* switch options

Switch/Parameter	Purpose
[*volume*] (such as C:)	Specifies that *chkdsk* only check the designated volume
[*filename*] (such as* .dll)	Enables a check of the specified file or files only
/c	For NTFS only, *chkdsk* uses an abbreviated check of the folder structure
/f	Instructs *chkdsk* to fix errors that it finds and locks the disk while checking
/i	For NTFS only, *chkdsk* uses an abbreviated check of indexes
/L:*size*	For NTFS only, enables you to specify the size of the log file created by the disk check
/r	Searches for bad sectors, fixes problems, and recovers information (if possible, or use the recover command afterwards)
/v	On FAT, shows the entire path name of files; on NTFS, shows clean-up messages associated with errors
/x	Dismounts or locks a volume before starting (/f also dismounts or locks a volume)

Hands-on Project 3-9 enables you to run *chkdsk* in Windows 2000/XP/Server 2003.

TIP

In Windows 2000/XP/2003, *chkdsk* runs automatically at boot up if it detects that the operating system was previously shut down with a file system problem, or shut down before the operating system had the opportunity to clean up temporary files on the disk.

```
Command Prompt                                              _ □ ×
C:\>chkdsk
The type of the file system is NTFS.

WARNING!  F parameter not specified.
Running CHKDSK in read-only mode.

CHKDSK is verifying files (stage 1 of 3)...
File verification completed.
CHKDSK is verifying indexes (stage 2 of 3)...
Index verification completed.
CHKDSK is recovering lost files.
Recovering orphaned file 00010006.ci (55321) into directory file 17854.
Recovering orphaned file 00010006.dir (55325) into directory file 17854.
Recovering orphaned file CiFLfffc.001 (55329) into directory file 17854.
Recovering orphaned file CiFLfffc.002 (55330) into directory file 17854.
CHKDSK is verifying security descriptors (stage 3 of 3)...
Security descriptor verification completed.
CHKDSK is verifying Usn Journal...
Usn Journal verification completed.
Correcting errors in the master file table's (MFT) BITMAP attribute.
Correcting errors in the Volume Bitmap.
Windows found problems with the file system.
Run CHKDSK with the /F (fix) option to correct these.

   39029917 KB total disk space.
    9694332 KB in 54121 files.
      15224 KB in 2945 indexes.
          0 KB in bad sectors.
     141425 KB in use by the system.
      65536 KB occupied by the log file.
   29178936 KB available on disk.

       4096 bytes in each allocation unit.
    9757479 total allocation units on disk.
    7294734 allocation units available on disk.

C:\>_
```

Figure 3-8   Running *chkdsk* in Windows XP Professional

If *chkdsk* finds any problems, it either fixes them (depending on the error) or displays an error message. Or, you have the option of letting it fix all problems automatically by using the /f, or Fix option. The most common problems are files with 0 sizes, caused when a file is not properly closed, or chains of clusters (file allocation units) that have no directory entries attached. When *chkdsk* finds lost allocation units or chains, it prompts you with a yes or no question: Convert lost chains to files? Answer "yes" to the question so that you can save the lost information to files. The files that *chkdsk* creates for each lost chain are labeled Filexxx.chk, and can be edited with a text editor, such as Microsoft Word, to determine their contents. The presence of some bad sectors is normal. Many disks have a few bad sectors that are marked by the manufacturer during the low-level format on which data cannot be written. If there are hundreds of bad sectors, however, this indicates a problem with the disk.

TIP

If you frequently see errors when you run *chkdsk*, you should look for a bigger problem. Sometimes the operator is to blame. Systems that are not used properly—for example, because software is not closed correctly—can cause problems in the file system. Often, disks that are about to fail will show small glitches (*chkdsk* errors) a long time before they finally fail, so be alert for possible future system failure if you see frequent errors.

From the Trenches...

A customer who purchased a newly manufactured computer ran *chkdsk* on the hard drive to verify its condition. *chkdsk* showed that nearly half of the disk had bad clusters that were quarantined via the low-level format so they could not be used. Because the customer ran *chkdsk* right after receiving the computer, he was able to discover the problem right way and returned the computer for a more functional hard drive.

Windows 2000, XP, and Server 2003 all have a built-in disk defragmenting tool. Over time, disk space becomes fragmented with pockets of open space. For example, when one of these operating systems writes a file to disk, it looks for the first place in the first empty disk location and uses the cluster (allocation unit) indicated there. It continues to use the next empty cluster until there are no more clusters free immediately following the last cluster. At that point, it skips ahead to find the next open cluster. As a result, files written to disk may be scattered all over the disk. Imagine a scenario where four small files are written—we'll call them A, B, C, and D. On an empty disk, these files will occupy sequential clusters on the disk. If files A and C are removed, there will be some open clusters on the disk. If file E, which is larger than A and C combined, is written to the disk, it will start using the clusters formerly occupied by A, then use those formerly used by C, and then continue beyond the clusters occupied by D. When a disk is highly fragmented, the read heads have to work harder to obtain data, wasting time and creating more wear. For this reason, it is wise to periodically defragment your disks. A **defragmenter** is a tool that rearranges data on the disk in a continuous fashion, ridding the disk of scattered open clusters.

Windows 2000, XP, and Server 2003 all have Disk Defragmenter, which is initiated by clicking Start, pointing to Programs (in Windows 2000) or All Programs (in Windows XP/ Server 2003), pointing to Accessories, pointing to System Tools, and clicking Disk Defragmenter (see Figure 3-9). The Disk Defragmenter can be used on volumes formatted for FAT16, FAT32, and NTFS. Hands-on Project 3-10 enables you to use the Disk Defragmenter. You also learn more about defragmenting disks in Chapter 10.

Windows XP and Windows Server 2003 both come with a Disk Cleanup utility that deletes temporary Internet files, temporary program files, program files that are not used, and files in the Recycle Bin. To start this utility, click Start, point to All Programs, point to Accessories, point to System Tools, and click Disk Cleanup.

Care should be taken to use only utilities designed to work with NTFS; serious damage can occur if other utilities are used. If utilities designed for MS-DOS or Windows 95/98/Me are used on NTFS file systems, they may reach incorrect conclusions regarding file system layout. This can result in loss of data, damaged files, or even destruction of the complete file system and all of its contents.

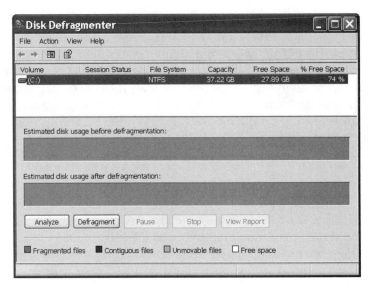

Figure 3-9   Disk Defragmenter in Windows XP

CDFS and UDF

Windows 2000, XP, and Server 2003 recognize two additional file systems used by peripheral storage technologies. The CD-ROM File System (CDFS) is supported so that these operating systems can read and write files to CD-ROM disk drives. CD-ROM capability is important for loading the operating systems, and sharing CD-ROM drives on a network. The **Universal Disk Format (UDF)** file system is also used on CD-ROM and large capacity DVD-ROM media, which are used for huge file storage to accommodate movies and games.

THE UNIX FILE SYSTEM

The UNIX file system works a little differently from anything discussed up to this point. "UNIX file system" is really a misnomer. There are, in reality, many different file systems that can be used, but some file systems are more "native" to specific UNIX/Linux operating systems than others. Most versions of UNIX and Linux, support the **UNIX file system (ufs)**, which is the original native UNIX file system. ufs is a hierarchical (tree structure) file system that is expandable, supports large storage, provides excellent security, and is reliable. In fact, many qualities of NTFS are modeled after ufs. ufs supports journaling so that if a system crashes unexpectedly, it is possible to reconstruct files or to roll back recent changes for minimum or no damage to the integrity of the files or data. ufs also supports hot fixes to automatically move data on damaged portions of disks to areas that are not damaged.

In Linux, the native file system is called the **extended file system(ext** or **ext fs)**, which is installed by default. ext is modeled after ufs, but the first version contained some bugs, supported files to only 2 GB, and did not offer journaling. However, in Linux, ext provides an advantage over all other file systems because it enables the use of the full range of built-in Linux commands, file manipulation, and security. Newer versions of Linux use either the second (ext2) or third (ext3) versions of the extended file system. ext2 is a reliable file system that handles large disk storage. ext3 has the enhancements of ext2 with the addition of journaling.

TIP

If you are not sure what file systems are incorporated in UNIX/Linux, you can determine them by viewing the contents of the /proc/filesystems file, or use the *mount* command to display the mounted file systems. Table 3-5 lists a sampling of file systems that are compatible with UNIX/Linux systems. Also, try Hands-on Project 3-11 to determine what file systems are loaded in a Linux installation.

Table 3-5   Typical file systems supported by UNIX/Linux

File System	Description
Extended file system (ext or ext fs) and the newer versions, second extended file system (ext2 or ext2 fs), and third extended file system (ext3 or ext3 fs)	File system that comes with Linux by default (compatible with Linux and FreeBSD)
High-performance file system (hpfs)	File system developed for use with the OS/2 operating system
msdos	File system that offers compatibility with FAT12 and FAT16 (does not support long filenames); typically installed to enable UNIX/Linux to read floppy disks made in MS-DOS or Windows
International Standard Operating system (iso9660 in Linux, hsfs in Solaris, cd9660 in FreeBSD)	File system developed for CD-ROM use; does not support long filenames
Proc file system	File system that presents information about the kernel status and the use of memory (not truly a physical file system, but a logical file system)
Network file system (nfs)	File system developed by Sun Microsystems for UNIX systems to support network access and sharing of files (such as uploading and downloading files) and supported on virtually all UNIX/Linux versions as well as by many other operating systems
Swap file system	File system for the swap space; swap space is disk space used exclusively to store spillover information from memory, when memory is full (called virtual memory) and used by virtually all UNIX/Linux systems

Table 3-5 Typical file systems supported by UNIX/Linux (continued)

File System	Description
UNIX file system (ufs; also called the Berkeley Fast File System)	Original file system for UNIX that is compatible with virtually all UNIX systems and most Linux systems
uMS/DOS	File system that is compatible with extended FAT16 as used by Windows NT, 2000, XP, and Server 2003, but it also supports security permissions, file ownership, and long filenames
vfat	File system that is compatible with FAT32 and supports long filenames
ntfs	File system used by Windows 2000/XP/ Server 2003

The main difference between native UNIX/Linux file systems, such as ufs and ext and those covered earlier in the chapter, lies in the way information is physically stored on the disk. Because ufs and ext are the most popular file systems across UNIX/Linux platforms we detail them here and lump them into the reference—"UNIX/Linux file system." Both file systems use the same structure, which is built on the concept of information nodes, or **inodes**. Each file has an inode and is identified by an inode number. Inode 0 contains the root of the folder structure (/) and is the jumping-off point for all other inodes. This concept is shown in Figure 3-10.

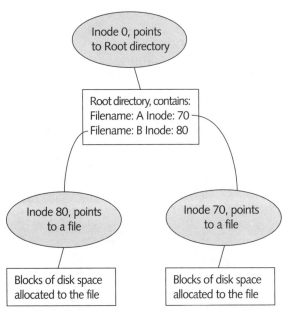

Figure 3-10 UNIX/Linux information nodes (inodes) design

3

You can display inode information for directories and files by using the *ls -l* command. Also, note that in most UNIX/Linux systems a directory is technically just a file that can hold other files.

TIP

An inode contains 1) the name of a file, 2) general information about that file, and 3) information (a pointer) about how to locate the file on a disk. In terms of general information, each inode indicates user and group ownership, access mode (read, write, execute security permissions), the size and type of the file, the date the file was created, and the date the file was last modified and read.

The pointer information is based on logical blocks. Each disk is divided into logical blocks ranging in size (depending on the version of UNIX/Linux) from 512 to 8192 bytes or more (but blocks can also be divided into multiple subblocks or fractions as needed by the file system). The inode for a file contains a pointer (number) that tells the operating system how to locate the first in a set of one or more logical blocks that contain the specific file contents (or it specifies the number of blocks or links to the first block used by the folder or file). In short, the inode tells the operating system where to find a file on the hard disk.

Groups of blocks are allocated to specific cylinders on a disk. Also, to handle large files, the file system can assign these files to one or more cylinders. The end of files or small files are stored in fragmented blocks. A block can be divided by two repeatedly until the smallest fractional block size is reached, which is typically equal to the size of a single sector on the disk.

NOTE

When the file system is created, a fixed number of inodes is created. Because every unique file uses an inode on the file system, the number of inodes needs to be set high enough so that the system can hold enough files. It is not possible to increase or decrease the number of inodes, so, by default, a very conservative scheme is used, which allocates an inode for each 4 KB of disk space. Note that everything in the UNIX/Linux file system is tied to inodes. Space is allocated one block, or fraction of a block, at a time. The directories in this file system are simple files that have been marked with a directory flag in their inodes. The file system itself is identified by the superblock. The **superblock** contains information about the layout of blocks, sectors, and cylinder groups on the file system. This information is the key to finding anything on the file system, and it should never change. Without the superblock, the file system cannot be accessed. For this reason, many copies of the superblock are written into the file system at the time of file system creation. If the superblock is destroyed, you can copy one of the superblock copies over the original, damaged superblock to restore access to the file system.

Note that the inode does not contain a filename; the filename is stored in a directory, which in itself is no more than a file. In it is stored the names of the files and the inode to which they are connected. Several directory entries can point to the same inode. This implements a hard link, which makes it possible to have one file appear in several directories, or in the same directory under several names, without using a lot of disk space. You can see how this works in Figure 3-11.

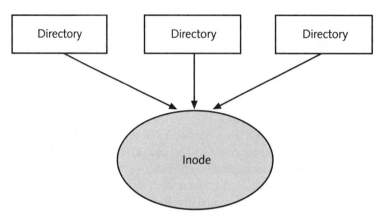

Figure 3-11   Multiple directory entries point to the same inode

The inode keeps a counter that tells how many directory entries point to a file. Deleting a file is achieved by deleting the last directory entry, which brings the inode link count down to 0, meaning the file has effectively been removed.

A UNIX/Linux system can have many file systems. Unlike the MS-DOS and Windows environment where each file system must have a letter of the alphabet assigned to it to enable access, UNIX/Linux mounts file systems as a sub file system of the root file system. In UNIX/Linux, all file systems are referred to by a path (see Figure 3-12).

The path starts out with /, which indicates the main root directory of the root file system. If other file systems are to be used, a directory is created on the root file system—for example, we will call it "usr." Then, using the *mount* command, the UNIX/Linux operating system is told to associate the root inode of another file system to the empty directory. This process can be repeated many times, and there is no hard limit to the number of file systems that can be mounted this way, short of the number of inodes in the root file system. Every file in every file system on a computer is thus referred to by a long directory path, and jumping from one file system to another is seamless. The *mount* command has several options; typing it without parameters results in a display of the disks (and file systems) that are currently mounted. For each disk, you will see the name of the partition and the path on which it was mounted. A typical *mount* listing for UNIX/Linux is shown later in this chapter in Hands-on Project 3-11.

Directories in the file system contain a series of filenames, and as mentioned earlier, directory names themselves are no more than filenames. UNIX/Linux allows you to use extremely long filenames, which may include any character that can be represented by the ASCII character set, including spaces.

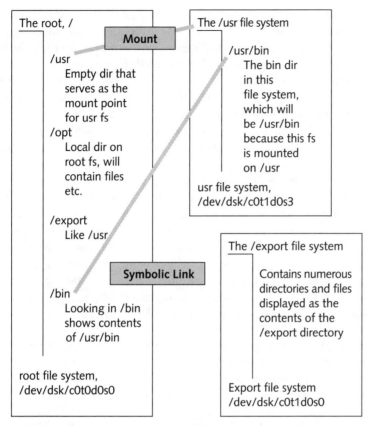

Figure 3-12   UNIX/Linux file system path entries

NOTE

The UNIX/Linux operating system and file system treat uppercase and lower-case characters as different characters; a file named HELLO is a different file from a file named hello, which is in turn different from one named Hello. It is, therefore, extremely important to type UNIX/Linux filenames exactly as they appear.

As we already mentioned, a directory is nothing more than a special file. There are several other special files in the UNIX/Linux file system. Disks themselves are, for example, referenced by a special inode called a device. There are two types of devices: **raw devices** and **block devices**. A raw device has no logical division in blocks, whereas a block device does. Every device the UNIX/Linux computer uses must be represented by a device inode, whether it is a disk, a serial port, or an Ethernet (network) card. These devices have special parameters in the inode that enable the OS to figure out how to get to them. All partitions of all disks appear as devices. For example, an ext3 partition on a hard disk may be represented as /dev/hda1. Devices are normally kept in the /dev or /devices directory. When you look at the output of the *mount* command, you will see your disks referenced this way (refer to Figure 3-22 in the Hands-on Projects).

There is another special feature of the UNIX/Linux file system we should mention here, the symbolic link. As we previously indicated, it is possible to link multiple directory entries to one inode. For this to work, the inode and the directory entry must be on the same partition. If you want to link a directory entry to a file that is on a different partition, you must use a feature known as a **symbolic link**. This is a special file that has a flag set in the inode to identify it as a symbolic link. The content of the file is a path that, when followed, leads to another file. Whenever one of these symbolic links is accessed, the operating system reads the contents of the symbolic link file and interprets that as if it were the filename typed, referencing the directory entry, and then in turn the inode to which the symbolic link refers. Note that a hard link, when created, must point to a valid inode and will therefore always be valid. A symbolic link is merely a pointer to a file. It is possible to create symbolic links that point to files that do not exist, or to remove the file to which a symbolic link points without removing the link. Doing this can result in having a symbolic link that, when looked at in a directory, appears to be a valid file, but when opened returns a "no such file" error. Another interesting effect of using symbolic links is that it is possible to create loops. You can make a Directory A, which contains a Directory B, which contains a link back to Directory A. This is a feature that is nice, but it can end up being extremely confusing. Links are made with the *ln* command, and the *-s* option is used to make a symbolic link. The first option is the name of the existing file, followed by the name of the link you wish to create.

TIP   One way to save time in typing is to create a link to a directory that has a long path. For example, assume that you store many files in the /user/bus/inventory directory. Each time you want to perform a listing of that directory, you must type *ls /user/bus/inventory*. If you enter *ln -s /user/bus/inventory* to create a link to that directory, in the future you only have to type *ls inventory* to see its contents. To learn more about the *ln* command type *man ln* and press Enter. *man* is the command for displaying the contents of the online manual pages for a specific command, such as *ls*.

As with all other operating systems discussed so far, you first have to partition a disk to use the UNIX/Linux file system. The command used to partition the disk differs slightly from one version of UNIX/Linux to another. In most UNIX/Linux systems, either *fdisk* or *format* does the job. The utility is generally text based, and it requires you to type commands. Typing *man fdisk* or *man format* and pressing Enter at the command prompt gives you an overview of available commands. In the *format* utility, you can type *partition* to display a screen with partition information. The *print sub* command shows you current partition information, while the other menu commands can be used to adjust individual partitions on the disk.

TIP   Great care should be taken when changing partitions. UNIX/Linux lets you make any changes you want without the extensive warnings found in operating systems like Microsoft Windows. This is because you make these changes using the root account for the system administrator, which gives you full access to the operating system.

After making your changes, the *write* command saves the disk label to the disk (recall that a disk label is the UNIX/Linux equivalent to a Windows partition table). Most versions of UNIX/Linux allow you to write a backup label in addition to the main disk label; this is a good idea, as it can be used to restore the original label if something goes wrong with the disk. The *fdisk* utility is similar to the partition section of the *format* utility. It usually has a *print* command that shows you the contents of the partition table and other commands to edit partition information and write the disk label and backup label. The same caution applies here that applies to the partition editing tools in *format*. Linux uses an *fdisk* utility, but Solaris uses *format*, for example.

Once a partition is made, it is time to create the file system. To do this, you must know the device name of the partition on which you wish to create a file system. This name can be obtained from the *print partition table* command in *fdisk* or *format*. The most convenient way to create a new file system is the *newfs* command. Simply type *newfs*, followed by the name of the device. After you confirm that you wish to create a new file system, you will see a progress report showing you where copies of the superblocks are written, as well as some information about the cylinder group and the number of inodes. When *newfs* is completed, you can make a mount point for the new file system (note that a mount point in UNIX/Linux is nothing more than an empty directory which is at the disk location in which the file system contents will appear) using the *mkdir* command. If, for example, you want to mount the new file system you just created on /dev/rdsk/c0t0d0s1 on the /test mount point, you type *mkdir /test*. Next, you mount the file system by typing *mount /dev/rdsk/c0t0d0s1 /test*, and now you are ready to use the new file system. *newfs* is available in many versions of UNIX, such as in Solaris UNIX, but it is not available in all versions of Linux, including Red Hat Enterprise Linux. The *newfs* command in turn uses the *mkfs* program to actually create the file system. In UNIX/Linux varieties where *newfs* is not available, *mkfs* should be used instead (available in Red Hat Enterprise Linux). Use of *mkfs* is less desirable because it requires the user to specify many parameters, such as the size of the file system, the block size, number of inodes, number of superblock copies and their locations, and a few others, depending on the version of UNIX/Linux. The *newfs* utility takes care of all these details automatically.

UNIX/Linux is very picky when it comes to file system consistency. If it finds problems on the file system in the inodes, superblock, or directory structures, it will shut down. When you save a file to disk, the system first stores part of the data in memory, until it has time to write it to disk. If for some reason your computer stops working before the data is written to disk, you can end up with a damaged file system. This is why UNIX/Linux machines should always be shut down using the proper shutdown commands, which ensure that all data is stored on disk before the machine is brought down. In normal operation, all data waiting to be saved to disk in memory is written to disk every 30 seconds. You can manually force a write of all data in memory by using the *sync* command. When the system is properly shut down, the file systems are unmounted. A flag is set in the superblock of each file system to indicate that the file system was properly closed, and does not need to be checked at startup. Whenever the machine starts up, UNIX/Linux checks the file systems to make sure they are all working properly. To do this, the operating system verifies the integrity of the super-block, the inodes, all cluster groups, and all directory entries. The program that performs this operation is the file system checker, also known as *fsck*.

CAUTION

You can manually run *fsck* at any time to perform file system checks after the system is up, but take great care when doing this. If data on the disk is changed while an *fsck* is in progress, the results may be disastrous. The most common problems found when *fsck* is run are unlinked inodes, directory entries with no associated inodes, and wrong free block counts. All of these can be a result of a system that was not properly shut down. If these errors occur frequently, hardware failure may be imminent.

Typically, ufs/ext file systems can be up to 4 GB in size, but by using larger block sizes, the systems can be made much larger. Depending on the implementation of UNIX/Linux being used, and the exact ufs/ext version in use, it is possible to create file systems in excess of 32 exabytes. Typically, the maximum file size is 2 GB, but in some versions of UNIX/Linux it is possible to use special libraries that allow for the creation of larger files. Check your UNIX/Linux manuals to find out more about the particular file systems your implementation supports. Most of these systems use the standard commands discussed here. Table 3-6 presents a summary of useful commands for managing UNIX/Linux file systems.

Table 3-6   UNIX/Linux file system commands

Command	Description
cat	Displays the contents of a file to the screen
cd	Changes to another directory
cp	Copies a file to another directory (and you can rename the file at the same time)
fdisk	Formats and partitions a disk in some UNIX systems, such as Linux
format	Formats and partitions a disk in some UNIX systems, such as Solaris
ls	Lists contents of a directory
mkdir	Creates a directory
mkfs	Creates a file system (but requires more parameters than *newfs*)
mount	Lists the disk currently mounted; also mounts file systems and devices (such as a CD-ROM)
mv	Moves a file to a different directory
newfs	Creates a new file system in some versions of UNIX/Linux
rm	Removes a file or directory
sync	Forces information in memory to be written to disk
touch	Creates an empty file
umount	Unmounts a file system

THE NETWARE FILE SYSTEM

The NetWare file system is built to enable the NetWare server services over a network. In NetWare 6.x, the file system has evolved into **Novell Storage Services (NSS)**, which is a file system that uses disk partitions, storage pools, and volumes. NSS is in version 3 at this writing. One of the hallmarks of NSS is its great flexibility in terms of managing files and folders through a wide range of attributes and user rights. You learn much more about these qualities in Chapter 9; however, this chapter provides a basic introduction to NSS.

When you use NSS, you begin by creating one or more disk partitions. NSS enables you to create a nearly unlimited number of disk partitions to match the needs of your organization. In a basic setup, there is one 200-MB or larger FAT (DOS) partition that is needed for the installation of the operating system. A minimum of 200 MB is needed for the installation, but some organizations make a FAT partition up to 1 GB for extra space and in which to store DOS-based utilities. Also needed is an NSS partition for the SYS volume, which contains system, login, and other important files. A typical size for this partition is 5 GB or more. Additional partitions are used for creating user home folders and for storing files and databases. For example, there might be a 20-GB NSS partition for user home folders and a 20-GB NSS partition for shared files or database files. Also, some organizations leave unpartitioned (free) disk space available so there is space reserved for future expansion.

The next step after partitioning is the creation of storage pools. **Storage pools** offer additional ways to divide the use of a disk and can be a superset of disk partitions because one storage pool can house one or more disk partitions. For example, the SYS partition might be one storage pool. A partition for user home folders and another partition for databases might be combined into one storage pool.

After storage pools, volumes are created to enable users to access directories and files. In NetWare 6.0 and above, you can create either traditional volumes or NSS volumes. The traditional volumes are offered for backward-compatibility to earlier operating system versions and have some limitations when compared to NSS volumes. For example, the maximum number of volumes housed on a server with traditional volumes is 64, while the maximum number of volumes on a server using NSS volumes is 255. The amount of memory required to mount a traditional volume is 10 times the memory required to mount an NSS volume. Further, traditional volumes can have up to 16 million files, while NSS volumes can have an unlimited number of files. Finally, traditional volumes use the FAT structure, which takes longer to mount and has slower file access. NSS volumes use the **balanced-tree (b-tree)** file structure that enables fast file access through creating an internal file system tree structure off of the root that is more horizontally oriented than vertically oriented. Thus, instead of indexing the directory and file structure several layers deep—for example, root directory to a directory under a directory under a directory under a directory and finally to the file—the indexing of directories and files is just off of the root directory—root directory to a directory to a file, for instance.

NOTE Two Web sites that provide background about b-tree concepts are *www.semaphorecorp.com/btp/algo.html* and *www.bluerwhite.org/btree*.

Other features of NSS include:

- File compression
- Hot fixes when a damaged disk area is detected
- Journaling to enable data error correction and recovery, such as after a system crash from a power failure
- Ability to have user disk quotas
- Automatic flushing of files so they are written from memory to disk immediately after creation
- Ability to expand storage pools
- Data shredding, so that deleted files are immediately purged and cannot be salvaged (for security)
- Improved techniques for backing up files

NSS is managed through tools such as ConsoleOne, which is a system manager's tool that can be started from the server console or can be used remotely from a workstation (with the proper security access), such as from Windows XP Professional. For example, a system manager might have a ConsoleOne icon on the desktop from which to start this management tool. Another tool available for managing NSS is the NetWare Remote Manager.

THE MACINTOSH FILE SYSTEM

The original **Macintosh Filing System (MFS)** of 1984 was limited to keeping track of 128 documents, applications, or folders. This was a reasonable limit when the only storage device was a 400 KB floppy disk drive. As larger disks became available, the need for directories and subdirectories became obvious, and Apple responded with the **Hierarchical Filing System (HFS)** in 1986.

Like FAT16, HFS divides a volume (the Mac term for a disk or disk partition) into, at most, 2^{16} (65,536) units. On PC systems, these units are called clusters or allocation units. On the Mac, they are called **allocation blocks**, but the principle is the same. Interestingly, while UNIX/Linux and Windows operating systems report file sizes in terms of their actual physical size, the Macintosh operating system in some places reports file sizes in terms of logical size, based on the number of allocation blocks occupied by the file. The best way to view the actual physical size of a file is to use the Mac's Get Info option. The Get Info screen shows all types of information about a file, including its physical file size.

3

In 1998, Apple released Mac OS 8.1, which introduced a new disk format, Hierarchical Filing System Extended Format—variously referred to as Mac OS HFS+, Mac OS Extended, or Mac OS Extended (HFS+)which is used today in Mac OS X. Like NTFS for Windows 2000/XP/Server 2003, the newer HFS+ format increases the number of allocation blocks per volume to 2^{32}. This creates smaller allocation blocks (clusters) and more efficient disk utilization. Systems using Mac OS 8.1 or later can format disks in either Mac OS Standard (HFS) or Mac OS Extended (HFS+) formats. However, Macintoshes with pre-8.1 versions of the OS can't read disks in Extended format. Floppy disks and other volumes smaller than 32 MB must continue to use Standard format.

In Mac OS X version 3.0, Mac OS Extended (HFS+) includes several new features, which are:

- A case-sensitive format to make the file system more compatible with other UNIX/Linux systems (optional)

- Journaling, which is turned on by default (see Figure 3-13) so that data can be recovered from a journal file if there is a disk or system problem that occurs while data is being updated or modified

- Ability to store up to 16 TB of data (particularly important for the Mac OS X Server version)

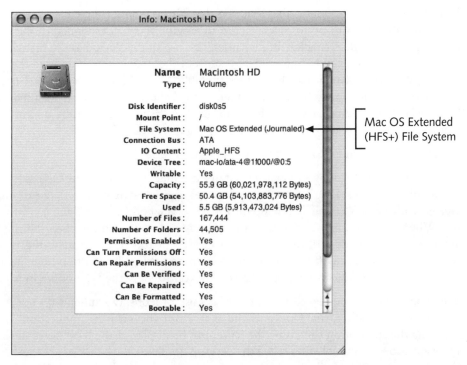

Figure 3-13   Mac OS X using the Mac OS Extended (HFS+) file system

The first two sectors of a Mac-formatted disk are the boot sectors, or boot blocks in Macintosh terminology. The boot blocks identify the filing system, the names of important system files, and other important information. The boot blocks are followed by the **volume information block**, which points to other important areas of information, such as the location of the system files, and the catalog and extents trees.

The **catalog b-tree** is the list of all files on the volume. It keeps track of a file's name, its logical location in the folder structure, its physical location on the disk surface, and the locations and sizes of the file's data fork and resource forks (discussed later in the chapter). The **extents b-tree** keeps track of the location of the file fragments, or extents.

Macintoshes can read and write to disks from other operating systems. For instance, Macs can read iso9660 CD-ROMs using the iso9660 CD-ROM driver. Macs can read all manner of MS-DOS- and Windows-formatted disks from floppy and Zip disks to almost any kind of SCSI device thanks to pre-Mac OS X tools, such as the PC Exchange control panel and to various Mac OS X tools, such as ones offered through System Preferences and as disk utilities. In Mac OS X, floppy disks can be formatted in non-Mac OS X formats, such as for MS-DOS and Windows by using the Disk Utility. Prior to Mac OS 8.5, disk reading/ writing utilities assumed that PCs used short filenames and truncated Mac filenames to 8.3 format when writing to DOS/Windows-formatted media. Beginning with Mac OS 8.5, the Mac writes files with long names to PC disks without truncation.

In terms of filename length, the Mac OS has always supported what might be called **medium filenames** of up to 31 characters in length. Mac OS Extended (HFS+) volumes can support Unicode characters in filenames. The use of the period as the first character in a filename is discouraged because older versions of the operating system used the period as the first character of invisible driver files (notably ".sony" for the Sony 3½" floppy disk drives). Any character may be used in a filename except the colon, which is used internally by the Mac OS as a directory separator, equivalent to slashes in other OSs. It's for this reason that Macintosh paths are written as colon-separated entities like this:

Hard Drive:System Folder:Preferences:Finder Prefs

UNIX/Linux and Windows operating systems use filename extensions such as .txt and .gif to identify file types. The Mac uses **type codes** and **creator codes**. As an example, files created with Apple's SimpleText text editor have a type code of APPL and a creator code of ttxt. When a user double-clicks such a file, the Mac knows it must open the file with an application (type code APPL) with a creator code of ttxt. You can view the type of file (creator code), such as a tiff file for a graphic, by using the Get Info option for a file, as shown in Figure 3-14. Hands-on Project 3-12 enables you to view the type of file in Mac OS X.

The type and creator codes facilitate the Mac's use of icons. Documents do not store their own icons, but rather, the Mac gets the icon from the creating application. Instead of accessing the application each time the icon must be displayed, the Mac stores the icons and file associations in invisible files called the desktop databases. Each disk or volume has its own desktop databases. "Rebuilding the desktop" on a Macintosh rebuilds these database files and is a common troubleshooting step when icons appear incorrectly. You can rebuild the

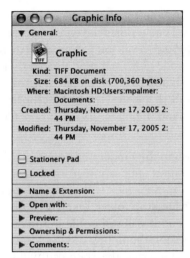

Figure 3-14   Using Get Info in Mac OS X

desktop on a disk at startup by holding the command and option keys. For removable media, hold down the command and option keys before inserting the disk.

One way in which Macintosh files are unique is that Mac files can contain two parts, or forks: the data fork and the resource fork. The **data fork** contains frequently changing information (such as word-processing data), while the **resource fork** contains information that is fixed (such as a program's icons, menu resources, and splash screens). One advantage of resource forks for programmers is that they modularize the program. For instance, it becomes very easy to change the text of a warning dialog or the name of a menu item without having to change the underlying code, so customization and internationalization are easier. Most Mac documents contain only a data fork. Traditionally, Mac applications contained only a resource fork, but programs written for PowerPC-equipped Macintoshes store PowerPC code in the data fork.

One clever use of the data and resource forks is to store style information in a plain text file. The text is stored in the data fork, while the style information (font face, color, font size, italics, etc.) is stored in the resource fork. The advantage of this system is that the text file can be read by any Mac text editing program, even if it doesn't understand the style information, and by any text editor on another operating system. This system is used by Apple's SimpleText program, America Online's text editor, and some other Mac programs.

Apple's free ResEdit utility can edit file resources. Using ResEdit, a programmer can modify a program's version number, splash screens, default memory allocation, icons, menu items, window resources, dialog text, and many other properties. Users can also use ResEdit to modify the way programs operate.

The fact that Mac files have type and creator codes and two forks can create problems when storing files on non-Macintosh servers (such as on a Windows 2000 or 2003 server), or transferring files over the Internet. The need to store Mac files on non-Mac computers has led to several Mac file formats for online services and the Internet. One of these formats is **MacBinary**, which joins the two forks into one, and safely stores the type and creator codes and finder flags. For files that must be transferred through seven-bit gateways (such as Usenet news), the preferred format is **BinHex**. Like uuencode (a format used frequently in e-mail applications to convert binary files into text files transferable in e-mail systems), BinHex transforms all files into seven-bit files using the ASCII character set. Like MacBinary, BinHex preserves the two forks, the type and creator codes, and the finder flags. BinHex files can be identified by the .hqx filename extension.

Folders can be created using the New Folder option in the Finder's File menu (at the top of the desktop) and in the Save and Save As dialogs in most applications. All volumes have two special, invisible folders: Trash and Desktop. If you move a file's icon from a floppy disk to the desktop, the file still resides in the floppy disk's Desktop folder. Likewise, you can move the file's icon to the Trash can without deleting it, and it will still reside in the floppy disk's Trash folder. You can prove this to yourself by ejecting the floppy disk and inserting it in another Macintosh. The files will appear on the desktop, and the Trash can will bulge.

Apple's equivalent of the UNIX/Linux symbolic link and Windows shortcut is the **alias**, introduced in System 7.0 in 1991. Files, folders, applications, and disks can be aliased. The system-level Alias Manager keeps track of the original, even if it is moved or renamed. The word "alias" is tacked onto the filename when the alias is created, and the filename is presented in italicized text. Beginning in OS 8.5, aliases also have small arrows on their icons, similar to shortcuts in Windows-based operating systems. Hands-on Project 3-12 enables you to create an alias.

Mac OS X comes with two important disk utilities: Disk Utility for managing disk drives and Disk First Aid for repairing disk problems. Mac OS X also comes with the Sherlock program. **Sherlock** can search disks for filenames and text within files. These operations are extremely fast because Sherlock pre-indexes local disks, just as search engines index Web pages. Because indexing takes significant processor time, indexing can be scheduled for times when the computer is not heavily used. Sherlock also functions as a program for querying multiple Internet search engines or the site search engines available on many Web sites.

When the Mac is shut down normally using the Apple menu's Shut Down option, a flag is set on the hard drive. In the event of a crash or forced reboot, this flag is not set. If the flag is not set, at the next startup, the Mac will see that the computer was not shut down properly and will run a disk integrity check.

The Mac is extremely versatile at booting from different devices. Like other operating systems, the Mac will boot from a floppy disk inserted during the boot sequence. If the floppy disk does not contain a valid System Folder, the Mac spits it out and continues searching for a bootable device. The Mac will also boot from various SCSI devices (Zip drives, Syquest drives, etc.), and since the early nineties, Macs have been able to boot from a CD-ROM drive. To boot from a CD-ROM, press the "C" key while booting up. Pressing the Shift-Option-Delete-Apple (SODA) keys during the boot sequence will bypass the internal hard drive and boot from the next drive in the SCSI chain.

CHAPTER SUMMARY

- ❑ For the user, files are the "bread and butter" of an operating system. Besides containing the operating system kernel, files hold documents and programs on which users rely.

- ❑ Files are made possible by a file system that enables them to be created, written, managed, and stored on disk media. All operating systems must have a file system that provides a file-naming convention, a way to store files, and a means to partition and format disks.

- ❑ Besides creating and modifying files, the file system also should offer the ability to defragment files, compress file contents, ensure file and data integrity, secure files, and control removable storage media, such as floppy and Zip disks.

- ❑ The file systems used in Windows 2000/XP/Server 2003 are extended FAT16, FAT32, and NTFS.

- ❑ In FAT16/32 the file system creates a file allocation table to store information about files.

- ❑ FAT32 is more robust than FAT16, providing for the use of more clusters and larger partitions.

- ❑ NTFS is the native file system for Windows 2000/XP/Server 2003 with the advantage of better security, larger disk and file sizes, better management tools, and greater stability than FAT16/32.

- ❑ *chkdsk* is an important disk verification and repair utility that works for FAT16/32 and NTFS.

- ❑ UNIX and Linux support many different file systems but typically employ ufs or ext.

- ❑ ufs and ext use information nodes (inodes) to organize information about files. Also, a UNIX/Linux system can have many file systems mounted as subdirectories of the root.

- ❑ Different varieties of UNIX/Linux use different file system utilities, such as *fdisk* and *format* to partition and format disks. The *fsck* (file system checker) utility is used to verify the integrity of UNIX/Linux file systems.

- ❑ NetWare 6.0 and 6.5 use NSS which structures the file system by partitions, storage pools, and volumes.

- ❑ Mac OS X uses the Mac OS Extended (HFS+) file system which is an enhancement of HFS and was introduced in 1998 with Mac OS 8.1. Like NTFS, the Mac OS Extended file system makes more efficient utilization of disk space and supports larger disk sizes, and in Mac OS X version 10.3 offers a case sensitive capability, journaling, and support for 16 TB disk storage.

- ❑ Two important Mac OS X disk tools include the Disk Utility and Disk First Aid.

KEY TERMS

8.3 filenames — Older-style file name format in which the name of the file can be up to eight characters long, followed by a period and an extension of three characters. See *extension*.

active partition — The logical portion of a hard disk drive that is currently being used to store data. In a PC system, usually the partition that contains the bootable operating system.

alias — In the Macintosh file system, a feature that presents an icon that represents an executable file. Equivalent to the UNIX/Linux link and the Windows shortcut.

allocation block — In the Macintosh file system, a division of hard disk data. Equivalent to the Windows disk cluster. Each Macintosh volume is divided into 216 (65,535) individual units.

bad clusters — On a hard disk drive, areas of the surface that cannot be used to safely store data. Bad clusters are usually identified by the *format* command or one of the hard drive utilities, such as *chkdsk*.

balanced-tree (b-tree) — A way of structuring a file system that enables fast file access through creating an internal file system tree structure off of the root that is more horizontally oriented than vertically oriented.

BinHex — In the Macintosh file system, a seven-bit file format used to transmit data across network links that do not support native Macintosh file formats.

block allocation — A hard disk configuration scheme in which the disk is divided into logical blocks, which in turn are mapped to sectors, heads, and tracks. Whenever the operating system needs to allocate some disk space, it allocates it based on a block address.

block device — In the UNIX/Linux file system, a device that is divided or configured into logical blocks. See also *raw device*.

boot block — The UNIX/Linux and Mac OS X equivalent of the DOS/Windows Master Boot Record (MBR), the area of the hard disk that stores partition information for the disk. For example, on a Mac-formatted disk, the first two sectors are boot blocks that identify the filing system, the names of important system files, and other important information. See also *volume information block*.

catalog b-tree — In the Macintosh file system, a list of all files on a given volume. Similar to a directory in the Windows file system.

CD-ROM File System (CDFS) — A 32-bit file system used on CD-ROMs.

cluster — In Windows-based file systems, a logical block of information on a disk containing one or more sectors. Also called an allocation unit.

creator codes — Hidden file characteristics in the Macintosh file system that indicate the program (software application) that created the file. See *type code*.

cylinder — Tracks that line up from top to bottom on the platters in a hard disk drive (like a stack of disk tracks).

data fork — That portion of a file in the Macintosh file system that stores the variable data associated with the file. Data fork information might include word-processing data, spreadsheet information, and so on.

3

defragmenter — A tool that rearranges data on a disk in a continuous fashion, ridding the disk of scattered open clusters.

directory — Also called a folder in many file systems, an organizational structure that contains files and may additionally contain subdirectories (or folders) under it. In UNIX/Linux, a directory is simply a special file on a disk drive that is used to house information about other data stored on the disk. In other systems, a directory or folder is a "container object" that houses files and subdirectories or subfolders. A directory or folder contains information about files, such as filenames, file sizes, date of creation, and file type.

disk label — The UNIX/Linux equivalent of a partition table in MS-DOS or Windows-based systems. The disk label is a table containing information about each partition on a disk, such as the type of partition, size, and location. Also, the disk label provides information to the computer about how to access the disk.

disk quota — Allocating a specific amount of disk space to a user or application with the ability to ensure that the user or application cannot use more disk space than is specified in the allocation.

Distributed Link Tracking — A technique new to NTFS 5 so that shortcuts, such as those on the desktop, are not lost when files are moved to another volume.

extended file system (ext or ext fs) — The file system designed for Linux that is installed, by default, in Linux operating systems. ext enables the use of the full range of built-in Linux commands, file manipulation, and security. Released in 1992, ext had some bugs and supported only files up to 2 GB. In 1993, the second extended file system (ext2 or ext2 fs) was designed to fix the bugs in ext and support files of up to 4 TB in size. In 2001, ext3 (or ext fs) was introduced to enable journaling for file and data recovery. ext, ext2, and ext3 support filenames of up to 255 characters.

extension — In MS-DOS and Windows-based systems, that part of a filename that typically identifies the type of file associated with the name. File extensions traditionally are three characters long and include standard notations such as .sys, .exe, .bat, and so on.

extents b-tree — Keeps track of the location of the file fragments or extents in the Mac OS HFS file system.

file allocation table (FAT) — A file management system that defines the way data is stored on a disk drive. The FAT stores information about file size and physical location on the disk.

file attributes — File characteristics stored with the filename in the disk directory, which specify certain storage and operational parameters associated with the file. Attributes are noted by the value of specific data bits associated with the filename. File attributes include Hidden, Read-only, Archive, and so on.

file system — A design for storing and managing files on a disk drive. File systems are associated with operating systems such as UNIX/Linux, Mac OS X, and Windows.

folder — See *directory*.

hard link — In Windows 2000/XP/Server 2003 and UNIX/Linux, a file management technique that permits multiple directory entries to point to the same physical file.

Hierarchical Filing System (HFS) — An early Apple Macintosh file system storage method that uses a hierarchical directory structure. Developed in 1986 to improve file support for large storage devices. Mac OS Extended (HFS+) file system was released in 1998 with Mac OS 8.1 and is the file system used in Mac OS X.

high-level formatting — A process that prepares a disk partition (or removable media) for a specific file system.

hot fix — A procedure used by a file system that can detect a damaged disk area and then automatically copy information from that area to another disk area that is not damaged.

inode — Short for "information node." In UNIX/Linux, a system for storing key information about files. Inode information includes: the inode number, the owner of the file, the file group, the file size, the file creation date, the date the file was last modified and read, the number of links to this inode, and information regarding the location of the blocks in the file system in which the file is stored.

journaling — The ability of a file system or software (such as database software) to track file changes so that if a system crashes unexpectedly, it is possible to reconstruct files or to roll back changes for minimum or no damage.

linked list — Used in FAT file systems so that when a file is written to disk, each cluster containing that file's data has a pointer to the location of the next cluster of data. For example, the first cluster has a pointer to the second cluster's location, the second cluster contains a pointer to the third cluster, and so on.

logical drive — A software definition that divides a physical hard drive into multiple drives for file storage.

long filename (LFN) — A name for a file, folder, or directory in a file system in which the name can be up to 255 characters in length. Long filenames in Windows-based, UNIX/Linux, and Mac OS systems are also POSIX compliant in that they honor uppercase and lowercase characters.

low-level format — A software process that marks tracks and sectors on a disk. A low-level format is necessary before a disk can be partitioned and formatted.

MacBinary — A format for Mac OS files that joins type and creator codes so that Mac files can be transferred over the Internet, or used via online services.

Macintosh Filing System (MFS) — The original Macintosh filing system, introduced in 1984. MFS was limited to keeping track of 128 documents, applications, or folders.

Master Boot Record (MBR) — An area of a hard disk in MS-DOS and Windows that stores partition information about that disk. MBRs are not found on disks that do not support multiple partitions.

Master File Table (MFT) — In Windows NT, 2000, XP, and Server 2003, a file management system similar to the FAT and directories used in MS-DOS and earlier versions of Windows. This table is located at the beginning of the partition. The boot sector is located ahead of the MFT, just as it is in the FAT system.

medium filenames — In the Macintosh file system, the 31-character filename length that Macintosh OS has supported from the beginning.

New Technology File System (NTFS) — The 32-bit file storage system that is the native system in Windows NT, 2000, XP, and Server 2003.

Novell Storage Services (NSS) — The NetWare file system fully implemented in NetWare 6.0 and above that uses disk partitions, storage pools, and volumes.

partition table — Table containing information about each partition on a disk, such as the type of partition, size, and location. Also, the partition table provides information to the computer about how to access the disk.

partitioning — Blocking a group of tracks and sectors to be used by a particular file system, such as FAT or NTFS. Partitioning is a hard disk management technique that permits the installation of multiple file systems on a single disk. Or, the configuration of multiple logical hard drives that use the same file system on a single physical hard drive.

physical drive — Hard drive in a computer that you can physically touch and that can be divided into one or more logical drives.

Portable Operating System Interface (POSIX) — A UNIX standard designed to ensure portability of applications among various versions of UNIX.

raw device — In the UNIX/Linux file system, a device that has not been divided into logical blocks.

resource fork — In the Macintosh file system, that portion of a file that contains fixed information, such as a program's icons, menu resources, and splash screens.

root directory — The highest-level directory (or folder), with no directories above it in the structure of files and directories in a file system.

sector — A portion of a disk track. Disk tracks are divided into equal segments or sectors.

Sherlock — In the Macintosh file system, a file search utility that can find filenames or text within files.

status bits — Bits used as part of a directory entry to identify the type of filename contained in each entry. The status bits in use are Volume, Directory, System, Hidden, Read-only, and Archive.

storage pool — In the NetWare file system, a way to divide the use of a disk that can be a superset of disk partitions because one storage pool can house one or more disk partitions.

superblock — In the UNIX/Linux file system, a special data block that contains information about the layout of blocks, sectors, and cylinder groups on the file system. This information is the key to finding anything on the file system, and it should never change.

switch — An operating system command option that changes the way certain commands function. Command options, or switches, are usually entered as one or more letters, separated from the main command by a forward slash (/).

symbolic link — A special file in the UNIX/Linux file system that permits a directory link to a file that is on a different partition. This is a special file, which has a flag set in the inode to identify it as a symbolic link. The content of the file is a path that, when followed, leads to another file.

track — Concentric rings that cover an entire disk like grooves on a phonograph record. Each ring is divided into sectors in which to store data.

type code — In the Macintosh file system, embedded file information that denotes what applications were used to create the files. Mac OS type codes are used in much the same way as Windows file extensions that identify file types with .txt, .doc and other extensions. See *creator codes*.

Unicode — A 16-bit character code that allows for the definition of up to 65,536 characters.

Universal Disk Format (UDF) — A removable disk formatting standard used for large-capacity CD-ROMs and DVD-ROMs.

UNIX file system (ufs) — A file system supported in most versions of UNIX/Linux that is a hierarchical (tree structure) file system which is expandable, supports large storage, provides excellent security, and is reliable. ufs employs information nodes (inodes).

volume information block — On a Mac-formatted disk, the sector after the boot blocks. See also *boot block*. The volume information block points to other important areas of information, such as the location of the system files and the catalog and extents trees.

volume label — A series of characters that identifies a disk drive or the file system it is using.

REVIEW QUESTIONS

1. As you are using some files on a workstation running Linux, you determine that a few of the files seem to be corrupted. What should you do? (Choose all that apply.)

   a. Close all files and applications and run *fsck*.

   b. Start DiskScan to check for file links.

   c. Reformat your disk.

   d. Use the Disk Check utility, which can be run at any time.

2. You are installing Windows XP Professional on a new disk that has only been low-level formatted. What is the first thing you need to do to prepare the disk?

   a. Use Disk Scrub to ensure there are no bad spots on the disk.

   b. Format the disk for FAT16.

   c. Partition the disk.

   d. Initialize the disk with the root directory.

3. You need to create a new directory in a Linux system and you choose to do this from a terminal window. Which of the following commands enables you to create a directory?

   a. *fdisk*

   b. *mkdir*

   c. *touch*

   d. *dir*

4. What file system is used on a hard disk in a computer running Mac OS X?

   a. Macintosh Filing System (MFS)

   b. Macintosh Network File System (MNFS)

   c. Extended file system (ext)

   d. Mac OS Extended (HFS+) file system

5. Your assistant has documentation showing how to modify a device file in Linux, but the documentation omits information about in what folder to find the file. You suggest looking in the _____ folder.

   a. /mnt

   b. /var

   c. /dev

   d. /proc

6. On a Windows-based system, which of the following are contained in the Master Boot Record? (Choose all that apply.)

   a. disk signature

   b. boot program

   c. end-of-MBR marker

   d. partition table for the active partition

7. Which of the following are elements of Novell Storage Services? (Choose all that apply.)

   a. volumes

   b. disk partitions

   c. dynamic disks

   d. storage pools

8. You need to copy files in UNIX to a floppy disk so that the disk is compatible with extended FAT16 and can be read by Windows XP Professional. Which of the following enables you to do this?

   a. Mount the floppy disk to use ufs.

   b. Format the floppy disk for ext.

   c. Initialize the floppy disk using nfs.

   d. Mount the floppy disk to use UmsMS/DOS.

9. You need to find out more about the *fdisk* utility and the commands associated with it before you set up a new Linux system in addition to the one you are already using. What command can you use on your present system to find out more about *fdisk*?

    a. *man fdisk*

    b. *fdisk /?*

    c. *fdisk /help*

    d. *find fdisk*

10. Mac OS X files can contain which of the following? (Choose all that apply.)

    a. application generator

    b. data fork

    c. extension marker

    d. resource fork

11. Users on your organization's Windows 2003 Server are beginning to take up excessive disk space on the NTFS volumes. You have plenty of disk space now, but you're worried about the future. What can you do?

    a. Enforce stronger security so it is harder for users to write files to their home directories.

    b. Establish disk quotas.

    c. Encrypt portions of their home directories so that these can only be used by the Administrator account.

    d. Use bigger blocks for the partition.

12. You find the Master File Table in _____ .

    a. FAT12

    b. NFS

    c. NTFS

    d. ufs

13. What command in Windows 2000 can you use to format a disk for FAT32?

    a. *fdisk:FAT32*

    b. *format/fs:FAT32*

    c. *part /FAT32*

    d. *mkdisk FAT32*

3

14. Your colleague is trying to install NetWare 6.5 but is not having success. Which of the following might be the problem?

    a. The disk is set up to use blocks instead of clusters.

    b. There must be an MFS partition on the disk.

    c. The disk is too big for NSS.

    d. There must be a 200-MB or larger FAT partition on the disk, and one does not exist now.

15. In what file system(s) would you find inodes? (Choose all that apply.)

    a. FAT16

    b. ufs

    c. ext3

    d. NTFS

16. The president of your company uses Mac OS X and wants to find out more about a file, such whether or not the file is a TIFF document. What tool should she use?

    a. The Get Info option for that file

    b. Explorer

    c. Nautilus

    d. The Window options for the file

17. _____ is a process that marks the location of tracks and sectors on a disk.

    a. Disk tracking

    b. A low-level format

    c. A high-level format

    d. Etching

18. In FAT32, file characteristics such as Hidden and Read-only are examples of _____ .

    a. cluster designations

    b. formatting properties

    c. file attributes

    d. properties applied only to files and folders in the root

19. You run a computer support business and one of your customers calls to say he formatted his hard drive because it seemed to contain lots of bad clusters. The problem is that now the operating system won't start. What might be the problem?

    a. He performed a quick format that does not fix bad clusters.

    b. A hard disk can only be formatted once.

    c. He formatted using the wrong driver.

    d. Formatting the disk destroyed all files that were on the disk, including the operating system files.

20. The _____ holds information about the layout of blocks and sectors in the UNIX file system.

    a. root

    b. file allocation table

    c. superblock

    d. directory flag

Hands-On Projects

HANDS-ON PROJECTS

Project 3-1

File systems store and manage files like a personal assistant to the file system user. In this project, you employ My Computer to view folders and files in **Windows 2000/XP/Server 2003**. Also, you view the information that is stored for and can be displayed about a file.

To view folders and files and their associated information:

1. In Windows 2000, double-click **My Computer** on the desktop; or in Windows XP and Windows Server 2003, click **Start** and click **My Computer**.

2. What information do you see displayed? Record your observations.

3. Double-click **Local Disk (C:)** to view folders and files on the hard drive.

4. Record some examples of folders that you see. Are there any files displayed?

5. Double-click **Documents and Settings** to view more folders.

6. In Windows 2000 only, click the **View** menu and click **Details**. Next, click the **View** menu and click **Choose Columns**. Use the scroll bar to view all of the information that can be displayed in columns for a folder's contents (for each file). Click **Cancel** to close the Column Settings dialog box. In Windows XP and Windows Server 2003, click the **View** menu and click **Choose Details**. You should see a dialog box similar to the one shown earlier in Figure 3-2. Use the scroll bar to view all of the information stored about a folder's contents. Click **Cancel**.

7. Close the Documents and Settings window.

Project 3-2

There are two common ways to view and manage folders and files in Red Hat Enterprise Linux: from the command line and from the Nautilus tool in the GNOME desktop. In this project, you use both tools in **Red Hat Enterprise Linux 3.0** (or in many UNIX/Linux systems). Log on using your own account and note the root account for this project.

To view folders and files from the command line:

1. Access the command line, such as from a terminal window. To open a terminal window, click **MainMenu**, point to **System Tools**, and click **Terminal**.

2. Type **ls –a** and press **Enter** to view the folders and files in your home folder, including those that are hidden. How many folders and files do you see?

3. Type **ls –l /** and press **Enter** to view the main folder structure in the system (see Figure 3-15).

4. If you are using a terminal window, type **exit** and press **Enter** to close it.

```
mpalmer@localhost:~                                              _ □ ✗
File   Edit   View   Terminal   Go   Help
.bash_history   .gconfd          .gtkrc-1.2-gnome2   .rhn-applet.conf
.bash_logout    .gnome           .ICEauthority       .Xauthority
.bash_profile   .gnome2          .kde                .xsession-errors
.bashrc         .gnome2_private  .metacity
[mpalmer@localhost mpalmer]$ ls -l /
total 193
drwxr-xr-x    2 root     root        4096 Dec 20 10:53 bin
drwxr-xr-x    4 root     root        1024 Dec 20 11:28 boot
drwxr-xr-x   21 root     root      118784 Dec 22 10:40 dev
drwxr-xr-x   58 root     root        4096 Dec 22 10:39 etc
drwxr-xr-x    3 root     root        4096 Dec 20 11:40 home
drwxr-xr-x    2 root     root        4096 Jan 24  2003 initrd
drwxr-xr-x   11 root     root        4096 Dec 20 11:21 lib
drwx------    2 root     root       16384 Dec 20 03:43 lost+found
drwxr-xr-x    2 root     root        4096 Sep  8 09:29 misc
drwxr-xr-x    5 root     root        4096 Dec 20 11:28 mnt
drwxr-xr-x    2 root     root        4096 Jan 24  2003 opt
dr-xr-xr-x   73 root     root           0 Dec 22 03:39 proc
drwxr-x---   11 root     root        4096 Dec 22 12:02 root
drwxr-xr-x    2 root     root        8192 Dec 20 11:00 sbin
drwxrwxrwt    9 root     root        4096 Dec 22 12:02 tmp
drwxr-xr-x   15 root     root        4096 Dec 20 10:51 usr
drwxr-xr-x   21 root     root        4096 Dec 20 11:24 var
[mpalmer@localhost mpalmer]$
```

Figure 3-15   Viewing the main system folder structure from the Red Hat Enterprise Linux command line

To access folders and files in Nautilus:

1. Double-click your account's home folder icon, such as mpalmer's Home, or click **Main Menu** and click **Home Folder**.

2. What information do you see? Use the scroll bar to view all of the home folder's contents if there are too much to fit in one window.

3. Click the **View** menu and notice the options that you can set.

4. Close the View menu and close your home folder window in Nautilus.

Project 3-3

In this project, you learn to use the Macintosh HD desktop icon in **Mac OS X** to access files and folders.

To access files and folders in Mac OS X:

1. Double-click the **Macintosh HD** icon on the desktop. What folders do you see in the Macintosh HD window?

2. Double-click the **Users** folder. What folders appear in the Users window?

3. Double-click your account's home folder, which is in the shape of a small house. Your home folder contains a combination of folders and files. Typically documents that you create using this account are placed in the Documents folder. There are also folders in which to store Music, Pictures, Programs, Movies, and so on, as shown in Figure 3-16.

4. Close the window for your home folder.

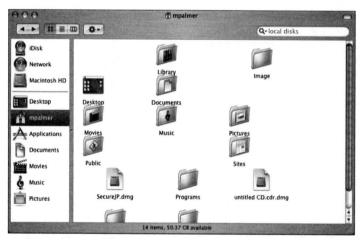

Figure 3-16 Displaying the contents of an account's home folder in Mac OS X

Project 3-4

When you use an operating system, there are many times in which you need to create a new folder. In this project, you learn how to create a new folder in **Windows 2000/XP/Server 2003** using My Computer.

To create a new folder:

1. Double-click **My Computer** on the Windows 2000 desktop; or in Windows XP and Windows Server 2003, click **Start** on the taskbar and click **My Computer**.

2. Double-click **Local Disk (C:)**.

3. Double-click the **Documents and Setting**s folder.

4. Click the **File** menu, point to **New**, and click **Folder**.

5. For the new folder's name, type in your initials, plus the word Folder, such as "JPFolder". Press **Enter**. (Don't delete this folder because you use it later in Hands-on Project 3-8.)

6. Right-click the folder you just created and click **Properties** to view the properties associated with the new folder. What tabs do you see? Click each tab to quickly get an overview of the kinds of properties you can configure for the folder.

7. Click **Cancel**.

8. Close the Documents and Settings window.

HANDS-ON PROJECTS

Project 3-5

In **Red Hat Enterprise Linux 3.0**, you can create a folder by using the Nautilus tool. Or, in virtually all UNIX/Linux systems, including Red Hat Enterprise Linux 3.0, you can create a folder from the command line. In this project, you learn both approaches.

To create a folder:

1. Click **Main Menu** and click **Home Folder** or click the icon for your home folder on the desktop.

2. Click the **File** menu and click **New Folder**.

3. What appears in the window? Record your observations.

4. Enter your initials plus the word Folder1, such as MPFolder1, and press **Enter**.(As you start typing, the default entry *untitled folder* is replaced with your entry.)

5. Right-click the new folder and click **Properties**.

6. What tabs appear? Click each tab to briefly see the properties it configures.

7. Click **Close**.

8. Close the window for your home directory.

9. Access the command line, such as by opening a terminal window (click **Start**, point to **System Tools**, and click **Terminal**).

10. Type **ls** and press **Enter**. Do you see any subdirectories listed in your home directory?

11. Type **mkdir** plus a space, then your initials and the word Folder2, such as MPFolder2 (see Figure 3-17). Press **Enter**.

12. Type **ls** and press **Enter** to verify that you successfully created the new folder (or directory in other UNIX/Linux systems).

13. Type **exit** and press **Enter** to close the terminal window.

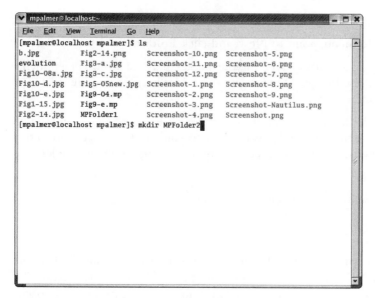

Figure 3-17   Creating a directory in the Red Hat Enterprise Linux terminal window

HANDS-ON PROJECTS

Project 3-6

In this project, you create a folder in **Mac OS X** using the graphical user interface (GUI) window and also from the command line.

To create a folder:

1. Double-click **Macintosh HD** on the desktop.

2. Double-click the **Users** folder.

3. Double-click your home folder (indicated by the house icon).

4. Click the **File** menu at the top of the desktop and click **New Folder**. What do you see in the window?

5. Type your initials appended to Folder1, such as MPFolder1, and press **return**.

6. Close the window for your home folder.

7. Click the **Go** menu at the top of the desktop.

8. Click **Utilities**.

9. Double-click **Terminal**.

10. Type **ls** and press **return** to view the contents of your home folder. Do you see the folder you created in Steps 4 and 5?

11. Type **mkdir**, press the **spacebar**, and type your initials plus Folder2 (see Figure 3-18). Press **return**.

12. Type **ls** and press **return** to make sure your folder was created.

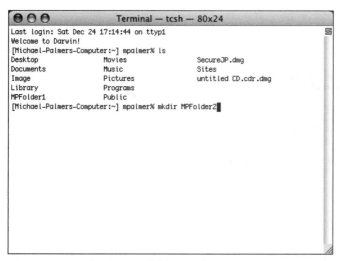

Figure 3-18   Creating a folder in the Mac OS X terminal window

13. Close the terminal window. Also, click the **Terminal** menu at the top of the desktop and click **Quit Terminal**.

14. Close the Utilities window.

Project 3-7

A sudden power failure or a bad spot on a disk can cause the Master Boot Record to become corrupted, preventing a computer from booting. In **Windows 2000**, **Windows XP**, and **Windows Server 2003**, you can fix the Master Boot Record using the Recovery Console. This project gives you the opportunity to start the Recovery Console to see how to fix the Master Boot Record in these operating systems. For this project, you'll need the installation CD-ROM for the operating system. Also, you will need the password for the Administrator account.

To view how to fix the Master Boot Record:

1. Make sure all files are saved (and users are logged off of a server). Shut down the operating system and computer.

2. Insert the CD-ROM for your operating system.

3. Power on the computer, enabling it to boot from the CD-ROM.

4. After the Windows Setup program starts, continue with the installation process until you reach the Welcome to Setup screen. Press **R** (for repair) on that screen. In Windows XP and Windows Server 2003, this action takes you to the Recovery Console. Figure 3-19 shows the Welcome to Setup screen in Windows Server 2003. The screen sequence is somewhat different in Windows 2000. First, on the Welcome to Setup screen in Windows 2000, press **R** for repair, which leads to a second screen on which you press **C** to start the Recovery Console.

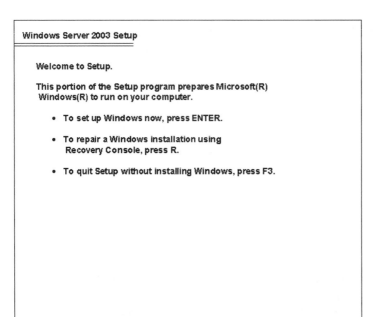

Figure 3-19   Starting the Windows Server 2003 Recovery Console

5. Select the drive containing the \Winnt or \Windows folder, such as by typing 1 to access the appropriate folder on drive C. Press **Enter**. (Windows 2000 uses the \Winnt folder, as does Windows Server 2003 when upgraded from Windows 2000. When Windows Server 2003 is installed from scratch, it uses the \Windows folder.)

6. Enter the Administrator account password and press **Enter**.

7. The *fixmbr* command is used to fix the Master Boot Record from the command line. Type **help fixmbr** and press **Enter** to view the help information for this command. IF YOU HAVE PERMISSION FROM YOUR INSTRUCTOR ONLY, type *fixmbr* and press **Enter**.

8. Type **exit** and press **Enter** to leave the Recovery Console and reboot.

HANDS-ON PROJECTS

Project 3-8

In this project, you learn how to compress files in **Windows 2000/XP/2003**. You need a computer with a drive formatted for NTFS.

To compress files in a folder:

1. In Windows 2000, double-click **My Computer** on the desktop; or in Windows XP/Server 2003, click **Start** and click **My Computer**.

2. Double-click **Local Disk (C:)**.

3. Double-click the **Documents and Settings** folder.

4. Browse to the folder you created in Hands-on Project 3-4, such as JPFolder and double-click it.

5. Click the **File** menu, point to **New**, and click **Folder**.

6. For the new subfolder's name, type in your initials plus the word SubFolder, such as "JPSubFolder". Press **Enter**.

7. Click the **Back** (arrow) button (under the File menu by default) to go back to the main folder, such as JPFolder.

8. Right-click the folder (such as JPFolder) and click **Properties**.

9. Click the **Advanced** button to view a dialog box similar to Figure 3-20. Notice and record the advanced attributes you can configure. Which attribute is important for backing up files?

Figure 3-20   Advanced Attributes dialog box in Windows XP Professional

10. Click **Compress contents to save disk space**.

11. Click **OK** to save your change to the advanced attributes.

12. Click **OK** to exit the folder's Properties dialog box.

13. In the Confirm Attribute Changes dialog box (which is displayed when a folder contains subfolders or files), click **Apply Changes to this folder, subfolders, and files**, if this option is not already selected.

14. Click **OK**.

15. Close the Documents and Settings window.

You cannot compress a folder that is encrypted.

NOTE

Project 3-9

chkdsk is an important utility included in **Windows 2000/XP/2003** that verifies the integrity of a disk and its file system—and can fix problems that it encounters. In this project, you run *chkdsk* to see how it works.

To use *chkdsk*:

1. Click **Start**, point to **Programs** (in Windows 2000) or **All Programs** (in Windows XP/2003), point to **Accessories**, and click **Command Prompt**.

2. Type **chkdsk** and press **Enter**. What information does *chkdsk* verify as reported in the Command Prompt window? What other information is displayed? Also, did *chkdsk* fix any problems on your disk?

3. Close the Command Prompt window.

NOTE

Another way to have *chkdsk* start is to save all of your work and simply turn off the computer without properly shutting it down. When you reboot, if the system detects a problem with the way the computer was shut down, it will run *chkdsk*. (In most cases this is a safe test because it is unlikely that you will cause damage to files or the file system if all of your work is saved and programs are closed.)

Project 3-10

In this project, you run the Disk Defragmenter in **Windows 2000/XP/2003**. You need access to an account with Administrator privileges to run this utility.

To use the Disk Defragmenter:

1. Click **Start**, point to **Programs** (in Windows 2000) or **All Programs** (in Windows XP/2003), point to **Accessories**, point to **System Tools**, and click **Disk Defragmenter**.

2. To determine if a disk or volume needs to be defragmented, click it under Volume and click the **Analyze** button.

3. After the analysis is done, click the **View Report** button. Notice that at the top of the Analysis Report box there is a recommendation about whether or not you need to defragment the disk (see Figure 3-21). What does your report say?

4. Click **Close**.

5. Click the **Defragment** button whether or not defragmentation is recommended so that you can view the process.

6. Click **View Report**. Were there any files that could not be defragmented?

7. Click **Close**.

8. Close the Disk Defragmenter window.

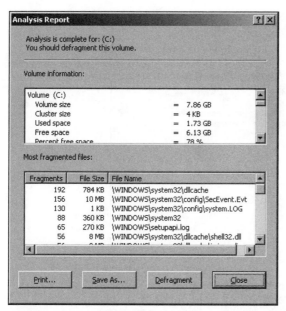

Figure 3-21 Analysis Report box in Windows Server 2003

Project 3-11

In this project, you determine what file systems are incorporated in a system running **Red Hat Enterprise Linux 3.0**. (Note that these commands work in many UNIX/Linux versions.)

To view the file systems:

1. Access the command prompt or a terminal window, such as by clicking **Main Menu**, pointing to **System Tools**, and clicking **Terminal**.

2. At the command prompt, type **manmount** and press **Enter**. Continue pressing **spacebar**, as necessary, to view the documentation for the -t parameter for the mount command. (If you are using a terminal window you may need to press Q to exit the text display mode when you are finished.) What file systems can be mounted?

3. Next, type **mount** and press **Enter** to determine what file systems are actually mounted (see Figure 3-22). What file systems do you see mounted on your system?

4. If you are in a terminal window, type **exit** and press **Enter**.

Figure 3-22   Mounted file systems in Red Hat Enterprise Linux

**HANDS-ON
PROJECTS**

Project 3-12

Mac OS X includes the Get Info option to view the type of file. Also, aliases are among the useful Macintosh file system features. Like shortcuts in Windows, aliases let you create custom icons and names to place on your desktop, menus, or elsewhere to point to other applications. Aliases give you multiple ways to access the same application and let you easily place these access points at various locations to help you get to them when you need them. In this project, you view the file type of an application and you create an alias.

To view the file type and create an alias:

1. Click the **Go** menu at the top of the desktop and click **Applications**.

2. Click **Address Book**.

3. Click the **File** menu and click **Get Info**. What information is provided for Kind?

4. Close the Address Book Info window.

5. Make sure **Address Book** is still selected or click it if it is not selected.

6. Click the **File** menu and click **Make Alias**.

7. Click to move the cursor to the box under the Address Book icon and change the text to have your initials in front of Address Book, such as JP Address Book alias.

8. Click and drag the new alias to an open spot in the Applications window, as shown in Figure 3-23.

9. Close the Applications window.

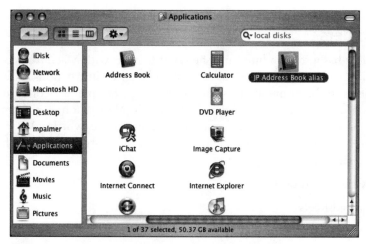

Figure 3-23   Creating a new alias in Mac OS X

NOTE   Although an alias only points to the actual application, you can treat an alias like an application. For example, you can drag a file onto an alias icon to open the file with the application to which the alias points. You can also create an alias for a folder instead of an application. This lets you save files into a folder by choosing its alias. Further, you can create an alias from a network connection so you can open the server it represents by simply double-clicking the alias icon wherever it resides.

CASE PROJECTS

Tasty Freeze is a company that produces ice cream and sells it to distributors in North America. The company's headquarters are in a large downtown building in Chicago. All of the senior management—the president and all vice presidents—use Macintosh computers with the Mac OS X operating system. The Marketing Department uses Windows XP Professional as does the Accounting Department. The Manufacturing and Operations Department uses workstations running Linux, which have specialized software for their area, including a complex inventory and distribution client/server system. The servers used by the company include a combination of Windows Server 2003 and NetWare 6.5 servers. There has been some turnover in the Computer Support area of the company and they have hired you as a consultant to provide help.

Case Project 3-1: Training a New Vice President in Using Mac OS X Folders

A new vice president has just been hired and she is not familiar with Macintosh computers. You have been asked to provide her with a set of simple written instructions about how to access the documents in the home folder, which were left by her predecessor. Also, provide instructions about how to create a new folder in Mac OS X. Note that both the predecessor and the new vice president are using the same user account name, which is VP Financials. Finally, the vice president needs your advice for creating a folder structure under her home folder. She wants a separate location for each of the following:

- ❑ Rulings by the board of directors
- ❑ Financial spreadsheets
- ❑ Word-processed documents that pertain to her division
- ❑ Word-processed documents that relate to senior management activities
- ❑ Marketing reports

Explain how you would set up the folder structure and what you would name the folders.

Case Project 3-2: Determining Whether a File System is Mounted for a CD-ROM Drive

An inventory specialist in the Manufacturing and Operations Department needs to determine what file systems are mounted on his Linux computer because he is not sure that the CD-ROM drive is properly mounted. Explain the steps he should use to determine the mounted file systems, and also note which file system should be mounted for the CD-ROM.

Case Project 3-3: Choosing a File System for Windows XP Professional

A new computer has just been purchased for the accounting manager. The company purchased the computer without an operating system because they already have extra licensed copies of Windows XP Professional. They ask you to set up the computer. What Windows XP Professional file system do you implement, recognizing that the accounting manager needs a system that can be secure? Explain your decision and briefly discuss the advantages of this file system. Also, the accounting manager asks you to set up a preliminary folder structure to contain:

- ❑ Accounting reports
- ❑ Word-processed documents

3

<ul>
<li>Department memos</li>
<li>Personnel evaluations</li>
</ul>

Explain where you would set up this folder structure and show how you would name the new folders.

Case Project 3-4: Summarizing the Advantages of the NetWare File System

Tasty Freeze has just hired a new person who is training to be a NetWare 6.5 system administrator. She has worked with computers in many capacities, but has never managed a NetWare server. You are asked to train her and as part of the orientation to NetWare, you decide to give her a background in the advantages of its file system. Create a short report that you can give her that summarizes the advantages you discuss in your training.

Case Project 3-5: Repairing a File Problem

The Windows XP Professional computer used by a copywriter in the Marketing Department is experiencing some problems. Each time the copywriter accesses certain files, he sees an error message. He is concerned because these are files to be used for an upcoming catalog that will go into print soon. Explain the steps to take to fix these files.

4

Installing and Upgrading Operating Systems

> ## After reading this chapter and completing the exercises, you will be able to:
>
> ♦ Understand the overall process of operating system installation and upgrading
>
> ♦ Prepare for operating system installation and understand the factors involved in making the decision to upgrade
>
> ♦ Install and upgrade the following operating systems and understand the various options presented in:
>   - Windows 2000 Server and Professional
>   - Windows XP
>   - Windows Server 2003
>   - NetWare 6.0 and 6.5
>   - Mac OS X
>
> ♦ Install Red Hat Enterprise Linux 3.0 and understand the basic differences between UNIX-type installations and those of other operating systems covered in this chapter
>
> ♦ Review upgrading from one version to the next

For many, the installation or upgrade of an operating system seems like a complex and worrisome task. This chapter takes the mystery out of the process by showing you, step by step, how to install or upgrade each operating system described in the book. An overview is given in the text portion of the chapter, and you can step through actual installations and upgrades in the Hands-on Projects at the end of the chapter. By the end of the chapter, you know how to prepare for an operating system installation or upgrade, what to expect, what to watch for and what to avoid during the process, and how to update your operating system once it is installed. It is beyond the scope of this book to cover all possible options and settings, so only usual installations and upgrades are presented.

INSTALLING AN OPERATING SYSTEM

There are two basic types of operating system installations: clean installations on a machine that has no operating system installed (a new hard drive or one that has been formatted), and upgrade installations on systems that already have an operating system installed.

The process of installing operating systems varies from one operating system to another, but there are certain features common to all installations. Operating system installation can be divided into three general stages: preparation for installation, the installation itself, and any required or optional steps following installation.

Preparing for installation involves the following:

- Checking the computer on which you will install the operating system to make sure it meets or exceeds the hardware and/or software requirements for the operating system.

- Ensuring that all equipment (computer and peripheral devices) is powered on and operating correctly.

- Having the appropriate floppy disks or compact discs (CDs) on hand, including those for the operating system installation, and any floppy disks needed during the installation to create startup disks.

- Understanding the general features of the operating system you are installing so you can decide which modules to install and which to omit.

- Having the most up-to-date device drivers for your compact disc read-only memory (CD-ROM), Small Computer System Interface (SCSI) devices, printers, modems, and so on, usually from the manufacturer's disk that came with the device, or downloaded from the manufacturer's Web site. Make sure you have the correct information for the operating system you are going to install or upgrade.

- Having pertinent information available about your computer and peripheral devices.

During the installation, you may need to provide some or all of the following information:

- Where (in which directory/folder or path) to install the operating system and what to name the directory/folder

- What type of installation you wish to perform (Typical/Default, Portable, Compact, or Custom, for example)

- Information about you, your company, and your computer (your name, company name, computer or workgroup name)

- Licensing information (usually a license key or ID number), verifying your right to install the operating system

- Which components of the operating system you want to install

After you complete an installation, keep the license key, ID number, or activation number in a safe place so you can reinstall the operating system in the event that your computer or hard drive fails. Some operating systems (Windows 2000/XP/Server 2003, Mac OS X, and some versions of UNIX) can automatically detect and configure devices, such as monitors, keyboards, printers, mice, network cards, video cards, and sound cards. However, these operating systems also let you specify a device type or model that is different from the one they detect, in case the automatic detection made a mistake.

Installation programs can be primarily text based. Some versions of UNIX, for example, use a combination of text-based and graphical user interface (GUI) (most Windows-based systems when booted from floppy disks or CD-ROMs), or use an automated "wizard" to step you through the process (all Windows-based systems when upgraded from a previous version of Windows, and Mac OS). Operating systems are usually installed from CD-ROMs, and, in many cases, can be installed over a network. (Network installations are not covered in this book.)

The installation itself consists of some or all of the following general functions:

- Loading/running the installation program

- Gathering system information

- Determining which elements of the operating system are to be installed

- Configuring devices and drivers

- Creating a floppy disk used to boot the operating system in an emergency

- Copying operating system files onto your computer

- Restarting the system and finalizing configuration of devices

Not all of these functions are performed in every operating system installation. For some operating systems, such as Microsoft Disk Operating System (MS-DOS), devices and drivers are installed after the operating system installation. For others, device/driver configuration is part of the operating system installation. Operating systems from Windows 95 on have the Plug and Play (PnP) feature that automatically configures internal and external devices as part of the installation and at startup whenever a new device is added.

Even with a PnP capable operating system, you may have to configure memory for optimum performance or configure devices to work with the operating system.

For example, in some operating systems, if your machine contains a CD-ROM drive, you must install a CD-ROM driver, or appropriate file system, before you can use the CD-ROM. In the following section, you will learn how to prepare for installation. After that, each operating system installation will be covered in more detail.

Preparing for Installation

Before you can install any OS, you must make a few advance preparations. First, and most important, the machine must be working correctly. If you have defective hardware, such as a disk drive, CD-ROM drive, or bad section of memory, the operating system installation can be extremely difficult. Most operating systems interface with the hardware on many levels. Many of the operating systems covered in this book try to automatically detect the hardware connected to your computer. The result of non-working hardware can be a failed installation.

Checking the Hardware

Before you begin an installation, you should be sure that all hardware is actually turned on and ready for use, including the computer and any external peripheral devices such as SCSI devices, tape drives, disk drives, modems, and scanners.

It is recommended that you remove any tapes or removable media that contain important data from tape and other drives. In general, an operating system installation will not destroy data on tapes or removable media, unless it is specifically instructed to do so. However, if important data is backed up, and removable media are out of the drives, there is no chance of losing anything.

You should also have available information about your hardware. This means that you should know how many hard disks you have, what size they are, and how they are connected to the machine. You should also know how much memory you have in your machine. For any expansion cards, such as your video card, network card, sound card, and SCSI cards, you should know the make and model. If you have a printer, modem, scanner, plotter, or other device, you should keep the device driver disks handy, and know their types. For some symmetric multiprocessing (SMP) systems, make sure that you have the multiprocessor driver, such as the HAL.dll (hardware abstraction layer driver). Table 4-1 is an example of how you might organize this information to have it available during installation.

Table 4-1   Hardware component information

Component	Description/Setting
CPU (type)	The system basic input/output system (BIOS) knows this information, and the operating system should automatically adjust anything required (unless you are using an SMP computer, in which case you should have the multiprocessor driver provided by the manufacturer).
Amount of RAM	Your operating system should automatically detect the amount of random access memory (RAM) in your system. However, guidelines supplied with your operating system tell you how much RAM is recommended. You should know how much you have to ensure that the operating system installs and operates properly.
Type of buses	You'll need this information if you install new expansion cards.
Hard disk(s)	Type, size, connection. Most new hardware includes BIOS routines to automatically detect the type of hard drive installed, as well as critical drive settings. It's also a good idea to write down hard drive statistics, such as number of cylinders, capacity, and number of heads. This information may be available in your owner's manual, on the case of the hard drive, or on the BIOS setup screen. Try Hands-on Project 4-1 to learn more about the BIOS setup.
Keyboard	Unless your keyboard has special features that require custom drivers, the type of keyboard you have should not be a factor during operating system installation.
Mouse	Standard, three-button, wheel mouse? Is a custom driver required? Does the mouse use a serial, a parallel, or a Universal Serial Bus (USB) port?
Video card	Most modern operating systems will detect your video card and automatically include required drivers. However, special features of your video card may become available only with the use of a special driver provided by the manufacturer.
Floppy drive type	Your operating system automatically detects this information.
Sound card	Some operating systems include drivers for common sound card hardware. If your card isn't one of the really popular models, make sure you have the required drivers supplied by the card's manufacturer.
Network interface card (NIC)	Windows 95 and later Windows operating systems, Red Hat Linux, and Mac OS probably will automatically detect your NIC. However, it may still be a good idea to use the manufacturer's custom drivers for best performance.
Printer	You should have custom drivers from your printer manufacturer.
Modem	Use manufacturer drivers, or those supplied with your operating system. You should know at least the manufacturer of your modem's basic chip set in case you must choose it during installation. If you have custom driver software that came with your modem, use it.
Other input/output (I/O) devices	If your operating system doesn't detect other hardware during the installation, you must understand hardware basics and have access to any custom drivers required to make it function properly with your operating system.

4

Chapter 5, "Configuring Input and Output Devices" and Chapter 6, "Using and Configuring Storage Devices," give more detailed information on devices and device drivers.

NOTE

Many cards installed in the machine include settings on the card. In the Intel PC architecture, these cards often must be configured to interface with the computer in a certain way. Windows 95 and later Windows products use the PnP system to do this. If you install a PnP operating system, card configuration is automatic. If you do not use a PnP operating system, or if your machine does not support the PnP system, you may be in for a few surprises. Many PnP cards come with a utility (usually included on the manufacturer's disk with the drivers) that lets you configure them to work in non-PnP mode. Currently, Windows 95 and later Windows products, other than Windows NT, support PnP mode. Interface cards in the Macintosh architecture usually don't need any special configuration for the hardware to work properly because the Macintosh operating system is specifically designed for the Macintosh hardware.

With newer hardware, there may be BIOS settings that can turn PnP compatibility on or off. PnP should be enabled by default. If it isn't, check your computer's BIOS documentation to find out how to turn it on before installing a new operating system.

NOTE

Checking Drivers

Many devices such as CD-ROM drives, SCSI drives, software-driven modems, and scanners, require special drivers to work correctly. In general, drivers are on the disks that come with the devices, but often these disks do not include drivers for all possible operating systems, or the most up-to-date drivers. Also, your device may not be on the list of drivers that come with the operating system, which can result in some installation problems.

If you install drivers that came with your hardware, the hardware should operate properly. However, in some cases (particularly with modems), you may experience significantly better performance by installing later drivers that you secure from the manufacturer. There are a few strategies to obtain the latest drivers for your particular device and operating system. If you have access to the Internet, simply go to your hardware manufacturer's Web site for drivers and support information. Or, contact the manufacturer and ask for the latest driver disks for your device. You don't want to have to abort an installation because you don't have the driver files.

Even though you may have driver disks on hand, it is best to get the most recent drivers because driver updates often fix bugs in older driver versions.

TIP

You should also check the documentation that came with any hardware you want to use with your new operating system. In many cases, the manufacturer includes a disclaimer indicating which operating systems are certified for use with particular hardware.

Ensuring Hardware Compatibility

Because of the wide range of hardware available today, you will find that many operating systems have certain minimum hardware requirements. These are usually listed on the box or in a section of the manual. More advanced operating systems often include a **hardware compatibility list (HCL)**. This is usually a list or book that contains brand names and models for all hardware supported by the operating system. Windows XP uses the **Windows Catalog** (found at *www.microsoft.com/windows/catalog*) and Windows Server 2003 uses the Windows Server Catalog (found at *www.microsoft.com/windows/catalog/server*). Nearly all advanced Microsoft Windows, and some UNIX systems, for example, include an HCL in one form or another. For Microsoft Windows–based operating systems, look on the installation CD-ROM for the HCL, or search on HCL at the Microsoft Web site at *www.microsoft.com*. Red Hat Linux lists hardware partners on its Web site at *www.redhat.com*.

If you have hardware that is not on the HCL for the operating system you want to install, all is not lost. If the hardware comes with appropriate drivers for the operating system you are about to install, your installation should be successful. However, if you do not have drivers, and your hardware is not on the HCL, you are probably asking for trouble.

CAUTION
If the hardware you plan to use is a clone, or an original equipment manufacturer (OEM) version of hardware that is on the list, proceed as if it is the hardware in question. If your hardware is not on the list of compatible hardware, or you do not have drivers, beware. The installation of the operating system could fail, or it could become unstable after installation. Stick with compatible devices and drivers.

Each operating system vendor also publishes minimum hardware requirements for running the operating system. However, these "minimum" recommendations are often so minimal that you might be able to install the operating system, but you probably won't be able to use it. Therefore, in the tables in this chapter that describe hardware requirements for installing an operating system, you'll find both minimum requirements and recommended specifications.

NOTE
If you need to partition and format the hard disk before you start, run *fdisk* from MS-DOS. When *fdisk* is finished, format the partition by running the MS-DOS command *format c: /s/u* (where c: is the drive letter) to unconditionally format the partition, and place the system files on it so that you can boot from that partition. Refer to Chapter 3 for a discussion of the *fdisk* command. Most of the current versions of operating systems provide for partitioning and formatting the hard drive as part of the installation procedure.

Making Time to Do the Job

Last of all, make sure you have enough time to complete the operating system installation. Nothing is more frustrating than not being able to finish an install or upgrade because you have some other obligation at an inconvenient moment. Coming back to the process later often turns out to be extremely confusing.

UPGRADING AN OPERATING SYSTEM

No matter how comfortable you are with an operating system, there comes a time when you must upgrade to the next version. For instance, you may find that your current operating system version does not support new software or certain devices. Also, older versions of operating systems don't have the security features required for network and Internet access, or to protect e-mail systems. Whether it is a small upgrade to fix bugs, or a larger upgrade to introduce a new operating system, many of the upgrade procedures are similar to those required for an initial installation. In this section, you'll learn about general upgrade considerations, backup and safety procedures, and finally, the specific steps (and possible pitfalls) involved in upgrading computer operating systems.

Preparing for an Upgrade

Before you upgrade, the first thing to consider is whether an upgrade is truly necessary. If you are certain that an upgrade is necessary and desirable, then you must make sure that you have the necessary hardware and software (including device drivers) to perform the upgrade, as well as information about your system that may be needed during the upgrade. You should also make a complete backup of your current system and data before upgrading. If you are upgrading more than two or three computers at once, you may want to perform a test upgrade on one or two before doing a complete upgrade. These and other general upgrading considerations are discussed in the following sections.

Deciding to Upgrade

When new versions of operating systems are released that promise new features, bug fixes, enhanced capabilities, and more speed, it is tempting to jump immediately on the upgrade bandwagon. However, before taking such a step (especially in a large production environment), you should carefully consider (1) whether you need to upgrade, and (2) whether the time is right to upgrade. Although newer versions of operating systems promise great new features, you should ask yourself whether you actually need the new functionality. Objective analysis of the situation may show that an upgrade may not be cost effective. In other cases, such as upgrading a work environment from Windows NT to Windows 2000 or Windows Server 2003, the upgrade can be used to significantly lower the total cost of ownership (TCO) because Windows 2000 and Windows Server 2003 enable you to manage users via group policies.

In some cases, upgrades to operating systems have little immediate effect on the functions performed by the computers and users for which you are responsible. You may also find that software or hardware that ran without difficulty on the older version of the operating system will not run on a newer version. Check with your software and hardware vendors before attempting an upgrade to ensure that the software and hardware will be compatible with the upgrade. Never assume that all of your current software and hardware will work flawlessly with the upgrade.

Sometimes operating system vendors publish a list of the software tested on the upgraded operating system. These tests may not be comprehensive enough to ensure that all features of the software work properly, or that they work on all types of computers. Install the new operating system and the software your organization uses on a test computer so that you can personally verify the operating system and software before implementing it on a large scale.

Experience also has shown that it is best not to upgrade shortly after a new operating system is released. If you can put off an upgrade for several months, maybe even a year, you gain the benefit of the experiences of thousands of other users solving problems that might have been yours. If you wait, you will have access to many patches and bug fixes that are not available for early releases. If you feel you must upgrade soon after a new version is released, consider using the test upgrade strategy covered later in this chapter.

Some operating system vendors offer prerelease or **beta software** for you to try. Microsoft, for example, typically offers prereleases in the form of **alpha software**, beta, and **release candidate (RC)** versions. Never upgrade production computers to anything other than an official release of an operating system. Prerelease or beta operating system versions are in the preliminary to final test stages before release. They can have many bugs and may be unstable. A **production computer** is any computer used to perform real work, and which, if it were to become unusable for any reason, would cause an inconvenience, hinder workflow, or cause data to be lost.

If you plan to implement an upgrade, consider obtaining a prerelease or beta version, and put it on a machine that is not a production computer. Use this computer for training and investigation to learn about the new features of the operating system and how they will affect your work environment, particularly your existing software.

Checking Hardware and Software

As with an original installation, before you decide to upgrade, you should carefully check the computers you wish to upgrade against the requirements of the new operating system. In many cases, newer operating systems require more hardware including increased memory, disk space, central processing unit (CPU) speed, and sometimes even improved display properties. For Windows 2000 and Windows XP, you can use the **Upgrade Advisor**, a tool available on the operating system CD or via the Internet, to check if your system hardware and software are ready for upgrade (try Hands-on Project 4-6). Take special note of the hardware installed in the computer, such as network cards, scanners, sound cards, and other devices that require special drivers. If your organization supports many computers, consider obtaining network software that can automatically inventory the hardware components of the computers on your network. Or, you can develop a checklist so that you can inventory your hardware, as illustrated in Table 4-2.

Also, before you upgrade to a new operating system, make sure that the current drivers for I/O devices and storage media work with the new version, or that there are drivers available for these devices for the new operating system. It is a good idea to contact hardware vendors and get some assurance that their devices will continue to work properly after the upgrade. Do not leave this to chance; older or discontinued hardware may not be supported in newer operating system versions.

TIP

The existence of drivers is another reason to delay your upgrade until an operating system has been on the market for several months. Sometimes operating system vendors release a system before hardware manufacturers have had time to develop and test new drivers. Waiting to upgrade usually means there will be more drivers—and hardware—available to use with an operating system.

Table 4-2   Hardware checklist for multiple computers

Computer ID	CPU/ Clock Speed	RAM	Disk Capacity	CD-ROM/ DVD	Video	Special Devices
CFNP9012	1.8 GHz	256 MB	20 GB	CD-ROM	On board	None
D3FX1931	3.06 GHz	512 MB	60 GB	CD-ROM/ DVD combo drive	AGP	Tablet
...	...	...	...	...	...	...

Make sure that you have all the device drivers needed for the hardware available on floppy disk, Zip disk, or CD-ROM. If there are drivers that exist only on the hard disk of the computer, copy them to a floppy disk, or some other safe place. Otherwise, if the upgrade fails, you will not have the drivers you need to get the computer back to work. If there are new drivers for the new version of the operating system, keep those handy, as well as copies of your current drivers. This will enable you to reinstall the old operating system if, for some reason, you are unable to complete the upgrade.

It is also a good idea to keep detailed records of custom software settings—changes in the defaults for the operating system and other software—so that these custom settings can be restored, if necessary, after any operating system or other software upgrade. For example, it is not uncommon for users to modify display or other settings after they run an operating system for a while; they may use an automated backup program, run special disk tools on a regular basis, or have customized network settings. Upgrade installations may reset some settings to their defaults, which may not be what you want.

Determine what software is used on systems prior to an upgrade so that you can check to see if there are any compatibility problems. For example, not all software written for Windows 95 can run in Windows XP, and the Windows 95 software that can run in Windows XP is run in Windows 95 compatibility mode (in Windows XP click Start, point to All Programs, point to Accessories, and click Program Compatibility Wizard). Further, some databases may not be accessible, or there might be access problems, such as with **Open Database Connectivity (ODBC)** drivers, when you upgrade. ODBC is a set of rules developed by Microsoft for accessing databases. Table 4-3 illustrates a checklist that you can make before upgrading software. Also, try Hands-on Project 4-7 to learn how to assess what software is loaded on an operating system.

Table 4-3   Software checklist

Software	Vendor/ Version	Operating System	Location	Future Software Upgrade Plans
Accounting				
Publishing				
Word process- ing				
Spreadsheet				
Database				
E-mail				
Inventory				
Manufacturing				
Human resources				
Custom-built				

Making Backups Before Upgrades

A **backup** involves copying files from a computer system to another medium, such as tape, Zip disk, another hard drive, or a removable drive. It is essential to have a complete backup of your old operating system, software, and data before beginning an upgrade. Some operating systems, in particular Windows, can change many configuration files, even those not used exclusively by the operating system. As a result, some applications may not be able to locate data. There are cases in which operating system installers have altogether destroyed parts of application programs. As you learned earlier in the book, the operating system is responsible for, among other things, the management of files and disks, and at the same time it provides many services to application software. With this level of complexity, a change in even one file during an upgrade can drastically change the way the new operating system works.

Making backups of software and data also is a very important part of day-to-day computer operation because unexpected things happen, such as hard disk crashes or unintentional file deletions. As operating systems and computers get more complicated, failures can even happen for unexplainable reasons during normal computer operation. If you use computers long enough, eventually you will lose critical information. Backups are essential to recovering from such a loss.

Most operating systems have a backup utility. Figure 4-1 shows the Backup tool in Windows NT 4.0, which you use to back up a computer before upgrading to Windows Server 2003 or Windows XP, for example.

NOTE If a program is lost, you may be able to simply reinstall it. But when data files are lost, the damage may take hours or days to repair. For this reason, regular backup of your system during normal operations and full backup prior to an upgrade are necessities.

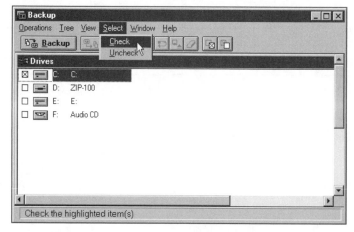

Figure 4-1   Windows NT 4.0 Backup tool

The following are some points to consider when backing up your information:

- Close all open windows, programs, and files before starting a backup because most backup tools do not back up open files (on systems that use swap files—most systems—the swap file is always open, but it is acceptable to omit the swap file contents in the backup).

- Make sure that you have the software needed to restore the backups under both the old and new operating systems. There is nothing more frustrating than having a backup, but not being able to restore it. Even though you tested the backup and restored software with the old operating system, there is no guarantee that it will work properly with the new one. Before you perform an upgrade, you should test the restore software, preferably by making a backup and restoring it to the computer you set up to test the new operating system.

- Make sure that you actually make a full backup. Sometimes important files are not included in the backup process because of program error or human oversight. In addition, you should make a backup of all the contents of all fixed disks connected to the computer, not just the boot drive. If a disaster happens, it can save you a lot of time. You then only need to restore backup tapes, instead of having to find installation disks for software programs.

NOTE When you perform a backup, make sure that you back up critical system files, such as the system state data in Windows 2000/XP/Server 2003, which includes the registry. In the backup utility that comes with these operating systems (and for some third-party utilities), you must manually select to back up these files. Another way to make sure that you have a backup of all files, including system files, is to perform an image (binary) backup by using tools in your backup or third-party software, such as Symantec Norton Ghost, or Power-Quest Drive Image.

- If you upgrade to a new version of backup software on your new operating system, make 100 percent sure, preferably by a test you perform yourself, that the new system will be able to read your backup without problems. For example, a Windows 95 backup is not compatible with a Windows XP backup.

Some computers that you upgrade will not have a built-in drive, such as a tape drive, that is suitable to make a full backup. If the computer is connected to a network, you may be able to use another computer on the network, which is equipped with an appropriate backup device, to make your backup. Alternatively, backup devices, such as tape drives or large removable disk drives, are now relatively inexpensive; almost all operating systems support easily removable external drives that connect to the parallel, USB, FireWire, or SCSI port on a computer. It is worth the money to have one of these devices handy to make full backups of computers before an upgrade installation.

NOTE   Upgrading an operating system can be very simple; it may take only 20 minutes, and you may never need those backup tapes that took two hours to create, or that test upgrade that took two weeks. However, if that 20-minute job turns into a three-week project, or if you must give up the upgrade and start from scratch, you will be very happy to have the backups. The time spent doing a test upgrade, including testing the backup, can prevent many headaches and problems with your larger system upgrade.

Conducting a Test Upgrade

You should plan to test an upgrade before you apply it to a production computer. If you have only one or two computers to upgrade, this may not be an option. But when you have five or more computers to upgrade, it can be beneficial to perform an upgrade test on a sample computer, or on several computers.

The purpose of an upgrade test is to simulate what would happen in a real upgrade. You can discover any problems that might occur, either with the upgrade itself, or with running hardware and software after the upgrade. To do this, you need a working computer that closely resembles the computers you will be upgrading. Choose a computer that resembles the "lowest common denominator" of the computers you are upgrading, in terms of the amount of memory, speed of the CPU, size of the hard disk, and any devices connected to the computer. You should also install all software that is typically found on a production computer in your situation. If you are in a network environment, connect the computer to the network and make sure everything is fully functional. You should be able to use this machine as if it were a production computer. At the beginning of the test, this computer will run the old version of the operating system, the version you currently run on your production computers. Part of the test is to practice upgrading this operating system.

NOTE   If the test computer is also a production computer (because that is the only option available to you), it is important to back up all files—data, system, and software—before you start. Operating system upgrades can destroy application configuration files and data during the upgrade. See the "Making Backups Before Upgrades" section in this chapter for more information about backing up a computer.

When the test computer is fully functional, you can perform the upgrade. During this first upgrade, it is very helpful to take specific notes describing the steps of the installation and any problems that arose, and what you did about them. Also note any questions you had about the installation, and any information you had to look up to complete the installation. Write down drivers that you needed. These notes will serve as a guide in later installations.

When there are many computers to upgrade, it is common to upgrade them over a period of several weeks or months, so having notes on the exact steps of the upgrade process will help you remember the information you need, and the problems you found. Another approach is to create a written "script" that documents the upgrade process step by step, including how to handle problems, or special driver and software installations and configu-rations. Figure 4-2 illustrates a sample upgrade script for upgrading from Windows 98 to Windows XP using the Windows XP CD-ROM.

Windows 98 to XP upgrade script:

1. Obtain a software license for each system to be upgraded.
2. Make sure that the hardware fulfills the Windows XP hardware requirements.
3. Make sure that the hardware is on the Windows XP HCL or is listed in the Windows XP Catalog.
4. Determine if the BIOS needs to be upgraded and obtain any BIOS upgrades on floppy or CD-ROM (particularly for portable computers that are part of the upgrade).
5. Determine if there are new drivers for XP, such as for SCSI devices, modems, etc., and obtain them.
6. Make sure that there is a key code available for each installation (associated with the individual license).
7. Be sure that a password is already selected for the Administrator account.
8. Before upgrading, get a fresh startup by rebooting and then closing any open windows.
9. Insert the Windows XP CD-ROM and use the Autorun option to start the installation.
10. Use the option to check for system compatibility.
11. Use the option to upgrade rather than to install a new system (so existing settings are retained).
12. Prior testing shows there is no need to download updated setup files. Thus choose No when this option is displayed.
13. Choose the option to save existing operating system files, so it is possible to uninstall if there are problems.
14. Click Next and OK as appropriate to the setup dialog boxes.
15. Log in after you are finished to make sure that the installation worked.
16. Obtain a product activation code via the Internet.

Figure 4-2   Sample upgrade script

Once you complete the upgrade on the test computer and immediately deal with any software issues that arise, test the computer for a couple of days. Perform tasks that you would normally perform, and take note of anything that changed in the way the computer, and in particular the user interface, works.

If you find no apparent problems, the next step is to ask an informed computer user, whose computer is on the list to be upgraded, to use this computer for day-to-day work for a few days. Keep in close communication with this person, taking note of any problems experi-enced, and anything that does not work properly. After any operating system upgrade, one of the first things to check is whether all application software functions normally. Sometimes after upgrades, particular functions in software packages do not work, or work differently. If there are problems, chances are that the problems will not surface until a user tries to access a certain function that you never think to test.

During the testing phase, ensure that the upgrade did not change any settings, or move or remove files or programs. If you do encounter significant problems with hardware or software, consider delaying the upgrade until these problems are resolved. Just as a prerelease test will uncover major and minor problems with a new operating system design, an upgrade test can uncover conflicts between the new operating system and your particular system configuration.

After resolving any problems, repeat the test installation process starting with a **clean computer** (a computer from which all unnecessary software and hardware have been removed). Install the old operating system, then all software, then upgrade the operating system (using your initial set of notes), and make the changes you think will resolve the issues you encountered earlier. Test the computer yourself for a couple of days, and then let a user test the upgraded computer. In this way, you have another chance to test the upgrade and your installation notes.

These pre-upgrade tests can be time consuming; you may need a week or longer to get through them. In some cases, you may perform many test installs before you get every detail worked out. Or, you may decide after repeated tries that the upgrade will not work, and decide not to upgrade. Either way, the test results, when carefully documented, will tell you what to expect from your upgrade. Obviously it is better to find out in a test situation that an operating system upgrade won't work for you. Your test results also can be used as a tool to explain to employees and management why an upgrade should or should not be carried out. If you decide the upgrade should proceed, you will know the steps, you will know what to expect, and you will be efficient in performing the upgrade. A test upgrade is well worth your time.

Installing and Upgrading Windows 2000

Windows 2000 is available in Server and Professional options, and is built on Windows NT technology. There are several ways to install Windows 2000, including CD-ROMs, over the network, and in unattended mode.

Hardware Requirements

At the very least, you will need the hardware recommended in Table 4-4. It is important that your hardware is listed on the HCL for Windows 2000.

Table 4-4   Windows 2000 hardware requirements

Hardware	Minimum	Recommended
CPU (Server or Professional)	Pentium 133	Pentium 200 or faster
RAM (Server)	128 MB	256 MB
RAM (Professional)	64 MB	64 MB or more
Storage (Server)	1 GB	2 GB
Storage (Professional)	650 MB	1 GB

Your installation time should be between 45 and 120 minutes.

Installing Windows 2000

Two common ways to install Windows 2000 are by booting from the Windows 2000 CD-ROM, or by booting from the Setup disks. Both methods first go into a character-based screen that is actually started by the Winnt program.

NOTE

If you upgrade from an existing Windows NT installation, another way is to boot Windows NT, insert the Windows 2000 CD-ROM, and run Winnt32— which is an all-GUI install, but does not follow all of the steps here.

The two common ways discussed in Hands-on Project 4-2 will work every time, no matter what operating system is on the PC.

Hands-on Project 4-2 addresses how Windows 2000 Setup provides a way to install a special mass storage driver, or HAL, for SMP computers. **HAL** is the **hardware abstraction layer** consisting of the code that talks directly to the computer's hardware. This allows an application to use multiple processors if the need arises for additional processing power.

Other Considerations

If you install the Server version, you have two licensing options, depending on what you purchased. **Per-seat licensing** (a license for each workstation) makes sense in larger settings where you have more than one Windows 2000 server, because one client can be connected to multiple servers with only a single per-seat license. In smaller settings with only one server, however, **per-server licensing** with a single server and a set number of workstations may make more sense.

If you install Windows 2000 Server, you must specify how this machine fits in the domain structure. Recall from Chapter 2 that a domain is a group of computers that share a common security database. If you install a single Windows 2000 server and do not plan to have other servers, or if you want it to participate only in a workgroup or exist as a standalone server in an existing domain, you should choose the standalone server option during installation. If you want multiple Windows 2000 servers and want to keep user and permission information consistent among all of them, put them all in a domain.

Windows 2000 also gives you the option to create a startup disk, called the **emergency repair disk (ERD)**. It is strongly recommended you make one. You will need one blank floppy during installation to make your ERD. This disk is unique to the machine on which you are installing, and you should make an ERD for every Windows 2000 computer you have. Also, plan to update the ERD each time that you make a change, such as after adding a new device (and driver), installing new software, or adding many user accounts.

 Never use the ERD from another computer! Doing so is likely to result in loss of data, and in many cases, require a new installation of Windows 2000.

If your computer is connected to a network, you must answer questions about network connections and protocols. You can also install Remote Access Service (RAS) either during or after the Windows 2000 installation. RAS setup is covered in greater detail in later chapters.

You can also confirm or change **network bindings**, part of the Windows 2000 Server system, which are used to coordinate software communications among the NIC, network protocols, and network services. (Network binding is covered in more detail in Chapter 8.) Setup automatically configures network bindings for protocols and services you select.

Upgrading to Windows 2000

There are several upgrade paths to Windows 2000, such as from Windows 95, Windows 98, and Windows NT. The most common paths are to upgrade from Windows 95/98 or from Windows NT 4.0.

 There is no upgrade path from Windows Me to Windows 2000 because in order to upgrade, you must purchase a full non-upgrade copy of Windows 2000 and install it from scratch.

When you upgrade from Windows 95/98, you will upgrade to Windows 2000 Professional. If you upgrade Windows NT Workstation 4.0 (or earlier), you will upgrade to Windows 2000 Professional. Windows NT Server 4.0 is upgraded to Windows 2000 Server or higher (Advanced Server or Datacenter Server).

For users who upgrade from Windows 95/98, there are several issues to consider:

- Determine if your computer meets the minimum system requirements for Windows 2000, listed in Table 4-4.

- Determine if you need to obtain new drivers for the devices in your computer, such as for a modem or NIC. Visit the Windows 2000 Home Page site at *www.microsoft.com/windows2000/default.asp* (click or search for the link for compatibility) to check on compatible devices.

- Decide if you want to upgrade to NTFS from FAT16 or FAT32. It is recommended that you wait to upgrade to NTFS until after the installation is completed, and you have an opportunity to make sure your computer is working properly. Keep in mind that once you convert from FAT16 or FAT32 to NTFS, you cannot convert back without reformatting the hard disk and performing a restore.

- You will need a password for the Administrator account. Decide on a password before you start the installation.

4

When you are ready to upgrade from Windows 95/98 to Windows 2000 Professional, start Windows 95/98, close any open windows, and then insert the Windows 2000 Professional CD-ROM. The first box you see queries whether you want to upgrade to Windows 2000. Click Yes to view the Welcome to the Windows 2000 Setup Wizard dialog box. In this box, select the option to Upgrade to Windows 2000 (Recommended), as shown in Figure 4-3.

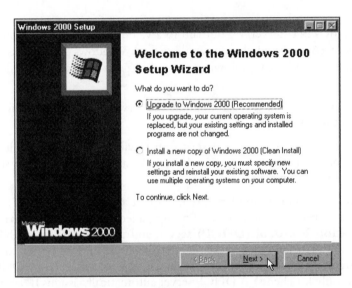

Figure 4-3   Windows 2000 Setup Wizard

After you select the upgrade option, you are on your way to upgrading to Windows 2000 Professional. The installation takes from 45 minutes to about an hour and a half. One way to save time during the installation is to go to the Windows 2000 Home Page site in advance and make sure that your system and peripherals are compatible with Windows 2000 Professional. Also, obtain any new drivers or BIOS updates for Windows 2000 before you start. You may also need to obtain Windows 2000 updates for some of your software. Consult your software vendors' Web sites for Windows 2000 update information. You can install these software updates after you install Windows 2000 and determine that you need them. Try Hands-on Project 4-9 to upgrade from Windows 98 to Windows 2000 Professional.

The preparations for upgrading from Windows NT 4.0 to Windows 2000 are the same as those for upgrading from Windows 95/98, with a few exceptions. First, Windows NT 4.0

only uses FAT16 or NTFS, and not FAT32. If you are using FAT16 and want to continue using the FAT file system, the Windows 2000 Setup program upgrades your disk to FAT16 if it is 2 GB or smaller; it upgrades to FAT32 if your disk is more than 2 GB. If your disk is already formatted for NTFS version 4, Windows 2000 Setup converts it to NTFS version 5. Second, make sure that you obtain Windows 2000 drivers for your Windows NT-supported devices. Third, the protocol of preference for Windows 2000 is Transmission Control Protocol/Internet Protocol (TCP/IP). If you are using the legacy NetBIOS Extended User Interface (NetBEUI) protocol, convert your Windows NT system to use TCP/IP before you upgrade (for a smoother upgrade path).

NOTE The actual upgrade steps from Windows NT Workstation to Windows 2000 are similar to those for Windows 98, which means that you can apply what you learn in Hands-on Project 4-9 to a Windows NT Workstation upgrade.

If you upgrade a Windows NT Server 4.0 domain to a Windows 2000 Server domain, the upgrade steps are more complicated than upgrading from Windows NT Workstation to Windows 2000 Professional. Use the following general steps to upgrade a Windows NT Server domain:

1. Coordinate a time when you can upgrade the servers and domain while no one is accessing them but you.

2. Back up each Windows NT 4.0 server that will be upgraded, including its registry, before you start an upgrade. Also, make an ERD before you start, and again just after you finish.

3. If TCP/IP is not already implemented, upgrade the servers to TCP/IP before you start, or consider setting up the first upgraded server as a **Dynamic Host Configuration Protocol (DHCP)** server, and use the default TCP/IP configuration for each upgraded server (generally, however, it is better to give all servers a static Internet Protocol (IP) address that is not assigned by DHCP, and use DHCP only for clients). A DHCP server automatically assigns IP addresses to network clients. Also, set up the first upgraded server to work as a **Domain Name Service (DNS)** server if one does not already exist on the network, such as via a UNIX server. A DNS server resolves domain and computer names to IP addresses (and vice versa).

4. If you are upgrading more than one server in a domain, start by upgrading the Windows NT 4.0 **Primary Domain Controller (PDC)**, the server that contains the master copy of the domain information, to the first Windows 2000 domain controller. Next, and one at a time, upgrade each Windows NT 4.0 **Backup Domain Controller (BDC)**, the servers that contain backup copies of the domain data, to be a Windows 2000 domain controller.

5. To begin the upgrade, use the Winnt32 program on the Windows 2000 Server CD-ROM by clicking Start, clicking Run, entering the path to the CD-ROM plus Winnt32, such as *D:\i386\Winnt32* (or use the browse option on the CD-ROM window that is displayed by the Autorun program when you insert the CD-ROM).

NOTE To view the command switches for Winnt32, click Start, click Run, enter the CD-ROM path plus *\i386\Winnt32 /?*.

6. Select Upgrade to Windows 2000 (Recommended) on the first screen when the Setup program starts so that you can retain existing settings, including the Windows NT Security Account Manager (SAM) database information about accounts, groups, and software.

7. Follow the directions in the Windows 2000 Setup.

8. During the upgrade, the Active Directory Wizard starts and provides the opportunity for you to specify if you want to join an existing domain tree or forest, or start a new one. Specify that you want to start a new one if you are upgrading the PDC. Specify that you wish to join an existing one if you are upgrading a BDC, and provide the name of the domain.

9. The Active Directory Installation Wizard upgrades the PDC or BDC to have Windows 2000 Server directory services and Kerberos authentication services. Also, it converts the SAM in the Windows NT registry to the database used by Active Directory so that accounts, groups, and security information are retained.

10. After you upgrade a PDC, it is still recognized by any Windows NT BDC as the domain master, and can synchronize with live BDCs until they are upgraded. Leave a BDC running until all servers are upgraded (except for the last server to be upgraded, of course) because this gives you a backup alternative if there is a problem. (If you are concerned about upgrade problems, create an extra BDC to match the last BDC before it is converted. Remove the backup BDC from the network, and store it in a safe place until you feel assured the upgrade process is fully successful.)

11. Establish security policies for the domain via Active Directory, including logon restrictions.

12. After all servers are upgraded and there are no Windows NT servers connected to the domain, convert the domain (or all domains) to native mode, which reflects that there are no longer any Windows NT PDCs or BDCs on the network. You can do this by clicking the Start button, pointing to Programs, pointing to Administrative Tools, and clicking Active Directory Domains and Trusts. Right-click the domain you want to convert and click Properties. Click the Change Mode button.

After you finish upgrading any system to Windows 2000, connect your computer to the Internet (if you have access), and use the **Windows Update** option to obtain the latest patches and upgrades. To access the Windows 2000 Windows Update option, click Start, and click Windows Update at the top of the Start menu (or click Start, point to Settings, click Control Panel, double-click Add/Remove Programs, click Add New Programs in the left pane, and click the Windows Update button).

TIP

When you are done with the Windows Update, you should make a new ERD.

Installing and Upgrading Windows XP

Windows XP, which stands for "experience," has Home and Professional versions. The two versions are very similar, but the Professional version has more features, such as the ability to host up to 10 clients. Recreational users will probably use the Home version. Intended for office and networked environments, the Professional version adds support for multiple processors, software administration for the whole organization, and advanced security, to name just a few of the features provided.

Hardware Requirements

At the very least, you will need the hardware recommended in Table 4-5. It is important that your hardware is listed in the Windows Catalog for Windows XP.

Table 4-5   Windows XP hardware requirements

Hardware	Minimum	Recommended
CPU (Home and Professional)	Pentium 233	Pentium 300 or faster
RAM (Home and Professional)	64 MB	128 MB or more
Storage (Home and Professional)	1.5 GB	5 GB or more

See Hands-on Project 4-3 to practice installing Windows XP. Your installation time will be about 60 to 120 minutes.

Installing Windows XP

Windows XP, both Home and Professional, combines features of Windows NT, Windows 2000, and Windows Me. You will notice several underlying similarities in Windows XP that remind you of features in these operating systems.

One new feature implemented in Windows XP is the concept of activation. Once you finish the setup and reboot your computer, you have 30 days to activate your copy of Windows XP. This can be done either by phone or online. Almost all new PCs with Windows XP installed have their activation linked solely to the BIOS. As long as the BIOS is not replaced, there should be no need for a reactivation.

Included with Windows XP is a new utility called the Files and Settings Transfer Wizard (see Figure 4-4). This allows you to transfer your files from your old computer to your new one via a direct cable or a network connection, if you are connected. You can transfer your display settings, browser favorites, desktop icons, and many other items to your new computer. This wizard is activated by clicking Start, clicking Accessories, clicking System Tools, and then clicking Files and Settings Transfer Wizard.

Figure 4-4   Files and Settings Transfer Wizard

After you install Windows XP, use the Windows Update feature to download and install any critical updates along with any optional updates you want to use (make sure your computer is connected to the Internet, then click Start, All Programs, Windows Update). Hands-on Project 4-3 enables you to practice a Windows XP installation.

Upgrading to Windows XP

You can upgrade to Windows XP from any of the following Microsoft operating systems:

- Windows 98
- Windows Me
- Windows NT
- Windows 2000

Before you start an upgrade, keep in mind that you cannot upgrade Windows 95 or earlier operating systems to Windows XP. Also, as is true for any upgrade: (1) back up your system before you start, including the registry, (2) make sure that your hardware matches the recommended hardware requirements for Windows XP, (3) check hardware compatibility in the Windows Catalog on Microsoft's Web site, and (4) obtain any drivers that you may need before you start.

If you have older hardware, such as a Pentium I or Pentium II computer, the manufacturer may offer a BIOS upgrade that makes the computer more compatible with Windows XP. Contact the computer manufacturer or visit its Web site to check on a possible BIOS enhancement that you can download or obtain on CD-ROM.

There is not room to explain how to upgrade from all possible operating systems to Windows XP, but it is not necessary because the upgrade process is virtually identical for Windows 98, Me, NT, and 2000. In this section, we provide the general upgrade steps for all of these systems.

Microsoft considers Windows XP to be a "minor" upgrade from Windows 2000 because Windows 2000 and XP are built on nearly the same kernel. The primary differences are in the introduction of a relatively new GUI in Windows XP, and Windows XP has more functionality for multimedia applications, including photos, music, and video clips. Because Windows XP is a minor upgrade, some organizations may choose to upgrade their servers from Windows 2000 to Windows Server 2003, retaining Windows 2000 on client computers, or upgrading clients to Windows XP.

To upgrade to Windows XP (Home or Professional) from Windows 98, Me, NT, or 2000, begin by closing all open windows, or reboot the computer and then close any windows that you don't need. Insert the Windows XP CD-ROM and wait for the Autorun program to automatically start the Setup program. Use the option to check system compatibility (see Figure 4-5) before you start the actual installation, and then select the option to check your system automatically. If you see the message "Windows XP upgrade check found no incompatibilities or problems" (see Figure 4-6), your system is ready for the upgrade. Click

Finish and then click Back so you can continue with the upgrade. If there is an incompatibility, stop the upgrade and check with your computer manufacturer for Windows XP updates.

Figure 4-5   Option to check compatibility with Windows XP

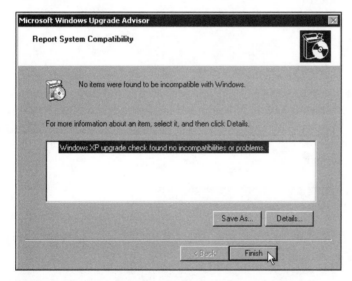

Figure 4-6   Viewing the compatibility test results

Next, begin the Windows XP installation, and specify that you want to use the upgrade option so that the settings you already have in Windows 98, Me, NT, or 2000 are carried into Windows XP. Read the license agreement, enter your product key, and complete the remaining steps in the Windows XP Setup program. The upgrade takes from 30 to 90 minutes to complete. Try Hands-on Project 4-10 to practice upgrading to Windows XP.

For all systems that you upgrade to Windows XP, you must obtain a product activation code by going to the Microsoft Web site. Also, keep in mind that if your computer stops working and you need to move Windows XP to another system, such as through a tape restore, you must obtain another product activation code for the new computer.

Finally, after you upgrade to Windows XP, use the Windows Update feature to link to Microsoft's Web site for additional features and special upgrade options. To access Windows Update, click Start, select All Programs, and click Windows Update.

INSTALLING AND UPGRADING WINDOWS SERVER 2003

Windows Server 2003 is the next generation in the Windows 2000/Windows XP line of operating systems. The family of Windows Server 2003 products includes the following editions:

- Standard Edition
- Enterprise Edition
- Datacenter Edition
- Web Edition
- Small Business Server

We will discuss the Enterprise Edition as that is the edition used in most businesses and institutions of higher education. The installation and upgrades of the other editions are very similar. Once you are familiar with the Enterprise Edition, you will be able to perform an install or upgrade on any of the other editions. Figure 4-7 shows the initial screen for updating to Windows Server 2003.

Figure 4-7   What do you want to do? Windows Server 2003 dialog box

Hardware Requirements

At the very least, you will need the hardware recommended in Table 4-6. It is important that your hardware is listed in the Windows Server 2003 Catalog.

Table 4-6   Windows Server 2003 hardware requirements

Hardware	Minimum	Recommended
CPU	Pentium 133	Pentium 733 or faster
RAM	128 MB	256 MB or more
Storage	1.5 GB	5 GB or more

See Hands-on Project 4-12 to practice updating Windows 2000 Server to Windows Server 2003, Enterprise Edition.

Installing Windows Server 2003

To install Windows Server 2003, place the CD-ROM in the drive and turn your computer on. Because Windows Server 2003 is strongly related to Windows 2000 Server, the installation is very similar and many of the features are the same. In fact the steps are almost identical, so please review the installation information earlier in this chapter on Windows 2000. Also, try Hands-on Project 4-2, substituting Windows Server 2003 for Windows 2000 Server. As with Windows 2000 and Windows XP, you should run Windows Update after installation to get the latest patches and updates.

Upgrading to Windows Server 2003

You can update from the Windows 2000 Server family to the Windows Server 2003 family of operating systems. Windows 2000 Server will upgrade to the Windows Server 2003 Standard Edition. Windows 2000 Advanced Server will upgrade to the Windows Server 2003 Enterprise Edition, and the Windows 2000 Datacenter Server will upgrade to the Windows Server 2003 Datacenter Edition. The Windows Server 2003 Web Edition has no equivalent version in the Windows 2000 Server family.

Before you start an upgrade: (1) back up your system, including the registry, (2) make sure that your hardware matches the recommended hardware requirements for Windows Server 2003, (3) check the hardware compatibility information on Microsoft's Web site, and (4) obtain any drivers that you may need before you start.

To upgrade to Windows Server 2003 from Windows 2000, begin by closing all open windows, or reboot the computer and then close any windows that you don't need. Insert the Windows Server 2003 CD-ROM and wait for the Autorun program to automatically start the Setup program. Use the option to check system compatibility before you start the actual installation, and then select the option to check your system automatically. If you see the message "Windows Server 2003 upgrade check found no incompatibilities or problems," your system is ready for the upgrade. Click Finish and then click Back so you can continue with the upgrade. If there is an incompatibility, stop the upgrade and check with your computer manufacturer for Windows Server 2003 updates.

For all systems that you upgrade to Windows Server 2003, you must obtain a product activation code by going to Microsoft's Web site. Also, keep in mind that if your computer stops working and you need to move Windows Server 2003 to another system, such as through a tape restore, you must obtain another product activation code for the new computer.

INSTALLING AND UPGRADING UNIX: LINUX

And now for something completely different: UNIX. This section discusses installing one UNIX version—Red Hat Enterprise Linux 3.0—on the Intel PC platform. There are numerous other versions of UNIX designed for different hardware platforms. If you understand how Linux installs on the Intel platform, you should have no problem installing other versions of UNIX.

Hardware Requirements

The Red Hat Enterprise Linux 3.0 operating system requires at least the hardware shown in Table 4-7.

Table 4-7   Red Hat Enterprise Linux 3.0 hardware requirements

Hardware	Minimum	Recommended
CPU	386 DX 40	Pentium II series or faster
RAM	8 MB	64 MB or more
Storage (Server)	1 GB (minimal install)	4 GB (full install)

Installing Linux

Linux is available in many shapes and forms. This section focuses on installing a commercial version of Linux, although there are shareware versions, such as Fedora. In the business environment, most companies choose to use operating systems for which they can get support. Using a commercial version of Linux guarantees support. Red Hat Enterprise Linux 3.0 is the most recent commercial version at this writing. The steps to install any Linux variety will be similar, but not identical, to the steps described here.

NOTE For specific instructions on installing Red Hat Fedora, see Appendix B, "Using Fedora with This Book."

You will get a set of CD-ROMs in the package if you buy Red Hat Linux Enterprise 3.0, or you can download the files from the Internet. For information on Red Hat Enterprise Linux 3.0, point your browser to *www.redhat.com*. You can also search for "linux download" (use any Web search engine) to find many sites where you can download versions of Linux.

If your machine can boot from the CD-ROM drive, you will be able to boot Red Hat Enterprise Linux 3.0 from the CD-ROM. You will need between 15 minutes to over one hour to install Red Hat Enterprise Linux 3.0. You do not need to make partitions or format your disk ahead of time. Step-by-step instructions for installing Red Hat Enterprise Linux 3.0 are included in Hands-on Project 4-4 at the end of this chapter.

Linux comes with the complete source code for the kernel, all the drivers, and most of the utilities. This is helpful if you are a computer programmer who wants to change code and make it do exactly what you want. This is probably the strongest advantage of Linux; because thousands of people worldwide are doing this kind of development, you will find a wide variety of programming tools and toys on the Internet. How well they work, and how well they are supported, is a different story. Linux is not for everyone!

Upgrading Linux

The upgrade process described here is based on the Red Hat Enterprise Linux 3.0 installer. Although the installers have changed significantly in appearance over the years, the functionality has not changed much. Upgrades from any version of Linux to this version should work, but in many cases the installer cannot determine the exact features installed on the previous version of Linux. It's recommended that you upgrade to Red Hat Enterprise Linux 3.0 only from Red Hat version 3.0 or up. If you used a different Linux version, back up your data and perform a clean install, then restore your data.

Under Linux, the upgrade process works similarly to the installation process. You start the installation as described in the previous section, then choose to perform an upgrade. The installer asks for some basic system information, such as which language and keyboard to use. Also, it checks to determine what hard disks to use for the installation. It then gets most system information previously stored on the hard disk by the old operating system. The appropriate system files are replaced, and the installer asks if you want to customize the package installation. If you select Yes, you can choose specific elements to install or update for each previously installed package. Note that many libraries and programs will be replaced, and if you add software to the computer, you should check carefully to ensure that everything still works as expected after installation.

CAUTION

An important caveat in UNIX upgrades is that many configuration files are overwritten during the upgrade. The mail system, printing system, window system, and network services such as File Transfer Protocol (FTP) and the World Wide Web server may be reconfigured. You should make sure you have backups of these files before you begin an upgrade, and double-check configuration files on these services to make sure they did not change.

Installing and Upgrading NetWare 6.5

The steps for installing NetWare 6.0 and NetWare 6.5 are very similar. This section presents only the steps for NetWare 6.5.

Hardware Requirements

The NetWare 6.5 operating system requires at least the hardware shown in Table 4-8.

Table 4-8   NetWare 6.5 hardware requirements

Hardware	Minimum	Recommended
CPU	Pentium II	Server class PC (Pentium III or greater)
RAM	512 MB	1 GB or more
Storage (Server)	2.4 GB	5 GB (full install)

You will also need at least one network card, a bootable CD drive, and a mouse.

Installing NetWare 6.5

Novell NetWare 6.5 steps you through the installation process in a very logical manner. Novell has made evaluation kits available so you can download a trial copy. Their Web site gives you step-by-step instructions on how to download and burn the CDs. They also give you instructions for ordering a demo/evaluation set of CDs from them for a nominal fee. To check this out, visit *www.novell.com* and search using the terms "evaluation" and "download."

Novell also has very good documentation available on their Web site. To access this information, go to the Novell Web site and search on "NetWare 6.5 documentation." Hands-on Project 4-13 takes you through the steps of loading a basic NetWare 6.5 installation.

Upgrading to NetWare 6.5

You can upgrade to NetWare 6.5 if your current server is running one of the following NetWare versions:

- NetWare 4.2 with Support Pack 9
- NetWare 5.1 with Support Pack 6
- NetWare 6 with Support Pack 3

If you are running NetWare 4.2 and want to upgrade to NetWare 6.5, you will need to do a down server upgrade. This type of upgrade is outside the scope of this book, but you can go to the Novell Web site and follow the instructions in the NetWare 6.5 Overview and Installation Guide.

Using the Novell Migration Wizard 6 you can migrate a Windows NT 3.51/4.0 server to NetWare 6.5. The wizard can be downloaded free from *www.novell. com/downloads*.

TIP

INSTALLING AND UPGRADING MAC OS X

The installation of Mac OS X uses a graphical interface and a Setup Assistant that functions similarly to the Microsoft setup wizards. Mac OS X requires a Macintosh with a PowerPC processor chip. It also requires at least 128 MB of RAM.

Hardware Requirements

The Mac OS X operating system requires at least the hardware shown in Table 4-9.

Table 4-9   Mac OS X hardware requirements

Hardware	Minimum	Recommended
CPU	PowerPC G3	PowerPC G3, G4, or G5
RAM	128 MB	128 MB or more
Storage (Server)	2.0 GB (minimal install)	3.5 GB (full install)

Installing Mac OS X

The Mac OS X installer can be installed from a CD-ROM or over an AppleTalk network. The easiest way to install Mac OS X is directly from the CD-ROM. The installation process has three parts: booting the CD-ROM, running the installer, and restarting from the hard drive. Complete, step-by-step instructions for installing Mac OS X are given in Hands-on Project 4-5 at the end of this chapter.

Booting from the CD-ROM

A Macintosh will boot from the CD-ROM drive only if instructed to do so. This may be done either by selecting the CD-ROM icon on the desktop, or by holding down the C key on the keyboard at the very beginning of the startup process (put the CD-ROM into the machine, restart, and immediately hold down the C key).

At the end of the boot process, the CD-ROM icon appears in the upper-right corner of the screen, just below the menu bar, and the Mac OS X window opens, showing you the contents of the CD-ROM, as shown in Figure 4-8.

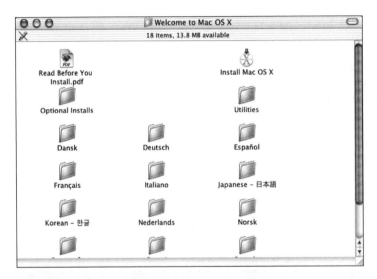

Figure 4-8 Mac OS X CD boot initial screen

You may want to read the Mac OS X Read Before You Install PDF file before starting the installation.

NOTE

Running the Installer

To proceed with the installation, double-click the Install Mac OS X icon. Select the option to Restart and the installer launches after the computer reboots. You are presented with the opening screen, which lists the steps for installation.

During this phase, you select a destination drive, read important information, agree to the software license, and then the installer copies operating system files to your hard drive. Depending on your computer, copying files takes from about six minutes to over 45 minutes.

Restarting from the Hard Drive

When the installer finishes copying files, you are prompted to restart the computer. If you did a clean install, the operating system software that's appropriate for your Macintosh will appear on your hard drive, along with AppleTalk and TCP/IP networking software, and drivers for almost all Apple-brand printers.

Upgrading to Mac OS X

Before attempting to upgrade to Mac OS X, you should perform three basic steps:

1. As with other operating systems, you must back up all data and configuration files on the hard drive. This includes the entire System Folder, which may contain the user's browser bookmarks, and Eudora address book and mail files.

2. Check the disk for errors using a utility like Norton Disk Doctor (part of Symantec's Norton Utilities for Macintosh) or Apple Disk First Aid. Otherwise, the installation could aggravate existing directory damage and cause new problems, including data loss. Newer versions of Apple installers perform a basic check automatically.

3. Always upgrade the hard disk drivers. Skipping this step can result in a loss of data if the old disk drivers are incompatible with the new operating system. If you are using an Apple drive formatted with an Apple driver, newer versions of the installer handle this automatically. For third-party drives, contact the publisher of your disk-formatting utility for new disk drivers. If new disk drivers have not shipped, postpone the upgrade until the necessary software is available.

When you upgrade from Mac OS 9.x to Mac OS X, the old Mac OS 9.x applications are treated as "classic applications" because they are not written to use the new interface, and they do not run as fast as the applications written for Mac OS X. When you open a Mac OS 9.x application, it automatically starts the classic applications environment for that application. Also, try Hands-on Project 4-11 to manually start and stop the classic applications environment.

To make the most out of the information in this chapter, try the Hands-on Projects that follow, and practice installing various operating system functions. Nothing can replace experience in performing these installations.

UPDATING OPERATING SYSTEMS

Every operating system vendor provides a mechanism to provide bug fixes, security patches (for threats such as worms and viruses), and interim upgrades between major releases of their operating system. You've already been introduced to the Windows Update feature, which should be used following a Windows installation or upgrade. This section briefly reviews the update features of the operating systems covered in this book.

Windows Updates

Beginning with the Windows 98 release, Microsoft includes Windows Update, a Web-based function that allows you to download and install fixes, updates, and enhancements to your Windows operating system.

The initial screen in Windows Update (see Figure 4-9) provides you the opportunity to scan your computer. When you click Scan for updates, Windows Update will automatically scan your computer to determine your operating system and check on the installed updates. It then provides you with a list of components that you can choose to download and install on your computer.

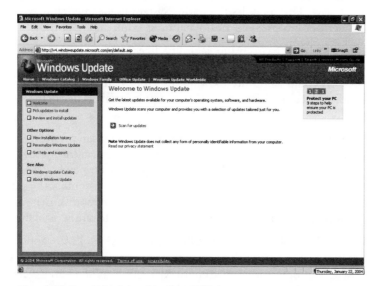

Figure 4-9 Windows Update initial screen

 NOTE Critical Updates and Service Packs listed for your system should be downloaded and installed. These will fix known bugs, security issues, and other problems that should be addressed as soon as possible. Click the View installation history button to view a listing of all updates previously performed on your computer.

NetWare Updates

Novell issues Consolidated Support Packs approximately twice a year. These packs are a collection of patches and updates for various Novell products. You can order a copy of these packs on digital video disc (DVD) or download them from the Novell Web site.

There is also a beta program for these Consolidated Support Packs. If you are interested in being a beta test site, visit *www.novell.com* and look up the Novell Beta program.

Linux Updates

Red Hat Linux provides the Red Hat Network Update Module. This module, which is included with your subscription to Red Hat Enterprise Linux 3.0, gives you access to software updates. This module provides timely and automatic updates to your Red Hat system.

NOTE Fedora includes a tool called up2date that can be accessed from the Panel in a way that is similar to accessing updates in Red Hat Enterprise Linux 3.0.

Mac Updates

Apple releases free software updates on a fairly regular basis. The Mac OS X operating system automatically checks for these software updates on a weekly basis, or you can check for updates on a manual basis. You will need an Internet connection to check for these updates.

CHAPTER SUMMARY

- There are two basic types of installations: clean installations on a machine with no operating system installed, and upgrade installations on systems that already have an operating system installed. The process of installing operating systems varies from one operating system to another, but all installations can be divided into three general stages: preparation for installation, the installation itself, and any required or optional steps following installation.

- Before installing or upgrading to a new operating system, make sure that it is necessary. Also, when you decide to install or upgrade, check that your hardware meets the requirements for the new operating system, and make sure you have the correct, most up-to-date drivers for the various devices on your system. Gather and document information about your system.

- Before you upgrade, make sure that you have a working backup of the current operating system and data. Check your backup after it is made to make sure that you can perform a restore from it if the install or upgrade is unsuccessful, or if you need to retrieve data that was overwritten by the installation.

- The installations of and upgrades to Windows 2000 (Server and Professional), Windows XP (Home and Professional), Windows Server 2003, Red Hat Enterprise Linux 3.0, Novell NetWare 6.5, and Mac OS X are overviewed in the chapter text and described step by step in the Hands-on Projects.

- After installation, and at regular intervals thereafter, it is a good idea to check for and download operating system updates. Windows versions after Windows 98 provide the Windows Update tool, and other operating systems provide their own update tools.

KEY TERMS

alpha software — An early development version of software in which there are likely to be bugs, and not all of the anticipated software functionality is present. Alpha software is usually tested only by a select few users to identify major problems and the need for new or different features before the software is tested by a broader audience in the beta stage.

backup — A process of copying files from a computer system to another medium, such as a tape, Zip disk, another hard drive, or a removable drive.

Backup Domain Controller (BDC) — A server in the domain that has a copy of the domain's directory database, which is updated periodically by the PDC. The BDC also can authenticate logons to the domain.

beta software — During software development, software that has successfully passed the alpha test stage. Beta testing may involve dozens, hundreds, or even thousands of people, and may be conducted in multiple stages: beta 1, beta 2, beta 3, and so on.

clean computer — A computer from which all unnecessary software and hardware have been removed. A clean computer is useful during software upgrade testing because a minimum number of other software and hardware elements are in place, making it easier to track down problems with new software.

Domain Name Service (DNS) — A TCP/IP application protocol that resolves domain and computer names to IP addresses, or IP addresses to domain and computer names.

Dynamic Host Configuration Protocol (DHCP) — A network protocol that provides a way for a host to automatically assign an IP address to a workstation on its network.

emergency repair disk (ERD) — A startup disk in Windows 2000 for emergency repairs.

hardware abstraction layer (HAL) — Code in a Windows operating system that talks directly to the computer's hardware.

hardware compatibility list (HCL) — A list of brand names and models for all hardware supported by an operating system. Adherence to the HCL ensures a more successful operating system install. HCLs can often be found on operating system vendors' Web sites.

network bindings — Part of an operating system that coordinates software communications among the NIC, network protocols, and network services.

Open Database Connectivity (ODBC) — A set of rules developed by Microsoft for accessing databases and providing a standard doorway to database data.

per-seat licensing — A software licensing scheme that prices software according to the number of individual users who install and use the software.

per-server licensing — A software licensing scheme that prices software according to a server configuration that permits multiple users to access the software from a central server.

Primary Domain Controller (PDC) — A server in the domain that authenticates logons, and keeps track of all changes made to accounts in the domain.

production computer — Any computer used to perform real work, which should be protected from problems that might cause an interruption in workflow or loss of data.

release candidate (RC) — The final stage of software testing by vendors before cutting an official release that is sold commercially. A release candidate is usually tested by a very large audience of customers. Some vendors may issue more than one release candidate if problems are discovered in the first RC.

Upgrade Advisor — A tool available on the Windows operating system CD or via the Internet to check if your system hardware and software are ready for upgrade.

Windows Catalog — A list that contains brand names and models for all hardware and software supported by the Windows XP operating system. The Windows Server 2003 Catalog lists compatible hardware and software for Windows Server 2003.

Windows Update — A Web-based function that allows you to download and install product updates for your Windows operating system.

REVIEW QUESTIONS

1. Windows Catalog provides which of the following?

   a. A list of screen savers and backgrounds for your Windows XP operating system.

   b. A list of brand names and models for all hardware supported by the operating system.

   c. A list of vendors who sell software for your operating system.

   d. A list of alternative office type programs.

2. A PnP operating system eliminates the need to understand operating system hardware requirements and limitations before installing the system. True or False?

3. Software driver requirements change as you add new hardware or install new software. Perhaps the best resource for updated drivers for any manufacturer's hardware is _____ .

4. Windows 2000 ships in four configurations. Two of these configurations are Advanced Server and Datacenter Server. What are the other two?

   a. Home and Professional

   b. Server and Professional

   c. Home and Workstation

   d. Server and Workstation

5. Before installing the Red Hat Enterprise Linux 3.0 operating system, you must partition and format the hard drive. True or False?

6. Windows XP is supplied in two configurations. What are they?

7. Why would you choose a commercial version of Linux over a shareware version?

   a. You have the money and don't want to take the time to download the shareware version.

   b. The source code for Linux comes with the commercial version.

    c. The commercial version comes with support for your company.

    d. The commercial version comes with a GUI interface, but no shareware versions have a GUI.

8. The HCL helps ensure that you have the proper hardware available during some Windows and UNIX installs. HCL stands for what?

9. To boot a Mac from the CD-ROM, you hold down what key during the bootup process? How do you know that it actually booted from the CD-ROM?

10. Choosing the Customize button during a Mac OS X install allows you to:

    a. select which operating system to install

    b. choose the install location

    c. choose various OS components you want to install

    d. None of the above.

11. Windows Update is available in Windows 95 and later operating system releases. True or False?

12. What utility can you use in Windows XP to transfer Internet Explorer settings, Outlook Express settings, desktop settings, the My Documents folder, dial-up connections, and display settings to your new computer?

13. What three operating systems form the foundation for Windows XP?

14. Each operating system upgrade is somewhat unique, but there are some general steps you should conduct with every upgrade. Which of the following apply? (Choose all that apply.)

    a. Test the upgrade on a non-production computer.

    b. Physically disconnect from the network in case you have to change protocols during the upgrade.

    c. Back up all data and applications before starting the upgrade.

    d. Test backup and restore software before committing to the new software version.

    e. Completely remove the old operating system before starting the upgrade.

15. You only need to back up application files because an operating system upgrade won't touch your data files. True or False?

16. What backup utility are you likely to use when making a pre-upgrade backup in Linux?

    a. *ls*

    b. *vms*

    c. *tar*

    d. *grep*

    e. *mount*

17. You have Windows 95 and are trying to upgrade to Windows XP, but the upgrade won't work. What is the problem?

   a. You must first make a change to the Windows 95 registry to allow upgrades.

   b. You cannot upgrade to Windows XP from Windows 95.

   c. Your Windows 95 system is using NetBEUI, and you must first convert to TCP/IP before starting the upgrade.

   d. Windows 95 is not compatible with the Windows XP Active Directory.

18. During installation of some versions of Windows, the installer may access the Internet. What is the purpose of this access? Is it desirable, or should you stop this process in the interest of local system security?

19. You upgraded from Mac OS 9.1 to Mac OS X, but some of your applications do not run using the new Mac OS X interface. What can be done?

   a. Stop using those old applications because they may damage your new system.

   b. Purchase the Mac application converter program that converts these applications to run in Mac OS X.

   c. Contact the old application vendors to obtain special .dll files.

   d. Use the classic environment to run these applications.

20. One advantage to upgrading to Mac OS X compared to other operating systems is that you do not need to make a backup. True or False?

HANDS-ON PROJECTS

Be sure to read the text sections on installing these operating systems before attempting the Hands-on Projects. The text contains important background information, such as hardware requirements, which you need to know before attempting the installations.

CAUTION

HANDS-ON PROJECTS

Project 4-1

Your hardware system BIOS controls many basic functions of your computer. This chapter discusses the need for being able to boot from a CD-ROM disk. You can find out how your system BIOS handles CD-ROM booting by displaying the Setup or Configuration screen on your computer.

To display your current booting options by looking at your BIOS:

   1. Display your computer's BIOS Setup screen. How you do this varies with the machine, but common techniques are to press **F8** or **F2** during the system bootup process. Other keystrokes or combinations may be used, such as **Del**, **Ctrl+Alt+Esc** simultaneously, or **F1**. Another way is to hold down a key on the keyboard while booting. The BIOS often sees the error and gives you the option

to go into Setup. If none of these works, study your computer's documentation, or carefully read all screens during system boot.

2. Look for settings for boot order. This usually involves using the cursor keys to position the cursor over a field, then pressing the space bar or Page Up/Page Down to step through the settings.

3. Step through the choices available on your machine.

4. If available, choose a CD-ROM boot, and save and exit the Configuration screen.

5. Insert your operating system CD-ROM disk and reboot the computer. Did the CD boot your computer? What error messages did you see, if any? Can you reconfigure your system to boot from your hard disk drive?

Project 4-2

Please read the section on installing **Windows 2000** earlier in this chapter for important hardware requirements.

To install the Windows 2000 Server operating system:

If you start from the floppy disk method:

1. Make sure the computer's BIOS is set to boot first from floppy drive A:.

2. Power off the computer.

3. Insert Setup Disk #1 into drive A: and the CD-ROM into the CD- ROM drive.

4. Turn on the computer, allowing it to boot from Setup Disk #1.

5. This method automatically starts Winnt.exe, and you follow the instructions on the screen, such as inserting Setup Disk #2 next.

If you start by booting from the CD-ROM (if your computer supports this):

1. Make sure the computer's BIOS is set to boot first from the CD-ROM drive.

2. Insert the Windows 2000 Server CD-ROM in the CD-ROM drive.

3. Power off the computer.

4. Turn on the computer, allowing it to boot from the CD-ROM. On some computers, you may be prompted to press Enter to boot from the CD-ROM.

5. This method automatically starts Winnt.exe and you follow the instructions on the screen.

When Winnt starts, the first screens are character based and you use the following steps:

1. Setup inspects the hardware configuration and loads the drivers and other files to get started. Next, Windows 2000 Server Setup provides a screen with three options: set up Windows 2000, repair an existing Windows 2000 installation, and quit Setup (see Figure 4-10). Press **Enter** to begin the installation, but also make a note that you can later access the repair option at any time. The repair option enables you to access diagnostic and repair functions on the ERD.

4

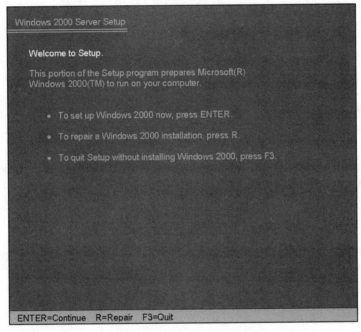

Figure 4-10   Beginning Setup options

TIP

Setup provides a way to install a special mass storage driver, or special HAL, for SMP computers, in case the Windows 2000 Server CD-ROM does not contain the driver, or in case Setup cannot find storage devices when it inspects the computer. For special mass storage, press **F6** as soon as possible when Setup begins inspecting the hardware. Setup provides a special screen that enables you to install new drivers. Press **S**, insert the driver disk, and press **Enter**. Also, if Setup does not recognize the type of computer because it is an SMP computer, obtain a HAL driver from the vendor, press **F5** as soon as possible when Setup starts, select **Other** on the menu, and install the HAL driver from a floppy disk or CD-ROM.

2. Setup presents the license agreement for Windows 2000. Use the Page Down key to read the agreement and when you are finished reading, press **F8** to indicate that you agree.

3. Setup scans the hard drive(s) to determine if there are any previous versions of Windows 2000 Server. If it finds one, you have the choice to repair it if it is damaged, or to install a new copy of Windows 2000 over the current version. If you see this screen, press **Esc** to install a new copy.

4. The hard drive scan also determines if any FAT16, FAT32, or NTFS partitions are already in place. Use the up and down arrow keys to select the unpartitioned space, or an existing partition, on which to install Windows 2000, and press **Enter**. If you use an unpartitioned space, Setup displays another screen to confirm the selection, and enables you to specify the size of the partition. If you select to write over an existing partition, Setup displays a warning screen on which you can enter **C** to continue.

5. Use the up and down arrow keys to select a file system, NTFS or FAT (a third option is to leave the existing file system, if the drive is already formatted). On the next screen, Setup warns that files will be deleted if you are formatting over an existing partition. Press **F** to format the partition. Or, if you change your mind at this point, press **Esc** to go back and select a different partition. After you start the format, a screen appears to show the progress of the format.

6. After the disk is formatted, there is a file copy stage and then Setup automatically reboots into the Windows 2000 graphical mode. If your computer is set up to boot first from a CD-ROM, depending on the computer, you may need to remove the Windows 2000 Server CD-ROM before it reboots, and then put the CD-ROM back in after it reboots.

After the system reboots, it goes into the Windows GUI mode. In this mode, you make selections with a mouse or pointing device by clicking buttons at the bottom of dialog boxes, such as Back and Next.

The steps from the GUI mode are as follows:

1. The first dialog box is used to gather information about the computer, which includes the keyboard and pointing device. Click **Next**. An action bar in the next dialog box shows you the progress of the detection process, and automatically goes to the following dialog box when it finishes.

2. In the next dialog box, you have options to change regional and keyboard settings, such as to customize the server to use a specific language, or to customize a language for your locale. For example, you may be set up to use English, but want to use the United Kingdom locale English. Complementing the language, you can customize number, currency, time, and date formats. Use the Customize buttons to make adjustments, and click **Next**.

3. Enter your name and the name of your organization in the Personalize Your Software dialog box. Click **Next**.

4. Enter the Product Key and click **Next**. You can find the key on a sticker attached to the reverse side of the Windows 2000 Server CD-ROM jewel case.

5. If you are installing a server, you will see a Licensing Modes dialog box. In the Licensing Modes dialog box, select the licensing mode (per-server or per-seat), and enter the number of licenses. You can add licenses later as needed, so only add the number of licenses you have now. Click **Next**.

6. Enter the name of the computer and provide a password for the Administrator account. Confirm the password, and click **Next**.

Windows 2000 passwords are case sensitive.

7. Enter checks in the boxes of the components that you want to install. Windows 2000 Server offers more choices than Windows 2000 Professional. For example, you might install Message Queuing Services or Other Network File and Print Services (for UNIX and Macintosh communications). When you first install Windows 2000, it is recommended that you select only the services you need immediately and install others later, to minimize configuration difficulties. To view information about a particular component, click the component name, and click **Details**. Click **Next** after you make the selections.

8. If there is a modem installed in your computer, you must provide your region and country information, telephone area code, number you dial for an outside line (optional), and telephone line type (tone or pulse) in the Modem Dialing Information dialog box. This information is used to establish dial-up networking. Click **Next**.

9. Verify the accuracy of the date and time in the Date and Time Settings dialog box and make any needed changes. Also, make sure the time zone is correctly set, such as for Mountain Time. Click **Next**.

10. Setup next displays a dialog box to show it is configuring your network settings and then enables you to select the Typical or Custom settings. Click **Typical settings** if you want to use Client for Microsoft Networks, TCP/IP, and Print Sharing for Microsoft Networks. Otherwise click **Custom settings** to establish a different setup, such as to install for connectivity to an older NetWare server. To keep the installation simple, it is recommended that you use the Typical settings and make adjustments later. If you are not using dynamic IP addressing, you should configure the TCP/IP protocol manually. Click **Next** after you make your selection.

11. If the computer is not currently on a network, or if you want to specify a workgroup for the computer, click the **No** radio button, or click **Yes** if the computer will join a domain. Enter the workgroup or domain name in the text box. Click **Next**. If you join a domain, you must enter the domain account and the password of the account you already created to enable the server to join the domain. Setup now installs the components you specified (see Figure 4-11), sets up Start menu items, and removes the temporary files created by the installation process.

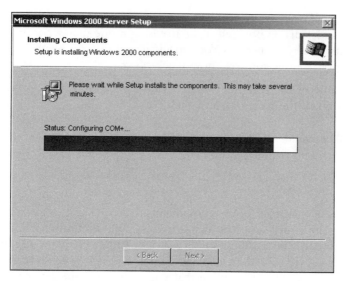

Figure 4-11   Installing components

12. Click **Finish**, remove the Windows 2000 Server CD-ROM, and wait for the computer to restart.

13. Run Windows Update as described in this chapter.

Project 4-3

In this project, you install **Windows XP Professional** using the CD-ROM installation method. Before you start, you will need the Windows XP Professional CD-ROM. Please read the section on Installing Windows XP in this chapter for important hardware requirements. The installation of Windows XP will take approximately 60 to 90 minutes. Similar to Windows 2000, the first part of the installation is in a text-based format and the second part is in a GUI-based format. (Ask your instructor for the name of a workgroup or domain to join. If you join a domain, you will need to obtain an account name and password from your instructor.)

To start the first phase, the text-based installation:

1. Insert the Windows XP Professional CD-ROM and boot the computer from scratch so that it boots from the CD-ROM. Windows XP Setup briefly inspects hardware components and then loads files onto the disk.

2. Press **Enter** if you see a Setup Notification screen (for evaluation copies).

3. Press **Enter** on the Welcome to Setup screen (see Figure 4-12).

4. Read the Windows XP Licensing Agreement and press **F8** to accept the agreement.

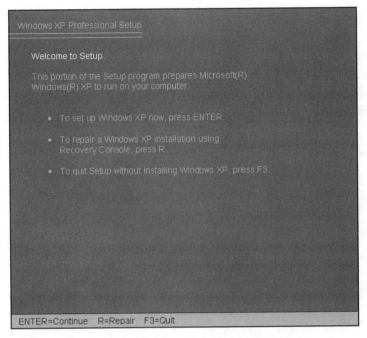

Figure 4-12 Windows XP Welcome to Setup screen

5. Use the up and down arrows to select the disk space on which to install Windows XP Professional and press **Enter**. Note that if there is already an operating system on the computer, such as Windows 98 or 2000, you can create a dual boot system by placing Windows XP Professional on another partition. Figure 4-13 shows the Setup screen on a computer that has two disk drives, one with Windows 98 (drive C) and one with unpartitioned space (drive D). In this situation, you can (1) select to install Windows XP Professional on drive C, thus erasing Windows 98 or (2) install Windows XP on the unpartitioned space on drive D, resulting in a dual boot system.

6. Use the up and down arrows to select **Format the partition using the NTFS file system** (which is selected by default). Press **Enter**. Setup takes a few minutes to format the partition and then it examines your disks.

NOTE

Avoid selecting the (Quick) format option, because this will not check the disk for errors and set aside bad spots on the disk so that they are not used.

Next, Setup copies files to the installation folders and then initializes the installation. Finally, Setup restarts the computer. If a floppy disk is loaded, remove it before the computer restarts.

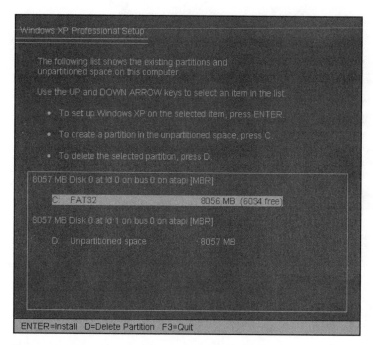

Figure 4-13 Selecting the partition for Windows XP

To complete the GUI-based second phase of the installation:

1. Windows XP Professional restarts and immediately begins the installation. The first portion of the installation will take a few minutes. You will see an overview of Windows XP features in the right pane and the installation steps in the left pane. Also, the moving green square across the green dots in the bottom right side of the screen means that Setup is working.

2. Notice the bar that eventually appears in the bottom portion of the left pane that shows what is happening during the installation, such as installing devices.

3. When you see the Regional and Language Options dialog box, click **Customize** to review the regional options. Make sure that your format preferences are selected, such as **English (United States)**. Also, select your present location, such as **United States**. Click **OK**.

4. Click **Next**.

5. Enter your name and the name of your organization. Click **Next**.

6. Enter the product key (look on the back of your Windows XP Professional CD-ROM's jewel case) and click **Next**.

7. Enter the name of your computer, such as XP plus your last name (such as XPWalters). Also, enter the password for the Administrator account and then enter it again to confirm it. Click **Next**.

8. If there is a modem already installed in the computer, enter the country/region in which you reside, the area or city code, and a number to access an outside line (if necessary). Also, click the radio button for the type of phone system (tone or pulse dialing). Click **Next**.

9. Verify the date and time settings. For example, you may need to select the time zone (click the Time Zone list box down arrow). Click **Next**. Setup continues the installation, starting with the installation of the network configuration.

10. On the Network Settings dialog box for this project, select **Typical settings** (the default) to configure for a Microsoft-based network using the TCP/IP transport protocol. Click **Next**.

11. Select whether to make the computer a member of a workgroup or a domain (check with your instructor, or enter a workgroup name that consists of your initials plus "workgroup"). Click **Next**. (If you select to join a domain, another dialog box appears in which to provide the name of the account and password that you will use in the domain. Click OK after you enter the account and password.) The installation proceeds, such as copying files to the newly formatted partition.

12. A display settings dialog box appears stating "To improve the appearance of visual elements, Windows will automatically adjust your screen resolution." Click **OK** to continue. Then a verification dialog box appears verifying that the new resolution is readable to the user. Click **OK** if you can read the information. When the installation is finished, Setup restarts the computer so that you can access Windows XP Professional.

13. After the computer restarts, click **Next** on the Welcome to Microsoft Windows screen.

14. Windows XP checks your Internet connectivity. Click the appropriate radio button for how the computer will connect to the Internet. For this project, use the default option, **Yes, this computer will connect through a local area network or home network**. Click **Next** (or you can click **Skip** if you do not wish to configure Internet access at this time).

15. The next dialog box that appears deals with IP and DNS information. Check with your instructor for the exact information you need to enter on these screens.

16. Select whether or not to activate Windows over the Internet or to wait until another time. For example, if you have Internet access, click **Yes, activate Windows over the Internet now**. Click **Next**.

17. Select whether or not to register online. For this project, click **No, remind me every few days**. Click **Next**.

18. Enter your name and click **Next**.

19. Click **Finish**.

20. Run Windows Update as described in this chapter.

HANDS-ON PROJECTS

Project 4-4

This project enables you to install **Red Hat Enterprise Linux 3.0** using the graphical mode installation.

To install the Red Hat Enterprise Linux 3.0 operating system:

1. Boot the system from Disc 1 of the Red Hat Enterprise Linux 3.0 installation CD-ROM.

2. Press **Enter** to use the graphical mode installation.

3. For this project, select **Skip** (use the right arrow key) and press **Enter**. (Choosing Skip bypasses the test of the CD media from which you are performing the installation.)

4. Click **Next** on the Welcome to Red Hat Enterprise Linux screen.

5. Use the up or down arrow key to select the language, such as English (English). Click **Next**.

6. Use the arrow keys to select the keyboard configuration (such as U.S. English). Click **Next**.

7. Select the mouse configuration (or use the default selection), such as Wheel Mouse (PS/2), and click **Next**.

8. Select **Automatically partition**, if this is not already selected, and click **Next**.

9. Choose the method of partitioning from: Remove all Linux partitions on this system, Remove all partitions on this system, Keep all partitions and use existing free space. (For this installation, we are using Remove all partitions on this system.) Click **Next**. Click **Yes** to proceed.

10. Examine the disk setup. For this project, use the setup automatically created by the installation process and click **Next**.

11. For this project, the GRUB boot loader is located on the default partition. Notice that you can set a password for the boot loader, but for this project we bypass this option. Click **Next**.

12. The next screen enables you to configure a NIC (if one is installed). You can set the hostname at either: automatically via DHCP or by providing an IP address manually. Use the default **automatically via DHCP** unless your instructor provides information about configuring the IP address manually. Click **Next**.

13. On the next screen you can configure a firewall. Click **Enable firewall**, if it is not already selected. Choose the services that you want to allow through the firewall from: WWW (HTTP), FTP, SSH, Telnet, and Mail (SMTP). Click **Next**.

14. Choose the default language for the system, such as English (USA). Click **Next**.

15. Select the time zone and click **Next**.

16. Enter the root password (use six characters or more). Confirm the password and click **Next**.

17. For this project, install the default packages by selecting **Accept the current package list**, if it is not already selected. Click **Next**.

18. Click **Next** on the About to Install screen. The installer formats the disk(s) and begins installing packages.

19. Insert additional installation CD-ROMs as requested (the number of CD-ROMs required depends on the packages you have selected to install). Click **OK** after inserting each installation CD-ROM.

20. Use the default display adapter selected by the installer or choose a different one from the list. Click **Next**.

21. Use the default monitor selected or choose a different one. Click **Next**.

22. Use the Graphical login type and click **Next**.

23. Remove any CD-ROMs or floppy disks and click **Exit**. The system automatically reboots.

24. A screen displays stating "There are a few more steps to take before your system is ready to use. The Red Hat Setup Agent will now guide you through some basic configuration. Please click the "Next" button in the lower right corner to continue". Click **Next**.

25. Read the License Agreement and, if you agree, click **Yes, I agree to the License Agreement** and click **Next**.

26. Reconfigure the date and time, if necessary. Click **Next**.

27. Enter the Username, Full Name, Password, and Password Confirmation to create an account that you can use in addition to the root account. Click **Next**.

28. You can choose to test the sound card if one is installed. For this project, however, skip the test and click **Next**.

29. Typically, you register your system with Red Hat at this time. However, for this project, click **No, I do not want to register my system**. Click **Next**.

30. You can select to install additional CD-ROMs, such as one for documentation. For this project, omit this process and click **Next**.

31. On the Finish Setup screen, click **Next**.

32. Log on to your new systems using the root account or the additional account you created and proceed to use the system.

33. Run the Red Hat Enterprise Linux 3.0 updates as described in this chapter.

Project 4-5

Please read the section in this chapter on Installing and Upgrading **Mac OS X** before completing this project.

To install/upgrade Mac OS X:

1. Start your current version of the Mac OS.

2. Insert the Mac OS X Install Disc 1 (CD-ROM).

3. If you have questions about the installation or want to find out more before you begin, double-click the folder entitled, **Read Before You Install.pdf** and then close the window when you are finished.

4. Double-click **Install Mac OS X**.

5. Click the **Restart** button to restart the computer so that the installation process can be started.

6. If you see the Authenticate window, enter the username of an account that has administration privileges and enter the password. Click **OK**.

7. Select (click) the language you want to use, such as Use English for the main language. Click **Continue**.

8. Click **Continue** on the Welcome to the Mac OS X Installer screen.

9. Read through the Important Information screen which provides information about the following main topics:

    ◻ System requirements

    ◻ Updating your computer's firmware

    ◻ Quitting the Installer

    ◻ Hardware compatibility

    ◻ Installing Mac OS X

10. Click **Continue**.

11. Read the Software License Agreement. Click **Continue**. Click **Agree** to continue the installation.

12. Click the hard drive on which to install the operating system, such as Macintosh HD (which is what you will usually select for most systems with one hard drive). Click **Continue**.

13. Perform a basic installation by clicking **Upgrade**.

14. The Installer takes a few minutes to verify the installation disk. (You can click the Skip button if you are certain that your installation CD-ROM is fully intact and readable.)

15. Next the Installer prepares the disk for the installation process, install software, and optimize the system for performance.

16. The computer automatically restarts when the basic installation is completed.

4

17. After the computer restarts, it ejects Install Disk 1 and requests Mac OS X Install Disc 2.

18. Insert Install Disc 2. The Installer installs files and software.

19. When the Installer finishes, it ejects Install Disc 2. Remove the disc. Click **Quit** or simply wait for the installer to quit automatically.

20. If the Registration Information screen displays, provide the following information:

    ▫ First Name

    ▫ Last Name

    ▫ Address

    ▫ City

    ▫ State

    ▫ Zip Code

    ▫ E-mail Address

    ▫ Area Code

    ▫ Phone Number

    ▫ Company/School

    Or, you can use the default information about you if provided on the screen. Click **Continue**.

21. A dialog box displays with "A Few more Questions; Where will you primarily use this computer? What best describes what you do? Would you like to receive news?" Click **Continue**, click **Continue** one more time, and then click **GO**. The Mac OS X desktop is displayed for you to start using.

22. Run the Mac OS updates as described in this chapter.

Project 4-6

In this project, you learn how to determine if a computer has the proper hardware configuration for an upgrade to **Windows 2000** or **Windows XP**. You need the Windows 2000 or Windows XP (any version of these operating systems) CD-ROM.

To check the computer's hardware prior to an upgrade:

1. Start any of the following computer operating systems: Windows 95, Windows 98, Windows NT, Windows 2000 (for an upgrade to Windows XP), or Windows XP (if you do not have an earlier operating system).

2. Insert the Windows 2000 or Windows XP CD-ROM in the CD-ROM drive.

3. Click **Start**, and then click **Run**.

4. Enter the drive letter and path of the winnt32.exe file (on the CD-ROM) in the Open box, and enter **/checkupgradeonly**. Enter the command as in: **D:\i386\winnt32.exe /checkupgradeonly** (winnt32 is located on the CD-ROM in the \i386 folder for Intel-based computers). Click **OK**.

5. If you are connected to the Internet, you can use the Microsoft Windows Upgrade Advisor (which starts automatically) to obtain upgrade updates from Microsoft's Web site. To use the advisor after it starts, click **Yes, download the updated Setup files (Recommended)**, and then click **Next**. View the information about incompatibilities and problems, and then click **Finish**. If you are not connected to the Internet, click **No, skip this step and continue installing Windows**, and then click **Next**. Examine the report and click **Finish**. (In some versions of Windows 2000 you may not see the Microsoft Windows Upgrade Advisor. In these cases the Microsoft Windows 2000 Readiness Analyzer creates the report and you click **Finish** after you review it.)

Project 4-7

Before upgrading an operating system, it is important to know what software will be affected. In this project, you learn one place in which to look for the software installed on different operating systems.

To determine the software installed on Windows-based systems:

1. Begin by observing the application icons that are on the desktop. What software application icons or shortcuts do you see?

2. Click **Start** on the taskbar, and point to **Programs** (or select **All Programs** in Windows XP). What programs are listed?

3. In Windows 95, 98, or NT, click **Windows Explorer** (or **Windows NT Explorer** for Windows NT). In Windows Me, 2000, or Windows XP, point to **Accessories**, and then click **Windows Explorer**.

4. Locate the main drive on the computer (most desktop computers have only one drive—also in some versions of Windows, you may need to open My Computer to see the drive). Double-click that drive, such as drive **(C:)**, if its contents do not appear under the drive.

5. Double-click the **Program Files** folder. (In some Windows versions the sub-folders and files are not displayed until you elect to display them.) What subfolders or programs do you see (such as Microsoft Office)?

6. Close Windows Explorer.

7. Next, in Windows 95/98/NT/2000, click **Start**, point to **Settings**, click **Control Panel**, and click **Add/Remove Programs**. Or, in Windows XP, click **Start**, click **Control Panel**, and double-click **Add or Remove Programs**. What programs are listed as already installed?

8. Close the Add/Remove (or Add or Remove) Programs dialog box. Also, close the Control Panel if it still appears.

To determine the software installed in Mac OS X:

1. Double-click **Macintosh HD**. Notice that there are two folders for Applications—*Applications (Mac OS 9)*, which is for Mac OS 9.x-compatible applications, and *Applications*, which is for Mac OS X-compatible applications.

2. Select **Applications** and determine what applications are available.

3. Close the Applications window by clicking the X in the upper left corner.

To determine the software installed in Red Hat Enterprise Linux 3.0 (with the GNOME interface):

1. Click the **Main Menu** icon in the Panel.

2. Point to **Accessories**. What applications do you see?

3. Point to **Office**. What applications do you see?

4. Point to **System Tools**. Write down a couple of the tools displayed.

To see a list of all of the software packages installed in UNIX:

1. At the Red Hat Enterprise Linux 3.0 command line (or in the terminal window in the GNOME interface), type **rpm –qa**. Press **Enter**. What are some examples listed of software? (The list will be quite long.)

2. If you opened a terminal window to access the command line, type **exit** and press **Enter** to close the window.

The command to view installed software packages is different in various UNIX systems. For example, you enter *pkginfo* in Solaris, *swlist* in HP UNIX, *pkg_info -a* in FreeBSD, and *lslpp -L all* in IBM's AIX.

NOTE

HANDS-ON PROJECTS

Project 4-8

Plan to back up system and application files prior to conducting an operating system upgrade. In this project, you back up files in **Windows 98**, such as in preparation to upgrade to Windows Server 2003 or Windows XP. You also back up files in **Red Hat Enterprise Linux 3.0** and restore files in Windows 98.

The backup process is very similar for Windows Me, Windows 2000, and Windows XP. With the guidance from these steps, you can find your way through nearly any Windows-based backup—begin by clicking Start, pointing to Programs, pointing to Accessories, pointing to System Tools, and clicking Backup. To start a backup in Windows NT, click Start, point to Administrative Tools (Common), and click Backup. (Windows 2000 and XP offer wizards to help you complete a backup.)

TIP

You need a medium on which to write the backup, such as a tape, Zip disk, network drive, or floppy disk—consult your instructor about which to use. Also, the Windows 98 Backup utility should already be installed. If it is not (see Step 1), obtain the Windows 98 CD-ROM and insert it in the CD-ROM drive. Click Start, point to Settings, and click Control Panel. Double-click Add/Remove Programs, and open the Windows Setup tab. Double-click System Tools, and click the box in front of Backup. Click OK and click OK again.

To back up specific directories or files in Windows 98:

1. Click **Start**, point to **Programs**, point to **Accessories**, point to **System Tools**, and click **Backup**.

2. If the Backup program does not detect any backup hardware installed on your computer, it will ask if you want AutoDetect to try to find it. If this occurs, click **No**.

3. On the opening Backup screen, choose **Create a new backup job**, and click **OK**.

4. Choose **Back up selected files, folders and drives**. You can use this choice to back up to floppy disks or a removable high-density disk such as a Zip or Jazz drive. If you have a tape backup system, choose **Backup My Computer** to back up everything on your hard drive. Click **Next**.

5. Navigate to the folder(s) or file(s) you want to back up, and click the check boxes beside the entries you want to back up.

6. Click **Next**, and choose **All selected files** from the following dialog box.

7. Click **Next** and specify the backup location. This is where you choose the destination drive for the backup files. Note that you can back up to a network hard drive, or even to a file on a local hard drive, if you wish.

8. Click **Next** to continue the Backup Wizard, and choose whether you want to use file compression.

9. Click **Next** and name the backup job. This lets you repeat this process later, or modify the job for later backups.

10. Click **Start** to complete the backup process. A dialog box informs you when the operation is complete. Click **OK**.

11. Click **OK** in the Backup Progress window, and then close the Microsoft Backup window.

Before you upgrade to a new version of UNIX, it is crucial to make a backup of important UNIX configuration files so that it will be easy to restore your old system, if necessary. Many systems have important files in the /etc directory and also in the /usr/local directory. In this project, you'll back up the Red Hat Enterprise Linux 3.0 configuration files.

NOTE

To complete this project, you must have root privileges on the system.

To back up UNIX configuration files:

1. To make a backup to a disk:

   a. Use the *df* command to find a partition that has enough space to hold your backup. Type **df**, and locate a directory on your file system that has enough space. DO NOT use the TEMP or root (/) directory!

   b. Use the *tar* command to create a compressed format backup file. The syntax for *tar* is *tar -[command][options][parameters]*. For example, to back up the /etc and /usr/local directories and all their subdirectories to a file called *archive.tar* in the /home directory, you enter:

   tar −cvf /home/archive.tar /etc /usr/local.

   The command *c* is used to create a new tar file; the *v* and *f* options are for verbose and file (to show you what is happening, and to indicate that what follows next is the path and filename of the file to be saved); and the parameters include the file or directory name(s) you are backing up.

2. To make a backup of /etc and /usr/local and all of their subdirectories to a tape drive using built-in compression:

a. Load an empty tape in your tape drive.

b. Enter the command **tar –cvf /dev/rmt/0c /etc /usr/local**.

(If necessary, replace "rmt/0c" with the proper designation for your tape drive.)

No data backup is useful if the restore software or the backup media fail. Many critical failures occur during data restoration because of bad media and incompatibilities between the restore software and new system software. That's why backup and restore testing is critical during operating system upgrades. In this project, you'll practice a restore from the backup that you just created.

TIP

As in the backup portion of this project, you can use similar steps for Windows Me, Windows 2000, and Windows XP. To start a restore in Windows NT, click Start, point to Administrative Tools (Common), and click Backup.

Make sure that you obtain permission from your instructor for the restore. If you do not have permission, only complete Steps 1 through 8.

To test the backup created above:

1. Click **Start**, point to **Programs**, point to **Accessories**, point to **System Tools**, and click **Backup**.

2. From the opening Backup screen, choose **Restore backed up files**, and click **OK**.

3. Choose the source for the restored data from the next wizard screen. Click **Next**.

4. Choose from the list of backup sets displayed in the next dialog box. Click **OK**.

5. Click the check boxes beside the items within the backup set to select individual items to restore, and click **Next**.

6. Choose a restore location from the next dialog box. During testing, you should choose a destination other than the original, in case you encounter problems. Click **Next** to continue the wizard.

7. Choose the type of restore operation if the program finds existing files at the destination location. You can tell the program not to replace existing files, to replace files only if the ones on your computer are older, or to always replace existing files. (Close the Backup tool after this step if you do not have permission to complete the restore.)

8. Click **Start** to begin the restore. You are prompted for the backup media originally used. Insert the requested media, and click **OK**.

9. Click **OK** in the Operation Completed dialog box, then click **OK** in the Restore Progress dialog box. Close the MSBackup window.

10. Test the restored data to make sure everything was restored properly.

Project 4-9

In this project, you upgrade **Windows 98** to **Windows 2000 Professional**. Make sure that your computer is compatible with Windows 2000 Professional before you start.

To upgrade from Windows 98 to Windows 2000:

1. Start Windows 98 and close any windows that are opened automatically at startup.

2. Insert the Windows 2000 Professional CD-ROM.

3. An opening box displays:"This CD-ROM contains a newer version of Windows than the one you are presently using. Would you like to upgrade to Windows 2000?" Click **Yes**.

4. In the Welcome to the Windows 2000 Setup Wizard dialog box, make sure that **Upgrade to Windows 2000 (Recommended)** is selected, and then click **Next**. (Refer back to Figure 4-3.)

5. Read the license agreement by using the scroll bar. Click the radio button for **I accept this agreement**, and then click **Next**.

6. Enter your product key (see Figure 4-14), which is usually found on the back of the jewel case or paper envelope for the CD-ROM (you can use the Tab key to advance from field to field). Click **Next**.

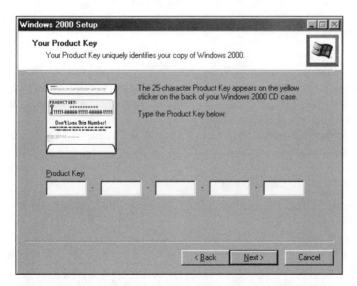

Figure 4-14   Windows 2000 Product Key dialog box

7. In the Preparing to Update to Windows 2000 dialog box, you can select **Click here** to go to the Windows Compatibility Web site to check for the latest hardware and software compatibility information. For the sake of this project, and because your computer may not be connected to the Internet, click **Next**. (If you do select **Click here**, the Internet Connection Wizard is used to set up your Internet connection before you can connect to the Windows Compatibility Web site. Also, when you use the Internet Connection Wizard, if you have TCP/IP file and printer sharing enabled, you will see a warning box to disable it. Click **OK** if you see this warning box.)

8. The next dialog box queries whether or not you have upgrade packs for your programs. These are upgrades so that the programs will work with Windows 2000. Since you can apply upgrade packs later, click the radio button **No, I don't have any upgrade packs** (which is the default), and then click **Next**.

9. You are given the option to upgrade from FAT16 or FAT32 (whichever is currently on your system) to NTFS (see Chapter 3). Although you will likely want to use NTFS in the future (there is a Convert program included with Windows 2000), for now, select **No, do not upgrade my drive** (the default)—the prudent selection. It is best to keep the upgrade process simple so that it is easier to troubleshoot problems. After you are certain that your system is working properly, then consider upgrading to NTFS for better file and workstation security. Click **Next**.

10. Windows 2000 Setup begins to prepare the Upgrade Report and prepares to install the operating system. If the Setup program detects hardware drivers that may need to be updated, particularly for PnP, it provides a list of the hardware that may need new drivers in order to work with Windows 2000. Make a note of the hardware on the list, and then click **Next**. (After the upgrade, if you determine that this hardware is not working properly, contact the hardware manufacturers for new drivers. Or, if you have the drivers now, click **Provide Files** to install them.)

11. Depending on your version of Windows 2000 (you may not see this screen), the next screen enables you to access the Upgrade Report about possible installation issues concerning your hardware and software. You can click **Save As** to save the report as a file, or click **Print** to print it now (if your computer is connected to a printer). Determine which option you want, and complete the parameters for that option (provide a filename if you save it to a file, or select a printer if you print it). Examine the report, if you printed it, or plan to examine the report file after the installation. Click **Next**.

12. In the Ready to Install Windows 2000 box, Setup informs you that it is ready to begin the upgrade, which will take 30 to 45 minutes (see Figure 4-15). Click **Next**. (Setup will reboot three times. Also, the first part of the process is in character mode, while the remaining setup process is in a GUI Windows mode.) *Make sure that you let Setup work automatically; you do not need to click any buttons, including the Next button, because Setup handles all of the work.*

NOTE If you did not have a workgroup or domain previously specified before upgrading Windows 98 to Windows 2000, you will see an additional dialog box after Step 12 that enables you to select whether or not to join a workgroup or domain. If the computer is not currently on a network or if you want to specify a workgroup for the computer, click the **No** option button; or click **Yes** if the computer will join a domain. Enter the workgroup or domain name in the text box. Click **Next**. If you join a domain, you will need to enter the domain account and the password of the account you already created to enable the server to join the domain.

4

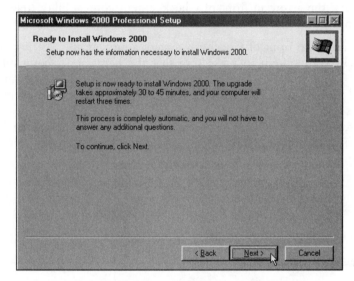

Figure 4-15 Beginning the Windows 2000 upgrade

13. Enter a password for the Administrator account, and then enter it again to confirm it. You might want to write the password down in a secure place in case you forget it. Click **Next**.

14. Log on to Windows 2000 using the Administrator account and your new password. After you enter the account and password, click **OK** in the Log On to Windows box. Note that after you log on, the Getting Started with Windows 2000 window appears. From this window you can:

   □ Register your copy of Windows 2000

   □ Discover more about Windows 2000

   □ Connect to the Internet

15. Run Windows Update as described in this chapter.

Project 4-10

In this project, you upgrade **Windows Me** to **Windows XP Professional**.

To upgrade from Windows Me to XP:

1. Reboot your computer so you have a fresh system running. After it reboots, close all programs and windows.

2. Insert the Windows XP CD-ROM in the CD-ROM drive.

3. Wait for the Autorun feature to start up the Welcome to Microsoft Windows XP screen. Click the arrow in front of Check system compatibility (refer back to Figure 4-5).

4. Click the arrow in front of Check my system automatically (see Figure 4-16). This checks your system to make sure that the hardware is compatible with Windows XP. If you see a screen to enable you to connect to the Internet to download more setup files, click **No, skip this step and continue installing Windows** (or if you have Internet connectivity, click **Yes** and be prepared to supply information about how to configure for an Internet connection). Check for any incompatibilities, and if there are none, click **Finish** (refer back to Figure 4-6).

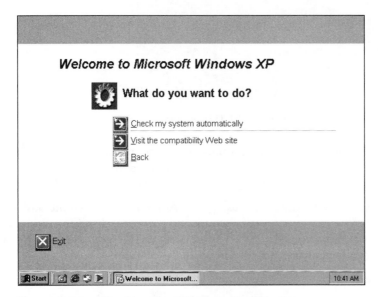

Figure 4-16   Checking the system automatically

5. Click the **Back** arrow to return to the first screen. Now you are ready to begin installing Windows XP.

6. Click **Install Windows XP**.

7. The Welcome to Windows Setup screen displays. Click the down arrow in the Installation Type list box to view two choices for the setup: Upgrade (Recommended) and New Installation (Advanced). For this project, choose **Upgrade (Recommended)** as in Figure 4-17, and then click **Next**.

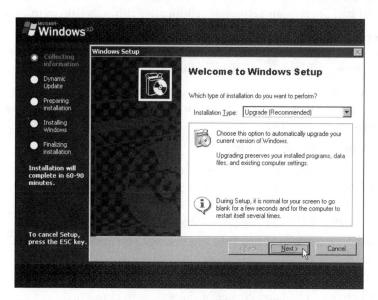

Figure 4-17   Selecting to upgrade to Windows XP

8. The License Agreement screen displays. Read the agreement using the Page Down key to move through the agreement. If you accept the agreement, click **I accept this agreement**. Click **Next**.

9. Enter the unique product key for Windows XP. This 25-character product key usually is found on the back of the CD-ROM jewel case. Type in the key and click **Next**.

10. The Get Updated Setup Files screen enables you to obtain new setup files. If you have Internet connectivity and already downloaded the setup files in Step 4 or if you do not have Internet connectivity, click **No, skip this step and continue installing Windows**. If you have Internet connectivity, but did not download the new setup files—and want to now—click **Yes, download the updated Setup files (recommended)**. Click **Next** to continue. You may need to configure your Internet connection if you select to download the files. Ask your instructor for the configuration information.

11. Setup now analyzes your computer to collect information. This may take several minutes. During this time, information about new features and enhancements in Windows XP appears. After Setup analyzes the computer, it goes through additional steps. The green bar in the lower-left corner shows the progress for this section of the installation.

12. While it is preparing for the installation, Setup copies files from the CD-ROM to your computer. Once this is completed there will be an automatic reboot.

13. Next the Preparing installation step is highlighted along with additional information on Windows XP. You can watch the progress of this step in the green progress bar. There is an automatic reboot after this step has completed.

14. After the Installing Windows step starts, the screen may flicker, which is normal because Setup is installing and testing your screen type. What steps do you see being executed in the Installing Windows stage?

15. When you see the Finalizing installation screen, there is still more information for you to read along with the progress bar. Also, what steps do you see executed in this stage of the process?

16. Setup now reboots your computer.

17. After the computer reboots, a Display Settings dialog box appears informing you that Windows will automatically adjust your screen to improve the appearance of visual elements. Click **OK** to continue. (Depending on the display parameters set up before you started the upgrade, you may not see this step or Step 18.)

18. The Monitor Settings dialog box appears, and you should click **OK** if you can read it.

19. Next, the Welcome to Microsoft Windows screen displays. Click the **Next** arrow in the bottom right-hand corner of the screen to continue.

20. The Ready to register with Microsoft? screen displays. Click **Yes** if you have permissions from your instructor or register now or click **No** to register later. Click the **Next** arrow in the bottom right-hand corner.

21. The Who will use this computer? screen appears. Enter the name of each person that will use this computer in the appropriate box and click the **Next** arrow.

22. The Thank you! screen now appears. Click the **Finish** arrow in the bottom right-hand corner of the screen to continue.

23. The Password Creation screen enables you to enter a password for your account and the administrator's account. The password is the same for both accounts. You are asked to retype the password to make sure it is entered correctly the first time. Click **OK**. After the upgrade, you can change the password for either account by opening the Control Panel (click **Start** and click **Control Panel**) and selecting the User Accounts option.

NOTE

When upgrading from Windows NT or Windows 2000, Setup uses the Administrator password that you set up prior to the upgrade, so you do not go through Step 23. For these systems, enter the Administrator password in Step 24.

24. Next you will see the Login screen. Enter your password (the one that you just configured), and then click the **arrow**. Windows XP now welcomes you and applies your personal settings. After this is completed, you are ready to begin using Windows XP.

Windows XP will notify you about how many days you have left to complete the product activation.

25. Run Windows Update as described in this chapter.

Project 4-11

When you upgrade to **Mac OS X**, applications written for previous versions of the operating system must run in the classic environment. This project shows you how to start and stop that environment.

To start the classic applications environment:

1. Open the Apple menu and click **System Preferences**.
2. Click **Classic**.
3. Click **Start**. What message appears now?
4. Close the Classic window.

To stop the classic environment:

1. Open the Apple menu and click **System Preferences**.
2. Click **Classic**.
3. Click **Stop**. What happens to the Mac OS 9.x applications?
4. Close the Classic window.

Project 4-12

In this project, you upgrade **Windows 2000 Server** to **Windows Server 2003**. Make sure that your computer is compatible with Windows Server 2003 before you start.

To upgrade from Windows 2000 Server to Windows Server 2003:

1. Start Windows 2000 Server and close any windows that are opened automatically at startup.
2. Insert the Windows Server 2003 CD-ROM.
3. An opening box displays "Welcome to Microsoft Windows Server 2003, What do you want to do?" Click the arrow before "Install Windows Server 2003, Enterprise Edition." (See Figure 4-7.)

4. In the Welcome to Windows Setup dialog box, make sure that **Upgrade (Recommended)** is selected, and then click **Next**.

5. Read the license agreement by using the scroll bar. Click the radio button for **I accept this agreement**, and then click **Next**.

6. Enter your product key, which is usually found on the back of the jewel case or paper envelope for the CD-ROM. Click **Next**.

7. In the Get Updated Setup Files dialog box, you can select **Yes, download the updated Setup files (Recommended)** and then click **Next** to go to the Windows Web site to check for the latest setup files and information. For this project, and because your computer may not be connected to the Internet, click **No, skip this step and continue installing Windows** and then click **Next**.

8. The next dialog box you may or may not see is the Report System Compatibility box. It reports any software from Windows 2000 Server that will not be compatible in Windows Server 2003. Click **Next**.

9. Next the system copies installation files to the hard drive and reboots.

10. Now the system begins Installing Windows. Once this step has been completed, the system reboots again.

11. The Windows Server 2003 login screen displays. Hold down the **Control, Alt**, and **Delete** keys (**Ctrl+Alt+Del**) to cause the system to prompt you for the password to the Administrator login account. Enter the password you entered earlier in this upgrade process.

12. You should now be successfully logged on to Windows Server 2003, Enterprise Edition. The next screen you see is the Manage Your Server dialog box. In this dialog box you have the opportunity to add, delete, and edit roles for your server. Your server is automatically set up as a file server and an application server. (See Figure 4-18.)

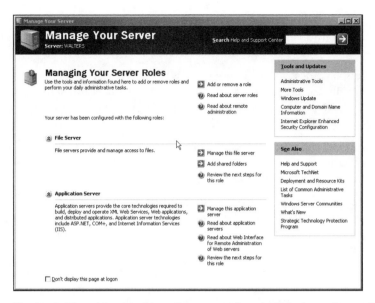

Figure 4-18   Manage Your Server window in Windows Server 2003

13. Run Windows Update as described in this chapter.

Project 4-13

In this project, you install **NetWare 6.5** on your server. Please read through the installation completely and make sure you have the necessary information from your instructor. If you are installing NetWare 6.5 on a standalone server, the information you need is included within the steps.

To install NetWare 6.5:

1. Make sure your server is set up to boot from a CD-ROM.

2. Insert the Novell NetWare 6.5 CD 1 into the CD-ROM drive and turn the computer on.

3. Starting Caldera DR-DOS will be displayed.

4. Three choices display: "I" to install a new server, "R" to run the existing server, and "C" to create a boot floppy. Choose **I** to install a new server.

5. Next three more choices display: "A" to search for a CD-ROM driver, "I" to search for an IDE CD-ROM driver, and "S" to search for a SCSI CD-ROM driver. Choose **A** to search for a CD-ROM driver.

6. Now four choices display: "A" to Auto Terminate (try B, C, then D), "B" to Terminate all drive emulation, "C" to Terminate A: drive emulation, and "D" to Switch A: with floppy drive letter. Choose **A** to Auto Terminate (try B, C, then D).

7. Finally, two choices display: "A" for Auto Execution of Install.bat or "M" for Manual Execution of Install.bat which allows optional parameters to be used. Choose **A** for Auto Execution of Install.bat.

8. Several display lines appear showing items that have been loaded, etc. followed by a red Novell 6.5 screen and then the NetWare Installation screen. Next, seven options allow you to choose the language you want to use to perform the installation. Highlight the first line to choose English. Press the **Enter** key.

9. Next you select the regional settings for the server. The defaults are USA for the Country, United States English for the Code page, and United States for the Keyboard. Highlight **Continue** and press **Enter**.

10. Now the NetWare 6.5 Novell Software License Agreement displays. Use the arrow keys to scroll through the agreement. Once you have read the agreement and agree to the terms, press the **F10** function key to accept the license agreement.

11. The License Agreement for JREPORT Runtime displays. Use the arrow keys to scroll through the agreement. Once you have read the agreement and agree to the terms, press the **F10** function key to accept the license agreement.

12. It is now time to decide whether to do a Default or Manual installation. The Default option automatically detects everything and performs the installation. The Manual option lets you make choices about settings and drivers. Choose **Default** installation and use the down arrow to highlight **Continue** and press **Enter**.

13. The installation is now ready to create a 4 GB volume SYS, detect LAN and disk drivers, and choose Super VGA Plug N Play for the video. Highlight **Continue** and press **Enter**.

14. If the installation detects a copy of NetWare already installed, it will notify you of that and ask you whether to continue or not. Highlight **Yes** and press **Enter**.

15. The installation now copies files to your hard drive. A percentage completion bar appears.

16. System files are installed and the screen flashes. Please wait while it loads files and utilities.

17. The installation now copies additional files and displays a status of the copy bar.

18. Next a Copying Files dialog box displays.

19. Choose one of three options for the type of server you want or select one of five preconfigured server types. For this installation, choose **Basic NetWare File Server** and then click **Next**.

20. The Basic NetWare File Server pattern detail appears. Click **Copy files** to proceed.

21. The installation routine now requests that the CD 1 be removed and CD 2 be inserted in the CD-ROM drive. Once this is done, click **OK**. The files being copied appear with a progress bar displaying the percent completed. Additional information about features of NetWare 6.5 displays.

22. Next enter a name for the server and click **Next**.

23. Insert the NetWare 6.5 License/Cryptography diskette in the floppy drive and point the path to the .NFK file, then click **Next**.

24. Enter information about the protocols IP and IPX including the IP address, subnet mask, and router (gateway) addresses if you are using IP. For this example installation, do not select IPX. Check with your instructor for the appropriate IP address, subnet mask, and gateway address to enter. On a standalone server, you could enter 192.168.1.1 for your IP address, 255.255.255.0 for your subnet mask, and you can leave the router blank. The router is optional, and because you are loading NetWare 6.5 on a standalone server, there is no connection to a router. Click **Next**.

25. Next enter the Host Name and Domain along with the IP address for Name Server 1. Get this information from your instructor, or if this is a standalone server, you can use any name and domain you choose along with 192.168.1.254 for Name Server 1. Click **Next**.

26. Scroll down and highlight the appropriate time zone for your location. If you live in an area that has daylight savings time and would like the server to adjust for it, check the box for this. Click **Next**.

27. Next enter eDirectory information provided by your instructor. If this is a standalone server, select Create a new eDirectory tree. Click **Next**.

28. Enter a tree name such as Novell University. For the Context, click on the box at the end of the blank window. Next click **Add** to add a container to the tree. You might type in Students. Click **OK** and then click **OK** again.

29. Under Administration Information, enter a password and enter it again in the retype password box. Click **Next**.

30. The Tree name, Server context, and Administrator name display. Record this information and the password for future reference. Click **Next**.

31. The next screen refers to the license diskette. You have already loaded the information from the diskette, so click **Next**.

32. Click **Next** on the NDS context screen. If this is a standalone server, the context will be Students.

33. A number of choices display for Novell's Modular Authentication Service (NMAS). For our purposes, NDS is already selected, so click **Next**. If you are interested in any of the other options, place your mouse pointer over the method to display information about it. NetWare 6.5 continues to configure the server

and the percentage completed progress bar displays. Next it will close all the installation files. These steps may take some time depending on the speed of your server.

34. Remove any CDs and diskettes from your server and click **Yes** to reset your server. The server reboots itself and Netware 6.5 Server is now operational. The Novell NetWare 6.5 screen displays while the server finishes configuring itself. When everything has been configured, a large red "N" displays along with a task bar at the bottom of the screen. You have successfully installed NetWare 6.5 on your server.

CASE PROJECTS

Merlinos Mills is a company that produces flours and grains for grocery stores. It owns mills and distribution centers in the northwestern and midwestern United States. The headquarters in Bend, Oregon employs more than 400 people, most of whom use computers. Also, the headquarters has 28 servers, all running either Microsoft Windows NT 4.0, Windows 2000, or Red Hat Linux 7.2. The company employees use a full range of operating systems, including Windows 95, Windows 2000, Windows XP, Red Hat Linux 7.2 (Workstation), and Mac OS 9.

The management of Merlinos Mills wants each department to upgrade to the newer operating systems. Also, they are very concerned about network security, and they want to install new servers and upgrade their current servers to operating system versions that take better advantage of security features. Your role in the process is to work with each department to help ensure that the installations and upgrades go smoothly.

CASE
PROJECTS

Case Project 4-1: Determining Preliminary Steps

The master distribution center in Bend, Oregon has 42 people, including 9 Windows 95 diehards, 22 people using Windows 2000, and 11 people using Windows XP Professional. The distribution center is slated to upgrade the rest of its computers to Windows XP Professional. What preliminary steps should be taken before starting the upgrades on these computers? In general, are there any problems involved in upgrading to Windows XP from each of these operating systems?

CASE
PROJECTS

Case Project 4-2: Deciding to Upgrade or Not?

The 11 people in the distribution center who are running Windows 2000 Professional are currently able to use all software, such as office software, customized distribution software, and inventory software that is integrated with the distribution software. They are resisting the upgrade to Windows XP Professional, and the distribution manager asks for your opinion about whether or not to upgrade these computers. Should they upgrade from Windows 2000 Professional to Windows XP Professional?

Case Project 4-3: Installing Windows XP

The distribution center is getting new computers to replace the old Windows 95 computers. Although they have Windows XP already installed, it is the Home version. You have decided to start from scratch and install a fresh copy of Windows XP Professional. The user support person for the distribution center has not performed an installation for Windows XP. Tell her generally what to expect when performing this installation.

4

Case Project 4-4: Upgrading Steps from Windows 2000 to 2003

The IT Department already has been testing Windows Server 2003, and some time ago purchased licenses to upgrade all of its Windows NT and Windows 2000 servers to Windows Server 2003. Explain the general process it must follow to upgrade to Windows Server 2003, recognizing that there's already one Windows NT domain called merlinosmills.

Case Project 4-5: Upgrading Linux

For the IT Department, review the general steps it must follow to upgrade Red Hat Linux servers to Red Hat Enterprise Linux 3.0.

Case Project 4-6: Upgrading Mac OS

The Marketing Department strictly uses computers running Mac OS 9, and plans to upgrade to Mac OS X. What steps must it follow for the upgrade?

5

CONFIGURING INPUT AND OUTPUT DEVICES

After reading this chapter and completing the exercises, you will be able to:

♦ Understand how operating systems interface with input and output devices

♦ Explain the need for device drivers and install devices and drivers

♦ Describe popular input device technologies

♦ Discuss the types of printers and install printers

♦ Explain display adapter technologies

♦ Install circuit boards for new devices

♦ Explain the use of sound cards and other output devices

Input and output devices bring a computer to life for the user—enabling that user to communicate with the computer. The keyboard is an example of an input device through which you issue commands and enter text. A computer monitor is an output device that enables the computer to communicate back, showing the results of your work in text or rendering eye-catching graphics. A printer lets you output your work on the printed page.

This chapter describes how operating systems interface with input and output devices, such as through device drivers. You learn general techniques for installing devices and device drivers for each operating system. You also learn about many types of input and output devices, such as keyboards, mice, monitors, scanners, printers, and others. Further, you learn how to install printers in operating systems.

OPERATING SYSTEMS AND DEVICES: AN OVERVIEW

As you learned in Chapter 1, one of the primary functions of any operating system is to provide basic input/output (I/O) support for application software—that is, to translate requests from application software into commands that the hardware can understand and carry out. For example, the operating system must:

- Handle input from the keyboard, mouse, and other input devices.

- Handle output to the screen, printer, and other output devices.

- Control information storage and retrieval using various types of disk and optical drives.

- Support communications with remote computers, such as through a network or dial-up connection.

There are two ways that an operating system accomplishes these tasks: through software (device driver code within the operating system itself, as well as accessing third-party device driver software) and through hardware (controllers and adapter boards for specific input or output devices) controlled by the operating system. Device drivers perform the actual communication between the physical device and the operating system. Adapters, which are circuit boards that plug into a slot on the motherboard of the computer, are the interface between hardware components (such as display adapters to produce video output, or sound cards to produce audio output). The particular configuration of device drivers and adapters varies from operating system to operating system, but they function in the same way in each operating system.

Likewise, setting up or installing input, output, or storage devices involves three general steps across operating systems:

1. Install any software drivers that are required.

2. Install the input, output, or storage device.

3. Set up the hardware.

 Installing and configuring storage devices is covered in Chapter 6.

NOTE

USING DEVICE DRIVERS

A device driver is software that enables the operating system and application software to access specific computer hardware, such as a monitor or disk drive. A separate device driver is often needed for each input or output device used on the computer. The operating system provides the basic I/O support for the parallel, serial, bus, or other ports your printer and other hardware use, but it doesn't support specific features of individual devices you may connect to these ports. For that, you need a driver, which may be supplied by the hardware manufacturer or the producer of the operating system. (See the discussion of driver software in Chapter 1.)

Computer monitors, printers, and disk drives are so common today that it might be surprising that a device driver is necessary for each type of device. However, when you consider that there are hundreds of devices and device manufacturers, it makes sense. If all computer operating system vendors attempted to incorporate code for all of the possible devices, the operating system kernel would be huge and probably slow. Also, the operating system kernel would have to be updated each time a new device or manufacturer came on the market. The advantages of using device drivers are:

- Only essential code is necessary to build into the operating system kernel for maximum performance.

- Use of specific devices does not have to be linked to a single operating system.

- In a competitive marketplace, the number of I/O devices can expand in virtually unlimited directions to offer the computer user a broad range of device selections, functions, and features.

- New devices can come on the market without requiring extensive updates to operating systems.

Many hardware manufacturers supply a floppy disk or compact disc read-only memory (CD-ROM) with drivers for current operating systems. In general, you should use the manufacturer's driver, if available, instead of the driver supplied with your operating system. Although many operating system drivers for specific hardware were developed by the hardware manufacturer in cooperation with the operating system producer, they may be generic—designed to support a range of hardware models—or they may be older than the specific hardware you are installing. Using the driver shipped with your particular printer or other device gives you a better chance of having the latest version designed for your specific hardware.

TIP

Even if your hardware is brand new, it is good practice to check with the manufacturer for newer driver software. Drivers usually are designated by version number, and sometimes with a date. Drivers with later version numbers and dates may contain fixes for problems identified with earlier releases, and they sometimes enable or improve the performance of some hardware features. The best source of new driver software is the World Wide Web. Check the documentation that came with your hardware for a Web site for new drivers, or simply point your browser to the manufacturer's main Web site and look for downloads, product support, software updates, or pages with a similar title.

For example, at this writing, to find drivers for a broad range of Epson hardware products, point your browser to *www.epson.com*, click your country, and click the link for Drivers & Downloads. Here are some other examples of Web support addresses:

- For Hewlett-Packard devices, visit *www.hp.com/country/us/en/support.html*. Select See support and troubleshooting information, provide the name of the product, and click the arrow to execute your selection. Next, follow the links for the specific model and for driver downloads for that model (or if the Web site has changed, follow the links to select a device and to download drivers for that device).

- For Lexmark devices, visit *www.lexmark.com*. Select the country and choose the link for Drivers and Downloads.

- For SoundBlaster audio cards, go to *us.creative.com*. Navigate to the Creative Labs (SoundBlaster) pages to find drivers and review other support material.

- For Matrox graphics display devices, visit *www.matrox.com/mga/support/drivers/home.cfm*. Select the Latest drivers link.

TIP

Remember that you can usually guess the home page for major companies. Simply type *www.companyname.com* in the address line of your browser where *companyname* is the actual name of the manufacturer of your hardware product. If you don't find the page you want, try a variation of the company name. If this doesn't work, go to a Web search engine and search for information about a particular company or product.

The procedure for installing drivers varies slightly with the source of the driver and the operating system you are using. If you download a new driver from a manufacturer's Web site, you'll probably have to uncompress the file before you can use it.

For example, many PC users use the PKZIP or WinZip compression/decompression utilities. Many software producers distribute software bundled and compressed with the PKZIP/WinZip format. Compression software not only reduces the size of the supplied files by removing redundant information, it also groups multiple files into a single distribution file or archive. Distribution files may be supplied in self-extraction format, an executable file that decompresses the archive and expands individual files. PC-executable files normally use an .exe file extension. If you download a driver archive that includes this extension, it is a self-extracting file. If the file includes a .zip extension, on the other hand, you'll need a program such as PKZIP or WinZip to expand the archive before you can install the driver software.

NOTE

If you don't have the PKZIP or WinZip software, you can download it from the Internet at a variety of sites. There also are other programs that perform similar functions. One resource for a wide variety of shareware, freeware, and low-priced software is *www.tucows.com*.

Mac OS X users can use ZIP-format archives, but a more common format is StuffIt, a utility similar to PKZIP, which also bundles multiple files into a single distribution archive. StuffIt products are actually available for the Windows, Linux, and Mac OS X operating systems (and some versions of UNIX). StuffIt files can be self-extracting, or you can use StuffIt Expander or another utility to expand the archive into its individual components. To obtain this utility visit *www.stuffit.com*. StuffIt also supports ZIP format, and it lets you retrieve compressed or archived files from Macintosh users. For a small fee, you can purchase the full-blown StuffIt software so you can create archives for Mac and Windows environments. The ZIP utilities available for the Mac don't always produce files that are compatible with Windows systems. The StuffIt Expander software, on the other hand, works both ways quite well.

UNIX/Linux system users may retrieve drivers and other software in a *tar* format. **tar** files also are archives that group multiple files into a single distribution file. *tar* doesn't compress the files; it merely groups files to make it easier to copy and distribute multiple files together. You may find that a *tar* archive is also zipped. You can use StuffIt or a UNIX/Linux version of unzip to expand the compressed *tar* archive into an uncompressed file, then you issue a UNIX/Linux *tar* command to extract individual files from the archive.

Once you locate the driver you want to use, you generally have three choices for installation, depending on the source of the driver: you can use your operating system's install utility, the Plug and Play (PnP) feature of Windows operating systems, or the install utility provided by the hardware manufacturer. Procedures are slightly different among different operating systems, and precise steps differ with different equipment (a printer installs differently from a sound card, for example), but the general process is very similar. The following sections discuss manufacturer driver installation and specific steps for installing devices in operating systems.

From the Trenches...

An IT professional was called to help a company president's administrative assistant with a network printer problem during a board of directors meeting. She tried all types of troubleshooting steps from turning the printer off and on to testing the network to looking for a paper jam in the printer. After working on the problem for quite some time (and resulting in delays in the meeting) the IT professional realized that the printer driver had gotten removed from the operating system used to print the documents.

Manufacturer Driver Installation

When you use a hardware manufacturer's install utility, the process is usually fully automatic and well documented. In fact, newer printers, plotters, and other devices frequently come with extensive support material on CD-ROM. You might be presented with video or animated training material to teach you how to install or use the device. Certainly, you shouldn't have to know much about the way your operating system installs drivers or interfaces with the device you're installing because the manufacturer's install routine handles it all for you. Because each manufacturer has a different procedure with different devices and different operating systems, it is difficult to document each system and device type.

In general, however, the procedure is to insert a CD-ROM (usually) or floppy disk (for some systems) into a drive and either wait for a program to start automatically, or run a setup or install utility. Then, simply follow on-screen prompts. If you run into problems, look for a disk-based tutorial, or go to the manufacturer's Web site to search for more information. Some software suppliers also include .txt files on install disks to present new information or tips for the installer. You can use Notepad or any text program to look for these files and read them.

Windows 2000/XP/Server 2003 Device and Driver Installation

There are several ways to install drivers in Windows 2000/XP/Server 2003. The easiest way to install a driver for a new system is to use the PnP capability to automatically detect the new hardware and install drivers. Another way to install new devices and drivers is to use the Add/Remove Hardware Wizard in Windows 2000 or the Add Hardware Wizard in Windows XP/Server 2003. Yet a third way is to use a specialized icon on Control Panel. Finally, a fourth way is to use Device Manager. With Device Manager, you can install a new driver or update an existing one. Each of these methods is explained in the next sections.

Using PnP to Install a Device and Driver

You can quickly install a new printer, for example, by following these general steps:

1. Shut down the operating system by choosing Shut Down from the Start menu.
2. Turn off the power to the computer and the printer.
3. Connect the printer to the computer's printer port.
4. Plug the printer into a power outlet and turn it on.
5. Turn on the computer.

When the operating system boots, it recognizes that a new piece of hardware is attached to the printer port and tries to locate the drivers for it. If Windows 2000/XP/Server 2003 already has a built-in driver for this device, these operating systems find the driver on the Windows distribution disk or CD-ROM. Otherwise, you must insert the manufacturer's disk or CD-ROM into an appropriate drive when the operating system asks for it.

Using a Windows 2000/XP/Server 2003 Wizard to Install a Device and Driver

If Windows 2000/XP/Server 2003 doesn't recognize newly installed hardware, if you simply want to conduct an installation manually, or to start automatic procedures to detect a hardware device (because PnP did not work initially), use the Add/Remove Hardware Wizard in Windows 2000 or the Add Hardware Wizard in Windows XP/Server 2003. To get started:

- In Windows 2000, click Start, choose Settings, click Control Panel, and double-click the Add/Remove Hardware icon.

- In Windows XP (using the Category View), click Start, click Control Panel, click Printers and Other Hardware, and click the Add Hardware link in the left pane to start.

- In Windows Server 2003, click Start, point to Control Panel, and click Add Hardware to start the Add Hardware Wizard shown in Figure 5-1.

Figure 5-1   Add Hardware Wizard in Windows Server 2003

Notice in Figure 5-1 there is an informational message suggesting that if your device comes with an installation CD, you should close the Wizard and use the CD instead. If you have an installation CD (or floppy disk) from the device manufacturer, it is always better to use it so that that the latest drivers are installed. When you use the Wizard, the drivers may not be the most current ones because Windows 2000/XP/Server 2003 use the drivers from their respective operating system installation CD-ROMs. (Note, however, that in many cases if you continue with the installation using the Wizard, it gives you the opportunity to access Microsoft's Web site for updated drivers or to install drivers from a manufacturer's CD-ROM.)

Hands-on Project 5-1 enables you to use the Add/Remove Hardware Wizard in Windows 2000 and Hands-on Project 5-2 employs the Add Hardware Wizard in Windows XP and Windows Server 2003.

Using Control Panel to Install a Device and Driver

Many devices can be configured directly through Control Panel. This includes the following devices:

- Display (monitor)
- Game controllers
- Keyboard
- Mouse
- Network interfaces
- Phone and modem connections
- Uninterruptible power supply (UPS)
- Printers and faxes
- Scanners and cameras
- Audio devices

Figure 5-2 shows Control Panel options in the menu format in Windows Server 2003. If you use the Category View in Windows XP, the options are separated out by activity. For example, the display installation options are accessed from the Appearance and Themes category and network interfaces are configured from the Network and Internet Connections category. Figure 5-3 illustrates the Category View options. If you want to view the Windows XP Control Panel options using icons instead, click Switch to Classic View in the left panel.

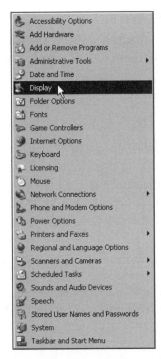

Figure 5-2   Control Panel options in Windows Server 2003

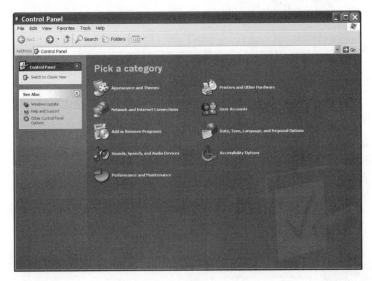

Figure 5-3   Control Panel Category View options in Windows XP

Using Device Manager to Install or Update a Driver

If you need to install a device driver or to update one for a device that is already installed, Device Manager offers a convenient way to accomplish the task. You can also use Device Manager to:

- Determine the location of device driver files.
- Check to make sure a device is working properly.
- Determine if there is a resource conflict for a device.

The advantage of determining the location of a device file is that you not only verify that the driver is installed, but you can check the version of the device driver. For example, if you suspect that you have an old driver, check with the manufacturer for the version level or date of the most current driver and then use Device Manager to compare with the version you have installed.

When you access a device through Device Manager, you can determine if the device is installed in two ways. The most obvious way is that Device Manager places a question mark on the device if there is a problem with the installation or if the driver is not installed. Also, when you access a device through Device Manager that has a driver set up, the utility checks to verify that the device is working properly. Figure 5-4 shows an example of a keyboard that is working properly.

Figure 5-4   Device Manager verification that a keyboard is working in Windows XP

A device uses the computer's resources to enable it to function and communicate with the computer. A computer's resources include the **interrupt request (IRQ) line** and one or more I/O address ranges. (See Chapter 2 for more information about IRQs.) The IRQ line is a channel within the computer that is used for communications with the central processing unit (CPU). Usually a separate channel, such as IRQ 01, is allocated for a specific device, such as the keyboard (see Figure 5-5). The **I/O address range** is memory reserved for use by a particular device. If more than one device is assigned the same IRQ line or I/O address range, then those devices become unstable or may not work altogether. Device Manager not only shows the IRQ line and I/O address ranges for a device, but also lets you know if it detects a conflict.

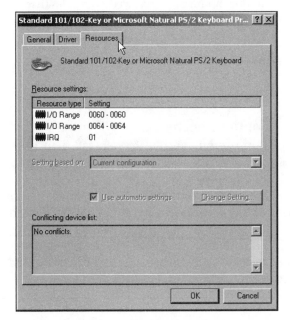

Figure 5-5   Resource settings for the keyboard in Windows Server 2003

Hands-on Project 5-3 gives you the opportunity to use Device Manager in Windows 2000/XP/Server 2003.

Configuring Driver Signing

When you install an I/O device under Windows, such as a pointing device or a new sound card, you have the option to make sure that the driver for that device has been verified by Microsoft. When a driver is verified by Microsoft, a unique digital signature is incorporated into that driver, in a process called **driver signing**. After you install Windows 2000/XP/Server 2003, you can choose to be warned that a driver is not signed, to ignore whether or not a driver is signed, or to have the operating system prevent you from installing a driver that is not signed. The warning level is assigned by default so that you are made aware of when a driver you are installing is unsigned, but you can still select to install or not to install that driver. Using driver signing helps to ensure that the driver works properly with the device and in conjunction with other devices. It is also a security feature to ensure that no one has tampered with the driver you are using, such as incorporating malicious code or a virus.

When you configure driver signing, you configure it to apply to all new software installations, as well as device drivers, because besides drivers, many critical operating system files are also signed. Each time you install a word processor or spreadsheet application, there is a risk that an important operating system file, such as a .dll (dynamic-link library) file may be overwritten by a file that is unsigned. If you have selected the Block option, this means that drivers and operating system files cannot be modified or overwritten by files that do not have the appropriate digital signature. No software installation can inadvertently install a driver or system file that is inappropriate for your version of Windows.

Hands-on Project 5-4 shows you how to configure driver signing in Windows 2000/ XP/Server 2003.

From the Trenches...

Many Windows operating system users have had to reinstall their operating systems because important drivers and other files used by the operating system have been overwritten, such as by newly installed software. A Windows 2000 user who purchased a new printer and downloaded new drivers from the manufacturer loaded a virus in the process because one of the manufacturer's driver files was infected and the driver was unsigned. The user had to reinstall his operating system and all of his software and data files—losing valuable time and some information along the way. If he had configured driver signing, the problem would not have occurred.

UNIX/Linux Driver Installation

The concept of drivers in UNIX/Linux is slightly different from that in other operating systems. The central portion of the UNIX/Linux operating system, the kernel, is where most of the UNIX/Linux device drivers are loaded. Device drivers are either in the form of kernel modules, which are pieces of code that must be linked into the kernel, or loadable modules, similar pieces of code that are not linked into the kernel, but are loaded when the operating system is started. Device support in most UNIX/Linux versions is limited compared to other operating systems; manufacturers of devices often provide drivers for special hardware, which are then linked or loaded into the kernel.

UNIX/Linux devices are managed through the use of **device special files**, which contain information about I/O devices that is used by the operating system kernel when a device is accessed. In many UNIX/Linux systems there are three types of device special files:

- **Block special files**, which are used to manage random access devices that involve handling blocks of data, including CD-ROM drives, hard disk drives, tape drives, and other storage devices.

- **Character special files**, which handle byte-by-byte streams of data, such as through serial or Universal Serial Bus (USB) connections, including terminals, printers, and network communications. USB is a relatively high-speed I/O port found on most modern computers. It is used to interface mice, keyboards, monitors, digital sound cards, disk drives, and other external computer hardware such as printers and digital cameras.

- **Named pipes** for handling internal communications, such as redirecting file output to a monitor.

When you install a UNIX/Linux operating system, device special files are created for the devices already installed on the system. On many operating systems, including Linux, these files are stored in the /dev directory. Table 5-1 provides a sampling of device special files.

Table 5-1   UNIX/Linux device special files

File	Description
/dev/console	For the console components, such as the monitor and keyboard attached to the computer (/dev/tty0 is also used at the same time on many systems)
/dev/fd*n*	For floppy disk drives where *n* is the number of the drive, such as fd0 for the first floppy disk drive
/dev/hd*xn*	For Integrated Drive Electronics (IDE) and Enhanced Integrated Drive Electronics (EIDE) hard drives where *x* is a letter representing the disk and the *n* represents the partition number, such as hda1 for the first disk and partition
/dev/modem	Symbolic link to the device special file (typically linked to /dev/ttys1) for a modem
/dev/mouse	Symbolic link to the device special file (typically linked to /dev/ttys0) for a mouse or pointing device
/dev/sd*xn*	For a hard drive connected to a SCSI interface (described later in this chapter) where *x* is a letter representing the disk and the *n* represents the partition, such as sda1 for the first SCSI drive and first partition on that drive
/dev/st*n*	For a SCSI tape drive where *n* is the number of the drive, such as st0 for the first tape drive
/dev/tty*n*	For serial terminals connected to the computer
/dev/ttys*n*	For serial devices connected to the computer, such as ttys0 for the mouse

If you need to create a device special file for a new device, you can do so by using the *mknod* command as in the following general steps:

1. Log on to the root account.

2. Access a terminal window or the command prompt.

3. Type *cd /dev* and press Enter to switch to the /dev folder.

4. Use the *mknod* command plus the device special file name, such as ttys42, and type of file, such as character (c) or block (b), and a major and minor node value used by the kernel (check with the device manufacturer for these values). For example, you might type, *mknod ttys20 c 8 68*, and press Enter for a new serial device.

TIP

Some versions of UNIX/Linux also support the *makedev* command for creating a device special file (not supported in current versions of Red Hat Enterprise Linux and Fedora). To determine which commands are supported in your UNIX/Linux version and to learn the syntax, use the *man mknod* or *man makedev* command to view the documentation.

To view the I/O device special files already on your system, use the *ls* command to see all of the files in the /dev folder. Also, Red Hat Enterprise Linux and Fedora offer the Hardware Browser from the GNOME desktop for viewing installed hardware. To access this browser, click Main Menu, point to System Tools, and click Hardware Browser. Try Hands-on Project 5-5 to view the device special files.

Managing Devices in NetWare 6.x

Devices in NetWare are typically managed through **NetWare Loadable Modules (NLMs)** which extend the capabilities and services of the operating system. There are hundreds of modules that can be loaded for all kinds of purposes from running a Web server to establishing security to managing a device such as a mouse or a hard drive. The NLMs work with device drivers provided by a manufacturer or by Novell. A device often can be configured through an NLM, depending on the type of NLM and commands that can be used with an NLM. Table 5-2 lists examples of NLMs that are used for devices.

Table 5-2   NetWare NLMs for devices

NLM	Device Supported by the NLM
_COMPORT.NLM	Serial port
_FIO.NLM	Disk file I/O
_LPTPORT.NLM	Parallel port
AIOCOMX.NLM	Asynchronous serial port
CDROM.NLM	CD-ROM
CIOS.NLM	Consolidated I/O management
KEYB.NLM	Keyboard

Table 5-2 NetWare NLMs for devices (continued)

NLM	Device Supported by the NLM
NSSMU.NLM	Disk storage management utility
PS2.NLM	PS/2 mouse
SETXKBMAP.NLM	Keyboard mapping of keys
UKBDSHIM.NLM	USB keyboard
UMSSHIM.NLM	USB mouse
UPS_AIO.NLM	UPS serial port connection
XMODMAP.NLM	Built-in keyboard device

NLMs are automatically loaded when a NetWare server boots. You can load or configure an NLM at the NetWare server console by entering the name of the NLM, along with any parameters that are appropriate for what you want to do. Because NLMs are critical to the function of NetWare, make sure you have instructions about how to use a particular NLM before you load or unload it. When you obtain a new device, always consult the device manufacturer's instructions for implementing that device and its drivers in NetWare. Hands-on Project 5-6 allows you to view the NLMs loaded on a NetWare server.

Mac OS X Driver Installation

Mac OS X systems come with device drivers for most hardware that connects to these systems. When you obtain new hardware, make sure that you have an installation CD-ROM from the manufacturer for that hardware. The general steps for installing new hardware on a Mac OS X system are:

1. Shut down the operating system and turn off the computer.

2. Attach the new hardware.

3. Restart the computer and operating system.

4. Insert the CD-ROM for the hardware.

5. Run the installer program on the CD-ROM for that hardware.

TIP

If you are having problems with hardware in Mac OS X, it may be necessary to reinstall the operating system. Depending on your version of Mac OS X, you can do this by inserting the Mac OS X Install Disk 1 CD-ROM, select the Mac OS X disk as the destination, click Options, and select to perform Archive and Install (in earlier versions of Mac OS X); or in Mac OS X v10.3, insert the installation disk and double-click Install Mac OS X (the installation will retain your previous settings and software).

Now that you're familiar with device drivers and with the basic process of installing devices and drivers in various operating systems, it's time to survey the types of input and output devices and how they relate to operating systems in more depth.

STANDARD INPUT DEVICES

There are two standard and universal computer input devices: the keyboard and the mouse. The keyboard is the single most important input device, and the second most important is the mouse (or one of the mouse alternatives such as a trackball, stylus, touch pad, or pointing stick). As universal as the mouse is today, it is a relatively new addition in the history of computer operating systems. Macintosh computers have used the mouse from the beginning, of course, but it was several years later before Microsoft-based computers routinely were supplied with a mouse. Today you wouldn't consider computing without a mouse—even if your preference is UNIX—assuming that you're a user of the X-Window graphical interface with a desktop such as GNOME or KDE, which is the norm on these platforms.

Mouse and Keyboard Drivers

Because the I/O routines for the mouse and keyboard are highly standardized across operating systems, it is unlikely that you will need to interact with the operating system to set up these devices. Although mice and keyboards do use device drivers, unlike printers and other output devices, these drivers are standard and, in most cases, included as part of the operating system. The operating system provides only general support for output devices like printers (it includes routines to send data out a parallel port, for example, and to receive data sent to the computer from a device connected to this port, but has no intrinsic routines to support specific printer brands, models, or capabilities). For keyboards and mice, however, most operating systems contain intrinsic routines to handle these devices.

The mouse and keyboard use special ports—serial or USB ports, basically—in a way similar to the way a printer uses a parallel port. Like a printer or other output device, the keyboard and mouse also need additional software to support specific functionality. However, the main difference between your mouse and keyboard and another device you may connect to your computer is virtually universal standardization. You can plug in a keyboard supplied with your computer, use a cheap replacement from a discount store, or pay the difference for a high-quality custom design, and, in most cases, you won't need any drivers beyond what is supplied with your operating system. For the most part, individual differences among keyboards are handled inside the keyboard itself. All the operating system cares about is the set of standard signals presented to the keyboard port when individual keys or key combinations are pressed. Different keyboards may include different hardware designs—switches or membranes for the keys, for example, and unique electronics for processing keystrokes. Some keyboards even include specialty keys that replace complex keystroke combinations or sequences. As long as these special keys send standard keystroke sequences to the keyboard port, the operating system doesn't really care how the codes are generated. These key closure codes or encoded sequences are captured at the port by intrinsic operating system routines and passed to higher level operating system applets and applications (word processing, spreadsheet, etc.) running under the operating system. No special drivers are required; the ones that install as part of your standard operating system generally will work just fine.

Some operating systems include fairly sophisticated keyboard driver routines and custom configuration utilities, such as the one from Windows XP, shown in Figure 5-6 (the AccessDirect tab in this figure is proprietary to a vendor and offers specialized keyboard programming options). Try Hands-on Project 5-7 to view basic keyboard configuration settings.

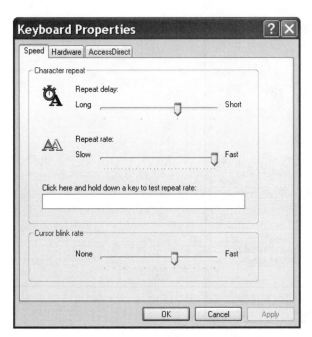

Figure 5-6   Windows XP Control Panel keyboard configuration utility

As you can see from this figure, the degree of configuration is minimal. This simply points out the standard nature of the keyboard itself, and the drivers that support it. Earlier operating systems—particularly non-Windows systems—may have even more limited keyboard configuration options. You plug it in and it either works or it doesn't.

A mouse is a pointing device with a ball on the underside that rotates as you move the mouse across a desk or mouse pad, and one, two, or three buttons on top. As the ball rolls, it moves two potentiometers (variable resistors) positioned at 90-degree angles to each other. As this movement changes these resistor values, the operating system records the direction of movement, the distance moved, and even the speed of movement. The top-mounted buttons are connected inside the mouse housing to microswitches that close when the buttons are pressed. Operating system drivers capture this switch closure and send the information to other operating system routines and application programs for interpretation.

NOTE There are also mice that use optical sensors rather than a ball to determine movement. These mice are referred to as optical mice. Other mouse alternatives include the trackball, touch pad, stylus, or pointing stick.

As with the keyboard, the intrinsic operating system mouse drivers may offer customization options to the user. Mouse options for Windows XP are shown in Figure 5-7. Try Hands-on Project 5-8 to view the basic mouse settings in Windows 2000/XP/Server 2003.

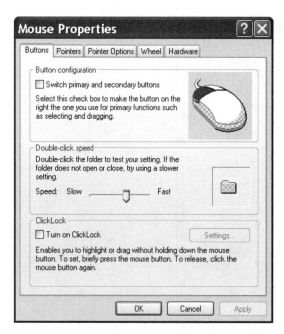

Figure 5-7   Windows XP mouse configuration options

Typically, the configuration routines let you set the double-click speed, calibrate mouse movement and direction (based on how you hold the mouse as you roll it around the desk), and customize the pointer graphic and a variety of other features. In addition to adding special features to the function of the mouse itself, manufacturers' drivers usually provide additional levels of user configuration, such as options to help quickly find the cursor on the screen or to select a window by just pointing to the title bar.

One thing most PC users notice about the Macintosh right away is the single mouse button on the Mac or a single clicking motion on optical mice, whereas the PC mouse has at least two. In Windows, you can right-click, which means you click with the rightmost button on your mouse. That's something a Mac user has never done; the right button doesn't exist. Mac users use keyboard shortcuts for most of the same functions that the right-click serves in the PC world. Additionally, Apple added contextual menus to Mac OS X that are strikingly similar to the PC's properties menus. If you want second-button functionality on a Mac, you can add a third-party two-button mouse, or you can use a trackball or joystick with two or more buttons. Generally, these extra buttons are programmable with software that ships with the hardware.

5

Hands-on Project 5-9 shows you how to maintain a mouse.

OTHER INPUT DEVICES

The keyboard and mouse are ubiquitous and standard. If your computing needs stop with fairly common business applications such as word processing, spreadsheets, and databases, you probably won't need anything more. On the other hand, if you do graphics design, Web page development, digital photography, or movie or sound editing, then you will use one or more specialty input devices, such as digital tablets, scanners, joysticks and gamepads, digital sound input, or digital picture and video input/output. The following sections introduce these devices.

Digital Tablets

A **digital pad** or **digital tablet** is really a different kind of mouse. A mouse is an excellent input tool for normal operations: choosing from a menu, selecting an icon or other graphic object, or dragging text or graphics to a new screen location. However, when you need to draw pictures, sign your name, color a detailed graphic image, or conduct other tasks that require a high degree of manual dexterity, then a digital pad or tablet is a useful addition to your computer hardware.

The same technology used in digital tablets is also used in **personal digital assistants (PDAs)** and tablet PCs. PDAs are handheld devices, which, because of their size (about the size of a hand), are easily transported. Features include daily planner functions and the ability to synchronize this information with your desktop computer. **Tablet PCs** are larger (about the size of a sheet of paper or a notebook-sized computer), and contain a complete computer within a touch screen. Windows XP comes in a special version for tablet PCs, but that version is not covered in this book.

A digital pad plugs into your computer via a standard or custom serial port, or through a USB port. After you install custom drivers (usually supplied by the pad manufacturer), then you can use the pad to conduct usual mouse operations, such as selecting menu items or moving objects. In addition, you can use the pad's electronic stylus for finer tasks, such as object drawing, capturing signatures, or manipulating specialty graphics programs, such as CorelDRAW or Adobe Photoshop. If you've ever tried to use even a simple drawing program with a mouse as your only input device, you can appreciate the value of a digital pad that lets you write and draw in much the same way you would with a pen or pencil.

The digital pad, like the mouse, can range from fairly standard, simple hardware to specialty devices that include liquid crystal display (LCD) panels that mirror your computer's video display. Even the simplest pads require some custom software and a unique installation process. Refer to earlier sections in this chapter for general information on installing drivers (operating system support software) for specialty devices such as the digital pad.

Scanners

A **scanner** is like a printer in reverse, or maybe like an office photocopier that "prints" to your computer instead of onto plain paper. Instead of accepting digital data from the computer and converting it to hard copy like a printer, a scanner starts with hard copy—a photograph, negative or slide, newspaper article, book page, even a solid object—and creates a digital image, which is then transmitted to the computer. Once in the computer, this digital image can be saved in a variety of graphics image formats, edited, merged with other images or text, transmitted over the Internet or other network connection, or, of course, printed.

Scanners can also be used with **optical character recognition (OCR)** software. Instead of scanning the text into a digital graphic image, which does not allow for text manipulation, imaging software scans each character on the page as a distinct image. Then you can import the scanned results into a word-processing document to work with the text.

Most scanners use some form of **Small Computer System Interface (SCSI)** hardware or the USB port. SCSIs are fast because they use wide data paths and rely less on the main system CPU, freeing the CPU for other work. Some scanners come with their own SCSI card, but you don't have to use this interface. If you have any standard SCSI port already installed in your computer, chances are your scanner can use it. You will need drivers to enable the scanner to use any SCSI port. The Mac OS has supported SCSI ports from the earliest days, while SCSI port support came later to Windows. SCSI manufacturers implement the standard SCSI protocols in different ways, making it important to be sure you have the correct drivers for your operating system.

If you're using a USB scanner with Windows 2000/XP/Server 2003, for example, installation and configuration should be automatic through PnP. Figure 5-8 shows the Windows XP Scanner and Camera Installation Wizard, which is accessed by clicking Start, clicking Control Panel, clicking Printers and Other Hardware, clicking Scanners and Cameras, and clicking Add an imaging device. You answer several questions about the scanner and the wizard completes the installation.

Figure 5-8   Windows XP Scanner and Camera Installation Wizard

For the most part, you'll install custom drivers, and, in many cases, custom interface software supplied by the scanner manufacturer when you install the hardware. In most cases, the driver software—usually a driver with user interface and scanner control—links automatically with a variety of graphics software. If you're using Photoshop, for example, the scanner may show up as an add-in; if you're using a Microsoft product such as Publisher or Photo Editor, you'll see a scanner icon on your toolbar. When you click the icon, the custom scanner software will load so you can use your scanner. These drivers and the user interface interact with the operating system to control the SCSI or USB port and capture data supplied by the scanner.

Windows and other operating systems generally ship with several SCSI drivers—in much the same way as they ship with printer drivers—and you can probably find an intrinsic driver that will enable input and output through your SCSI port. However, to get the best and most reliable performance from any SCSI device, you should install the drivers supplied by the manufacturer of the device itself. Again, you should check the vendor's online site to determine whether there are later versions of the required drivers for your hardware. This is true even if you just bought the hardware. Chances are the manufacturer has posted the very latest driver versions on the Web page, which you can download and install on your computer.

Joysticks and Game Pads

If your computer application is strictly business, you'll have no need for **joysticks** and **game pads**. On the other hand, if some part of your computer experience includes an occasional game, then one of these alternative input devices could be part of your hardware collection.

A joystick is more like a mouse than a digital pad. Like a mouse, the joystick uses a mechanical device to rotate one or more potentiometers. Changing resistance tells the joystick driver what value to feed to the operating system and any associated application software. You use the joystick for three-dimensional movement of an onscreen cursor or other object, such as a car, airplane, or cartoon character. Just as the digital pad makes it easier to input handwriting, picture retouching, and the like, the joystick offers a lot more control than a mouse when it comes to detailed movements of graphical screen objects. Although games are the primary application for joysticks, Mac users sometimes use them to supplement the mouse functionality. Joysticks can be used for virtually any application input task, given the proper driver.

In addition to the three-dimensional movements of the vertical joystick, this input device usually includes one or more push-button switches that can be associated with gun firings, boxing swings, menu selection, and so on. Like the digital pad, the joystick can use a conventional serial port, including the Mac's ADB or the PC and Mac's USB. Potentiometer settings or switch closures are sent through the I/O port as positive/negative pulses or as variable values on a scale. The operating system's basic port I/O routines grab this data, and then it is up to the associated application—a game, for example—to interpret this data in a meaningful way.

Game pads come in a wide variety of designs. As the name suggests, they are primarily designed for interaction with games, and include multiple buttons, wheels, or balls to effect movement of a variety of onscreen objects. As with the joystick, the game pad sends standard signals to a serial port where the operating system I/O routines take the data and pass it off to an application program or custom driver for interpretation.

Digital Sound Input

Almost every Mac, PC, and even workstation computer is supplied with some kind of analog sound card for sound input and output. For most of us, this sound capability is used pretty frivolously: software startup sounds, beeps when e-mail arrives, or playing music CDs. There are more serious applications for sound hardware, however. You can connect a microphone to an input port on your sound card and record voice mail that you can include with electronic mail, for example, or for narration of slide presentations. You can record custom sounds or music from a CD player or tape deck for use within software applications. Voice input to word processing and other programs is important for those unable to use a keyboard or mouse.

For more professional applications, such as editing music or voice for electronic writing or training applications, you may want to add a digital I/O card. This lets you capture digital sound from a digital audio tape (DAT) recorder or digital camera directly into the computer, without having to convert to analog in the process. A digital card lets you copy digital audio directly from a recorder to your hard drive in much the same way as you would copy digital information from one hard drive to another. There is no loss of quality; you can edit the sound files in native digital format, and then copy the finished files back to tape, or burn them onto a CD for distribution or presentation.

There are multiple professional audio I/O standards, both optical and copper. Which one you use depends on the external hardware you will interface with your computer. Some DAT machines and digital cameras include more than one digital I/O port, so you can choose which format to use based on personal preference, your need to interface with other users, or which interface you can find. Most cards require custom driver software. And, like scanners, these cards usually can be controlled and accessed from inside application software, such as digital audio or video editing packages. Once the driver is installed, you can transfer audio information through the digital sound card from inside the application you are using to manipulate the audio files.

Most digital audio interfaces plug into the computer's internal bus—usually Peripheral Component Interconnect or PCI—but there also are devices that use a USB port. If you need to transfer audio into multiple computers, the USB interface is a good choice because USB is self-configuring for the most part, and most USB devices are external to the computer. By installing the required drivers on a second computer, you can easily add digital audio I/O capabilities by using the USB device.

Digital Picture and Video Input/Output

Digital picture and video I/O works similarly to digital audio I/O. You need a digital I/O interface and drivers to allow your operating system to recognize and use the card. And, as with digital audio, you import digital images into whatever application software you are using for picture or video editing. In some cases, you use a utility supplied by the interface manufacturer to import the digital image, then launch another application, such as Adobe Premier or Photoshop, to conduct the actual editing. On the other hand, some card manufacturers include the ability to link their hardware drivers directly into editing software so you can import and export digital files from an external camera and edit the video or still images, all from the same application.

1394 Technology

IEEE 1394 (or 1394a) is the original specification for a high-speed digital interface that supports data communication at 100, 200, or 400 megabits per second (Mbps). The newer 1394b specification enables communications at 800 Mbps, 1.6 Gbps, and 3.2 Gbps.

IEEE 1394a and 1394b are technologies currently targeted at multimedia peripherals, which include digital camcorders, music systems, digital video discs (DVDs), digital cameras, and digital TVs. The IEEE 1394b standard also enables data transfer over regular twisted-pair (copper wire) network cable, and glass and plastic fiber-optic cable.

FireWire, an IEEE 1394 implementation for bus communications, was developed by Apple Computer and Texas Instruments and is used in computers built by those companies. IEEE 1394 is also known as i.Link (Sony) and the High Performance Serial Bus (HPSB).

NOTE The **Institute of Electrical and Electronics Engineers (IEEE)** is an international organization of scientists, engineers, technicians, and educators that plays a leading role in developing standards for computers, network cabling, and data transmissions—as well other electronics areas, such as consumer electronics and electrical power. Also, visit the Web site *www.1394ta.org* for links to information and vendors that support 1394 technologies.

PRINTERS

A printer is an important part of nearly every computer installation. The following sections outline the most popular types of printers and printer connections. You also learn how to install printers.

Printer Types

The following types of printers are the most popular today:

- **Dot-matrix printers** produce characters by slamming a group of wires (dots) from a rectangular grid onto a ribbon and then onto paper to produce characters (thus the designation "impact printer"). Dot-matrix printers tend to be noisy, and the quality of the characters is not as good as laser and ink-jet printers. Although dot-matrix printers are declining in popularity, you'll still find them behind sales counters to support point-of-sale (POS) computers, in many businesses, anywhere a computer is used to fill out forms, or where multiple copies of the same document are needed simultaneously.

- **Ink-jet printers** create characters by squirting tiny droplets of ink directly onto the page. Whereas impact dot-matrix printers may be capable of printing a few hundred dots per inch, some ink-jet designs can lay down 2880 dots per inch. Full color—even near-photographic quality—printing with ink jets is quite common today. Small, quiet, and inexpensive, these printers are popular personal printers in many offices, and dominate the bulk of the printer market for schools and homes. Models that deliver color and high resolution are used for proofing by graphics designers and printers, as well as home and office users. With the popularity of digital electronic cameras, high-resolution ink-jet printers are used increasingly to produce photograph-like output on heavy, slick paper, much like photographic paper stock.

- **Laser printers** use an imaging technology similar to copiers to produce computer output, and are probably the most popular printer design for business text and graphics. A typical laser printer contains its own CPU and memory because printed pages are first produced electronically within the printer. Laser printer prices have declined sharply over the past several years, so that even small businesses, home offices, and individuals now can afford them. Color laser printers are popular in medium- and large-scale companies. They are quickly gaining popularity in small offices and home offices as prices continue to drop.

The cost of printing is more than just the expense of the printer. Ink and laser cartridges add to printing costs. Depending on the cost for the cartridges, and the number of pages you are able to print with each one, many people are finding that a less expensive printer may cost more in the long run. For example, if you print a high volume of documents, it can be cheaper to use a laser printer than an ink-jet printer because one laser cartridge can print thousands of sheets while one ink-jet cartridge may only print hundreds.

Aside from these three major printer types, there are some other printer designs that are used in specialized arenas.

- **Line printers**, generally used on older mainframes, are impact printers that print an entire line at a time rather than a character at a time. Line printers are fast but extremely noisy, because the "line" is usually a metal chain. They use some form of tractor feed or pin feed. Line printers are rare these days; you may see them in government agencies, colleges or universities, or other venues that require large amounts of paper output, particularly paper output with multiple copies.

Vestiges of the line printer still remain: the main printer port on a PC is designated **LPT1**, which stands for line print terminal 1. It is doubtful that very many PCs ever were connected to a true line printer, but this big machine terminology stays with us.

- **Thermal-wax transfer** printers. Two basic thermal-wax transfer designs exist. One uses rolls of plastic film coated with colored wax, which is melted onto the page, one primary color at a time. A second type, known as phase change, melts wax stored in individual colored sticks and sprays the molten, colored wax onto the page. These printers generally produce very high-quality color output, but they also are relatively slow. In addition, these printers frequently require special paper, which adds to the cost of the printed output.

- **Dye sublimation** (sometimes shortened to dye sub) printers. The dye sublimation design takes the concept of atomizing waxy colors onto the paper a step further. Dye sub printers don't just melt pigments and spray them onto the paper, they vaporize them. This colored gas penetrates the surface of the paper to create an image on the page. Dye sub printers produce high-quality output. Moreover, they can mix and blend colors to produce output at near-photographic quality. Thermal-wax transfer and dye sublimation printers are used in many graphics applications where very high-quality, color printed output is required.

- **Imagesetter** printers, high-quality output devices frequently used in the printing industry to produce final output or page masters for offset printing. Imagesetters frequently produce output directly to film rather than paper. The film is used in a printing press to produce the final output. In color printing, a separate piece of film is produced for each of the colors cyan, magenta, yellow, and black.

High-speed copiers, printers, and most other printing devices found in a printing shop are now connected to the network. This allows the device to receive materials electronically from any computer connected to the network. The operator of these printing devices schedules printing in accordance with the instructions submitted electronically with the materials.

In addition to traditional printers, another printer-like device called a **plotter** is popular in engineering, architecture, and other fields where hard copy output (such as blueprints) won't fit on standard paper sizes, or can't be produced by standard character or graphics printers. Plotter design is even more complex than printers, using pen and control mechanisms. As with printers, plotters require special drivers to enhance the operating system's intrinsic capabilities, but the process of installing plotter hardware and software is similar to that for printers. Likewise, plotters can be installed on a computer's parallel and serial ports in much the same way as printers (see the next section on Printer Connections).

Printer Connections

In the early days of computing, nearly all printers were connected to a **serial port**—the same port where you may connect your modem or mouse today. A serial port manages communications between the computer and devices in a one-bit-after-the-other (asynchronous) stream. Today, the most common PC printer connection is a **parallel port**, which manages communications between the computer and peripherals, in which data flows in parallel streams. Because more data can be sent at the same time (synchronously) in a parallel connection, it is generally a higher speed connection than a serial connection. The parallel port is sometimes called a **Centronics interface**, after the printer manufacturer that made it popular. The original Centronics interface used a 36-pin connector. Current PC platforms and most UNIX computers use a 25-pin (**DB-25**) connector because some of the original Centronics lines aren't necessary.

Besides the parallel port, USB port connections are also popular for today's printers. Almost all printers now come with a USB port built into the printer. External disk drives, cameras, scanners, modems, and other devices also use this interface. Apple computers are also supplied with USB connectivity, but older Apple machines use a slower, similar technology, the **Apple Desktop Bus (ADB)**. The ADB is used for keyboard, mouse, printer, and other device connections in much the same way as the newer USB interface.

Some printers are designed with some combination of parallel, serial, and USB interfaces so you can connect in more than one way.

TIP

In general, a parallel printer connection is best because it provides a fast data path and better two-way communication between the computer and the printer. However, if you need to locate the printer more than 10 feet (3 meters) or so from the computer, a serial or USB connection is the better choice. For example, you can place a printer up to 50 feet (15 meters) from the computer if you use a serial connection.

Parallel printer communication is achieved in one of three ways. The first is compatibility or Centronics, which is one-way communication between the computer and printer. The second form of communication is referred to as nibble. This is a form of two-way communication, but it only allows communication one way at a time. The final way is usually referred to as **Extended Capabilities Port** (**ECP**; also called Enhanced Capabilities Port) communication, which allows for higher speed bidirectional communication between the computer and printer, as well as the printer and computer.

NOTE

The printer cable must be bidirectional and the parallel port set to bidirectional communications in order for ECP communication to work properly. If the printer cable is not bidirectional, you must turn off this feature on the port.

Printer manufacturers are increasingly offering alternative connection methods. Printers designed for corporate environments, for example, frequently have a direct network connection option that lets you place the printer virtually anywhere on a local area network (LAN), where it can be shared among all of the computers attached to the LAN. If a particular printer doesn't include a networked option, you can purchase a network printer interface from a third party. These interfaces have one or more network ports plus one or more printer ports. You connect the network on one side and plug in the printer on the other. It is generally more efficient to use a direct network-attached printer rather than a printer attached to a computer and configured for sharing on the network. Using a printer attached to a computer can be a drain on that computer's resources when others are using the printer, and a network interface is always on, making the printer always available to network users.

Installing Printers

Operating systems provide one or more ways to install printers because printing is vital to outputting documents from word processors, spreadsheets, graphics programs, and other software. In the following sections, you learn how to install a printer in the operating systems that are the focus of this book.

Installing Windows 2000/XP/Server 2003 Printers

In Windows 2000/XP/Server 2003, many printers can be installed by connecting the printer to the computer (shut down the operating system and turn off the computer first) and then letting PnP initiate the installation, as discussed earlier in this chapter. Another option is to connect the printer and use the Add/Remove Hardware Wizard (in Windows 2000) or the Add Hardware Wizard (in Windows XP/Server 2003), which was presented earlier. However, if an installation CD-ROM comes with the printer, the best approach is to connect the printer and use the CD-ROM for the installation. Finally, another alternative, if you need to perform a manual installation or to initiate automatic detection and setup of a new printer, is to use the Add Printer Wizard from Control Panel, as shown in Figure 5-9 for Windows XP (using Category View).

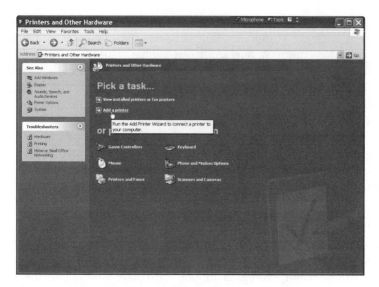

Figure 5-9   Starting the Add Printer Wizard in Windows XP

The steps used by the Add Printer Wizard are similar (but in slightly different order) to those used in Hands-on Projects 5-1 and 5-2 by the Add Hardware Wizard. The main difference is in how you start the Add Printer Wizard. Hands-on Project 5-10 gives you the opportunity to use the Add Printer Wizard for Windows XP to install a printer.

Installing UNIX/Linux Printers

Because UNIX/Linux is a multiuser, multitasking operating system, it uses a print queue. When a print job is sent from an application, a **print queue** or **print spooler** temporarily stores the print job, from which it is sent to the printer. In order to configure a printer on a UNIX/Linux system, you first must define the printer parameters and the print queue. All definitions of printers and queues are kept in the file /etc/printcap. This file is maintained in plain American Standard Code for Information Exchange (ASCII) text and can be edited with any text editor. However, there are UNIX/Linux utilities to make this job easier and it is a good idea to take advantage of these tools.

For example, Red Hat Enterprise Linux uses a printer configuration (printconf) utility called *printtool*. You can start this tool from a terminal window using the *printtool* command, which starts a GNOME-based Printer configuration window, as shown in Figure 5-10. Another option is to open the same Printer configuration window from the GNOME Main Menu by clicking Main Menu, pointing to System Settings, and clicking Printing.

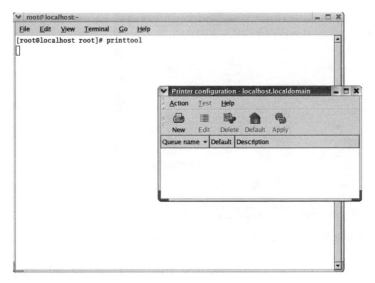

Figure 5-10   Using the *printtool* command in Red Hat Enterprise Linux

Hands-on Project 5-11 enables you to use Red Hat Enterprise Linux printer-related tools.

NOTE

In UNIX/Linux, a printer connected to one computer can be used to print jobs from another computer. Every computer that wants to use a printer, whether remotely or locally, must first create a print queue for that printer. If there is one computer with the printer connected, and three other UNIX computers want to use the printer, a print queue for that printer must be created on all four computers. When a print job is submitted, it is queued in the local print queue. From there, it is submitted to the print queue of the computer to which the printer is connected, and then it spools to the printer.

Installing NetWare Printers

Installing NetWare printers is a relatively complex process that can be accomplished in two general ways. One is to use separate utilities to set up printers and print queues. The more modern way is to use Novell Distributed Print Services. You learn more about NetWare printing and printer installation in Chapter 9.

Installing Mac OS X Printers

In Mac OS X, most printer drivers are already installed when you install the operating system. If they are not installed through these means, make sure that the printer you buy has a CD-ROM to install the new printer driver. To set up a printer, use the Printer Setup Utility, which is started from the Utilities window (see Figure 5-11) or from Print & Fax in System Preferences, and click Add to select the printer that you want to install.

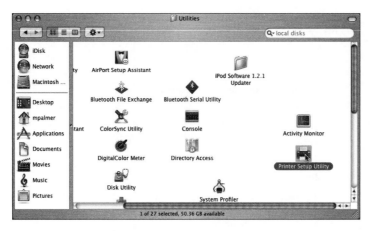

Figure 5-11   Opening the Mac OS X Printer Setup Utility

Depending on the setup of your computer, you can configure the following types of printers:

- AppleTalk
- LPR
- IP
- Firewire
- USB
- FAXstf

AppleTalk is used to connect to a shared network printer for Apple computers. LPR is another option for connecting to a shared network printer that uses the traditional UNIX-based LPR configuration and can be a computer shared through a Mac, Windows-based, or UNIX/Linux computer (or a network print server device). IP is for printing through a Transmission Control Protocol/Internet Protocol (TCP/IP) printer (or print server) on a network. You learn more about shared network printers in Chapter 9. Firewire is for connecting a printer through an IEEE 1394 interface that is on the Mac computer. USB is the most typical type of printer connection and, of course, is through a USB port on the computer. Finally, FAXstf is for sending a print file to a fax machine.

 If your printer is not manufactured by Apple, you must follow the instructions provided with that printer, and it might also be a good idea to check the printer manufacturer's Web site. Many printers include driver versions significantly older than the currently available downloadable versions, and these older versions can cause problems when used with the latest version of Mac OS.

NOTE

Try Hands-on Project 5-12 to learn more about how to use the Mac OS X Printer Setup Utility.

DISPLAY ADAPTERS

Once wildly diverse in design and features, display adapters today are reaching a common ground across operating systems and hardware platforms. The general industry acceptance of the **Accelerated Graphics Port (AGP)** bus standard has enabled adapter manufacturers to supply one hardware product, or a line of hardware products, to a variety of hardware platforms. The AGP bus enables high-performance graphics capabilities.

Basic Display Adapter Technology

If you are using a PC with a monitor, you have a display adapter card already installed in your computer. The display adapter is part of a standard computer package. No matter what computer platform you are using, the basic display (and the baseline standard in most cases) consists of 640 pixels horizontally and 480 pixels vertically. A **pixel** is a picture element, actually a small dot of light that represents one small portion of your overall screen display. Depending on the display adapter in your computer and how the operating system detects the display adapter through PnP, your display may be at 800 × 600 or greater. There also is a minimum resolution associated with many operating systems. Top-end display adapters today are easily capable of displaying 1280 × 1024 pixels, 1600 × 1280, or even 2048 × 1536 in some cases.

In general, as you display more pixels on the screen, you'll need a larger monitor to comfortably read the displayed data. For a given size of screen, higher resolution displays can present more data at a time on the screen, but this data is presented in a smaller format. A 1024 × 768 display on a 15-inch monitor works okay, but is better on a 17-inch monitor. And if you prefer 1280 × 1024 or higher resolution for the applications you use, for how far you sit from the screen, and to fit more on your desktop, you should consider at least a 19-inch monitor (a 21-inch monitor is a better choice).

Current operating systems support devices with the full range of resolution, so the major considerations in choosing an adapter are the adapter's resolution capabilities, the amount of memory included onboard the adapter (more memory on the adapter generally means faster performance when rendering screen images), type of video processor (display adapters may have their own CPU or accelerator to speed things up), and cost. As noted previously, you should also consider what kind of monitor you need as you decide on the screen resolution.

There's another aspect of screen resolution that isn't often discussed: the density of the displayed image, or bit density. A resolution of 640 × 480 simply means that images are displayed with 640 dots of light from left to right and 480 dots of light top to bottom. However, there is a third consideration to the display, the bit density—how many of these dots of light can be crammed into an inch of display. All computer displays have a bit density of 72 **dots per inch (dpi)**, and this is probably why so many books and articles about computer graphics ignore this important aspect of image display. When you consider graphics programs (such as Photoshop or CorelDRAW), or choose a digital camera or other image source, this aspect of resolution becomes important. A high-quality photograph, for example, may contain 4000 dots per inch. Books are can be printed at 133 dpi but to ensure good quality, files are usually produced at 200 dpi or greater; brochures may be printed at 1200 dpi, for example.

TIP   When you view graphics on your computer monitor, you see only 72 dpi because that's all your monitor is capable of showing. However, your printer may be able to reproduce 600 dpi, 1200 dpi, 1440 dpi, 2880 dpi, or more for some applications. It is important to know this third dimension when you spec printers, plotters, scanners, digital cameras, video editing software, and graphics programs. Print resolution, for example, may be more precise than the resolution of the monitor. The printer may show imperfections that the monitor does not display.

Although 640 × 480 is the basic **Video Graphics Array (VGA)** resolution, the majority of new computers ship with 800 × 600 or better set as the default. Today's computer display technology is called by a variety of names (depending on the manufacturer)—**Super VGA (SVGA)**, **Ultra VGA (UVGA)**, and **Ultra Extended Graphics Array** (**UXGA**, based on the early IBM XGA technology). All of these refer to display technologies that provide 1600 × 1200 and higher resolution.

Standard video adapters also have standard color rendition capabilities that range from 16 colors, at the very low end, to 16.5 million colors for SVGA/UVGA/UXGA. At the mid range is a 256-color setting that lets you reproduce color material with reasonably good quality; that setting is compatible with the broadest range of display adapters. World Wide Web page designers frequently design their images for 256 colors to ensure the broadest possible compatibility with computer hardware in use by Web browsers. A 256-color setting is pleasing to the eye, but still very low quality compared to the higher 16.5 million colors setting.

Larger monitors also are the norm. For example, a 17-inch display or larger is now common. With the 17-inch monitor, you can routinely set a resolution of 1024 × 768 and still see everything you need to see. Also, many computers ship with a flat panel monitor, which takes up less space and can provide a flicker-free image.

Installing Display Adapters

Unless you're building a computer from scratch, or you want to upgrade your existing video capabilities, there should be no reason for you to install a display adapter yourself. The computer should come from the manufacturer with a display adapter installed. The original adapter should last for the life of the computer.

However, there can also be good reasons for upgrading display hardware. Technology changes, software changes, and our personal needs change, all leading to potential upgrade situations.

By far, the majority of display adapters are supplied as cards that plug into the AGP slot on the motherboard. The AGP bus has become a popular standard among computer hardware manufacturers, including Intel-based computers, Macintosh computers, and workstations designed for UNIX, Sun Solaris, and other systems. As with printers and other hardware, display adapters are installed in two phases, hardware and software.

Installing any display adapter card is similar to installing circuit boards, as detailed in the last section of this chapter. And, thanks to the industry's adoption of the AGP bus standard and similarities among computer case designs, the installation procedure should be the same across platforms.

5

Sound Cards

In the past, computer support for sound and other multimedia devices was rare. Today there's hardly a computer that doesn't include high-end audio support. Multimedia, sound output, and even quality recording capabilities have become more important to a broader range of users. Businesses use sound as part of documentation or training, sales presentations, and even for music and motion video productions.

You'll find that support for a sound card is automatic with newer computers. The sound card comes preinstalled, and the operating system includes integral support for sound input and output. However, there are drivers for individual pieces of sound hardware that must be installed, as described earlier in the chapter. Also, if you format your hard drive (or replace it with a new one), you must install the proper drivers for your sound hardware for everything to work properly.

Sound devices are of two general types: bus cards (which are installed into a bus slot in the same way as a display adapter; see the last section of this chapter) and hardware integrated with the motherboard. Increasingly you will see sound cards built into the motherboard. This provides the easiest installation because the hardware is always there, and all you might need to do is install or configure drivers. The downside to motherboard sound hardware, as with built-in disk controllers, video adapters, and other devices, is that it may be harder to update or change the hardware.

Other Output Devices

In today's computer marketplace, there are so many output options that it would be impossible to cover them all here. Digital video, for example, is a popular consumer and professional computer-based feature. Adapter cards that let you capture and output digital video to a camera or VCR are available, coupled with capable, low-cost video editing software to help you use them.

Enhanced sound output is also now reasonably priced. Instead of living with analog output, for a few dollars more, you can output (and input) a digital audio stream to minidisk or DAT recorders. Multiport sound cards are available that permit a computer to serve as a fully digital, multichannel recorder for sound studio applications.

As you interact with a variety of computer systems and read specifications for products from a variety of industries, be aware of what hardware and software may be driving the features you are using or reading about. And, be aware that there's probably some specialty software required to make everything work properly.

The next section outlines the general steps for installing all types of cards.

INSTALLING CIRCUIT BOARDS

Today's computer hardware is pretty rugged. Still, perhaps the biggest enemy of the devices supplied on circuit boards or cards is static (high-voltage, low-current charges that can exist between any two devices, including human bodies). Static discharges are obvious when the voltage is high enough to cause a spark to jump between objects, or from an object to your finger. However, you can damage delicate computer parts with voltage levels below this sparking level.

To avoid damage to circuit boards during installation, follow these simple guidelines:

- Leave the card inside its protective cover until you are ready to install it.

- Disconnect all power to the computer.

- Prepare the computer by removing the case and any slot covers for the slots you will use.

- Position the card inside its cover, near the computer.

- Touch a grounded part of the computer. The power supply case is a good choice. Now, without removing your hand from the computer, open the bag and remove the card you are about to install. If you must swap hands as you move the card into position, just be sure you keep touching the computer case. This is easier than it sounds. You can use your elbow, wrist, the back of your hand, and so on, to maintain contact with the computer as you handle the card.

NOTE
Electrostatic discharge (ESD) straps can be used to prevent damage to your computer and cards. An ESD strap usually consists of a wrist strap with a grounding cord to clip to the computer's metal frame.

- Insert the card carefully into the chosen slot and press it firmly into place. It is helpful to wiggle the card into position, pressing first one end, then the other, until it is firmly seated. You'll quickly get the hang of it as you work with more cards.

Just remember that the card itself is quite rugged. Except for static discharge, it isn't likely that you'll hurt a modern computer card during installation (see Figure 5-12).

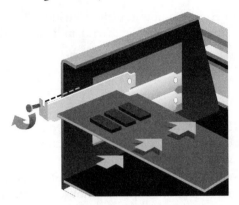

Figure 5-12   Typical card being placed in a computer

CHAPTER SUMMARY

- An operating system handles input and output device communications through device drivers (software) and through hardware such as controller and adapter boards.

- Device drivers are often provided with an operating system, but the most up-to-date device drivers come directly from each device manufacturer.

- Manufacturer device and device driver installations typically are performed from a manufacturer's CD-ROM or floppy disk. Up-to-date drivers can usually also be downloaded from the manufacturer's Web site.

- Installing devices and drivers in Windows 2000/XP/Server 2003 can be done using PnP, the Add Hardware Wizard, Control Panel options, and Device Manager. Also, plan to configure driver signing to ensure successful and secure device driver installations.

- UNIX/Linux systems use device special files for managing input and output devices.

- NetWare uses a combination of device drivers and NLMs for managing devices.

- For Mac OS X devices, most drivers come with the operating system or can be installed from an installation CD-ROM provided by the device manufacturer.

- Standard input devices include a mouse, keyboard, digital pad, scanner, joystick, game pad, digital sound devices, digital picture devices, and devices that use 1394a or 1394b technology.

- Printers are common output devices. The most common types are ink-jet and laser, while dot-matrix printers are still used in some business situations.

□ Most operating systems include tools for installing printers, such as Add Printer Wizard in Windows XP/Server 2003, printtool in Red Hat Enterprise Linux, and the Printer Setup Utility in Mac OS X.

□ Besides printers, other examples of common output devices include display adapters and sound cards. Today, many other output devices for high-end audio and video processing are available.

KEY TERMS

Accelerated Graphics Port (AGP) — A bus standard that has enabled adapter manufacturers to supply one hardware product to a variety of hardware platforms. Display adapters are typically plugged into the AGP slot on a motherboard.

Apple Desktop Bus (ADB) — A serial bus common on older Apple Macintosh computers. ADB is used to connect the Macintosh keyboard, mouse, and other external I/O devices.

block special file — In UNIX/Linux, a file used to manage random access devices that involves handling blocks of data, including CD-ROM drives, hard disk drives, tape drives, and other storage devices.

Centronics interface — An industry standard printer interface popularized by printer manufacturer Centronics. The interface definition includes 36 wires that connect the printer with the computer I/O port, though all of these pins aren't always used, particularly in modern desktop computers, which usually use a DB-25 connector.

character special file — A UNIX/Linux I/O management file used to handle byte-by-byte streams of data, such as through serial or USB connection, including terminals, printers, and network communications.

DB-25 — A 25-pin D-shaped connector commonly used on desktop computers, terminals, printers, modems, and other devices.

device special file — File used in UNIX/Linux for managing I/O devices. Can be one of two types: *block special file* or *character special file*.

digital pad or **digital tablet** — An alternative input device frequently used by graphic artists and others who need accurate control over drawing and other data input.

dot-matrix printer — An impact character printer that produces characters by arranging a matrix of dots.

dots per inch (dpi) — Used to measure the resolution of a printer or a video screen, the number of dots contained in an inch.

driver signing — A digital signature that Microsoft incorporates into driver and system files as a way to verify the files and to ensure that they are not inappropriately overwritten.

dye sublimation — A printer technology that produces high-quality, color output by creating "sublimated" color mists that penetrate paper to form characters or graphic output.

Extended Capabilities Port (ECP) — Also called Enhanced Capabilities Port, a form of communication that allows for higher speed bidirectional communication between the computer and printer, and the printer and computer.

game pad — An input device primarily designed for interaction with games. Includes multiple buttons, wheels, or balls to effect movement of a variety of on-screen objects.

imagesetter — A high-end printer frequently used for publishing. Capable of producing film output.

ink-jet printer — A character printer that forms characters by spraying droplets of ink from a nozzle print head onto the paper.

Institute of Electrical and Electronics Engineers (IEEE) — An international organization of scientists, engineers, technicians, and educators that plays a leading role in developing standards for computers, network cabling, and data transmissions—as well as other electronics areas, such as consumer electronics and electrical power.

interrupt request (IRQ) line — A channel within the computer that is used for communications with the CPU. Intel-type computers have 16 IRQ lines, with 15 of those available to be used by devices, such as the keyboard.

I/O address range — A range of memory addresses that is used to temporarily store data that is transferred between a computer device or component and the CPU.

joystick — An input device shaped like a stick that allows for three-dimensional movement of an on-screen cursor or other object, such as a car, airplane, or cartoon character.

laser printer — A high-quality page printer design popular in office and other professional applications.

line printer — A printer design that prints a full line of character output at a time. Used for high-speed output requirements.

LPT1 — The primary printer port designation on many desktop computers. Also designated line print terminal 1.

named pipe — In UNIX/Linux, a device special file for handling internal communications, such as redirecting file output to a monitor.

NetWare Loadable Module (NLM) — Program code that is loaded in NetWare to extend the capabilities of the operating system, such as for configuring a hard drive, managing the mouse connection, or setting up a USB port.

optical character recognition (OCR) — Imaging software that scans each character on the page as a distinct image and is able to recognize the character.

parallel port — A computer I/O port used primarily for printer connections. A parallel port transmits data eight bits or more at a time, using at least eight parallel wires. A parallel port potentially can transmit data faster than a serial port.

personal digital assistant (PDA) — Handheld devices, which, because of their size, are easily transported wherever you go. They include features to assist you in organizing your time, such as a calendar, to-do lists, contacts, etc.

pixel — Short for picture element. The small dots that make up a computer screen display.

plotter — Computer hardware that produces high-quality printed output, often in color, by moving ink pens over the surface of paper. Plotters are often used with computer-aided design (CAD) and other graphics applications.

print queue or **print spooler** — A section of computer memory and hard disk storage set aside to hold information sent by an application to a printer attached to the local computer or to another computer or print server on a network. Operating system or printer drivers and control software manage the information sent to the queue, responding to printer start/stop commands.

scanner — Creates a digital image from a hard copy that is then transmitted to the computer.

serial port — A computer I/O port used for modem, printer, and other connections. A serial port transmits data one bit after another in serial fashion, as compared to a parallel port, which transmits data eight bits or more at a time.

Small Computer System Interface (SCSI) — A computer I/O bus standard and the hardware that uses this standard. There are many types of SCSI in use today, providing data transfer rates from 5 Mbps to 320 Mbps.

Super VGA (SVGA) — Sometimes called **Ultra VGA (UVGA)**, a display technology based on VGA that provides a 1600 × 1200 or higher resolution and up to 16.5 million colors. See *VGA*.

tablet PC — A complete notebook-sized computer within a touch screen enabling the user to enter handwritten text via a digital pen device.

tar — A UNIX/Linux file archive utility.

thermal-wax transfer — A printer technology that creates high-quality color printed output by melting colored wax elements and transferring them to the printed page.

Ultra Extended Graphics Array (UXGA) — A display technology based on IBM's older eXtended Graphics Array (XGA) technology that provides a 1600 × 1200 or higher resolution and up to 16.5 million colors.

Video Graphics Array (VGA) — A video graphics display system introduced by IBM in 1987.

REVIEW QUESTIONS

1. The *tar* format for retrieving drivers is used in which of the following? (Choose all that apply.)

   a. Windows 2000

   b. Windows XP/Server 2003

   c. UNIX/Linux

   d. NetWare 6.x

2. A newly trained technician who works for you has obtained and installed a 36-pin interface in a computer for parallel printer communications. However, he has found that none of the printer cables on hand in your organization will work with that interface. What is the problem?

   a. The interface has a broken pin.

   b. Modern parallel printer cables that connect to a PC use a 25-pin connector.

c. Most parallel printer cables now have a USB connector.

d. Typical parallel cables use a 9-pin connector.

3. You need to check a printer parameter for a Linux printer. In what file can you look for information about the printer configuration?

a. /dev/ptr

b. /bin/ptr

c. /usr/printer

d. /etc/printcap

4. You have been asked to order a type of printer for the Geography Department that uses pens and produces fine images for maps. What type of printer do you need to order?

a. plotter

b. laser

c. dot matrix

d. line printer

5. You support the Windows XP computers in your organization and a new network interface driver has been issued to plug a security hole. Which tool would you use to quickly install this driver update?

a. Device Manager

b. Add Network Interface Wizard

c. PnP

d. Registry editor

6. On a Mac OS X computer, 1394 technology is implemented as
_____ .

a. a Centronics port

b. Fire wire

c. RS232

d. USB

7. You have been unloading NetWare NLMs that you believe are not needed so that you can return more memory for the operating system to use. After you do this, your mouse no longer works. What NLM should you reload?

a. KEYB.NLM

b. MOUSE.NLM

c. REMOTE.NLM

d. PS2.NLM

8. Which of the following might be attached to a computer through a USB port? (Choose all that apply.)

   a. mouse

   b. keyboard

   c. printer

   d. video display adapter

9. What type of port is typically used for a scanner? (Choose all that apply.)

   a. serial

   b. parallel

   c. USB

   d. SCSI

10. You have just installed a new printer in Red Hat Enterprise Linux, but when you print the test page, several of the characters are not printing correctly. Which of the following should you do first?

    a. Use a different printer cable.

    b. Obtain the latest printer drivers from the printer manufacturer's Web site.

    c. Reconfigure the speed of the printer port.

    d. Return the printer for a refund.

11. Your organization often receives long forms from the state to complete and return. Which of the following tools can you use to convert these forms so that you can complete them faster using a word processor? (Choose all that apply.)

    a. SCSI interpreter

    b. scanner

    c. digital picture I/O

    d. OCR software

12. After you install a new sound card and its related device drivers, your monitor frequently pauses or stops working until you reboot. Which of the following is most likely to be the problem?

    a. You need a new monitor.

    b. You need a new display adapter.

    c. There is an I/O address range conflict.

    d. Your system has run out of IRQ lines.

13. You are the computer support person in your small company. One of the employees has installed an off-brand network interface card (NIC) and its drivers on his Windows XP Professional computer. Now the operating system will not run several network-related programs, such as e-mail, a calendar scheduling program, and programs used for remote database access. The problem is severe enough that you back up the system, reinstall Windows XP Professional, and restore the user's files. How can you prevent this from happening the next time this user installs a device?

   a. Configure driver signing.

   b. Remove Administrator privileges for that user.

   c. Set up a device block.

   d. Configure a firewall.

14. The _____ tool in Linux enables you to create a device special file.

   a. tty

   b. mknod

   c. mkspc

   d. devmake

15. When you create a device special file, in what folder should it be stored in Linux?

   a. /etc

   b. /dev

   c. /sbin

   d. /tmp

16. On what type of computer would you find ADB ports? (Choose all that apply.)

   a. one running the Mac OS

   b. one running Linux

   c. one running Windows 2000

   d. one running Windows Server 2003

17. You have a new computer support employee who has never installed one of the specialized ergonomic keyboards used by your company. What Windows XP tool(s) can you teach her to use to install these keyboards? (Choose all that apply.)

   a. Add Hardware Wizard

   b. Keyboard Manager

   c. Start menu Accessories option

   d. Keyboard option available through Control Panel

18. The types of sound devices include which of the following? (Choose all that apply.)

   a. bus cards

   b. hardware integrated with the motherboard

    c. chips that supplement the CPU

    d. buffers built into disk drive components

19. A friend of yours was installing a circuit board and damaged it due to a static discharge at the time of installation. How can this be avoided? (Choose all that apply.)

    a. Remove all batteries from circuit boards prior to installation.

    b. Scrape the contacts on the circuit board before you install it.

    c. Turn the computer off, then ground yourself by continuously touching the power supply.

    d. Only purchase self-grounding circuit boards.

20. In UNIX and Linux, which of the following is (are) true about device drivers? (Choose all that apply.)

    a. They must be written in C or Pascal.

    b. They can be loadable modules.

    c. They can be NLMs.

    d. They must never be kernel modules.

HANDS-ON PROJECTS

HANDS-ON PROJECTS

Project 5-1

The Add/Remove Hardware Wizard in Windows 2000 Professional and Server and the Add Hardware Wizard in Windows XP/Server 2003 are valuable tools for installing all types of devices and drivers. This project enables you to use the Add/Remove Hardware Wizard in **Windows 2000 Professional and Server**. Use an account that has Administrator privileges. Also, for the sake of practicing all of the steps, your computer should not have newly installed hardware.

To add hardware and install drivers using the Add/Remove Hardware Wizard:

1. Click **Start**, choose **Settings**, click **Control Panel**, and double-click the **Add/Remove Hardware** icon.

2. Click **Next**. What options can you select? Record your observations.

3. Click **Add/Troubleshoot a device**. Click **Next**. What does the wizard do at this point?

4. Scroll through the list of hardware that is already installed and record some examples.

5. Click **Add a new device**, as shown in Figure 5-13. Click **Next**.

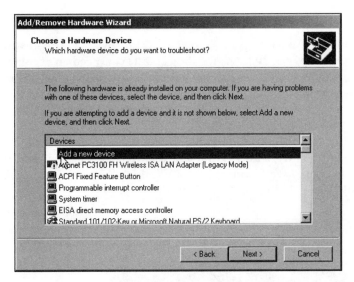

Figure 5-13   Adding a new device in Windows 2000 Server

6. Click **No, I want to select the hardware from a list**. Click **Next**.

7. Scroll through the list to view what types of hardware can be installed.

8. Click **Printers**. Click **Next**.

9. Use the default port selection, which is LTP1 Printer Port and click **Next**.

10. Select **HP** as the Manufacturer and **HP Color LaserJet** as the Printer. Click **Next**.

11. Provide a name for the printer, such as your initials plus "TestPrinter."

12. Click **No** so this is not used as a default printer (the printer that software on this computer defaults to for printing documents). Click **Next**.

13. Make sure that **Do not share this printer** is selected. (Note that this is where you could choose to share the printer with others on the network.) Click **Next**.

14. Normally you would select Yes to print a test page, but because you may not have an HP Color LaserJet actually connected to your computer for this project, click **No**. Click **Next**.

15. Review your printer settings and click **Finish**.

16. Close Control Panel.

Project 5-2

In this project, you use the Add Hardware Wizard in **Windows XP** (**Professional** and **Home**) and in **Windows Server 2003**. As for Project 5-1, you need an account that has Administrator privileges. And, your computer should not have newly installed hardware, so that you can manually practice the full range of steps.

To add hardware and install drivers using the Add Hardware Wizard:

1. In Windows XP (Professional or Home using Category View) click **Start**, click **Control Panel**, click **Printers and Other Hardware**, and click the **Add Hardware** link in the left pane (see Figure 5-14). In Windows Server 2003, click **Start**, point to **Control Panel**, and click **Add Hardware**.

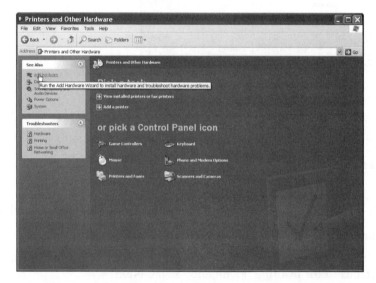

Figure 5-14   Starting the Add Hardware Wizard in Windows XP

2. Click **Next** after the Wizard starts. What does the wizard do at this point?

3. Click **Yes, I have already connected the hardware**. Click **Next**.

4. Scroll through the list of hardware that is already installed and record some examples.

5. Click **Add a new hardware device**. Click **Next**. What options do you see? Record your observations.

6. Select **Install the hardware that I manually select from a list (Advanced)**. Click **Next**.

7. Click **Printers** (see Figure 5-15). Click **Next**.

8. Use the default port selection, which is LTP1: (Recommended Printer Port), and click **Next**.

Figure 5-15   Adding a Printer in Windows XP

9. Select **HP** as the Manufacturer and **HP Color LaserJet** as the Printer. Click **Next**.

10. Notice that you can select whether or not to use this printer as the default printer. For this project (because it is practice and your system may already have a preferred default printer), select **No**. Click **Next**.

11. In Windows Server 2003, provide a name for the printer, such as your initials plus "TestPrinter." Click **Next**.

12. Make sure that **Do not share this printer** is selected. (Note that this is where you could choose to share the printer with others on the network.) Click **Next**.

13. Normally you would select Yes to print a test page, but because you may not have an HP Color LaserJet actually connected to your computer for this project, click **No**. Click **Next**.

14. Review your printer settings and click **Finish**. Close any open windows, such as the Printers and Other Hardware window in Windows XP.

Project 5-3

In this project, you use Device Manager to view where to install or update a driver in **Windows 2000/XP/Server 2003**. You also use this utility to determine if a device is working properly and to view the resources used by a device.

To use Device Manager:

1. In Windows 2000, right-click **My Computer** on the desktop and click **Manage**. In Windows XP and Windows Server 2003, click **Start**, right-click **My Computer**, and click **Manage**.

2. Click **Device Manager** in the left pane (tree) under Computer Management (Local) and System Tools (see Figure 5-16).

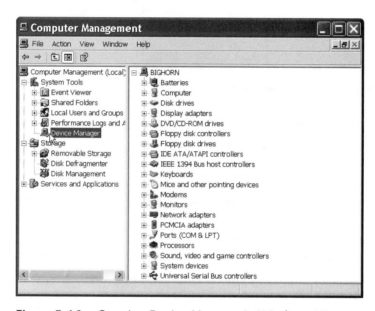

Figure 5-16   Opening Device Manager in Windows XP

3. Double-click **Display adapters**.

4. Double-click the specific adapter under Display adapters.

5. Make sure that the General tab is displayed. What is the device status of the display adapter? How would you troubleshoot the device?

6. Click the **Driver** tab (see Figure 5-17). Notice that you can use the Update Driver button to either install a driver if one is not already installed or to obtain an updated driver. Also, the Roll Back Driver button (not available in Windows 2000) goes back to a previously installed driver if there is a problem with updating a driver. And, you can use the Uninstall button to remove a driver.

Figure 5-17   Viewing driver information in Windows XP

7. Click the **Driver Details** button. How many driver files are used for this device? In what folder (or folders) are the driver files?

8. Click **OK**.

9. Click the **Resources** tab. What IRQ line (Interrupt Request in the window) is used by the device, and are there any reported conflicts?

10. Click **Cancel** and then close the Computer Management window.

Project 5-4

Driver signing helps ensure that the device drivers you use are compatible with Windows operating systems and enables you to avoid unauthorized drivers or ones that are out of date. Many users set driver signing at the warning level or at the level to prevent unsigned drivers from being installed. In this project, you set driver signing at the Block level in **Windows 2000/XP/Server 2003**, which prevents an unsigned driver from being installed. You need to use an account with Administrator privileges.

To configure driver signing:

1. In Windows 2000, click **Start**, point to **Settings**, click **Control Panel**, and double-click **System**. In Windows XP, click **Start**, click **Control Panel** (using Category View), click **Performance and Maintenance**, and click **System**. In Windows Server 2003, click **Start**, point to **Control Panel**, and click **System**.

2. Click the **Hardware** tab and click **Driver Signing** (see Figure 5-18).

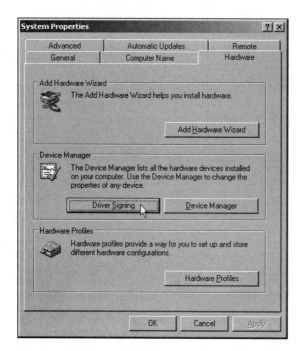

Figure 5-18   Accessing driver signing in Windows Server 2003

3. What options are available for driver signing? How can you make the option that you select apply to all users who log on to the operating system and attempt to install software? Record your observations.

4. In Windows 2000/XP, click **Block – Never install unsigned driver software** if this option is not already selected. In Windows Server 2003, click **Block – Prevent installation of unsigned files**, if this is not already selected.

5. Click **OK** in the Driver Signing Options dialog box.

6. Click **OK** in the System Properties dialog box.

7. Close any open windows, such as Control Panel in Windows 2000 or the Performance and Maintenance window in Windows XP.

HANDS-ON PROJECTS

Project 5-5

As you learned earlier, in many UNIX/Linux systems, the device special files are contained in the */dev* folder. In this project, you examine the contents of that folder using **Red Hat Enterprise Linux 3.0** (the same command can be used in many versions of UNIX/Linux).

To view the files in the */dev* folder:

1. Access the command line, such as by clicking **Main Menu**, pointing to **System Tools**, and clicking **Terminal** in Red Hat Enterprise Linux.

2. Type **ls /dev | more** and press **Enter**. (The more command enables you to view the file listing a screen at a time.) Figure 5-19 illustrates the first screen of the listing of files.

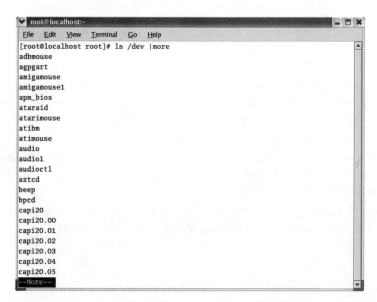

Figure 5-19   Viewing device special files in Red Hat Enterprise Linux

3. Press the **spacebar** to scroll through each screen and record examples of files that you see on your system. (Note that you can press q at any time to exit the listing and go back to the command prompt.)

4. If you are using the command prompt from a terminal window, type **exit** and press **Enter** to close the window.

Project 5-6

Devices and their associated device drivers are often managed in **NetWare** through the use of NLMs. In this project, you view the NLMs loaded on a server. You need access to the System Console for this project (ask your instructor for help accessing the System Console).

To view the loaded NLMs:

1. At the System Console, type **modules** and press **Enter**.

2. Notice the modules that are loaded and record some of the modules you see listed.

NOTE

The command to load a module is LOAD plus the name of the module (or you can simply type the name of the module). To unload a module, use the UNLOAD command plus the name of the module. You might unload a module, for example, when you want to configure a specific device and then reload the module to configure it.

Project 5-7

Many of us never view or change the configuration settings for our computer's keyboard. However, whether you are using a standard keyboard or an enhanced version, such as a Microsoft Natural Keyboard, configuration software is readily available to you. In this project, you view the keyboard settings in **Windows 2000/XP/Server 2003**.

To view basic keyboard configuration settings:

1. In Windows 2000, click **Start**, point to **Settings**, and click **Control Panel**. In Windows XP, click **Start** and click **Control Panel** (using Category View). And, in Windows Server 2003, click **Start** and point to **Control Panel**.

2. In Windows 2000, double-click the **Keyboard** icon to open the Keyboard dialog box. In Windows XP, click **Printers and Other Hardware**, and click **Keyboard**. In Windows Server 2003, click **Keyboard**. What tabs are available for your keyboard? What options do you see on each tab?

3. Click **Cancel** and close any open Windows, such as the Printers and Other Hardware window in Windows XP and Control Panel in Windows 2000.

Project 5-8

Just as you can configure the settings for your keyboard, you can also configure them for a mouse. In this project, you view the settings available for your mouse in **Windows 2000/XP/Server 2003**.

To view the settings you can change for your mouse:

1. In Windows 2000, click **Start**, point to **Settings**, and click **Control Panel**. In Windows XP, click **Start** and click **Control Panel** (using Category View). And, in Windows Server 2003, click **Start** and point to **Control Panel**.

2. In Windows 2000, double-click the **Mouse**. In Windows XP using Category View, click **Printers and Other Hardware**, and click **Mouse**. In Windows Server 2003, click **Mouse**. What tabs are available for your mouse?

3. Click each tab to view the properties you can set.

4. Click **Cancel** and close any open Windows, such as the Printers and Other Hardware window in Windows XP and Control Panel in Windows 2000.

Project 5-9

Mouse hardware is fairly standard, even between very inexpensive models and high-end devices. For the most part the mouse just works. However, a mechanical mouse does require periodic cleaning. In this project, you examine a mechanical mouse and clean it.

To view basic mouse hardware design and clean mechanical parts:

1. Turn over the mouse.

2. Notice the plastic ring or cover around the mouse ball. In most cases, it is marked with clockwise and counterclockwise arrows.

3. Apply pressure on the cover in the direction the counterclockwise arrow points. The cover should slide a fraction of an inch to enable you to remove it.

4. Set the cover aside.

5. Place your hand over the bottom of the mouse and turn over the mouse. The mouse ball will fall into your hand. Set the ball aside.

6. Notice the internal components. You should see two horizontal rollers. In cheaper mice these are plastic. More expensive mice use stainless steel rollers. These connect to potentiometers that send mouse movement information to your operating system. A third roller is a tensioning device that helps keep the ball in place and rolling smoothly.

7. Is there any lint, hair, or other residue on any of these rollers? If so, that could explain why you have had difficulty positioning the mouse pointer accurately.

8. Use a soft rag or tissue and a little rubbing alcohol to clean the rollers.

9. Clean the ball by rubbing it with a soft cloth (rubbing the ball on your clothing works well as long as you don't use a sweater or other garment that might produce lint).

10. Turn over the mouse and drop the ball into the hole.

11. Set the cover in place, rotate it clockwise until it clicks, and reposition the mouse on its pad or your desktop.

HANDS-ON PROJECTS

Project 5-10

The Windows Add Printer Wizard works in similar fashion to the Add Hardware Wizard that you used in Hands-on Projects 5-1 and 5-2. This project uses the Add Printer Wizard in **Windows XP Home** or **Professional** to illustrate the Add Printer Wizard for comparison. You need access using an account that has Administrator privileges (but you don't need a printer actually attached to the computer). As you go through this project, compare the steps to those for Windows XP described in Hands-on Project 5-2, and record your general observations about the differences.

To use the Add Printer Wizard:

1. Click **Start** and click **Control Panel**.

2. Click **Printers and Other Hardware**.

3. Click **Add a printer**.

4. Click **Next** after the Add Printer Wizard starts.

5. Make sure that **Local printer attached to this computer** is selected. Also, for this project, uncheck **Automatically detect and install my Plug and Play printer**, if it is checked. Click **Next**.

6. Use the default port selection, which is LPT1: (Recommended Printer Port) as in Figure 5-20, and click **Next**.

Figure 5-20   Selecting a printer port in Windows XP

7. Select **Epson** as the Manufacturer and **Epson ActionLaser 1600** as the Printer. What button could you use to check for a more recent printer driver available through Microsoft? What button could you use to employ a driver from a CD-ROM or floppy disk provided by the manufacturer? Click **Next**.

8. Provide a name for the printer, such as your initials plus "EpsonPrinter." Also, click **No** so this is not designated as the default printer. Click **Next**.

9. For this project, click **Do not share this printer** (to set up a printer that will not be available to network users). Click **Next**.

10. Click **No** so that a test page is not printed (unless you have an Epson ActionLaser 1600 printer actually attached to the computer). Click **Next**.

11. Review the printer setup parameters and click **Finish**.

12. Close the Printers and Faxes window.

HANDS-ON PROJECTS

Project 5-11

The UNIX/Linux environment offers several kinds of tools for viewing and managing printer functions. In this project, you use the *printtool* utility in **Red Hat Enterprise Linux 3.0** to learn from where to configure a printer. Also, you employ the *lpc* command from the command line to view printers connected to your computer. Log on to the root account for this project.

To learn from where to configure a printer:

1. Start *printtool* in either of two ways: 1) click **Main Menu**, point to **System Settings**, and click **Printing** or 2) access the command prompt from a terminal window, type **printtool**, and press **Enter**.

2. Click **New**.

3. Click **Forward** on the Add a new print queue screen.

4. In the Name box enter your initials plus "printer," such as JPPrinter. Click **Forward**.

5. Open the **Select a queue type** box at the top of the dialog box to view the options. What options do you see?

6. Click **Locally connected**.

7. If you have a printer connected to the computer, you can click the **Rescan devices** button to detect it. If you do not have a printer connected, click the **Custom device** button and enter the device name. For example, for the device name specify /dev/lp0 if you are setting up a parallel printer or /dev/usblp0 for a USB printer. Click **OK**.

8. Make sure a device is selected, such as /dev/lp0, and click **Forward**.

9. In the Printer model dialog box, select **Text Only Printer** (for this project, or ask your instructor what to select if you have a printer actually attached). Click **Forward**.

10. Click **Apply**.

11. Click **No** so that a test page does not print (for this project), or if you have a printer connected, click **Yes**. You should now see the print queue name you entered in Step 4.

12. Close the Printer configuration window.

13. Click **Save**.

To find out the status of printers in Red Hat Linux (and many other UNIX systems):

1. Access the command line or a terminal window (in Red Hat Enterprise Linux, click **Main Menu**, point to **System Tools**, and click **Terminal**).

2. Type **lpc status** and press **Enter**. (Note that in some versions of UNIX/Linux you type *lpc status all* to view the status of all print queues.)

3. Printer and print queue information displays, as shown in Figure 5-21.

Figure 5-21   Viewing printer and print queue information in Red Hat Enterprise Linux

4. If you opened a terminal window, type **exit** and press **Enter** to close it.

Project 5-12

In this project, you learn how to start the **Mac OS X version 10.3** Printer Setup Utility to install a printer. (This project is intended for practice using Print Center without requiring you to have a printer connected.)

To install a printer using the Printer Setup Utility:

1. Click the **Go** menu and click **Utilities**.

2. Double-click **Printer Setup Utility**. Are any printers already installed?

3. Click the **Add** button.

4. Open the top box in the Printer List screen and scroll through the printer options. Record two or three options.

5. Click **USB**. Note that if you had a USB printer connected, you would now click Add to finish the installation steps. Also, if you were configuring a network printer, such as by using AppleTalk, you would click Add and the Printer Setup Utility would enable you to open System Preferences to configure AppleTalk network parameters if they are not already configured.

6. Click **Cancel**.

7. Click **Printer Setup Utility** on the menu at the top of the desktop and click **Quit Printer Setup Utility**.

8. Close the Utilities window.

To start the Printer Setup Utility from System Preferences, open System Preferences from the Dock (or by clicking Go, clicking Applications, and double-clicking System Preferences), double-click Print & Fax, and click the Set Up Printers button.

CASE PROJECTS

Hard Rock makes all types of hard candies that are sold worldwide. One of their specialties is making fruit flavored candies, such as papaya, guava, grapefruit, kiwi, orange, banana, watermelon, and many others. Hard Rock employs 328 people and makes extensive use of computers and networks in their business. Users in the business office have Windows XP Professional and Windows 2000 Professional computers. The candy kitchen staff all use Mac OS X, while the shipping unit prefers Red Hat Enterprise Linux (workstation or WS). The IT unit uses Red Hat Enterprise Linux WS for their own desktop computing needs as well as supporting eight Windows 2003 servers.

Case Project 5-1: Installing Printers in Windows XP Professional

The business office has just received 12 new laser printers for installation and wants you to train their printer support coordinator to install the printers, but only on computers running Windows XP Professional. Develop a set of instructions for installing the printers, using the Add Printer Wizard (because PnP is not supported for the printers). What other tool besides the Add Printer Wizard could they use? Note that these printers will not be shared over a network.

Case Project 5-2: Resolving a Hardware Installation Conflict in Windows XP Professional

Hard Rock's business manager has installed a new trackball to use with his portable computer that is running Windows XP Professional, and now there seems to be a conflict between the trackball and the touchpad on the portable. Explain the tool that he might use to solve the problem as well as how to use the tool to solve the problem.

Case Project 5-3: Checking the Printer Status for Troubleshooting in Red Hat Enterprise Linux

The shipping unit has a Red Hat Enterprise Linux computer to which they have connected three printers for different uses. One is a color laser printer, one is an ink-jet printer, and a third is a dot-matrix printer. They are having trouble with the laser printer and want to check its status. What tools might they use for this purpose in troubleshooting the problem and how do they use these tools?

Case Project 5-4: Reinstalling a Printer in Mac OS X

A cook in the candy kitchen is assigned to use a computer running Mac OS X. He needs to reinstall a printer on this computer because his supervisor uninstalled the printer to temporarily replace the broken printer attached to another computer used for inventory and supplies. Explain how to use the tool to reinstall the printer in Mac OS X.

Case Project 5-5: Setting Up a Fax Machine in Windows 2003 Server

The IT unit has been asked to connect a fax machine to a USB port on a Windows 2003 server. Explain two tools that they can use to set up the fax machine, including the general steps to start these tools.

6

USING AND CONFIGURING STORAGE DEVICES

After reading this chapter and completing the exercises, you will be able to:

♦ Understand basic disk drive interface technologies

♦ Compare the different types of CD-ROM and DVD storage

♦ Explain the differences between a storage area network (SAN) and network attached storage (NAS)

♦ Discuss various removable storage options

♦ Describe tape drive options and their advantages and disadvantages

♦ Briefly discuss storage management options in different operating systems

Regardless of what you do with your computer, you must be able to save information to disks or other storage devices so that all of your changes are not lost when your computer experiences a power failure, and so that you can make backup copies of important data. This chapter describes how major storage components work, how to install and configure them, and how various operating systems work with them.

DISK STORAGE OPTIONS

Storage devices are somewhat different from the input/output (I/O) devices discussed in the previous chapter, but they also are an integral part of a functioning computer system and its associated operating system. This section briefly discusses various storage technologies.

Today, most computer systems are supplied with a single 3½" floppy drive, perhaps a high-density floppy or Zip disk, one or more internal, fixed hard drives, and a CD-ROM or DVD drive. These storage devices are mounted in the computer case and connect to the computer hardware through the cable system.

NOTE

Many computer manufacturers are now selling computers without a floppy drive, but you can add a floppy drive to the system for an additional charge.

Floppy and hard disk drives along with CD-ROM and DVD drives include internal electronics and an interface to connect the drive to the computer. In modern computers, these devices may plug into the same bus interface card, which includes separate connectors and separate controllers that share some common components. The operating system acts as an interface between this controller and the rest of the computer. The operating system also provides services to application software that needs to read from and write to the drive. There are many controller designs. When they comply with the standards required by the operating system, what goes on inside the hard drive or the hard drive controller is not significant in terms of the user or the operating system.

Hard Drive Interfaces

The most popular hard drive interface in the Intel PC architecture is the **Integrated Drive Electronics (IDE)** interface. **Enhanced IDE (EIDE)** supports higher transfer speeds and is found in most modern PCs, although sometimes the interface is still referred to as simply IDE. This interface is often built into the main board (mother board) of the computer, or it is otherwise present in the form of an interface card. A single IDE interface can support two devices, one so-called **master** (the first or main drive) and one **slave** (secondary storage device). The cable usually has three 40-pin header connectors. One connector plugs into the IDE card or into the appropriate connector on the main board. The other two can be used to connect to the IDE devices. Figure 6-1 shows two IDE cables with master and slave connections.

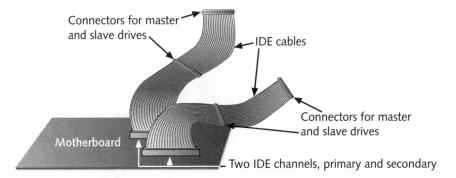

Figure 6-1   IDE cables with connectors

IDE has many subtypes that control the speed of data transfers between the devices and the computer. An advantage of IDE is that the controller and the devices are able to determine which of the various substandards they support, and normally, you, as the user, do not have to worry about the details. Today's computer systems generally include dual EIDE controllers, usually built into the system motherboard. The primary controller interfaces the boot drive to the system. The secondary controller may be used for a CD-ROM drive, a second hard disk, DVD drive, and so on.

Another type of drive interface, which can be used on all PC platforms mentioned in this book, is the Small Computer System Interface (SCSI) introduced in the last chapter. SCSI is a relatively fast interface, and it tends to be more expensive than IDE. Each SCSI interface can support up to 8 or 16 devices (including the controller), depending on the type of SCSI. The disks or other SCSI devices are connected to each other and to the controller by a single cable. Each end of the cable must be electrically terminated to prevent echoes and ghost signals on the cable. Either a disk drive or an external terminator typically terminates the other end of the chain. Figure 6-2 shows an example of a SCSI configuration.

Advances in the SCSI industry have resulted in several enhancements. These include the Ultra SCSI, wide Ultra SCSI, Ultra2 SCSI, wide Ultra2 SCSI, Ultra3 SCSI (Ultra160), and now the Ultra320 SCSI, which is the seventh generation of SCSI technology. It transfers at a rate of 320 Mbps, has a 16-bit bus, handles 16 devices, and is especially well positioned for servers and network storage.

Serial Attached SCSI is the latest in SCSI technology and it supports up to 4032 devices per port. It is a high-speed technology with initial speeds in the 3 Gbps range. Information on current developments in the SCSI industry can be found at the SCSI Trade Associations Web page at *www.scsita.org*.

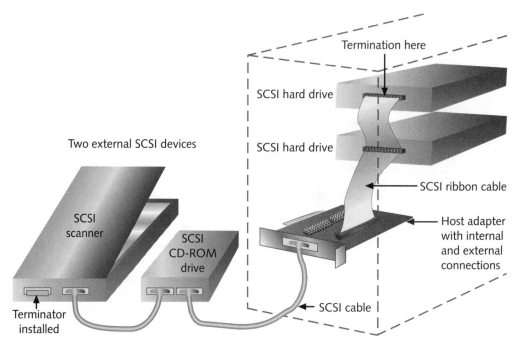

Figure 6-2   SCSI configuration

NOTE

It is important to make sure each device connected to the SCSI has a unique address, with the first device addressed as 0. Problems occur if two devices have the same address. Also, when troubleshooting SCSI problems, make sure that the SCSI cable is properly terminated at both ends. Omitting the cable terminator at the last device in the daisy chain is a common problem when connecting several devices to one SCSI adapter. If your operating system experiences difficulty recognizing SCSI devices, check to make sure the terminator is connected to the last device on the SCSI cable.

The number of platters, heads, tracks, and sectors per track varies widely from hard disk to hard disk. This information is often stored in an area of non-volatile memory in the computer. In addition, many operating systems keep a table somewhere on the disk that describes the disk in great detail. EIDE and SCSI provide ways for the controllers to communicate with the electronics on the disk, which enables the controllers to retrieve this information. However, this exchange of information does not always work correctly, and it is a good idea to have the information about a disk on hand. This data is known as the **disk geometry**. Try Hands-on Project 6-4 to view the properties of a Windows XP hard drive, and try Project 6-11 to use the Windows XP System Information utility to study your hard drive configuration.

Storage capacity of a single hard disk can be a few megabytes to hundreds of gigabytes. Hard disks are fast and allow the user to store large amounts of data and programs. In many computers, they are used to store the operating system, the application software, and all the data.

Because of the delicate mechanisms inside the disk, it is not uncommon for a hard disk to fail. Hard disks seem stable, and many users do not make copies of data stored on hard disks. As a result, hard disk failures are often catastrophic for a user or an organization. Backing up data contained on hard disks is an essential practice. Hands-on Project 6-3 shows you how to use the Windows XP/Windows Server 2003 Backup Utility Wizard.

Universal Serial Bus (USB) and FireWire interfaces can also be used to connect hard drives and storage devices to computers. This technology was discussed in Chapter 5 as it related to I/O devices, but it also can be used to hook up storage devices.

Basic and Dynamic Disks

A **basic disk** is a physical hard drive. It contains primary partitions, extended partitions, or logical drives which are known as basic volumes. Basic volumes are only available on basic disks. Partitions and drives were discussed in Chapter 3.

Beginning with Windows 2000 and included in Windows XP Professional and Windows Server 2003, the concept of **dynamic disks** was introduced. With dynamic disks you can create volumes that span multiple disks. Fault tolerant volumes are also supported. Similiar to basic disks, volumes on dynamic disks are referred to as dynamic volumes. Dynamic disks make it possible to set up to 2000 dynamic volumes on one disk, but Microsoft recommends 32 or less volumes per disk. Dynamic disks also have the ability to extend volumes onto additional physical disks. You can convert basic disks to dynamic disks by using the Disk Management tool. Hands-on Project 6-5 takes you through the steps to convert a basic disk to a dynamic disk.

RAID Arrays

Although hard disks can store large amounts of data and are relatively fast and fairly reliable, there is room for improvement on all three points. To address some of these issues, a group of researchers at the University of California in Berkeley introduced the concept of a **redundant array of inexpensive disks (RAID)** to use multiple disks in a storage array. They defined various levels of RAID technology; a brief discussion follows. (A more detailed discussion of RAID levels is found in Chapter 10.)

RAID arrays serve three purposes: increased reliability, increased storage capacity, and increased speed. Different levels of RAID focus on different purposes, and there is no RAID level that can be declared superior for all situations. Because RAID array implementation tends to be costly, they are used primarily on network servers, with network operating systems (NOSs).

RAID is implemented as a combination of hardware and software. The hardware can consist of simply a few hard disks connected to one controller, or something as complicated as a very large set of hard disks connected to several disk controllers equipped with processors to assist in running RAID software. The RAID software is typically a low-level device driver that works with any RAID hardware and provides an interface to the operating system to provide access to the special RAID features offered. Some systems are presented to the operating system as if they were simple drives; the RAID hardware interacts with the OS as if it were a hard disk. Try Hands-on Project 6-1 to find out more about RAID options.

CD-ROM AND DVD

Two more recent storage options are based on optical rather than magnetic technology: the **compact disc read-only memory (CD-ROM)** and its newer sibling, the **digital video disc (DVD)**.

Compact Disc (CD) Technology

CD-ROMs are very important in today's operating system environment because most software and documentation are distributed on these media. CDs are also increasingly being used to back up and store data. These disks are different from floppies and hard disks for many reasons, including the way data is stored. Instead of using a system of tracks and sectors like floppy and hard disks, CD-ROMs use a big "spiral" that starts at the inside of the disc and winds itself slowly toward the outside of the disc (see Figure 6-3). Whenever data is needed from the disc, a laser pickup is pointed at a part of the disc surface.

Figure 6-3   How data is stored on a CD

For additional technical information on how CDs work, visit *www.pcguide.com/ref/cd/index.htm*.

TIP

When a disc is read, laser light is emitted by the CD-ROM head and reflected off the disc surface onto an optical pickup. The surface of the disc is covered with little indents or "pits," which shift the position of the reflected laser light as it is returned to the pickup. Depending on the size of the pits, ones or zeroes are returned. You are probably familiar with the

CD-ROM disc itself, a silverish disc about four inches in diameter. The surface of the CD-ROM reflects light during a data read operation. Although CD-ROM discs are extremely reliable, the large number of dents make this surface very sensitive to scratches and other kinds of damage that can hinder optical readout.

Because it is almost inevitable that the CD-ROM surface will become damaged through frequent use, the CD-ROM drive and disc are equipped with extensive mechanisms to protect the user from critical data errors. The data on the CD-ROM has **cyclical redundancy check (CRC)** bits encoded in it as other disks do, and it also has error-correction bits encoded on the disc. As long as there is not too much damage to the disc surface, the reading mechanism will recover from reading errors. Although the CD-ROM is one of the more delicate media, its built-in error detection and correction make it one of the most reliable.

About 650 MB of data can be stored per disc. CD-ROMs are single-sided discs. The rotational speeds of CD-ROM drives range from as little as twice the normal audio speed, or 2X, to as high as 72 times that speed (72X). High-speed CD-ROM drives can reach data transfer rates of several megabytes per second, some as much as about 10 MB. This kind of performance is very close to what you would expect from some hard disks, but in most practical situations, CD-ROM drives appear to be a lot slower.

Digital Video Disc (DVD) Technology

The digital video disc, also referred to as digital versatile disc, or DVD, works a lot like the CD-ROM. It is also an optical drive, and it has the data written on the disc in the form of a spiral of blocks. All data is read from the disc with the use of a laser and an optical pickup. The storage capacity and data transfer rate of a DVD are much higher than a CD-ROM, but the size of the disc is the same. Almost all DVD drives can read CD-ROMs and DVDs. There is a physical similarity between the DVD and CD-ROM discs and drives.

The DVD can have two sides with up to two layers per side. All data on a hard disk, floppy disk, or CD-ROM is stored on one layer of material. On the CD-ROM, when laser light hits the layer, it is reflected. On a DVD, the same thing happens, but in addition to the first layer, which is a spiral that moves from the middle of the disc to the outside like a conventional CD-ROM, the DVD has a second layer. This layer is read by using light that hits the disk at a different angle. The second layer is also a spiral, this one written from the outside of the disk to the inside. Each side of a DVD may contain up to two layers, and each layer can hold 4.7 GB of data. The result: on each DVD, you can store roughly 17 GB of data. The trend toward more graphics and multimedia as part of operating systems and application programs is certain to continue the popularity of the DVD format.

TIP

Look for much more DVD software in all forms in the future. DVD is fast enough to run applications directly from the DVD disc as you would from a hard disk. This could change the way application software is used, and it may significantly increase the number of applications at your disposal at any given time.

Recordable and Rewritable CD and DVD

For some time it has been possible to record and rewrite CD-ROMs using compact disc-recordable (CD-R) and compact disc-rewritable (CD-RW) devices. You can also record and rewrite DVD-ROMs using several technologies (see Table 6-1). CD-R, digital video disc-recordable (DVD-R), and digital video disc+recordable (DVD+R) can record data once on the media, and then it can be read many times. CD-RW, digital video disc-rewritable (DVD-RW), and digital video disc+rewritable (DVD+RW) can write on the media thousands of times.

Table 6-1   DVD devices

DVD Device	Description
DVD-ROM	Read-only device. A DVD-ROM drive can also read CD-ROMs.
DVD-R	DVD recordable. Uses a similar technology to CD-R drives. Can read DVD-ROM discs.
DVD-RAM	Recordable and erasable. Multifunctional DVD device that can read DVD-RAM, DVD-R, DVD-ROM, and CD-R discs.
DVD-RW or DVD-ER	Rewritable DVD device, also known as erasable, recordable device. Media can be read by most DVD-ROM drives.
DVD+RW	A technology similar to and currently competing with DVD-RW. Can read DVD-ROM and CD-ROM discs but it is not compatible with DVD-RAM discs.

As you might be able to tell from the number of different DVD types, the industry's inability to agree on DVD standards has been a challenge. The main group developing these standards is the DVD Forum. High Definition–Digital Video Disk (HD-DVD), developed to meet the needs of the HDTV technology, has the ability to store up to 27 GB of data or the equivalent of approximately 13 hours of regular TV or 2 hours of HDTV. A couple of vendors have demonstrated 50 GB models.

CD-ROM and DVD-ROM Interfaces

CD-ROM and DVD-ROM drives are typically connected to the computer using a hard disk interface. Many PCs use the EIDE interface with SCSI as a close second. Because these discs have a distinctively different organization from hard disks, typically an operating system requires a special driver to read from them. The latest PCs have drivers for CD-ROM and DVD-ROM drives built into the read only memory (ROM) basic input/output system

(BIOS), which allows them to use the drives without special drivers. This enables these machines to boot an operating system directly from a CD-ROM or DVD-ROM. Mac OS, Windows NT 4.0/2000/XP/Server 2003, and many flavors of UNIX can boot an operating system directly from the CD-ROM or DVD-ROM for initial installation.

Connecting Drives

All of the drives discussed in this chapter connect to the computer in much the same way as hard disks, typically through an EIDE or SCSI interface, or a USB or FireWire port. The drivers needed for these drives are often quite specialized, so it is important to make sure you have the drivers required for the operating system with which you want the drives to function. Do not assume that any drive can be used with any operating system. Always make sure the drive you wish to use is supported by your operating system.

6

NETWORK STORAGE

Many organizations today are dealing with massive amounts of data, whether from e-commerce transactions, corporate databases, or other applications with lots of data, and they need a method to manage this data. Backups, disaster recovery, and availability of data are just a few of the reasons organizations have turned to **storage area networks (SANs)** or **network attached storage (NAS)**.

SAN technology directly connects servers and storage systems without sending data over the corporate network. This is accomplished by tying the servers and storage systems together via a switched, full-duplex (data goes in both directions at the same time) **Fibre Channel** connection. All data transfer between the servers and storage systems takes place on the Fibre Channel. The Fibre Channel runs between 1 Gbps and 2 Gbps, with 4 Gbps and 10 Gbps in the works. Figure 6-4 shows a configuration for a SAN.

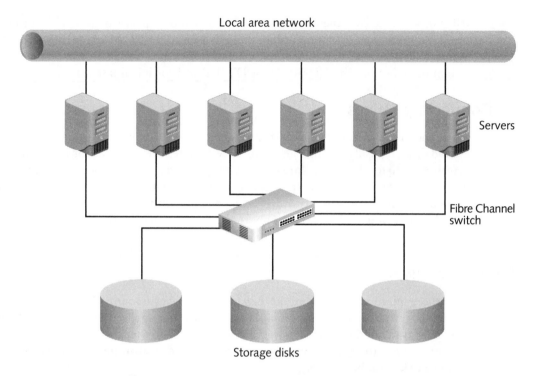

Figure 6-4   Storage area network (SAN)

A NAS is a way to directly attach storage to a local area network (LAN). NAS devices may work with multiple operating systems like UNIX/Linux, Microsoft Windows, Netware, and Mac OS. This allows most clients to access the storage on the network. Transmission Control Protocol/Internet Protocol (TCP/IP), Internet Packet Exchange/Sequence Packet Exchange (IPX/SPX), and AppleTalk are three of the protocols that many NAS vendors support. A NAS is different from a SAN in that the servers communicate with the storage over the LAN rather than a Fibre Channel connection. Figure 6-5 shows an example of a NAS setup.

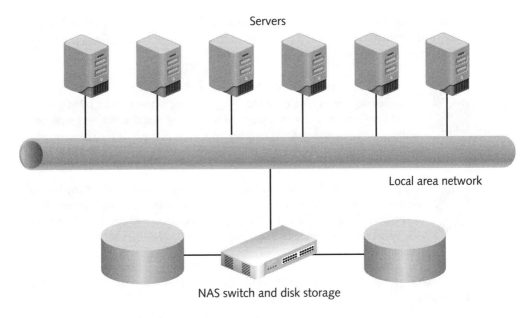

Figure 6-5   Network attached storage (NAS)

REMOVABLE DISKS AND MOBILE STORAGE

Removable disks, in most cases, are hard disks with a twist. These also come in many shapes, sizes, and formats, and we will briefly take a look at some of the more popular drives and disks available today. The first type of drives are those that use flexible magnetic disks, such as Iomega **Zip disks**. The second group consists of drives that use hard platters, much like a hard disk. Castlewood's ORB drives are examples of these technologies.

Removable Large-Capacity Floppy Drives

The Zip disk is addressed by the system like a hard disk, and offers a storage capacity of 100, 250, or 750 MB. Zip drives are available in both external and internal varieties with printer port, SCSI, EIDE, or USB connections. The newest generation of external Zip drives has a port that connects to a printer port, a SCSI port, or a USB port. It automatically adapts to the port to which it is connected. The disk consists of a cartridge that contains a magnetic disk. The medium is much like a floppy, and the size is similar to a 3½" floppy. When connected to a native disk interface such as SCSI, EIDE, or USB, most operating systems do not need any special drivers to use a Zip drive. It is generally recognized as another hard disk connected to the system.

There are, however, special drivers for the Zip drive, which enable some additional functions. As is generally the case with removable drives, some of the features the special drivers offer are related to change notification. This means that the operating system is notified when the disk is inserted or removed. More advanced operating systems typically store some information about the disk in memory. It may be as little as the table of contents, or as much as some of the data stored on the disk.

If the operating system is not told when a disk is swapped, the results can be rather disastrous. For example, the operating system could blindly write data to an area on a disk that it assumes is empty, but if a disk was swapped without the operating system being notified, some of the data may be damaged beyond repair.

It is possible to use Zip drives with many operating systems without any special drivers, but it is not recommended, particularly with operating systems that cache part of the disk, such as Mac OS X, UNIX/Linux, Windows 95, Windows 98, Windows Me, Windows NT, Windows 2000, Windows XP, and Windows Server 2003.

Zip drives are available for many platforms. Some commercial computers, even some laptops, now have a built-in Zip drive.

You can connect Zip drives to a computer's printer or USB port, which is a great feature. In many cases, a Zip disk can hold enough information to install an entire operating system from one disk. This is convenient for fixing problems on computers that do not have a CD-ROM drive. In addition, disks that connect to the printer or USB port can be easily connected and disconnected, and used on more than one computer.

The price you pay for connecting to the parallel port versus the USB port is speed. When connected to the printer port, the speed at which the disk can be accessed is greatly reduced. Throughput may go down to as little as 140 Kbps. In addition, much of the central processing unit (CPU) time may be used in making the drive work.

Removable Rigid Cartridges

The second class of removable disks have a disk made out of a solid material inside the cartridge, much like the platters found in a hard disk. The heads in these systems, much like the heads in a hard disk, are not in contact with the disk surface. Instead, they float above the surface at a very close distance. This has some advantages and some disadvantages. A very big advantage is that there is no mechanical contact between the heads and the disk, which means that both the heads and the disk last a lot longer. They suffer no wear and tear from the read/write head. A big disadvantage is that it is not easy to make a head float very close to a platter in a system where the platter is in a removable cartridge.

Castlewood Systems, Inc. makes the ORB 2.2 GB and the ORB 5.7 GB drives. The ORB drives come in EIDE, SCSI, USB, and FireWire models. These drives are used for applications that require the storage of large amounts of data.

From the Trenches...

At a college teaching Microsoft Certification classes, students needed to load several different server operating systems on the lab computers. The challenge was to find a way to allow multiple classes to use the same set of computers. The ORB drive was a solution. Each student purchased an ORB disk and used it to load the operating system. When class was over for the day, the student ejected the disk and took it home. The next student using that computer would insert his or her own disk into the drive and continue on from their last class session. The students could purchase multiple disks so they had one for each operating system.

Mini USB Drives

Several companies produce mini or thumb drives that plug into a USB port on your computer. These drives don't require additional drivers and are recognized by Plug and Play (PnP) operating systems. Thumb drives come in sizes ranging from 64 MB to 1 GB or more with transfer speeds of 3 to 9 Mbps. They are very handy for easily moving information from computer to computer. Vendors manufacturing this type of drive include Iomega, Lexar, SanDisk, Sony, and others. Most vendors support the Windows, Mac, and Linux operating systems. Many of the newer computer cases have one or more USB ports on the front panel to facilitate using these drives and other USB devices like digital cameras.

From the Trenches...

A college student used computers in several of her classes, and used a mini USB drive to store her class work and transport it to her home computer. At home, she was able to plug the USB drive into her computer and continue working on her assignments. She was able to transport her files easily between several campus computers and her home computer.

Table 6-2 shows some of the major storage devices and their respective capacities.

Table 6-2 Storage media capacities

Storage Medium	Capacity
Castlewood ORB	2.2 or 5.7 GB
CD-ROM	650 MB
CD-R	650 MB
CD-RW	650 MB
DVD-ROM	4.7, 8.5, 9.4, or 17 GB
DVD-R	4.7 GB

Table 6-2 Storage media capacities (continued)

Storage Medium	Capacity
DVD-RW	4.7 GB
DVD+RW	4.7 GB
Iomega Zip disk	100, 250, or 750 MB
Mini USB drive	64 MB to 1 GB

TAPE DRIVES

Tape backup systems have traditionally been the choice for backing up large amounts of data. They are relatively inexpensive and can hold large amounts of data. The disadvantage of tapes is that they use serial access, which means that to access a piece of information, you have to search through all the material on the tape that precedes the item. This is in contrast to hard disks, CD-ROMs, and DVDs, which use direct access to go directly to the piece of information you want. Thus tape drives are most popular for long-term storage such as backups. With the size of disk drives growing to the tens of gigabytes, there is a constant need to develop tape drives that will store more and more data on a single tape. The following sections briefly describe four main types of tape drive systems. Table 6-3 lists tape media and their capacity.

Table 6-3 Tape media capacities

Tape Medium	Capacity
Digital audio tape (DAT)	2 GB to 72 GB
Digital linear tape (DLT)	10 GB to 80 GB
Super digital linear tape (SDLT)	160 GB to 2.4 TB
Advanced intelligent tape (AIT)	35 GB to 1.3 TB
Linear tape open (LTO)	160 GB to 1.6 TB

DAT Drives

Digital audio tape (DAT) drives use a 4-mm tape. The most common is the digital data storage (DDS) format. The first DDS standard had a capacity of 2 GB. The current standard is DDS-4 at 20 GB (40 GB compressed) or DDS-5 which has a storage capacity of 36 GB (72 GB compressed). The DDS format standard is backward-compatible so you can, for example, upgrade to a DDS-4 tape drive and still read the DDS-3 tapes.

DLT and SDLT Drives

Digital linear tape (DLT) drives use half-inch wide magnetic tapes to record the data. These tapes record data in tracks that run the whole length of the tape. Each tape contains 128 or 208 tracks and the data is recorded on the first track from beginning to end of the tape. Then the tape is reversed and the data is written from the end to the beginning. This continues until all the tracks are full. Using this track system with high-speed search capability, a file can be found in about 45 seconds on an average tape of 20 GB. DLT-III tapes start at 10 GB (20 GB compressed) and go up to DLT-IV tapes which have a storage capacity of 40 GB (80 GB compressed). DLT tape drives are used in many automated tape backup systems.

Super digital linear tape (SDLT) drives use both magnetic and optical recording methods. This along with laser technology more accurately writes the data to the tape and allows for greater density of information. The SDLT 320 drive starts at 160 GB of data (320 GB compressed). The next generation of drives will be the SDLT 640 with 320 GB of data (640 GB compressed) and should be available in 2004. The SDLT 1280 is scheduled for 2005 with 640 GB of data recording (1.28 TB compressed), and the SDLT 2400 with 1.2 TB of data (2.4 TB compressed) is scheduled to be released in late 2006 or 2007.

AIT and S-AIT Drives

Advanced intelligent tape (AIT) drives were first introduced in 1996 and are used mainly in midrange servers. The tapes for this drive have an erasable memory chip inside the cartridge that stores the information normally written at the beginning of a tape. This provides the information necessary to fast forward and pinpoint the desired information. The AIT drives started out with a capacity of 35/90 GB (native/compressed) of recorded data. Today the **super advanced intelligent tape (S-AIT)** has a capacity of 500 GB/1.3 TB and is good for 500,000 hours.

LTO Drives

The **linear tape open (LTO)** drive is most widely accepted in the high-end server market. The Ultrium format has a 100 GB cartridge with a 16 Mbps data transfer rate. Future plans call for a capacity of 1.6 TB with a transfer rate of 320 Mbps.

WINDOWS REMOVABLE STORAGE OPTIONS

Microsoft introduced the Removable Storage system in Windows 2000. The Removable Storage system tracks removable storage media such as tapes, CD-ROMs, DVD-ROMs, optical disks, and even high-capacity disk drives, which might be contained in changers and jukeboxes. Applications such as backup software manage the actual data stored on these removable media. Removable Storage provides the mechanism for multiple applications to share the same media. All applications using the Removable Storage system must run on the same computer.

Figure 6-6 shows the Removable Storage section under Computer Management in Windows 2000.

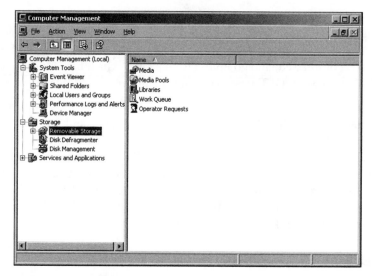

Figure 6-6   Removable Storage in Windows 2000

STORAGE MANAGEMENT TOOLS

This section covers some of the operating system tools and commands used to manage storage devices. Also, you will find step-by-step instructions for using some of these tools in the end-of-chapter Hands-on Projects.

Windows 2000/XP/Server 2003

Windows Disk Management snap-in is a tool used to view and manage the hard disks associated with a computer. You can create partitions, format those partitions with the FAT, FAT32, or NTFS file systems, delete partitions, and so on. Chapter 3 introduced the *fdisk, chkdsk,* and *format* commands along with the file system options FAT16, FAT32, and NTFS. Figure 6-7 shows using the Disk Management snap-in to format a partition called drive D: for the NTFS file system.

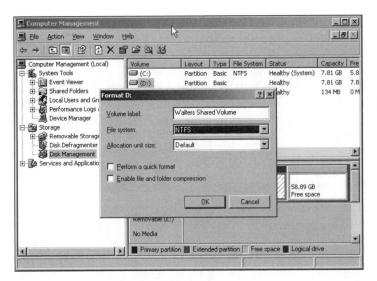

Figure 6-7   Formatting a partition in Windows Server 2003

You can also convert basic disks to dynamic disks using the Windows Disk Management snap-in tool. Hands-on Project 6-5 shows you how to do this.

Other storage management tools that you might find useful are the Disk Defragmenter (Hands-On Project 6-2 shows how to defragment a disk in Windows Server 2003), the Event Viewer, and the Performance Logs and Alerts. You can go to Start, Administrative Tools, and Computer Management to see what is available. Click on several of these to see what is available. You can right-click on the item and then click Help to see a description of each one.

To see which devices are installed on a Windows XP/Server 2003, and how they are configured, you can use the Device Manager in the System applet in the Control Panel, as shown in Hands-on Project 6-9.

UNIX/Linux

Three common command-line utilities for managing, formatting, and partitioning disks on UNIX/Linux system are *fdisk*, *format*, *sfdisk*, and *cfdisk*. You learned about *fdisk* and *format* in Chapter 3. *sfdisk* and *cfdisk* are utilities that enable you to verify partitions, list information about partitions, such as the size of a partition, and to repartition a disk. Red Hat Enterprise Linux 3.0 offers both *fdisk* and *sfdisk*, but not *format* or *cfdisk*. Hands-on Project 6-6 shows you how to view partitions in Red Hat Enterprise Linux 3.0.

Further, UNIX/Linux systems offer the *mount* command-line utility, introduced in Chapter 3, to mount a file system so that you can use a disk partition, CD-ROM drive, or floppy drive. Normally, when you boot UNIX/Linux, the main file systems are mounted as part of the boot process, such as the ext3 file system in Linux. However, you may need to manually mount file systems for CD-ROM or floppy drives. For example, to mount a CD-ROM drive you would use the following command:

mount -t iso9660 /dev/cdrom /mnt/cdrom

The "-t iso9660" portion of the command mounts the iso9660 (CD-ROM) file system. Further, this command mounts the device, /dev/cdrom, to the mount point, /mnt/cdrom, so that after the CD-ROM file system is mounted, you can view its files by viewing the contents of /mnt/cdrom.

In another example, you can mount a floppy disk by using the command:

mount -t vfat /dev/fd0 /mnt/floppy

In this example, you mount the vfat file system (so the floppy disk can be read by Windows and DOS file systems) and connect the /dev/fd0 device for the floppy disk to the mount point, /mnt/floppy. After you mount a floppy disk using this command, you can read files in the /mnt/floppy folder and you can write or delete files, as well. (Hands-on Project 6-10 steps you through mounting and unmounting floppy drives and CD-ROM drives in Red Hat Enterprise Linux 3.0.)

Use the *umount* command to unmount a file system. For example, you would enter:

umount /mnt/floppy

to unmount the file system for the floppy disk.

In the Red Hat Enterprise Linux 3.0 GNOME and Bluecurve desktop, you can also use graphical user interface (GUI) tools to manage disk storage. For example, to mount or format a disk, click Main Menu, point to System Tools, and click Disk Management. This action starts the User Mount Tool (see Figure 6-8). To mount, unmount, or format a disk, you highlight it in the User Mount Tool and click the appropriate button (Format, Mount, Unmount).

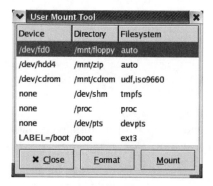

Figure 6-8   Red Hat Enterprise Linux 3.0 User Mount Tool

Also, the GNOME-based Hardware Browser enables you to view current disk partition information. To view the partition information, click Main Menu, point to System Tools, click Hardware Browser, and click Hard Drives in the left pane. The Hardware Browser shows the following (Figure 6-9):

- Device name

- Start and end points

- Partition size

- Type of partition, including file system

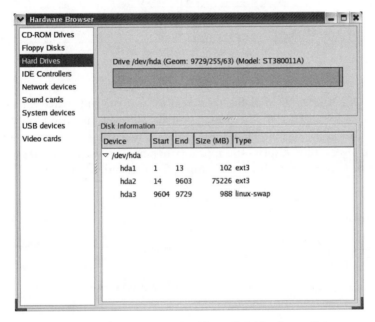

Figure 6-9   Red Hat Enterprise Linux 3.0 Hardware Browser

NetWare 6.x

Novell Storage Services (NSS) is a storage management system that allows you to configure, mount, and maintain volumes. Networks by their nature continue to grow and NSS allows for this growth. This is the default storage and file system for NetWare 6.x. Hands-on Project 6-7 shows how to mount and dismount volumes in NetWare 6.5.

Do not run *vrepair* on NSS volumes. NSS keeps a transaction journal so it can recover after a crash.

CAUTION

Table 6-4 shows several NSS commands and describes what they do.

Table 6-4   NSS commands

NSS Command	Description
nss /help or nss /?	Accesses Help
nss /modules	Lists the providers, loadable storage subsystems, and semantic agents
nss /status	Lists the current NSS status
nss /volumes	Lists all NSS volumes
nss /salvage	Enables salvage of deleted files on volumes
nss /space	Shows the amount of space on pools and their associated volumes

Mac OS X

The Mac OS X Disk Utility is available to partition, format, and manage hard drives, CD-Rs, CD-RWs, floppy disks, and other storage media. To open the Disk Utility, click the Go menu, click Utilities, and double-click Disk Utility. When you select a storage medium in the left pane, the Disk Utility displays the appropriate tabs for the actions you can perform on that disk, as shown in Figure 6-10. For example, for a hard disk you can:

- Repair the disk using the First Aid option
- Erase the contents
- Partition and format the disk
- Set up RAID on the disk
- Restore a disk image or volume using another disk as the source

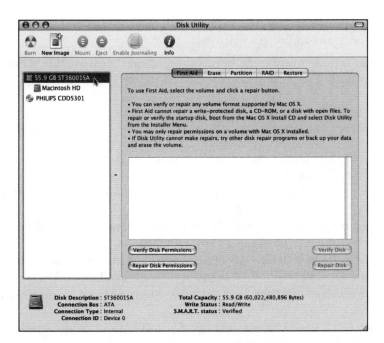

Figure 6-10   Mac OS X version 10.3 Disk Utility

Because Mac OS X is a UNIX-based system, you can also open a terminal window and use the *mount* command to manage storage media. To learn the specific mount options available, type *man mount* and press Enter at the command line.

Hands-on Project 6-8 shows how to use the Mac OS X Disk Utility to manage storage, and Hands-on Project 6-12 enables you to view the mount documentation for Mac OS X.

CHAPTER SUMMARY

- This chapter provides a conceptual overview of how operating systems interface with storage devices and gives an overview of various storage device technologies.

- Popular computer storage technologies include hard disk drives, RAID arrays, CD-ROMs, and DVD drives. These storage devices interface to the computer hardware through the operating system and device drivers.

- Removable storage devices such as the Zip disk and ORB drives provide several options for portable storage. Depending on the device, these devices can store between 120 MB and 5.7 GB. Tables 6-1 and 6-2 list storage media and their respective capacities.

- There are two primary types of network storage: storage area networks (SANs) and network attached storage (NAS). SANs use a Fibre Channel connection to transfer large amounts of data without using the corporate network. NAS servers communicate with storage devices over the LAN rather than a Fibre Channel connection.

❏ There are many tape drive options such as DAT, DLT, SDLT, AIT, S-AIT, and LTO drives. Table 6-3 lists tape media and their capacities.

❏ Operating systems include many tools for managing storage, such as Disk Management, Disk Defragmenter, the Event Viewer, and the Performance Logs and Alerts.

KEY TERMS

advanced intelligent tape (AIT) — A tape drive that has an erasable memory chip and has a capacity between 35 and 90 GB.

basic disk — A physical hard drive. It contains primary partitions, extended partitions, or logical drives which are known as basic volumes.

compact disc read-only memory (CD-ROM) — A non-volatile, digital data storage medium used for operating system and other software distribution.

cyclical redundancy check (CRC) — An error-correction protocol that determines the validity of data written to and read from a floppy disk, hard disk, CD-ROM, or DVD.

digital audio tape (DAT) — A tape drive that uses 4-mm tape and has a capacity of up to 72 GB.

digital linear tape (DLT) — A tape drive that uses half-inch magnetic tapes and has a capacity of up to 80 GB.

digital video disc (DVD) — A high-capacity CD-ROM-like hardware device used for high-quality audio, motion video, and computer data storage. This is also referred to as digital versatile disc.

disk geometry — Critical information about a hard drive's hardware configuration. This information is often stored in an area of non-volatile memory in the computer.

dynamic disk — With dynamic disks you can create volumes that span multiple disks.

Enhanced IDE (EIDE) — A more modern, faster version of IDE used on most current computers.

Fibre Channel — A means of transferring data between servers, mass storage devices, workstations, and peripherals at very high speeds.

Integrated Drive Electronics (IDE) — A storage protocol in some desktop computer systems. IDE is significant because it simplifies the hardware required inside the computer, placing more of the disk intelligence at the hard drive itself.

linear tape open (LTO) — A tape drive used in the high-end server market with a capacity between 100 GB and 1.6 TB.

master — In an EIDE drive chain, the main or first drive. Most EIDE interfaces can support two drives. One is the master (Drive 0) and the second drive is the slave. See *slave*.

network attached storage (NAS) — A way to directly attach storage to a network.

redundant array of inexpensive disks (RAID) — A relatively inexpensive, redundant storage design that uses multiple disks and logic to reduce the chance of information being lost in the event of hardware failure. RAID uses various designs, termed Level 0 through Level 5.

removable disks — A class of relatively high-capacity storage devices that use removable cartridges. These devices are used for data backup, long-term offline storage, and data portability among multiple computer systems.

slave — In an EIDE drive chain, the secondary storage device. See *master*.

storage area network (SAN) — Technology that provides for interconnection between servers and storage systems without sending data over the corporate network.

super advanced intelligent tape (S-AIT) — A tape drive that has an erasable memory chip in the tape and a capacity between 500 GB and 1.3 TB.

super digital linear tape (SDLT) — A tape drive that uses both magnetic and optical recording and has a capacity between 1.2 and 2.4 TB.

Zip disk — A removable high-capacity floppy disk design from Iomega. Zip disks store a nominal 100 to 750 MB of data.

REVIEW QUESTIONS

1. An IDE cable has both a master and a slave connection. True or False?

2. SCSI stands for Serial Computer Systems Interface? True or False?

3. The latest DVD drive is the HD-DVD where a hard drive (HD) and a DVD player are merged together? True or False?

4. CD-ROM discs can store up to
   a. 150 MB of data
   b. 4.7 GB of data
   c. 650 MB of data
   d. 17 GB of data

5. The rotational speed on a CD-ROM is referred to in terms like 72X where the X is:
   a. the speed of the first CDs
   b. the X factor defined as the baseline speed of a single sided CD
   c. the normal audio speed of a CD
   d. just a place holder in the counting scheme

6. There are four ways to connect a drive to your computer. They are
   _____ , _____ , _____ ,
   and _____ .

7. The largest Zip drive from Iomega is the 250 MB model. True or False?

8. The DAT in DAT drive stands for
   a. digital advanced tape
   b. digital audio tape

    c. digital accelerated tape

    d. disk and tape

9. Microsoft introduced the Removable Storage system in Windows Server 2003. True or False?

10. Mini USB drives require drivers to be installed in the operating system. True or False?

11. Zip drives are only available in external models as they are too large to fit inside a desktop computer case. True or False?

12. List the five models of DVDs.

13. A SCSI cable needs to be terminated on both ends. True or False?

14. Which interface is not one that can be used to hook up a DVD device to your computer?

    a. SCSI

    b. IDE

    c. RAID

    d. EIDE

15. Disk geometry is:

    a. the size of platters and space between them

    b. the curve of the coated surface of a platter

    c. the number of platters, heads, tracks and sectors on the disk

    d. the thickness of the coating on a platter

16. NAS technology differs from a SAN in that the servers communicate with the storage devices over _____ .

17. RAID is a technology for

    a. eliminating programming bugs during application development.

    b. using multiple hard drives in various configurations to provide data security through redundancy and error checking.

    c. storing data in a redundant access integrated drive arrangement.

    d. communicating configuration information between the computer and a remote user interface.

18. Describe the major design differences between DVD and CD-ROM that enable the much larger storage capacities of DVD.

19. The Removable Storage system manages the actual data stored on the removable media. True or False?

20. A SAN interconnects servers and storage systems via:

 a. Ethernet

 b. token ring

 c. Fibre Channel

 d. Category 5e cable

HANDS-ON PROJECTS

Project 6-1

In this project, you use the Internet to research RAID options.

To use the Internet to learn about RAID options:

1. Open your Web browser.

2. Search for information on RAID options. You might start with *www.webopedia.com*.

3. Describe RAID levels 0 and 5. Why would you use one over the other?

Project 6-2

In this project, you defragment a disk in **Windows Server 2003**.

To defragment a disk in Windows Server 2003:

1. Click **Start**, highlight **Administrative Tools**, and then click **Computer Management**.

2. Next, in the console tree, click **Disk Defragmenter**. The disks and volumes display.

3. Click on the drive you want to defragment.

4. Click the **Defragment** button at the bottom left corner of the window. You can also click the **Analyze** button to have the system check out the drive and report to you if it needs to be defragmented.

5. When the defragmentation is complete, a dialog box with two buttons displays. Click **View Report** to see a report showing what was done and then click **Close**. If you do not want to see the report, click **Close** to leave the disk defragmentation process.

Project 6-3

In this project, you use the Backup Utility Wizard to back up files and folders in **Windows XP** or **Windows Server 2003**.

To back up files and folders in Windows XP or Windows Server 2003:

1. Open up the Backup Utility Wizard by clicking **Start**, highlighting **All Programs**, highlighting **Accessories**, highlighting **System Tools**, and then clicking **Backup** (see Figure 6-11).

Figure 6-11   Backup Utility Wizard

2. Click **Advanced Mode**.

3. Click the **Backup** tab.

4. Select the drives, files, and folders you want to back up by clicking the check boxes.

5. Click **Start Backup**. You can type in a description as well as a label.

6. Click **Start Backup**. You may also schedule the backup for a later time or select **Advanced options**.

7. Backup will determine available devices and whether they have been used before. Answer the questions to back up your drives, files, and folders selected earlier.

Project 6-4

In this project, you view the properties of a hard drive in **Windows Server 2003**.

To view the properties of a hard drive:

1. Click **Start**, click **Control Panel**, click **Performance and Maintenance**, click **Administrative Tools**, and then double-click **Computer Management**.

2. In the tree on the left, click **Disk Management**.

3. Right-click the drive you wish to view the properties for and then click **Properties**. The disk type, file system, used space, free space, and capacity along with a number of tabs showing additional information display (see Figure 6-12).

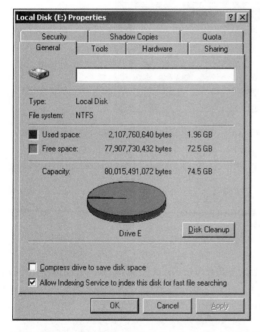

Figure 6-12   Disk properties in Windows Server 2003

Project 6-5

In this project, you view how to convert a basic disk to a dynamic disk in **Windows Server 2003**.

To view how to convert a basic disk to a dynamic disk in Windows Server 2003:

1. Click **Start**, highlight **Administrative Tools**, and then click **Computer Management**.

2. In the console tree, click **Disk Management**. The disks and volumes display in the right pane (see Figure 6-13 for an example).

3. In the gray area that contains the title of the disk (**Disk 0** for example), right-click the title and then click **Convert to Dynamic Disk**.

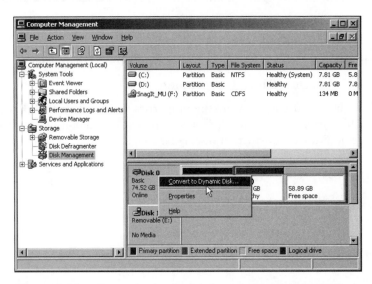

Figure 6-13 Convert a basic disk to a dynamic disk in Windows Server 2003

4. Select the disk to be converted by selecting the check box and clicking **OK**.

5. Click **Convert**.

6. If you are prompted to, confirm the conversion.

Project 6-6

In this project, you use the *fdisk* and the *sfdisk* commands to view partition information in **Red Hat Enterprise Linux 3.0** (or in most Linux or UNIX operating systems) from the command line. You need to use the root account for this project.

To view partition information:

1. Access the command line or a terminal window, such as by clicking **Main Menu**, pointing to **System Tools**, and clicking **Terminal**.

2. Type **sfdisk –s** and press **Enter** to view partition information, as illustrated in Figure 6-14. How many partitions are on your system and what is the size of each?

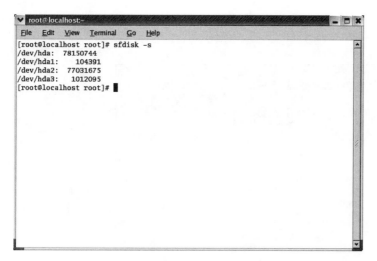

Figure 6-14 Partition information in Red Hat Enterprise Linux 3.0

3. Next, type **fdisk –l** and press **Enter**. How does the information from the *fdisk* command sequence compare to the information displayed for the *sfdisk* command sequence?

4. If you opened a terminal window in Red Hat Enterprise Linux 3.0, type **exit** and press **Enter** to close it.

Project 6-7

In this project, you learn to mount and dismount a volume in **Netware 6.5**.

To mount or dismount a volume in Netware 6.5:

1. At the prompt, type **mount *volume_name*** to mount a volume. To mount the SYS volume and make it available to users, type **mount sys**.

2. To dismount a volume, type **dismount *volume_name*** *a*t the prompt. To dismount the SYS volume and make in unavailable to users, type **dismount sys**.

Project 6-8

Mac OS X provides the Disk Utility for working with disk storage. In this project, you use the Disk Utility to view information about a disk and see from where to partition a disk.

To use the Disk Utility:

1. Click the **Go** menu and click **Utilities**.

2. Double-click **Disk Utility**.

3. Select a disk in the left pane. What tabs are displayed for the disk?

4. Click the Info icon (the "I" in the blue circle), to view information about the disk (see Figure 6-15).

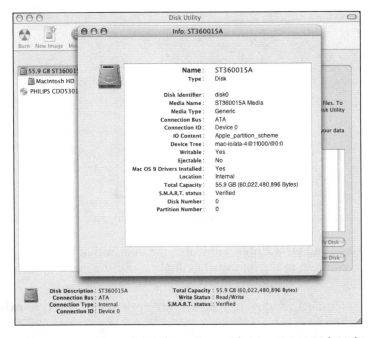

Figure 6-15   View disk information with Mac OS X Disk Utility

5. Close the Info window.

6. Click the **Partition** tab. What information is displayed about the partition? Note that on many systems, this display is deactivated because it is locked (see the small locked padlock in the window). DO NOT unlock the padlock for this project. Also, DO NOT try partitioning the disk, but note that an unlocked and non–write protected disk can be partitioned by using the Partition button.

7. Click the **Disk Utility** menu and click **Quit Disk Utility**.

8. Close any remaining open windows, such as the Utilities window.

HANDS-ON
PROJECTS

Project 6-9

Does your computer include any specialty input hardware? You can physically view the back of your computer to find special devices, or you can check the drivers installed on your system to see what devices are in there.

To review installed devices in Windows Server 2003:

1. Click **Start** on the taskbar.

2. Choose **Control Panel** and click the **System** icon to open the System Properties dialog box.

3. Click the **Hardware** tab.

4. Click the **Device Manager** button to display installed devices (see Figure 6-16).

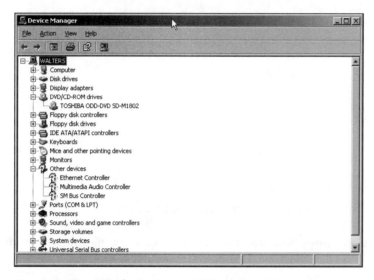

Figure 6-16   Windows Server 2003 Device Manager

5. If necessary, click the plus sign to display additional information about any entry.

6. Right-click an entry and click **Properties** to display detailed information about any entry in this list.

7. Cancel the Device Manager dialog box, and close all open windows.

Project 6-10

This project enables you to mount a floppy disk and a CD-ROM drive in **Red Hat Enterprise Linux 3.0** (or in most UNIX/Linux systems). You need to be logged on as root for this project, and you need a FAT-formatted floppy disk (ideally already containing some files) and a formatted CD-ROM.

To mount a floppy disk and CD-ROM:

1. Access the command line or a terminal window, such as by clicking **Main Menu**, pointing to **System Tools**, and clicking **Terminal**.

2. Insert the floppy disk.

3. Type **mount -t vfat /dev/fd0 /mnt/floppy** and press **Enter**, as shown in Figure 6-17. (Note that you typically will not see a message after you press Enter, unless there is an error in your mount command.)

Figure 6-17 Mount a floppy in Red Hat Enterprise Linux 3.0

4. Type **ls -l /mnt/floppy** and press **Enter**. Do you see any files already on the floppy disk?

5. Type **umount /mnt/floppy**, press **Enter**, and remove the floppy disk.

6. Insert the CD-ROM.

7. If the CD-ROM mounts automatically, and you see a Question box about running /mnt/cdrom/autorun, click **No**. Next, in the terminal window (or command line) type **umount /mnt/cdrom** and press **Enter**.

8. Type **mount -t iso9660 /dev/cdrom /mnt/cdrom** and press **Enter**. Because the CD-ROM is write protected, you will likely see a brief message warning that it is or that it is mounted as read-only (or both).

9. If a cdrom (Nautilus) window opens, close it and return to the terminal window.

10. Type **ls -l /mnt/cdrom** and press **Enter**. Do you see files and folders listed on the CD-ROM?

11. Type **umount /mnt/cdrom**, press **Enter**, and remove the CD-ROM.

HANDS-ON PROJECTS

Project 6-11

Windows XP includes some useful system-level utilities that can help you find out more about your hard drive.

To use the Windows XP System Information utility to study your hard drive configuration:

1. Click **Start**, point to **All Programs**, point to **Accessories**, and point to **System Tools**.

2. Click **System Information**. The Microsoft System Information dialog box opens, as shown in Figure 6-18. Next click the '+' sign in front of Components, then the '+' sign in front of **Storage**, and then click **Drives**.

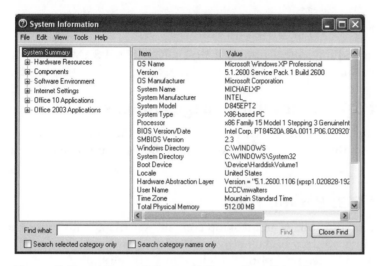

Figure 6-18   Microsoft System Information dialog box

3. Note the size of your hard drive and the amount of space used.

4. Click **File** and then click **Exit** on the menu to close this dialog box, and return to your desktop.

Project 6-12

Mac OS X also provides a standard UNIX *mount* command that you can use. In this project, you view the documentation for the *mount* command.

To view the documentation for the *mount* command:

1. Click the **Go** menu and click **Utilities**.

2. Double-click **Terminal**.

3. Type **man mount** and press **Enter**. If you were to enter the command mount -a -t nonfs,mfs, what would this do?

4. Type **q** to exit the manual information.

5. Click the **Terminal** menu and click **Quit Terminal**.

6. Close the Utilities window.

CASE PROJECTS

As the MIS manager for a small business network, you are asked to research additional storage options for the company. The business has been growing and more information is being stored on the network. It has become apparent that you will run out of storage in the next six months.

Case Project 6-1: NAS and SAN

Research the costs and implementation challenges for NAS and SANs. Weigh the options and make your recommendations.

Case Project 6-2: Removable Storage Options

Several of the employees want to easily carry data from their office computer to their home computer so they can continue working at home. Recommend a method to accomplish this.

Case Project 6-3: Backup Plans

With the growth in your storage and desktop computers arriving with larger hard drives, you see a need to improve your backup plans for servers, networks, and desktop computers. Prepare a proposal with recommendations on how to accomplish this.

7

MODEMS AND OTHER COMMUNICATIONS DEVICES

After reading this chapter and completing the exercises, you will be able to:

♦ Explain analog modem architecture

♦ Use the classic Hayes AT modem command set with computer communications applications

♦ Describe digital modem architecture for high-speed communications through ISDN, cable, DSL, and satellites

♦ Explain the basics of telephone-line data communications

♦ Configure modem and Internet communications in different operating systems

Modems open a vast world of communications to the computer user. Through a modem, a student can access the Internet for educational research and communicate her discoveries with a teacher using e-mail. A modem enables a parent to order products over an Internet connection and to quickly catch up on the day's news. Grandparents send family pictures to friends and relatives using modem connections. Employees use these connections to telecommute or to stay in touch with their organizations while traveling with a portable computing device. By employing modems, all of these computer users become members of a wide area network (WAN) for communications.

This chapter reveals how modems and other essential long distance communications devices work. You start by learning about analog modems, which are now built into most computers purchased for home or office use. You also learn how digital modems work in the context of high-speed communications services, including ISDN, DSL, and cable modems. Finally, you learn how modems interact with operating systems and how to configure an operating system to use a modem to connect to the Internet.

ANALOG MODEM ARCHITECTURE

Computers handle information in a digital format. Everything the computer understands is stored as a series of 1s and 0s, represented as the presence of voltage (a digital 1) or the absence of voltage (a digital 0). Information is sent over a telephone line in analog format—the rising and falling sounds produced when you speak into the telephone handset. The computer doesn't recognize the telephone system's analog data, and the telephone system—at its most commonly used level—can't use the computer's digital data format. A **modem** is a piece of hardware and associated software that connects these two incompatible systems in a way that lets them communicate with each other.

The analog modems that you are most likely to use work over copper or fiber-optic telephone lines. Typically these are called **Plain Old Telephone Service (POTS)** lines, which is the old term, or **Public Switched Telephone Network (PSTN)** lines, which is the modern term. Also, because analog modems are used over telephone lines, they are often called dial-up modems. Further, the connections using analog modems are often called dial-up connections (because access is initiated through "dialing" a telephone number).

NOTE Communications over modern telephone lines are typically governed by the communications devices at either end. When you use a POTS/PSTN line, you use an analog device, such as a telephone or modem that communicates over the line with an analog device at the telecommunication company, such as a switch. When you use ISDN or DSL (discussed later in this chapter), digital devices are used between the subscriber and the telephone company.

Analog Modem Hardware Basics

An analog modem consists of three basic electronic hardware or software components: the data pump, the controller, and the UART. The name modem comes from a description of what the modem does. A modem is a *modulator/demodulator*. It modulates digital signals from the computer into analog signals that can be sent over the phone line and demodulates incoming analog signals back into digital signals the computer can understand. The component that performs basic modulation/demodulation is sometimes called a **data pump**. Basic modem concepts are illustrated in Figure 7-1.

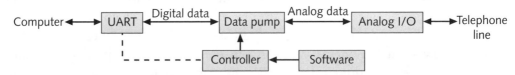

Figure 7-1   Basic analog modem concepts

The **controller** is like the modem's management center because it handles communications tasks and interprets commands. For example, this is where protocols for modulation (V.34, V.90, and V.92, for example), error correction (V.42), and data compression (V.42bis) are stored. A **protocol** is an established guideline that specifies how networked data, including data sent over a telephone network, is formatted into a transmission unit; how it is transmitted; and how it is interpreted at the receiving end. The controller also interprets commands to configure and operate the modem using a special command set called Attention (AT) commands that are discussed later in this chapter.

Modem protocols define some of the basic operational parameters of your modem and determine how compatible it is with other modems with which it communicates. Modem protocol standards are established by the **International Telecommunications Union (ITU)** and compose the International Telecommunication Union-Telecommunication Standardized Sector (ITU-T) standards. The latest standards, V.90 and V.92, define a 56,000 bits per second (56 Kbps) communications protocol. These are by far the most popular analog modem choices for data communications requirements such as browsing the World Wide Web. For more information about modem speed and testing your modem's performance, see Hands-on Projects 7-1, 7-2, 7-3, and 7-4 at the end of this chapter.

Modem protocols are not presented in detail in this chapter, but it is important for you to understand the basics of modem protocols and how their development has paralleled the development of modem technology. Historically, modem protocols have been a determining factor in modem speed and compatibility. Also, modems are the basis of the simplest and most common WANs—connecting a personal computer to the Internet, or to other computers through modems at both ends, joined by a telecommunications line. Table 7-1 presents the common standards and protocols that you may see as you read and learn about modems. The V.90 and V.92 standards popular today generally incorporate most of the earlier technologies and protocols listed in the table.

NOTE

Even though modem technology currently seems stopped at the 56 kilobits per second (Kbps) used by the V.90 and V.92 standards, theoretically, PSTN can support up to 64 Kbps for standard analog modem communications.

CAUTION

Sometimes modems, particularly older modems, will not communicate because of how their settings are configured. For example, a 2400/4800 bps V.27ter modem cannot establish communications with a 36.6 Kbps V.42 modem if the 36.6 Kbps modem is not set to negotiate to a slower speed. When you set up network modems or work to solve modem communication problems, make sure that the modem standards used by a modem at one end are compatible with the modem standards used by a modem at the other end.

Table 7-1 Modem standards and protocols

ITU-T Modem Standard	Description
V.21	300 bps data transmission for dial-up lines
V.22	1200 bps data transmission for dial-up and leased lines
V.22bis*	2400 bps data transmission for dial-up lines
V.23	600/1200 bps data transmission for dial-up and leased lines
V.26	2400 bps data transmission for leased lines
V.26bis	1200/2400 bps data transmission for dial-up lines

Table 7-1   Modem standards and protocols (continued)

ITU-T Modem Standard	Description
V.26ter	2400 bps data transmission for dial-up and leased lines
V.27	4800 bps data transmission on leased lines
V.27bis	2400/4800 bps data transmission on leased lines
V.27ter	2400/4800 bps data transmission on dial-up lines
V.29	9600 bps data transmission on leased lines
V.32	9600 bps data transmission on dial-up lines
V.32bis	14.4 Kbps data transmission on dial-up lines using synchronous communications
V.33	14.4 Kbps data transmission on leased lines
V.34	28.8 Kbps data transmission on dial-up lines with the ability to drop to slower speeds when there are line problems
V.34 (new)	Enhancement of the previous V.34 standard to reach 33.6 Kbps
V.35	48 Kbps data transmission on leased lines
V.42	Error detection and correction on noisy telephone lines
V.42bis	4:1 data compression for high-capacity transfer
V.90	56 Kbps data transmission on dial-up lines (actually is 33.6 Kbps upstream from the modem to the remote site and 56 Kbps downstream from the remote site to the modem)
V.92	56 Kbps data transmission (offering enhanced upstream transmissions at 48 Kbps)—also can temporarily stop data transmissions to take a voice communication

*   The "bis" suffix is derived from the Latin word for "repeat" and means that this is the second updated version of the standard. The suffix "ter" means "three times" in Latin and indicates the third update of the standard.

 NOTE   Prior to the ratification of the ITU V.90 standard, 56 Kbps analog modem communications were made possible by two proprietary methods, K56flex offered by Rockwell and X2 offered by U.S. Robotics/3COM.

When a computer is connected to a modem, the data transfer speed is the **Data Terminal Equipment (DTE)** communications rate. A desktop computer with a modem is an example of a DTE because it prepares data to be transmitted. The modem is called the **Data Communications Equipment (DCE)** and its speed is the DCE communications rate. The computer's port setup for the modem (DTE rate) should be the same or higher than the DCE rate of the modem. For example, if you have a 56 Kbps modem, select a maximum port speed of 57.6 Kbps (the closest setting) in Windows 2000/XP/Server 2003 when you configure the computer for that modem. Hands-on Projects 7-1 and 7-3 enable you to check the port speed.

When two modems communicate over a telephone line, such as the modem on a remote workstation communicating with a modem on a network, they may not truly communicate at the maximum speed for both modems. For example, two V.90 modems may negotiate to transmit at 33.6 Kbps instead of 56 Kbps because of noise detected on the line. **Line noise** is interference from any source, such as from electromagnetic interference (EMI) caused by electric motors or radio frequency interference (RFI) from radio wave communications. Hands-on Project 7-4 enables you to test the actual speed of a modem.

From the Trenches...

Sometimes users can cause their own line noise. A busy marketing executive experienced this problem because he ran his telephone cable from the modem in his computer over a power supply contained in a large printer in his office. After he moved the cord off the power supply, his modem speed increased significantly (and so did his Internet access speed).

7

Computer modems can be classified in several ways. One distinction is whether the modem is located inside the computer (an internal modem) or outside the computer (an external modem). Internal modems usually are built on expansion cards that plug into the computer's expansion bus, most commonly the Peripheral Component Interconnect (PCI) bus. They may also be part of the computer's main circuit board.

External modems are circuit boards that are placed inside a standalone case with its own power supply. External modems usually plug into the computer via a serial port or, with newer modems, the Universal Serial Bus (USB) port. An external USB modem is an excellent choice for several reasons. For one thing, the USB port is a high-speed port that can supply power to peripheral devices, obviating the need for external power supplies. USB devices are self configuring. When you plug in a USB modem, the operating system recognizes the presence of the new device and automatically launches a configuration utility. To some users, external modems are preferable to internal modems because they include status lights that indicate when the modem is connected, what state it is in, and whether data is being transferred. In addition, an external modem is a universal device that can be used with Windows, UNIX/Linux, NetWare, or Mac OS.

The **UART** (pronounced "you art"), short for universal asynchronous receiver-transmitter, is an electronic chip that converts data from the computer into data that can be sent to serial ports. The UART reads in one byte of data at the computer's bus speed, adds a **start bit** at the beginning, a **stop bit** at the end, generates an interrupt, and feeds the bits to the serial port at a slow speed that won't overwhelm the peripheral (a modem in this case, but the same system applies to other serial devices). External modems use whatever UART is attached to the serial port. Internal modems use their own UART, bypassing the computer's serial I/O port. (In Figure 7-1, you can see this internal UART concept. An external modem has serial port hardware and uses the computer's internal UART.)

Computers communicate with external serial devices in two basic modes: synchronous and asynchronous. These terms refer to the method used to keep the data streams on the local and remote devices aligned so proper data transfer can occur. **Asynchronous**

communication is the most common method for today's desktop computers. Asynchronous communication uses fairly accurate clocks (timers) at both ends of the connection to synchronize data. The transmitting device sends a start bit, which is captured by the receiving device. The next eight bits are assumed to be data, and the final two bits are stop bits. The start and stop bits help the receiving device interpret data and stay in sync. In a sense, the start and stop bits show the start and stop points of a specific communication so that communication makes sense to both the sender and the receiver. This might be likened to two people agreeing to not interrupt each other in the middle of a sentence, and instead waiting until the speaker finishes talking.

Synchronous communication, on the other hand, sends information in blocks (frames) of data that include embedded clock signals. Alternately, the clock data can be sent over a separate, dedicated clock line that is part of the connection. Synchronous data transfer usually is more efficient, but it requires more processing at both ends of the link. Synchronous communication is normally used to send data over very high quality, digital lines.

Software-Based Modems

All modems need the functions of the data pump, controller, and UART. However, some modems do not implement the controller functions in a microchip, but instead implement them in software functions handled by the PC. Other modems implement both the controller and data pump functions in software and not in microchips. Software-based modems are often referred to as **Winmodems** after the trademarked name of 3Com/U.S. Robotics popular models.

The 3Com/U.S. Robotics Winmodem is a controllerless modem that retains a hardware data pump (a **Digital Signal Processor** or **DSP**), but implements the controller functions in software. So-called **Host Signal Processor (HSP)** modems dispense with the controller and data pump hardware entirely. Instead of using their own signal processors, HSP modems use the host's central processing unit (such as the Pentium or PowerPC), along with special software, to handle the same jobs.

One disadvantage of implementing modem functions with software rather than hardware is that such software takes up memory and processor cycles, although these cycles are now quite inexpensive. The biggest disadvantage of software-based modems is their dependence on particular operating systems. A Winmodem won't work on a Mac, or even on a PC running Linux, and the Mac OS version of a software modem, Geoport Express, won't work on a PC operating system. In addition, some communications software packages simply aren't compatible with a software modem design because they expect to find a serial or USB port and modem hardware at traditional locations, while many software modem designs use nonstandard address locations. Newer communications software can find such address locations, but older software won't always work properly with software-based modems.

In contrast, an external hardware modem can be used on virtually any computer. All that is required is a serial or USB port on the computer that's compatible with the modem's serial or USB connection and communications software that's capable of using compatible commands between the computer and the modem.

The advantages of using a software modem are cost savings and upgradeability. By eliminating physical parts, the unit cost falls dramatically. In a completely software-based modem, drastic upgrades are possible by rewriting the software. In addition, many multimedia features, such as voice mail or speakerphones, are easier to implement in a software-based modem design. Today, software modems are often used in portable/laptop computers because they do not require as much power as hardware modems—saving battery time.

HAYES AT COMMAND SET FOR ANALOG MODEMS

7

In the 1970s, modems were sold for specific purposes—such as connecting a particular remote dumb terminal (monitor and keyboard with no CPU) to a specific mainframe computer—and commanded high prices. Dennis Hayes devised a way to create a general-purpose modem that could be configured using a command language he invented, the **Hayes command set**, also called **Attention (AT) commands**. AT commands are still used for analog modems. When a modem is said to be Hayes-compatible, it simply means that the modem supports all or part of the Hayes AT command set. Most chipset vendors support the standard Hayes command set and supplement it with additional commands.

Hayes commands begin with the letters AT, which tells the modem to interpret the next character string as a command. A Hayes-compatible modem is equipped with software that acts as a command interpreter. The command interpreter ignores spaces and dashes (which people are accustomed to using to separate area codes, exchanges, and extensions). Table 7-2 summarizes many commonly used AT commands. The commands are not case sensitive and can be issued in uppercase or lowercase. Although many modem manufacturers extend the basic AT command set or use proprietary commands, most modern modems still respond to the basic commands in the traditional ways. This command set is used extensively to set up and control modems so that they are compatible with a variety of host hardware. Hands-on Project 7-5 enables you to view how some AT commands are used on a UNIX/Linux computer that employs the commonly used Minicom program.

Table 7-2 AT command set summary

AT Command	Description
DT and DP	Dial the phone number that follows. DT is for touchtone phones. DP is for pulse dial phones. A complete touchtone dialing sequence is: ATDT 555-5555 (the phone number you wish to dial).
, (comma)	Cause a delay before executing the next command. Often used to make sure the phone switch has recovered before dialing, as when dialing a 9 to get an outside line: ATDT 9,555-5555
W	Wait for the dial tone before dialing: ATDT 9W555-5555
+++	Escape from online mode into command mode. In command mode, AT commands can be sent to the modem.

Table 7-2   AT command set summary (continued)

AT Command	Description
H	Hang up. A typical hang-up sequence is: +++ ATH.
O	Go from command mode back to online mode. This is the only occurrence of the letter "o" in the Hayes AT command set. All other occurrences of o-like shapes are zeroes.
S0=n	Answer incoming calls after n rings. Setting n to zero tells the modem not to answer incoming calls.
Mn	Turn modem speaker off (n=0) or on (n=1).
Ln	Set speaker volume for values of n equal to 0 (lowest volume), 1 or 2 (medium volume), or 3 (highest volume).
&Fn	Set modem to the default settings from the factory.
Z	Reset modem to defaults.

DIGITAL MODEMS

The name digital modem is a misnomer because there is no actual modulation or demodulation (of analog signals), but the usage persists. A digital modem performs the same basic function as an analog modem: it moves data out of a computer, across a telephone line, cable, or other medium, and into another computer at a remote location. The major difference is that the data is digital from start to finish. **Digital modems** are digital devices that use digital transmission media. Digital modems can be network devices (connected directly to the network), serial devices (connected to the serial port), or USB devices. When connecting to Transmission Control Protocol/Internet Protocol (TCP/IP) networks, they connect via Point-to-Point Protocol (PPP), which is a popular communications protocol for Internet communications (see Chapter 8).

Today there are four popular telecommunications networks, which each use different types of digital communications and digital modems:

- ISDN
- Cable networks
- DSL
- Satellite

ISDN

Integrated Services Digital Network (ISDN) uses digital communications over a telecommunications line for high-speed computer communications, videoconferencing, Internet connections, and so on. This technology has been around for more than 20 years, but only with the rise in Internet usage and videoconferencing has it gained much market penetration. ISDN uses standard copper telephone line pairs with digital equipment on either end of the connection to encode and transmit the information—an ISDN router (to route the transmission to the right place) and **terminal adapter (TA)**, a type of digital modem.

ISDN routers and TAs typically include analog telephone jacks so you can plug in a conventional telephone or modem for use over the digital line. With most ISDN hardware, you connect to a single telephone line copper pair (the same kind of wire that brings telephone service into your home or office consisting of two wires twisted together), but you get separate channels for computer data and analog telephone lines. You can use one analog line and one data line simultaneously, or two digital lines, or two analog lines.

Two interfaces are supported in ISDN: basic rate interface and primary rate interface. The **Basic Rate Interface (BRI)** has an aggregate data rate of 144 Kbps. The BRI consists of three channels: two are 64 Kbps Bearer (B) channels for data, voice, and graphics transmissions; and the third is a 16 Kbps Delta (D, sometimes called Demand) channel used for communications signaling, packet switching, and credit card verification. The primary function of a D channel is for ISDN call setup and teardown for starting and stopping a communication session. BRI is used for videoconferencing, Internet connectivity, and high-speed connectivity for telecommuters and home offices. Multiple BRI channels can be "bonded" together for even faster communications. For example, one BRI line with two 64 Kbps channels can be bonded to achieve a 128 Kbps connection for actual data throughput. With the 16 Kbps D channel added, plus 48 Kbps for maintenance and synchronization, the total rate is 192 Kbps. Another example is the bonding of three BRI lines consisting of six 64 Kbps channels for an aggregate data throughput speed of 384 Kbps.

TIP

Windows 2000/XP/Server 2003 and many UNIX/Linux systems support bonding ISDN lines using Multilink PPP. Also, if you subscribe to BRI ISDN, some telecommunications companies implement download capabilities through the D channel, thus creating an additional 16 Kbps for downstream communications.

The **Primary Rate Interface (PRI)** has faster data rates, with an aggregate of switched bandwidth equal to 1.544 Mbps. In the United States and Japan, PRI consists of twenty-three 64 Kbps B channels and one 64 Kbps D channel for signaling communications and packet switching (plus 8 Kbps for maintenance). European PRI ISDN is thirty 64 Kbps channels and one 64 Kbps signaling or packet-switching channel. The PRI is used for LAN-to-LAN connectivity, Internet service provider (ISP) sites, videoconferencing, and corporate sites that support telecommuters who use ISDN.

NOTE

A third type of ISDN is broadband or B-ISDN, which currently supports 1.5 Mbps, but theoretically has a limit of 622 Mbps.

ISDN is generally more expensive (it could be twice as expensive or more depending on your area) than DSL and cable modems, which are discussed in the next sections. It is, however, a good alternative for those who need faster access than asynchronous modems can provide, particularly in areas that do not have DSL or cable modem access. Also, ISDN can be very economical for small businesses because it is possible to connect multiple digital devices (usually up to eight) to one incoming line, such as several digital telephones, computers, and faxes.

Cable Modems

In some areas, cable TV providers also offer data services to businesses and homes. A **cable modem** is used to attach to cable data services. This type of modem is usually an external device that plugs into a USB port or network interface card (NIC) in your computer, and is connected to the coaxial cable used for the cable TV (CATV) system. The cable modem communicates using upstream and downstream frequencies (channels) that are already allocated by the cable service. The upstream frequency is used to transmit the outgoing signal over a spectrum (contiguous range) of frequencies that carry data, sound, and TV signals. The downstream frequency is used to receive signals, and is also blended with other data, sound, and TV downstream signals. Depending on the modem, upstream and downstream data rates may or may not be the same. For example, one vendor's modem provides a 30 Mbps maximum upstream rate and a 15 Mbps maximum downstream rate. Another vendor offers a modem that has 10 Mbps for both the upstream and downstream rates. However, even though cable modems are built for high speeds, at this writing, a single modem user is likely to have access (bandwidth) in the range of 256 Kbps to about 3 Mbps. The actual speed is partially dependent on how many of your neighbors are using their cable modems at the same time because one cable run that connects a group of subscribers to the cable hub can handle a maximum of 30 Mbps of bandwidth. Also, a cable service provider may establish a limit on your bandwidth (how fast you can transmit and receive) so that the provider can give more users access to the cable network.

The cable modem industry has been working to provide a set of standards with accompanying certification to govern cable modem communications in a project called the **Certified Cable Modem Project**. This project is more commonly referred to as **Data Over Cable Service Interface Specification (DOCSIS)**. Most cable communications companies support this project and are replacing older cable modems with modems certified to meet the DOCSIS standards. The following DOCSIS standards are in use:

- *DOCSIS 1.0*: Accepted in 1999, this standard enables 5 Mbps upstream and downstream communications for standard Internet access.

- *DOCSIS 1.1*: Accepted in 2001, this standard doubles the speed of DOCSIS 1.0 to achieve 10 Mbps, plus it includes data encryption security.

- *DOCSIS 2.0 (also called Adv PHY)*: Accepted in 2002, this standard is especially targeted for direct point-to-point communications between two organizations, for example. It is intended to compete with current T-carrier telecommunications applications. DOCSIS is capable of three times the upstream speed of DOCSIS 1.1 (up to 30 Mbps) and provides better insurance against sources of signal interference.

Cable modems are manufactured as either internal or external devices. When you purchase an internal device, it looks similar to a modem card that fits into an expansion slot in your computer. External cable modems are more common and typically connect to your computer in one of two ways. One way is to connect the cable modem directly to a conventional NIC that is already in your computer using twisted-pair wire (similar to telephone wire), an RJ-45 connector, and Ethernet communications. The second type of cable modem connects directly to a USB port on your computer. Once the cable modem is installed at the computer, the other end is connected to broadband (carries several communications at once) coaxial wire used for CATV communications.

If you are purchasing a cable modem, make sure you purchase one that is certified to meet at least the DOCSIS 1.1 standard; and if you have a cable modem that is not certified or that is certified for DOCSIS 1.0, strongly consider upgrading to one that is certified for the DOCSIS 1.1 standard or higher. Besides the extra speed built into a DOCSIS 1.1 certified cable modem, you also get encryption security, which helps prevent others from having access to your data. At this writing, more than 20 million DOCSIS modems have already been distributed worldwide and there are more than 70 manufacturers of certified DOCSIS cable modems.

NOTE To ensure that a DOCSIS 1.0 or 1.1 certified modem will work on your cable system, the cable provider must have certified Cable Modem Termination Systems (CMTSs) at the headend (centralized cable operator's site). Most cable operators have or are implementing CMTSs.

The advantage of cable modem communications is that currently unallocated bandwidth can be allocated to you, even for a millisecond or two, when you are downloading a large file, for example. This means that even when the cable is busy because you and your neighbors are all using TV, radio, or computer communications, the system is always dynamically allocating unused cable bandwidth. If your neighbor is connected via her cable modem, but is not sending or receiving, then you are allocated some of her bandwidth when you are downloading a file, for example.

CAUTION Because you share the same cable with your neighbors, it is possible for a knowledgeable user to view or access the files on your computer, particularly if your modem is not certified or only certified for DOCSIS 1.0. For this reason, if you use a cable modem, it is vital that you protect your files and access to the computer through file security and personal firewalls. Windows XP, Red Hat Enterprise Linux 3.0, and Mac OS X, for example, enable you to set up a personal firewall via built-in software functionality. For even more security help with Windows XP, visit Microsoft's Web site at *www.microsoft.com* to obtain their Security Tool Kit. For more information on cable security, visit *www.cablemodem.com*, which is the Web site of CableLabs, a consortium of cable telecommunications companies that engages in research and development of cable telecommunications technologies.

DSL Modems

Another high-speed digital data communications service that has gained popularity in relation to ISDN and cable modems is **Digital Subscriber Line (DSL)**. DSL is a digital technology that works over copper wire that already goes into most residences and businesses for telephone services (newer forms of DSL can be used over fiber-optic telephone lines). To use DSL, you must install an intelligent adapter in your computer, which is connected to the DSL network (see Figure 7-2). The adapter can be a card similar in appearance to a modem, but that is fully digital, which means it does not convert the DTE's (computer or network device's) digital signal to analog, but instead sends a digital signal over the telephone wire. Two pairs of wires are connected to the adapter and then out to the telephone pole. Communication over the copper wire is simplex, which means that one pair is used for outgoing transmissions, and the other pair for incoming transmissions, thus creating an upstream channel to the telephone company (telco) and a downstream channel to the user. The maximum upstream transmission rate is 2.3 Mbps, while downstream communications can reach 60 Mbps. Also, the maximum distance from user to telco without a repeater (to amplify and extend the distance of the signal) is 5.5 kilometers (3.4 miles, which is similar to ISDN).

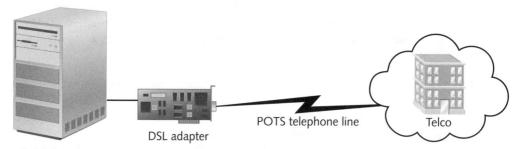

POTS telephone line   Telco

DSL adapter

Figure 7-2   Connecting to DSL

The actual transmission rate is determined by several factors, including the type of DSL service used, the condition of the cable, the distance to the telco, and the bus speed in the user's computer.

NOTE

Like a cable modem, a DSL adapter offers high-speed data transmissions, but it also has some advantages over a cable modem. For example, a cable modem uses a line shared by other users, which means its signal can be tapped and read by another user. A DSL line is dedicated to a single user, which means that there is less likelihood that the signal can be tapped without the telco being alerted. Also, the DSL user employs the full bandwidth of his or her line, in contrast to the cable modem user who shares bandwidth with others.

On networks, DSL is connected by means of a combined DSL adapter and router. A router is a device that can be used to direct network traffic and create a firewall so that only authorized users can access network services. This type of connection enables multiple users to access one DSL line, and it protects the network from intruders over the DSL line. Usually this type of connection comes with management software that enables you to monitor the link and perform diagnostics, such as Cisco's Commander software, as shown in Figure 7-3.

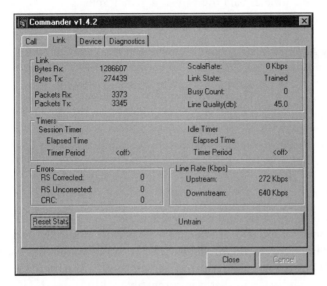

Figure 7-3   DSL monitoring and management software

There are eight types of DSL services:

- Asymmetric Digital Subscriber Line (ADSL)

- G.lite Asymmetric Digital Subscriber Line (G.lite ADSL)

- Integrated Services Digital Network Digital Subscriber Line (IDSL)

- Rate Adaptive (Asymmetric) Digital Subscriber Line (RADSL)

- High Bit-Rate Digital Subscriber Line (HDSL)

- Symmetric High Bit-Rate Digital Subscriber Line (SHDSL)

- Very High Bit-Rate Digital Subscriber Line (VDSL)

- Symmetric Digital Subscriber Line (SDSL)

There are other all-proprietary versions of DSL that are not discussed in this book due to limited use and the lack of standardization. These include EtherLoop from Nortel Networks, Consumer Digital Subscriber Line (CDSL) from Rockwell International, and Consumer Installable Digital Subscriber Line (CiDSL) from Globespan.

ADSL is the most commonly used version of DSL. Aside from traditional data and multimedia applications, ADSL also is well suited for interactive multimedia and distance learning. Before transmitting data, ADSL checks the telephone line for noise and error conditions in a process called forward error correction. When it was first established, ADSL upstream transmissions were 64 Kbps, and downstream transmissions were 1.544 Mbps. Currently, those transmission rates are 576–640 Kbps for upstream, and up to 6 Mbps for downstream. ADSL also can use a third communications channel for 4 KHz voice transmissions that occur at the same time as data transmission, which means that the user can be on the Internet and the telephone at the same time.

CAUTION

When you employ ADSL for simultaneous computer and telephone use, it is necessary to place an inexpensive filtering device between the ADSL line that comes in from the telco and the telephone. The filter is used to block line noise that can diminish telephone conversations. However, do not place the filter between the incoming line and the DSL digital modem.

G.lite ADSL is a variation of ADSL that is developed for compatibility with Plug and Play (PnP), which enables computer operating systems and hardware to automatically configure new hardware devices. G.lite ADSL enables upstream communications to 500 Kbps and downstream up to 1.5 Mbps.

Many new residential and business areas deploy a telephone network device called a Digital Loop Carrier that is intended to improve the techniques used to physically distribute the telephone cable—but that interferes with DSL delivery. **IDSL** was developed to enable DSL to be used in these areas. IDSL enables upstream and downstream communications of up to 144 Kbps. IDSL has another advantage in that it is compatible with exiting ISDN terminal adapters.

Originally developed for on-demand movie transmissions, **RADSL** applies ADSL technology, but enables the transmission rate to vary depending on whether the communication is data, multimedia, or voice. There are two ways that the transmission rate can be established. One is by the telco setting a specific rate per each customer line based on the anticipated use of the line. Another is for the telco to enable the rate to automatically adjust to the demand on the line. RADSL is an advantage to customers because they pay only for the amount of bandwidth they need, and it helps the telco by allowing it to allocate unused bandwidth for other customers. Another advantage of RADSL is that line length can be greater in situations where not all of the bandwidth is used, so it can accommodate customers who are more than 5.5 kilometers from the telco. The downstream transmission can be up to 7 Mbps, and the upstream transmission can be up to 1 Mbps.

Originally, **HDSL** was designed for full-duplex communications (simultaneous two-way communications) over two pairs of copper telephone wires at a fixed sending and receiving rate of either 1.544 Mbps or 2.3 Mbps for distances up to 3.6 kilometers (2.25 miles). Another HDSL implementation has been created to use one of these two pairs of telephone wires, but with a full-duplex transmission rate of 768 Kbps. One limitation is that HDSL does not support voice communications as well as ADSL and RADSL, in part because it requires the installation of specialized converters and adapters for voice transmission. However, HDSL is particularly useful for businesses needing to join two or more local area networks (LANs) into a WAN.

SHDSL, also called G.shdsl, can be used over one or two wires. When two wires are used the maximum distance is about 4 miles, longer than the 3.4 mile maximum for other DSL versions. The extra distance is achieved by eliminating more of the signal reflection on the wire. The upstream and downstream rates are within the range of 192 Kbps to 2.3 Mbps. One limitation is that SHDSL is intended for data communications rather than combined data and voice.

VDSL is intended as an alternative to networking technologies that use coaxial or fiber-optic cable. The VDSL downstream speed is 51–55 Mbps and upstream is 1.6–2.3 Mbps. Although it offers very high bandwidth, VDSL's range, or maximum distance from the telco, is relatively short at 300–1800 meters (980–5900 feet), which limits how it can be applied. VDSL works in a fashion similar to RADSL in that bandwidth can be automatically allocated to meet the existing demand, and it is similar to ADSL because it creates multiple channels over the twisted-pair wires and enables voice transmission at the same time as data.

SDSL is similar to ADSL, but it allocates the same bandwidth for both upstream and downstream transmissions at 384 Kbps. SDSL is particularly useful for videoconferencing and interactive learning because of the symmetrical bandwidth transmissions. Table 7-3 provides a summary of the DSL technologies.

Table 7-3 DSL technologies

DSL Technology	Upstream Data Transmission Rate	Downstream Data Transmission Rate
Asymmetric Digital Subscriber Line (ADSL)	576–640 Kbps	Up to 6 Mbps
G.lite Asymmetric Digital Subscriber Line (G.lite ADSL)	Up to 500 Kbps	Up to 1.5 Mbps
Integrated Services Digital Network Digital Subscriber Line (IDSL)	Up to 144 Kbps	Up to 144 Kbps
Rate Adaptive (Asymmetric) Digital Subscriber Line (RADSL)	Up to 1 Mbps	Up to 7 Mbps
High Bit-Rate Digital Subscriber Line (HDSL)	Fixed rate at 1.544 Mbps or 2.3 Mbps	Fixed rate at 1.544 Mbps or 2.3 Mbps
Symmetric High Bit-Rate Digital Subscriber Line (SHDSL)	192 Kbps to 2.3 Mbps	192 Kbps to 2.3 Mbps
Very High Bit-Rate Digital Subscriber Line (VDSL)	1.6–2.3 Mbps	51–55 Mbps
Symmetric Digital Subscriber Line (SDSL)	384 Kbps	384 Kbps

Satellite

Satellite networks for Internet access are available in more and more rural areas and in metropolitan areas that do not offer ISDN, cable, or DSL services. Similar to ISDN, cable, and DSL, satellite connectivity is digital and designed to be faster than access through an analog modem and POTS. The connection speeds through a satellite network are currently up to about 500 Kbps for download speeds and up to 50 Kbps for uploading data. The actual speed depends on factors such as weather, signal strength of the user's equipment, and most particularly, amount of use experienced on the satellite. For example, the use of some satellites is divided between military and commercial communications. If military communications are heavy at particular times, and because they take precedence over commercial uses, communications may be slower for the commercial user at those times. Some satellite network providers offer equipment that combines network access with satellite TV access using one dish, which can involve high initial expenses. Others offer network access using a dedicated dish.

The user equipment needed for satellite communications typically includes the following (see Figure 7-4):

- A satellite dish about 2 or 3 feet in diameter and that is usually a little larger than a dish used for satellite TV

- A digital modem to transmit the signal and another digital modem to receive the signal (these may be in separate boxes or both housed on one box)

- Coaxial (TV-like) cables from the modems to the dish

- A serial or USB (usually USB) cable from the modems (usually attached to the receiving modem) that connects to a serial or USB port on your computer (or it can connect to a router on a network for sharing the satellite access)

- Software from the satellite provider to enable the computer setup (in some cases it is also necessary to have an analog modem for the initial setup because the installation software "provisions" or verifies the satellite connection with the satellite provider via a one-time modem/telephone line communication)

Older communications satellites orbit in the atmosphere at approximately 22,300 miles above the Earth's surface. The extreme distance of these satellites, and high atmospheric disturbances, can cause transmission delays that are unacceptable for time-sensitive communications involving data transfers and multimedia. Several companies are currently sending up newer low Earth orbiting (LEO) satellites, which orbit at a distance of between 435 and 1000 miles above the Earth's surface, resulting in faster two-way transmission of signals. LEO satellite technology is working to offer up to 720 Kbps downlink communications and up to 128 Kbps uplink communications. Currently, satellite networks are used for:

- Broadband (high-speed) Internet communications

- Around the world video conferencing

- Classroom and educational communications

- Other communications involving voice, video, and data

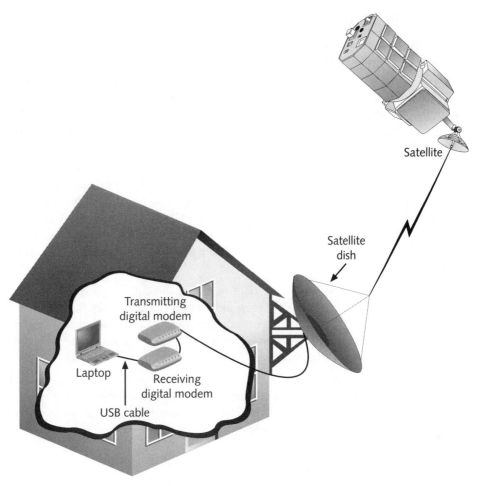

Figure 7-4   Satellite communications setup

A limitation of satellite communications is that they can experience interference during severe rain and snow storms. For snow storms, the remedy is often to brave the elements and simply clear the snow from your dish.

DATA COMMUNICATIONS TECHNIQUES

When two analog or digital modems communicate, they must have a way to halt and resume the flow of data. Otherwise, data buffers would fill and then overflow, resulting in lost data. The buffers are prevented from getting too full through the use of **flow control**, which is accomplished using software or hardware.

Software Flow Control

A popular software flow control method from the early days of modems is called **Xon-Xoff**. Xon-Xoff uses the Ctrl+S character (ASCII 19) to stop the flow of data (Xoff), and Ctrl+Q (ASCII 17) to resume (Xon). When the receiving computer needs time to process the data in the buffers, perform disk I/O, and so on, it can send an Xoff request to the remote modem to stop the flow of data. Once it processes the data in its buffer, it can send an Xon to begin receiving data again. This receive, stop, resume process continues repeatedly throughout the data transfer or communications session.

In the days before online services had graphical user interfaces (GUIs), you could manually type Ctrl+Q and Ctrl+S from the keyboard to issue the Xon-Xoff control signals to suspend and resume the flow of on-screen text. This was a common technique for users of dumb terminals connected to central computers as well. Some software in those days wasn't sophisticated enough to manage the dumb terminal screens automatically. Also, communications software running on early PCs or Macs simply emulated a dumb terminal to access text-based host computers.

One problem with Xon-Xoff flow control is that the data being transferred may contain Ctrl+S or Ctrl+Q characters, which can interrupt the data transfer. Another problem is that Xon-Xoff is a form of signaling that uses the bandwidth of the data stream to pass data about the condition of the data stream. This is inefficient because it reduces the amount of user data that can move over the phone line.

Xon-Xoff is not as commonly used today in modem communications as hardware flow control, but it is still included as a configuration option in most operating systems. The advantage of Xon-Xoff flow control is that in serial communications, the serial cable requires fewer wires inside the cable.

Hardware Flow Control

With the advent of faster modems, the industry moved to hardware flow control. Hardware flow control halts and resumes the movement of data by changing the voltage on specific pins in the communications interface. Controlling data flow with hardware eliminates the problem of the modem confusing data with control signals. If you are given a choice in configuring your modem for data communications, always use hardware flow control instead of Xon-Xoff. It is more reliable and permits faster modem performance. Figure 7-5 demonstrates the flow control options for a modem set up in Windows XP.

Error Correction

Sometimes errors are introduced into the data stream by the telephone lines or other equipment. Modems must check for these errors and resend bad blocks of data to ensure that the receiving modem gets the information exactly as it was transmitted.

Modems transfer bits (ones or zeroes). Three possible errors can occur: a bit can be lost, an extraneous bit can be introduced, or a bit can be flipped (changed from zero to one or from

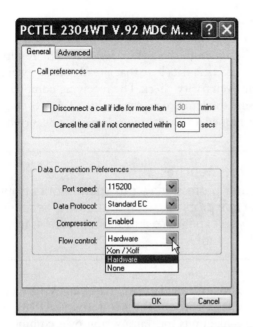

Figure 7-5 Flow control options in Windows XP

one to zero). The most basic form of error correction involves the start and stop bits. Each eight-bit byte is framed by a start bit at the beginning and a stop bit at the end (see Figure 7-6).

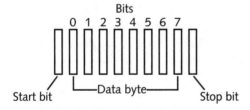

Figure 7-6 Data byte framing with start and stop bits

The start and stop bits always have the same value. If a bit is added or lost, the start and stop bits won't be in the right place. The receiving modem will notice this and request that the sending modem resend that block of data. The modem's UART adds start and stop bits to outgoing data and strips them from incoming data.

There are always eight bits between the start and stop bit, even when communicating with systems that only require seven bits. That makes it possible to use the eighth bit for another form of error checking: parity checking. **Parity checking** is a data verification process that ensures data integrity through a system of data bit comparisons between the sending and receiving computer.

Parity can be either even or odd (or none, if parity checking is turned off). For example, assume that the seven bits are 0100101. Adding up the 1s yields 3. If parity is set to even, then an extra parity bit with a 1 value must be added to this byte: 01001011. The resulting byte + parity combination has an even number of 1s. A data byte that already has an even number of 1s gets a parity bit of 0 to maintain the even parity check. The receiving computer checks the number of 1s in each byte to make sure they sum to an even value (2, 4, 6, 8, etc.). If they are odd, the computer knows that a bit flipped, or that some other error occurred.

From the Trenches...

Sometimes users and even computer professionals can spend hours trouble-shooting an analog modem connection problem when the cause is as simple as checking the parity setting. When you experience a modem problem, trouble-shoot the simple causes first, such as parity.

Most modems use the ITU's V.42 standard to provide error checking. V.42 employs an error-checking protocol called **Link Access Protocol for Modems (LAPM)**, which is used to construct data into discrete frame-like units for transmission over communications lines. Each frame is given a sequence number and is stuffed with a fixed or variable amount of data (depending on the V.42 version used) and a checksum. When the frame is received by the remote modem, that modem verifies the sequence number and checksum. If the data is received out of sequence, or the received checksum is in error, then the data is retransmitted. V.42 comes in three versions: (1) Full V.42 uses a variable-length frame, (2) V.42-Lite uses a fixed-length frame and less error-detection coding in modems and smaller buffer sizes, and (3) V.42-Relay is used over digital TCP/IP networks and some high-speed networks. All versions of V.42 enable the communicating modems to detect the presence of noise on the communication line, which can lead to errors. When noise is detected through using V.42, the communicating modems can decide to transmit at a slower speed so that fewer retransmissions are required.

Data Compression

In addition to error correction, modems usually compress the data they send. The concept behind data compression is fairly simple. Consider a screen displayed on your computer, for example. There may be several icons, an application dialog box, and a solid blue background. A data compression routine can study this picture and see that there's a lot of repetitive blue in the picture. The "compressed" representation of the screen shows a blue dot and a number that represents the number of times the blue dot is repeated. This takes a lot less room than physically representing each blue dot.

Other file types are compressed using this same—very simplified—approach. Text usually contains repetitive data, as does program code. Virtually any computer file can be compressed to reduce the overall size of the file that must be transmitted. If you are familiar with compression utilities, such as PKZIP or WinZip for the PC, or StuffIt for the Mac, then you have seen the results of data compression. Compression can reduce the size of a TIFF (Tag Image Format) file, for example, by more than 90 percent. In fact, many people compress large files before sending the files to their modems.

 Using file compression software prior to sending your file is one way to speed modem communications so that the modem does not have to perform the compression.

Modem data compression uses a similar technique to reduce the total number of data bytes that must be transferred over the connection, but it does it "on the fly," compressing the data while you send it. Data compression is one way in which modem manufacturers are able to achieve some of the high-speed data transfers expected today.

Compression is typically accomplished by using the V.42bis standard, which employs the Lempel-Ziv-Welch (LZW) compression method. This method works "on the fly" in two important respects. One is that it compresses data as it is sent rather than waiting for all of the data to be prepared in a buffer, compressed, and sent. The second is that it can detect when the data is already compressed, such as a file that is compressed using PKZIP, and it does not attempt to compress this type of file. In ideal conditions, data can be compressed on a 4:1 basis, which means that optimal data transmissions are up to four times faster when data can be fully compressed (as long as there are no transmission errors because of line noise).

MODEMS AND THE OPERATING SYSTEM

All operating systems include a communications component, such as for communicating through modems. In fact, data communications is one of the most basic operating system duties. Data moves along the internal computer bus from the CPU to memory, and to peripheral devices that may be connected to the internal bus or external ports. Part of the data communications software that is vital to the operating system was already presented in Chapter 5. Keep in mind that monitors, keyboards, storage devices, and modems all have a cumulative affect on the software components of the operating system that manage the flow of data through the serial and parallel ports, and they work with the features of vendor-specific drivers.

Sometimes when you configure an analog modem connection, you will receive an installation CD-ROM, such as for configuring an Internet connection, but that is not always the case for every dial-up communications situation. For this reason, the following sections show you how to configure dial-up connections in operating systems.

For digital communications connections, the installation requirements typically vary by the provider for each connection. For these communications, you typically receive an installation CD-ROM tailored to the operating system and the provider. The CD-ROM is used for the setup and usually involves steps for you to provide the user account and password information that applies to your connection. After the setup, you typically see an addition in the operating system's network configuration information. For example, when you view the network connections in Windows XP, you may see a DSL connection under a category called Broadband or under LAN or High-Speed Internet.

Configuring Dial-up Connections in Windows 2000/XP/Server 2003

In Windows 2000, there is a Network and Dial-up Connections tool that can be opened by clicking Start and pointing to Settings, or by opening Control Panel. To set up a modem combined with Internet access in Windows XP, click Start, click Control Panel, click Network and Internet Connections, click Network Connections (see Figure 7-7), and choose the link to Create a new connection. In Windows Server 2003, click Start, point to Control Panel, point to Network Connections, and select the New Connection Wizard. One advantage of the Windows XP/Server 2003 setup is that you can configure an Internet Connection Firewall to help discourage intruders from accessing your computer and to filter possible viruses from coming in over the Internet or through FTP downloads. You should certainly configure this option if you are connecting through a cable modem. Hands-on Projects 7-6, 7-7, and 7-8 enable you to configure a dial-up connection in Windows 2000, Windows XP, and Windows Server 2003.

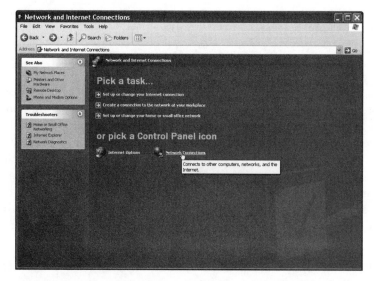

Figure 7-7 Accessing network connections in Windows XP

In Windows 2000/XP/Server 2003, you can set up modems individually. For example, in Windows 2000, open the Phone and Modem Options icon in Control Panel by clicking Start, pointing to Settings, clicking Control Panel, and double-clicking Phone and Modem Options. In Windows XP, click Start, click Control Panel, open Printers and Other

Hardware, and click Phone and Modem Options. And, in Windows Server 2003, click Start, point to Control Panel, and click Phone and Modem Options. Hands-on Project 7-1 enables you to access and configure the properties of a modem.

When you configure dial-up access in Windows 2000/XP/Server 2003, these operating systems will automatically start the modem configuration process if your modem has not already been configured by automatic PnP detection.

External communications programs can include simple terminal emulators (Microsoft Terminal), World Wide Web browsers (Microsoft Internet Explorer, Netscape Navigator or Communicator), e-mail programs (Outlook, Outlook Express, Eudora), audio and video communications applications (Microsoft NetMeeting), or anything that uses a modem link to exchange data with a remote computer or remote computer network.

Configuring Dial-up Connections in UNIX/Linux

In UNIX/Linux, and in some configurations of Windows, an analog modem has two purposes. It can either be a dial-in device, or a dial-out device. When a modem is used as a dial-in device, it is treated like a terminal connected to the computer using a serial connection. Any such terminal is still referred to as a teletype, from the old paper-based terminals that were used many years ago. In keeping with this tradition, the device port used for a modem is referred to as a TTY port, an abbreviation for teletype. To support dial-in connectivity on one of these TTYs, UNIX/Linux uses a **daemon** (an internal, automatically running program) called *getty*. There are numerous versions of *getty*. Some simply answer a call and let a user use the TTY as if on a terminal. More advanced versions are capable of using fax modems, detecting when a fax is received on the modem line, and automatically invoking fax software. The first modem in the computer is usually ttys0 or ttys1 and the path to the device file in many UNIX/Linux versions is /dev/ttys0 or /dev/ttys1. On many UNIX/Linux systems it is common to create a symbolic link to the device file so that you can refer to the modem as /dev/modem. You can do this by using the command *ln -s /dev/ttys1 /dev/modem*.

Keep in mind that *getty* is very picky when it comes to what the modem will report, both in the form of control lines used and the messages sent to the computer. In general, a modem should be used in factory settings with UNIX, with Data Carrier Detected (DCD) signaling enabled, with DTR set to drop the phone line, and with DSR and DTS set to normal.

You should set the modem to Auto Answer mode for use with *getty*. This means the modem automatically answers the phone when there is an incoming call and makes the connection to the other modem.

From the command line, many UNIX/Linux systems offer access to a modem through one of several possible programs, with Minicom as one of the most popular. Minicom is included in many versions of UNIX and nearly all versions of Linux, including Red Hat Enterprise Linux. The first step in using Minicom is to create a modem configuration file using the options shown in Figure 7-8. You configure the file by entering *minicom -s* from the root account, selecting Modem and dialing (see Figure 7-8), and then selecting the options that you want to configure (you must use AT commands for some parameters). After the file is configured, connect via the modem by entering *minicom* at the command line. Once Minicom is started, you can use the AT commands shown in Table 7-2. Hands-on Projects 7-3 and 7-5 demonstrate how to use Minicom.

Figure 7-8   Configuring a modem using Minicom in Red Hat Enterprise Linux

To learn more about Minicom and the most current version under development, visit *alioth.debian.org/projects/minicom*.

NOTE

Red Hat Enterprise Linux also simplifies modem setup and Internet setup by offering the Network Configuration tool and the Internet Configuration Wizard. The Network Configuration tool enables you to configure a modem. If you are connecting to an ISP, you can use the Network Configuration tool to configure the modem and your Internet connection; or you can use the newer Internet Configuration Wizard. To start the Network Configuration tool from the combined Bluecurve and GNOME desktop, for example, click Main Menu on the Panel, point to System Settings, and click Network. Click New to start a wizard to configure a new network connection, as shown in Figure 7-9. Notice in Figure 7-9 that you can configure an ISDN or xDSL connection as well as a regular dial-up modem connection. Or, to start the Internet Configuration Wizard, click Main Menu, point to System Tools, and click Internet Configuration Wizard. You need access to the root account to use either tool; or if you start it from your own account, you will need to provide the password for the root account. Both the Network Configuration tool and the Internet Configuration Wizard enable you to configure access to an Internet provider through different means, such as ISDN, analog modem, and DSL. For example, when you use the Internet Configuration Wizard, you can configure the following for an analog modem:

- Device file
- Communications speed
- Flow control
- Modem sound configuration
- Country of the ISP
- Telephone access number of the ISP
- Name of the ISP
- ISP user account name and password
- Use of TCP/IP and PPP for communications

Figure 7-9   Configuring a new connection from the Red Hat Enterprise Linux 3.0 Network Configuration tool

UNIX/Linux supports many software packages that can use the modem to dial out. The earliest packages were for message exchange using the **UNIX to UNIX Copy Protocol**, or **UUCP.** These packages are found on almost all UNIX/Linux versions, and one example is the very simple terminal program *tip* (Telephone Interface Program).

Many UNIX/Linux operating systems, including Red Hat Enterprise Linux, now run Mozilla as the Web browser and use Ximian Evolution for e-mail. Also, there are some advanced terminal emulation programs available as third-party add-ons to most UNIX/Linux operating systems, such as x3270, Kermit, and C-Kermit. Remember that Minicom provides terminal emulation (or you can use a third-party emulator with Minicom).

TIP

To learn more about x3270, go to the X Window Web site at *www.X.org*, or you can obtain it from *ftp://ftp.x.org/contrib/applications* (download the most recent x3270 zipped file in the main directory listing). To find out more about Kermit and C-Kermit, visit *www.columbia.edu/kermit*.

Some *gettys* don't want to see any progress information from the modem. To achieve this, consider using the following initialization string on most modems:

AT&F&C1&D2E0V0Q1S0=2&W

This string has the following components and meanings:

- *AT*—Modem command prefix
- *&F*—Resets the modem to factory settings
- *&C*—Turns on Request To Send/Clear To Send (RTS/CTS) control
- *&D2*—Sets DCD control to follow carrier
- *E0*—Enables the modem to forgo echoing commands sent to it back to the computer
- *V0*—Instructs the modem to send numeric, as opposed to verbal, error and progress messages
- *Q1*—Tells the modem not to return any error or progress messages
- *S0=2* —Tells the modem to answer the phone after two rings
- *&W*—Writes these settings to the modem's NVRAM (Non-Volatile Random Access Memory that stores configuration information), so the new settings are used the next time the modem is power cycled

Dial out can be done with the same modem, but, in general, a different device name is used. This is done because UNIX/Linux does not normally operate with a modem that does not have the DCD line raised. The initialization string for most dial-out applications is very similar to that for dial-in applications. The only change for most software is to use a Q0 instead of a Q1 setting and for some software to use the V1 setting instead of V0. Some modems may differ, so consult your modem manual.

Configuring Modems and Scripts in NetWare 6.x

Modems are often used in NetWare 6.x in association with the installation of Novell Internet Access Server. When Novell Internet Access Server is installed, the components for managing modems are also installed in the SYS:SYSTEM directory. These components include the following:

- WMDMMGR.EXE
- MODEMMGR.DLL
- Modem configuration files
- A sample PPP login script

WMDMMGR.EXE is a script-editing tool that is typically located in the directory SYS:SYSTEM\UTILS and needs MODEMMGR.DLL, a utility file, to properly run. The utility file along with help documentation for WMDMMGR.EXE are found in the directory SYS:SYSTEM\UTILS\NLS\ENGLISH. WMDMMGR.EXE is used to create new or edit exiting modem configuration files and PPP login scripts.

There are typically two or three modem configuration files that are provided by default. These files contain information about modem manufacturers, specific modem models, and configuration parameters for each model. NIASMDM1.MDC contains modem configurations for modems whose names start with A through L. NIASMDM2.MDC contains configurations for modems whose names start with M through Z. Finally, your system may also include the file NIASCERT.MDC, which contains configuration information for modems that have been certified by Novell to work with NetWare 6.x. The modem configuration files are typically located in the SYS:SYSTEM directory and always have the .MDC extension. Also, the combined three modem configuration files define several hundred modems that are on the market.

The ISPLOGIN.LSC file contains one or more sample PPP login scripts. A PPP login script defines the sequence of steps and commands that are necessary to access an ISP. You can use WMDMMGR.EXE to edit the sample login scripts or to create scripts of your own. ISPLOGIN.LSC is found in the SYS:SYSTEM directory. Figure 7-10 illustrates using WMDMMGR.EXE to edit the "sample" PPP login script, which is included in the IPSLOGIN.LSC file by default.

The recommended steps for modifying a modem configuration file or a PPP login script are generally as follows:

1. As administrator, copy the WMDMMGR.EXE and MODEMMGR.DLL modem configuration files (.MDC files) and PPP login script files (.LSC files) to the same folder on a workstation you use to manage the NetWare server, such as one running Windows XP Professional.

2. Make backup copies of the original .MDC and .LSC files in case the changes you make do not work properly.

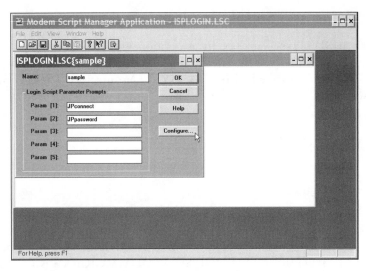

Figure 7-10   Editing a PPP login script for NetWare 6.x

3. Start WMDMMGR.EXE.

4. Click the File menu, click Open, and select the .MDC or .LSC file you want to edit.

5. Complete the desired actions and change the desired parameters as provided in the options of WMDMMGR.EXE.

6. Save the file via WMDMMGR.EXE (click File and click Save or click the Save button).

7. Copy the edited file back to the SYS:SYSTEM directory on the NetWare 6.x server.

Hands-on Project 7-9 enables you to use WMDMMGR.EXE.

Configuring Modems in Mac OS X

Many Macintosh computers come with an internal modem. There are two tools you can use to configure the modem for Internet access: Internet Connect and System Preferences. For example, to use Internet Connect click the Go menu, click Applications, and double-click Internet Connect, as shown in Figure 7-11. Select Internal Modem as the device to configure. You can provide information about:

■ The telephone number for the ISP

■ The user name for the ISP account

■ The password for the ISP account

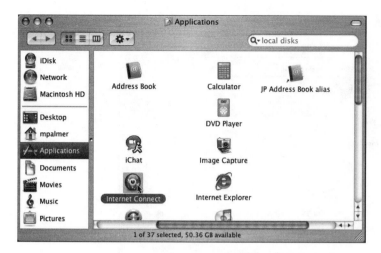

Figure 7-11   Using Internet Connnect in Mac OS X

In addition to this information, you can select to display the modem status on the menu bar, and you can choose to connect to the Internet.

The Network option in System Preferences is the second tool you can use for configuring the modem and Internet access. To access this tool, click System Preferences on the dock, double-click Network, and select to configure Internal Modem, as shown in Figure 7-12. Using this tool provides a wider range of parameters to configure than the Internet Connect tool, including:

- PPP and dial-up information
- TCP/IP information
- Proxy parameters
- Detailed modem parameters

Hands-on Project 7-10 enables you to configure an internal modem using System Preferences.

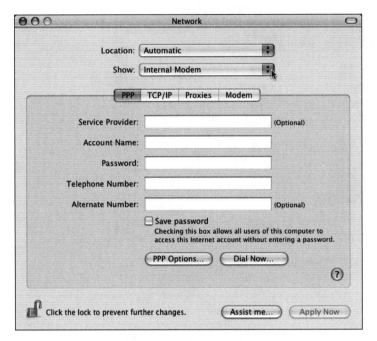

Figure 7-12   Using System Preferences to configure a modem connection in Mac OS X

Chapter Summary

◻ Modems open WAN communications to millions of users so they can access the Internet and communicate with servers for information sharing, education, and work.

◻ Most computers sold today come with a built-in analog modem, which converts the digital language of the computer to analog signals that can be used over regular telephone lines. The conversion process is called modulation/demodulation.

◻ Analog modems have a three-part architecture consisting of a data pump, controller, and UART. These components may be implemented completely in hardware, or partially in software.

◻ The most common way to communicate through analog modems is by using the Hayes AT modem command set to control modem settings and establish WAN connections.

◻ Digital modems are not actually modems at all because they are entirely digital and do not perform the modulation/demodulation required for analog devices. They are called modems because they perform the same basic functions as analog modems, allowing communications between computers over a WAN connection, such as a telecommunication line.

◻ Digital modems work with digital telephone systems, cable systems, and satellite systems—most commonly, ISDN, CATV networks, DSLs, and wireless satellite networks. Table 7-4 reviews analog and digital remote access speeds.

❑ Both analog and digital modems communicate by using communications protocols, software flow control, hardware flow control, error correction, and data compression. Each of these techniques conforms to standards, such as the ITU-T standards, so that one type of modem can successfully communicate with a different modem or WAN communications device at the other end.

❑ Windows 2000/XP/Server 2003 enable the configuration of modems and Internet connections through dial-up and Control Panel utilities built into the operating system.

❑ Modem and Internet configuration tools are available for UNIX/Linux systems, such as the commonly used Minicom program. Red Hat Enterprise Linux 3.0 also offers the GUI-based Network Configuration tool and the Internet Configuration Wizard.

❑ When Novell Internet Access Server is loaded in NetWare 6.x, the WMDMMGR.EXE program is available to configure modems and create modem scripts.

❑ Mac OS X comes with the Internet Connect and System Preferences tools for configuring modem and Internet connections.

NOTE For urban areas, it is likely that cable modem and DSL access will continue to grow and provide subscribers access to high-speed alternatives. Also, as satellite communications grow through TV providers, there will be continued improvements in options and services for urban and rural customers.

Table 7-4 Summary of analog and digital remote access speeds

Access Mode	Upstream Transmission Rate	Downstream Transmission Rate	Relative Expense
Analog modem	Up to 48 Kbps	Up to 56 Kbps	Relatively inexpensive (the cost of a modem and regular telephone line)
ISDN	Up to 128 Kbps for BRI and up to 1.544 Mbps for PRI	Up to 128 Kbps for BRI and up to 1.544 Mbps for PRI	Relatively expensive (the TA is relatively inexpensive but the monthly digital line fee is relatively expensive)
Cable modem	Up to about 3 Mbps for a single user (but rates vary depending on the provider)	Up to about 3 Mbps for a single user (but rates vary depending on the provider)	Relatively inexpensive (the cost of a cable modem and a monthly cable fee which can be combined with a TV access fee)

Table 7-4   Summary of analog and digital remote access speeds (continued)

Access Mode	Upstream Transmission Rate	Downstream Transmission Rate	Relative Expense
DSL	Up to 640 Kbps for the commonly used ADSL (VDSL, which is less commonly available, offers rates up to 2.3 Mbps)	Up to 6 Mbps for ADSL (VDSL offers rates up to 55 Mbps)	Relatively inexpensive (the cost of a DSL adapter or router and a monthly DSL telephone line fee)
Satellite	Transmission rates are not guaranteed, but typically can be up to about 50 Kbps (LEO satellites are working to offer up to 128 Kbps)	Transmission rates are not guaranteed, but typically can be up to about 500 Kbps (LEO satellites are working to offer up to 720 Kbps)	Relatively expensive (the cost of a dish, modems, and a monthly access fee; these expenses are going down with new technologies and can be combined with dish TV in some areas)

KEY TERMS

Asymmetric Digital Subscriber Line (ADSL) — A high speed digial subscriber line technology that can use ordinary telephone lines for downstream data transmission of up to 6 Mpbs and 576–640 Kbps for upstream transmission.

asynchronous communication — Communications that occur in discrete units in which the start of a unit is signaled by a start bit at the front, and a stop bit at the back signals the end of the unit.

Attention (AT) commands — A modem control command set designed by the Hayes company. This standard modem command set begins each command with AT (for Attention) and allows communications software or users to directly control many modem functions.

Basic Rate Interface (BRI) — An ISDN interface that consists of three channels. Two are 64 Kbps channels for data, voice, video, and graphics transmissions. The third is a 16 Kbps channel used for communications signaling.

cable modem — A digital modem device designed for use with the cable TV system providing high-speed data transfer. It may include an analog modem component that is used with a conventional telephone line connection for information sent from the user to the ISP.

Certified Cable Modem Project — Also called Data Over Cable Service Interface Specification (DOCSIS). A project sponsored by the cable modem industry to provide a set of standards and equipment certification to provide stability to cable modem communications.

controller — A hardware or software component of a modem that defines an individual modem's capabilities. The controller interprets AT commands and handles communications protocols, for example.

daemon — An internal, automatically running program, usually in UNIX/Linux, that serves a particular function such as routing e-mail to recipients or supporting dial-up networking connectivity.

Data Communications Equipment (DCE) — A device, such as a modem, that converts data from a DTE, such as a computer, for transmission over a telecommunications line. The DCE normally provides the clock rate/clocking mechanism necessary for communications.

Data Over Cable Service Interface Specification (DOCSIS) — See *Certified Cable Modem Project*.

data pump — The hardware or software portion of a modem that is responsible for converting digital data into analog signals for transmission over a telephone line and for converting analog signals into digital data for transmission to the computer.

Data Terminal Equipment (DTE) — A computer or computing device that prepares data to be transmitted over a telecommunications line to which it attaches by using a DCE, such as a modem.

digital modem — A modem-like device that transfers data via digital lines instead of analog lines.

Digital Signal Processor (DSP) — A software data pump used in software-driven modems such as the 3Com Winmodem.

Digital Subscriber Line (DSL) — A technology that uses advanced modulation technologies on existing telecommunications networks for high-speed networking between a subscriber and a telco and that offers communication speeds up to 60 Mbps.

flow control — A hardware or software feature in modems that lets a receiving modem communicate to the sending modem that it needs more time to process previously sent data. When the current data is processed successfully, the receiving modem notifies the sending modem that it can resume data transmission.

G.lite Asymmetric Digital Subscriber Line (G.lite ADSL) — A Plug and Play compatible version of ADSL that transmits at 500 Kbps upstream and 1.5 Mbps downstream.

Hayes command set — See *Attention (AT) commands*.

High Bit-Rate Digital Subscriber Line (HDSL) — A form of high-speed digital subscriber line technology that has upstream and downstream transmission rates of up to 1.544 Mbps.

Host Signal Processor (HSP) — A software approach to handling data pump duties in software-based modems such as the 3Com Winmodem.

Integrated Services Digital Network (ISDN) — A digital telephone line used for high-speed digital computer communications, videoconferencing, Internet connections, and telecommuting.

Integrated Services Digital Network Digital Subscriber Line (IDSL) — A DSL version that is compatible with a Digital Loop Carrier device that may be used on some telephone networks. IDSL provides upstream and downstream communications at 144 Kbps.

International Telecommunications Union (ITU) — An international organizationthat sets telecommunications standards for modem and WAN communications, for example.

line noise — Communications interference from any source, such as from electromagnetic interference (EMI) from electric motors or radio frequency interference (RFI) from radio-wave communications.

Link Access Protocol for Modems (LAPM) — An error-checking protocol used in the V.42 standard that constructs data into discrete frame-like units for transmission over communications lines. Error checking is made possible because each unit is given a sequence number and a checksum. If a received unit is out of sequence or has the wrong checksum, this signals an error in the transmission.

modem — A hardware device that permits a computer to exchange digital data with another computer via an analog telephone line or dedicated connection.

parity checking — A data communications process that ensures data integrity through a system of data bit comparisons between the sending and receiving computer.

Plain Old Telephone Service (POTS) — Regular voice-grade telephone service (the old terminology).

Primary Rate Interface (PRI) — An ISDN interface that consists of switched communications in multiples of 1.544 Mbps.

protocol — An established guideline that specifies how networked data, including data sent over a telephone network, is formatted into a transmission unit, how it is transmitted, and how it is interpreted at the receiving end.

Public Switched Telephone Network (PSTN) — Regular voice-grade telephone service (the modern terminology).

Rate Adaptive (Asymmetric) Digital Subscriber Line (RADSL) — A high-speed data transmission technology that offers upstream speeds of up to 1 Mbps and downstream speeds of up to 7 Mbps. RADSL uses ADSL technology (see *ADSL*), but enables the transmission rate to vary for different types of communications, such as data, multimedia, and voice.

start bit — In data communication, an extra bit inserted by the sending modem at the beginning of a data byte to help ensure that the received data is correct.

stop bit — In data communication, an extra bit inserted by the sending modem at the end of a data byte to help ensure that the received data is correct.

Symmetric Digital Subscriber Line (SDSL) — A form of digital subscriber line technology that is often used for videoconferencing or online learning. It offers a transmission speed of 384 Kbps for upstream and downstream communications.

Symmetric High Bit-Rate Digital Subscriber Line (SHDSL) — Also called G.shdsl, a DSL technology that can be transmitted over one or two wires and that can reach up to about 4 miles (over two wires). The upstream and downstream rates can vary in the range of 192 Kbps to 2.3 Mbps.

synchronous communication — Communications of continuous bursts or blocks of data controlled by a clock signal that starts each burst or block of data.

terminal adapter (TA) — A digital modem that permits computer-to-computer data transfer over a digital line, such as ISDN.

universal asynchronous receiver-transmitter (UART) — An electronic chip that handles data flow through a serial port or modem.

UNIX to UNIX Copy Protocol (UUCP) — A protocol used by UNIX computers for communicating through modems. UUCP can also be used on networks, but for these applications, it is usually replaced by the faster TCP/IP technology.

Very High Bit–Rate Digital Subscriber Line (VDSL) — A digital subscriber line technology that works over coaxial and fiber-optic cables, yielding 51–55 Mbps downstream and 1.6–2.3 Mbps upstream communications.

Winmodem — A software-driven modem from 3Com Corporation that uses minimal hardware and the computer's CPU with software to conduct data communications.

Xon-Xoff — A software flow control protocol that permits a receiving modem to notify the sending modem that its data buffers are full, and it needs more time to process previously received data.

7

REVIEW QUESTIONS

1. In a Winmodem, the controller functions are based in _____ .
   a. a serial port
   b. a USB port
   c. software
   d. hardware

2. Your boss has asked you to research DSL options for the company. Her concerns are to implement a version of DSL that is compatible with automatic configuration techniques in Windows XP Professional but that also provides communications faster than 400 Kbps. What do you recommend to her?
   a. IDSL
   b. G.lite ADSL
   c. AutoDSL
   d. SDSL

3. Your assistant is attempting to configure a modem in Red Hat Enterprise Linux. When he types *minicom* at the command line and presses Enter, he does not see any options for configuring the modem. What might be the problem?
   a. He needs to type *minicom -s* and press Enter.
   b. He must type *miniconfig* and press Enter.
   c. There is no modem installed in the computer.
   d. Minicom only works for USB modems and his computer has a serial modem.

4. A new employee on your staff has been explaining to a group of computer users that digital modems use modulation/demodulation to convert digital signals to carrier signals on computer lines. What is your reaction? (Choose all that apply.)
   a. You commend this employee for helping others understand digital modems.
   b. You add that digital modems are typically slower than other kinds of modems because modulation/demodulation takes extra time.

c. You share with the group that digital modems use octal signals for communications.

d. You add a correction by noting that digital modems are actually not modems because they use digital data transmissions from start to finish.

5. For which operating system would you use WMDMMGR.EXE to configure modems? (Choose all that apply.)

   a. Windows Server 2003

   b. NetWare 6.x

   c. Mac OS X

   d. Windows 2000 Professional

6. One of your customers is having trouble because modem communications seem to pause unexpectedly and then start again. Which of the following would you try first?

   a. Change the modem setup to use hardware flow control because it is currently set for software flow control.

   b. Replace the UART in the modem.

   c. Change the modem's speed to 24 Kbps because 56 Kbps is too fast.

   d. Reduce the size of the incoming data buffer to 8 bytes.

7. Which of the following tools can you use in Windows XP Professional to adjust the port speed for a serial modem?

   a. Modem Event Viewer

   b. Phone and Modem Options which is available through the Control Panel

   c. Add/Remove Software tool

   d. Local Area Connection tool

8. _____ is a basic but important form of error correction used by modems.

   a. Bitmapped error correction

   b. Start bit/stop bit error correction

   c. UUENCODE

   d. Port modulation

9. Your 56 Kbps modem does not seem to have as fast upstream communications as the one in your roommate's computer, which uses the same telephone line (but you both do not use the telephone line at the same time). Which of the following are possible explanations? (Choose all that apply.)

   a. The software in your modem that governs V.42bis communications has some bugs.

   b. The V.21 functions in your modem are not set for fast upstream communications.

   c. You have a V.90 modem and your roommate has a V.92 modem.

   d. Your modem does not have a "ter" certification.

10. You've purchased a cable modem from a friend who no longer needs hers. When you set it up, it does not properly communicate on your cable network. Which of the following is a likely explanation of the problem? (Choose all that apply.)

    a. Your cable network uses analog modems and not cable modems.

    b. The cable modem you purchased has more channels than are available from your cable provider.

    c. Your cable provider requires DOCSIS 1.1 or above compatibility and your modem does not conform to these standards.

    d. The distance from the cable connection in your house to the pole in the alley exceeds the signal strength of the cable modem you purchased.

11. Which of the following can you configure in the MAC OS X system preferences for an Internet and internal modem connection? (Choose all that apply.)

    a. PPP information

    b. TCP/IP information

    c. Proxy parameters

    d. Line signal strength

12. You are troubleshooting the modem setup for a client who has a POTS pulse dial line in an older part of the city. The command for dialing the number of his ISP is set up as ATDT 821-1244. You have checked and 821-1244 is the number to reach the ISP. What might be the reason that this command is not successfully connecting to the ISP?

    a. The command should be changed to ATDP 821-1244.

    b. The command should be changed to AT S0=10 821-1244.

    c. The ATDT command hangs up the phone line rather than initiating a call.

    d. There must be a W before DT as in ATWDT 821-1244

13. DSL _____ . (Choose all that apply.)

    a. is an entirely wireless broadband technology

    b. works over the copper wire already used in lines for telephone service

    c. in contrast to cable modem technology, gives the user a dedicated line rather than one that is shared

    d. doesn't allow the user to take a phone call on the same line as is used for data communications

14. What is the function of a data pump?

    a. It performs modulation and demodulation functions.

    b. It provides a modem with speaker services.

    c. It places a modem in sleep mode when the modem is not in use.

    d. It pumps up or amplifies the signal strength on a 64 Hz telephone line.

7

15. Your client's company is exploring ISDN for shared Internet access by employees. What type of ISDN do you recommend in this situation?

    a. Rate Adaptive (RA)

    b. Basic Rate Interface (BRI)

    c. Primary Rate Interface (PRI)

    d. National Public Rate (NPR)

16. One of the Windows XP computer users that you support in your company has a 56 Kbps modem, but he complains that it typically communicates with his ISP at 24 Kbps or slower. Why is this? (Choose all that apply.)

    a. The maximum speed setting for the modem's serial port is 24,000.

    b. The modem does not have a controller.

    c. The modem is negotiating down to a slower speed because there is noise on his telephone line.

    d. The modem is not using the faster AT command set.

17. Which of the following equipment is typically involved in an Internet connection via satellite? (Choose all that apply.)

    a. a dish for Internet connectivity

    b. a terminal adapter

    c. an analog satellite frequency tuner

    d. a digital modem for sending and a digital modem for receiving

18. In UNIX/Linux, which of the following would represent a typical modem device file?

    a. /etc/comm/modem

    b. /usr/comm

    c. /bin/mode/modem.1

    d. /dev/ttys0

19. Your NetWare 6.0 server assistant has been deleting files she believes to be unnecessary because disk space is running a bit low. In the process she has deleted all MDC files. What problem(s) might this cause?

    a. modem communications problems

    b. problems for editing PPP login scripts

    c. inability to communicate with the server using TCP/IP over both local area network and modem connections

    d. inability to access USB ports

20. When you configure the parity while setting up a modem, which of the following might be parity values you can set? (Choose all that apply.)

    a. 7-bit

    b. 8-bit

    c. even or odd parity

    d. no parity or none

HANDS-ON PROJECTS

HANDS-ON PROJECTS

Project 7-1

In Windows-based systems, it is important to make sure that the port speed (the speed setup for the serial or parallel port to which the modem is connected) is the same as or higher than the speed capability of the modem. If it is not, then you will not be using the full-speed capability of the modem. This project enables you to check the modem port speed setup in **Windows 2000/XP/Server 2003**. For this project, there should be a serial or parallel modem already installed in the computer. Also, before you start, check with your instructor to learn the maximum speed of the modem in the computer you are using.

To check the modem port speed setup:

1. In Windows 2000, click **Start**, point to **Settings**, click **Control Panel**, and double-click **Phone and Modem Options**. In Windows XP, click **Start**, click **Control Panel**, click **Printers and Other Hardware**, and click **Phone and Modem Options**. Or, in Windows Server 2003, click **Start**, point to **Control Panel**, and click **Phone and Modem Options**.

2. Click the **Modems** tab in the Phone and Modem Options dialog box.

3. How many modems are installed in your computer and what models do they represent? Can you tell which port(s) the modem(s) are using? Make certain that a modem is selected.

4. Click the **Properties** button (see Figure 7-13).

5. Click the **Modem** tab. What is the value in the Maximum Port Speed box? Is it higher than the actual speed of the modem? How can you change the port speed?

6. Click the **Diagnostics** tab. You use this tab to test the modem in case you are having communications problems.

7. Click **Cancel** to close the modem Properties dialog box. Click **Cancel** to close the Phone and Modem Options dialog box. Close the Printers and Other Hardware window in Windows XP, or close **Control Panel** in Windows 2000 and Windows Server 2003.

Figure 7-13 Selecting to configure the modem properties in Windows XP

Project 7-2

In this project, you check for the presence of a modem in **Red Hat Enterprise Linux 3.0** (or in many versions of UNIX and Linux), using the *wvdial* utility. Log onto the root account for this activity.

To check for the presence of a modem:

1. Access the command prompt or open a terminal window, such as by clicking **Main Menu**, pointing to **System Tools**, and clicking **Terminal**.

2. Type **wvdial**, as shown in Figure 7-14, and press **Enter**.

3. If there is a modem already configured, the *wvdial* program lists the device special file associated with the modem, usually the /dev/modem file, and it lists information about the modem. If a modem is not configured, you will see several error messages, including one or more lines, such as "Cannot open /dev/modem: No such file or directory." What information do you see on your display?

4. Close the terminal window.

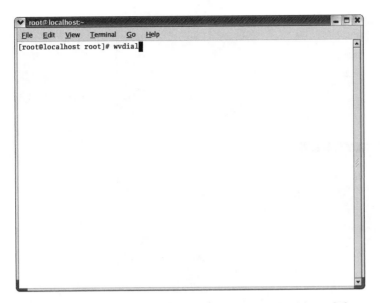

Figure 7-14   Using *wvdial* in Red Hat Enterprise Linux 3.0

Project 7-3

This project enables you to use the Minicom program in **Red Hat Enterprise Linux 3.0** to check the port speed setup. (Minicom is widely available in UNIX and Linux systems and is run from the command line.) You need to log on using the root account for this project.

To check the port speed setup:

1. Open a terminal window, such as by clicking **Main Menu**, pointing to **System Tools**, and clicking **Terminal**.

2. Type **minicom –s** and press **Enter**. You'll see a graphics-based display in the terminal window, similar to the one in Figure 7-15.

3. Press the **down arrow** on your keyboard until **Serial port setup** is highlighted.

4. Press **Enter**. What happens? Record you observations. What is the value for Serial Device (the device file used for the modem)? What is the setting for Bps/Par/Bits, which is the setup (bits per second, parity, and start/stop bits) for the port?

5. Type the option for Bps/Par/Bits, such as **E**. What happens?

6. Select the option for 57600, such as **H**. Notice that the Current: line at the top changes to show 57600 for the speed.

7. Press **Enter**.

8. Press **Enter** again.

9. Move the down arrow to select **Exit from Minicom**.

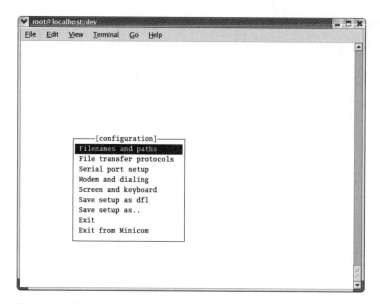

Figure 7-15 Using the Minicom program in Red Hat Enterprise Linux 3.0

10. Press **Enter**.

11. Close the terminal window.

Project 7-4

In this project, you use an Internet resource to test the speed of your modem. You can use a Web browser in any of the operating systems discussed in this book, such as Internet Explorer for **Windows 2000/XP/Server 2003/Mac OS X** or Mozilla for **UNIX/Linux** systems. You need access to the Internet via your modem for this project.

To test the speed of your modem:

1. Point your browser to *www.dslreports.com*.

2. Click the link for **Test+ Tools**.

3. Click the link for **Speed Tests**.

4. Click one of the speed test links, such as speakeasy, MegaPath, linkLine, or any others listed.

5. Review the information and instructions about the test.

6. Begin the speed test by clicking the **Start** button (sometimes the speed test site you select is too busy and you may need to go back a screen to select another site, or keep trying on the current site).

7. Do not use the connection until the test is finished. What upload and download speeds did you achieve through the test? Do the speeds match the top speeds of the modem or are they lower?

8. Close the Web browser.

TIP   There are many other Web sites you can use to perform speed tests if this Web site has moved or is too busy. Alternatives include *homepage.eircom.net/ ~leslie/testpage.htm, www.bandwidthplace.com/speedtest/, speedtest.clover. net, home. earthlink.net/~ttesla/spdtstlinks.htm* (for a list of speed test links). Note that any of these sites, too, may be temporarily unavailable because they can be busy from many people performing tests.

7

Project 7-5

HANDS-ON PROJECTS

In this project, you use the Minicom program in UNIX/Linux, such as in **Red Hat Enterprise Linux 3.0**, to view the use of Hayes AT commands for a modem's dial-up properties.

To view the use of AT commands:

1. Access the command line or open a terminal window, such as by clicking **Main Menu**, pointing to **System Tools**, and clicking **Terminal**.

2. Type **minicom –s** and press **Enter**.

3. Press the **down arrow** until **Modem and dialing** is highlighted.

4. Press **Enter**. Figure 7-16 illustrates a sample display. Which of the configurable options on your screen use AT commands?

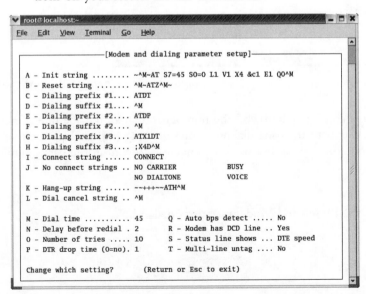

Figure 7-16   Viewing the modem and dialing properties in UNIX/Linux using Minicom

4. Press **Esc** to exit without changing any parameters.

5. Use the down arrow to select **Exit from Minicom**.

6. Press **Enter**.

7. Close the terminal window if you opened one to access the command line.

Project 7-6

In this project, you learn how to configure a dial-up connection in **Windows 2000 Professional**. You need access to an account that has Administrator privileges.

To configure dial-up networking in Windows 2000 Professional:

1. Click **Start**, point to **Settings**, and click **Network and Dial-up Connections**.

2. Double-click **Make New Connection** (see Figure 7-17).

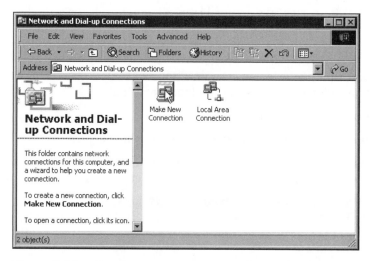

Figure 7-16   Creating a new connection for modem access in Windows 2000 Professional

3. Enter your area code (required) and the number to dial an outside line (if necessary). Also, select whether to use tone dialing or pulse dialing (most telephone lines have tone dialing). (If you see the Network Connection Wizard in the background, ignore it for now.)

4. Click **OK**.

5. Click **OK** in the Phone and Modem Options dialog box.

6. Click **Next** when you see the Network Connection Wizard. What connection options appear?

7. Click **Dial-up to the Internet** and click **Next**.

8. For this project, select **I want to set up my Internet connection manually, or I want to connect through a local area network (LAN)** (see Figure 7-18).

Figure 7-18   Determining how to access the Internet in Windows 2000 Professional

9. If your modem is not already installed, the wizard now installs it. Click **Next** if you see the Add/Remove Hardware Wizard. (If your modem is enabled for PnP, the wizard automatically configures it; otherwise, you must specify the type of modem and the port to which it is attached.) Click **Finished** when the Add/Remove Hardware Wizard is finished.

10. Click **I connect through a phone line and a modem**. Click **Next**.

11. Enter the telephone number for the connection (or make one up for practice) and click **Next**.

12. Enter the account or username and password used for the connection (or you can also make these up for practice).

13. Provide a name for the connection, such as the name of your ISP, or simply enter your initials to identify the connection.

14. Click **Next**.

15. Click **No** so that you do not set up an Internet mail account at this time. Click **Next**.

16. Click **Finish**.

17. If you are connected to a telephone line, you can click **Connect** now to test your connection. If you are not connected to a telephone line, close the Dial-up Connection box.

> When you use the Network Connection Wizard to set up an Internet connection, it automatically sets up to use TCP/IP and PPP. You can verify this by clicking Start, pointing to Settings, and clicking Network and Dial-up Connections. Right-click the connection that you just created and click Properties.

Project 7-7

This project enables you to configure dial-up networking in **Windows XP** (**Home** or **Professional**). You need access to an account that has Administrator privileges. Also, ask your instructor for the name of an ISP and an access telephone number (or you can make these up for practice).

To configure dial-up networking:

1. Click **Start**, click **Control Panel**, and click **Network and Internet Connections** (using the Category View).

2. Click **Set up or change your Internet connection** (see Figure 7-19).

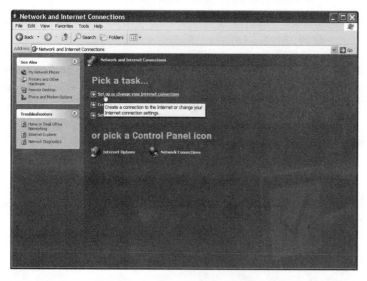

Figure 7-19   Configuring dial-up networking for Internet access in Windows XP

3. Click the **Setup** button in the Internet Properties dialog box.

4. The New Connection Wizard starts. Click **Next**.

5. What network connection options do you see? Record your observations.

6. Select **Connect to the Internet**, and click **Next**. What options are in the Getting Ready dialog box?

7. Click **Set up my connection manually**, and then click **Next**.

8. Click **Connect using a dial-up modem** if this option is not already selected. Notice that this option includes the ability to connect using an analog modem or an ISDN phone line (and TA). There are also options in this dialog box to connect using DSL and cable modems (for broadband connectivity). Click **Next**.

9. If your computer has more than one modem installed, you see a Select a Device dialog box that enables you to select which modem to configure. Select a modem if you see this dialog box (consult with your instructor if you are unsure which modem to select), and click **Next**.

10. Enter the name of the ISP (or use your initials to identify the connection), and then click **Next**.

11. Enter the phone number to use for accessing the ISP (or make up a phone number for practice). Click **Next**.

12. Enter the user/account name for the ISP connection and the password (or make these up for practice). Enter the password again to confirm it. Also, make sure that the following are checked:

    ❑ **Use this account name and password when anyone connects to the Internet from this computer.**

    ❑ **Make this the default Internet connection.**

    ❑ **Turn on Internet Connection Firewall for this connection.**

13. Click **Next**.

14. Review the parameters that you entered and click **Finish**.

15. On the Network and Internet Connections window, click **Network Connections**.

16. Right-click your new connection (under Dial-up), and click **Properties**.

17. Click the **Networking** tab. Notice that PPP and Internet Protocol (TCP/IP) are automatically configured for this connection. Also, what other option is configured by default?

18. Close the Properties dialog box and then close the Network Connections window.

7

Project 7-8

In this project, you configure a dial-up connection in **Windows Server 2003**. You will need access to an account that has Administrator privileges. Also, ask your instructor for the name of an ISP and an access telephone number (or you can make one up for practice).

To configure dial-up networking in Windows Server 2003:

1. Click **Start**, point to **Control Panel**, point to **Network Connections**, and click **New Connection Wizard**. (Or if there are other connections already created and you do not see New Connection Wizard as an option, click Start, point to Control Panel, double-click Network Connections, and click Create a new connection.)

2. Click **Next** after the New Connection Wizard starts. What network connection options do you see?

3. Select **Connect to the Internet** and click **Next**.

4. Notice that there are options for: *Connect using a dial-up modem, Connect using a broadband connection that requires a username and password,* and *Connect using a broadband connection that is always on.* For this project, select **Connect using a dial-up modem** and click **Next**.

5. Enter the name of the ISP provided by your instructor, or simply enter your initials plus "connection" to set up a practice connection. Click **Next**.

6. Enter the telephone number provided by your instructor, or provide a number for practice. Click **Next**.

7. Click **Anyone's use** so that any server users can access this dial-up connection.

8. Enter the user/account name for the ISP connection and the password (or make these up for practice). Enter the password again to confirm it. Also, make sure that the following are checked:

   ◻ **Use this account name and password when anyone connects to the Internet from this computer.**

   ◻ **Make this the default Internet connection.**

   ◻ **Turn on Internet Connection Firewall for this connection.**

9. Click **Next**.

10. Review the parameters that you entered and click **Finish**.

11. Click **Start**, point to **Control Panel**, point to **Network Connections**, right-click the connection you just created, and click **Properties**.

12. Click the **Networking** tab. Notice that PPP and Internet Protocol (TCP/IP) are automatically configured for this connection. (See Figure 7-20.)

13. Close the Properties dialog box and then close the Network Connections window.

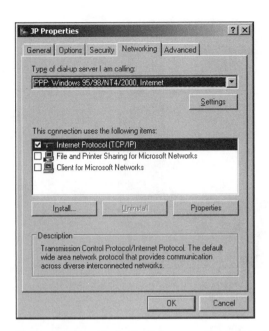

Figure 7-20 Default dial-up configuration in Windows Server 2003

Project 7-9

In this project, you practice using the **NetWare 6.x** WMDMMGR.EXE program to access a PPP login script. You need access to a workstation, such as one running Windows 2000 Professional or Windows XP (Home or Professional) that has a folder containing WMDM-MGR.EXE, MODEMMGR.DLL, and the ISPLOGIN.LSC file or, if you can connect to a NetWare server, you can run the WMDMMGR.EXE program from the server. (WMDM-MGR.EXE can be copied from the SYS:SYSTEM\UTILS NetWare directory, MODEM-MGR.DLL is usually in the SYS:SYSTEM\UTILS\NLS\ENGLISH directory, and ISPLOGIN.LSC is typically in the SYS:SYSTEM directory in NetWare.)

To access the PPP login script:

1. Start the WMDMMGR.EXE program. For example, in Windows 2000/XP, click **Start**, click **Run**, browse to the **WMDMMGR.EXE** program so it appears in the Open box, and click **OK**. (Or, if you are connected to a NetWare server, use My Computer to browse to and start SYS:SYSTEM\UTILS\WMDMMGR.EXE.)

2. Click the **File** menu and click **Open**, if necessary.

3. Select **Login Script Files (*.lsc)** in the List files of type box.

4. Browse to the drive and folder containing the ISPLOGIN.LSC file (on a NetWare server it should be in the SYS:SYSTEM directory) and select that file. Click **OK**.

5. Select a login script, such as **sample**, and click the **Modify** button, as shown in Figure 7-21.

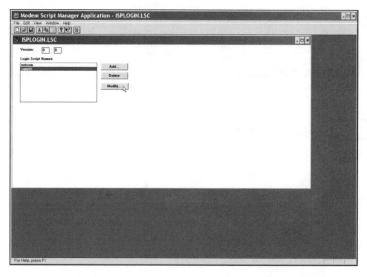

Figure 7-21   Modifying a PPP login script for NetWare 6.x

6. Notice the values for the Login Script Parameter Prompts and record them.

7. Click the **Configure** button. What information do you see?

8. Click **Cancel** and click **Cancel** again.

9. Close the Modem Script Manager.

Project 7-10

In this project, you use System Preferences in **Mac OS X** to configure an internal modem to access the Internet.

To configure the internal modem:

1. Click the **System Preferences** icon in the dock or click **Go**, click **Applications**, and double-click **System Preferences**.

2. Click the **Network** icon.

3. Select **Internal Modem** in the Show box if it is not already selected.

4. Make sure that the **TCP/IP** tab is selected.

5. What are the options available in the Configure IPv4 box? Choose **Using PPP** in the Configure IPv4 box if it is not already selected. How is the IP address determined? Note that you also have the option to provide DNS information and/or information for connecting to a specific domain, such as *www.apple.com*

6. Click the **PPP** tab. What information can you configure on this tab?

7. Click the **PPP Options** button to review the options that you can configure. Click **Cancel**.

8. Click the **Modem** tab. What type of modem is installed? What parameters can be configured for the modem?

9. Click the **System Preferences** menu and click **Quit System Preferences**.

10. Click **Don't Apply** if you see the Apply configuration changes box.

11. Close the Applications window if you opened it to access System Preferences.

CASE PROJECTS

Wilderness Supply is a 38-person company that makes outdoor clothing such as parkas, jackets, backpacks, hats, gloves, bags, and other equipment. The management group, sales representatives, purchasing agent, and inventory and shipping specialists all use computers that must be connected to the Internet to communicate with distributors, suppliers, a payroll preparation company, and for many other purposes. Currently, all of the computers have V.92 modems and access to telephone lines for outside communications. Also, the computers are connected to one another through a LAN. The company is contacting you to consult about ways in which to support modem access and to improve these communications.

Case Project 7-1: Comparing ADSL and Cable Modem Alternatives

Several members of the company have learned that ADSL is now available through a local telecommunications company. Cable modem access is also available. Compare these two alternatives and prepare a report for the company's management so they can consider these as replacements for analog modem access.

Case Project 7-2: Verifying the Serial Port Speed in Red Hat Enterprise Linux 3.0

The owner of the company uses Red Hat Enterprise Linux 3.0 on his workstation. He wants to check the serial port speed of his internal modem. Explain how he can check the speed.

Case Project 7-3: Finding a Communications Alternative for a Backcountry Research Team

Wilderness Supply has a contract with a two-person research team in Alaska that field tests new clothing and equipment. The research team has access to a telephone line, but the noise problems are so severe on the line into their backcountry residence that often they cannot use it to access the Internet. What is another alternative they can use to quickly exchange information via computers with the Wilderness Supply home office? Briefly describe the alternative you recommend along with the equipment that is necessary.

Case Project 7-4: Setting Up Modems for Mac OS X Computers

Four of the managers have just gotten MAC OS X computers. Create a short document that describes how to set up the internal modems for Internet access.

Case Project 7-5: Addressing a Telecommunications Line Problem

One week ago, a building contractor was working in the area of the Wilderness Supply offices and disrupted telephone service with his backhoe (the telephone lines are buried underground). Service has been restored, but ever since the mishap, all of Wilderness Supply's modem users have reported very slow access. The telephone company would like documentation of the access speed because they believe that all the problems with the damaged lines have already been addressed. What do you recommend to Wilderness Supply as a way to demonstrate to the telephone company that there is still a problem?

CHAPTER 8

NETWORK CONNECTIVITY

After reading this chapter and completing the exercises, you will be able to:

♦ Explain networking basics, such as network topologies, networking hardware, packaging data to transport, and how devices connect to a network

♦ Describe network transport and communications protocols, and determine which protocols are used in specific computer operating systems

♦ Explain how to integrate different operating systems on the same network

♦ Describe how network and workstation operating systems are used for remote networking

Computer networking is an extension of the desire to share information instantly. This information may take the form of word-processed documents, messages, graphs and charts, pictures, maps, x-rays, electronic mail, or full-motion video. Using networks, a physician in New York City can help diagnose a patient who is with another physician in Los Angeles. Using networks, an engineer can coordinate the design of a new supersonic airplane by electronically sharing design diagrams with other engineers working on the same project in the same building. Students now use networks to obtain assignments from teachers and to submit their completed work. They also chat, make phone calls, and send instant messages over the Internet. Other students take entire classes or programs of study using the Internet.

As you learned in the last chapter, modems provided one of the first and most basic ways to build a network. Today there are many new and evolving options to connect computers. Strong interest in setting up computers to communicate has spurred the development of an array of network technologies. In this chapter, you learn about basic networking theory and architectures and how computers communicate through network protocols. You discover the differences between local, metropolitan, and wide area networks, and what hardware is involved in these networks. Most importantly, you learn about networking features that are included in operating systems. These features make it possible for even the most diverse combination of operating systems to be partners in shared network communications.

NETWORKING BASICS

A **network** is a system of computing devices, computing resources, information resources, and communication devices that are linked together with cables or wirelessly with radio waves or light. The basic principle of networking is similar to connecting telephones (see Figure 8-1). In a telecommunications system, each telephone can communicate with other telephones by linking to the local main cable or trunk line, which in turn links to a local telephone switch that connects to other trunk lines. Computer networking is similar in that each computer is linked to the network by cable or a wireless connection, which connects to a network device such as a hub or wireless access point that allows the computers to communicate with one another. (Hands-on Projects 8-2 and 8-3 show how to view the computers connected to a network.)

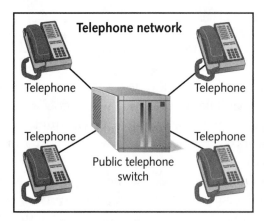
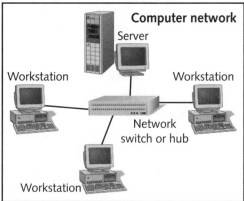

Figure 8-1   Telephone and computer networks compared

Networks have hardware and software elements. The hardware components of a computer network are computers, printers, communication cables, and networking devices such as network interface cards, hubs, bridges, switches, routers, and access points. Computer networks also have software components that include client and server operating systems, device drivers, and various networking protocols (rules for network communications).

Windows 98, Windows NT 4.0 Workstation, Windows 2000 Professional, and Windows XP Professional are examples of client operating systems. A **client operating system** is one that enables a workstation to run applications, process information locally, and communicate with other computers and devices over the network. A **workstation** is a computer that has a central processing unit (CPU) and can run applications locally or obtain applications and files from another computer on the network.

Sometimes the term *workstation* is confused with the term *terminal*. The difference is that a **terminal** has no CPU or local storage for running programs independently. The main use of a terminal is to access a mainframe, minicomputer or terminal server, and run programs on that computer.

A **server operating system** is a network operating system (NOS) that coordinates network activities and enables client workstations to access shared network resources such as printers, files, or software. Windows 2000, Windows Server 2003, UNIX/Linux, and Novell NetWare are examples of server operating systems. Another important function of a server operating system is to administer network security.

One way that server operating systems can save time and money is by centralizing installation of software and operating systems on client workstations. Windows 2000 Server and Windows Server 2003 use **Remote Installation Services (RIS)** to install client operating systems, such as Windows XP Professional, on a mass scale. When you use RIS to install a client operating system, you create an operating system image containing specific settings, and then the image is downloaded and installed on the clients. For example, if all clients must have a particular desktop appearance, the image can be created to set up that desktop appearance on all computers.

Windows 2000 Server and Windows Server 2003 also enable Windows 2000 Professional or Windows XP clients to install custom configured application software from a central Windows 2000 Server or Windows Server 2003 via their local Control Panels. This is called **publishing an application**. **Assigning applications** is another Windows 2000 Server/ Windows Server 2003 feature that enables a client to automatically start a particular version of software, such as Microsoft Word XP, through a desktop shortcut or menu selection, or by clicking a file type. An example is starting Word XP when the user clicks a document with a .doc extension. A Windows 2000 Server or Windows Server 2003 with Active Directory implemented can assign applications for a particular group, several groups, or all Windows 2000 or Windows XP Professional clients. If the user inadvertently deletes the shortcut or menu selection (or even the software), it is automatically reinstalled the next time the user logs on to the network.

The Development of Network Operating Systems

UNIX was the first operating system designed for networks, developed at AT&T Bell Laboratories. It began to be available to researchers, universities, government, and individuals in the early 1970s. Introduced in 1982, Novell NetWare was one of the first commercial operating systems to emphasize network capabilities and was the most popular network operating system for businesses in the late 1980s and early 1990s. In 1993, Microsoft incorporated peer-to-peer networking capability in Windows 3.11, also called Windows for Workgroups (WFW). WFW constituted a significant step up in Windows network connectivity with expanded workgroup capabilities and more support for connecting to servers (often NetWare servers). Peer-to-peer networking enables basic PCs or workstations to share resources, such as files, with other computers. **Workgroups** (predefined groups of member computers) provide the ability to limit resource sharing on the basis of group membership.

Windows 95 expanded peer-to-peer networking capabilities, and Windows 98/Me added even more client networking features, such as the ability to connect to very high-speed networks, as well as enhanced multimedia capabilities and easier Internet connectivity. Windows XP Home Edition is the most recent Windows client operating system, designed to be fully integrated into a multimedia, networked environment. It is a scaled-down version of Windows XP Professional.

Windows NT 3.1 Advanced Server, the first Microsoft server operating system, was released just a little later than Windows 3.1, and was intended for industrial-strength networking from the beginning. Windows NT 3.1 Advanced Server was targeted to compete with NetWare, but it wasn't until 1994 with Windows NT version 4.0 that Microsoft had a truly competitive product. Windows NT 4.0 came in two versions, Windows NT Workstation and Windows NT Server. Windows NT evolved into Windows 2000 Server and Windows 2000 Professional.

Today, Windows 2000 has evolved into two products, Windows XP and Windows Server 2003, both based on the core elements of the Windows 2000 kernel. Windows XP is the desktop version of the new operating system, while Windows Server 2003 is the server version. These operating systems offer better Internet security through a built-in firewall, and the ability to remotely control the computer over an Internet connection via a tool called Remote Desktop.

Windows 2000/XP/Server 2003 have built-in options to configure home and small office networks consisting of 10 or less computers, such as sharing one Internet connection between multiple computers. As you learned in Chapter 7, Windows 2000/XP/Server 2003 also have configuration options to enable novice users to quickly set up Digital Subscriber Line (DSL) or cable modem connections.

Local and Wide Area Networks

Networks are often classified by their scope or reach. A **local area network (LAN)** is one in which the service area is relatively small, such as a network in an office area, or contained on one floor or within one building. On a college campus, the Accounting Department computers might be connected to a LAN in the top floor of a classroom building, and the English Department computers might be on a different LAN on the main floor of the same building. Networking devices such as switches or routers might be used to connect these LANs.

A **wide area network (WAN)** is one that offers networking services over a long distance, such as between cities, states, or countries. WANs often connect LANs over a long distance, such as a documentary film company in Chicago that has a LAN that connects through a telecommunications line to the LAN of a film distribution company in St. Louis. The LANs and the telecommunications link compose a WAN. An example of a simple WAN is using a modem and telephone line at your computer to dial into your Internet service provider, which connects you to other computers worldwide.

Network Topologies

Networks are designed in three basic patterns, or architectures: bus, ring, and star. Each of these is called a network topology. A **topology** is the physical design of the network, or the path data takes when it goes from one computer to another. (You can practice identifying network topologies in Hands-on Project 8-1.)

A network that uses a **bus topology** is designed with a single central cable, to which all computers and other network devices attach. A bus topology has two end points. Each end point has a terminator to keep the electronic data signal from reflecting back along the path it just traveled. Figure 8-2 shows a simple bus network.

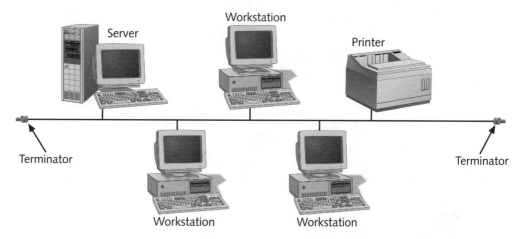

Figure 8-2   Bus topology

A **ring topology** is one in which the data-carrying signal goes from station to station around the ring, until it reaches the target destination. There is no beginning or end point, so there are no terminators (see Figure 8-3).

In the **star topology**, all of the computers or devices (nodes) on the network connect to a central device such as a hub or switch, as shown in Figure 8-4. The hub sends the signal onto each segment, which has a computer at the end. Every segment is terminated inside the hub at one end and inside the computer at the other end (when it is used for **Ethernet** communications, discussed later in this chapter). The star topology is the most popular network topology because it has the most flexibility in terms of providing for future growth and adding high-speed networking capability.

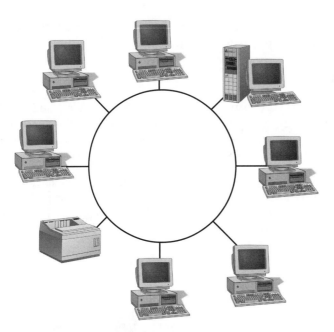

Figure 8-3   Ring topology

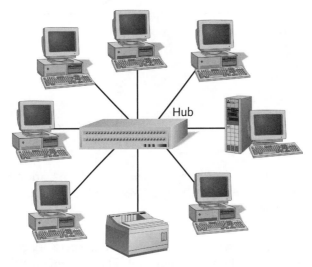

Figure 8-4   Star topology

Networking Hardware

The hardware that supports networking includes network interface cards, communications media such as cables or wireless media, and various devices that control the flow of information through and beyond the network such as hubs, switches, bridges, and routers.

NICs

Computers and other devices connect to a network through a **network interface card (NIC)**. A NIC is usually a card that goes into a computer's expansion slot, or that is built into a network device or a computer. The NIC is equipped with a connector that enables it to attach to the network communications cable, or an antenna that enables it to communicate via radio waves. Each NIC has a unique hexadecimal address, assigned by the manufacturer, called a device or physical address, which identifies it to the network. It is also called the **Media Access Control (MAC) address**. This address is used much like a postal address because it enables communications to be sent to specific destination computers on the same network (see Figure 8-5). Another type of address used to identify computers, called the IP address, is determined by software and protocols, and is discussed later in the chapter.

8

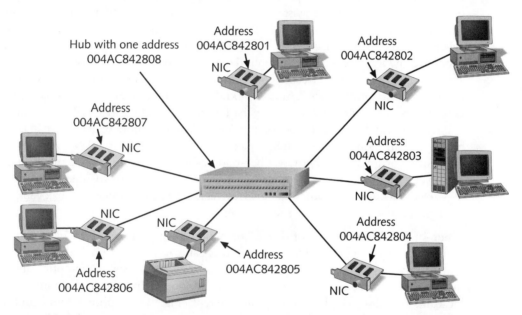

Figure 8-5   Devices on a network with unique physical addresses

The software logic on a NIC consists of one or more programs called **firmware** because it resides in a programmable chip on the card. Communication between the operating system and its NIC, like communication between the operating system and various input, output, and storage devices, is controlled by driver software written by the manufacturer of the device (in this case the NIC). Drivers are installed as part of the firmware on the NIC, and into the operating system on the computer when the NIC is installed.

NOTE One important step related to installing a NIC is to make sure you have the most recent software drivers for that NIC and for the operating system that is running on its host computer, such as NetWare, Windows 2000/XP/Server 2003, UNIX/ Linux, Mac, or Windows 95/98/Me. Network communications are complex, and early versions of NIC drivers often contain errors that impede the NIC's performance. Most manufacturers offer the latest versions of drivers on their Web sites.

Cables and Wireless Media

A communications medium is anything through which data is transmitted. Networking media include "guided" media such as twisted-pair cable, coaxial cable, and fiber-optic cable, or "unguided" media such as air and space that allow wireless transmission. **Twisted-pair cable** consists of one or more pairs of twisted copper wires bundled together within a plastic outer coating. The wires are twisted to reduce electromagnetic interference or noise. Twisted pair cable comes in two configurations, unshielded twisted pair (UTP) and shielded twisted pair. Shielded twisted pair is designed to be faster and more reliable than UTP, but it is more expensive and less flexible. Most telephone networks originally used twisted pair, and LANs often use UTP. Twisted pair cable comes in several categories, with Category 5e, or Cat5e, being the most common for LANs. **Coaxial cable**, often referred to as **coax**, consists of a copper wire surrounded by several layers: a layer of insulating material, a layer of woven or braided metal, and a plastic outer coating. Coaxial cable is more expensive than twisted pair, but its transmission rate is greater. Coax is not often used for LANs because it is more expensive, nor for WANs because fiber-optic cable transmits signals at much higher rates. However, coax is frequently used for home Internet connections. Cable television (CATV) uses coax cable, and companies that provide cable television service use coax cable and cable modems to link subscribers to the Internet.

Fiber-optic cable consists of dozens or hundreds of thin strands of glass or plastic that transmit signals using light. Fiber-optic cables can carry more signals than wire cables, are significantly faster, and are less prone to electrical interference. Fiber-optic cables are also much more difficult and expensive to install and modify. In spite of these limitations, most local and long-distance phone companies are replacing existing phone lines with fiber-optic cables. Businesses also use fiber-optic cables on high-traffic network **backbones**, the main connecting links between networks, such as between floors in a building or between buildings. **Wireless media** are becoming increasingly popular, especially where it is inconvenient, impractical, or impossible to install wires or cables. Wireless transmissions are carried by light (infrared) or radio frequencies (RF) including radio waves and microwaves. Cell phones also use wireless technology but broadcast in a different frequency range than wireless LANs.

Hubs, Access Points, Switches, Bridges, and Routers

Networks use several types of devices to connect computers and network-attached devices like printers to each other and to connect networks to each other. Each computer or device (node) connected to a network must have a NIC, which connects through a cable or a wireless antenna to a hub, switch, bridge, router, or wireless access point, which in turn connects to a LAN or WAN. A **hub** is a common device often used in bus and star LANs to connect computers or devices to a local network. A **switch** is like a hub, except that it is more "intelligent." Communications that go through a hub are broadcast to all segments attached to the hub; a switch only transmits the information to the segment where the destination device resides. A **wireless access point** is a device that connects wireless devices to a wired network. A **bridge** is used to link network segments that are close together, such as on different floors of the same building. Another use for bridges is to extend segments, such as when more stations must be added, but the primary segment already contains the maximum length of cable or number of stations permitted by network standards. Bridges are also used to segment a network into smaller networks as a way to control traffic and reduce bottlenecks at busy network intersections. Finally, bridges can be used to link segments that use different cable types, such as linking a segment that uses twisted-pair cable to one that uses fiber-optic cable. Most network administrators today use switches instead of bridges. Switches provide additional logic that enables them to move network traffic more efficiently than the old-style bridges. Modern switches use a Web-style interface for managing switch functions. Statistics and reports are also generated through this same Web interface.

A **router** is also used to connect networks. It can connect dissimilar networks and it can be programmed to act as a firewall to filter communications. Routers keep tables of network addresses that identify each computer on the network along with the best "routes" to other network addresses. Bridges are not designed to route packets from one network to another because they ignore routing information.

> ### From the Trenches...
> A college familiar to the authors set up a switched network. The campus consists of multiple buildings spread out across a large area. The Network Department installed switches in each building and connected all the offices, labs, and classrooms to these switches located in the main wiring closet of each building. The speed from the switches to the desktops was 100 Mbps and the cabling was Cat5e. Then the Network Department connected the building switches to the main campus switch with fiber-optic cabling at 1 Gbps. The switch they installed is capable of running at 10 Gbps so there is plenty of expansion available when they need a faster backbone.

Packets, Frames, and Cells

Each computer or network device translates data into individual units, and then places the units onto the network cable or transmits them wirelessly. For example, if you obtain a file from a server and transport it to your workstation, the file is broken into hundreds of small data units, transmitted one unit at a time from the server to your workstation. Each data unit is called a **packet** or **frame**. These terms are sometimes used interchangeably, but they are not the same. Both consist of data and transmission control information contained in a header that is appended to the front of the data. The difference is that a packet contains routing information that allows packets to be forwarded to specific networks. The actual data is placed after the header information and followed by a footer or trailer that enables detection of a transmission error. Figure 8-6 shows a basic packet format.

Figure 8-6   Basic packet format

Older networks transmit at speeds of 4 Mbps, 10 Mbps, and 16 Mbps. Newer networks transmit at 100 Mbps to 10 Gbps and faster, or consist of segments that transmit at 10 Mbps, 100 Mbps, 1 Gbps, or 10 Gbps. Network backbones typically run at 100 Mbps or higher.

Some networks require extra capacity for high-speed transmissions more than 100 Mbps, such as networks that have a high proportion of multimedia applications, or on which large files (1 MB and more) are regularly transmitted. On these networks, data may be transported in cells. A **cell** is a data unit designed for high-speed communications; it has a control header and a fixed-length payload (see Figure 8-7). The **payload** is that portion of a frame, packet, or cell that contains the actual data, which might be a portion of an e-mail message or word-processing file. One element of the cell header is path information that enables the cell to take the route through the network that is most appropriate to the type of data carried within the cell. For example, a large graphics file that holds a medical x-ray might take a different network path than a cell transmission containing streaming video for a movie clip.

Figure 8-7   Basic cell format

The exact format of a frame, packet, and cell is determined by the type of protocol used on a network.

NETWORKING PROTOCOLS

A protocol is a set of formatting guidelines for network communications, like a language, so that the information sent by one computer can be accurately decoded by another. Protocols also coordinate network communications so that data is transported in an orderly fashion, preventing chaos when two or more computers want to transmit at the same time. A network may use several different protocols, depending on the NOS and the types of devices that are connected.

Protocols are used for many types of network communications, including the following:

- Coordinating transport of packets and frames among network devices

- Encapsulating data and communication control information

- Providing communications to accomplish a specific function, such as enabling the destination computer to tell the source computer to slow its transmission speed because it is too fast for the destination computer

- Enabling communications over a long-distance network, such as the Internet

- Enabling remote users to dial into networks or access them wirelessly

Two of the most important types of protocols are those that coordinate transport and those that communicate and coordinate how data is encapsulated and addressed.

Transport Protocols

The most commonly wired transport protocols are Ethernet and token ring. Ethernet is in more installations than token ring because there are more network equipment options for it, and because modern Ethernet network designs are most easily expanded for high-speed networking. Token ring, an IBM-proprietary protocol, is used because it is reliable, and network problems were initially easier to troubleshoot on token ring networks than on early Ethernet networks. Wireless networks are also becoming more common, and they use their own type of transport protocols.

 Improved design options and equipment now make the complexity of trouble-shooting Ethernet problems on a par with troubleshooting token ring problems.

NOTE

Standards for Ethernet, token ring, and wireless networking are defined as part of the standards established by the Institute of Electrical and Electronics Engineers (IEEE) through its 802 standards committee. The 802 standards are followed by network administrators and manufacturers to ensure consistent network communications and the ability for one network to connect to another. IEEE specifications for Ethernet are found in 802.3, token ring in 802.5, and wireless in 802.11. The IEEE Web site at *www.ieee.org* is a good place to obtain additional information on the 802 standards.

Ethernet

In Ethernet communications, only one station on the network should transmit at a given moment. If two or more stations transmit at the same time, frames collide. The transmission control method used by Ethernet is called **carrier sense multiple access with collision detection (CSMA/CD)**. In CSMA/CD, the NICs of computers and devices check the network communications cable for a carrier signal that contains an encoded frame. If the device's NIC detects a carrier signal, and if the NIC decodes its own device address within the frame, it forwards that packet to its firmware for further decoding. If the frame does not contain its device address, then the NIC does not process the signal any further.

When the detected carrier signal is twice (or more) the strength of a normal carrier signal, this indicates that at least two network stations transmitted at the same time. In this situation, a collision occurred, and a transmitting station sends a "jam" signal to warn all other stations. After the jam signal is sent, every station waits a different amount of time before attempting to transmit again. The amount of time that a particular station waits is determined by generating a random number for the wait period on the assumption that each station will generate a different random number. If two stations generate the same random number and transmit simultaneously, then the collision recovery process starts again.

Networks that use Ethernet are designed in a bus topology, or a star-bus topology in which the networking devices are arranged in a physical star topology, but actually use a logical bus topology. Ethernet star-bus networks are very common in modern network design.

Originally, the speed of Ethernet was 10 Mbps. Newer Ethernet standards now include 100 Mbps and 1 Gbps versions that are called Fast Ethernet and Gigabit Ethernet, respectively. 10 Gbps is now delivered by several vendors. Fast Ethernet is becoming commonplace, and most Ethernet NICs are designed to handle either 10 or 100 Mbps communications. Gigabit Ethernet is finding acceptance on busy network backbones in which even Fast Ethernet does not provide enough capacity.

All versions of Ethernet are compatible with popular operating systems such as:

- UNIX/Linux
- NetWare
- Windows NT, Windows 2000, and Windows Server 2003
- Windows 98/Me
- Windows XP
- Mac OS

Token Ring

In most versions of **token ring**, only one network station transmits at a time. The sequence of frame and packet transmissions is controlled by the use of a specialized frame, called a **token**. A token without data is transmitted around the network until it is captured by a station that wants to transmit. When the token is captured by a station, no other station can transmit until the station that has the token is finished (see Figure 8-8). The transmitting station packages data inside the token so that part of the token is used as the frame header to indicate the beginning of a frame, and the other part of the token is used as the frame trailer to indicate the last sequence of bytes in the frame.

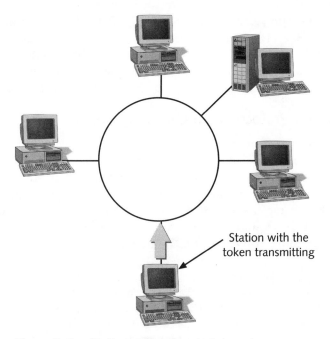

Station with the
token transmitting

Figure 8-8   Station with token in token ring

As the name suggests, token ring networks use the ring topology. Thus, the frame is transmitted from station to station around the ring until it reaches the destination station. The destination station removes the frame from the network and decodes the frame's contents for local use. It also replicates the frame back onto the network to be forwarded around the ring to the sender, but changes two bits inside the frame indicating that the frame was successfully received and decoded at the destination.

Older token ring networks transmit at 4 Mbps and newer networks transmit at 16 Mbps. IBM developed 100 Mbps fast token ring technology that is compatible with existing 4 Mbps and 16 Mbps networks. Fast token ring got off to a slow start in the market and, as a result, manufacturers discontinued production of internetworking devices that support it.

Token ring is compatible with the same mainstream network operating systems that are used with Ethernet.

Wireless

A wireless network can be described by its MAC (medium access control) protocol. The most prevalent protocol used in a wireless LAN is **carrier sense multiple access with**

collision avoidance (CSMA/CA). This is a variation of the CSMA/CD method used in Ethernet communications. A wireless station that wants to transmit, listens for other transmissions. If there are transmissions, it will wait a specified amount of time and then listen again. If there are no transmissions, the station will begin transmitting.

There are three main IEEE wireless specifications today. They are 802.11a, 802.11b, and 802.11g. In the 802.11b standard, wireless operates in the 2.4 GHz spectrum with a bandwidth of 11 Mbps. In 802.11a, wireless operates in the 5 GHz frequency with a bandwidth of 54 Mbps. Finally, 802.11g is for wireless operating in the 2.4 GHz frequency at 54 Mbps. 802.11b and 802.11g make up the majority of wireless with approximately 23 percent and 76 percent respectively. 802.11g is backward-compatible with 802.11b.

Implementing a Transport Protocol in an Operating System

A transport protocol is interfaced with an operating system through three elements: a network driver specification built into the operating system, a NIC, and a NIC driver. Network operating systems are built to offer special elements, which programmers call "hooks" in the operating system kernel (program code), that enable the operating system to interface with a network. For example, Microsoft designed the **Network Device Interface Specification (NDIS)** and Windows-based NDIS drivers for this purpose. Similarly, NetWare uses the **Open Datalink Interface (ODI)** and ODI drivers.

 NOTE One way to think of networking "hooks" in an operating system, and how a NIC driver links into those hooks, is by using the analogy of a lock and key. The combined hooks are like a lock, and the NIC driver software is similar to a key that is specially cut to exactly match the unique configuration of the lock.

When you set up an operating system to work on an Ethernet, token ring, or wireless network, the first step is to purchase an Ethernet, token ring, or wireless NIC for the computer running the operating system. If the NIC is for a wired network, the NIC cable interface must also match the type of cable used on the network. After the NIC is installed in an open expansion slot in the computer, the next step is to boot the operating system and install the NIC driver software, which links the NIC into the network computing hooks in the kernel. For example, if you install an Ethernet NIC in a computer running Windows XP, then you must obtain an NDIS-compatible driver for that NIC, which is written for Windows XP Ethernet communications (the NIC usually comes with a CD or disk containing such drivers).

After the NIC setup is complete, and the computer is connected to the network, the operating system, NIC, and driver handle the work of converting data created at the computer to an Ethernet, token ring, or wireless format for transport over the network. The same three elements also enable the computer to receive packets or frames and convert them to data that the computer can interpret.

Communications Protocols

The development of communications protocols (the protocols that carry data between two communicating stations, and are encapsulated in Ethernet, token ring, or wireless transport protocols) is related to the network operating systems in which they are used. For example, the **Internet Packet Exchange (IPX)** and **Sequence Packet Exchange (SPX)** protocols (usually referred to as IPX/SPX) were developed in the early 1980s to enable a NetWare file server to communicate with its client workstations. In another setting, also in the early 1980s, researchers implemented and combined two protocols for use on the U.S. Department of Defense Advanced Research Projects Agency Network (ARPANET), the long-distance network that became the foundation of the Internet. The protocols developed for ARPANET, **Transmission Control Protocol (TCP)** and **Internet Protocol (IP)** or the combination called TCP/IP, are now used worldwide over the Internet and on many other networks. Because many of the original ARPANET servers ran UNIX, this operating system was quickly adapted to employ TCP/IP. Two other important communication protocols are **NetBIOS Extended User Interface (NetBEUI)**, a protocol developed for Microsoft networks, and **AppleTalk**, developed for Macintosh networks.

IPX

Although it was developed in the early eighties, IPX is still used in many NetWare environments because it is tailored for NetWare, and because it can be routed, which means that it can transport packets to specific networks, as designated in the packet addressing information. The limitation of IPX/SPX is that it is a "chatty" protocol. Servers and clients configured for IPX frequently broadcast their presence on the network, even when there are no requests to exchange actual data or information. IPX is the default communications protocol in all versions of NetWare up to version 5. The default protocol in NetWare 5 and Netware 6 is TCP/IP, although they still support IPX.

IPX encapsulates data and transports it within a host transport protocol format—Ethernet or token ring, for example. IPX is a connectionless protocol, which means that it does minimal checking to ensure that a packet reaches its destination, leaving this task for the Ethernet or token ring communications layer within the packet. When there is a need for more reliable data transport, such as for data from a database, an application running via NetWare can use SPX, a protocol that provides connection-oriented communications. In addition to Ethernet and token ring, IPX relies upon SPX to provide reliable, error-free communication. SPX is similar to TCP and IPX is similar to IP. The IPX/SPX combination is similar to TCP/IP, which is discussed in further detail later in this chapter.

IPX works with other specialized service and NetWare protocols as follows:

- *Link Support Layer (LSL)*: Enables one NIC to transmit and receive multiple protocols, such as IPX and TCP/IP
- *NetWare Core Protocol (NCP)*: Used to access applications between a server and its client

- *NetWare Link Services Protocol (NLSP)*: Enables routing information to be added to an IPX packet

- *Routing Information Protocol (RIP)*: Enables a NetWare server to build tables of routing information about the location of particular network stations

- *Service Advertising Protocol (SAP)*: Enables NetWare client computers to identify servers and the services offered by each server

NetBEUI

NetBEUI was introduced in the early nineties as the main protocol for LAN Manager, a network server operating system developed by Microsoft and IBM, and the forerunner of Windows NT Server. NetBEUI became a widely implemented communications protocol as the use of Windows NT Server on small networks grew through the mid nineties. The role of NetBEUI in Windows 2000 Server is diminished in favor of using the more versatile TCP/IP. Microsoft does not include support for NetBEUI in Windows XP and Windows Server 2003.

TCP/IP

As mentioned earlier, TCP/IP is an older set of protocols, initially developed for long-distance networking on ARPANET, and now used on most networks. One of the strongest influences on TCP/IP use has been the growth of the Internet. UNIX has always used TCP/IP as its main network communications protocol. NetWare versions 5 and 6, Windows 2000 Server, Windows 2000 Professional, Windows XP, and Windows Server 2003 also have adopted TCP/IP as the default protocol. Further, Mac OS X comes installed with TCP/IP (as well as with AppleTalk) for Internet and network communications, and TCP/IP is compatible with Windows 95/98, Windows Me, and Windows NT.

TCP was developed for extremely reliable point-to-point communications between computers on the same network. This protocol establishes communication sessions among applications on two communicating computers, making sure there is a mutually agreeable "window" of transmission characteristics. TCP performs some of the following communication functions:

- Establishes the communication session between two computers

- Ensures that data transmissions are accurate

- Encapsulates, transmits, and receives the payload data

- Closes the communication session between two computers

The IP portion of TCP/IP is used to make sure that a frame or packet reaches the intended destination. IP performs the following complementary functions with TCP:

- Handles packet addressing

- Handles packet routing

- Fragments packets, as needed, for transport across different types of networks

- Provides simple packet error detection in conjunction with the more thorough error detection provided by TCP

IP uses a dotted decimal notation that consists of four 8-bit binary numbers (octets) separated by periods to produce an **IP address** used to identify a computer or network device and the network it is on. The format is as follows: 10000001.00000101.00001010.00000001, which converts to the decimal value 129.5.10.1. Part of the address designates a unique identifier for a network, called the network identifier (NET_ID). For example, a school or corporation has its own NET_ID, which distinguishes its network from all others. Another part of the address is the host identifier (HOST_ID), which distinguishes a computer or network device from any other computer or device on a network. There are five IP address classes. Table 8-1 shows each class and the range of addresses.

Table 8-1   IP address classes

Class	Beginning Address	Ending Address
A	0.0.0.0	127.255.255.255
B	128.0.0.0	191.255.255.255
C	192.0.0.0	223.255.255.255
D	224.0.0.0	239.255.255.255
E	240.0.0.0	255.255.255.255

In Class A through Class E, each is used with a different type of network. The address classes reflect the size of the network, and whether the packet is unicast or multicast. In the **unicast** method of transmission, one copy of each packet is sent to each target destination. If there are eight workstations designated to receive a packet, such as a portion of a video clip, then it is transmitted eight times. In the **multicast** method, the recipients are placed in a group, such as a group of all eight workstations. Only one packet is sent to the group, via a router or switch, which then sends the packet to each group member.

Class A is used for the largest networks composed of up to 16,777,216 nodes. Class A networks are identified by a value between 1 and 126 in the first position of the dotted decimal address. The network ID is the first 8 bits, and the host ID is the last 24 bits. Class B is for medium-sized networks composed of up to 65,536 nodes, and it is identified by the first octet of bits ranging from decimal 128 to 191. The first two octets are the network ID, and the last two are the host ID. Class C addresses are used for network communications on small networks of 256 nodes or less. The first octet translates to a decimal value in the range of 192 to 223, and the network ID is contained in the first 24 bits, while the host ID is contained in the last 8 bits.

Class D addresses do not reflect the network size, only that the communication is a multicast. Unlike Classes A through C, the four octets are used to specify a group of nodes to receive the multicast, which consists of those nodes that are multicast subscription members. Class D addresses are in the range from 224.0.0.0 to 239.255.255.255. A fifth address type, Class E, is used for experimentation, and addresses range from 240 to 255 in the first octet.

Besides class addressing, there are some special-purpose IP addresses, such as 255.255.255.255, which is a broadcast packet sent to all network locations. Packets that begin with 127 in the first octet are used for network testing. An entire network is designated by providing only the network ID and zeroes in all other octets, such as 132.155.0.0 for a Class B network, or 220.127.110.0 for a Class C network.

A newer way of addressing ignores address class designation by using **classless interdomain routing (CIDR)** that puts a slash (/) after the dotted decimal notation. CIDR provides more IP address options for medium-sized networks because there is a shortage of Class B and Class C addresses. The shortage is due to the proliferation of networks, combined with the finite number of addresses numerically possible in the basic four-octet address scheme. For example, a CIDR network addressing scheme for a network that needs up to 16,384 (2^{14}) nodes might be 165.100.0.0/14.

Some network administrators also designate a **subnet mask** within the IP address, which enables them to uniquely identify smaller networks or subnetworks within the larger network setup. For example, using a subnet mask enables the network administrator at a college or university to limit how much network traffic goes to certain networks on campus as a way to reduce congestion and implement network security. In Figure 8-9, implementing a subnet mask enables a packet to be sent from one campus network to Station A on another network, without flooding all networks with traffic. The exact allocation of the IP address into NET_ID, HOST_ID, and subnet masks depends on factors unique to each network, such as its size, the number of computers connected to it, and the overall design of the network.

Consider a college or university's IP address of 129.72.22.124, in which the first half (first two octets) of the address is the NET_ID and the last octet is the HOST_ID. The first three octets are used to specify the subnet. In this address, the 129.72 identifies the (NET_ID), 129.72.22 identifies the subnet on which the station is located within the college or university, such as the network in the English building, and 124 is the HOST_ID of a particular computer on that subnet. In this designation, the subnet is useful in several ways. One is that data, such as e-mail intended for English faculty, can be directed to the English building subnet so that it does not saturate other parts of a busy network. Another advantage is that the English Department can set up its own private Web site containing salary, budget, and human resources information, and limit access to only those with the correct subnet as part of their IP addresses.

NOTE   By Internet convention, an IP address in which the first octet translates to a decimal number between 128 and 191 signifies a medium to large network consisting of 257 to 65,536 stations.

Computers and devices that use IP addressing actually have two addresses: a MAC address and an IP address. The use of two addresses provides better insurance that a packet will reach the right destination, while expending the fewest network resources. For example, on a large network, a packet might be able to follow any of several paths to its destination, but some

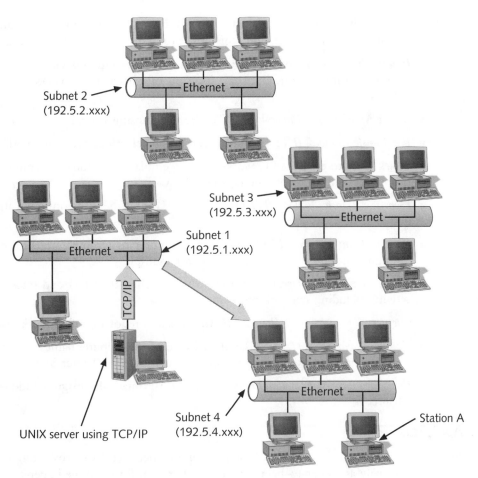

Figure 8-9   Using TCP/IP subnet masks

paths will be longer, or will involve using more expensive resources, such as high-speed backbone links. IP addressing makes it possible to send a packet along the best or fastest route for the type of information it contains.

Today IP version 4 (IPv4) is in use on nearly all networks, but its 32-bit (four-octet) addressing capacity is a problem. The explosive growth of networks and the Internet has created an address shortage. IP version 6 (IPv6; there is no version 5), or IP Next Generation, is a newer standard that is one way to solve the address shortage by using 128-bit addresses and providing more specialized networking implementations, including voice, video, and multimedia applications. Vendors are slowly releasing their implementations of IPv6, but it will be several years before IPv6 is broadly available. Microsoft released updates for Windows 2000, and Windows XP/Server 2003 has IPv6 as part of the operating system. Also, Red Hat Enterprise Linux 3.0 supports IPv6 as does Mac OS X.

TCP/IP works with a range of associated protocols that make this a powerful combination for networks of all sizes and types. Some of those protocols include the following:

- *Routing Information Protocol (RIP)*: Enables network routing devices to build tables of routing information about the location of particular networks and network stations

- *Simple Mail Transfer Protocol (SMTP)*: Used to transmit e-mail

- *File Transfer Protocol (FTP)*: Used to send and receive files over a network

- *Telnet*: Used to enable a PC workstation to emulate a terminal for connections to mainframes and minicomputers over a network

- *Hypertext Transfer Protocol (HTTP)*: Used for World Wide Web communications (for network browsers)

- *Point-to-Point Protocol (PPP)*: Enables a computer to remotely access a network, through a dial-up modem connection, for example

- *Simple Network Management Protocol (SNMP)*: Used to detect and track network activity, including network problems

- *Internet Control Message Protocol (ICMP)*: Enables reporting of network errors

- *Domain Name Service (DNS)*: Resolves domain and computer names to IP addresses and IP addresses to domain and computer names (see Chapter 5)

- *Dynamic Host Configuration Protocol (DHCP)*: Automatically assigns IP addresses (see Chapter 5)

AppleTalk

AppleTalk is a network communications protocol used between Macintosh computers. It is designed primarily as a peer-to-peer protocol, rather than for combined peer-to-peer and client-to-server communications. As a peer-to-peer protocol, AppleTalk establishes equal communications between networked Macintosh computers, without the need for a server. Most mainstream network operating systems, such as Windows NT/2000/Server 2003 and NetWare, support AppleTalk as a means to communicate with Macintosh computers. For example, disk space can be specially configured on a Windows NT/2000/Server 2003 server for access by Macintosh computers. Network communications are then configured by installing AppleTalk (and Services for Macintosh) in Windows NT/2000/Server 2003.

AppleTalk performs three essential services: remote access to files over a network, network print services, and access to computers running MS-DOS or Windows operating systems. Examples of protocols designed for use with AppleTalk are as follows:

- *AppleTalk Address Resolution Protocol (AARP)*: Converts computer names to IP addresses and vice versa for network and Internet communications

- *AppleTalk Data Stream Protocol (ADSP)*: Ensures that streams of data are sent and received reliably

- *AppleTalk Session Protocol (ASP)*: Used to ensure reliable network communications between two stations

- *Datagram Delivery Protocol (DDP)*: Used for routing packets

- *Name-Binding Protocol (NBP)*: Enables network services to be associated with specific computer names

- *Printer Access Protocol (PAP)*: Used to communicate with network printers

- *Routing Table Maintenance Protocol (RTMP)*: Enables routing table information to be built for routing packets

Early versions of AppleTalk are not very compatible with large networks that use multiple combinations of protocols, such as TCP/IP, IPX/SPX, and NetBEUI, over the same communication cable. AppleTalk Phase II is a newer version that is designed to work smoothly on large networks.

Implementing Communications Protocols in an Operating System

Most computer operating systems are designed to support one or more communications protocols. Those that support multiple communications protocols are able to do so through the same kernel interface hooks intended for transport protocols, such as NDIS for Windows-based operating systems and ODI for NetWare communications.

In general, there are two steps involved in setting up a communications protocol in an operating system. The first is to install the protocol software that is written for that operating system. For example, in Windows NT or 2000, you can install AppleTalk, IPX/SPX, NetBEUI, TCP/IP, or all four. The Windows-based software for each of these protocols is written to work in conjunction with NDIS so that these protocols can be carried over Ethernet, token ring, or wireless networks. The next step is to bind the protocol with the NIC. **Binding** the protocol enables the NIC to format data for that protocol, and identify the most efficient methods for transporting it. When two or more protocols are used, binding also enables the NIC to set a priority for which protocol to process first. The protocol priority has a direct impact on how fast the computer and its NIC process network communications, and it also affects network performance.

 In most modern operating systems, such as Windows XP, the protocol binding occurs automatically (although you can still manually bind or unbind a protocol).

For example, consider a workstation that is configured for IPX/SPX, NetBEUI, and TCP/IP, and on which TCP/IP represents 80 percent of the communications. If its binding priority is set so that TCP/IP packets are processed after IPX/SPX and NetBEUI, then that workstation will take longer to process network communications than if TCP/IP is given the first priority. The end result is that the network must wait longer on that workstation, delaying communications to other workstations.

Adjusting the priority of the network binding for workstations that support this, such as Windows NT/2000/XP, can make a significant difference in network performance. Figure 8-10 illustrates the screen used in Windows XP for setting the binding order.

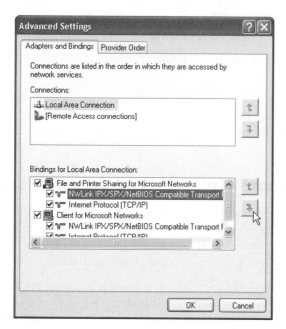

Figure 8-10   Setting the binding priority

Mac OS up through version 9.x provides one of the easiest methods for setting up communications protocols. In this earlier version of the Mac OS, you use a Control Panel to designate a port for network communications associated with the NIC. After designating the port, you simply turn on AppleTalk from the Chooser window. Binding takes place without user intervention.

In Mac OS X, setting up network communications is also simplified, but with more options than in Mac OS 9.x. You set up network connectivity through the Network option that is accessed via System Preferences. This is the same option that enabled you to configure network and Internet connectivity in Chapter 7. Through the Mac OS X Network option, you can fully configure your Mac to use TCP/IP and TCP/IP network services, including the following:

- Manual configuration of IPv4 or IPv6 address and subnet mask
- Automatic configuration of the IPv4 or IPv6 address using DHCP
- Identification of the nearest router by IP address

- Identification of DNS servers by IP address
- Identification of search domains by IP address

Most UNIX/Linux systems have TCP/IP networking support built in, and some of these automatically run a network configuration program when you first boot the computer with an installed NIC. NIC device drivers are loaded in the kernel. When the configuration program runs, you must supply information about the network connection, such as the IP address. If TCP/IP networking is not automatically configured when you first boot, it can be configured later by using the *ifconfig* command (for all versions of UNIX except HP-UX, which uses the *lanscan* command), when you log on as root. *Ifconfig* is a utility typically found in the /etc or /sbin directories (the /sbin directory in Red Hat Enterprise Linux 3.0), which enables you to assign an IP address, turn on the network interface, and assign a subnet mask.

TIP

In most versions of UNIX/Linux, including Red Hat Enterprise Linux 3.0, Fedora, and Solaris, type *ifconfig* to view the current IP and NIC settings (in HP-UX, type *lanscan -v*).

For some versions of UNIX/Linux, including Red Hat Enterprise Linux 3.0, you must configure a loopback device, which is used to provide your computer with an internal IP address, even when it is not connected to the network. The IP address of the loopback device should be 127.0.0.1.

In the Red Hat Enterprise Linux 3.0 GNOME interface, you can configure a network connection by clicking the Main Menu on the Panel, pointing to System Tools, and clicking Network. The Network Configuration tool enables you to set up host and domain name, IP addressing (manual or automatic), interface information, routing and gateway information, and so on. See Hands-on Project 8-8.

Communications protocols in NetWare, such as IPX and TCP/IP, can be set up in a window that appears when NetWare is installed. If TCP/IP is used, the setup process requires the IP address and subnet mask. Before version 5, NetWare uses IPX/SPX as the protocol of preference. In versions 5 and 6, TCP/IP is the preferred protocol, but NetWare can be configured to interoperate with TCP/IP and IPX/SPX (there is no support for NetBEUI).

Communications protocols are set up in Windows 95, Windows 98, Windows Me, and Windows NT 4.0 through the Network icon in the Control Panel. In Windows 95, Windows 98, and Windows Me, you open the Network icon in the Control Panel and click the Configuration tab. Next, click the Add button and then double-click Protocol in the Select Network Component Type dialog box (see Figure 8-11 for the resulting dialog box). Windows NT 4.0 adds a slight variation in that you open the Network icon in the Control Panel, click the Protocols tab, and click Add to add a new protocol.

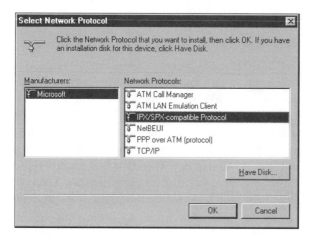

Figure 8-11   Installing IPX/SPX in Windows Me

Windows 2000 Server and Windows 2000 Professional use yet another method to set up a new protocol. In these versions of Windows, you open the Control Panel in the same way as in Windows 95, Windows 98, Windows Me, and Windows NT. Next, double-click the Network and Dial-up Connections folder. Use the Make New Connection Wizard to add a new setup for a NIC. Or, if there is already a connection, right-click it and select Properties (see Figure 8-12). Click Add and then click Protocols to add a new protocol.

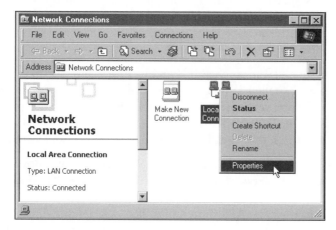

Figure 8-12   Installing a protocol in Windows 2000 Server

Finally, the network connection setup in Windows XP is performed through the New Connection Wizard (see Figure 8-13), or manually via the Control Panel. To start the wizard, click Start, click Control Panel, click Network and Internet Connections, click Network Connections, and click Create a new connection. To configure the connection manually, open the Control Panel, click Network and Internet Connections, click Network

Connections, right-click Local Area Connection, and click Properties. (Try Hands-on Projects 8-6 to practice installing a protocol in Windows 2000, Windows XP, and Windows Server 2003. Try Hands-on Project 8-9 to practice installing a protocol in Windows XP.)

Figure 8-13   New Connection Wizard

Integrating Different Operating Systems on the Same Network

The key to implementing multiple operating systems on one network is to select a transport protocol and communications protocols that are supported in all of the operating systems that must be connected. Ethernet is particularly well suited to a network that has different operating systems. It is supported by Mac OS, UNIX/Linux, Windows-based operating systems, server operating systems, and mainframe operating systems. Also, the TCP/IP communications protocol is supported by most operating systems.

TIP
Ethernet is also a strong choice for mixed networks because there are more equipment, NICs, and driver options for it than for token ring. Also, there are more tools for troubleshooting problems. In general, Ethernet is also less expensive to implement than token ring. Most importantly, however, Ethernet has become the de facto standard for all modern networks.

In situations where TCP/IP is not supported by all operating systems, then multiple protocols can be configured, such as a combination of AppleTalk, TCP/IP, and IPX/SPX. For example, consider a network that has a combination of computers running Macintosh, Windows 98, Windows XP, Windows Server 2003, and UNIX/Linux. This network might use AppleTalk and TCP/IP. AppleTalk might be used for communications among the Macintosh computers, and to enable them to access Windows Server 2003 resources.

TCP/IP might be used for communications between the Windows-based computers, the server, and the UNIX/Linux computers. Another example is a small network of 120 computers in which the workstations run Windows 95, and Windows Me and access Windows NT 4.0 and NetWare 5 and 6 servers. This network might use both NetBEUI and IPX/SPX to enable communications among all of the workstations and servers.

USING OPERATING SYSTEMS FOR DIAL-UP ACCESS

As you learned in Chapter 7, users on remote computers can access host computers and networks through dial-up networking and modem connections. For example, a specialized Novell server can be configured, with the appropriate software, to be a NetWare Access Server (NAS) on a LAN. A user who wants to access the LAN from home or while traveling simply dials up the NAS through software on the computer and a modem connection. Through the NAS, that user can gain access to files and software on one or more NetWare servers connected to the remote LAN.

Windows NT/2000/Server 2003 offers a similar option for dialing into a LAN through a **Remote Access Services (RAS)** server. RAS is a set of network services that can be installed on any Windows NT/2000/Server 2003 server connected to one or more modems. Once the services are installed and started, a remote user can dial into one or more Windows NT/2000/Server 2003 servers, and also access NetWare servers on the same network through a single RAS connection.

Besides setting up a RAS server, there must be a way to set up remote access capability on client workstations. Windows 95/98/Me and Windows NT/2000/XP all have a dial-up networking service that can be configured to access a remote network, as shown in Hands-on Projects 6, 7, and 8 in Chapter 7. The dial-up service is set up by specifying the telephone number used to access the remote network, the communication protocol (TCP/IP, IPX/SPX, or NetBEUI), and the remote communication protocol. Most users configure dial-up networking to use the **Point-to-Point Protocol (PPP)**, which can encapsulate packets already formatted in TCP/IP, IPX/SPX, and NetBEUI for transmission over a telecommunications line (try Hands-on Projects 8-10 and 8-11). A close relative, **Point-to-Point Tunneling Protocol (PPTP)** can also be configured for making a remote connection to a LAN over the Internet. Another protocol, **Serial Line Internet Protocol (SLIP)** is sometimes used in UNIX/Linux for remote communications that transport TCP/IP.

Security for dial-up remote access is a very important topic because of potential threats from viruses or hackers. Two ways to enhance the security surrounding the use of remote access are with authentication and encryption. **Authentication** is the way you identify and validate whom you are to the server. **Encryption** is the encoding of the data between you and the server so that only you and the server can decode the information.

For further information on firewalls, authentication, and encryption, see Michael Palmer's book, *Guide to Operating System Security* (Course Technology 2003, ISBN 0-519-16040-3).

NOTE

CHAPTER SUMMARY

❑ A network is a system of information resources and productivity tools that facilitates our human need to communicate. Networks were invented because they enable us to share information and information resources over short and long distances. Today, networking is a vital part of society that enables us to communicate by e-mail, order products rapidly, and accomplish work without leaving our homes or offices.

❑ Networks are roughly categorized as LANs or WANs, depending on their areas of service. LANs are smaller networks that run throughout an office area or a floor in a building. WANs are long-distance networks that can span states and continents to join LANs and individual users.

❑ Networks are designed in standardized topologies (bus, star, and ring) and use standardized communication means, such as frames, packets, and protocols, with the end result that a network in Jackson, Wyoming can be connected to another in Denver, Colorado or Montreal, Canada. Protocols are particularly important to networking because they act as a common language for communication. Some protocols are used to provide orderly transport of data between computers. Other protocols package data so that it can be decoded and checked for errors when it arrives at its destination. Protocols make communications reliable, enable the delivery of e-mail, and monitor networks for problems.

❑ Modern computer operating systems use a variety of network protocols for communication, such as TCP/IP, IPX/SPX, and NetBEUI. Even computers running very different operating systems, UNIX/Linux and Windows XP for example, are able to communicate and exchange information over networks. Network operating systems such as Windows NT, Windows 2000/Server 2003, NetWare, and UNIX/Linux offer a wide spectrum of services to client computers, including file sharing, printer services, backing up files, access to software applications, and access to databases.

❑ Tables 8-2, 8-3, and 8-4 provide a summary of the transport, communications, and remote protocols introduced in this chapter, and the operating systems that support those protocols.

Table 8-2 Summary of transport protocols

Transport Protocol	Communications Protocols Transported	Operating Systems That Support the Protocol
Ethernet	IPX/SPX, NetBEUI, TCP/IP, AppleTalk	Mac OS, NetWare, UNIX/Linux, Windows 3.1, 3.11, 95, 98, Me, NT, 2000, XP, and Server 2003
Token ring	IPX/SPX, NetBEUI, TCP/IP, AppleTalk	Mac OS, NetWare, UNIX/Linux, Windows 3.1, 3.11, 95, 98, Me, NT, 2000, XP, and Server 2003

Table 8-3 Summary of communications protocols

Communications Protocol	Operating Systems That Support the Protocol
AppleTalk (native to Mac OS)	Mac OS, NetWare, Windows NT, 2000, and Windows Server 2003
IPX/SPX (native to early versions of Netware)	NetWare, Windows 3.1, 3.11, 95, 98, Me, NT, 2000, XP, and Server 2003
NetBEUI (native to early versions of Windows-based systems)	Windows 3.1, 3.11, 95, 98, Me, NT, and 2000
TCP/IP (designed for Internet and general networking and native to most current NOSs)	Mac OS, NetWare, UNIX/Linux, Windows 3.1, 3.11, 95, 98, Me, NT, 2000, XP, and Server 2003

Table 8-4 Summary of remote communications protocols

Remote Communications Protocol	Communications Protocols Transported over Remote Links	Operating Systems That Support the Protocol
SLIP	TCP/IP	NetWare, UNIX/Linux, Windows 95, 98, NT, 2000, XP, and Server 2003
PPP	IPX/SPX, NetBEUI, and TCP/IP	Mac OS, UNIX/Linux, Windows 95, 98, Me, NT, 2000, XP, and Server 2003

❑ Networking devices such as hubs, bridges, switches, and routers enable network connectivity. Bridges, switches, and routers can be employed for network security and to control network traffic patterns. Each of these devices is used to achieve different connectivity goals, based on its capabilities.

❑ Ethernet is a good choice where there is a need to implement multiple operating systems on one network. It is supported by all of the popular operating systems including Mac OS, UNIX/Linux, Windows-based systems, and NetWare

❑ Also called dial-up access, modem communications with a LAN are made possible through remote communications protocols, such as SLIP and PPP. PPP is most commonly used because it can transport a combination of protocols, such as TCP/IP and IPX/SPX.

KEY TERMS

AppleTalk — Used for communications with Macintosh computers, this protocol is designed for peer-to-peer networking.

assigning applications — A feature in Windows 2000, Windows XP, and Windows Server 2003 that enables an Active Directory group policy to be set up so that a particular version of software is automatically started on a client (Windows 2000 or XP) through a desktop shortcut, via a menu selection, or by clicking a file with a specific file extension.

authentication — A scheme to identify and validate the client to the server.

backbone — A main connecting link or highway between networks, such as between floors in a building or between buildings. Main internetworking devices, such as routers and switches, are often connected via the network backbone.

binding — When binding the protocol, it enables the NIC to format data for that protocol, and identify the most efficient methods for transporting it.

bridge — A network device that connects two or more segments into one, or extends an existing segment.

bus topology — A network that is designed with a single central cable, to which all computers and other network devices attach. A bus topology has two end points. Each end point has a terminator to keep the electronic data signal from reflecting back along the path it just traveled.

carrier sense multiple access with collision avoidance (CSMA/CA) — A variation of CSMA/CD and the most prevalent protocol used in a wireless LAN.

carrier sense multiple access with collision detection (CSMA/CD) — A transmission control method used by Ethernet.

cell — Format for a unit of data that is transported over a high-speed network, usually at speeds of 155 Mbps to more than 1 Gbps.

classless interdomain routing (CIDR) — A way to ignore address class designation by using addressing that puts a slash (/) after the dotted decimal notation.

client operating system — Operating system on a computer, such as a PC, that enables the computer to process information and run applications locally, as well as communicate with other computers on a network.

coaxial cable — Often referred to as **coax**, consists of a copper wire surrounded by several layers: a layer of insulating material, a layer of woven or braided metal, and a plastic outer coating.

encryption — The encoding of data between the client and the server so that only the client or server can decode the information.

Ethernet — A network transport protocol that uses CSMA/CD communications to coordinate frame and packet transmissions on a network.

fiber-optic cable — Consists of dozens or hundreds of thin strands of glass or plastic that transmit signals using light.

firmware — Software logic that consists of one or more programs, which reside in a programmable chip on a card.

8

frame — A data unit sent over a network that contains source and destination, control, and error-detection information, as well as the data.

hub — A device often used in bus and star LANs to connect computers or devices to a local network.

Internet Packet Exchange (IPX) — Developed by Novell, this protocol is used on networks that connect servers running NetWare.

Internet Protocol (IP) — Used in combination with TCP, this protocol handles addressing and routing for transport of packets.

IP address — Used to identify a computer or network device and the network it is on.

local area network (LAN) — A series of interconnected computers, printing devices, and other computer equipment in a service area that is usually limited to a given office area, floor, or building.

Media Access Control (MAC) address — A unique hexadecimal address assigned by the manufacturer, called a device or physical address, which identifies a NIC to the network.

multicast — A transmission method in which a server divides recipients of an application, such as a multimedia application, into groups. Each data stream is a one-time transmission that goes to one group of multiple addresses, instead of sending a separate transmission to each address for every data stream. The result is less network traffic.

NetBIOS Extended User Interface (NetBEUI) — A protocol used on Microsoft networks that was developed from NetBIOS and is designed for small networks.

network — A system of computing devices, computing resources, information resources, and communications devices that are linked together by communications cable or radio waves.

Network Device Interface Specification (NDIS) — Special elements, which programmers call "hooks" in the operating system kernel (program code), that enable the operating system to interface with a network. NDIS is from Microsoft.

network interface card (NIC) — A device used by computers and internetworking devices to connect to a network.

Open Datalink Interface (ODI) — An interface developed by Novell that allows the same NIC to carry data for different protocols.

packet — A data unit sent over a network that contains source and destination, routing, control, and error-detection information, as well as data (related to the network layer of network data communications between two stations).

payload — That portion of a frame, packet, or cell that contains the actual data, which might be a portion of an e-mail message or word-processing file.

Point-to-Point Protocol (PPP) — Enables a computer to remotely access a network through a dial-up modem connection.

Point-to-Point Tunneling Protocol (PPTP) — Used to make a remote connection to a LAN over the Internet.

publishing an application — Available in Windows 2000 Server and Windows Server 2003, setting an Active Directory group policy so that Windows 2000 and Windows XP Professional clients can install preconfigured software from a central server by using Add/Remove Programs (or Add or Remove in Windows XP) via the Control Panel.

Remote Access Services (RAS) — A set of network services that can be installed on any Windows NT/2000/Server 2003 server connected to one or more modems.

Remote Installation Services (RIS) — Services in Windows 2000 Server and Windows Server 2003 that enable clients to download an operating system over the network, such as downloading and installing Windows 2000 Professional on a client computer via RIS on a Windows 2000 Server.

ring topology — One in which the data-carrying signal goes from station to station around the ring until it reaches the target destination. There is no beginning or end point, so there are no terminators.

router — A device that joins networks and can route packets to a specific network on the basis of a routing table it creates for this purpose.

Sequence Packet Exchange (SPX) — A protocol used on Novell networks that provides reliable transmission of application software data, usually in combination with IPX.

Serial Line Internet Protocol (SLIP) — A protocol sometimes used in UNIX/Linux for remote communications that transport TCP/IP.

server operating system — A network operating system that enables client workstations to access shared network resources such as printers, files, software applications, or CD-ROM drives, and allows administrators to manage the network.

star topology — All of the computers or devices (nodes) on the network connect to a central device such as a hub or switch. The hub sends the signal onto each segment, which has a computer at the end. Every segment is terminated inside the hub at one end and inside the computer at the other end.

subnet mask — A designated portion of an IP address that is used to divide a network into smaller subnetworks as a way to manage traffic patterns, enable security, and relieve congestion.

switch — A network device that connects LAN segments and forwards frames to the appropriate segment or segments. A switch works in promiscuous mode, similar to a bridge.

terminal — A device that has a keyboard but no CPU or storage and is used to access and run programs on a mainframe or minicomputer.

token — A specialized frame that is transmitted without data around the network until it is captured by a station that wants to transmit.

token ring — A network that uses a ring topology and token passing as a way to coordinate network transport.

topology — The physical design of a network and the way in which a data-carrying signal travels from point to point along the network.

Transmission Control Protocol (TCP) — A communications protocol that is used with IP; it facilitates reliable communications between two stations by establishing a window tailored to the characteristics of the connection.

twisted-pair cable — Consists of one or more pairs of twisted copper wires bundled together within a plastic outer coating. The wires are twisted to reduce electromagnetic interference or noise.

8

unicast — A transmission method in which one copy of each packet is sent to every target destination, which can generate considerable network traffic compared to multicasting, when the transmission is a multimedia application.

wide area network (WAN) — A system of networks that can extend across cities, states, and continents.

wireless access point — A connection point between a wired network and a wireless one.

wireless media — Any form of communication that works where it is inconvenient, impractical, or impossible to install wires or cables.

workgroup — A predefined group of member computers, which provides the ability to limit resource sharing on the basis of group membership.

workstation — A computer that has a CPU and usually storage to enable the user to run programs and access files locally.

REVIEW QUESTIONS

1. A network operating system (NOS) is the part of a desktop computer that allows it to talk with the network. True or False?

2. Packet collisions occur in _____ networks, but never in _____ networks.

3. Gigabit Ethernet communications are at _____ Mbps.

4. The Internet Protocol (IP) handles _____ on networks.

5. Fast Ethernet refers to what speed?

   a. 10 Mbps

   b. 100 Mbps

   c. 1 Gbps

   d. 10 Gbps

6. The Media Access Control (MAC) address is a unique hexadecimal address found on all of the multimedia cards in a computer. True or False?

7. Which of the following operating systems cannot be used on an Ethernet network?

   a. Mac OS X and UNIX/Linux

   b. Windows XP

   c. NetWare 6.0

   d. All of the above can be used on Ethernet networks.

8. Dialing into a networked server at work from your home computer is a simple example of what type of network?

   a. Ethernet

   b. LAN

   c. WAN

   d. Token ring

9. A Remote Access Services (RAS) server for remote dial-in access runs on which of the following operating systems?

   a. NetWare

   b. Windows Server 2003

   c. IBM MVS

   d. DEC VMS

10. You are setting up a UNIX/Linux server for communications on a network. Which of the following protocols are you most likely to implement in the UNIX/Linux operating system for communications?

   a. NetBEUI

   b. IPX

   c. TCP/IP

   d. SNMP

11. By Internet convention, an IP address in which the first octet translates to a decimal number between 128 and 191 signifies a medium to large network consisting of 257 to 65,536 stations. True or False?

12. Bridges are used to extend segments. This may occur when more stations must be added, but the primary segment already contains the maximum length of cable. True or False?

13. IPX and SPX are new protocols found in Windows Server 2003. True or False?

14. You are setting up a workstation running Windows XP so that it can access your network. To enable the computer to connect to the network cable, you need to install a hardware card in the computer called a(n) _____, and then you need to install software into the operating system called a(n) _____, which enables the hardware card to communicate with Windows XP.

15. Hypertext Transfer Protocol (HTTP) is used in association with which of the following protocols?

   a. TCP/IP

   b. XNS

   c. IPX

   d. NetBIOS

16. One problem with AppleTalk is that it cannot be used for network print services. True or False?

17. Two ways to enhance the security for remote access are with _____ and _____ .

8

18. Routers keep tables of network addresses that identify each computer on the network along with the best "routes" to other network addresses. True or False?

19. A network that has a combination of NetWare and Windows Server 2003 servers can be either Ethernet or token ring. True or False?

20. 144.79.22.122 is an example of a(n) _____ address.

HANDS-ON PROJECTS

Project 8-1

In this project, you examine a network to see if you can determine its topology.

To view a network topology:

1. Arrange to examine the network in a lab located in your school.

2. With the help of your instructor (or on your own), determine how each workstation is connected to the network. For example, are workstations connected directly to each other, to a wall outlet, or directly to a hub or switch? What type of cabling or wireless access is used?

3. If the workstations are connected to a wall outlet, ask if the connection eventually goes to a network device, such as a hub or switch.

4. Ask your instructor if the network employs Ethernet or token ring communications.

5. Determine if you can see any visible terminators.

6. Using the information that you gathered and the information you learned in this chapter, attempt to identify the network as a bus, ring, or star topology.

Project 8-2

In this project, you examine the computers connected to your school's network. You will need a workstation running **Red Hat Enterprise Linux 3.0** and one with **Mac OS X** that has access to your school's network.

To observe the computers on your network from the Red Hat Enterprise Linux 3.0 workstation:

Many versions of UNIX and Linux can use the Samba software that supports Server Message Block (SMB) protocol. SMB is a resource sharing protocol used in Windows-based networking. Samba, as used in Red Hat Enterprise Linux 3.0, employs SMB to contact and connect to Windows operating systems as long as it can find a master browser (a Windows NT/2000/Server 2003 server in this role). In this project, you learn how to view computers running Windows that are attached to the same network as Red Hat Enterprise

Linux 3.0—through the use of Samba. (Samba should already be installed on your Red Hat Enterprise Linux 3.0 computer.) Also, you learn more about Samba and SMB in Chapter 9.

1. Click **Main Menu** and then click **Network Servers**. Once Red Hat Enterprise Linux 3.0 contacts the Windows Master Browser, you will see other computers on the network. What computers can you view? If there is no computer running the Master Browser, you will see a Can't Display Location box.

2. If you succeeded in contacting the Master Browser, close the Nautilus display of network computers. Or, if you see the Can't Display Location Box, close it.

3. Next, you view documentation about Samba. Click **Main Menu**, point to **System Tools**, and click **Terminal**.

4. Type **info Samba** and press **Enter**.

5. Read the brief documentation about Samba, pressing the **spacebar** to advance from screen to screen. Can Samba enable printing services between networked computers?

6. Press **q** to exit the documentation when you are finished with it.

7. Type **exit** and press **Enter** to close the terminal window.

To observe the computers on your network from the Mac OS X workstation:

Mac OS X also supports viewing Windows-based computers on a network using SMB. In this project, you view the Windows-based computers on your network from Mac OS X.

1. Click the **Go** menu at the top of the desktop and click **Connect to Server**. The Connect to Server window enables you to enter the IP address of a server or to use the Browse button to locate one (see Figure 8-14).

2. Click the **Connect To Server** window (you learn more about using this capability in Chapter 9).

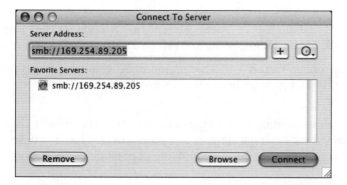

Figure 8-14   Mac OS X Connect To Server Window

8

Project 8-3

In this project, you again examine the computers connected to your network. You will need a workstation running **Windows XP** that has access to your network.

To observe the computers on your network:

1. Point to **Start**, click **My Computer**, click **My Network Places**, then click **View workgroup computers**. Observe the number of computers on the network and their computer names. Notice if there is any apparent naming scheme for computers, or if users have a wide range of options in selecting their computer names.

2. Right-click one of the visible computers, and click **Properties**.

3. Look for the General tab in the dialog box and review the types of information displayed. Close the dialog box.

4. Repeat Steps 2 and 3 to view other computers and their information.

5. Click **View workgroup computers** and then click the **Up** button on the toolbar.

6. Notice if you see options, such as Microsoft Windows Network, NetWare, or Compatible Network. If you do, first double-click one of the options to view its member computers. Click the **Up** button. Then double-click the other option to view its contents.

7. Close the open windows.

Project 8-4

UNIX and Linux use TCP/IP and other protocols for network communications. In this project, you use the *netstat* command to view the protocols currently in use and network activity associated with these protocols. (Note that they can do this from any account.)

To view protocols currently in use:

1. Access the command line, such as by opening a terminal window in Red Hat Enterprise Linux 3.0 (click **Main Menu**, point to **System Tools**, and click **Terminal**).

2. Type **netstat —s** and press **Enter**. For what protocols do you see information displayed? How many IP packets have been received and how many have been delivered?

3. TCP and IP leave open communication channels called sockets. To view the number of open and connected sockets type **netstat** and press **Enter**. How many sockets are open (not connected)? Note that these can provide opportunities for hackers to access a system.

4. Type **exit** and press **Enter** to close the terminal window.

Project 8-5

In this project, you view the IP address information configured for a computer running **Mac OS X**.

To view the IP address information:

1. Click the **Go** menu and click **Applications**.

2. Double-click **System Preferences** in the Applications window.

3. Click the **Network** icon under Internet and Network. Click the up and down arrows in the Open box and make sure that the Ethernet card (NOC) is selected, such as Built-in Ethernet. Figure 8-15 illustrates the information you see for the TCP/IP configuration. Note that in this figure the IP address information is automatically assigned by selecting *Using DHCP* (Dynamic Host Configuration Protocol), a network protocol that provides a way for a server to automatically assign an IP address to a workstation on its network or for a workstation to use a self-assigned IP address), which users can choose if they do not have an officially assigned IP address and when they work from an internal network not directly connected to the Internet.

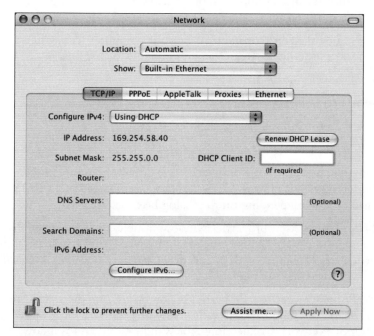

Figure 8-15 TCP/IP address information for Mac OS X

4. What are the IP Address and Subnet Mask configurations for your computer? Record your observations.

5. Click the up and down arrows for the Configure **IPv4** box. What options are available for configuring the network information?

6. Click in an open part of the desktop to close the option box.

7. Close the Network window. Click **Don't Apply**, if you see an Apply configuration changes box.

8. Close the Applications window.

HANDS-ON PROJECTS

Project 8-6

In this project, you practice installing TCP/IP in **Windows 2000**, **Windows XP**, or **Windows Server 2003**.

To install TCP/IP in Windows 2000, Windows XP, or Windows Server 2003:

1. Click **Start**, point to **Settings** (Windows 2000 only), and click **Control Panel**.

2. Double-click the **Network and Dial-up Connections** icon (applet) in Windows 2000, or click **Network and Internet Connections**, then click **Network Connections** in Windows XP and Windows Server 2003. If you are in Classic View, the **Network Connections** options will be available without having to navigate through Network and Internet Connections.

3. Double-click the **Local Area Connection** or your computer icon. Click the **Properties** button in the Local Area Connection Status dialog box.

4. Click the **Install** button in the dialog box.

5. Click **Protocol**, and then click **Add**.

6. After you view the protocol selections, click **TCP/IP**.

7. Click **OK**.

8. If the setup program asks for a path from which to install the protocol software, insert the Windows 2000, Windows XP, or Windows Server 2003 CD-ROM. Then click **Continue** or **OK** (depending on the dialog box that appears).

9. In the Local Area Connection properties window, double-click **Internet Protocol (TCP/IP)** to open the TCP/IP Properties window. Make sure the General tab is displayed (particularly for Windows XP) and that *Obtain an IP address automatically* is checked as the default. Click **Cancel**.

10. Close the Local Area Connection Properties dialog box. Close the Local Area Connection Status dialog box, and then close the Network and Dial-up Connections (for Windows 2000) or Network Connections (for Windows XP and Windows Server 2003) window.

Project 8-7

The *ifconfig* utility provides lots of information about how a UNIX/Linux computer is configured for networking. In this project you use this utility in **Red Hat Enterprise Linux 3.0** to determine address information about your network connection. You will need to log on using the root account for this project. Be sure to log off when you are finished.

To determine address information about your network connection:

1. Click **Main Menu**, point to **System Tools**, and click **Terminal**. Type **ifconfig** and press **Enter**. The Ethernet connection to your network is indicated by "eth0" in the left part of the display. What value is displayed for inet addr, which is your IP address? What value is displayed for Mask, which is the subnet mask in the TCP/IP protocol setup? What is the value for HWaddr, which is the device address burned into your network interface card?

2. Type **exit** and press **Enter** to close the terminal window.

3. Click **Main Menu**, click **Log Out**, and click the option button for **Log Out**.

Project 8-8

In this project, you learn how to use the Network Configuration tool in **Red Hat Enterprise Linux 3.0** to view or edit the properties for an Ethernet card (NIC) that is already configured. You need to log on as root for this project.

To view information about an Ethernet NIC using the Red Hat Enterprise Linux 3.0 Network Configuration tool:

1. Before you start, obtain information about your NIC from your instructor, such as the type of adapter, device type, and IRQ used in the computer.

2. Click **Main Menu**, point to **System Settings**, and click **Network**.

3. Find and click the Ethernet card (where the Device name is eth0).

4. Click the **Edit** button (with the wrench).

5. Click each of the **General Route** and **Hardware Device** tabs to view the current configuration. Notice that you can configure IP and DHCP (or automatic IP addressing) information on the General tab.

6. Click **Cancel**.

7. Click the **Hardware** tab and click **Edit** (see Figure 8-16). Notice that you can configure hardware parameters such as IRQ, MEM, and others. Click **Cancel**.

8

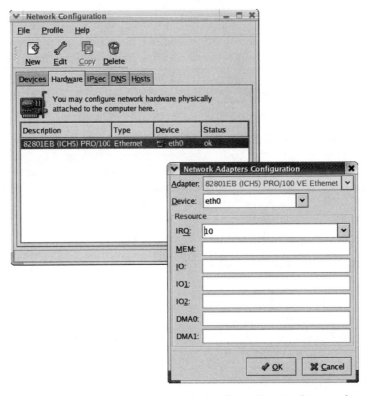

Figure 8-16   Using the Network Configuration tool to configure a NIC

8. Close the Network Configuration window.

9. Click **No**, if you are asked whether to save your changes.

Project 8-9

In this project, you set up **Windows XP** to use IPX/SPX communications with a NetWare server.

To set up IPX/SPX in Windows XP:

1. Point to **Start** and click **Control Panel**.

2. Double-click the **Network Connections** icon.

3. Double-click the **Local Area Connection.**

4. Click the **Properties** button.

5. On the General tab, click the **Install** button.

6. Click the **Protocol** icon, and then click the **Add** button.

7. Click **NWLink IPX/SPX/NetBIOS Compatible Transport Protocol**, then click **OK**.

8. Click **Close**.

Project 8-10

In this project, you find out how to set up PPP for remote networking in **Windows Server 2003**. Ask your instructor for an account and password into Windows Server 2003. Also, Dial-up Networking should already be installed.

1. Click **Start**.

2. Point to **Control Panel**.

3. Point to **Network Connections**.

4. Click on any of the dial-up icons. The Properties dialog box for the dial-up icon you clicked displays.

5. Click the **Networking** tab.

6. Notice the Type of dial-up server I am calling box to see if **PPP: Windows 95/98/NT/2000, Internet** is the selected protocol.

7. Also, on the Networking tab, notice that you can specify which protocols will be carried via PPP.

8. Click **Cancel** to close the dialog box.

Project 8-11

As an alternative to Project 8-10, or in addition to that project, check the remote protocol setup in **Windows 2000**.

Note that Dial-up Networking should already be installed.

To check the remote protocol setup:

1. Double-click **My Computer**.

2. Double-click **Control Panel**, and then double-click **Network and Dial-up Connections**.

If Dial-up Networking is not already installed on your computer, see Chapter 7 for information about how to install it.

3. Right-click an existing dial-up networking icon.

4. Click **Properties**.

5. Click the **Networking** tab.

6. Notice which protocol is set up in the Type of dial-up server I am calling list box.

7. Observe which network protocols are checked for transport over a remote connection.

8. Click **Cancel** in the Dial-up Connection Properties dialog box.

9. Click **Close** in the Network and Dial-up Connections dialog box.

CASE PROJECTS

You are the network administrator for a group of 18 groundwater hydrologists who work in two adjacent buildings. Their company works with new housing construction all over the United States to determine if there is enough local ground water to support new housing developments. Each hydrologist has his or her own computer workstation. Two use computers running Linux, three use Macintosh computers, and the rest use computers running Windows XP or Windows 2000. These hydrologists work with a variety of software, including word-processing, research databases, spreadsheets, mapping software, and mathematical calculation software. The buildings in which the hydrologists work are not networked, but the company plans to network each building and connect both networks. The company also decided to purchase a Linux server and a NetWare server for all of the hydrologists to access. Both servers will be in a secure computer room in one of the buildings. Also, the company plans to connect to an Internet service provider so that each hydrologist can easily access the Internet. Explain how you would handle the following immediate concerns:

Case Project 8-1: Type of Network

What type of network, Ethernet or token ring, do you believe should be implemented? Why?

Case Project 8-2: Topology

What topology should be installed?

Case Project 8-3: Equipment

What equipment must be purchased in order for each hydrologist's computer to be connected to the network?

Case Project 8-4: Protocols

What protocols will you need to set up on each server and on all of the workstations? Why will you need these particular protocols?

Case Project 8-5: Portable Computers and Dial-in Access

Ten of the hydrologists travel frequently and need remote access to the network from portable computers that run Windows XP or Windows 2000 Professional. What must be set up on the network for them to dial into it? What must be set up on each portable?

Case Project 8-6: Internetworking Devices

What internetworking device would you use to connect the networks in each building? Do you anticipate a need for routing capability on this network?

8

Case Project 8-7: Protocol Functions

As you work to set up the network, two of the hydrologists are curious about the function of protocols. Briefly explain to them the function of network protocols.

RESOURCE SHARING OVER A NETWORK

After reading this chapter and completing the exercises, you will be able to:

◆ Explain the principles behind sharing disks, files, and printers on a network

◆ Set up accounts, groups, security, and disk and file sharing on network server operating systems

◆ Set up disk and file sharing on client operating systems

◆ Set up printer sharing on server and client operating systems

◆ Discuss how network and Internet servers are used for vast information-sharing networks

The power of networks and network-capable operating systems lies in their ability to share resources, such as folders, programs, printers, compact disc read-only memory (CD-ROM) drives, tape drives, modems, and fax machines. A cartoon showing two network experts attempting to connect an air conditioning unit to share its cooling capabilities over the network cable appeared several years ago in a popular computer magazine. The cartoon is a humorous illustration of the real trend toward sharing more types of resources over a network. In keeping with this trend, newer operating system releases offer more ways to accommodate resource sharing.

In this chapter, you learn how to share resources in Windows 2000/XP/Server 2003, UNIX/Linux, NetWare, and Mac OS X. You learn about deploying user accounts, groups, and security to manage and protect shared resources—such as folders and printers—on servers and on client operating systems. And finally, you learn how these capabilities enable network server operating systems to propagate information for businesses, schools, and government organizations.

SHARING DISKS, FILES, AND PRINTERS

Most modern and many older computer operating systems can share files, directories, and entire disks on a network. The same operating systems also usually offer the ability to share printers. Sharing files was one of the first reasons for linking a workstation's operating system onto a network, and it remains one of the most important reasons for networking. In terms of network operating systems, NetWare was early on the scene at the start of the 1980s to enable file sharing through a server. This was possible through two methods: (1) by downloading a file from a file server to a workstation, and (2) by purchasing third-party software to create a special shared drive for other computers or workstations to access over a network. Downloading a file directly from a file server was one of the first methods for sharing files, and it was incorporated in the first version of NetWare.

When network operating systems such as Windows NT (now evolved into Windows Server 2003), NetWare, and UNIX became available, it was difficult for many users of mainframe computers to grasp the idea that entire applications could be loaded as files onto a networked workstation, instead of running on the mainframe. For instance, a word-processing package could be loaded onto the server and accessed by workstations. Each workstation would simply download the executable files, and perhaps a document file from a server, and run them in the local workstation's memory. Only one version of the word-processing software was needed at the server, which could be downloaded multiple times by authorized workstations, eliminating the need for the software on each workstation. In this arrangement, each workstation housed a specialized setup file for the word-processing software, but the executable files were always loaded from the server. Of course, it was still necessary, as it is today, to have the appropriate licenses, as mandated by the software vendor.

Although it was common to download application software from a server and run it in memory on a workstation, it is less common today because many applications are too large to download every time a workstation needs them. However, Microsoft Terminal Services enable users to log onto a Windows 2000/2003 server and run applications on the server. An explanation of Microsoft Terminal Services is beyond the scope of this book, but to find out more visit *www.microsoft.com/windowsserver2003/techinfo/overview/termserv.mspx*, *www.microsoft.com/windows2000/technologies/terminal/default.asp*, and *www.microsoft.com/windows/embedded/devices/tc/tcservertech.asp*.

Another complexity is that as software applications have grown in size, downloading them each time you want to run them on a workstation creates excessive network traffic. For example, early versions of word processors might have had executable files in the range of a few thousand kilobytes, but today, executable files and associated components can be in the range of 1 MB and more because they contain many more functions. Consider a business where 100 employees arrive at work at 8 a.m., and all access the WordPerfect or Microsoft

Word executable files from the server simultaneously. The resulting network traffic would be enough to bring the network to a standstill.

The concept of sharing resources quickly blossomed into other ways to access files, such as making shared drives available on a network, and making each shared drive look just like another local drive at the client. When a workstation accesses a shared drive, the process is called mapping. **Mapping** is a software process that enables a client workstation to attach to the shared drive of another workstation or server, and assign it a drive letter. The network drive that is attached is called a mapped drive in Windows-based operating systems. In UNIX/Linux and Mac OS X, a mapped drive is called a **mounted volume**.

TIP Medium-sized and large organizations often prefer to share drives from a server because this enables stricter management of access and security to company information. Small offices may use a server or simply share resources from clients. No matter how resources are shared, it is important to use the security techniques described in this chapter to ensure that documents do not end up in the wrong hands.

Sharing files also opened the way for printer sharing over a network. Organizations now save money on printer purchases because it is not necessary for each person in an office to have a printer. Where it is feasible given the office structure and individual duties of employees, one printer connected to a network server operating system or network client operating system can be used by others in the same office area or location.

From the Trenches...

In the interest of saving paper and focusing expenses on programming, a programming group in a large corporation decided to share two fast laser printers among the 22 programmers in their common work area, instead of purchasing printers for each programmer. The programmers focused on exchanging more documents and programs electronically, instead of exchanging hard copy. The savings in time, paper, and hardware enabled their manager to budget more for the programming tools that the programmers wanted.

SECURING SHARED RESOURCES

Sharing disks, files, and printers is a potential security risk because it is then possible for non-authorized users to access a file or use a printer. This presents problems, for example, when a shared file contains sensitive employee or company information, or when a shared printer is overtaxed because more people are using it than was originally intended.

Fortunately, all of the operating systems discussed in this book offer security measures for protecting shared resources. For example, access to a file, directory, or disk can be denied to those who are not authorized. In some instances, you want people to be able to read a file (document) but not change it. Or, you want only specific people to be able to execute a file (program). For these situations, a file, directory, or disk can be assigned security privileges that limit users to only these capabilities, such as only read or only execute a file.

Similarly, access to a shared network printer can be given to only a specific group of people. Also, permission to manage print jobs, such as to delete or prioritize the jobs submitted by coworkers, can be granted only to one or two qualified people who have that responsibility.

In the sections that follow, you'll learn how to set up shared resources and protect them so that they are used in the ways intended by your organization.

SHARING DISKS AND FILES THROUGH SERVER NETWORK OPERATING SYSTEMS

Windows 2000 Server, Windows Server 2003, UNIX/Linux, NetWare, and Mac OS X Server are prime examples of server network operating systems that can share disks and files over a network. Each of these operating systems offers a way for client workstations to access a combination of disk, file, and other shared resources. Further, each operating system enables the network administrator to establish security through techniques such as assigning accounts, account passwords, groups, and access privileges. Windows 2000 Server, Windows Server 2003, UNIX/Linux, NetWare, and Mac OS X Server are described in the next sections in terms of their capabilities to share disk and file resources, combined with the ability to secure those resources on a network.

Windows 2000 Server and Windows Server 2003

Windows 2000 Server and Windows Server 2003 use accounts, groups, and permissions; in this respect, they are similar to NetWare, UNIX/Linux, and Mac OS X Server. The steps involved in sharing Windows 2000 Server and Windows Server 2003 resources over a network include setting up the following:

- Groups
- Account policies
- User accounts
- Permissions
- Shared disks and folders

Managing Groups to Prepare for Shared Resource Access

In Windows 2000 Server and Windows Server 2003, you use groups to manage resources and permissions to resources in a way that is similar to NetWare and UNIX/Linux. Groups are important because they reduce the amount of work on the part of the server administrator for managing user accounts and security. In Windows 2000 Server and Windows Server 2003, the following types of groups can be used:

- *Local*: Used on standalone servers that are not part of a domain; the reach or "scope" of this type of group does not go beyond the local server on which it is defined.

- *Domain local*: Used when there is a single domain or to manage resources in a particular domain so that global and universal groups can access those resources

- *Global*: Used to group accounts from the same domain so that those accounts can access resources in the same and other domains

- *Universal*: Used to provide access to resources in any domain within a forest

On a Windows 2000/2003 server, all of these groups are also defined as security or distribution groups. **Security groups** are used to enable access to resources on a standalone server or in Active Directory. **Distribution groups** are used for e-mail or telephone lists, to provide quick, mass distribution of information. In this chapter, the focus is on security groups.

When Active Directory is not installed, such as in a small office setting, only local groups can be created to manage access to an individual server. A local group usually contains resources, such as the server or a printer, and user accounts that are given access to those resources.

When Active Directory is implemented, Windows 2000 Server and Windows Server 2003 add the ability to have container objects that include domains, trees, and forests. A **container object** is an entity that is used to group together resources in a directory service, such as Microsoft Active Directory. A **domain** is a fundamental component or container that holds information about all network resources that are grouped within it—servers, printers, and other physical resources, users, and user groups. For a medium-sized or large organization, a domain might be used to represent offices in a specific geographic location, for example. A **tree** consists of one or more domains, and a **forest** houses one or more trees. Figure 9-1 illustrates an Active Directory design using three general models: single domain, multiple domains in a single tree, and multiple trees in a forest.

9

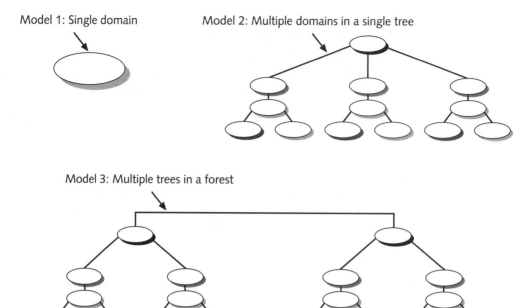

Figure 9-1 Sample domain and tree models

For example, in a large organization, domains that are in the same geographic location can be organized into trees. Further, trees that represent specific geographic regions, such as the eastern United States, can be organized into a forest. Although the concepts of domains, trees, and forests can be confusing, these organizational containers are a way to better manage multiple servers and computers in a very large organization, consisting of hundreds of servers and thousands of desktop computers.

Consider, for example, a large telecommunications company that has big offices in each state, regional offices in California and New Jersey, and headquarters in Pennsylvania. In this case, each state office might be set up as a domain of computer resources—servers, desktop computers, and printers. The domains in the midwestern and western states might be organized into one tree in the California regional office, and the domains in the eastern states organized into another tree housed in the New Jersey regional office. Finally, a forest consisting of both trees would be set up at the headquarters, where general security and group policies could be set for all domains in both trees. For each region, more specific security and group policies could be set in each tree, while specific security and group policies that apply to each state office can be set in its domain. As you are probably thinking, managing security for this large organization of thousands of users and hundreds of servers can be complex. This is why Windows 2000 Server and Windows Server 2003 have three types of groups available when Active Directory is set up.

NOTE

Besides domains, trees, and forests, Windows Active Directory uses a container object called an organizational unit (OU), which is smaller than a domain. In the telecommunications company example, each department in each state office might be organized into a separate OU, such as an Accounting OU, a Research OU, a Sales OU, and so on.

On a standalone server without Active Directory installed, a local group is used to manage both users and their access to shared resources, such as shared disks, folders, files, and printers. When Active Directory is installed on servers, a domain local group is typically assigned access to specific resources, but does not usually contain user accounts. A global group usually consists of user accounts and can be made a member of a domain local group that is in the same or a different domain—thus giving the accounts in the global group access to resources because the global group is a member of the domain local group.

As an example of working with domain local and global groups, consider a college that has a domain for students, a domain for faculty and staff, and a domain for research organizations that are associated with the college. The college's executive council, consisting of the college president and vice presidents, needs access to resources in all three domains. One way to enable the executive council to have access is to create a domain local group called LocalExec in each domain that provides the appropriate access to folders, files, and other resources. Next, create a GlobalExec global group in the faculty and staff domain that has the president's and vice presidents' user accounts as members (see Figure 9-2). These steps enable you to manage security for all of their accounts at one time from one global group. If the president or a vice president leaves to take another job, you simply delete (or disable) that person's account from the global group and later add an account (or rename and enable the old account) for her or his replacement. You also can manage access to resources in each domain one time through each domain local group, resulting in much less management work. If a new printer is added to a domain, for example, you can give the domain local group full privileges to the printer.

9

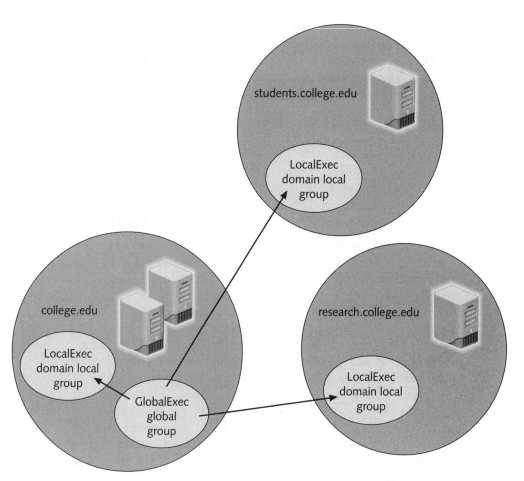

Figure 9-2   Managing security through domain local and global groups

In an Active Directory context in which there are multiple hierarchies of domains, trees, and forests, universal security groups provide a means to span domains and trees. Universal group membership can include user accounts from any domain, global groups from any domain, and other universal groups from any domain.

Universal groups are offered to provide an easy means to access any resource in a tree or among trees in a forest. If you carefully plan the use of universal groups, then you can manage security for single accounts with minimal effort. That planning is done in relation to the scope of access that is needed for a group of user accounts. The following are some guidelines to help simplify how you plan to use groups:

- Use global groups to hold user accounts as members. Give accounts access to resources by making the global groups to which they belong members of domain local groups or universal groups or both.

- Use domain local groups to provide access to resources in a specific domain. Avoid placing user accounts in domain local groups, but give domain local groups access to resources in the domain, such as shared folders and printers.

- Use universal groups to provide extensive access to resources, particularly when Active Directory contains trees and forests, or to simplify access when there are multiple domains. Give universal groups access to resources in any domain, tree, or forest.

- Manage user account access by placing accounts in global groups and joining global groups to domain local or universal groups, depending on which is most appropriate to the scope required for access.

In the example of setting up access for the executive council in the college that has three domains, an alternative is to create one universal group that has access to all resources in the three domains—create one global group containing the president and vice presidents, and make that global group a member of the universal group. In this model there are only two groups to manage, as shown in Figure 9-3.

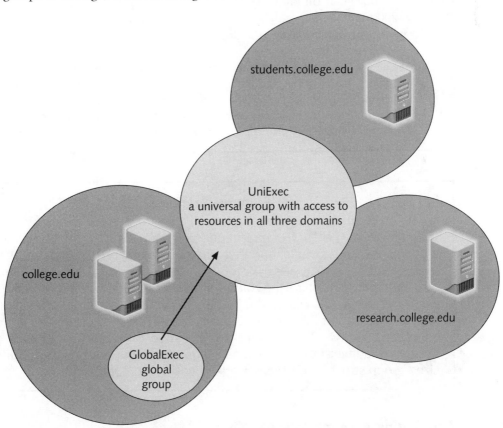

Figure 9-3   Managing security through universal and global groups

For group relationships to work between domains and trees, trust relationships are established when domains and trees are created. Thus, resources in one domain, for example, can be accessed by user accounts and groups in another domain. In Figure 9-3, for example, all three domains are both trusting and trusted. A **trusted domain**, such as college.edu, is given access to resources in another domain, such as to research.college.edu. And, a **trusting domain**, in this example, research.college.com, allows the access to its resources, such as to college.edu. You might think of this as simply a mutual relationship of trust between domains, which is managed by an Active Directory administrator or a security specialist.

When Active Directory is not installed, you create a local group or a user account by right-clicking My Computer on the desktop (in Windows 2000 Server) or from the Start menu (in Windows Server 2003), clicking Manage, and clicking Local Users and Groups (if Local Users and Groups is disabled, this means Active Directory is installed). When Active Directory is installed, you create user accounts and domain local, global, and universal groups by clicking Start, pointing to Programs (in Windows 2000) or All Programs (in Windows Server 2003), pointing to Administrative Tools, and opening the Active Directory Users and Computers tool. Hands-on Project 9-1 enables you to view the groups already created on a Windows 2000/2003 server with Active Directory installed. Also, in Hands-on Projects 9-2 and 9-3 you create domain local and global groups.

 By now you understand that groups are a valuable tool for managing shared resources, but they can also introduce complexity in resource management when too many groups are used, and there is no documentation. As a rule, in NetWare, UNIX/Linux, and in Windows 2000/2003 servers, keep resource management simple by planning groups in advance and keeping their numbers to a minimum.

From the Trenches...

In one medium-sized company, a new IT director performed an inventory of security groups on that organization's NetWare and Windows servers. He found there were over a hundred groups created on the fly and with no documentation. Also, it was risky to simply delete a group, because often it was difficult to fully determine the consequences for specific users. To make matters worse, security was so lax that a former employee was able to access sensitive folders through the Internet, just to demonstrate she could do this with little effort. Because the IT director urgently wanted to tighten security, he asked two server administrators to spend hours unraveling and fixing the disorganized group structure on the servers—a costly and complex task.

Configuring Account Policies

Before you set up user accounts and populate global groups with accounts, it is important to configure account policies on Windows 2000/2003 servers. Account policies are used to set restrictions and security to help ensure that an authorized user is accessing an account. For example, the parameters you can configure through account policies on Windows 2000/2003 servers include (see Figure 9-4):

- Password security
- Account lockout
- Kerberos security

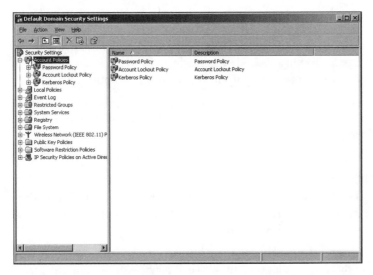

Figure 9-4 Account policy options in Windows Server 2003

Password security enables you to stipulate requirements for how users set their passwords, which can enhance security for server systems. For instance, one option is to set a password expiration period requiring users to change passwords at regular intervals. Many organizations use this feature, for example, and require that users change their passwords every 45 to 90 days. Another option is to require a minimum password length so that passwords are harder to guess. The following are password security options that you can configure through account policies:

- *Enforce password history*: Enables you to require users to choose new passwords when they make a password change because the system can remember the previously used passwords
- *Maximum password age*: Permits you to set the maximum time allowed until a password expires
- *Minimum password age*: Permits you to specify that a password must be used for a minimum amount of time before it can be changed
- *Minimum password length*: Enables you to require that passwords are a minimum length

- *Passwords must meet complexity requirements*: Enables you to create a filter of customized password requirements that each account password must follow

- *Store password using reversible encryption*: Enables passwords to be stored in reversible encrypted format

Account lockout is the ability to lock out an account (including the true account owner) after a number of unsuccessful tries. The lockout can be set to release after a specified period of time or by intervention from the server administrator.

A common policy is to have lockout go into effect after 5 to 10 unsuccessful logon attempts. Also, an administrator can set lockout to release after a designated time, such as 30 minutes. The 30 minutes creates enough delay to discourage intruders, while giving some leeway to a user who might have forgotten a recently changed password. The following are the account lockout parameters that you can configure in the account lockout policy:

- *Account lockout duration*: Permits you to specify in minutes how long the system will keep an account locked out after reaching the specified number of unsuccessful logon attempts

- *Account lockout threshold*: Enables you to set a limit to the number of unsuccessful attempts to log on to an account

- *Reset account lockout count after*: Enables you to specify the number of minutes between two consecutive unsuccessful logon attempts to make sure that the account will not be locked out too soon

As you learned in Chapter 2, Kerberos security involves the use of tickets that are exchanged between the client who requests logon and network services access and the server or Active Directory that grants access. On a network that does not use Active Directory, each standalone Windows 2000/2003 server can be designated as a Kerberos key distribution center, which means that the server stores user accounts and passwords. When Active Directory is used, each domain controller is a key distribution center. When a user logs on, the client computer sends an account name and password to the key distribution center. The key distribution center responds by issuing a temporary ticket that grants the user access to the Kerberos ticket-granting service on a domain controller (or standalone server), which then grants a permanent ticket to that computer. The permanent ticket, called a service ticket, is good for the duration of a logon session (or for another period of time specified by the server administrator in the account polices) and enables the computer to access network services beginning with the Logon service. The permanent ticket contains information about the account that is used to identify the account to each network service it requests to use. You might think of a Kerberos ticket as similar to one you would purchase to enter a concert; the ticket is good for the duration of that event and for entry to refreshment and merchandise booths, but you must purchase a new ticket to attend a concert on another date.

The following options are available for configuring Kerberos:

- *Enforce user logon restrictions*: Turns on Kerberos security, which is the default

- *Maximum lifetime for a service ticket*: Determines the maximum amount of time in minutes that a service ticket can be used to continually access a particular service in one service session

- *Maximum lifetime for a user ticket*: Determines the maximum amount of time in hours that a ticket can be used in one continuous session for access to a computer or domain

- *Maximum lifetime for user ticket renewal*: Determines the maximum number of days that the same Kerberos ticket can be renewed each time a user logs on

- *Maximum tolerance for computer clock synchronization*: Determines how long in minutes a client will wait until synchronizing its clock with that of the server or Active Directory it is accessing

When Active Directory is installed, the account policies enable Kerberos, which is the default authentication. If Active Directory is not installed, Kerberos is not included by default in the account policies because the default authentication is through **Windows NT LAN Manager (NTLM)**. NTLM is the authentication used by all versions of Windows NT Server prior to Windows 2000 Server, and it is not as secure as properly configured Kerberos.

NOTE
Kerberos is not just an Active Directory feature; it is also available in most operating systems because it offers important logon security.

Hands-on Project 9-4 enables you to view where to configure account policies in Windows 2000/Server 2003.

Configuring User Accounts

After you have configured account policies it is time to create user accounts, which enable users to access servers and resources. Also, after user accounts are created, they are typically added to the appropriate global groups to make managing security for multiple accounts easier.

As mentioned earlier, when Active Directory is not installed, a user account is created by right-clicking My Computer via the Start menu (in Windows Server 2003) or from the desktop (in Windows 2000 Server), clicking Manage, and clicking Local Users and Groups (you can also use these steps to create accounts in Windows 2000 Professional and Windows XP).

When Active Directory is installed, use the Active Directory Users and Computers tool to create a new account. Hands-on Project 9-5 enables you to create an account and make that account a member of a global group.

Configuring Access Privileges

As you'll find is true for UNIX/Linux and NetWare, access privileges (permissions) are associated with a Windows 2000/2003 server's disks, folders, and files when you use NTFS (see Chapter 3). Permissions enable you to protect the contents of files and folders so that only authorized people can access them. For example, consider an instructor who creates a shared folder and subfolders in which students can deposit work. In this case, the instructor wants to set up the folder and subfolders so that students cannot view each other's work. Another example is a shared folder set up for the board of directors of a corporation. It is important to set up the shared folder so that only the board members and CEO can access the folder.

The ease with which you assign permissions is closely related to how the folder structure is set up. For example, it is easiest to share access for the installation of application programs by placing those programs in subfolders within a main folder intended for installing applications. The main folder might be called Program Files or Apps, and there might be subfolders such as MS Office, Accounting, Drivers, CAD, and so on.

Permissions on a file or folder in a Windows 2000/2003 server are set by accessing the file or folder using My Computer or Windows Explorer. After you locate the file or folder, right-click it, click Properties, and click the Security tab (see Figure 9-5). In Windows 2000 Server, permissions from a higher level folder can be automatically inherited by selecting *Allow inheritable permissions from parent to propagate to this object* (which is configured by default). And, in Windows Server 2003, inherited permissions are established through the *Allow inheritable permissions from the parent to propagate to this object and all child objects. Include these with entries explicitly defined here* option, which is the default. For example, notice the shaded (and deactivated) boxes in Figure 9-5, which mean that these permissions are inherited. Table 9-1 shows the NTFS permissions available for files and folders in Windows 2000 Server and Windows Server 2003.

Figure 9-5   Setting permissions in Windows Server 2003

Table 9-1   Windows 2000 Server/ Windows Server 2003 NTFS folder and file
permissions

Permission	Description	Applies To
Full Control	Can read, add, delete, execute, and modify files, plus change permissions and attributes, and take ownership	Folders and files
List Folder Contents	Can list (traverse) files in the folder or switch to a subfolder, view folder attributes and permissions, and execute files, but cannot view file contents	Folders only
Modify	Can read, add, delete, execute, and modify files, but cannot delete subfolders and their file contents, change permissions, or take ownership	Folders and files
Read	Can view file contents, view folder attributes and permissions, but cannot traverse folders or execute files	Folders and files
Read & Execute	Implies the capabilities of both List Folder Contents and Read (traverse folders, view file contents, view attributes and permissions, and execute files)	Folders and files
Write	Can create files, write data to files, append data to files, create folders, delete files (but not subfolders and their files), and modify folder and file attributes	Folders and files

Hands-on Project 9-6 enables you to configure permissions for a folder on a Windows 2000/2003 server.

Configuring Shared Disks and Folders

After groups, user accounts, and permissions are set up, disk volumes and folders can be accessed through the network by creating shares through a Windows 2000/2003 server. A **share** is an object—a disk or folder, for example—that is given a name and made visible to network users, such as through Network Neighborhood in Windows 95, Windows 98, and Windows NT, or My Network Places in Windows Me, Windows 2000, Windows XP, and Windows Server 2003.

A drive or folder is shared through its properties. This is accomplished by accessing the drive or folder in My Computer or in Windows Explorer. Right-click the drive or folder and click Sharing. Click the option button to *Share this folder*, provide a name for the share, and configure how many people can access the share at the same time. Click the Permissions button to set share permissions (see Figure 9-6). The available share permissions are:

- *Read*: Permits groups or users to read and execute files
- *Change*: Enables users to read, add, modify, execute, and delete files
- *Full Control*: Provides full access to the folder including the ability to take control or change share permissions

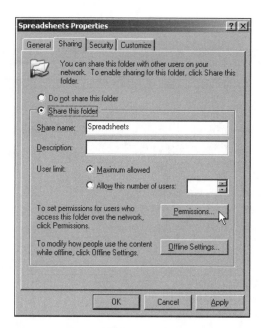

Figure 9-6   Configuring sharing in Windows Server 2003

Notice that the dialog box in Figure 9-6 has a button for Offline Settings in Windows Server 2003—Windows 2000 has a button for Caching. These options accomplish the same thing and enable you to set up a folder so that it can be accessed by a client, even when the client is not connected to the network. This capability is particularly useful for laptop users who travel away from the network. The contents of the folder can be stored on the client's hard drive while he or she is not on the network.

Also, Windows 2000/Server 2003 enable you to set up Web sharing, which makes files available on a Web server for Hypertext Markup Language (HTML) or File Transfer Protocol (FTP) access. Web sharing becomes available when Internet Information Services (IIS) is installed on a Windows 2000/2003 server. By using Web sharing, you can make the file available to a Web server, but set your own permissions on that file. Tables 9-2 and 9-3 show the two sets of permissions used for Web sharing: access permissions and application permissions.

Table 9-2   Web sharing access permissions

Access Permission	Description
Read	Enables clients to read and display the contents of folders and files via an Internet or intranet
Write	Enables clients to modify the contents of folders and files, including the ability to upload files through FTP
Script source access	Enables clients to view the contents of scripts containing commands to execute Web functions

Table 9-2   Web sharing access permissions (continued)

Access Permission	Description
Directory browsing	Enables clients to browse the folder and subfolders, such as for FTP access

Table 9-3   Web sharing application permissions

Application Permission	Description
None	No access to execute a script or application
Scripts	Enables the client to run scripts to perform Web-based functions
Execute (includes scripts)	Enables clients to execute programs and scripts via an Internet or intranet connection

One of the problems associated with permissions is that there can be permission conflicts, such as between the NTFS permissions granted to a user account, and those granted to a group to which the user belongs. Or, there can be a conflict between the NTFS permission granted to a user or group and the share permissions granted to the same user or group. When you assign or troubleshoot permissions, remember that NTFS permissions are cumulative with one another (except for No Access), but share permissions are not cumulative with NTFS permissions. An example of cumulative permissions in NTFS is if a user account has Read permission for a folder and belongs to a group that has Write permission, then that user has *both* Read and Write permissions. The exception is Deny. If the same user has Read permission on another folder and belongs to a group for which all permissions are denied to that folder, then that user does not have access to the folder.

NTFS and share permissions on the same folder are not cumulative, however. For example, if the Everyone group is granted NTFS Read access on a folder, but the share permissions for that folder are Full Control for the same group, the Everyone group still only has Read access to that folder. A summary of the permissions rules are:

- NTFS permissions are cumulative with the exception that if an account or group is denied access, this overrides other permissions.

- When a folder has both NTFS and share permissions, the most restrictive permissions apply.

You can practice setting up a shared folder in a Windows 2000/2003 server in Hands-on Project 9-7.

NOTE

Sharing resources through Windows 2000 Professional or Windows XP involves nearly the same processes as sharing resources through a Windows 2000/2003 server. The important differences are that Windows 2000 Professional and Windows XP support only local groups (not global groups), and these operating systems are only designed to support 10 or fewer users logged on simultaneously.

Troubleshooting a Security Conflict

Sometimes you will set up access for a user account but find that the account does not actually have the type of access you set up. Consider the example of Cleo Jackson, an English professor who maintains a shared subfolder on a Windows 2003 server called Assignments for his students from the account CJackson. Assignments is a subfolder under the parent folder English, which contains folders used by all English professors. CJackson needs to update files, copy new files, and delete files. As the server administrator, you have granted CJackson Modify access permissions to Assignments. However, you omitted the step of reviewing the groups to which CJackson belongs, such as the Paper group, which consists of Cleo Jackson and the student newspaper staff. The Paper group has been denied all access to the English folder and all of its subfolders. When Cleo Jackson attempts to copy a file to the Assignments folder, he receives an access denied message.

To troubleshoot the problem, you should review the folder permissions and share permissions for the CJackson account and for all of the groups to which CJackson belongs. In this case, because the Paper group is denied access, CJackson is also denied. The easiest solution is to remove CJackson from the Paper group and perhaps create a group of English professors, such as EngProfs, who all have access to the same resources as the Paper group.

Windows 2000 Server and Windows Server 2003 make determining a user's or group's effective permissions much simpler than previous versions of Windows. In these server operating systems, the properties of a folder or file include an Effective Permissions tab. To access this tab, right-click a folder or file, click Properties, click the Security tab, click the Advanced tab, and click the Effective Permissions tab. Using the Effective Permissions tab, you can view the effective permissions assigned to a user or group. The calculation will take into account group membership and well as permission inheritance. After the calculation is complete, a user's or group's effective permissions will be indicated with a checkmark beside them. Hands-on Project 9-8 enables you to examine the effective permissions on a folder in Windows Server 2003.

When you troubleshoot permissions, also take into account what happens when a folder or files in a folder are copied or moved. When a file is copied, the original file remains intact and a copy is made in another folder. Moving a file causes it to be deleted from the original location and placed in a different folder on the same or on a different volume. Copying and moving work the same for a folder, but the entire folder contents (files and subfolders) is copied or moved. When a file or folder is created, copied, or moved, the file and folder permissions can be affected in the following ways (depending on how inheritance is set up in the target location):

- A newly created file inherits the permissions already set up in a folder.

- A file that is copied from one folder to another on the same volume inherits the permissions of the folder to which it is copied.

- A file or folder that is moved from one folder to another on the same volume takes with it the permissions it had in the original folder. For example, if the original folder had Read permissions for the Users domain local group and the folder to which it is transplanted has Modify permissions for Users, that file (or folder) will still only have Read permissions.

- A file or folder that is moved or copied to a folder on a different volume inherits the permissions of the folder to which it is moved or copied.

- A file or folder that is moved or copied from an NTFS volume to a folder in a file allocation table (FAT) volume is not protected by NTFS permissions, but it does inherit share permissions if they are assigned to the FAT folder.

- A file or folder that is moved or copied from a FAT volume to a folder in an NTFS volume inherits the permissions already assigned in the NTFS folder.

UNIX and Linux

Access to directories and files on a UNIX/Linux server is also governed through user accounts, groups, and access permissions. Each user account in UNIX/Linux is associated with a **user identification number (UID)**. Also, users who have common access needs can be assigned to a group via a **group identification number (GID)**, and then the permissions to access resources are assigned to the group, instead of to each user. When the user logs on to access resources, the password file is checked to permit logon authorization. The password file (/etc/passwd) contains the following kinds of information:

- The username

- An encrypted password or a reference to the **shadow file**, a file associated with the password file that makes it difficult for intruders to determine the passwords of others (if the shadow file capability is turned on)

- The UID which can be a number as large as 60,000

- A GID with which the username is associated

- Information about the user, such as a description or the user's job

- The location of the user's home directory

- A command that is executed as the user logs on, such as which shell to use

Usually you will give users a unique UID; however, if there is more than one UNIX/Linux server on a network, you might create accounts on each server with the same account name and UID to simplify access and account administration.

In many UNIX/Linux systems, including Red Hat Enterprise Linux and Fedora systems, any account that has a UID of 0 automatically has access to anything in the system. Occasionally audit the /etc/passwd file to make sure that only the root account has this UID. You can view the contents of the /etc/passwd file from the root account by entering *more /etc/passwd* at the command line, and then pressing Enter to view each page.

The shadow file (/etc/shadow) is normally available only to the system administrator. It contains password restriction information that includes the following:

- The minimum and the maximum number of days between password changes
- Information on when the password was last changed
- Warning information about when a password will expire
- Amount of time that the account can be inactive before access is prohibited

Information about groups is stored in the /etc/group file, which typically contains an entry for each group consisting of the name of the group, an encrypted group password, the GID, and a list of group members. In some versions of UNIX/Linux, including Red Hat Enterprise Linux and Fedora, every account is assigned to at least one group, and can be assigned to more. User accounts and groups can be created by editing the password, shadow, and group files, but a safer way to create them is by using UNIX/Linux commands created for this purpose. If you edit the files, you run the risk of an editing error that can create unanticipated problems. Also, it is important to make sure that each group has a unique GID because when two or more groups use the same GID, there is a serious security risk. For example, an obvious risk is that the permissions given to one group also inappropriately apply to the other.

The *useradd* command enables you to create a new user. The parameters that can be added to *useradd* include the following:

- *-c* gives an account description
- *-d* specifies the user's home directory location
- *-e* specifies an account expiration date
- *-f* specifies the number of days the account can be inactive before access is prohibited
- *-g* specifies initial group membership
- *-G* specifies additional groups to which the account belongs
- *-m* establishes the home directory if it has not previously been set up
- *-M* means do not create a home directory
- *-n* means do not set up, by default, a group that has the same name as the account (in Red Hat Enterprise Linux)
- *-p* specifies the account password
- *-s* designates the default shell associated with the account
- *-u* specifies the UID

In Red Hat Enterprise Linux 3.0 and Fedora, for example, the command *useradd -c 'Lisa Ramirez, Accounting Department, ext 221"-p green$thumb -u 700 lramirez* creates an account called lramirez with a comment that contains the account holder's personal information, a password set to green$thumb, and a UID equal to 700 (see Figure 9-7). In Red Hat Enterprise Linux, a UID less than 500 is typically used for system-based accounts and user accounts have a UID of 500 or more. The parameters set by default, because they are not specified, are to create a group called lramirez, to create the home directory /home/lramirez (with lramirez as owner), and to set the shell as "bash" (Bourne Again shell). **Home directories** are areas on the server in which users store data. If you do not want a group automatically created at the time you create an account, use the *-n* parameter with the *useradd* command. When you use the *-n* parameter, the account is automatically assigned to a general group called users (with GID 100), instead of to a newly created group with the same name as the account. Setting up a default group with a name that is the same as the account name is a characteristic of Red Hat Enterprise Linux, but not generalized to other versions of UNIX. Hands-on Project 9-9 enables you to set up an account in Red Hat Enterprise Linux (although the same steps apply to most UNIX/Linux versions).

9

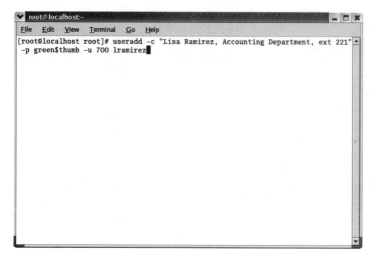

Figure 9-7   Creating an account in Red Hat Enterprise Linux

In many versions of UNIX/Linux, such as Red Hat Enterprise Linux, if no password is specified at the time the account is created, then the account is disabled by default. Also, for some versions of UNIX/Linux, including Red Hat Enterprise Linux 3.O, usernames should be entered in lowercase.

The parameters associated with an account can be modified by using the *usermod* command. For instance, to change the password for the account lramirez, you would enter *usermod -p applebuTTer# lramirez*. Also, account setup can be automated by writing a shell script that contains prompts for the desired information. Accounts are deleted through the *userdel* command, which enables you to specify the username and (optionally) delete the home directory and its contents. In Red Hat Enterprise Linux, Fedora, and Solaris, to delete an account, the home directory, and all files in the home directory, use the *-r* parameter instead of specifying the home directory, such as entering *userdel -r lramirez*.

Useradd, *usermod*, and *userdel* generally work in all versions of UNIX/Linux except IBM's AIX, which uses *mkuser*, *chuser*, and *rmuser*. Also, installations of Red Hat Enterprise Linux and Fedora, such as those for servers, include a GNOME graphical user interface (GUI) option to configure user accounts. In Red Hat Enterprise Linux 3.0, you can find this option by clicking Main Menu, pointing to System Settings, and clicking Users and Groups.

Information about groups is typically stored in the /etc/group file (see Figure 9-8), and group security information is in the /etc/gshadow file (or the /etc/security/group file in AIX and the /etc/logingroup file in HP-UX). Groups are created using the *groupadd* command. There are typically two inputs associated with this command. The *-g* parameter is used to establish the GID, and the group string creates a group name. For example, to create the auditors group, you would enter *groupadd -g 2000 auditors*. Once a group is created, it is modified through the *groupmod* command. Groups are deleted through the *groupdel* command. In Hands-on Project 9-10 you create a UNIX/Linux group.

Figure 9-8   Viewing the contents of the /etc/group file in Red Hat Enterprise Linux

AIX UNIX uses the commands *mkgroup*, *chgroup*, and *rmgroup* to add, modify, or delete groups.

NOTE

UNIX/Linux files are assigned any combination of three permissions: read, write, and execute. The permission to read a file enables the user to display its contents, and is signified by the letter *r*. Write permission entails the ability to modify, save, and delete a file, as signified by a *w*. The execute permission, indicated by an *x*, enables a user or group of users to run a program. For example, if you create a C++ program to perform database queries of customer service information for a business and want a group of customer service representatives to be able to run that program, you need to give the group the *x* permission. Also, when a directory is flagged with an *x*, that means a user or group can access and list its contents. Therefore, although a directory can be given read and write permissions for a user or group, these permissions have no meaning unless the directory is given the execute permission for that user or group.

Executable programs can have a special set of permissions called Set User ID (SUID) and Set Group ID (SGID). When either of these is associated with an executable, the user or group member who runs it can do so with the same permissions as held by the owner. This provides more access permissions than when the file is executed simply by the user.

Permissions are granted on the basis of four criteria:

- Ownership
- Group membership
- Other (or World)
- All (not used in every version of UNIX/Linux, but it is included in Red Hat Enterprise Linux and Fedora)

The owner of the file or directory typically has all permissions, can assign permissions, and has the designation of *u*. Group members, designated by *g*, are users who may have a complete set of permissions, one permission, or a combination of two, such as read and execute. The designation other, or *o* (sometimes referred to as World), consists of non-owners or non-group members who represent generic users. Finally, the all or *a* designation represents the combination of *u+g+o*.

For example, the owner of a file has read, write, and execute permissions, by default. A particular group might have read and execute permissions, while others might only have read permissions, or perhaps no permissions. In another example, if there is a public file to which all permissions are needed for all users, then you would grant read, write, and execute permissions to all.

Permissions are set up by using the *chmod* command in UNIX/Linux. *chmod* has two different formats, symbolic and octal. In the symbolic format, you specify three parameters: (1) who has the permission, (2) the actions to be taken on the permission, and (3) the permission. For example, consider the command *chmod go -r-w-x* * that is used on all files (signified by the *) in a directory. The *g* signifies groups and *o* signifies others. The - means to remove a permission, and *-r-w-x* signifies removing the read, write, and execute permissions (all three are removed; in some versions of UNIX/Linux, you might also enter *chmod go -rwx*). In this example, only the owner and members of the owner's group are left with read, write, and execute permissions on the files in this directory. In another example, to grant all permissions for all users to the data file in the /public directory, you would enter *chmod a+r+w+x /public/data* or *chmod a+rwx /public/data*. Hands-on Project 9-11 gives you practice configuring permissions in UNIX/Linux.

The octal permission format is more complex because it assigns a number on the basis of the type of permission and on the basis of owner, group, and other (World)—all is omitted from this scheme. Execute permission is assigned 1, write is 2, and read is 4. These permission numbers are added together for a value between 0 and 7. For instance, a read and write permission is a 6 (4 + 2), while read and execute is a 5 (4 + 1). There are four numeric positions (xxxx) after the *chmod* command. The first position gives the permission number of the SUID/SGID, the second position gives the permission number of the owner, the third gives group permissions, and the fourth position gives the permission number of other. For example, the command *chmod 0755 ** assigns no permissions to SUID/SGID (0); read, write, and execute permissions to owner (7); and read and execute permissions to both group and other (5 in both positions) for all files (*).

NetWare

When a Novell NetWare server is installed, one of the first projects is to use a directory structure (created by default when you install the system) that makes it easy to establish drive mappings. For example, important commands available to users are contained in a directory called PUBLIC. The SYSTEM directory contains operating system files and utilities that the server administrator uses to manage the server. The LOGIN directory has files that users can access before they log on to a server, such as the executable file (Login.exe) used to log on, and other startup files needed by clients. Other information important to users is contained in home directories set up for each user. Users typically have control over whether to enable other users to access their data. Also, on NetWare servers, there may be directories from which to install applications, such as WordPerfect or Microsoft Word, (or perhaps to run other applications that do not have much network overhead).

Consider, for example, a NetWare server set up for use by accountants. The main disk volume composing the root directory is the system volume, called the SYS volume. The server has default directories on the SYS volume created during installation, which are available to users, such as PUBLIC, LOGIN, HOME, APPS, and DATA (see Figure 9-9). The SYSTEM directory is also on the SYS volume, but full access is limited to the server administrator. If workstations access the server using a Windows-based client operating system, then the PUBLIC directory can have a subdirectory for utilities and programs related to a particular version of Windows, such as a subdirectory called WIN2K for Windows 2000 Professional or WINXP for Windows XP. The APPS directory might contain subdirectories for applications such as word processing, spreadsheets, and accounting software. The HOME directory has one subdirectory for each user, and the DATA directory contains database files for the accounting system.

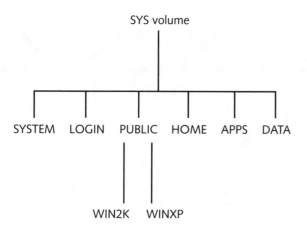

Figure 9-9   Sample NetWare directories available to users

Before users can access any shared directory, the network administrator performs several tasks to prepare the server before it is made available on the network. These tasks include the following:

- Set security on each directory, subdirectory, and on particular files
- Create an account and account password for each user who needs to access the server
- Set up groups as a way to provide shortcuts for managing security

After the server is prepared for network access, individual users log on to their accounts and map to particular drives. This can be done as a manual process by mapping each drive at the beginning of every login session, or it can be done using a login script. Table 9-4 illustrates how drives might be mapped at the client workstation, which might be running Windows 2000 or Windows XP, for example.

With an account and the appropriate security, a client can access directories and files within NetWare directories over the network. The directories that are mapped using a letter of the alphabet are available as shared drives for users to view and access files and copy files to their client workstations. The letters for these drives generally are those that follow letters allocated for local drives on the workstation, including local drive A: for a floppy drive, local drive C: for a hard drive, and local drive D: for the CD-ROM drive (depending on the number of hard drives installed).

Table 9-4   NetWare network drive mappings

Mapped Drive Letter at the Workstation	Mapped Directory at the Server	Purpose of the Mapped Directory
F	SYS volume root	Access to the main volume and logon utilities
H	SYS volume HOME directory and user's subdirectory (SYS:HOME\userdirectory)	Storing the user's files
P	SYS volume applications directory (SYS:APPS)	Accessing program files to download to the client
Q	SYS volume data directory (SYS:DATA)	Access to data files or a database
S1	SYS volume PUBLIC directory (SYS:PUBLIC)	Search access for NetWare utilities
S2	SYS volume, PUBLIC directory, and Windows 2000 subdirectory (SYS:PUBLIC\WIN2K)	Search access for clients using Windows 2000

NOTE

For legacy client systems—MS-DOS, Windows 3.x, Windows 95, and Windows 98, for example—the last drive letter allocated for a local drive can be specified in the Config.sys boot file using the *LASTDRIVE* command. Typically a computer that is not attached to a network is set up with the command *LASTDRIVE=E*; if it is connected to a network, *LASTDRIVE=Z* is used. Using this command occupies 40 KB of overhead in memory. When you do not use the command, these client operating systems default to using A: through E: for local drives, thus the first network drive is mapped as F:.

NetWare recognizes another type of network drive, called a **search drive**, which is given drive letters such as S1 for the first drive, S2 for the second drive, and so on. The difference between a mapped network drive and a mapped search drive is that NetWare can execute a file on a search drive, regardless of whether the file is in the main directory or in a subdirectory under the search drive. For example, if you want to execute a utility in a subdirectory under the S1 mapped directory for PUBLIC, you simply type the name of the program and NetWare searches all subdirectories under PUBLIC in order to execute it.

There are several ways to map a NetWare drive from a client workstation operating system. One way is to use the MAP command from the Windows 2000/XP Command Prompt window for Windows-based operating systems. The syntax of the MAP command is MAP drive:=volume:directory[\subdirectory] for regular network drives, and it is MAP S#: = volume:directory[\subdirectory] for search drives. For example, to map the PUBLIC directory as search drive S1, you type MAP S1:=SYS:PUBLIC (try Hands-on Project 9-12). Another way to set up the same search drive (so that you map it each time you log on to your account) is to put the MAP command in a NetWare login script. A **login script** is a file of commands that is stored on the NetWare server and associated with an account or a group of accounts. The login script runs automatically each time a user logs on to the account. The network administrator can set up login scripts and enable users to customize their own login scripts. Figure 9-10 is an example of a NetWare login script (the arrows in the figure point to the description of each command).

```
MAP DISPLAY OFF ──▶ Turns off the display of map commands as they are executed
CLS ──▶ Clears the screen
WRITE "Welcome to the First National Bank network server" ──▶ Displays a message
PAUSE ──▶ Requires that a key be pressed to continue
MAP F:=SYS: ──▶ Maps drive F: to the SYS: volume
MAP H:=SYS:USERS\HERRERA ──▶ Maps drive H: to the home directory location
MAP INS S1:=SYS:PUBLIC ──▶ Maps search drive S1 to the PUBLIC directory
MAP INS S2:=SYS:PUBLIC\WINXP──▶Maps search drive S2 to the WINXP subdirectory in PUBLIC
#CAPTURE Q=HPLASER ──▶ Directs printer files from a local printer port to a network printer
```

Figure 9-10 Sample NetWare login script

NOTE The MAP INS command is used to insert a search drive between two existing search drives. It is also used in login scripts to ensure that search drive mappings supercede those from another source.

NOTE To use the MAP and MAP INS commands from the Command Prompt window on a Windows 2000/XP client, there should already be a drive mapped to the NetWare server's SYS:PUBLIC drive, such as through a login script or the drive mapping tool in My Computer.

Access to a NetWare shared drive is granted through creating an account for each user. A user account can be set up using several kinds of restrictions. The restrictions include:

- Requiring a password
- Setting a minimum password length
- Requiring that a password is changed within a specified interval of time
- Requiring that a new password is used each time the old one is changed
- Limiting the number of unsuccessful attempts to log on to an account
- Setting time restrictions that specify when users can log on
- Setting intruder detection capabilities

User accounts and restrictions can be set up in the ConsoleOne utility for NetWare 6.x. ConsoleOne can be run at the server or from a client, such as a computer running Windows XP Professional connected to a NetWare server. When you set up account restrictions (similar to account policies on Windows server) you create a template (see Figure 9-11 in which ConsoleOne is run from Windows XP connected to a NetWare server as an administrator). Also, multiple accounts can be set up by using the UIMPORT utility.

UIMPORT is run in conjunction with an American Standard Code for Information Interchange (ASCII) text file that contains information about the accounts to be set up, such as the login name, the user's actual name, information about the location of a home directory, password restrictions, and other information pertinent to each account.

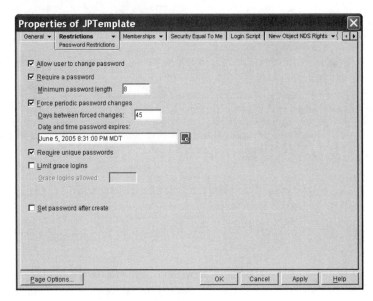

Figure 9-11   Using ConsoleOne to manage NetWare 6.x account restrictions

To set up an account in ConsoleOne:

1. Navigate to the organizational unit (a container for organizing NetWare resources) in which the account will reside.

2. Click the New User button on the ConsoleOne toolbar.

3. Complete the information for creating the account.

After accounts are set up, the network administrator can grant rights to access specific directories, subdirectories, and files. In general, the rights control the ability to:

- Perform a directory listing

- Create a new directory, subdirectory, or file

- Read the contents of a directory, subdirectory, or file

- Write to the contents of a file

- Delete a directory, subdirectory, or file

- Change the security associated with a directory, subdirectory, or file

- Copy a directory, subdirectory, or file
- Rename a directory, subdirectory, or file

Rights are assigned by making a user or group a directory or file trustee. Rights also can be inherited on the basis of the rights already assigned to higher level directories, and they can be inherited based on container objects. In NetWare, a container object is an entity that is used to group together resources, such as an organizational unit, an organization, or a country, as specified in the directory services of NetWare.

An effective way to manage the rights granted to accounts is by creating groups that need the same kinds of access. After a group is created, the network administrator assigns rights and accounts to the group. Likewise, a group can be assigned to a specific login script containing mapped drives and other network parameters, such as network printer assignments, applicable to each group.

User accounts, groups, printers, directories, subdirectories, files, and other resources in NetWare are considered **objects** (and the same is true for Windows a 2000/2003 server). Information about objects, such as rights that are associated with them, is stored in the **Novell Directory Services (NDS)**. NDS is a comprehensive database of shared resources and information known to the NetWare operating system. A portion of the NDS is used to store information about clients, which is one example of NDS **leaf objects** in an organization container, given various levels of authorization to access NetWare servers. The information that is stored in the NDS includes the client logon name, full name of the client, home directory location, and password information.

NDS and Windows Active Directory are examples of directory services. A **directory service** provides three important functions on a network: a central listing of resources, a way to quickly find resources, and the ability to access and manage resources.

In NetWare 6.x, groups can be created by using the ConsoleOne utility. To create a group, select the container to hold the group (such as an organizational unit), click the File menu, click New, click Group, and complete the information in the New Group dialog box (see Figure 9-12).

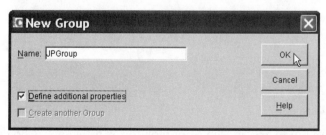

Figure 9-12   Creating a new group in NetWare 6.x using ConsoleOne

Mac OS X Server

Mac OS X Server is built on the Mac OS X foundation, but it is designed as a true server for file sharing, printer sharing, managing network users and groups, and providing Web services. A computer running Mac OS X Server can support up to several thousand users (depending on the network and computer hardware). You might deploy Mac OS X Server in a company that creates publications or advertising materials, for example. Or, Mac OS X Server might be deployed for a school laboratory consisting of Macintosh and other computers.

Mac OS X Server includes the Apache Web server software, which was originally designed for UNIX/Linux computers and has been adapted for Mac OS X Server. Through Apache, you can set up multiple Web sites and enable users to participate in Web authoring. Apache supports mainstream Web capabilities, including HTML documents, the Hypertext Transfer Protocol (HTTP) Web protocol, and scripts (command files).

As is true of Mac OS X, Mac OS X Server supports Transmission Control Protocol/Internet Protocol (TCP/IP) and AppleTalk. These network protocols open the door for communications with Mac OS computers and other computers that use TCP/IP. This also means that Mac OS X Server is compatible with the Internet e-mail protocol Simple Mail Transfer Protocol (SMTP). Out of the box, Mac OS X Server includes a Sendmail interface and program for e-mail communications. Also, Mac OS X Server comes with an FTP Service that can be used to transfer documents to or from the server over the Internet.

Two important tools are included with Mac OS X Server that enable server management: Server Admin and Macintosh Manager. Accounts and groups can be created and managed through the Server Admin tool. Through this tool, users can be set up with a login shell (similar to a login script of actions that occur before the user logs on) and a home directory on the server. File and print sharing can also be managed through Server Admin—for example, establishing sharing attributes (such as ownership of a share and group access to a share). Server Admin also establishes **share points**, which are simply shared resources on the server.

Through Server Admin, you can set up logging of events on a Mac OS X Server. The events log can include:

- Login and Logout events
- Opened files
- Newly created files
- Newly created folders
- Deleted files and folders

There is also a Printer Monitor in Server Admin, for monitoring print queues, holding print jobs, releasing print jobs, deleting jobs, setting printing priority, creating new printer queues, and so on.

The Macintosh Manager is a tool for managing users, groups, and computers that access the server. Through this tool, you can create users and groups by calling that part of the Server Admin tool that accomplishes these tasks. Also, a user account previously created through Server Admin can be imported into Macintosh Manager to fine-tune management of that account by establishing disk quotas to limit how much space that users can have to store files on the server, for example. Hands-on Project 9-13 enables you to create an account in Mac OS X.

ACCESSING AND SHARING DISKS AND FILES THROUGH CLIENT NETWORK OPERATING SYSTEMS

Many operating systems include the ability to act as clients to map to disks and directories on servers, for example. Some client operating systems can share files and folders as well. In the sections that follow, you learn about the capabilities of major client operating systems including:

- Windows 2000 Professional
- Windows XP
- UNIX/Linux
- Mac OS X

9

Accessing and Sharing Resources in Windows 2000 Professional

Windows 2000 Professional enables you to access a shared drive over the network, such as a drive shared by a Windows 2000/2003 server (or a NetWare or Mac OS X server) by mapping that drive via My Network Places. The general steps for mapping a drive in Windows 2000 are:

1. Double-click My Network Places on the desktop.
2. Double-click Entire Network.
3. Click the hyperlink for entire contents.
4. Double-click the network in which you want to look, such as Microsoft Windows Network.
5. Double-click the workgroup or domain in which to look.
6. Find the computer that offers the shared resource, and double-click it to view the folders and printers it shares.
7. Right-click the folder or printer that you want to access, and click Map Network Drive.
8. Specify a drive letter to assign to the network drive, and click Finish.

The process for sharing a drive in Windows 2000 Professional is the same as is used to share a drive in Windows 2000 Server, discussed earlier in the section about Windows 2000 Server. To disconnect a shared drive, find it in My Computer or Windows Explorer, highlight the drive, click Tools on the menu bar, and select Disconnect Network Drive.

Accessing and Sharing Resources in Windows XP

Windows XP uses My Network Places to locate and map network drives, but this tool offers more options in Windows XP than in Windows 2000. You can access My Network Places using several techniques, such as through Control Panel, My Computer, or Windows Explorer, but among the fastest is to use the following steps:

1. Click the Start menu, right-click My Computer, and click Map Network Drive.

2. Click the Browse button.

3. Find the workgroup, domain, or other network entity (such as Novell Connections) in which the computer sharing the drive resides, and click it (see Figure 9-13 in which a Microsoft Windows Network Workgroup is selected).

4. Click the folder that you want to access, and click OK.

5. Set the drive letter to which you want to map the network drive.

6. Click Finish.

Figure 9-13   Mapping a drive in Windows XP

Disconnecting from a shared drive in Windows XP involves the same steps as in earlier versions of Windows: find the drive in My Computer or Windows Explorer, right-click the drive, and then click Disconnect.

Sharing a drive or folder using Windows XP is the same process as sharing a driver or folder in Windows Server 2003. Review Hands-on Project 9-7 for the steps used to create a shared folder. For example, to share a folder, open My Computer or Windows Explorer, find the folder that you want to share, right-click it, and click Sharing and Security. Figure 9-14 shows the dialog box used to configure a shared folder called Data.

Figure 9-14   Configuring a shared folder in Windows XP

 NOTE   Another way to share a folder or file is to drag it to the Shared Documents folder in My Computer or Windows Explorer. Still another way to set up a shared folder is to click Start, right-click My Computer, click Manage, double-click Shared Folders, right-click Shares, click New File Share, and follow the steps in the Create a Shared Folder Wizard.

Accessing Shared Resources via UNIX/Linux and Specialized Utilities

UNIX/Linux systems also enable resource sharing by using **Network File System (NFS)**. NFS enables one computer running UNIX/Linux to mount a partition on another UNIX/Linux computer and then access file systems on the mounted partition as though they are local. Red Hat Enterprise Linux 3.0 (and Fedora) supports two versions of NFS: NFS version 2 (NFSv2) which is used on many UNIX/Linux systems and NFS version 3 (NFSv3) which is newer and offers better file and error handling than NFSv2.

When a client mounts an NFS volume on a host, both the client and host use **remote procedure calls (RPCs)**. An RPC enables services and software on one computer to use services and software on a different computer. To use NFS in Red Hat Enterprise Linux 3.0, the following services must be enabled:

- *portmap*: Establishes and manages the remote connections through designated User Datagram Protocol (UDP) ports
- *rpc.mountd*: Handles the RPC request to mount a partition
- *rpc.nfsd*: Enables the Linux kernel to manage specific requests from a client

The security that controls which clients can use NFS on a hosting computer is handled through entries in two files. The /etc/hosts.allow file contains the clients that are allowed to use NFS and the /etc/hosts.deny file contains computers that are not allowed to use NFS. Besides configuring the /etc/hosts.allow and /etc/hosts.deny files, the resources mounted through NFS are also protected by the permissions on the directories and files.

UNIX/Linux computers can access shared Windows 2000/XP/Server 2003 drives through the use of Samba. **Samba** is a utility that uses the Server Message Block (SMB) protocol, which is also used by Windows systems for sharing folders and printers. In Red Hat Enterprise Linux 3.0 (and Fedora), Samba is configured in the /etc/samba/smb.conf file. To access Windows shared drives from the Red Hat Enterprise Linux 3.0 GNOME desktop, for example, click Main Menu and then click Network Servers.

Accessing and Sharing Resources via Mac OS X

In Mac OS X, you connect to another computer that is sharing a disk or folder by using the Mac OS X desktop interface to Samba (because Mac OS X is really a UNIX operating system). To mount a shared drive, open the Go menu, select Connect To Server, and enter the address of the server to access or use the Browse button to find a server on the network (see Figure 9-15). Mac OS X regards both computers configured as servers and computers that share drives or folders as servers.

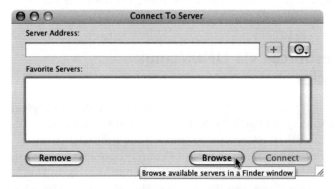

Figure 9-15   Connect To Server dialog box in Mac OS X

Like UNIX/Linux, Mac OS X uses the term *mount* instead of *map* when accessing a shared disk over the network.

NOTE

After you select the computer, click Connect, enter your account name and password, and click OK. Hands-on Project 9-14 enables you to mount a shared resource in Mac OS X.

In Mac OS X, you establish the network identity and turn on file sharing through System Preferences. Open System Preferences and select Sharing. The resources that you can configure for sharing are as follows (see Figure 9-16):

- *Personal File Sharing*: To share folders with other Mac OS X computers
- *Windows Sharing*: To share folders with Windows-based computers
- *Personal Web Sharing*: To share information on the Web
- *Remote Login*: To allow another computer to remotely log on to your computer
- *FTP Access*: To enable FTP file transfers
- *Apple Remote Desktop*: For remote access to the Apple desktop
- *Remote Apple Events*: So that other Mac OS X computers can send events to this computer
- *Printer Sharing*: To enable others to use your computer's printer

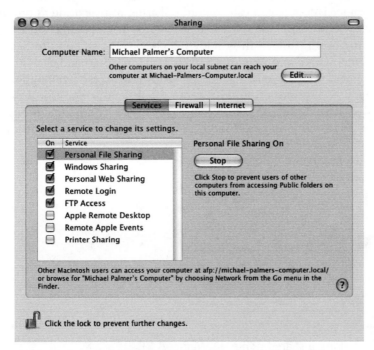

Figure 9-16   Configuring sharing options in Mac OS X

SHARING PRINTING DEVICES

All of the operating systems discussed in this book have the ability to share printers as well as disks, directories, and files. The sections that follow describe how printers are shared through these operating systems. (For more information on setting up printers in various operating systems, see Chapter 5.)

NOTE   Printers that have a built-in print server card and network interface card (NIC) (or that are attached to an external print server device on a network) can also be configured for sharing and accessed by computer operating systems. Explaining how to configure such a printer and print server combination is beyond the scope of this book. However, an operating system can connect to this type of printer by using the same network printer access tools as for other shared printers.

Windows-based Systems

Printing is configured in Windows-based systems by using the Add Printer Wizard to set up a printer. After a printer is set up, you can configure sharing in that printer's properties. In Windows 2000/XP/Server 2003, you share a printer by first opening the Printers (or Printers and Faxes) option or folder. In Windows 2000, click Start, point to Settings, and click Printers. In Windows XP and Windows Server 2003, click Start and click Printers and Faxes. Select the printer you want to share and right-click it to access menu options, such as those shown in Figure 9-17 (for a printer that is not the default printer) for Windows XP. Click Sharing and select the option to enable sharing of the printer, such as *Shared As* in Windows 2000, or *Share this printer* in Windows XP/Server 2003. Enter a name for the shared printer or use the default name.

Figure 9-17   Configuring a shared printer in Windows XP

To share a printer, file and printer sharing services may need to be installed. For example, in Windows XP, click Start, click Control Panel, click Network and Internet Connections, click Network Connections, right-click Local Area Connection, click Properties, click Install, and double-click Service. Also, the server, spooler, and workstation services should be running (you can check by right-clicking My Computer, clicking Manage, and clicking Services and Applications in the console tree).

When you configure sharing, make sure that you configure share permissions for the shared printer. To configure the share permissions in Windows 2000, click Start, point to Settings, and click Printers, right-click the printer, click Properties, and click the Security tab. In Windows XP/Server 2003, click Start, click Printers and Faxes, right-click the printer, click Properties, and click the Security tab.

For Windows 2000/XP/Server 2003, the following share permissions are checked for *allow* or *deny*:

- *Print*: Can send print jobs and manage your own jobs

- *Manage Documents*: Can send print jobs and manage yours or those sent by any other user

- *Manage Printers*: Can access the share, change share permissions, turn off sharing, configure printer properties, and delete the share

- *Special Permissions*: Shows whether special permissions are configured, and if they are allowed or denied (displayed on the Security tab only in Windows XP/Server 2003, although special permission can be configured in Windows 2000/XP/Server 2003)

If you use the Add Printer Wizard to configure and share a printer, make sure you later examine that printer's properties to ensure that sharing permissions are configured appropriately.

Mapping to a shared printer is an easy process in Windows 2000/XP/Server 2003. To map a printer, open My Network Places, find the computer that offers the shared printer, and double-click it. In the list of shared resources, right-click the printer, and click Install or Connect (depending on your version of Windows). Hands-on Project 9-15 enables you to access a shared network printer from Windows XP.

UNIX/Linux

UNIX/Linux printing in a networked environment is essentially the process of logging on to the UNIX/Linux server and printing to one of its printers. Typically, when a UNIX/Linux server is accessed through network connectivity, it is set up to use the Berkeley Software Distribution (BSD) or the System V Release 4 (SVR4) spooling systems, as described in Chapter 5. As a review, BSD uses three components for printing: the *lpr* print program, the *lpd* daemon, and the file /etc/printcap to specify printer properties. The file /etc/printcap is a text file that can be modified via a text editor. In SVR4, the spooling system consists of the *lp* print program and the *lpsched* daemon. SVR4 printer properties are stored in the file /etc/printcap, which is modified by using the *lpadmin* utility.

 If your version of UNIX/Linux can use either BSD or SVR4 spooling, note that administrators often consider BSD spooling to be more adaptable for network clients.

TIP

In Red Hat Enterprise Linux 3.0, you can set up a print queue by using the GNOME Print Manager tool. To access the tool in Red Hat Enterprise Linux 3.0, click Main Menu, point to System Tools, and click Print Manager. To configure a new queue, click the Action menu and click New queue, or to configure sharing, select the queue from which to share, click Action, and click Sharing.

NetWare

Shared printing in NetWare is accomplished by using two different approaches. Both approaches are relatively complex and are only summarized in this chapter. The first approach is to employ queue-based printing, which is used for MS-DOS or Windows applications. The second is **Novell Distributed Print Services (NDPS)**, which is used for Windows applications and printers that have options tailored to NDPS.

In queue-based printing, the network administrator performs several functions to set up a shared printer. The first is to install the printer and its driver in NetWare. The next step is to create a print queue for the printer. For versions of NetWare that use NDS, the next step is to set up an NDS printer object, which defines the printer to NDS. After the printer object is defined, a print server object is also defined, which links a printer to one or more print queues. The last step is to load the print server on the NetWare server so that the printer and its queue are shared through the NetWare server's operating system. After the printer is shared, clients access it by using the NetWare *capture* command, which captures the output from the client's designated printer port, such as line print terminal 1 (LPT1), to the network printer associated with the queue.

NDPS is a print service capability first added in NetWare 5.0. It is designed to work with printers that have built-in NetWare printer agent software. These printers are simply attached to the network as printing agents, and the NDPS on the NetWare server handles the details of directing client print requests to the correct printer. Because some printers do not come with printer agent software, NetWare provides a printer gateway that acts as printer agent and runs on the NetWare server. When printers without built-in agent software are attached, NetWare provides the NDPS Manager utility to manage their connectivity for client access.

Mac OS X

For Mac OS X, there are two ways to set up printer sharing. The steps for the first method are as follows. (See Chapter 5 to learn about installing a printer.)

1. Open System Preferences from the Dock or by clicking Go, clicking Applications, and double-clicking System Preferences.

2. Double-click Sharing.

3. Check the box for Printer Sharing (shown earlier in Figure 9-16).

4. Close the Sharing window.

The second method is to:

1. Open System Preferences from the Dock or by clicking Go, clicking Applications, and double-click System Preferences.

2. Double-click Print & Fax.

3. Check the box for Share my printers with other computers and close the window.

To use a shared printer on another networked computer, open System Preferences and double-click Print & Fax. Click the Set Up Printers button, and use the top two boxes to find a shared printer. For example, to use a Windows-based shared printer, select Windows Printing in the top box and select Network Neighborhood in the box under the top box (see Figure 9-18).

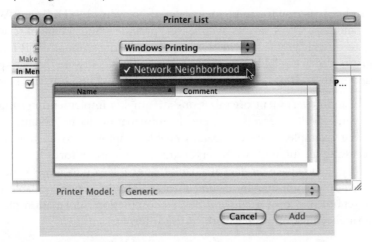

Figure 9-18   Accessing a shared printer via Mac OS X

NETWORK AND INTERNET RESOURCE SERVERS

NetWare, UNIX/Linux, Windows 2000/Server 2003, and Mac OS X servers can be set up as resource servers to provide network and Internet resources. All of these operating systems can act as servers for many kinds of functions. One of the most common is to handle e-mail. There is a wide range of programs that can turn a NetWare, UNIX/Linux, or Windows 2000/2003 server into an e-mail server. Also, Mac OS X Server can process e-mail through its Sendmail program. A close relative of e-mail is e-commerce, which consists of thousands of servers connected to the Internet conducting business, such as taking and fulfilling product orders. These servers process billions of dollars in business transactions.

Another area in which these operating systems participate as resource servers is in videoconferencing and multimedia. Many companies are implementing videoconferencing capabilities on servers and workstations as a way to save money by reducing travel expenses. Multimedia servers are also popular for business applications, education, government, and entertainment purposes. Many of these servers run NetWare, UNIX/Linux, Windows 2000 Server, Windows Server 2003, and Mac OS X Server. Another growing use for multimedia is to provide academic courses that you can access from a home computer over the Internet.

Client/server applications are also a reality and are made possible by networks and servers. A typical client/server application consists of three components: a workstation running a Windows-based operating system, a server from which to run applications, and one or more database servers. These applications are made possible because database software runs well on NetWare, UNIX/Linux, and Windows 2000/2003 servers. For instance, Oracle is a database system that can run on these operating systems. Informix is another database system designed for UNIX/Linux, and SQL Server is a database system designed for Windows 2000/2003 servers. All of these database systems are used frequently in client/server applications.

Web servers are another fast-growing implementation of NetWare, UNIX/Linux, Windows 2000/Server 2003, and Mac OS X servers. Web servers provide a huge range of services that include the ability to quickly access information and download it through FTP. This means that many Web servers also act as FTP servers. Before long, most software that you purchase will be downloaded from an Internet server instead of purchased in a box at a store.

Companies, schools, and government organizations are quickly implementing intranet and virtual private network (VPN) servers that enable information to be obtained through private networks. For example, some companies enable employees to change personnel information by accessing an intranet/VPN server and completing a form in a Web-based environment. You may already have services at a bank that enable you to access your account information from a home computer by dialing into an intranet server available over the Internet. Or, your school may post grade and degree completion information on a server that you access through your campus network or the Internet.

The uses for network servers are growing at an unimaginable rate. As networks are able to transport higher volumes of traffic at faster speeds, the implementation of servers grows reciprocally. Complementing the growth in the use of servers is equivalent growth in the capabilities of their operating systems and in the number of server programs written for them. For example, only a few years ago, most database systems were written for mainframe computers. Early versions of NetWare and Windows NT servers, in particular, were not considered robust enough to handle large databases. Today, major database systems run on NetWare and Windows 2000/2003 servers, and databases often grow to be multi-gigabytes in size.

Chapter Summary

❑ Resource sharing is why networks exist and are thriving. At first, networks were particularly designed to share files. One of the first methods of doing this was by using protocols such as FTP to upload and download individual files. Network file servers quickly followed with the ability to share disks, directories, and files. Before long, they were also sharing other services, such as printing and program services. Today, these functions on servers and workstations are commonplace and compose the vital network infrastructure of information and services.

❑ Whenever network resources, such as folders and printers are shared, it is important to secure these resources to make sure that only authorized users can access them.

❑ When you configure Windows 2000/XP/Server 2003 resources, the process typically involves creating security groups for easier management, establishing account policies and user accounts, setting permissions on the resources, and configuring sharing of the resources.

❑ UNIX/Linux systems also use groups, user accounts, and permissions to enable resource access and to protect resources.

❑ NetWare, like other server systems, enables sharing via groups and user accounts. Security policies for accounts are established through templates. Shared NetWare directories can be accessed by clients through drive mapping.

❑ Mac OS X Server is a server version of Mac OS X for providing more extensive access to resources through user accounts and sharing services.

❑ Client operating systems—such as Windows 2000/XP, UNIX/Linux, and Mac OS X—come with utilities to enable them to access shared resources over a network and to offer resources to share. For example, network drives can be mapped in Windows 2000/XP and network volumes can be mounted in UNIX/Linux and Mac OS X.

❑ All of the operating systems discussed in this book offer the ability to share printers and to access printers that are shared through a network. Printer sharing enables organizations to save money on the purchase of printers so that every user does not need a printer directly connected to their computer.

❑ Network server operating systems continue to offer more and more ways to share resources. Already, network server operating systems handle functions such as e-mail, e-commerce, network conferencing, multimedia distribution, database access, and education.

Key Terms

account lockout — A security measure that prohibits logging on to a user account, such as one on a server, after a specified number of unsuccessful attempts.

container object — An entity that is used to group together resources, such as an organizational unit, an organization, or a country, as specified in the directory services of NetWare; or an organizational unit, domain, tree, or forest in Microsoft Active Directory.

directory service — A large container of network data and resources, such as computers, printers, user accounts, and user groups, that (1) provides a central listing of resources and ways to quickly find specific resources, and (2) provides ways to access and manage network resources.

distribution group — A list of Windows 2000 Server or Windows Server 2003 users that enables one e-mail message to be sent to all users on the list. A distribution group is not used for security.

domain — In Active Directory, a grouping of resources into a functional unit for management. The resources can be servers, workstations, shared disks and directories, and shared printers.

forest — An Active Directory container that holds one or more trees.

group identification number (GID) — A unique number assigned to a UNIX/Linux group that distinguishes that group from all other groups on the same system.

home directory — A user work area in which the user stores data on a server and typically has control over whether to enable other server users to access his or her data. This is a term that can be applied to the Windows 2000/XP/Server 2003, NetWare, Linux/UNIX, and Mac OS X operating systems. Also called a home folder.

leaf object — An object, such as an account, that is stored in an organization or organizational unit container in the NetWare NDS.

login script — In NetWare, a file of commands that is stored on a NetWare server and is associated with an account or a group of accounts. The login script runs automatically each time a user logs on to the account.

mapping — The process of attaching to a shared resource, such as a shared drive, and using it as though it is a local resource. For example, when a workstation operating system maps to the drive of another workstation, it can assign a drive letter to that drive and access it as though it is a local drive instead of a remote one.

mounted volume — A shared drive in UNIX/Linux and Mac OS. See *mapping*.

Network File System (NFS) — Enables file transfer and other shared services that involve computers running UNIX/Linux.

Novell Directory Services (NDS) — A comprehensive database of shared resources and information known to the NetWare operating system.

Novell Distributed Print Services (NDPS) — Services used in NetWare version 5 and later that enable printers to attach to the network as agents, to be managed through a NetWare server, and to be accessed by NetWare and Windows-based clients.

object — An entity, such as a user account, group, directory, or printer, that is known to a network operating system's database, and that the operating system manages in terms of sharing or controlling access to that object.

remote procedure calls (RPCs) — Enables services and software on one computer to use services and software on a different computer.

Samba — Used by UNIX/Linux and Mac OS X systems, a utility that employs the Server Message Block (SMB) protocol, which is also used by Windows systems for sharing folders and printers. Samba enables UNIX/Linux and Mac OS X systems to access shared Windows resources.

search drive — A mapped NetWare drive that enables the operating system to search a specified directory and its subdirectories for an executable (program) file.

security group — A group of Windows 2000 Server or Windows Server 2003 users that is used to assign access privileges, such as permissions, to objects and services.

shadow file — With access limited to the root user, a file in UNIX that contains critical information about user accounts, including the encrypted password for each account.

share — An object, such as a folder, drive, or printer that an operating system or a directory service, such as Active Directory, makes visible to other network users for access over a network.

share points — Shared resources on a Mac OS X server.

tree — An Active Directory container that houses one or more domains.

trusted domain — A domain granted security access to resources in another domain.

trusting domain — A domain that allows another domain security access to its resources, such as servers.

user identification number (UID) — A number that is assigned to a UNIX/Linux user account as a way to distinguish that account from all others on the same system.

Windows NT LAN Manager (NTLM) — An authentication protocol used in Windows NT Server 3.5, 3.51, and 4.0 that is retained in Windows 2000 Server and Windows Server 2003 for backward-compatibility for clients that cannot support Kerberos, such as MS-DOS and Windows 3.1x.

9

REVIEW QUESTIONS

1. You have asked a new Windows Server 2003 administrator to create four new user accounts, but when he opens the Computer Management tool, the Local Users and Groups tool is disabled. Why is this and what can he do?

   a. This means that Active Directory is installed and he must use the Active Directory Users and Computers tool.

   b. He is not logged on to the User Creator account, so he must log off as an Administrator and access the User Creator account.

   c. The maximum number of user accounts have been created, so he must find and delete accounts that are no longer in use.

   d. He must first open Services and Applications in the Computer Management tool and start the User service.

2. In Windows 2000 Server, global groups typically contain which of the following? (Choose all that apply.)

   a. organizational units

   b. printers

   c. user accounts

   d. Active Directory information databases

3. You have found an old administrator's account on a computer running Red Hat Enterprise Linux 3.0 and determine that you should delete it because it is a security risk. What command can you use to delete the account?

   a. *userremove*

   b. *userdel*

   c. *chuser*

   d. *rmuser*

   e. *deleteuser*

4. While you are working on a NetWare 6.5 server at 3 a.m., you inadvertently delete the PUBLIC directory. What problems will occur if you do not restore this directory?

   a. Users cannot log on to the server.

   b. Login scripts will not properly map drives when users log on.

   c. The server cannot start UDP services for network access.

   d. No problems will occur for users other than administrators who access this directory exclusively to manage publicly shared resources.

5. Which tool(s) can you use to set up shared printing so that a Mac OS X system can offer a shared printer on a network? (Choose all that apply.)

   a. Print & Fax in System Preferences

   b. Printers and Faxes in Control Panel

   c. Printer Configuration in System Tools

   d. Sharing in System Preferences

6. The company president's administrative assistant has complained to you that the business manager sometimes ties up the shared printer in the president's office area, even though the business manager has been asked not to use this printer. What can you do to configure the printer so the business manager does not have access?

   a. Set special permissions for the printer to *No Printing*.

   b. Purchase separate printers for everyone in the president's office and do not set them up for sharing.

   c. Set up the printer so that all permissions to it are denied for the business manager's account.

   d. Set an account policy to deny access to the printer for the business manager's account.

7. What NetWare 6.5 tool can be used to create groups?

   a. ConsoleOne

   b. *addgroup*

   c. GROUP INS

   d. Users and Computers

8. Which of the following would you find in the /etc/passwd file in Red Hat Enterprise Linux? (Choose all that apply.)

   a. UID

   b. username

   c. user permissions to folders

   d. pointer information to the /usr/passwd file containing the passwords of all users

9. You have set up a folder for Web sharing on a Windows 2000 server with IIS installed. However, for security reasons you want to prevent users from running scripts. What folder permissions enable you to control the ability to run scripts?

   a. FAT attributes

   b. NTFS attributes

   c. share permissions

   d. Web sharing permissions

10. You are working with NTFS permissions on a Windows 2003 Server folder, but you discover you cannot change some permissions because they are already checked in shaded and deactivated boxes. What is the problem?

    a. The permissions have been locked because an intruder was detected on the server.

    b. Permissions can only be changed from the root account, and you are logged onto your own account.

    c. These permissions are inheritable permissions, so you must turn off this function before you can change them.

    d. For the sake of security, permissions can only be changed twice within 30 minutes and you have already changed these permissions twice, so you must wait 30 minutes.

11. A security audit of your company's NetWare 6.5 server shows that employees sometimes break into other employee's user accounts, because passwords are easy to guess. What steps can you take to improve security? (Choose all that apply.)

    a. Limit the number of times in a day that a user can log on and off, such as to two.

    b. Set a minimum password length on user accounts.

    c. Enable NTLM security.

    d. Require that passwords are changed at regular intervals, such as every 30 days.

12. Printer sharing on a computer running Windows XP can be configured as

    _____ .

    a. a printer property

    b. a service

    c. a container

    d. a printer driver for network sharing

13. Your small organization has just set up a network connecting Windows XP Professional and Mac OS X workstations. You recommend setting up a Windows 2003 server from which to share files. However, the manager of Customer Services complains in a meeting that his Mac OS X workstation won't be able to access Windows-based files. What is your response?

    a. Mac OS X users can access the files on the server by installing Client32 software.

    b. Mac OS X users can access the shared server files through the Connect To Server tool in Mac OS X.

    c. Mac OS X users cannot access files formatted for Windows-based systems, but they can store and share files formatted for Mac OS X systems on a Mac OS X partition created on the Windows 2003 server.

    d. Mac OS X systems cannot access a Windows 2003 server, so the organization should also purchase a Mac OS X server.

14. What happens when you execute *chmod 0755 calc.c*, where calc.c is a calculator program on a Red Hat Enterprise Linux server? (Choose all that apply.)

    a. Group members can execute the program as well as make programming changes to the program file.

    b. No one can execute the program other than the owner.

    c. Only non-group members can execute the program.

    d. The owner of the program file can execute it and change it.

15. When a NetWare server client uses the command MAP S2:=SYS:DATA, what does this accomplish?

    a. It maps a search drive to the DATA directory.

    b. It maps a trusted and trusting security setup between the user and the DATA directory.

    c. It sets up the DATA directory so that the user cannot mistakenly access it.

    d. It enables the server administrator to configure NetWare trustee rights on the client's computer to centrally manage network security.

16. Kerberos is an example of a(n) _____ on a Windows 2003 server. (Choose all that apply.)

    a. template

    b. password restriction

    c. system folder

    d. account policy

17. You are in charge of a group of server administrators who manage servers for an organization that uses Active Directory and has multiple domains and trees. What type of Windows Server 2003 security groups might you set up to simplify security access for the server administrators across all domains and trees?

    a. One global group that contains access to all resources and all of the server administrators' user accounts.

    b. A domain local group that enables access to resources in all domains and a global group of all server administrators' user accounts.

    c. A universal group that contains access to resources in all domains and a global group of all server administrators' user accounts.

    d. A global group that contains access to all resources and domain local groups in each domain which contain all of the server administrators' user accounts.

18. You have discovered that intruders are attempting to remotely access accounts on your organization's Windows 2003 server over the Internet. Which of the following should you configure to increase security?

    a. account lockout

    b. network timeout

    c. share inhibiting for remote access

    d. time duration monitoring

19. Which of the following enables a computer running Red Hat Enterprise Linux 3.0 to access a Windows 2000 Server that has shared folders?

    a. NTS

    b. My Network Places GUI interface

    c. SNMP

    d. Samba

20. What tool in Mac OS X enables the user to access and use a printer shared by a computer running Windows XP Professional on a network?

    a. Printer Configuration

    b. Printers and Faxes

    c. Print & Fax

    d. Print Chooser

9

HANDS-ON PROJECTS

Project 9-1

In this project, you view the existing global and local groups on a **Windows 2000/Server 2003**. You need access to an account that has Administrator privileges. Also, Active Directory should already be installed.

To view the global and local groups:

1. Click **Start**, point to **Programs** (in Windows 2000 Server) or to **All Programs** (in Windows Server 2003), point to **Administrative Tools**, and click **Active Directory Users and Computers**.

2. Double-click **Active Directory Users and Computers** (in Windows 2000 Server this has the name of the computer in brackets), and the domain, such as *jpcompany.com*, if the contents of these are not displayed in the tree in the left pane.

3. If necessary, click **Users** in the tree to view the contents of this folder in the right pane (see Figure 9-19).

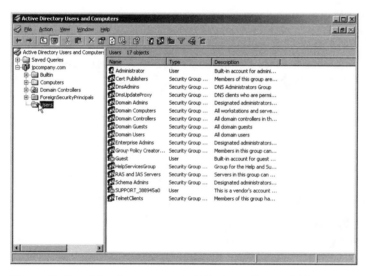

Figure 9-19   Viewing groups in Windows Server 2003

4. If necessary, expand the Name column to view the users and groups. How many security groups are already created?

5. Double-click the **Domain Admins** group. What is the Group scope?

6. Click **Cancel**.

7. Double-click another group to determine if it is a global or domain local group. Click **Cancel**.

8. Leave the Active Directory Users and Computers tool open for the next project. (If you do not have time to complete the project right away, close the tool.)

Project 9-2

In this project, you create a domain local group and a global group in **Windows 2000 Server**. You need access to an account that has Administrator privileges.

To create the groups in Windows 2000 Server:

1. Open Active Directory Users and Computers if this tool is not already open (click **Start**, point to **Programs**, point to **Administrative Tools**, and click **Active Directory Users and Computers**). Also, make sure that the Users folder is open in the tree.

2. Click the **Action** menu, point to **New**, and click **Group**.

3. Enter **DomainMgrs** plus your initials for the Group name.

4. Click **Domain local** for the Group scope (see Figure 9-20).

Figure 9-20   Configuring a domain local group in Windows 2000 Server

5. Make sure that **Security** is selected for the Group type.

6. Click **OK**.

7. Click the **Action** menu, point to **New**, and click **Group**.

8. Enter **GlobalMgrs** plus your initials for the Group name.

9. Click **Global** for the Group scope.

10. Click **OK**.

11. Double-click the domain local group you created.

12. Click the **Members** tab.

13. Click the **Add** button.

14. If necessary, scroll to find the global group you created, and then double-click that group.

15. Click **OK**. Is the global group displayed under Name on the Members tab?

16. Click **OK**.

17. Close the Active Directory Users and Computers tool.

Project 9-3

This project enables you to create a domain local and global group in **Windows Server 2003**. You need access to an account that has Administrator privileges.

To create the groups in Windows Server 2003:

1. Open the Active Directory Users and Computers tool if it is not open (click **Start**, point to **All Programs**, point to **Administrative Tools**, and click **Active Directory Users and Computers**). Make certain the Users folder is open in the tree.

2. Click the **Action** menu, point to **New**, and click **Group**.

3. In the Group name box, enter **DomainMgrs** plus your initials, for example DomainMgrsJP.

4. Click **Domain local** under Group scope, and click **Security** (if it is not already selected) under Group type.

5. Click **OK** and then look for the group you just created in the right pane within the Users folder.

6. Click the **Create a new group in the current container** icon on the button bar (with two heads).

7. In the Group name box, type **GlobalMgrs** plus your initials, for example GlobalMgrsJP.

8. Click **Global** under Group scope, and click **Security** under Group type if they are not already selected.

9. Click **OK** and then look for the group you just created in the right pane.

10. Find the domain local group that you created, for example DomainMgrsJP, and double-click it.

11. Click the **Members** tab.

12. Double-click the domain local group, such as DomainMgrsJP, and then click the **Members** tab. What members are shown?

13. Click **Add** then click **Advanced**.

14. Click **Find Now**.

15. Locate the global group you created, such as GlobalMgrsJP. Click that global group and click **OK**.

16. Verify that the global group is displayed in the Select Users, Contacts, Computers, or Groups dialog box, and then click **OK**.

17. Make sure the global group is listed under Name on the Members tab. Click **OK**.

18. Close the Active Directory Users and Computers tool.

Project 9-4

In this project, you view where to create account policies in **Windows 2000 Server** or **Windows Server 2003**. You need an account with Administrative privileges for the project.

To view where to create account policies:

1. Click **Start**, point to **Programs** (in Windows 2000 Server) or to **All Programs** (in Windows Server 2003), point to **Administrative Tools**, and click **Domain Security Policy**.

2. Double-click **Account Policies** in the tree if the items under it are not already displayed.

3. Click **Password Policy** in the tree and notice the policies that you can configure and how each is presently configured.

4. Double-click **Minimum password length** in the right pane. Be certain that *Define this policy setting* is checked. Set the characters text box to **8** and click **OK**, as shown in Figure 9-21.

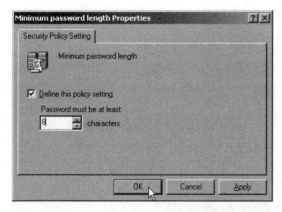

Figure 9-21   Configuring the minimum password length in Windows Server 2003

5. Click **Account Lockout Policy** in the left pane and notice the options in the right pane.

6. Click **Kerberos Policy** in the left pane. What options are available for Kerberos?

7. Close the Domain Security Policy window (in Windows 2000 Server) or the Default Domain Security Settings window (in Windows Server 2003).

Project 9-5

In this project, you use the Active Directory Users and Computers tool to create an account in **Windows 2000 Server** or **Windows Server 2003**. You need access using an account with Administrative privileges for this project.

To create an account:

1. Click **Start**, point to **All Programs**, point to **Administrative Tools**, and click **Active Directory Users and Computers**.

2. If necessary, double-click **Active Directory Users and Computers** in the left pane to display the elements under it. Double-click the domain name, such as *jpcompany.com* to display the elements under it, if necessary.

3. Click the **Users** folder in the left pane to ensure that it is opened. Are there any accounts already created?

4. Click the **Action** menu or right-click **Users** in the left pane, point to **New** and click **User**.

5. Type your first name in the First name box, type your middle initial (no period), and type your last name, with the word "test" appended to it, in the Last name box, for example: Peeletest. Enter your initials, with test appended to them, in the User logon name box, for example: JPTest. What options are automatically completed for you? Record your observations. Click **Next** (see Figure 9-22).

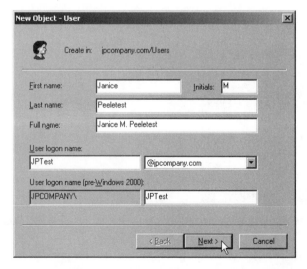

Figure 9-22 Creating a user account in Windows Server 2003

6. Enter a password and enter the password confirmation. (Make sure the password meets the password specifications set in the account policies, such as being at least eight characters long.) Click the box to select **User must change password at next logon**. This option forces users to enter a new password the first time they log on so that the account creator will not know their password. The User cannot change password option means that only the account administrator can change the user's password. Password never expires is used in situations in which an account must always be accessed, such as when a program accesses an account to run a special process. The Account is disabled option provides a way to prevent access to an account without deleting it. Click **Next**.

7. Verify the information you have entered and click **Finish**.

8. To continue configuring the account, in the right pane, double-click the account you just created, such as Janice M. Peeletest.

9. Notice the tabs that are displayed for the account properties and record them.

10. Click the **General** tab, if it is not already displayed, and enter a description of the account, such as Test account.

11. Click the tabs you have not yet viewed to find out what information can be configured through each one. Which tab enables you to record information about the user's e-mail address?

12. In this step, you make the account you've created a member of the global group that you created earlier. Click the **Member Of** tab. In Windows 2000 Server, click **Add**, double-click the global group you created in Hands-on Project 9-2, and click **OK**. Or, in Windows Server 2003, click the **Add** button, click the **Advanced** button, click **Find Now**, double-click the global group you created in Hands-on Project 9-3, and click **OK**.

13. Click **OK**.

14. Close the Active Directory Users and Computers tool.

**HANDS-ON
PROJECTS**

Project 9-6

In this project, you create a folder, and then configure permissions in **Windows 2000 Server** and **Windows Server 2003**. (The same steps apply to setting NTFS permissions in Windows 2000 Professional or Windows XP.) You will need to work on a disk formatted for NTFS. Note that in Windows XP, you should be a member of a Windows 2000 Server or Windows Server 2003 domain, or have Simple File Sharing turned off.

To create a folder and set NTFS permissions:

1. Double-click **My Computer** on the Windows 2000 Server desktop or in Windows Server 2003, click **Start** and click **My Computer**.

2. Double-click **Local Disk (C:)** (or another disk appropriate to your computer's setup).

3. Double-click the **Documents and Settings** folder.

4. Click the **File** menu, point to **New**, and click **Folder**.

5. Type your initials plus Test, such as JPTest, and press **Enter**.

6. Right-click the folder you created and click **Properties**.

7. Click the **Security** tab.

8. Click the **Add** button. In Windows 2000 Server, double-click the domain local group that you created in Hands-on Project 9-2 and click **OK**. In Windows Server 2003, click the **Add** button, click **Advanced**, click **Find Now**, and double-click the domain local group you created in Hands-on Project 9-3. Click **OK**. You should see a dialog box similar to Figure 9-23.

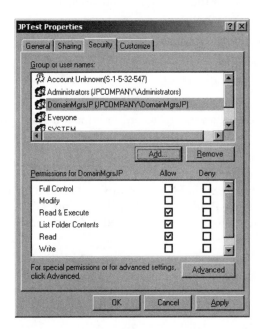

Figure 9-23   Configuring permissions in Windows Server 2003

9. Click the **Allow** box for **Full Control**. What other boxes are now checkmarked automatically?

10. Click **OK**.

11. Close the Documents and Settings window.

Project 9-7

In this project, you set up a shared folder in **Windows 2000 Server** and **Windows Server 2003**.

To set up a shared folder:

1. Double-click **My Computer** on the Windows 2000 Server desktop or in Windows Server 2003, click **Start** and click **My Computer**.

2. Double-click **Local Disk (C:)** (or another disk appropriate to your computer's setup).

3. Double-click the **Documents and Settings** folder.

4. Right-click the folder you created in Hands-on Project 9-6, such as JPTest, and click **Properties**.

5. Click the **Sharing** tab.

6. Click the option button for **Share this folder**.

7. Click the **Permissions** button. What permissions can you configure?

8. With the Everyone group already selected, click the **Allow** box for Change.

9. Click **OK**.

10. Click **OK** again and close the Documents and Settings window.

Project 9-8

This project enables you to learn how to use the effective permissions analysis tool on a **Windows Server 2003** to help troubleshoot a permissions conflict.

To use the effective permissions feature:

1. Use My Computer to browse to the folder you created in Hands-on Project 9-6, such as JPTest.

2. Right-click the folder and click **Properties**.

3. Click the **Security** tab.

4. Click the **Advanced** button.

5. Click the **Effective Permissions** tab.

6. Click the **Select** button, click **Advanced**, click **Find Now**, and double-click **Administrators**. Click **OK**.

7. Scroll through the Effective permissions box to practice looking for a permissions conflict.

8. Click **Cancel** and click **Cancel** again.

Project 9-9

In this project, you create an account in **Red Hat Enterprise Linux 3.0** by using the *useradd* command. (These steps also work in most versions of UNIX/Linux, other than AIX.) Log on to the root account to complete this project.

To create an account:

1. Access the command line by opening a terminal window. (Click **Main Menu**, point to **System Tools**, and click **Terminal** in Red Hat Enterprise Linux 3.0.)

2. When you set up the account, use your own name or initials, plus the word "test." For example, type *useradd -c 'Mac Arthur, practice account"-p practice -n marthurtest* , and press **Enter**. (Note that when you do not specify the UID, Red Hat Enterprise Linux will use the next available number over 500. Also, use all lowercase for the username.) What is the purpose of typing *-n*?

3. Type **more /etc/passwd** and press **Enter** to view the contents of the password file. Do you see the account that you created? (You may need to press the **spacebar** one or more times to go to the end of the file—you can press q to exit the file contents listing.)

4. Test your new account by logging off the root account and then logging on to the new account.

5. Leave the terminal window open for the next project (or close the window and log off root if you cannot proceed to the next project during this lab session).

If your instructor wants you to delete the account after you finish, log on to root and type *userdel -r* plus the name of the account.

NOTE

Project 9-10

For this project, you create a new group in **Red Hat Enterprise Linux 3.0** (but these steps also work in nearly all versions of UNIX/Linux, except AIX), change the group's name, and finally delete that group. Before starting, ask your instructor for a GID. For the group name, use the first and last initials of your name appended to test, such as jptest. You need to be logged on to the root account.

To create, modify, and delete a group:

1. Access the command prompt, such as through a terminal window.

2. At the command prompt, type *groupadd -g GID* (provided by instructor) *groupname* (your first and last initials + test), such as *groupadd -g 800 jptest* (see Figure 9-24), and press **Enter**. Note that if the GID is already in use, the system reports this information and does not create the group. If you omit the *-g* parameter, the system will use the next available GID. (Also, in some versions of UNIX/Linux, you will see a

return code of zero that indicates you successfully added the group. If a return code is displayed that is other than zero, make sure that you correctly typed the command, used a unique GID and group name, and that you have proper access to create groups; or, ask your instructor for help.)

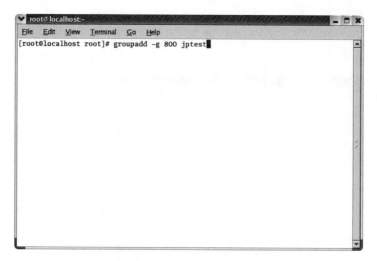

Figure 9-24   Creating a group in Red Hat Enterprise Linux

3. Change the group name by using your first and middle initial appended to test, using the command *groupmod -n newname oldname* , such as **groupmod –n jjtest jptest**, and press **Enter**. (Again, in some versions of UNIX/Linux, you will see a zero return code to indicate that you have successfully changed the group name.)

4. Type **more /etc/group** and press **Enter** to view the groups and verify that you successfully changed the group name. (You may need to press the spacebar several times to get to the end of the file, and press q to exit the listing.)

5. Delete the group by entering the *groupdel* command and the group name, such as **groupdel jjtest**, and press **Enter**.

6. Type **more /etc/group** and press **Enter** to verify that the group you created is truly deleted.

7. If you have a terminal window open, type **exit** and press Enter to close it.

8. Log off root when you are finished

Project 9-11

In this project, you give read permissions to a directory to all user accounts on a UNIX/Linux server. You will need access to a computer running **Red Hat Enterprise Linux 3.0** or **UNIX**, a user account, and a practice directory containing files.

To set the permissions:

1. Access the command line by opening a terminal window. (Click **Main Menu**, point to **System Tools**, and click **Terminal** in Red Hat Enterprise Linux 3.0.)

2. Switch to your home or practice directory if you are not in this directory by default, such as by typing **cd /home/mpalmer**, and pressing **Enter**.

3. At the command prompt, type **chmod a+r ***, and press **Enter** (see Figure 9-25.) (Note that there should be at least one file in the directory on which to set the permissions.)

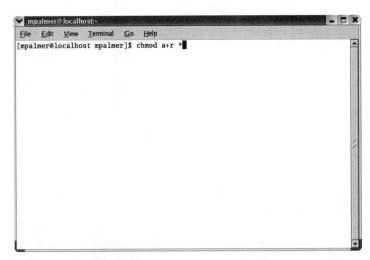

Figure 9-25   Configuring permissions in Red Hat Enterprise Linux

4. View the change by listing permissions via the command **ls –1**, and press **Enter**. How would you remove the permissions that you just set?

Project 9-12

In this project, you practice mapping a search drive to a **NetWare** server, and then delete the drive. You will need network access from Windows 2000 or Windows XP and an account on a NetWare server. Also, you need to obtain directions from your instructor about how to log on to the NetWare server for your particular network, such as using the Windows-based Client Service for NetWare or the Client32 software from Novell. (To use the map command, there should already be a drive mapping to the SYS:PUBLIC directory on the NetWare server, such as through a login script that runs automatically when you log on to the NetWare server; or by using My Computer in Windows 2000/XP to map to the NetWare server's SYS:PUBLIC directory, after you log on to NetWare via Client32.)

To map and then delete a search drive:

1. Log on to the NetWare server.

2. Open a Command Prompt window (in Windows 2000/XP), type **MAP** at the prompt, and then press **Enter** to view the current drive mappings.

3. Determine the last search drive in use from the list of mapped drives, which is the S# drive that has the highest number.

4. Using the next S# number (use S1 if no search drives are defined), map a search drive to the PUBLIC directory, or to another directory specified by your instructor. Type **MAP S1:=SYS:PUBLIC**, and press **Enter**.

5. Type **MAP** again to see if your drive is in the list of mapped drives.

6. Finally, type **MAP DEL S1:** (or S and the number of the drive you used in Step 4), and press **Enter** to delete the drive mapping.

7. Type **exit** at the command prompt to close the MS-DOS or Command Prompt window.

You may need to install Client Service for NetWare before you start. For example, to install Client Service for NetWare in Windows XP click Start, click Control Panel, click Network and Internet Connections, click Network Connections, right-click Local Area Connection, click Properties, click Install, double-click Client, and double-click Client Service for NetWare. Shut down and restart your computer to complete the installation.

Project 9-13

This project enables you to practice creating a new user in **Mac OS X**. (The ability to provide account password hints should be enabled by default.)

1. To create a new user in Mac OS X:

2. Click **System Preferences** in the Dock or click the **Go** menu, click **Applications**, and double-click **System Preferences**.

3. Double-click **Accounts**. What accounts are already created?

4. If the lock at the bottom of the screen is locked, click it to unlock it.

5. Click the **+** (Add) button.

6. Enter your name for the account plus "test," such as Janice Peeletest.

7. Enter a short name, such as JPeeletest.

8. Enter and verify a password for the account.

9. Enter a hint to help you remember the password (see Figure 9-26).

● ● ●	Accounts			◯

My Account
🦋 **Michael Palmer**
Admin

Other Accounts
🪲 **Tom Erickson**
Admin

⦿ Standard

Password | Picture | Security | Limitations

Name: Janice Peeletest

Short Name: JPeeletest

Password: •••••

Verify: •••••

Password Hint: Important event
(Optional)

🏠 Login Options

+ −

🔓 Click the lock to prevent further changes.

Figure 9-26   Configuring an account in Mac OS X

10. Click the **System Preferences** menu and click **Quit System Preferences**.

Project 9-14

In this project, you connect to shared resources on a Mac OS X or Windows-based computer from **Mac OS X** by using Samba.

To connect to another computer via Mac OS X:

1. Open the **Go** menu and select **Connect To Server**.

2. Click the **Browse** button.

3. Double-click Servers or a domain or a workgroup and select the shared resource to which to connect (or select the computer from which you are working).

4. Click **Connect**.

5. If you are accessing a computer other than your own, enter your username and password (or a name and password provided by your instructor).

6. Click **OK**.

7. Select the folder or shared resources to access.

8. Close the window from which you are working.

Project 9-15

In this project, you connect to network printers via **Windows XP**. Before you start, ask your instructor for the name of the computer that is offering the shared printer.

To connect to the shared printer:

1. Click **Start** and click **My Network Places**.

2. Click **Search** in the button bar at the top of the window.

3. In the Computer name box, enter the name of the computer that offers the shared printer and click **Search**.

4. Double-click the computer that offers the shared printer (you may need to provide an account and password if this is required by the computer).

5. Right-click the printer and click **Connect**.

6. Close the networked computer's window from which you selected the printer.

7. Click **Start** and click **Printers and Faxes**. Do you see the shared printer?

8. Close the Printers and Faxes window.

9

CASE PROJECTS

Parson's Lights manufactures natural lighting fixtures sold throughout North America. The users in the Manufacturing and Inventory Building are fully networked and use modern operating systems. The managers and accounting group use Windows XP Professional. Workstations on the manufacturing floor are equipped with Red Hat Enterprise Linux 3.0, and the inventory users have computers running Mac OS X. There is a secure computer room in the Manufacturing and Inventory Building that houses five Windows 2003 servers and two NetWare 6.5 servers. All of the computer equipment is recently set up because the company just reorganized and gave these users a large budget to fully network the building and upgrade operating systems.

Case Project 9-1: Considering the Merits of Using Active Directory

In the past, the building was only equipped with one Windows 2000 server and a NetWare 5.0 server. Now that they have five Windows 2003 servers, the IT support group is considering whether or not to install Active Directory. What advantages does Active Directory offer for managing user accounts?

Case Project 9-2: Developing Strategies for Managing User Accounts through Groups on Windows 2003 Servers

The old Windows 2000 server was set up so that all resources were managed through a confusing array of local groups. For example, the managers' user accounts were in one local group which was given full control access to all folders and files, printers, and other resources. What general suggestions do you have for creating a different way to manage user accounts and groups on the new Windows 2003 servers?

Case Project 9-3: Considering User Account Security for the NetWare 6.5 Servers

Security was lax on the previous NetWare 5.0 server; some users employed passwords and some did not. There must be better security associated with user accounts because the new NetWare 6.5 servers are connected to the Internet. What options can be used for user account security, and what tool can be used to configure these options?

Case Project 9-4: Reconsidering Root Account Access for Red Hat Enterprise Linux Users

Because there are three around-the-clock shifts of workers, all of the Red Hat Enterprise Linux computers on the manufacturing floor are shared by three people. In the past, they have all used the root accounts to access these computers, but there have been problems with unexpected changes to computer setups and files. Also, this has meant that no single user could secure specific files only for his or her use. What general suggestions do you have for doing things differently? Also, what tools do you recommend using to accomplish your suggestions?

Case Project 9-5: Enabling Sharing in Mac OS X

An inventory specialist has a new printer that is to be shared through the network with all other inventory users. Explain the steps she should take to enable sharing of this printer after it is connected and installed.

10

STANDARD OPERATING AND MAINTENANCE PROCEDURES

After reading this chapter and completing the exercises, you will be able to:

♦ Explain file system maintenance techniques for different operating systems

♦ Perform regular file system maintenance by finding and deleting unused files and directories

♦ Perform disk maintenance that includes defragmenting, relocating files and folders, running disk and file repair utilities, and selecting RAID options

♦ Set up and perform disk, directory, and file backups

♦ Explain how to install software for best performance

♦ Tune operating systems for optimal performance

Computer operating systems are similar to cars in that they need regular maintenance to achieve the best performance. A new car, like a new computer, delivers fast responses, and every component usually functions perfectly. To keep the car at its best, you must perform regular maintenance, such as changing the oil and performing tune-ups. If you neglect maintenance, the car's performance suffers and the wear shows quickly. Maintenance is as important for computers as it is for cars because it does not take long for an operating system, software, and hardware to degrade in performance. Computer operating system maintenance consists of deleting unnecessary files, tuning memory, regularly backing up files, defragmenting disks, and repairing damaged files. Maintenance is particularly important for computer systems connected to a network because a poorly responding computer has an impact on network operations.

In this chapter, you learn a variety of techniques for maintaining and tuning workstations and servers. One of the most important steps in making disk and file maintenance easy is to start with a well-designed directory structure, which makes finding unused files and folders a straightforward process. Two other important tasks are to perform regular backups and run disk maintenance utilities. How and where software is installed is also vital to how a computer performs. Finally, there are tuning options, such as adjusting virtual memory that can immediately enhance performance.

FILE SYSTEM MAINTENANCE

Successful file system maintenance is closely linked to the file structure on a computer. On both workstation and server operating systems, a well-planned file structure makes it easy to locate files, update files, share folders and files, back up and archive files, and delete unwanted files. In addition, on server operating systems, well-designed file structures favorably impact network performance and security.

Some basic rules for creating a file structure include:

- Keep a manageable number of directories in the root directory.
- Keep operating system files in the default directories recommended by the vendor.
- Keep different versions of software in their own directories.
- Keep data files in directories on the basis of their functions.
- Design home directories to match the functions of users in an organization.
- Group files with similar security needs within the same directories.

It does not take long for the number of directories in the root directory (often called the "root") to proliferate. Most vendors install their software in the default directory, Program Files. If you have many software applications, it makes sense to create one or two directories within the root that are intended for software applications, and then create subdirectories within each main applications directory to contain particular applications. Another technique is to create a general applications directory and separate directories for main software vendors. If you use Microsoft applications, consider using the Windows default directory, Program Files, or if you use other applications, such as the WordPerfect Office suite, use its default Corel directory. An example of a file structure in which you might use three directories for applications in the root of the main volume, Applications, Corel, and Program Files, is illustrated in Figure 10-1. The figure also shows two other directories usually found in the root. Depending on the version of Windows, the Windows directory may be called Windows, or a name that the installer chose, such as Win2003 or WinXP. Later versions of Windows create the Documents and Settings, or My Documents directories.

 TIP Some users and system administrators prefer to limit the number of entries in the root directory to only the number that can be displayed in one or two screens when you are at the command level in an operating system, or in a utility such as Windows Explorer. On a typical system, this might translate to a maximum of 10 to 15 directories per hard disk volume.

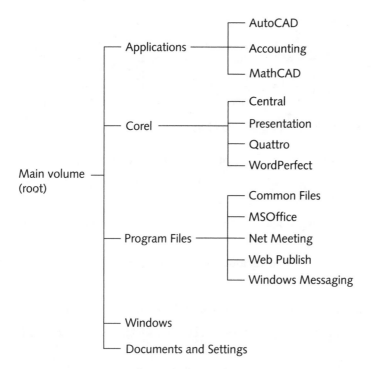

Figure 10-1   Example applications directories and subdirectories

Well-organized directories and subdirectories enable you to have a relatively small number of main directories in the root. Figure 10-2 illustrates a typical root directory structure in UNIX/Linux. The directories in this example are as follows:

- *bin* for user programs and utilities (binary files)
- *lib* for libraries
- *usr* for users' files and user programs
- *var* for files in which the content often varies, or that are only used temporarily
- *tmp* for files used only temporarily
- *dev* for devices
- *mnt* for floppy drives, CD-ROM drives, and other removable media that can be mounted
- *etc* for system and configuration files
- *sbin* for user programs and utilities (system binary files)
- *home* for users' home directories
- *proc* for system resource tracking

10

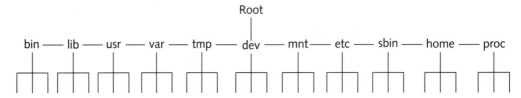

Figure 10-2   A typical UNIX/Linux root directory structure

Examples of important folders in the root of a Mac OS X system include:

- *Applications* for software applications (there is an Applications folder off the root, plus each user may have an Applications folder)

- *Documents* for storing documents (typically there is one off the root and one for each user)

- *Library* for library files that include fonts, preferences, and graphics, for instance

- *System* for system files

- *Users* for user accounts (containing a subfolder for each account)

In addition to folders off the root, each user account in Mac OS X may contain folders such as:

- *Music* for music files

- *Movies* for movies that can be played on the computer

- *Pictures* to sort picture files

- *Public* for files to share with others over the network

- *Applications* for applications used by the account

- *Library* for support files, such as fonts used by the account

- *Documents* for storing documents

- *Desktop* for files that are on the user's desktop

Operating system directories are typically placed in the root directory and have appropriate subdirectories under a main directory. For example, Windows XP operating system files are contained in the Windows folder (see Figure 10-3), which has subdirectories such as System and System32. Macintosh system files are likewise kept in the System folder. Table 10-1 illustrates typical locations for system files in various operating systems.

Figure 10-3   Windows XP operating system files in the Windows folder

Table 10-1   Operating system directories

Operating System	System Directory or Directories from the Root
Mac OS	System (in Mac OS X the *System* folder contains the system files, and the *System Folder* contains Mac OS 9.x system files for running the classic environment)
NetWare	System
UNIX/Linux	bin, etc, and sbin
Windows 2000 Professional and Server	Winnt
Windows Server 2003	Windows
Windows XP Home and Professional	Windows

There are several advantages to installing and leaving operating system files in the directories created by the operating system, instead of trying to hide these files, or use other directory locations (see the Caution that follows this paragraph). One reason is that it is easier for others to help with computer problems as they arise. For example, in organizations that have help desks or support centers, it is easier for support professionals to assist in solving problems with drivers and network access when system files are easy to find. Another reason for leaving system files in the default directories is that many software installations expect operating system files to be in the default locations, and they work best when it is easy for them to find specific subdirectories and key files related to the operating system.

10

CAUTION

When you install server operating systems, there may be a temptation to hide or rename default system directories as a way to protect them from intruders. However, most intruders will not be deterred by this attempt to hide files. A better approach is to understand and implement the security features available in the operating system. See Palmer, *Guide to Operating Systems Security*, Course Technology, 2004 (ISBN 0-619-16040-3).

In most Windows-based systems, installed software is also tracked in the registry, which contains configuration information, as well as information about individual components of a software installation. Thus, it is easier for the operating system to assist when it is necessary to uninstall or upgrade software because it is able to quickly identify and find the components to be deleted or upgraded. In Windows 2000/XP/Server 2003, these vital files are kept in the operating system's folder and subfolders. For example, in Windows Server 2003 and Windows XP, these files might be located in the \Windows, \Windows\System, or \Windows\System32 folders. In Windows 2000, they are found in the \Winnt and \Winnt\System32 folders. Table 10-2 lists some examples of typical Windows-based application software components. Application software and operating system enhancements are easier to install when these components are in known locations.

Table 10-2   Examples of Windows-based application software components

File Type	File Extension	File Type	File Extension
Application	.exe	Initialization	.ini
ActiveX Control	.ocx	Installation	.inf
Backup	.bak	Microsoft Common Console Document	.mcs
Bitmap image	.bmp	Microsoft Office Settings File	.pip
Compiled HTML help file	.chm	OLE common control	.ocx
Control Panel extension	.cpl	Precompiled setup information	.pnf
Configuration	.cfg	Screen saver	.scr
Data	.dat	Security catalog	.cat
Device driver	.drv	Temporary file	.tmp
Dynamic link library	.dll	Text	.txt
Help	.hlp	TrueType font	.ttf
Help context	.cnt	Virtual device driver	.vxd

Sometimes, particularly on network servers, it is necessary to keep several versions of a software application available for different uses. For example, an organization may have some users who still use earlier versions of WordPerfect or Microsoft Word. In a department or organization in which software applications are developed, it may be necessary to keep different versions of compilers or development tools available. Some users may have operating systems that only support 16-bit applications, whereas other users may have operating systems that support 32-bit applications. In these situations, one way to easily handle having more than one version of the same software is to put different versions in different subdirectories under a main applications directory. For example, in Windows 2000 Server, you can support different versions of Microsoft Word by having a Program Files directory, and subdirectories called Word97, Word 2000, Word XP, and Word 2003. In this case, one version is installed to run locally, and the other versions are available to clients for network installations (given appropriate licensing considerations).

From the Trenches...

When one organization studied the word-processing applications used in its various departments, it determined that most of the departments were using some form of Microsoft Office with a few using Corel WordPerfect. Management decided to bring all departments up to the latest version of either Microsoft Office or Corel WordPerfect. When the technicians went to install the new software, they were asked by some departments to not upgrade them. These departments relied on features in their version of software that were not available in the latest version. To assist the departments, the Information Technology Department set up multiple versions of the same software on their server. This was not the most ideal situation from the server side of the organization, but the departments were extremely happy that they could continue to perform their tasks without losing any functionality.

10

Some directory structures include special locations for data files. For example, if the computer contains files for word processing, spreadsheets, and databases, then those files might be stored as subdirectories under a root directory called Data. On a file server, the files might be stored on the basis of directories set up for departments. In a company that has a Business department and a Research department, the main directories might be Business and Research, with subdirectories under each for shared word-processing, spreadsheet, and database files.

Home directories on a server often reflect the organizational structure. In a college, the home directory might be called Home within the root directory. Under the Home directory, there might be subdirectories for each department in the college: Business, Registrar, Anthropology, Biology, Chemistry, English, Music, Psychology, and so on. Finally, under each department subdirectory, there would be subdirectories for that department's faculty and staff members.

FINDING AND DELETING FILES

A solid file structure on the computer makes it easier to find and delete unneeded files on a regular schedule. It does not take long on any computer system for such files to accumulate and occupy a large amount of disk space. One example is the temporary files created when you install new software and run many types of applications. Most installations create a temporary directory and a set of temporary files that are stored in the temporary directory. Some software applications do not completely delete temporary files when the application installation is finished. These files may be stored in a temporary directory in the root or operating system directory. Also, some software applications create temporary files that are not deleted when the application is improperly terminated. For example, many word-processing programs create temporary files that are used for backup purposes, or to save the most immediate changes. These files may not be completely deleted when the application is closed, or when the application is shut down improperly, such as because of a power failure.

Web browsers also write an impressive number of temporary Internet files that are not deleted, unless you set an expiration date, or delete them using an operating system utility or utility that comes with the Web browser. In most cases, the files can be deleted regularly, except for **cookies** that contain specialized information for accessing particular Web sites. Cookies are text files that have the preface *Cookie:*—for example, in many Windows operating systems, a cookie created after you access the Lycos Web site from your main (Windows XP) or Administrator (Windows Server 2003) account is *Cookie:administrator@lycos.com*. Temporary Internet files often have extensions such as .html, .htm, .jpg, and .gif.

It is a good practice to implement a regular schedule for finding and deleting these various types of unneeded files, using the methods available in different operating systems, detailed in the following sections.

TIP

Deleting files is vital as a means to make the best use of disk storage resources, and it can help extend the life of hard disks. One rule of thumb is that hard disk drives should be kept less than 80 percent full. Those that grow more than 80 percent full are subject to excessive wear, and are more likely to have problems or fail. This provides added incentive to make sure that files are regularly deleted as a means of keeping disk utilization less than 80 percent.

Deleting Temporary Files in Windows

Temporary files accumulate in Windows 2000/XP/Server 2003 systems, and can be deleted using utilities that are similar to those in other Windows-based systems. In Windows 2000, temporary files from applications are typically written to the \Temp, \Winnt\System32, and \Winnt\Temp folders. In Windows 2000, the temporary Internet files are stored in the \Documents and Settings\Administrator\Local Settings\Temporary Internet Files and \Documents and Settings*account*\Local Settings\Temporary Internet Files folders.

In Windows XP and Windows Server 2003, the temporary files are located in the \Temp, \Windows\Temp, and \Windows\System32 folders. Windows XP and Windows Server 2003 temporary Internet files are in the \Documents and Settings*account*\Local Settings\ Temporary Internet Files folder.

The best way to delete unneeded files in Windows 2000/XP/Server 2003 is to use the Disk Cleanup tool. Start it from Windows Explorer by opening Windows Explorer, right-clicking the disk you want to clean, clicking Properties, and clicking Disk Cleanup on the General tab (see Figure 10-4). (Practice using Disk Cleanup in Hands-on Project 10-1.) When you start Disk Cleanup, it scans your disk to determine the amount of space that can be restored after cleaning specific types of files. The types of files that you can select to delete are:

- Downloaded program files
- Temporary Internet files
- Recycle Bin
- Temporary files
- Compress old files (not really an option to delete, but to save space by compressing files)
- Catalog files for the Content Indexer
- WebClient/publisher temporary files (only in Windows XP)

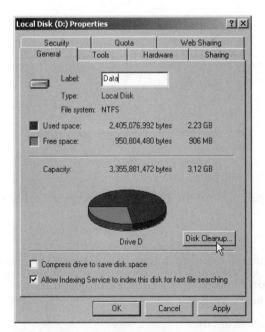

Figure 10-4   Windows 2003 Disk Cleanup tool

If you want to clean up only temporary Internet files, you can do this periodically when you start your Web browser, such as Microsoft Internet Explorer or Netscape's browser. For example, in Microsoft Internet Explorer, open the browser, click the View or Tools menu (depending on your version of Internet Explorer), click Internet Options, and click Delete Files.

Windows 2000/XP/Server 2003 all come with a Recycle Bin, which contains files that have been deleted, but that you can still restore unless the option to delete the files immediately has been set. Regularly open the Recycle Bin to delete its files, which purges them from the system. One way to delete files in the Recycle Bin is to use the Disk Cleanup tool in Windows 2000/XP/Server 2003. The fastest way to delete these files, however, is to open the Recycle Bin and delete selected files or all files. To delete all files, right-click the Recycle Bin, and click Empty Recycle Bin on the shortcut menu.

By default, the Recycle Bin can grow to occupy 10 percent of the available hard disk storage. Computers that are configured for two or more volumes have a Recycle Bin on each volume. You can resize the maximum allocation for the Recycle Bin by right-clicking its desktop icon, selecting Properties, clicking the Global tab, and moving the slider bar to the desired maximum size.

Another approach to deleting temporary files in Windows is to use Windows Explorer to search for and delete all files with a .tmp file extension.

UNIX/Linux

You can view UNIX/Linux files by using the *ls* command, along with one or more options for listing particular file qualities. Some of the options associated with this command in Red Hat Enterprise Linux 3.0 are as follows:

- *-a* lists all files
- *-C* formats the listing in columns for easier reading
- *-d* lists directories
- *-f* displays files in an unsorted list
- *-F* identifies the directory contents on the basis of directory, executable files, and symbolic links
- *-i* displays the inode number for each file
- *-l* presents a detailed information listing including permissions and file size
- *-n* displays user identification numbers (UIDs) and group identification numbers (GIDs) of those who have access to files
- *-r* sorts files in reverse alphabetical order
- *-s* displays the size of files (in kilobytes)

- *-t* displays files on the basis of the date they were last modified

- *-u* displays files on the basis of the time they were last modified

In the Red Hat Enterprise Linux 3.0 GNOME interface, you can view files and directories in the graphical user interface (GUI) windows-like Nautilus tool by double-clicking the Home icon on the desktop, such as root's Home, when you are logged on as root, and then use the Location box to specify a directory to display. Figure 10-5 shows the contents of the /bin directory in Nautilus.

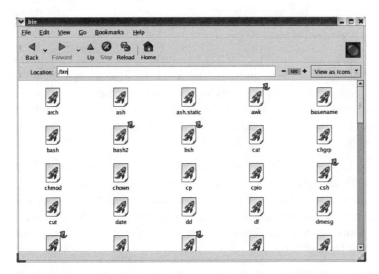

Figure 10-5   Viewing files and folders in the GNOME interface

Files and folders are deleted in UNIX/Linux by using the remove (*rm*) command. The two options commonly added to the command are *-i* and *-r*. The *-i* or interactive option results in a query about if you really want to delete the file or directory; the *-r* or recursive command is used to delete the entire directory contents, including all subdirectories and files within a directory.

In the Red Hat Enterprise Linux 3.0 GNOME Nautilus tool, you can delete a file by finding its folder (via the Location box) that contains the file, clicking the appropriate file in the display of the folder's contents, and pressing the Del key on your keyboard.

A file can be found by using the *find* command. This command enables files to be found on the basis of the filename, a wildcard character (*) associated with part of the name, the size of the file, and the last time it was accessed or modified. For example, to find and print a list of all temporary files modified in the last 30 days, you enter *find -name temp* -mtime -30 -print*. (Try Hands-on Project 10-2 to practice deleting temporary files in UNIX/Linux.)

Typical options used with *find* are as follows:

- *-atime* for last accessed time
- *-ctime* for last changed time
- *-mtime* for last modification time
- *-name* for the filename, including the use of wildcard searches
- *-print* to print the results of the find
- *-size* for file size (in blocks or bytes; with bytes specified by a "c" after the size value)
- *-user* to delete files by ownership

Similar to the Windows-based and Mac OS GUI interfaces, the Red Hat Enterprise Linux 3.0 GNOME interface offers a trash can from which deleted files can be retrieved. The trash can appears on the desktop containing papers when it contains files that can be retrieved or purged. Periodically view the contents of the trash can to purge files, which you can accomplish by double-clicking the trash can icon, clicking the File menu, and clicking Empty Trash.

UNIX/Linux provides commands to help you assess the allocation of disk space. One command is *df*, which enables you to view information on the basis of the file system. It provides statistics on the total number of blocks, the number used, the number available, and the percent of capacity used. While *df* provides gross file system statistics, the *du* command is used to display statistics for a given directory and its subdirectories, or for a subdirectory alone. (Try Hands-on Project 10-3.)

On a UNIX/Linux computer that acts as a server, the administrator can set up disk quotas. For example, a disk quota can be established in blocks for each user as a way to make sure that users do not occupy all of the disk space (see Figure 10-6). A quota is set by using the *edquota* command that opens the quota file for editing. The quota file must first be created by the administrator, or in some versions of UNIX/Linux, it is created automatically when you first use *edquota*.

TIP

It is easier to start off by establishing an agreed-upon disk quota for each user than to start with no quotas and attempt to impose them later. Disk quotas are a good reminder to server users that they must periodically delete temporary and unused files. Providing training at the time accounts are created, or when a new server is installed, is one way to help users learn to monitor disk usage before they receive notification that their disk quotas have been exceeded.

Mac OS X

One particularly important reason for deleting files in the Mac OS is to make sure that you do not run out of disk space. Regularly deleting files enables you to make sure there is enough disk space on hand for all needs. Mac OS X windows often have a list option that shows files and the size of each file. Click the List view button (a button showing five lines) in the window to see file sizes.

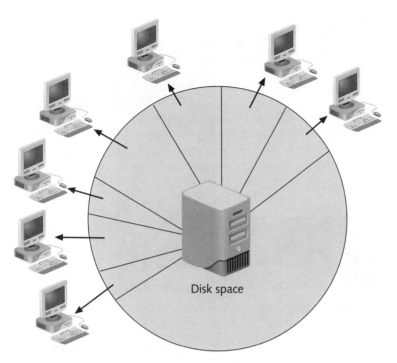

Disk space

10

Figure 10-6   UNIX/Linux disk quotas for server users

The Mac OS has a Find utility on the File menu that can be used to find files that are no longer needed. To use the Find utility, click the File menu, click Find, select the *Search in* value, such as Everywhere or Local Disks, specify the search parameters, and click the Search button. For example, if you want to find files to delete by date, you can use Date Modified or Date Created in the search parameters. Once an unneeded file is found, drag it into the Trash. The Mac OS is forgiving because the deleted item can be brought back from the trash by opening the Trash and moving the item back to a folder or the desktop. The Mac OS also has a Finder tool that can be used to display files and folders. For example, to access the Finder in Mac OS X, open the Finder icon (the icon at the far left) in the Dock (see Figure 10-7).

NOTE

Use the Sherlock utility, as described in Chapter 3, for complex search criteria including name, kind of file, creation date, modification date, size, version, and folder attribute. Sherlock also has the ability to index information for faster access.

TIP

Files are not truly deleted until they are purged by emptying the Trash. The Trash should be emptied on a regular schedule so that disk space occupied by deleted files is returned for use by other files. (Try Hands-on Project 10-4 to practice emptying the Trash.)

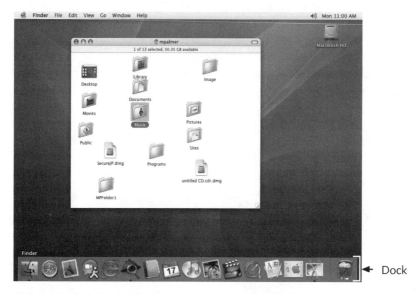

Figure 10-7   Mac OS X Finder icon is on the Dock

NetWare

There are several ways to manage files and folders in NetWare. NetWare Administrator is one tool that is available to view and manage directories and files on the server (see Figure 2-17 in Chapter 2 for an example of this). Another option for Windows-based NetWare clients is to use Network Neighborhood or My Network Places to view folder and file information, including information about properties. Starting with NetWare 6.0, you can also use NetWare Remote Manager to diagnose and manage NetWare servers (see Figure 10-8).

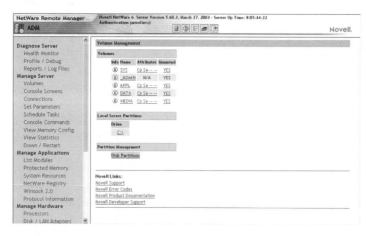

Figure 10-8   NetWare Remote Manager

NetWare Remote Manager allows you to manage servers, applications, hardware, etc. You can also access the server console. This is all accomplished through your Web browser. The following are some of the options of this utility found on the main screen:

- Diagnose Server
- Manage Server
- Manage Hardware
- Manage eDirectory
- Use Server Groups
- Access Other Servers

 NetWare Management Portal in NetWare 5.1 was renamed NetWare Remote
Manager, starting in NetWare 6.

NOTE

10

Another utility that can be very effective is called NDIR, and it is run from a NetWare DOS window. NDIR includes several commands that enable you to find files on the basis of specific criteria, such as date or owner. NDIR can also provide important information about directory space that is in use. The commands include the following:

- /AC BEF to view files not accessed since the date specified
- /DATE to view information based on date
- /DO to view all information on directories
- /OW to view files by owner
- /REV SORT SI to sort files listing the largest first
- /SPA to view how directory space is used
- /SORT SI to sort files on the basis of size
- /SORT OW to sort files on the basis of ownership
- /VOL to view the information by volume

You can delete directories and files by using NetWare Administrator or the delete (DEL) command in a DOS window. As is true for the Mac OS, NetWare files can be salvaged until they are purged. To salvage files from Network Neighborhood, for example, right-click the folder containing the files to be salvaged, and then click Salvage Files. Another option to salvage files is to use the Salvage command in the DOS window. Because file space is not returned until deleted files are purged, it is wise to establish a schedule for regularly purging them. For example, the deleted files in a directory called Data can be listed and purged by right-clicking the directory and clicking Purge Files. Next, click Purge all and click Yes. Another way to purge files is to open the DOS window, switch to the Data directory, and enter the PURGE command at the DOS prompt, such as PURGE *.* to purge all files, or

PURGE *.doc to purge word-processing files only.

When you create a home directory for a user, you can restrict the size of the directory by using NetWare Administrator. This technique ensures that there is a limit to the amount of disk space available to a single user. In fact, in some instances, users produce so many undeleted temporary files that they occupy all available disk space on a server. When this happens, no space is left to perform even the simplest functions until the administrator deletes these files.

Maintaining Large and Small System Disks

In addition to finding and deleting unneeded files, there are other disk maintenance tasks and techniques that are valuable in terms of maintaining the integrity of files and ensuring disk performance. These include the following:

- Defragmenting disks

- Moving files to spread the load between multiple disks

- Using disk utilities to repair damaged files

- Deploying redundant array of inexpensive disks (RAID) techniques that extend the life of disks and provide disk redundancy

Defragmenting Disks

Hard disks in any operating system are subject to becoming fragmented over time. **Fragmentation** means that unused space develops between files and other information written on a disk.

Some operating system file structures are more prone to fragmentation than others. File allocation table (FAT) files systems are very prone and NTFS systems are less prone. UNIX/Linux file systems are also less prone to fragmentation. It is a good idea to keep an eye on all operating system file systems to make sure they do not become fragmented.

When an operating system is first installed, disk files are positioned contiguously on a disk, which means there is little or no unused space between files. Figure 10-9 is a simple conceptual illustration of a hard disk without fragmentation. The shaded areas represent files that are arranged in contiguous fashion, and the white areas are unused disk space.

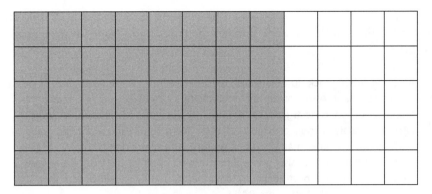

Figure 10-9   Files located contiguously on a disk

As the operating system deletes files, creates new files, and modifies files, the unused space between them grows and becomes scattered throughout the disk (see Figure 10-10). The greater the fragmentation, the more space that is wasted. Equally important, the disk read/write head begins to work harder to find individual files and data in files. When the disk read/write head must move over more disk area to find information, two problems result. One problem is that disk performance suffers because it takes the read/write head longer to find information, and it takes longer to find an appropriately sized unused location on which to write information. The second problem is that the read/write head works harder when there is more disk fragmentation, resulting in a possible hardware failure. The problem is apparent through excessive noise and hard disk activity.

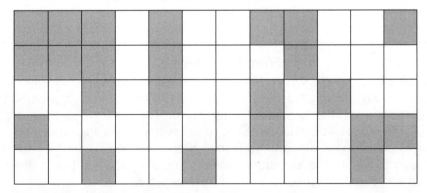

Figure 10-10   A fragmented disk

Defragmentation is the process of removing the empty pockets between files and other information on a hard disk drive. There are two ways to do this. The oldest method is to take a complete backup of a disk's contents and perform a full restore. Some administrators also run a **surface analysis** of a disk before performing the full restore as a means of finding damaged disk sectors and tracks. Some surface analysis tools are destructive to data and attempt to reformat the damaged area to determine if it can be recovered. Others are not

10

destructive to data because they relocate information from a damaged disk area to an undamaged location, and then mark the damaged area as off limits so that no files can be written there.

CAUTION

As a precaution, back up a hard disk before running a disk surface analysis or defragmenting it. Also, consult the documentation to make sure you know if a disk analysis tool is destructive to data before you run it. For example, sometimes disk analysis tools provided on the system troubleshooting disk made available by computer manufacturers perform a format along with the surface analysis of hard drives. Also, some disk troubleshooting tools that accompany hardware RAID are destructive to data because they initialize and format individual or all disks within the RAID.

A second option that is usually easier than backing up and restoring a hard disk is to run a disk defragmentation tool. Many operating systems come with a built-in tool to defragment disks. In some cases, it is necessary to purchase the tool from a third-party vendor. Some defragmentation tools can run in the background as you continue to use the operating system. Many also provide a quick analysis of the hard disk, and advise whether or not it is necessary to defragment it. For example, if disk fragmentation is 20 percent or less, the disk does not need to be defragmented immediately. Server operating systems often experience more rapid fragmentation than client operating systems. Server administrators should develop a regular schedule to defragment the hard disks. Some administrators defragment between once a week and once a month during times when no one is on the server other than the administrator. In some situations where a server is under constant and heavy use, such as one used for a client/server application, it can be necessary to defragment disks every few days.

From the Trenches...

At one business, a new server administrator checked the server and found the hard drive was severely fragmented. She felt it should be defragmented right away and started the process. To her horror, the defragmentation process caused the Microsoft Exchange Server process that was running on the computer to stop executing. All the e-mail processing was down for the time necessary to reboot the Exchange Server. She quickly learned that the defragmentation process must be run on an off-line server.

As introduced in Chapter 3, Windows 2000/XP/Server 2003 have built-in defragmentation utilities. Defragmentation is accomplished through the Start button, Programs menu (All Programs in Windows XP/Server 2003), Accessories menu, and System Tools menu. On the System Tools menu, select Disk Defragmenter. Next, highlight the drive you wish to work on, and then click Analyze to check fragmentation of the drive, or Defragment to actually defragment the drive. Figure 10-11 shows the Windows XP Disk Defragmenter dialog box. Also, try Hands-on Project 10-5 to run the Disk Defragmenter in Windows 2000/XP/ Server 2003.

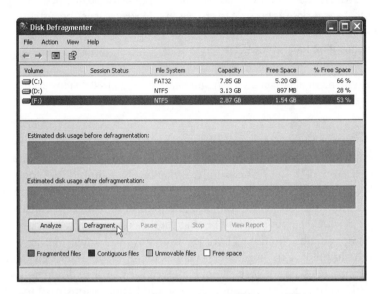

Figure 10-11   Disk Defragmenter in Windows XP

TIP

If a disk contains an error, the Disk Defragmenter detects the error and requires that it is repaired prior to defragmenting that disk. Errors can be repaired using the *chkdsk* utilities, discussed later in this chapter.

Defragmenting disks with Windows 2000 or Windows Server 2003 can be an effective way to enhance performance, depending on how the server is used. For example, a server that has frequent write and update activity may need to be defragmented every month.

CAUTION

When you defragment the drives on a server, make sure that you schedule a time when no users can access the server. Servers may be in 24/7 operation so notification of system down time will need to be made so everyone is aware that the server will not be available on a regular basis each week for system work.

Some versions of UNIX come with defragmenting tools, such as *defragfs*. The tools are limited in that they defragment and return to use existing empty space, but they may not rearrange files. Compunix, DEC (Compaq/HP), Eagle Software, and other companies offer full-feature UNIX/Linux disk defragmentation tools.

NOTE

Recent versions of Red Hat Enterprise and Fedora Linux use the ext2 and ext3 file systems, which are designed to keep disk fragmentation to a minimum. When this operating system writes files to disk in ext2 or ext3, it works to write them in consecutive space, or if consecutive space is not available, it writes to free blocks that are as close as possible to one another. However, if you are using other file systems with Red Hat Enterprise or Fedora Linux, consider purchasing a disk defragmenting tool for these file systems.

TIP

As for any system, an alternative to defragmenting disks on UNIX/Linux systems is to perform a full backup and restore.

The Mac OS is designed to minimize disk fragmentation, but third-party tools are available for systems that experience high use. For example, Symantec Norton Utilities for Macintosh includes a Mac OS version of SpeedDisk for defragmenting. One problem that is more likely to need attention in the Mac OS is memory fragmentation, in which pockets of unused space develop in memory. Receiving a message that there is not enough memory could be an indication of memory fragmentation. There are four ways to handle memory fragmentation. The first and simplest is to implement virtual memory, as described later in this chapter. Two other approaches are to close all open applications, or shut down and restart the computer. The fourth technique is to open your least-used applications first and the most used applications last; also, close the applications in the reverse order in which they were opened.

In NetWare, there are no built-in defragmentation tools. One third-party tool is Portlock Volume Defrag (*www.portlocksoftware.com*), which can be used to defragment and compress the hard drive. Before you use this tool, make sure everyone is logged off the server.

Moving Disk Files to Spread the Load

Another technique that can help extend the life of disk drives is to spread files evenly across disks when there is more than one disk. This technique is used mainly on computers with multiple-user access, such as servers, and on which there is frequent disk activity. Before files are moved, the server administrator examines disk and file activity to determine how to spread files across the disk drives to achieve even loading in terms of activity. Also, files must be moved on the basis of their functions so that files containing related information are on the same drive.

Disk activity is monitored in Windows 2000 and Windows Server 2003, for example, by using the System Monitor and monitoring the LogicalDisk and PhysicalDisk objects. Also, Windows 2000/XP/Server 2003 resources in use can be viewed by right-clicking My Computer, clicking Manage, and clicking Shared Folders under System Tools in the tree. (See Figure 10-12 and try Hands-on Project 10-6 to study users and resource use across disks in Windows 2000/XP/Server 2003.)

The *diskperf* utility must be started from the command prompt in Windows 2000 for LogicalDisk counters. PhysicalDisk counters are turned on by default. Windows Server 2003 enables both counters during startup.

NOTE

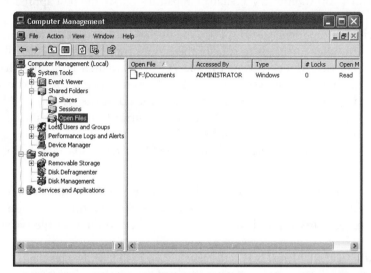

Figure 10-12   Studying resource use in Windows Server 2003 via the Computer Management tool

In Windows 2000 and Windows Server 2003, you can use the distributed file system (DFS) to share files across many computers and achieve load balancing.

TIP

Using Disk Utilities to Repair Damaged Files

Some operating systems have utilities that enable you to repair damaged files and file links. Four examples of these utilities are:

- First Aid in Mac OS X
- *fsck* and *p_fsck* in UNIX/Linux
- *chkdsk* in Windows 2000, Windows XP, and Windows Server 2003

Disk First Aid is a Mac OS X utility that verifies files, folders, and mounted disks. Before you verify a disk, it is necessary to turn off file sharing. In Mac OS X, Disk First Aid is combined with the Disk Utility. To access Disk First Aid, click Go, click Utilities, double-click Disk Utility, select a disk, and access the First Aid tab. You can use Disk First Aid to verify or repair a disk and disk permissions.

The *fsck* utility in UNIX/Linux is used to check one or more file systems. For example, it looks for orphaned files without names, bad directory pointers, inode problems, directories that do not exist, bad links, bad blocks, duplicated blocks, and pathname problems. It also makes other file system checks. If it discovers a problem with one or more files, it gives you the opportunity to fix or disregard the problem. Unless you have a reason not to (such as a database file on which you want to try a database repair tool first), the best approach is to fix any problem found. To use *fsck*, enter the command along with a file list, which is provided in one of two formats. One format is to specify the device name of the file system, such as /dev/devicename. Another format is to specify the mount point of a particular file system so that the utility can determine it from the file /etc/fstab, which contains a list of file systems. If you do not specify a file system to check, *fsck* assumes that it should check all file systems, or you can instruct it to check all file systems by including the -*A* option. Also, some versions of UNIX have a -*y* (-*a* in Red Hat Enterprise Linux 3.0) option that causes *fsck* to make its own decision about whether to fix a problem it finds, and a -*n* (–N in Red Hat Enterprise Linux 3.0) command to have *fsck* check the file system and report problems, but not fix them.

Besides *fsck*, there is the *p_fsck* utility in some UNIX versions. This utility checks two or more file systems simultaneously, instead of checking only one at a time, as is done by *fsck*. The drawback in using *p_fsck* is that it should not be applied to the root file system.

 In most UNIX/Linux systems, *fsck* starts automatically each time the operating system is booted. If *fsck* cannot run when you boot these systems, that means the root system is likely corrupted. To fix this problem, you must use the rescue **NOTE** disk or emergency boot disks for your version of UNIX/Linux to boot to a minimal system and restore the root system.

The *chkdsk* disk utility runs in the Command Prompt window in Windows 2000/XP/Server 2003. This utility is more powerful than the ones used in other versions of Microsoft Windows because it incorporates some of the features of the old ScanDisk. (Windows 2000/XP/Server 2003 do not have a ScanDisk utility.) Try Hands-on Project 10-7 to run *chkdsk* in Windows 2000/XP/Server 2003. Figure 10-13 shows *chkdsk* after it was run to check an NTFS volume on a Windows 2000 server.

Chkdsk can find and fix the following (depending on the version of Windows):

- Damage to the root directory or another directory
- Problems with the directory structure that cause *chkdsk* to be unable to process the full tree
- Indexes created by indexing (such as when you use the Index attribute in Windows 2000)
- Security descriptors
- Unallocated disk space
- Files that share the same allocation units
- A file pointer to an allocation unit that does not exist

```
Command Prompt                                                    _ 8 x
Microsoft Windows 2000 [Version 5.00.2195]
(C) Copyright 1985-1999 Microsoft Corp.

D:\>chkdsk
The type of the file system is NTFS.

WARNING!  F parameter not specified.
Running CHKDSK in read-only mode.

CHKDSK is verifying files (stage 1 of 3)...
File verification completed.
CHKDSK is verifying indexes (stage 2 of 3)...
Index verification completed.
CHKDSK is verifying security descriptors (stage 3 of 3)...
Security descriptor verification completed.
CHKDSK is verifying Usn Journal...
Usn Journal verification completed.
Windows found problems with the file system.
Run CHKDSK with the /F (fix) option to correct these.

   3277228 KB total disk space.
   2295208 KB in 10686 files.
      2692 KB in 581 indexes.
         0 KB in bad sectors.
     55808 KB in use by the system.
     18448 KB occupied by the log file.
    923520 KB available on disk.

      4096 bytes in each allocation unit.
    819307 total allocation units on disk.
    230880 allocation units available on disk.

D:\>
```

Figure 10-13   *Chkdsk* in Windows 2000

- Files assigned more allocation units than they need

- Directories without entries

- Damaged directories that cannot be repaired

- A full root directory (the limit is 512 files in some operating systems)

- Unreadable disk sectors

- Damaged subdirectory entries, such as damaged pointers to parent directories

- FAT entry problems or a damaged FAT

- Allocation units that contain partial information, but have no links to files

- Bad file attributes

Chkdsk only checks the first 640 KB of random access memory (RAM), and only for the purpose of determining how much of that is free for use by programs.

NOTE

Users frequently employ the */f* switch with *chkdsk*, which instructs it to repair errors without a yes or no interactive query. On FAT volumes, the */v* switch causes *chkdsk* to display all files as it checks them. The advantage to this is that you can see a particular file that is damaged, but the disadvantage is that you may have to watch it display hundreds of files. You can also instruct *chkdsk* to check a specific drive, directory, or file by using the drive letter or path after the *chkdsk* command. For example, *chkdsk D: /f* checks drive D and automatically fixes errors.

10

Use the */f* option with care: when *chkdsk* finds and fixes file errors, it may need to eliminate data that it cannot associate with a file; it fixes errors automatically and you may lose data. Also, in Windows 2000, XP, and Server 2003, you should dismount a volume before you check it—use the */f* or */x* switches to dismount a volume, but first make sure that all windows are closed, all programs are stopped, and that there are no users accessing the volume. See Chapter 3, Table 3-4 for more information about *chkdsk* switches.

If you do not specify the */f* option, *chkdsk* reports errors in terms of a query, such as: "*xx* lost allocation units found in *yy* chains. Convert lost chains to files (Y/N)?" If you automatically fix errors, or reply with yes to fix errors, *chkdsk* writes the lost data to one or more files in the root directory that have a .chk extension, as in Figure 10-14. Use an editor to examine the contents of the .chk files (some of the information consists of values you cannot read or interpret) in case there is information you want to retain. Once you extract the useful information, or determine that the information in the files is not needed, make sure that you delete the files to recover the space they occupy.

```
IMAGE      BAK      137,728 05-19-96   10:23p
TREEINFO IDX           871 10-10-96    1:28p
FILE0001 CHK        32,768 11-10-98   10:14p
FILE0002 CHK        98,304 11-10-98   10:14p
FILE0003 CHK        32,768 11-10-98   10:14p
FILE0004 CHK        32,768 11-10-98   10:14p
FILE0005 CHK        65,536 11-10-98   10:14p
FILE0006 CHK        98,304 11-10-98   10:14p
FILE0007 CHK        65,536 11-10-98   10:14p
FILE0008 CHK        65,536 11-10-98   10:14p
FILE0009 CHK        98,304 11-10-98   10:14p
FILE0010 CHK        32,768 11-10-98   10:14p
FILE0011 CHK        32,768 11-10-98   10:14p
FILE0012 CHK        32,768 11-10-98   10:14p
COLLWIN    <DIR>           03-04-99    3:45p
SCANDISK LOG           520 03-31-99   11:10a
DOSBAK     <DIR>           04-05-99   11:22a
DOSMJP     <DIR>           04-16-99    3:45p
WIN31      <DIR>           04-16-99    3:48p
CONFIG   SYS           305 04-17-99   12:08p
AUTOEXEC BAT           178 04-16-99    5:39p
        51 file(s)       1,031,178 bytes
                       973,766,656 bytes free

C:\>
```

Figure 10-14   Examples of .chk files

Two additional switches are available in the Windows 2000/XP/Server 2003 *chkdsk*: */r* and */l:size*. The */r* switch instructs *chkdsk* to look for bad sectors, and attempt to relocate information that it is able to read. The */l:size* switch is used to change the size of the log file in NTFS. Another difference between Windows 2000/XP/Server 2003 and some other versions of Microsoft Windows is that *chkdsk* runs automatically when the operating system boots, and determines if there might be disk or file corruption.

Deploying RAID Techniques

As you learned in Chapter 6, deploying RAID is a technique used by server operating systems, such as UNIX/Linux, NetWare, Windows 2000, and Windows Server 2003, for three purposes: increased reliability (providing data recovery when a disk drive fails and extending the useful life of disks), increased storage capacity, and increased speed. This section focuses on how RAID is used to extend the life of a set of disks. RAID does this by using **disk striping**, a technique for spreading data over multiple disk volumes. For example, when a file is written to a striped disk set, portions of that file are spread across the set. Striping ensures that the load resulting from reading and writing to disks is spread evenly across the set of disks. This means that the disks experience equal wear, rather than placing extra load on one or two disks that are then likely to wear out sooner.

There are six basic RAID levels:

- *RAID level 0*: Provides disk striping only, and requires the use of two or more disks.

- *RAID level 1*: Uses two disks that are mirror images of one another so that if one fails, the other one takes over; however, it does not use disk striping to extend the life of disks. A variation of RAID level 1 uses duplexing, which duplicates the controller card as well as the disk. This is not as common as mirroring.

- *RAID level 2*: Provides disk striping, and all disks contain information to help recover data in case one fails.

- *RAID level 3*: The same as RAID level 2, but error recovery information is on one disk only.

- *RAID level 4*: Provides disk striping, as in RAID level 2, and adds checksum verification information that is stored on one disk in the array.

- *RAID level 5*: The same as RAID level 4, except that checksum verification information is stored on all disks in the array, and level 5 includes the ability to replace a failed drive and rebuild it without shutting down the drive array or server.

There are two general ways to deploy RAID: hardware RAID and software RAID. Hardware RAID is controlled through a specialized RAID adapter that has its own RAID software on a chip, which usually provides extra redundancy, such as a battery backup for the RAID logic in the adapter. Software RAID is set up and managed by the server operating system, and it does not have as many redundancy features as hardware RAID. Generally speaking, software RAID is slower than hardware RAID.

TIP

When given the choice, most server administrators use hardware RAID because it enables them to bypass some restrictions that the operating system places on software RAID. For example, Windows 2000 Server does not permit boot and system files to reside on software RAID, but the restriction does not apply to hardware RAID. Also, most hardware and software RAID is deployed as RAID level 1, RAID level 5, or a combination of these, in order to achieve the best performance combined with optimal data protection.

10

MAKING BACKUPS

In Chapter 4, you learned that it is vital to back up your operating system and data files before an operating system upgrade. It is also essential to back up these files as a regular maintenance practice. Disk drives fail, files can be lost or corrupted, and database files can get out of synchronization on any workstation or server. The best line of defense is to develop a strong backup plan. Most computer operating systems have built-in backup utilities, or backup software can be purchased separately. Typically, backups are written to tape, but other backup options include floppy disks, Zip drives, CD drives, and DVD drives. USB/flash memory drives can be used to back up specific files, but for reliable long term storage, the other options listed are a better choice. USB/flash memory drives are too costly compared to these other media.

There are several types of backups. One type is called a **binary backup** because it backs up the disk contents in binary format to create an exact image of the disk contents. The advantages of this type of backup is that it is simple to perform, and includes everything on the disk. The disadvantages are that in many versions, you cannot restore individual files or directories, and when you perform a restore, the target disk drive must be the same size or larger than the disk drive from which the backup was made.

Another backup type is called a **full file-by-file backup**, in which all of the disk contents are backed up, but as individual directories and files. This type of backup is commonly used on workstations because it enables you to restore a single directory or a given set of files without restoring the entire disk contents. Full file-by-file backups also are performed on servers, depending on the backup scheme that is in place. Some backup schemes call for a full file-by-file backup to be performed at the end of each workday, as long as the total amount of information on the disks is not too prohibitive. If the disks hold lots of information, then it is common to perform a full file-by-file backup once a week and partial backups on the other days of the week. There are typically two kinds of partial backups—differential and incremental. A **differential backup** backs up all files that have an archive attribute (file attribute that indicates that the file needs to be backed up), but does not remove the archive attribute. An **incremental backup** backs up all files that have the archive attribute, and removes the attribute from each file after backup.

The differences between using differential or incremental backups between full backups are in the number of tapes required for these backups, and the number of days that must be restored when a complete restore is necessary. For example, assume that a business needs to restore all files because of a catastrophic disk failure during the day on Thursday. Also, assume that the business performs a full file-by-file backup each Saturday evening and differential backups Monday through Friday evenings. To recover after the disk drives are replaced, it first restores the full file-by-file backups from the previous Saturday, and then restores the differential backup from Wednesday night. If the same business had been performing incremental backups, it would restore the full file-by-file backup from Saturday, and then restore the incremental backups from Monday, Tuesday, and Wednesday.

Windows 2000, Windows XP, and Windows Server 2003 Backups

Windows 2000, Windows XP, and Windows Server 2003 have a Backup utility that allows different combinations of full and partial backups, along with the ability to restore backed up information. The options in the Backup utility are as follows:

- Normal backup (full file-by-file backup)
- Incremental backup
- Differential backup
- Daily backup for files that changed on the same day as the backup
- Copy backup that is performed only on specified files

Prior to backup, the backup media and the driver that integrates the backup media with the operating system must be installed. For example, if you back up to tape, it is necessary to have the tape adapter and tape device driver installed, and the tape drives detected by the operating system. With these installed, you are ready to start a backup by starting the Backup utility. To perform a backup in Windows 2000/XP/Server 2003, click Start, point to Programs (in Windows 2000) or All Programs (in Windows XP/Server 2003), point to Accessories, point to System Tools, and click Backup. In Windows 2000, select the button to use the Backup Wizard (see Figure 10-15). In Windows XP/Server 2003, the Backup or Restore Wizard starts automatically to guide you through a backup or restore (see Figure 10-16).

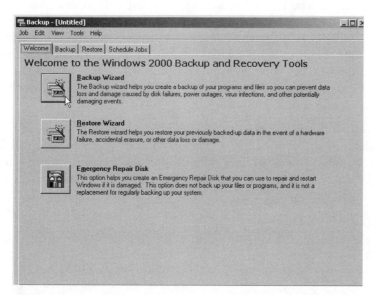

Figure 10-15   Starting with Windows 2000 Backup Wizard

Figure 10-16   Windows XP Backup or Restore Wizard

UNIX/Linux

Two main utilities in UNIX/Linux for backing up files are *volcopy* and *dump*. *Volcopy* (not available in Red Hat Enterprise Linux 3.0) is a binary backup that creates a mirror image of a disk onto the backup medium, such as a tape or Zip drive. The *volcopy* utility requires that you provide specifics about the length and density of the information to be backed up. It can write to one or multiple tapes, calling for additional tapes if the information does not fit on the first one. The utility also can back up to multiple tape drives. It is sometimes used with the *labelit* utility, which can label file systems or unmounted volumes to provide unique identification for each one copied in the backup.

The *dump* utility (used in Red Hat Enterprise Linux 3.0) is used for full or partial file-by-file backups. (These backups are often called "dumps.") The *dump* utility backs up all files, files that have changed by date, or files that have changed after the previous backup. Files can be backed up using a dump level that correlates a dump to a given point in time. For example, a Monday dump might be assigned level 1, Tuesday's dump level 2, and so on. Up to nine dump levels can be assigned. A dump is restored via one of three commands, depending on the flavor of UNIX: *restore* (in Red Hat Enterprise Linux 3.0), *ufsrestore*, and *restor*.

NOTE

A third backup utility called *tar*—available in most versions of UNIX, including Red Hat Enterprise Linux 3.0—is sometimes used in addition to *volcopy* and *dump*. The *tar* utility is designed for archiving tapes, and includes file information, as well as the archived files, such as security information and dates when files were modified. (You learned about *tar* in Chapter 4.) Also, there are several third-party utilities that employ *tar*-based backups and restores, which offer many added features. Two examples of these utilities are CTAR from UniTrends Software and BRU from the TOLIS Group. A comprehensive backup and restore solution for networked systems is available in Computer Associate's BrightStor ARCserve for Linux.

NetWare

NetWare uses its Storage Management System (SMS) to create backups. Typically, three NetWare Loadable Modules (NLMs) are loaded at the server console by using the *LOAD* command. They include the target server software (TSA410), the target NDS agent (TSANDS, to back up the NDS database), and backup device drivers (SBACKUP). Try Hands-on Project 10-8 to view loaded NLMs in NetWare 6.5.

After these NLMs are loaded, you highlight the Backup From or Restore To option on the SBACKUP menu at the console, and select the server to back up. Next, access the Backup menu, and provide a name and location for the backup log file. Specify the directories and files to back up using the Backup Selected Target selection, and provide a name for the backups. Use the Start backup now option to run the backups.

Mac OS X

Apple Computer provides backup capability with ES-Backup. You can download the latest ES-Backup version and other backup utilities from the Apple Web site, *www.apple.com*. Another option is to sign up for a backup service through Apple. Using the backup service, backups can be directed to the hard drive, CDs, DVDs, external hard drives, and network servers. There are also a number of third-party vendors that have developed backup utilities for the Mac OS. A quick search of the Internet will provide you a list of those vendors. The following is a list of four of those vendors:

- Symantec Norton SystemWorks for Macintosh (bundled with Retrospect Express by Dantz)
- Retrospect by Dantz
- FWB Backup Toolkit from FWB Software
- Tri-BACKUP from TRI-EDRE

10

Optimizing Software Installation

One aspect of software installation already discussed in this chapter is to plan and set up a well-organized directory structure. The directory structure influences the ease of the installation, provides the ability to keep different versions in separate places, and enables you to smoothly uninstall software. The following is a checklist of additional guidelines for software installation:

- Make sure that the software is compatible with your operating system.

- Check the central processing unit (CPU), RAM, disk storage, audio, and other requirements to make sure your computer is a match for the software.

- Find out if there are different installation options, such as one with or without tutoring applications to help you to learn the software.

- For Microsoft operating systems, determine if the software is DOS-based or Windows-based, and if any special drivers are required. Keep in mind that Windows 2000/XP/Server 2003 may not run some DOS-based software, games, and 16-bit Windows-based software.

- Check to determine if there are programs that attempt to directly manage hardware and peripherals because these may not be allowed to function in Windows 2000 and Windows Server 2003 because these functions must go through the system kernel.

- Use any utilities provided by the operating system for installing software. For example, Windows 2000/XP/Server 2003 use an Add/Remove Programs (or Add and Remove Programs in Windows XP) utility in the Control Panel.

- Look in the documentation, or ask your vendor, for software that is written to take advantage of the registry for Windows 2000/XP/Server 2003 applications.

- Check the vendor's "bug" list for the software to make sure there are no bugs that will impact the way you will use it. Bug lists are often posted on the vendor's Internet site in the software support area.

- Make sure that the software is well documented and supported by the vendor, and that the vendor can provide the required drivers, if applicable.

- Determine, in advance, how to back up important files associated with the software, and find out the locations and purposes of all hidden files.

- Determine if running the program requires adjustments to page or swap files used by the operating system. (Page files and swap files are discussed in the next section.)

- Find out what temporary files are created by the program, and where they are created.

- For Windows-based software, always install the latest versions of components, including .dll, .ocx, .ini, .inf, and .drv files. (These are generally available directly from the software vendor or on the vendor's Web site.)

- Do not mix .inf and driver files between different versions of Windows because some other software on the computer may no longer work.

- Always keep service patches up to date for all software. **Service packs** are issued by the vendor to fix software problems, address compatibility issues, and add enhancements.

Installing software on a network server requires some additional considerations, which include:

- Make sure there are enough licenses to match the number of users, or that you have metering software that limits simultaneous use to the number of valid licenses.

- Determine the network load created by software, such as client/server, database, and multimedia applications.

- Consider purchasing management software, such as Microsoft System Management Server, that can automatically update system-wide software when there is a new release. This ensures that all users are on the same version of word-processing or database software, for example.

- Determine if the software will be loaded from the server each time it is used, or if it will be installed permanently at workstations from the server. (Windows 2000 Server Terminal Services, for example, enables users to run software on the server.)

- Publish or assign software offered from Windows 2000 or Windows Server 2003.

- Determine if the server or client workstations must be tuned for the software in a particular way, such as by modifying page files or registry entries.

- For operating systems that support two or more file systems, make sure that the software is compatible with the file system used by the operating system.

10

Tuning the Operating System

After an operating system is installed, you may notice that its performance is not what you expected, or that performance seems to decrease with time. Just as a car needs periodic tuning, so do workstation and server operating systems. One critical reason for tuning operating systems is that slow workstations and servers have a cumulative impact on a network. Sometimes poor network performance is not the result of network problems or too little bandwidth, but instead, a preponderance of workstations and servers that cannot keep up with the network. This is an often overlooked area that can result in huge dollar savings for an organization. It is much less expensive to tune servers and workstations (often at no cost) than invest in faster and very expensive network devices such as routers and switches. There are many ways to tune operating systems to achieve better performance, including tuning virtual memory, installing operating system updates and patches, and tuning for optimal network communications.

Tuning Virtual Memory

Some operating systems supplement RAM by employing virtual memory techniques. **Virtual memory** is disk storage that is used when there is not enough RAM for a particular operation, or for all processes currently in use. The computer's CPU, in conjunction with the operating system, can swap to disk processes and data in RAM that temporarily have a low priority, or that are not in immediate use. When the operating system and CPU need to access the information on disk, they swap something else to disk, and read the information they need back into RAM, using a process called paging. The information that is swapped back and forth from RAM to disk and from disk to RAM is stored in a specially allocated disk area called the **page file** or paging file, or **swap file** (or swap file system in UNIX/Linux).

Some operating systems that use virtual memory and paging enable you to tune the page file by adjusting its size. Tuning the page file can result in better operating system performance.

Virtual memory in Windows 2000/XP/Server 2003 is adjusted to set an initial starting size and a maximum size to which it can grow. Generally, the rule for sizing the page file is to set the initial size to equal the amount of RAM (in megabytes), plus 12 MB. The maximum page file size should allow for adequate growth in order to handle the most active times. You can monitor RAM and page file activity through the Task Manager's Performance tab (see Figure 10-17 and try Hands-on Project 10-9), and System Monitor in Windows 2000 or Windows Server 2003.

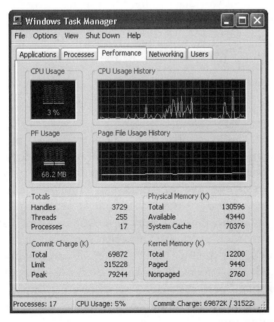

Figure 10-17   Monitoring memory and page file activity in Windows Server 2003

The default page file size in Windows 2000/XP/Server 2003 is determined by multiplying the amount of RAM by 1.5, with the maximum page file size being 4095 MB per volume.

For Windows 2000 and Windows Server 2003, you can configure the page file by opening the Control Panel, clicking the System icon, clicking the Advanced tab, clicking Performance Options, and clicking the Change button. To set the page file size in Windows XP, click Start, and click Control Panel. Click the System icon, click the Advanced tab, click the Settings button for Performance, click the Advanced tab, and click the Change button to view the screen in Figure 10-18.

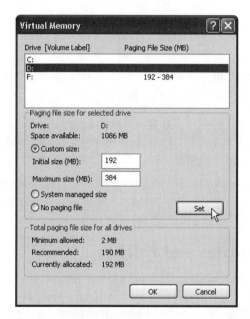

Figure 10-18 Creating page files in Windows XP

In UNIX, you can use the *vmstat* utility, recognized in all UNIX versions, to monitor paging (see Figure 10-19). Another tool that you can use to track disk activity is *iostat* (recognized in all UNIX versions except Linux). Paging in UNIX/Linux is accomplished by creating a swap file system using the "make file system" command appropriate to the flavor of UNIX (see Chapter 3), such as the *nsfs* or *mkfs* commands in Solaris and Linux. The swap file system is mounted like any other file system. If the swap file system is often more than 80 percent full, increase its size. Also, if there frequently is a high rate of swapping, consider spreading the swap space over multiple disks on different controllers. Try Hands-on Project 10-9 to monitor swap space in Linux, NetWare, and Windows 2000/XP/Server 2003.

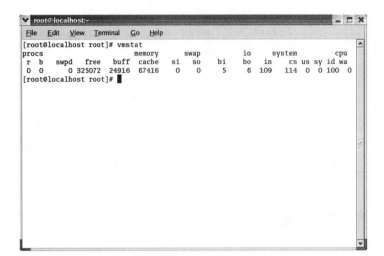

Figure 10-19   Monitoring virtual memory information in Red Hat Enterprise Linux 3.0

NetWare also provides a virtual memory system. The memory management subsystem monitors the memory requirements of the server and allocates the available memory. Use the NetWare Remote Manager to create, delete, view information about, and change parameters for the swap file.

In Mac OS X, there is no option for turning on virtual memory because it is always enabled. The use of virtual memory is built into the operating system, and it is not subject to user intervention.

Installing Operating System Updates and Patches

One of the most important ways to keep your operating system tuned is by installing operating system updates issued by the vendor. Often problems with an operating system are not fully discovered until it has been released and used by thousands, or even millions, of users. Once enough problems are discovered and reported, vendors create updates. For example, you can obtain updates by using the Windows Update capability in Windows 2000/XP/Server 2003 (see Chapter 4). System updates can be downloaded from the vendor's Web site, or ordered on the appropriate medium, such as on CD-ROM.

Red Hat Enterprise Linux 3.0 includes the Red Hat Network Alert Notification Tool as an icon in the Panel, which you can use to access *www.redhat.com* and obtain operating system updates via the Internet.

Apple Computers provides AppleCare Help Desk Support and AppleCare Protection Plan which provides you with tools that give you access to a dedicated Web site where you can obtain the latest patches and updates for the Mac OS.

Novell releases patches and consolidated support packs that are similar to Microsoft's service packs to solve problems in the NetWare operating system. These updates are available on the Novell Web site in the Product Updates section (Figure 10-20). Notice the Minimum Patch List hot link on the right side. Click this link to see a list of patches that can be downloaded.

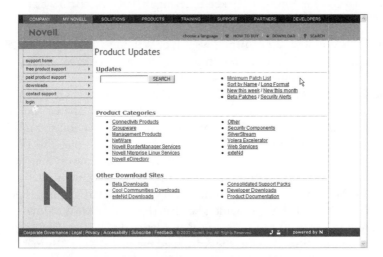

Figure 10-20   Novell Product Updates Web site

 Often when you call a vendor to get help for an operating system problem, the representative will ask what service releases, upgrades, or patches you have installed, and may request that you install them as the first step in problem **NOTE** resolution.

Tuning for Network Communications

Any computer connected to a network should be checked periodically to make sure that the connectivity is optimized. An obvious, but often ignored, step is to periodically inspect the cable and connector into the computer for damage. A crushed or severely bent cable, or one in which wires are exposed at the connector, should be replaced immediately. Also, make sure that the network interface card (NIC) connector is in good condition. When the NIC is purchased, it should be high quality, and designed for use in the fastest expansion slot in the computer.

Just as operating systems need periodic patches, so do NIC drivers. Periodically check the NIC vendor's Web site for updated drivers that you can download and use immediately. Another problem with NICs is that they occasionally experience problems that cause them to saturate the network with repeated packet broadcasts, called a broadcast storm. Network administrators can regularly monitor the network and individual nodes to make sure none are creating excessive traffic.

Sometimes an operating system is configured for protocols that are not in use on a network. An easy way to tune the operating system is to periodically check which protocols are configured, and eliminate those that are no longer used. On many networks, only Transmission Control Protocol/Internet Protocol (TCP/IP) is in use, but workstations and servers are still configured for Internet Packet Exchange (IPX), NetBIOS Extended User Interface (NetBEUI), or both.

A workstation running Windows 2000, Windows XP, or Windows Server 2003 enables you to specify the order in which the workstation handles protocols on a multiprotocol network—called the protocol binding order (see Chapter 8). One very effective way to tune the response time of the workstation and improve the network response is to set the protocol binding order so that the most frequently used protocol is handled first. For example, consider a network that uses peer-to-peer communications and server communications that involve TCP/IP, NetBEUI, and IPX, plus printer communications that use IPX. In this example, most of the peer-to-peer and server communications involve TCP/IP, then NetBEUI, and last IPX. The workstation owner in this situation should set the order of Network Providers in Windows 2000, for example, as TCP/IP, NetBEUI, and IPX. Also, he or she should set the order of Printer Providers so that IPX is first. In Windows 2000, you set the protocol binding order by right-clicking My Network Places, clicking Properties, selecting Local Area Connection, clicking the Advanced menu, clicking Advanced Settings, and selecting the Provider Order tab (see Figure 10-21).

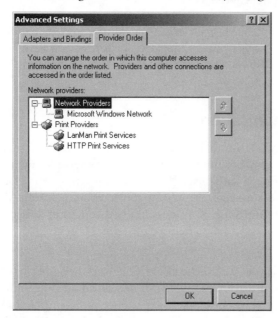

Figure 10-21   Windows 2000 network binding order

In Windows XP and Windows Server 2003 the screen to set the network binding order is nearly identical to that in Windows 2000, but you initially follow somewhat different steps to access it. Click Start, click Control Panel, click Network and Internet Connections, click Network Connections, select Local Area Connection, click the Advanced menu, click Advanced Settings, and select the Provider Order tab. (Try Hands-on Project 10-10 to set the binding order in Windows 2000, Windows XP Professional, and Windows Server 2003.)

Testing Network Connectivity

Often questions arise about whether the network is working, or whether a particular workstation's network connection is working. Anyone can poll another network device using the *ping* utility. Ping offers a simple and quick way to determine if a workstation or server's network connection is working. It also offers a fast means to determine if one network is communicating with another network because *ping* can be transported through network devices, such as routers. Ping displays statistics that include the number of packets sent, received, and lost. It also provides an approximate round trip time in milliseconds.

All of the operating systems covered in this book support *ping*. Many of these operating systems support *ping* as a command-line command. Others, such as Mac OS X, include a GUI interface from which to use the utility. In all of these operating systems, you can use *ping* by entering the command plus the IP address of another computer or network device that you want to poll. Many versions of *ping*, such as in Windows-based operating systems, also let you poll by using the computer name or computer and domain name of the device you want to poll—such as *ping antelope*, where *antelope* is the NetBIOS name of a computer on a Windows 2000 or Windows Server 2003 network.

If you poll a computer and receive a reply showing its address along with other information, that means your computer's connection is working. Also, if the computer that you poll is on another network or across the Internet, that means all of the network connections between your computer and the other computer are communicating. Try Hands-on Project 10-11 to use the *ping* utility in Mac OS X, Red Hat Enterprise Linux 3.0, Windows, and NetWare operating systems.

CHAPTER SUMMARY

❑ Maintaining an operating system is as important as setting it up. There are many procedures you can follow on a regular schedule to ensure that your operating system is at its best. One important technique for maintaining an operating system is to regularly find and delete unused files. Disk space is often at a premium, and there is no reason to leave unused files on a system, particularly because they are easy to delete. Designing a well-organized file structure is a vital part of this maintenance technique.

❑ Other ways to maintain disks include defragmenting disks, moving files to relatively unused disks, finding and repairing disk problems, and setting up RAID. Many operating systems have built-in utilities that can determine if disks are fragmented, and then defragment them. Regularly defragmenting disks is an inexpensive way to extend disk life and improve performance. Disk scan and repair tools are another inexpensive way to work on disk problems and prevent them from growing more serious. Equalizing the disk load by periodically moving files is another way to extend the life of disks. Also, RAID techniques are frequently used to extend longer disk life, as well as protect data when a disk fails.

❏ An important part of maintaining a system is to make regular backups. Backups are vital at times when a hard disk fails, or after you delete and purge files that you later wish you had retained. Backups can also be used to restore drivers or other operating system files that were damaged or overwritten.

❏ There are many considerations when installing software. Two of the most important are to make sure that the software is compatible with the computer hardware and operating system. Another is to use the software installation tools and features built into the operating system.

❏ Finally, all operating systems should be tuned periodically. Adjusting paging is one way to tune for better performance. Another way is to make sure that you keep current with operating system patches and updates. Networked systems should be tuned so that only the necessary protocols are in use, NIC drivers are current, and the network cable is in good condition. Also, TCP/IP-based network systems include the *ping* utility for testing a network connection.

Key Terms

binary backup — A technique that backs up the entire contents of one or more disk drives in a binary or image format.

cookie — A text-based file used by Web sites to obtain customized information about a user, such as the user's name, the user's password to access the site, and information about how to customize Web page display.

defragmentation — The process of removing empty pockets between files and other information on a hard disk drive.

differential backup — Backs up all files with an archive attribute, but does not remove that attribute after backup.

disk striping — A disk storage technique that divides portions of each file over all volumes in a set as a way to minimize wear on individual disks.

fragmentation — Developing more and more empty pockets of space between files on the disk due to frequent writing, deleting, and modifying files and file contents.

full file-by-file backup — A technique that backs up the entire contents of one or more disk drives on the basis of directories, subdirectories, and files so that it is possible to restore a combination of any of these.

incremental backup — A technique that backs up all files with an archive attribute, and then removes the attribute after backup.

page file — Also called the paging file or swap file, an allocated portion of disk storage reserved for use to supplement RAM when the available RAM is exceeded.

service packs — Software "fixes" issued by the vendor to repair software problems, address compatibility issues, and add enhancements.

surface analysis — A disk diagnostic technique that locates damaged disk areas and marks them as bad. Some surface analysis tools are destructive to data because they also format a disk. Others can run without altering data, except to move data from a damaged location to one that is not.

swap file — Also called the page file or paging file, an allocated portion of disk storage reserved for use to supplement RAM when the available RAM is exceeded.

virtual memory — Disk storage that is used when there is not enough RAM for a particular operation, or for all processes currently in use.

REVIEW QUESTIONS

1. The *ping* utility is used for _____ .

2. In disk striping _____ .
   a. a disk array is specially coated to reduce wear
   b. portions of files are spread over several disks in a set
   c. redundancy is not needed because mirrored data is stored on a chip in the disk adapter
   d. All of the above.

3. In which of the following operating systems can you adjust virtual memory?
   a. NetWare 6.5
   b. Windows XP and Windows Server 2003
   c. Red Hat Enterprise Linux 3.0
   d. All of the above.

4. How can you purge a file in Mac OS X?
   a. Right-click the file and click purge.
   b. Send the file to the trash can and then delete it from the trash can.
   c. Copy the file to another hard drive and then delete it.
   d. Mac OS X files are always purged as soon as they are deleted.

5. Performing a complete backup and then fully restoring a disk is one way to eliminate heavy fragmentation. True or False?

6. The swap or page file is used for _____ memory.

7. Which of the following utilities in Windows XP can be used to find and delete temporary files created by programs?
   a. Disk Tracker
   b. Recovery Console

10

    c. Disk Cleanup

    d. Control Panel System icon

8. _____ and _____ are examples of partial backups.

9. Which of the following backup utilities are available in Red Hat Enterprise Linux 3.0?

    a. NLMs

    b. *volcopy*

    c. *dump*

    d. All of the above.

10. Which of the following utilities would help you acquire information about paging in Windows 2000 or Windows XP?

    a. PageScan

    b. Task Manager

    c. ScanDisk

    d. None of the above.

11. UNIX/Linux has no built-in tools to fix file and directory problems, which means that you must always perform a complete system installation in these situations. True or False?

12. Which of the following are characteristics of RAID level 0?

    a. It involves disk striping.

    b. Four or more disks are required.

    c. It involves disk mirroring.

    d. only a and c

13. ScanDisk can repair file and directory problems in which of the following?

    a. Windows Server 2003

    b. NetWare 6.5

    c. Windows XP

    d. None of the above.

14. Which of the following is not a backup option in Windows 2003?

    a. normal

    b. incremental

    c. daily

    d. binary image

15. In most directory structures, the directory that contains the operating system is _____ .

    a. in the root

    b. hidden in a remote subdirectory for security

    c. in server operating systems, located as a subdirectory under the /usr directory, a technique used to enhance performance

    d. placed as a subdirectory in the main directory for all software applications

16. In Windows XP, you can optimize the network binding order as a way to improve network performance. True or False?

17. You are at the Red Hat Enterprise Linux 3.0 command prompt and have changed to a large directory in which you want to delete a file that you think begins with the letter "w," but you're unsure of the exact name. Which of the following *ls* command switches might help you find the file faster?

    a. *-F*

    b. *-l*

    c. *-r*

    d. *-n*

18. Your Windows 2000 Professional workstation's hard drive seems to be laboring to find files, possibly because you added and deleted hundreds of files without performing any special disk maintenance. To improve the hard drive's performance you should _____ .

19. You use the Internet frequently. What simple step should you perform on a regular basis to maintain your computer?

    a. Tune your Internet browser to automatically delete all cookies.

    b. Reset the protocol binding order in the Internet browser to give priority to IPX/SPX communications because accessing multiple sites can change the binding order.

    c. Check to make sure that your Internet browser's speed is always maintained between 128 Kbps and 20 Mbps.

    d. Use your Internet browser to delete temporary Internet files.

20. You need to restore two files from a backup. Fortunately, an image backup enables you to quickly restore only those two files. True or False?

10

HANDS-ON PROJECTS

Project 10-1

This project enables you to use the Disk Cleanup tool in **Windows 2000/XP/ Server 2003** to delete temporary Internet files and temporary files created by applications.

To use the Disk Cleanup tool:

1. Close all active windows and programs.

2. Click **Start**, point to **Programs** or **All Programs**, point to **Accessories**, point to **System Tools**, and click **Disk Cleanup**.

3. Select the drive to clean up if there is more than one, such as drive **(C)**, and click **OK**. What types of files can be deleted?

4. Make sure the **Disk Cleanup** tab appears. Check the boxes for **Temporary Internet Files** and **Temporary files**.

5. Click the **More Options** tab. What can you do on this tab?

6. Return to the **Disk Cleanup** tab and click **OK**.

7. Click **Yes** to verify that you want to delete the files.

Project 10-2

In this project, you create a couple of test files and then practice deleting them in **Red Hat Enterprise Linux 3.0**. Log on to your account for this project, rather than the root account.

To find and delete the files using the command line:

1. Access the command line, such as by opening a terminal window. (Click **Main Menu**, point to **System Tools**, and click **Terminal** in Red Hat Enterprise Linux 3.0.)

2. Create two files that you can practice deleting. First, type **touch practice1.tmp** and press **Enter**. Next, type **touch practice2.tmp** and press **Enter**.

3. Type **ls *.tmp** and press **Enter**. Do you see the files you just created?

4. Type **rm *.tmp** and press **Enter**. If prompted, type **Y** and press **Enter** to confirm removal.

5. Type **ls *.tmp** and press **Enter**. Do you see the message indicating there are no files associated with *.tmp thus verifying that you have deleted these files? (See Figure 10-22.)

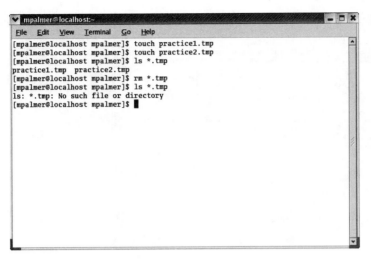

Figure 10-22   Deleting Red Hat Enterprise Linux 3.0 files

6. If you opened a terminal window, type **exit** and press **Enter** to close it.

Project 10-3

In this project, you use the *df* and *du* commands in **Red Hat Enterprise Linux 3.0** to examine disk space use.

To examine disk space use:

1. Access the command line, such as by opening a terminal window.

2. Type **df –a** and press **Enter** to view information about all mounted file systems.

3. Type df /*directory*, such as **df /var** and press **Enter** to view information about the file system in which that directory resides. What information do you see for your system? See Figure 10-23 as an example.

4. Switch to a directory of your choice (such as by typing **cd /usr** and pressing **Enter**).

5. Type **du |more** and press **Enter** to view how large each subdirectory is within the main directory. (Use the space bar to advance a screen at a time or type **q** to exit the listing of information.)

6. To view the total size of the directory you are currently in, plus the total size of each subdirectory, type **du –s |more** and press **Enter**.

7. If you opened a terminal window, type **exit** and press **Enter** to close it.

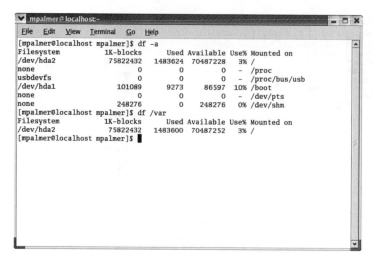

```
mpalmer@localhost:~
File   Edit   View   Terminal   Go   Help
[mpalmer@localhost mpalmer]$ df -a
Filesystem           1K-blocks       Used Available Use% Mounted on
/dev/hda2            75822432     1483624  70487228   3% /
none                        0           0         0    - /proc
usbdevfs                    0           0         0    - /proc/bus/usb
/dev/hda1              101089        9273     86597  10% /boot
none                        0           0         0    - /dev/pts
none                   248276           0    248276   0% /dev/shm
[mpalmer@localhost mpalmer]$ df /var
Filesystem           1K-blocks       Used Available Use% Mounted on
/dev/hda2            75822432     1483600  70487252   3% /
[mpalmer@localhost mpalmer]$
```

Figure 10-23   Disk space in Red Hat Enterprise Linux 3.0

Project 10-4

In this project, you empty the trash in **Mac OS X**.

To empty the trash in Mac OS X:

1. Click the **Trash** icon on the Dock to view its contents.

2. Make sure that there are no files you want to salvage from the trash. If there are items you want to salvage, drag them out of the trash and into the appropriate folder or folders.

3. Open the **Finder** menu.

4. Select **Empty Trash** as in Figure 10-24.

5. Click **OK**.

TIP

In Mac OS X, if there are no files in the trash can, it appears as an empty wire basket on the Dock; if it contains files to delete, the wire trash can shows papers inside.

Figure 10-24   Mac OS X trash

Project 10-5

In this project, you practice using Disk Defragmenter in **Windows 2000, Windows XP**, or **Windows Server 2003**.

To run the Disk Defragmenter in Windows 2000/XP/Server 2003:

1. Click **Start**, point to **Programs** (in Windows 2000) or **All Programs** (in Windows XP/Server 2003), point to **Accessories**, point to **System Tools**, and click **Disk Defragmenter**.

2. Highlight the desired disk and click **Defragment**.

3. Click **View Report** after the disk is defragemented. What type of information is in the report?

4. Click **Close** to close the report window.

5. Close the Disk Defragmenter tool.

Project 10-6

In this project, you use the Computer Management tool to view the resources available for sharing on a computer running **Windows 2000/XP/Server 2003**. This project works best if you have one or more shared drives already set up, and one or more clients accessing those drives.

To view the resources in use:

1. Log on as Administrator, or access an account that has Administrator privileges.

2. In Windows 2000, right-click **My Computer** and click **Manage** (or in Windows 2000 Server, click Start, point to Programs, point to Administrative Tools, and click Computer Management). In Windows XP/Server 2003, click **Start**, right-click **My Computer**, and click **Manage**.

3. Notice the options in the left pane. What kinds of tasks can be accomplished through the Computer Management tool?

4. Double-click **Shared Folders** in the tree (under System Tools).

5. Double-click **Shares** in the tree. Notice that the right pane displays the drives and folders that are shared from your computer.

6. In the tree, click **Sessions** to view the users connected to a share on your computer.

7. Click **Open Files** in the tree to view the files that have been opened by a client.

8. Close the Computer Management window.

Project 10-7

In this project, you run *chkdsk* in **Windows 2000**, **Windows XP**, and **Windows Server 2003**. On these systems, close all windows and programs before you run *chkdsk*. Also, make sure that no one is accessing a shared resource. (See Hands-on Project 10-6, for example.)

To run *chkdsk* in Windows 2000, Windows XP, or Windows Server 2003:

1. In Windows 2000, click **Start**, point to **Programs**, point to **Accessories**, and click **Command Prompt**. Or, in Windows XP/Server 2003, click **Start**, point to **All Programs**, point to **Accessories**, and click **Command Prompt**.

2. Type **chkdsk** at the command prompt, and press **Enter**.

3. Notice the information that appears, and whether or not any errors are found (refer back to Figure 10-13 for Windows 2000 Server, as an example). If errors are found, run **chkdsk /f**. The system informs you that the volume is in use by another process and asks to schedule this for the next time the system restarts. Type a **Y** for yes and press **Enter**.

4. Type **exit** and press **Enter** to close the Command Prompt window.

Project 10-8

In this project, you see how various NLMs are utilizing the server's processors in **NetWare 6.5**.

To monitor the loaded NLMs:

1. Start up the NetWare Remote Manager by opening a Web browser and pointing it to server's_TCP/IP_address**:8008**. The default port number is 8008. If you changed this on the NetWare configuration page, you should use that port number.

2. Accept the SSL certificate.

3. At the login dialog box, enter the appropriate information provided by your instructor.

4. Click the **Profile/Debug** option in the left navigation panel. What do you see about each NLM and its workload over the available CPUs?

5. Click the **Reports/Log Files** option in the left navigation panel. What NLMs are loaded on this server?

6. Close the browser window.

Project 10-9

This project enables you to view the virtual memory information in **Red Hat Enterprise Linux 3.0**, **NetWare 6.5**, **Windows 2000**, **Windows XP**, and **Windows Server 2003**.

To monitor the use of swap space in Red Hat Enterprise Linux 3.0 (and many other versions of UNIX/Linux):

1. Access the command line, such as by opening a terminal window.

2. Type **vmstat** and press **Enter** (see Figure 10-25). How much swap space is in use?

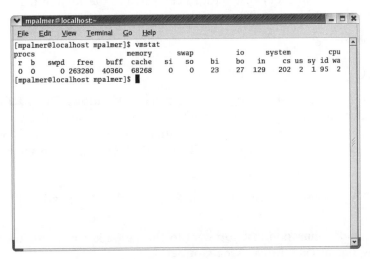

Figure 10-25   Red Hat Enterprise Linux 3.0 virtual memory

3. If you opened a terminal window, type **exit** and press **Enter** to close it.

To monitor virtual memory in NetWare 6.5:

1. Start up the NetWare Remote Manager by opening a Web browser and pointing it to server's_TCP/IP_address:**8008**. The default port number is 8008. If you changed this on the NetWare configuration page, you should use that port number.

2. Accept the SSL certificate.

3. At the login dialog box, enter the appropriate information provided you by your instructor.

4. Click **View Memory Config** in the navigation frame.

5. Click **Used by Virtual Memory System** on the View Memory Config page.

6. Click **To Virtual Memory Cache Pool**.

7. Report the statistics for each cache pool.

8. Click **To Virtual Memory Statistics**. What statistics are reported?

9. Close the browser window.

To monitor page file and memory use in Windows 2000/XP/Server 2003:

1. Right-click the **taskbar**.

2. Click **Task Manager**.

3. Click the **Performance** tab.

4. Notice the memory usage statistics and graphing information.

5. Notice the amount of memory that is paged compared to the amount that is not paged (see the Kernel Memory (K) section).

6. Close the Task Manager.

Project 10-10

In this project, you view where to set the binding order in **Windows 2000/XP/Server 2003**. For these three operating systems, you need access to an account with Administrator privileges. (This project works best if all of the operating systems are configured for at least two network providers [protocols such as TCP/IP and IPX/SPX] and two print providers.)

To view where to set the binding order in Windows 2000:

1. Right-click **My Network Places** on the desktop, and click **Properties** on the menu.

2. Click the network connection that you want to change—ask your instructor which connection to use, or click **Local Area Connection**.

3. Click **Advanced** on the menu bar in the Network and Dial-up Connections dialog box.

4. Click **Advanced Settings** on the Advanced menu.

5. Make sure the **Adapters and Bindings** tab is selected so that you can view the current bindings. What bindings exist on your computer?

6. Click the **Provider Order** tab (refer back to Figure 10-21). What is the network binding order for the providers?

7. Click **Cancel**. Close the Network and Dial-up Connections window.

To view where to set the binding order in Windows XP Professional and Windows Server 2003:

1. Click **Start** and select **Control Panel**.

2. Double-click **Network Connections**.

3. Select the network connection that you want to change—ask your instructor which connection to use, or click **Local Area Connection**.

4. Click **Advanced** on the menu bar.

5. Click **Advanced Settings** on the Advanced menu.

6. Make sure the **Adapters and Bindings** tab is selected so that you can view the current bindings. What bindings exist on your computer?

7. Click the **Provider Order** tab. What is the network binding order for the providers?

8. Click **Cancel**. Close the Network Connections window.

Project 10-11

In this project, you use *ping* in **Windows 2000/XP/Server 2003**, **Red Hat Enterprise Linux 3.0**, **NetWare 6.5**, and **Mac OS X**. Before you start, obtain an IP address from your instructor that you can poll across a network. If you don't have an address to *ping*, use the IP address of your workstation.

For example, in Windows XP, you can determine your own IP address by opening the Command Prompt window and typing *ipconfig* and then Enter. Or, in any operating system, you can determine your IP address by using the network configuration tools (but do not change the IP address).

To use *ping* and netstat utilities in Mac OS X:

1. Click the **Go** menu.

2. Click **Utilities**.

3. Double-click **Network Utility**.

4. Click **Ping** in the bar of tab options under the title bar.

5. Enter the IP address that you want to poll, such as **17.254.3.183** (the Apple Web site).

6. Select **Send only** _____ **pings** and enter **4**.

7. Click the **Ping** button (see Figure 10-26). You should notice that the address you specified is returned with other information. (If the *ping* failed, that means there is a problem with your connection to the network or that the site you pinged is down. Try a different network address to determine which is the case.)

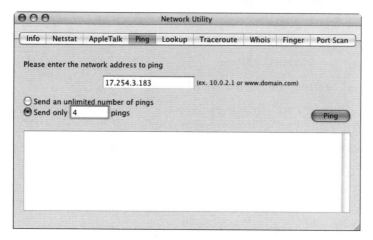

Figure 10-26   Mac OS X Network Utility Ping

8. Next, click **Netstat** in the bar of tab options.

9. Make sure that *Display comprehensive network statistics for each protocol* is selected.

10. Click the **Netstat** button. For what protocols do you see information displayed?

11. Click the **Network Utility** menu and click **Quit Network Utility**.

To use *ping* in Red Hat Enterprise Linux 3.0 (or virtually any UNIX/Linux system):

1. Access the command line, such as by opening a terminal window.

2. Type **ping –c 4** (-c limits the number of polls to four) plus the IP address you are polling, such as **ping –c 4 216.148.218.195** (the Red Hat Web site) and press **Enter**. What information do you see?

3. If you opened a terminal window, type **exit** and press **Enter** to close it.

To use *ping* in Windows 2000/XP/Server 2003:

1. Click **Start**, point to **All Programs**, point to **Accessories**, and click **Command Prompt**.

2. Type **ping** plus the IP address to poll, such as **ping 207.46.197.101** (for the Microsoft Web site). What information is returned? What does the information mean to you?

3. Type **exit** and press **Enter** to close the window.

To use *ping* in NetWare 6.5:

1. At the system prompt, type **LOAD PING**.

2. Enter the IP address to poll, such as **130.57.4.70** in the Host name field (for the Novell Web site).

3. To start sending packets, press **ESC**.

4. Type **exit** and press **Enter** to close the window.

CASE PROJECTS

The National Center for Weather Research (NCWR) is funded by 22 state universities and eight foundations to study all areas relating to weather patterns, forecasting, cloud seeding, and other weather phenomena. In NCWR's building, there is a network consisting of 295 workstations, supercomputers, and Red Hat Enterprise Linux 3.0, Windows 2000, Windows Server 2003, and NetWare 6.5 servers. The workstations run Red Hat Enterprise Linux 3.0, Windows 2000 Professional, Windows XP Professional, and Mac OS X. The network protocols are TCP/IP, AppleTalk, and IPX/SPX. You are one of 10 computer professionals who provide support to users on this network.

10

Case Project 10-1: Discussing Options for Additional Storage

CASE PROJECTS

More than 50 users who run Windows XP and Windows 2000 Professional are certain they need to purchase additional disks because they are nearly out of space. What options can you show them before their department heads order new disks?

Case Project 10-2: Solving the Problem of Slow Network Response

CASE PROJECTS

The executive director of NCWR is experiencing slow network response at her Windows XP Professional workstation, but the network administrator can find no apparent network problems after monitoring the network with a protocol analyzer. What alternatives might you examine to solve this problem?

Case Project 10-3: Repairing Disk and File Problems

CASE PROJECTS

Your boss hired a new computer professional who formerly worked as a database support specialist in the business office, but who is relatively inexperienced in operating systems. The boss assigned you to train your new colleague. One area that you are covering now is how to find and repair disk and file problems. Explain the tools available for the following operating systems:

❑ Red Hat Enterprise Linux 3.0

❑ Mac OS X

❑ Windows 2000/XP/Server 2003

Case Project 10-4: Avoiding Corrupted Files

As you discuss the progress of the new employee, your boss mentions that he has an important word-processing file that opens with a message that it is corrupted. Is there anything he might do to keep this from happening again in Windows 2000 Professional?

Case Project 10-5: Backing up Data on Another Computer

The chief financial officer (CFO) of NCWR keeps a huge number of reports, spreadsheets, and other critical financial information on his computer, which runs Windows 2000 Professional. As you walk by the CFO's office, you notice that the disk drive on his computer sounds like it might have some mechanical problems. The CFO does not have a tape drive, and has not backed up his computer in more than a year. However, you have a tape drive on your computer that runs Windows 2000 Professional, and there is a tape drive on one of the Windows 2000 servers in the computer room. Can you back up his computer on either of these computers? How?

Case Project 10-6: Outlining Maintenance Tasks on Mac OS X

The director of publications uses Mac OS X and has been working on so many projects for the past six months that she hasn't had time to perform maintenance tasks. She wants to spend some time tomorrow morning on these tasks. What maintenance tasks do you recommend?

Case Project 10-7: Adjusting Page File Size

Your new associate has not yet learned how to adjust the page file size in Windows XP Professional. Explain how this is done.

Case Project 10-8: Creating a Backup Plan

You have been asked to create a backup plan for this organization. It should include both desktop computers and servers. Develop a sequencing plan for the tapes. You should search the Internet on tape or media sequencing (grandparent, parent, and child). Address how long to keep each tape and the pros and cons of your proposal.

A

OPERATING SYSTEM COMMAND-LINE COMMANDS

You can accomplish many tasks by using commands in an operating system, such as creating a user account or configuring a network interface card (NIC). Many UNIX/Linux users prefer using commands instead of graphical user interface (GUI) utilities because the commands are so universal and are often quicker to execute. Commands are a staple in NetWare, particularly for server administrators. Windows and Mac OS X users also often find commands to be powerful and step-saving tools. For example, the Windows XP/Server 2003 *systeminfo* command provides an instant snapshot of the hardware and software used on a computer. The following sections provide tables for quick reference to the operating system commands. There are two tables presented for each operating system. For Windows 2000/XP/Server 2003, Red Hat Enterprise Linux (and Fedora), and Mac OS X, one table is for general commands and one is for commands that relate to network functions. For NetWare 6.x one table is a listing of commands for the Server Console and one table is for commands that can be used from a client, such as from Windows XP Professional.

Windows 2000/XP/Server 2003 Command Prompt Commands

Table A-1 presents the general Command Prompt window commands for Windows 2000, Windows XP Professional/Home, and Windows Server 2003. Table A-2 presents the Command Prompt window commands for network functions in these operating systems. The steps for opening the Command Prompt window are:

1. Click Start.

2. Point to Programs (in Windows 2000) or All Programs (in Windows XP/Server 2003).

3. Point to Accessories.

4. Click Command Prompt.

Also, many commands can be run by clicking Start, clicking Run, entering the command, and clicking OK. However, when you use commands in this way, the Command Prompt window often closes before you view the results of the command.

To find out more about a general command, type *help* plus the command, such as *help attrib*, and press Enter. To learn more about a network command, such as the *net* command, type *net /?* and press Enter, or type the full command set and */?*, such as *net accounts /?*, and press Enter.

Table A-1 Windows 2000/XP/Server 2003 general commands

Command	Description
assoc	Used to view and change file extension associations in Windows
at	Enables you to schedule one or more programs to run at a designated date and time
attrib	Enables you to view the attributes set for a file and to change one or more attributes
break	Causes the system to check for a break key only during standard operations, such as while making input or output (*break off*) or during all program execution options (*break on*)
cacls	Enables you to set, edit, or view the security permissions associated with a directory or file
cd or *chdir*	Enables you to change to a different folder or to view the name of the current folder
chcp	Used to view the currently active code page number or to set a different code page number
chkdsk	Used to report the disk file system statistics and to correct file system errors such as lost clusters (for FAT and NTFS)
chkntfs	Used to report the disk file system statistics and to correct file system errors such as lost clusters (for NTFS)
cls	Clears the information currently displayed on the screen
cmd	Used to start a new NT DOS Virtual Machine (NTDVM) session; a new command line session

Table A-1   Windows 2000/XP/Server 2003 general commands (continued)

Command	Description
color	Sets up the foreground and background screen colors
comp or fc	Enables you to compare the information in two files or in two sets of files to determine the differences in content
compact	Compresses files and subfolders within a folder or removes the compression attribute
convert	Converts a FAT formatted volume to NTFS at the time a server is booted
copy	Copies files from one disk location to another
date	Enables you to view the date and to reset it
del or erase	Deletes specified files on a volume
dir	Lists files and subfolders within a folder
diskcomp	Checks the contents of one floppy disk against the contents of another
diskcopy	Copies information on a floppy disk to another floppy disk
diskperf	Installs, starts, or stops the Performance/System Monitor disk counters
doskey	Starts the recall of previously used MS-DOS commands and is used to create command macros
echo	Shows an associated message or turns screen messages on or off
exit	Used to close the Command Prompt windows session
find	Used to find a designated set of characters contained in one or more files
findstr	Used to find one or more sets of characters within a set of files
format	Formats a floppy disk
ftype	Provides detailed information about file extension associations and it is used to change associations so as to link them with a designated program
graftabl	Displays characters and code-page switching for a color display monitor
help	Provides a list of command-line commands and is used to display help about a particular command
keyb	Enables you to set the keyboard language or layout
label	Modifies the label on a disk volume
md or mkdir	Used to set up a new folder
mode	Sets up parameters for a device or a communications port
more	Used to limit the display to one screen at a time so that information does not rush by faster than it can be read
move	Enables you to move files from one disk location to another on the same volume
path	Used to establish the path or list of folders to search in order to run a program or command
popd	Deletes a specified drive letter that was temporarily created by pushd
print	Prints a designated file
prompt	Modifies the format of the command prompt shown in the Command Prompt window
pushd	Changes the path and directory specified and stores the current path and directory for later reference; (also can be used to create a temporary drive letter to a network resource)
rd or rmdir	Deletes a folder or subfolder

Table A-1   Windows 2000/XP/Server 2003 general commands (continued)

Command	Description
recover	Enables you to try recovering files and data from a damaged or unreadable disk
regedit or *regedt32*	Starts the GUI-based registry editor
ren or *rename*	Renames a file or a group of files
replace	Compares files in two disks or folders and synchronizes the files in one to those on another
set	Shows a list of currently set environment variables and is used to modify those variables
setlocal	Used to start command process extensions via a batch file, such as for detecting error-level information
sort	Sorts lines input into a file, written to the screen, or sent to a printer from a file
start	Starts a new Command Prompt window in which to run a program or a command
subst	Used to link a path or volume with a designated drive letter
systeminfo	Provides a wealth of information about hardware and software (not available in Windows 2000)
time	Used to view the time of day and to reset it
title	Modifies the title in the title bar of the Command Prompt window
tree	Used to show a graphic of the folder and subfolder tree structure
type	Shows a file's contents on the screen or sends the contents to a file
ver	Shows the current version of the operating system
verify	Instructs the operating system to verify that each file is accurately written to disk at the time it is created, copied, moved, or updated
vol	Used to view the volume label, if there is one, and the volume serial number
xcopy	Designed as a fast copy program for files, folders, and subfolders

TIP

A very useful command that works from the Windows XP/Server 2003 Start menu Run option, but not from the Command Prompt window is *msconfig*. This command starts the System Configuration Utility, which enables you to configure files that automatically run when the operating system boots, specify which programs to run at startup, and to enable or disable services. (Note that *msconfig* is not available in Windows 2000.)

Table A-2   Windows 2000/XP/Server 2003 network commands

Command	Description
ipconfig	Displays information about the TCP/IP setup
net accounts	Used to change account policy settings and to synchronize BDCs
net computer	Adds or removes a computer in a domain

Table A-2   Windows 2000/XP/Server 2003 network commands (continued)

Command	Description
net config	Shows the started services that can be configured from this command, such as the Server and Workstation services
net continue	Resumes a service that has been paused
net file	Shows the currently open shared files and file locks and is used to close designated files or to remove file locks
net group	Shows the existing global groups and is used to modify those groups
net help	Displays help information for the net command
net helpmsg	Used to determine the meaning of a numeric network error message
net localgroup	Shows the existing local groups and is used to modify those groups
net name	Used to display, add, or remove computer names that can participate in the Messenger service
net pause	Pauses a service
net print	Used to view and manage queued print jobs by computer, share name, and job number
net send	Sends a message to designated users or to all users currently connected to the server
net session	Shows the users currently connected to the server and is used to disconnect designated user sessions or all user sessions
net share	Used to create, delete, or show information about a shared resource
net start	Shows the started services or is used to start a designated service
net statistics	Shows the accumulated statistics about the Server or Workstation service
net stop	Stops a network service on a server
net time	Used to synchronize the server's clock with that of another computer in the same or in a different domain, or to view the time as set on another computer in the same or in a different domain
net use	Shows information about shared resources or is used to configure, connect, and disconnect shared resources
net user	Used to view, add, or modify a user account set up on the server or in a domain
net view	Presents a list of domains, the computers and servers in a domain, and all resources shared by a computer in a domain
nbstat	Shows the server and domain names registered to the network (used only on server versions)
netstat	Used to display information about the Transmission Control Protocol/Internet Protocol (TCP/IP) session at the server
ping	Used to poll TCP/IP node to verify you can communicate with it
tracert	Used to view the number of hops and other routing information on the path to the specified server or host

Linux Commands

The commands presented in Table A-3 are general Linux commands and the commands in Table A-4 are network-related commands. If you are using the GNOME interface in Red Hat Enterprise Linux 3.0 or Fedora, open a terminal window using the following steps:

1. Click Main Menu.

2. Point to System Tools.

3. Click Terminal.

When you are ready to close the window, type *exit* and then press Enter. To access documentation on any of these commands, type *man* and the command, such as *man at* and press Enter. Press Enter to advance through lines in the documentation or press the space bar to view pages. Type *q* in the text window to leave it and return to the normal command prompt. Another way to find out about a command is to type *info* plus the command, such as *info at*, and press Enter. Press Enter or the space bar to read the information and press *q* to exit.

Table A-3   Linux commands

Command	Description
at	Runs a command or script at a given time
atq	Shows the jobs that are scheduled to run
atrm	Used to remove a job that is scheduled to run
batch	Runs a command or script and is really a subset of the *at* command that takes you to the at> prompt if you type only *batch*; in Red Hat Enterprise Linux and Fedora, it is intended to run a command or script when the system load is at an acceptable level that is determined by you or automatically determined by the system
cat	Displays the contents of a file to the screen
cd	Changes to another directory
chgrp	Changes the group associated with one or more files to a different group
chmod	Controls file security
chown	Changes file ownership
chsh	Sets your login shell
cmp	Used to compare two files
cp	Copies a file to another directory (and you can rename the file at the same time)
df	Shows a report of how the disk space is used
dump	Backs up files
edquota	Used to edit disk quotas associated with user accounts
fdisk	Formats and partitions a disk
file	Displays the file type

Table A-3   Linux commands (continued)

Command	Description
find	Used to find specific files
fsck	Performs a verification of the file system
grep	Searches for a particular string of characters in a file
groupadd	Creates a new group
groupdel	Deletes an existing group
groupmod	Modifies an existing group
info	Displays information and documentation about a command or a utility
kbconfig	Used to configure a keyboard
kbdrate	Sets the repeat rate for the keyboard
kill	Stops a process
less	Shows the contents of a file, with the ability to go back or move ahead in the file
ln	Creates symbolic file links
lpd	Configures a printer
lpq	Used to check a print queue
lpr	Prints a file
lprm	Removes print jobs from the queue
ls	Lists the contents of a directory
man	Displays documentation in Linux
mkdir	Creates a directory
mkfs	Creates a file system (but requires more parameters than newfs)
more	Displays text in a file one screen at a time
mount	Lists the disks currently mounted; also mounts file systems and devices (such as a CD-ROM)
mv	Moves a file to a different directory
newfs	Creates a new file system
passwd	Used to change a password
pr	Used to format a file into pages or columns for printing
printenv	Prints environment variables that are already set up
ps	Shows currently running processes
pwck	Checks the /etc/passwd and /etc/shadow files to make sure password authentication entries are valid
pwd	Shows the directory you are in
quota	Displays the disk quota for users
quotacheck	Verifies the disk quota files, including reporting disk usage
quotaon/quotaoff	Enables or disables disk quotas
repquota	Makes a report of disk quotas
restore	Restores files (from a dump)
rm	Removes a file or directory
rmdir	Deletes a directory that is empty
sort	Sorts the contents of a text file

A

Table A-3   Linux commands (continued)

Command	Description
swapon/swapoff	Turns page file devices on or off
sync	Forces information in memory to be written to disk
tar	Used to archive files
top	Shows a report of the main, current processes engaging the central processing unit (CPU)
touch	Creates an empty file
umount	Dismounts a file system
uname	Shows information about the operating system
useradd	Configures a new user account
userdel	Removes an existing user account
usermod	Modifies an existing user account
vmstat	Displays a report about virtual memory use
whereis	Used to locate information about a specific file, such as a program

Table A-4   Linux network commands

Command	Description
finger	Provides information about a user
ftp	Enables file transfers
ifconfig	Used to set up a network interface
ipchains	Used to manage a firewall
netstat	Shows network connection information
nfsstat	Shows statistics for Network File System (NFS) file upload and download activity
nslookup	Used to query information on Internet Domain Name System (DNS) servers
ping	Used to poll a TCP/IP node to verify you can communicate with it
route	Displays routing table information and can be used to configure routing
showmount	Shows clients that have mounted volumes on an NFS server
who	Shows who is logged on
wvdial	Controls a Point-to-Point Protocol (PPP)-based modem dialer

NetWare 6.x Commands

Two types of commands are listed here for NetWare 6.0 and 6.5. Table A-5 lists commands that can be used from the Server Console. To access the Server Console, if it is in GUI mode perform the following steps. If the Server Console is not in GUI mode, simply type the commands at the server.

1. At the server, click the Novell button.

2. Point to Utilities.

3. Click Server Console.

You can find out more about a Server Console command by typing *help* plus the command, such as *help modules* and pressing Enter. Table A-6 lists commands that you can use from a computer running Windows 2000/XP/Server 2003 and that is already logged on to a NetWare 6.x server, such as through Client32 and mapped to the SYS:SYSTEM and SYS:PUBLIC directories. Use these commands from a Command Prompt window. For help with one of these commands type the command plus */?*, such as *flag /?*.

Table A-5   NetWare 6.x Server Console commands

Command	Description
BIND	Configures a protocol to work with a NIC
CONFIG	Shows information about how a NIC is configured, including the device address and protocol used by the NIC
DISABLE LOGIN	Disables new attempts to log on to the server
DISMOUNT	Dismounts a volume so it is not available for use
DISPLAY SERVER	Shows available network servers
DOWN	Closes files, connections, and removes the server from online activity
ENABLE LOGIN	Enables new users to log on to the server
LOAD	Loads a module or NLM
MEMORY	Shows the free memory on the server
MODULES	Shows the currently loaded NLMs
MOUNT	Mounts a volume for use
PROTOCOLS	Lists the protocols in use by the server
SECURE CONSOLE	Implements stricter security for the Server Console
SET TIME	Configures the time and date
UNBIND	Disassociates (unbinds) a protocol from a NIC
UNLOAD	Unloads an NLM
VOLUMES	Shows which volumes are currently mounted

Table A-6   Client commands for NetWare 6.x

Command	Description
CAPTURE	Sends print requests to a NetWare printer
CX	Switches the logon context
FILER	Manages files
FLAG	Sets attributes on files and folders
FLAGDIR	Changes directory attributes
GRANT	Used for trustee assignments
MAKEUSER	Creates user accounts
MAP	Sets up logical drives for access to NetWare resources
NCOPY	Copies files and folders
NDIR	Provides directory listings
NLIST	Shows eDirectory resources

Table A-6   Client commands for NetWare 6.x (continued)

Command	Description
NWBACK32	Backs up and restores selected directories and files
PURGE	Removes files that have been deleted so they cannot be salvaged
REMOVE	Deletes a user or group from an access control list (ACL) associated with a directory or file
RENDIR	Renames a directory
REVOKE	Modifies rights to a directory or file associated with a user
RIGHTS	Manages rights to a directory
SALVAGE	Restores files that have been deleted, but not yet purged
SETPASS	Changes a user account's password

MAC OS X COMMANDS

The Mac OS X kernel (also called Darwin), is based on Berkeley Software Distribution (BSD) UNIX, which means that you can access a terminal window in which to execute UNIX commands. To open the Mac OS X terminal window:

1. Click Go.

2. Click Utilities.

3. Double-click Terminal.

Tables A-7 and A-8 list commands that you can use in the Mac OS X terminal window. Notice that these commands are nearly identical to those available in Linux, including the use of *man* to read manual pages and *info* to learn more about a command.

Table A-7   Mac OS X commands

Command	Description
cat	Displays the contents of a file to the screen
cd	Changes to another directory
chgrp	Changes the group associated with one or more files to a different group
chmod	Controls file security
chown	Changes file ownership
chsh	Sets your login shell
cmp	Used to compare two files
cp	Copies a file to another directory (and you can rename the file at the same time)
df	Shows a report of how the disk space is used
dump	Backs up files
edquota	Used to edit disk quotas associated with user accounts
fdisk	Formats and partitions a disk

Table A-7   Mac OS X commands (continued)

Command	Description
file	Displays the file type
find	Used to find specific files
fsck	Performs a verification of the file system
grep	Looks for a string of characters in a file
kill	Stops a process
less	Shows the contents of a file with the ability to go back or move ahead in the file
ln	Creates symbolic file links
lpq	Used to check a print queue
lpr	Prints a file
lprm	Removes print jobs from the queue
ls	Lists the contents of a directory
man	Displays documentation
mkdir	Creates a directory
more	Displays text in a file one screen at a time
mount	Lists the disks currently mounted; also mounts file systems and devices (such as a CD-ROM)
mv	Moves a file to a different directory
newfs	Creates a new file system
passwd	Used to change a password
pr	Used to format a file into pages or columns for printing
printenv	Prints environment variables that are already set up
ps	Shows currently running processes
pwd	Displays the directory you are in
quota	Displays the disk quota for users
quotacheck	Verifies the disk quota files, including reporting disk usage
quotaon/quotaoff	Enables or disables disk quotas
rcp	Performs a remote copy
repquota	Makes a report of disk quotas
restore	Restores files (from a dump)
rm	Removes a file or directory
rmdir	Deletes a directory that is empty
scp	Secure version of ftp or rcp (remote copy procedure)
sort	Sorts the contents of a text file
ssh	A secure version of ftp
sync	Forces information in memory to be written to disk
tar	Used to archive files
telnet	Used to remotely connect to another computer
top	Shows a report of the main, current processes engaging the CPU
touch	Creates an empty file
umount	Dismounts a file system

A

Table A-7 Mac OS X commands (continued)

Command	Description
uname	Shows information about the machine and operating system
vm_stat	Displays a report about virtual memory use
whereis	Locates a specific file

Table A-8 Mac OS X network commands

Command	Description
finger	Provides information about a user
ftp	Enables file transfers
ifconfig	Used to set up a network interface
netstat	Shows network connection information
nfsstat	Shows statistics for NFS file upload and download activity
nslookup	Used to query information on Internet DNS servers
ping	Used to poll another TCP/IP node to verify you can communicate with it
route	Displays routing table information and can be used to configure routing
showmount	Shows clients that have mounted volumes on an NFS server
who	Shows who is logged on

B

USING FEDORA WITH THIS BOOK

This text includes CD-ROMs that enable you to install the Fedora version of Linux to use for the Hands-On Projects at the end of each chapter. This appendix gives a brief introduction to Fedora and step-by-step instructions for installing it.

WHAT IS FEDORA?

Fedora is a project sponsored by Red Hat to (1) provide a free version of Linux and (2) to create a public testing environment for the Red Hat Enterprise Linux products. New options, software, and the latest versions of the GNOME and KDE X Window desktops are typically included in Fedora. The newly developed Fedora elements that are well received through public testing are considered for incorporation into future releases of Red Hat Enterprise Linux. However, the basic Linux operating system is retained in Fedora.

For readers of this book, Fedora offers a way to learn UNIX/Linux and use some of the most current UNIX/Linux applications—all for free. Also, through using Fedora, you learn the basic Linux skills that can be applied to Red Hat Enterprise Linux and other UNIX/Linux versions. For example, when you use Fedora for the GNOME-based Hands-on Projects in this book, typically the same steps apply in Fedora as in Red Hat Enterprise Linux. However, the appearance of some screens may be a little different. For instance, the word "Fedora" appears in the upper right corner of the Fedora desktop. In another example, in Red Hat Enterprise Linux 3.0, the title bar in the terminal window is left-aligned and in Fedora, the title bar is centered. Fortunately, the commands that you execute in the terminal window, such as *ls* or *cat*, work the same way in Fedora as in Red Hat Enterprise Linux (and virtually all other versions of Linux).

HOW TO INSTALL FEDORA

The Fedora installation discs accompany this book. Because Fedora is on a rapid development track, you can also download the latest version of Fedora at *fedora.redhat.com*. In this appendix you learn how to install Fedora for workstation functions, using GNOME as the primary desktop.

For many new users, one of the best ways to install Fedora is to put it on a computer already running some version of Microsoft Windows, such as Windows 98, Windows 2000, Windows Me, or Windows XP (Home or Professional). If you have 3 to 4 GB or more of unused disk space or a second hard drive, you can install Fedora in that space so that your computer can be booted either into your existing Windows version or Fedora. Another option is to let the Fedora installation completely overwrite the operating system you are currently using, so that the computer can only boot into Fedora. Consider all of the ramifications of these two choices before you start the Fedora installation.

Preparing for the Installation

There are several steps you should take prior to the Fedora installation:

- Back up your present system before you start. If you perform a dual-boot installation and there is a problem, you'll still have a way to restore your system. If you are planning to have a computer only with Fedora, backing up before you start enables you to restore your present files and applications, either later on the same computer or on a different computer.

- Gather information about your computer (see the complete list below).

- If your computer has a floppy drive, keep a blank floppy disk handy to make a Fedora boot disk.

- Configure the BIOS setup to boot from the CD-ROM or DVD drive (and change the configuration back to what it was after you complete the installation).

Fedora will do its best to identify your systems' components, but if you have very new components or ones that are proprietary, Fedora may need your help in identifying certain components (particularly the display card). Here is a list of information you should obtain before you install Fedora:

- The type and size of your hard drive(s)

- The amount of memory in your system

- The type of CD drive in your system (specifically if it has an IDE, SCSI, or other interface)

- The brand and model of your video card (very important to know)

- The amount of video memory on your video card

- The brand and model of your monitor, as well as the monitor's vertical and horizontal sync ranges (you can find this information in the monitor's manual)

- The type of mouse you are using (PS/2 or serial, two buttons or three)

- If your computer has a SCSI adapter, its brand and model

- The printer type you will use, if any. You also need to know how the printer connects to the computer. If you will print through a network, you need all the correct network connection information for the printer.

Also, if your computer is on a network, you need to know:

- The type of network card in your computer

- Your computer's IP address configuration information. You need to determine if your computer has a static IP address or if it uses BOOTP or DHCP. You also need to know the IP address of your default gateway and primary name server. (If you have a secondary and tertiary name server, you need their IP addresses as well.) Your network administrator can provide all this information.

Finally, for the version of Fedora included with this book, it is recommend that your computer have the following:

- 500 MHz CPU

- 128 MB or more RAM

- 3 GB or more disk space

- floppy drive
- CD-ROM or DVD drive
- Mouse or pointing device

Installing Fedora

The steps for installing Fedora are as follows:

1. Boot the system from disc 1 of the Fedora installation CD-ROMs.

2. Press **Enter** to use the graphical mode installation.

3. Select **Skip** (use the right arrow key) and press **Enter**. (Choosing Skip bypasses the test of the CD media from which you are performing the installation.)

4. Click **Next** on the Fedora Core screen.

5. Use the up or down arrow key to select the language, such as **English**. Click **Next**.

6. Use the arrow keys to select the keyboard configuration, such as **U.S. English**, and click **Next**.

7. Select the mouse configuration (or use the default selection), such as **Wheel Mouse (PS/2)**, and click **Next**.

8. Depending on how Fedora detects the hardware in your system, you might see the Monitor Configuration screen, particularly if the installation software cannot detect your monitor. Select your monitor from the list and click **Next** if you see this screen.

9. If you have an earlier version of Red Hat Linux installed on your computer, you see an Upgrade Examine screen on which to click *Upgrade an existing installation* or *Install Fedora Core*. For the sake of learning all of the options for an installation, select **Install Fedora Core** (if you see this screen) and click **Next**.

10. Notice there are different installation types: Personal Desktop, Workstation, Server, and Custom. Select **Workstation** and click **Next**.

11. Select **Automatically partition**, if this is not already selected, and click **Next**.

12. Choose the method of partitioning from: *Remove all Linux partitions on this system*, *Remove all partitions on this system*, and *Keep all partitions and use existing free space*. (If you want to keep an existing Windows system intact on your computer and have determined in advance that you have enough disk space for Fedora, select *Keep all partitions and use existing free space*.) After you make your selection, click **Next**. Click **Yes** to proceed.

13. If you selected *Remove all Linux partitions on this system* or *Keep all partitions and use existing free space* in Step 12, examine the disk setup that is displayed. For this project, use the setup automatically created by the installation process and click **Next**.

14. Notice that you will use the GRUB boot loader on the default partition. Also, you can choose to set a password for the boot loader (if you do, make sure you have a way to remember it). Click **Next**.

15. If you have a network interface card installed, the next screen enables you to configure network communications. You can set the hostname to either: *automatically via DHCP* or by providing an IP address *manually*. Use the option that applies to your situation. If you are on a network with a DHCP server, select *automatically via DHCP*. Or, chose *manually* if you have an IP address plus addressing information that includes at least the *Gateway* address and *Primary DNS* address. You can also supply the *Secondary DNS* and *Tertiary DNS* addresses, if you have them. Click **Next**.

16. On the next screen you can configure a firewall. Click **Enable firewall**, if it is not already selected. Choose the services that you want to allow through the firewall from: *WWW (HTTP), FTP, SSH, Telnet,* and *Mail (SMTP)*. Also, click **eth0** to allow traffic from your network card. Click **Next**.

17. Choose the default language for the system, such as **English (USA)**. Click **Next**.

18. Select the time zone and click **Next**.

19. Enter the root password (use six characters or more). Confirm the password and click **Next**.

20. Select **Install default software packages** and click **Next**.

21. Click **Next** on the About to Install screen. The Required Install Media screen displays which installation CDs you will need to have ready. Click **Continue**.

22. The installer formats the disk(s) and begins installing packages.

23. Insert additional installation CD-ROMs as requested (the number of CD-ROMs required depends on the packages you have selected to install). Click **OK** after inserting each installation CD-ROM.

24. Click **Yes**, I would like to create a boot diskette. Insert a floppy disk and click **Next**. Click **Make boot disk**. (If you do not have a floppy disk drive, you will have to skip this set of steps.)

25. Remove any CD-ROMs or floppy disks and click **Reboot**.

26. If you have configured a dual boot system, select the **Fedora Core** option.

27. On the Welcome screen, click **Next**.

28. Read the License Agreement and, if you agree, click **Yes, I agree to the License Agreement** and click **Next**.

29. Reconfigure the date and time, if necessary. Click **Next**.

30. Enter the Username, Full Name, Password, and Password Confirmation to create an account that you can use in addition to the root account. Notice you can also configure to use Kerberos, if your network already uses it for authentication. Click **Next**.

31. You can choose to test the sound card, if one is installed. Click **Next**.

32. At this point, you can select to install additional CD-ROMs, such as one for documentation. Click **Next**.

33. On the Finish Setup screen, click **Next**.

34. Log on to your new system using the root account or the additional account you created and proceed to use the system.

NOTE

Compare these steps to the ones in Hands-on Project 4-4 in Chapter 4 to install Red Hat Enterprise Linux 3.0 and you'll notice they are very similar.

MICROSOFT WINDOWS VISTA

Microsoft Windows Vista is the code name for the workstation operating system that follows Windows XP. Features in Windows Vista have grown out of Windows XP and out of the development process for Microsoft's new server system code-named Longhorn. While operating systems are under development, Microsoft often uses code names as a way to provide more time to decide on the actual name. The decisions about naming are influenced by current marketing approaches and the capabilities of the operating system. For example, Windows 2000 was named to signal advances for the year 2000, the new millennium. In Windows XP, the "XP" represents "experience" to signify the operating system was developed out of many years of experience—with the goal to enable users to do more things as though they are computer experts.

Windows Vista is geared to make desktop computing more intuitive and more reliable for users than previous versions of Windows. For example, every computer user has experienced difficulties in finding a specific document or file they know is buried in a folder somewhere. Windows Vista is designed to enable users to quickly find documents, files, and resources—even if they don't remember the exact location. This is accomplished through enhanced search facilities and new ways to organize information. It is also accomplished by enabling users to view a snapshot of the contents of a document or file, such as by quickly magnifying a Word document so the text can be read.

In terms of security and reliability, Windows Vista has more built-in security features than previous versions and requires less rebooting. For instance, the Windows Vista firewall is enhanced to monitor both incoming and outgoing communications. When used with Windows Vista, Internet Explorer has stronger security to avoid spyware and malicious software attacks. Further, when you install a software patch to enhance security or for other reasons, there are fewer instances requiring you to reboot the computer right away, which makes your system more reliable.

Code enhancements "under the hood" in Windows Vista make this operating system about a third faster than Windows XP and Windows 2000. In terms of what you see on the desktop, Windows Vista provides what Microsoft calls a "unified presentation subsystem for Windows," which means that the windows you see are consistently designed and offer many new features for quickly accessing information. The new desktop presentation, called AERO (Authentic, Energetic, Reflective, and Open), also enables organizations to more effectively manage user desktops for uniformity and to reduce common problems in computer use. To the developer, the unified subsystem means there is a more consistent set of application programming interfaces (APIs) for linking programs with the operating system. Visually, AERO can use 3D graphics accelerators to render transparent and other visual effects called "Glass" display effects.

For most users the reasons to upgrade to Windows Vista are for greater speed, more productivity through the use of intuitive features, uniformity of the desktop, and greater security and reliability. These are factors particularly important to users who rely on a computer for school, work, entertainment, and important functions in a home.

COMPARATIVE CHANGES

Windows Vista implements many new features that represent changes from earlier Windows operating systems. A sampling of new features includes:

- Hardware requirements
- Desktop and windows interface
- Virtual folders
- Folder resource sharing options
- Reliability features
- Security features
- Management options

Each of these is explained in the next sections.

Hardware Requirements

As is true for any new operating system, you can run Windows Vista on many kinds of computers, but you cannot take full advantage of the operating system's features unless you employ a relatively modern computer with advanced graphics. An important characteristic of Windows Vista is that it offers new visual features that can take full advantage of the high resolution and display abilities of systems with advanced graphics capabilities. If you employ a computer with an advanced graphics processor, Windows Vista can offer more productivity features, such as transparent icons and the ability to clearly stack multiple documents for instant thumbnails of their contents. Also, with a high-quality graphics processor, you can use a high resolution, such as 1600×1200 pixels, on a desktop or laptop computer and still clearly see all elements on the display. An example of a modern graphics system is Intel GMA 950 graphics.

Microsoft lists the following general guidelines for planning hardware compatibility with Windows Vista:

- Modern CPU (Pentium 4 or later)
- 512 MB or more RAM (1 GB is recommended)
- Graphics processor compatible with the Windows Vista Display Driver Model

Besides the graphics processor, you will get more out of the operating system with a computer that has a modern, fast processor, such as a Pentium 4 or equivalent AMD processor. For even faster performance consider a Pentium 4 processor with HT Technology 600 sequence processing and 2 MB L2 cache.

Another rule of thumb for using a new operating system is to deploy adequate RAM. By using more RAM, you reduce the amount of virtual memory (see Chapter 10) needed when there is an overflow of memory use. RAM is faster than virtual memory (disk) and enables data handling to keep up with the speed of the CPU and the speed of the operating system. Though you can run Vista on 512 MB of RAM, 1 GB works better for advanced features such as multimedia capabilities.

Desktop and Windows Interface

When you use Windows Vista, you'll notice there is still a Start button on the taskbar and the taskbar can contain icons for programs currently running or ones you can choose to run. There is still a notification area on the right side that contains the clock and other elements, such as the speaker volume. A new addition to the notification area under consideration by Microsoft is the Windows Search Engine icon that enables you to see the status of and rebuild the index for the Windows Search Engine.

TIP
The Windows Vista Beta screens are current as of this writing, but may change in appearance in later Beta or Release Candidate versions.

The Windows Search Engine is an important feature that enables fast searching for a specific document or file. Figure C-1 shows the Windows Search Engine screen for a search on the word "Microsoft." The Windows Search Engine provides very fast searches for resources. You can search using criteria such as the following:

- Music
- Documents

- Pictures

- Videos

- Messages

- Items of Any Type

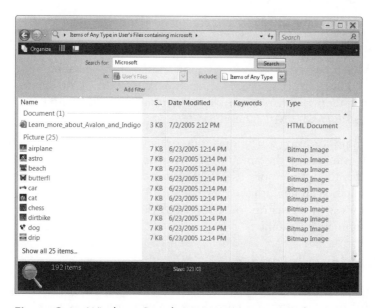

Figure C-1   Windows Search Engine screen in Windows Vista Beta

Windows Vista files can have associated information in the properties of a file, including comments, keywords, ratings, and information specific to that kind of file. For example, picture files can include information about where the pictures were taken and the equipment used to take them. Music files can have information about the album title, the year of production, rating, duration, and other information (see Figure C-2). The Windows Search Engine is designed to enable you to search on this information as well as the criteria listed above.

Figure C-2   Information associated with a music file in Windows Vista Beta

The Start button options and their arrangement have similarities and differences compared to Windows XP, as shown in Figure C-3 and Table C-1. There is an improved Start button option in Vista called Set Program Access and Defaults that is used to set program defaults, such as for sending e-mail, browsing the Internet, or using a media player.

Table C-1   Comparing Start button folders in Windows XP and Vista

Windows XP	Windows Vista
My Documents	Documents
My Pictures	Pictures
My Music	Music
My Computer	Computer
Set Program Access and Defaults	Set Program Access and Defaults

When you select All Programs from the Start button, the program selections in Windows Vista are displayed in the Navigation (left) pane of the Start button window instead of in a new window as is the case in Windows XP.

Windows Vista folders come with an Organize button for creating subfolders and to better organize the contents of a particular folder. There is also a Share button (which may be renamed Sharing) so you can share a folder without first displaying the folder's properties.

Figure C-3   Start button options in Windows Vista Beta

However, if you do display the folder's properties, you can still set up sharing from within the Properties dialog box.

The Documents, Pictures, Music, and Computer folders available from the Start button are actually explorer windows, similar to Windows Explorer and Internet Explorer in previous Windows versions. The Windows buttons are context sensitive when you open one of these explorers. For example, if you open the Documents explorer you see the Organize and Share (or Sharing) buttons. When you open the Music explorer, in addition to the Organize button you see a Play all button, another button to Shop for music online, a View button, and a Configure the Explorer's layout button. The Pictures explorer has buttons for Organize, Slide show, Print, Share (or Sharing), and Order prints online.

The Documents, Pictures, Music, and Computer explorers all include a Search box for rapidly finding an item within the folder or subfolder you are accessing. Search can search on file names and on labels. A label is a name, such as "Work" or "Sarah's" that enables you to organize files. For example, if you take work home, you can organize your work files under the label Work. Further, if Sarah has school files on the computer, these can be organized within Sarah's label. One or more labels can be associated with any file.

The Windows Vista Control Panel is the place to configure your computer, similar to previous versions of Windows. Control Panel still offers the Classic view, which is comparable to pre-Windows XP versions. You also can see Control Panel contents in the Category view introduced in Windows XP. When you use the Category view, the presentation of information is designed to more quickly address a specific task, such as to configure a network connection. Also, the Category view in Vista adds a category head called Security.

The categories in the Category view include:

- Security—to configure Internet, User Account, and Firewall security, check for security updates, and to assess the security status of a computer (see Figure C-4 to view the options associated with the Security category).

Figure C-4   Security options in the Windows Vista Beta Control Panel

- Accessibility—to customize the computer for people with particular visual or hearing needs
- Performance and Maintenance—to use the system restore feature, manage accounts, configure power management, and tune the computer
- Network and Internet—to configure network connections and the firewall
- Communications and Sync—to set up fax parameters, synchronize files (such as between a desktop and a laptop), and configure dialing rules for a phone/modem

- Hardware—to configure hardware connected to the computer, such as the mouse and keyboard, printers, portable devices, wireless devices, game controllers, and power options

- User Accounts and Parental Controls—to set up and manage user accounts and configure parental controls on accounts

- Programs—to install programs, install software updates, play and manage games and to set advanced features for programs

- Appearance and Themes—to configure many options, such as the display, mouse options, scanner options, folder options, fonts, the taskbar and Start menu, and other options

- Sound and Speech Recognition—to set up sounds associated with audio devices, speech options, and accessibility options

- Clock, Language, and Regions—to configure regional and language options and the date and time

- Additional Options—to add and remove programs, configure database sources, and other options

Try Hands-on Project C-1 to survey the Windows Vista desktop.

Virtual Folders

A *virtual folder* is a Windows Vista innovation for organizing files on the basis of information associated with those files, such as author, rating, date, and so on. A single association factor, such as author, can be used or a combination of factors, such as author, creation date, and a particular keyword.

For example, consider a company in which Taylor Hanson has authored spreadsheets in one shared folder, Word documents in another folder, and PowerPoint slides in still a different folder. Taylor has the option to create a virtual folder that organizes all of the files she has created using her name (author) as the basis for the virtual folder. In this way, when Taylor wants to work on a particular file she has created, it is easy to find that file in her virtual folder.

A virtual folder is not really a physical folder, such as Documents. It is a dynamic folder housing files from one or more different physical locations. The virtual folder is a concept similar to symbolic links used in UNIX/Linux, which are dynamic pointers in one partition with path information to the physical file on a different partition (see Chapter 3).

Folder Resource Sharing Options

Sharing folders over a network is a powerful tool for making information resources available to multiple network users (see Chapter 9). As mentioned earlier, in Windows Vista, you have the option to configure sharing a folder in one of two ways: (1) by selecting the folder and clicking the sharing button in the explorer that lists the folder or (2) by right-clicking the folder and clicking Share (or Sharing). After you select to share a folder, you see the Sharing Wizard that enables you to specify which users can access the folder. You can choose from a list of users presented on the screen who have accounts on the computer or you can use the Find button to locate other users on a network, such as those in Active Directory. At this writing there are three permission levels (see Figure C-5):

- Reader (with read permissions)—permissions to view and use the file

- Editor (with change permissions)—permissions to view, use, and change the file contents, and to remove the file (note that Microsoft may change the name Editor to Contributor)

- Co-owner (with full control permissions)—permissions to view, use, and change the file contents as well as change permissions on the file

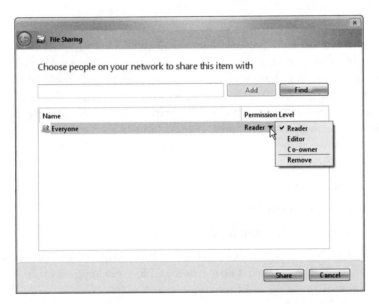

Figure C-5   Using the Sharing Wizard in Windows Vista Beta

As is true in Windows XP, a Vista folder or file also has file permissions that control who accesses a folder or file. If the file permissions deny access to a user or group, this means that person or group will not have share access. Also as in Windows XP, the file permissions are configured by right-clicking the folder or file, clicking Properties, and clicking the Security tab.

In addition to the Sharing Wizard, users can specify the use of a file on the basis of a personal or public profile established on their computers. Files not to be shared can be saved into a personal profile and files to be shared can be saved into a public profile.

Reliability Features

Windows Vista has new features for increased reliability so users experience fewer interruptions and information is kept intact. These features include the following:

- Startup Repair Tool
- New code to prevent interruptions
- Self-diagnosis for problems
- Restart Manager
- Service-failure recovery

Each of these features is discussed in the next sections.

Startup Repair Tool

Sometimes a system file is corrupted or missing on your system. In other instances, you may have reconfigured your system or added new software that can interfere with starting up the system. For these occasions, Windows Vista offers the Startup Repair Tool. Windows Vista automatically launches the Startup Repair Tool when a boot problem is detected. This tool is designed to assess the problem and repair it. The Startup Repair Tool begins by running diagnostics to determine the problem source. It even has the ability to check log files for clues to a problem. As soon as the Startup Repair Tool determines the problem, it works to repair it. Problems that the tool can address include:

- Driver inconsistencies
- Problems with startup settings
- Corrupted startup information on disk

The Startup Repair Tool logs its activities so that users and computer support professionals can determine what actions were taken. For the user and for user support professionals, this means less time is spent diagnosing and fixing problems.

New Code to Prevent Interruptions

Microsoft has strengthened the operating system code to prevent "crashes and hangs," particularly for known problems in earlier versions of Windows. Further, Windows Vista has better ability to notify program developers about system errors so they can improve application program code to eliminate sources of crashes and hangs.

Self-Diagnosis for Problems

Windows Vista has built-in diagnostics for common hardware problems, such as disk or memory failures. For example, the built-in diagnostics can detect a disk that may fail before the failure occurs. This capability can mean the user has advance warning about a disk failure so he or she can take proactive steps, such as saving data and replacing the disk.

Windows Vista also can identify memory problems so that users do not have to struggle with unreliable computer functions. Replacing bad memory can be an inexpensive way to increase reliability and productivity. As Microsoft mentions, in the past these diagnostics often required inserting a boot disk or had to be downloaded from the Internet. Also, the diagnostics are improved for easier use and interpretation.

Restart Manager

Windows XP reduced the number of times you have to restart a computer after installing particular software or reconfiguring the computer, such as for network connectivity. However, as Microsoft has offered more updates, fixes, and security patches, the number of situations requiring restarts in Windows XP has crept back up. If you run a virus or spyware checker, you most likely have noticed the need to restart the computer after updating to check for the latest viruses and spyware.

System restarts have often been necessary in Windows operating systems as a way to reinitialize particular services so they take advantage of updates and patches. Windows Vista offers the Restart Manager as a way to reduce the number of times you have to reboot your computer. The Restart Manager has the ability to determine which running processes and services are affected by an update or patch. Without interruption to the user, the Restart Manager can stop and restart an affected service in the background. This means you usually can keep working without having to reboot.

The update services listed by Microsoft to be compatible with Restart Manager at this writing include:

- Windows Update
- Automatic Update
- Microsoft Update
- Microsoft Software Installer
- Windows Server Update System
- Systems Management Server

Service-Failure Recovery

Sometimes a service, such as the Server or Workstation service, can fail while your computer is running. A service failure means there is an interruption in your work or you may have to reboot the computer to correct the problem. The service-failure recovery built into Windows Vista means that the operating system can automatically detect when a service has failed and attempt to restart it. In addition to restarting a particular service, Windows Vista can stop and restart services dependent on the one that has failed.

Security Features

Building a secure operating system means building in security from the ground up. If you are a user of pre-Vista Windows operating systems, you are probably aware of the continuous need to install security updates and patches. Because computer attackers use a multitude of ways to invade operating systems, manufacturers have had to plug all kinds of unanticipated holes. Today we know more about how systems are attacked and there are more available defenses. In Windows Vista, Microsoft is working to change coding structures at the foundation of the operating system to reduce the opportunities for attackers. Besides locking down the code, Microsoft has implemented additional security features, including:

- A more comprehensive firewall
- User Account Protection
- Built-in security software to find and eliminate malicious software
- Status information

The Windows Vista firewall monitors traffic going into and coming out of the computer. This is a capability initially implemented in Windows XP with Service Pack 2. Another firewall element used in Windows Vista is the ability to link it to the use of group policy settings. This means that a server manager can set up a group policy to have consistent desktop and system settings on that server's clients. In an office or organization, the group policy configuration can be used to ensure that all users have enabled the firewall and are using exactly the same security settings within the firewall. Even if a user changes his or her firewall settings, the group policy ensures the settings are back the next time that user logs on (or the group policy can be set to prevent users from changing firewall settings). Having consistent firewall settings is vital for an organization, because an organization's network is no more secure than the least secure client. Hands-on Project C-2 enables you to learn how to access and configure the firewall in either Windows XP with Service Pack 2 or Windows Vista (or use both operating systems to compare the differences).

Another feature of the Windows Vista firewall is that it is compatible with IP Security (IPSec). IPSec is a set of secure communications standards and standards for encryption to protect network communications between computers. IPSec is supported by Microsoft and other server systems, such as Windows Server 2003 and Linux.

User Account Protection (UAP) is a new feature in Windows Vista intended to make user accounts more secure. UAP enables the user account administrator to better protect accounts by controlling permissions and by limiting the software applications that can be run from an account. UAP protects the registry and specified folders so their contents are only available to a specific user. If you regularly use virus checking or other system protection software, you have probably noticed that the software often corrects changes to a computer's registry that have been introduced by malicious software. UAP is designed to address this important security problem.

C

Some users log onto their computers using an account that has Administrator permissions. Because this type of account can make significant changes to the operating system, there is a risk in running all applications with Administrator permissions in effect. UAP limits the permissions given to applications, so that system-wide changes are not made inadvertently or through malicious software. The downside to UAP is that some applications you could formerly run in Windows XP may not run in Windows Vista.

TIP At this writing, Microsoft does not have a listing of software compatible with Windows Vista. However, Windows Vista does have the Program Compatibility Wizard that enables you to troubleshoot problems encountered when running software that worked on an earlier version of Windows. To use the Program Compatibility Wizard, click Start, click All Programs, click Accessories, and click Program Compatibility Wizard.

In Windows Vista, Microsoft has integrated into the operating system programs to search for and eliminate malicious software, including viruses, worms, and Trojan horses. If the integrated programs cannot successfully delete specific malicious software they may instead be able to block the effect of the malicious software on the local computer.

Windows Vista also includes what Microsoft calls *Windows Service Hardening*. One common avenue for attackers is through an open service, such as through FTP. Windows Service Hardening limits the effect a service can have in Windows Vista, so attacks are limited or thwarted.

It can be difficult for a user to determine if new security patches and other updates are implemented on a computer. Windows Vista provides status information to show whether recent patches and updates have been installed. This is part of Microsoft's Network Access Protection initiative for networks using Windows Vista workstations and Longhorn servers. Longhorn servers will have the ability to set up network access protection that is enforced on all clients, such as maintaining security patches and updates.

Management Options

Windows Vista extends the lower total cost of ownership (TCO) initiatives of Microsoft to save on support costs experienced by users and organizations. Windows Vista comes with more group policy settings than Windows 2000 or Windows XP, which means that computers in an office, department, or organization can be standardized for easier use. For example, if all users in the customer service department in a business use the same order entry program, that program can be set up to start the same way on all department computers via group policy. A customer service representative can go to any computer in the department and access the program in a familiar way. By creating consistency in the way computer systems are used, group policy saves on support costs.

Sometimes one computer is used by many people, such as a public computer in a coffee shop or library. In this situation, one computer might have different group policies, depending on who logs on. Windows Vista includes the Group Policy Management Console (GPMC; see

Chapter 3 for information about the Microsoft Management Console). The GPMC enables the computer's administrator to configure different group policies for different kinds of users. To open the Microsoft Management Console to add group policy management in the console, you can open the Command Prompt window, type mmc, and press Enter.

In Windows Vista it is more difficult to change system settings and files, such as the registry, because the system can be configured so that only an authorized installer makes these changes—instead of users or software that do not have authorization. This system protection is accomplished through the Windows Resource Protection (WRP) feature of Windows Vista.

For more versatile management, Windows Vista brings back the Administrative Tools menu first introduced in Windows NT. At this writing, to access the Administrative Tools menu, click Start, click All Programs, and click Administrative Tools. The Administrative Tools that are available include:

- Authorization Manager—enables you to associate applications with this tool as a way to manage permissions based on the specific roles of users, such as having one set of permissions for the administrators of a human resources program and another set for regular users.

- Certification Authority—enables management of certificate services for security, such as for Internet security.

In future versions, Microsoft may omit Certification Authority from the list of tools, but add Group Policy Management and Microsoft Services for NFS.

NOTE

- Component Services—enables management of components, which includes specified software components, running processes, distributed transactions, and services. It also provides access to the computer's Event Viewer, which enables viewing of logs, such as the system and application logs (see Chapter 6).

- Computer Management—opens the Computer Management tool that provides access to many general management functions such as Event Viewer, Shared Folders, Local Users and Groups, Diagnostic Console, Device Manager, Disk Defragmenter, Disk Management, and Services and Applications (see Chapter 6).

- Performance—accesses the System Monitor and Diagnostic Console tools for monitoring the computer's performance and for gathering network use information.

- Scheduled Tasks—permits you to set up tasks or applications to run at a certain time, such as starting a backup at 6:00 p.m.

- Windows Event Viewer—enables you to access the computer system's logs to track activities and errors. Note there are more logs from which to choose than in Windows XP and the Event Viewer logs are reorganized into the categories, Global Logs and Application Logs.

NOTE There is a chance that all of these administrative tools will be removed from access through the Start menu by the time Windows Vista goes to production. If this happens, it is likely you will be able to access the same tools as snap-ins through Microsoft Management Console (open the Command Prompt window, type mmc, and press Enter). The advantage of using the MMC is that you can customize how you use and view these tools.

Try Hands-on Project C-3 to explore the Administrative Tools selections in Windows Vista.

UPGRADING TO WINDOWS VISTA

At this writing, you can upgrade to Windows Vista from Windows 2000 or Windows XP. In Windows Vista Beta, Microsoft has simplified the process of an upgrade or clean (from scratch) installation. You do not need to answer a host of questions about the computer hardware, language used, type of keyboard or display, time zone, and so on.

CAUTION If you install Windows Vista Beta for testing, first back up your computer. Plan to use a computer that can be used for testing and that does not play a critical mission, such as a personal computer used for school work or in a professional office. It is important to recognize that by definition, a beta version of an operating system is likely to have some bugs and the full range of features will not be implemented until the release to manufacturing version is created for public use.

The steps for an upgrade are as follows:

1. Start your computer.
2. Insert the Windows Vista Beta installation CD or DVD.
3. Click Install Now.
4. Click Next on the Install Windows Screen. If you see a choice to obtain the latest updates, choose Do not get the latest updates. (You can get these later.)
5. Enter your product key and click Next.
6. Click I accept the License Terms (required to use Windows) and click Next.
7. Click Upgrade (recommended). (Note that to upgrade, the destination disk must be formatted for NTFS. Also note that if you want to have a clean installation—in which your existing settings and files are not retained—you would click Custom. If you use the Custom option you can specify which partition and free disk space to use.)
8. If the Windows Setup Confirmation windows pops up, click Next. If requested, enter a computer name and click Next.

9. You now see the Windows screen which says: "That's all the information we need from you. Windows will now finish installing on its own. Note: your computer will restart during installation."

10. After the installation begins, you see a progress bar at the bottom of the screen.

11. Wait for your new system to reboot.

12. If you see the Supplemental Driver Pack Installation Wizard after the system reboots, click Next to install drivers for additional components on your computer, such as network components.

13. Click Finish.

Microsoft offers information to help with deployment of Windows Vista in organizations with many users. For technical information about deployment options visit: *www.microsoft.com/technet/windowsvista/deploy/depguide.mspx*.

TIP

HANDS-ON PROJECTS

In this section you have the opportunity to try out Windows Vista Beta. You'll need a computer that has Windows Vista Beta already installed and an account on that computer.

HANDS-ON PROJECTS

Project C-1

In this project you survey the desktop and Start button options in Windows Vista Beta.

To learn about the desktop and Start button options:

1. Log on to Windows Vista. Notice the icons on the desktop. What icons do you see?

2. What icons are, by default, near the Start button in the taskbar?

3. Are there icons near the clock in the taskbar?

4. Click the **Start** button and notice the options.

5. Click **Documents** to view the new explorer format. Notice the Organize button option at the top of the window.

6. Click the **Public** folder. What new button options appear to the right of the Organize button?

7. Close the window.

8. Click the **Start** button.

9. Click **Computer**. Notice the new explorer format showing disk drives.

10. Double-click an available hard drive, such as **Local Disk (C:)**. Observe the virtual and regular folders in the Navigation (left) pane.

11. Close the window

12. Click **Start** and click **Control Panel**. Notice the new look of Control Panel.

13. Click an item in Control Panel, such as **Security**, and view the contents.

14. Close the open Window.

15. Right-click the **taskbar** and click **Properties**. What tabs do you see? Note there are two tabs not available in Windows XP: Notification Area and Toolbars.

16. Close all open windows.

Project C-2

Because the current Windows Firewall is new to Windows XP (added by Service Pack 2) and to Windows Vista (essentially the same version as used in Windows XP Service Pack 2) it is important to know how to enable the firewall and configure it. This project shows you how for both operating systems.

If your Windows XP computer has another firewall enabled, such as Norton Personal Firewall, you'll need to disable that firewall before trying this hands-on project; or if you don't have the option to disable the other firewall it is better to omit this project so you don't create a conflict.

To access and configure the Windows Firewall:

1. Click **Start** and click **Control Panel**.

2. Using the Category View, click **Network and Internet Connections** in Windows XP and click **Network Connections**. In Windows Vista Beta click **Security**.

3. In Windows XP, click **Change Windows Firewall** settings (in the Navigation pane on the left). In Windows Vista click **Windows Firewall**.

4. Ensure that **On (recommended)** is selected (on the General tab) to enable the firewall.

5. Click the **Exceptions** tab. Note some of the exceptions you can select.

6. Click the **Advanced** tab. Notice the connections that can be selected to have the firewall.

7. Click **Cancel** and close any remaining open Windows, such as the Network Connections window in Windows XP or the Control Panel Security window in Windows Vista.

Project C-3

In this project you explore the Administrative Tools in Windows Vista Beta.

To access and explore the Administrative Tools:

1. Click **Start** and click **All Programs**.

2. Click **Administrative Tools** in the Navigation pane on the left to expand the tools under this option.

3. What tools do you see?

4. Click **Computer Management**. (Note that you can also start this tool by clicking Start, right-clicking Computer, and clicking Manage.)

5. Close the Computer Management tool.

6. Click **Start** and click **All Programs**.

7. Click **Administrative Tools**.

8. Click **Performance** (you may have to click System Monitor under Diagnostic Console in the Navigation pane). You'll see the System Monitor tool in action.

9. Click the **Add** button (the plus sign). In the Add Counters dialog box, view the elements you can monitor.

10. Close the Add Counters dialog box and the Windows Diagnostic Console box if necessary.

11. Click **Start** and click **All Programs**.

12. Click **Administrative Tools**.

13. Click **Windows Event Viewer**.

14. In the Navigation pane, click **Global Logs**. Notice that you see the same logs as are offered in Windows XP: Application, Security, and System. (New logs that may be added to Vista are: DFS Replication, Media Center, and Setup.)

15. Click **Application Logs** in the Navigation pane to see the new specialized application logs that are available.

16. Close Windows Event Viewer.

D

MAC OS X TIGER

Mac OS X version 10.4 or Tiger is the latest in the Mac OS X versions named for large cats; the predecessors are Puma, Cheetah, Jaguar, and Panther. There are over 200 new features in Tiger, most of them related to the user's software experience. Tiger retains the Aqua interface with a similar look and feel of its immediate predecessor, Panther. At its root, Tiger is still built on the fast and reliable Darwin operating system—based on BSD UNIX. As with previous Mac OS X versions, you can access a terminal window and execute common UNIX commands. With Tiger, Apple has added some new terminal window commands for using features.

In recent years, dollars for development on Windows-based systems have particularly gone into security. UNIX-based systems have traditionally been more "hardened" from security problems (although they are not immune), in part because UNIX got an early start in the late 1960s and early 1970s and so has enjoyed more time to perfect the kernel for security. Because it's built on UNIX, the development of Mac OS X has focused more on new software and less on hardening for security. That's why the focus of Tiger is on software initiatives.

These initiatives are detailed in this appendix, and include the following highlights:

- *Widgets*—Tiger offers many new software features for more versatile computing. These features include a host of new programs, called widgets, for accomplishing everyday tasks such as checking spelling, creating electronic sticky notes (no more sticky notes all over the outside of your computer), and quickly finding an address of a friend.

- *Spotlight*—Spotlight is Tiger's desktop search tool for quickly finding files, e-mail, contacts, and other information on your computer. It is based on indexing and maintaining a database of "metadata" elements associated with a file, such as author, creation date, location, and many others. Apple even offers a new terminal command to use Spotlight, called *mdfind*, so you can quickly find a file while you are configuring the system or writing a program at the command line. Because Mac OS X Tiger is already available, it is ahead of Windows Vista in offering a fast search tool.

- *Desktop graphics*—Apple is also ahead of Windows Vista in offering sophisticated graphics on the desktop. Apple's graphics initiative, though, is geared more for entertainment than productivity features. If you use your computer for cinema, photos, and audio entertainment, you'll appreciate the new graphics features. Tiger is also designed so that running OpenGL graphics does not slow down other things you are doing, such as working on a document. OpenGL is a 3D capable application interface that works with most operating systems.

- *Support for application development*—Tiger is geared to the programming professional who wants to develop new software. Tiger comes with Xcode, which provides a development environment for the C, C++, Objective-C, and Java programming languages. As is true of earlier versions of Mac OS X, developers can also create shell and Perl scripts. And speaking of UNIX shells, Tiger adds the Korn shell to the shell environments used from the command line.

COMPARATIVE CHANGES

There are both major and minor new software offerings in Mac OS X Tiger, but the operating system still runs on a variety of Macintosh computers. Software new to Tiger includes (but is not limited to) the following:

- Dashboard
- Spotlight
- Folder types
- Automator
- Built-in dictionary
- Universal Access and VoiceOver

- .Mac Sync
- Xcode 2.0
- Safari enhancements
- Screensavers and desktop backgrounds
- Terminal window configuration options
- Command-line commands

In the sections that follow, you learn about the hardware requirements for Tiger and then you explore the new software offerings.

Hardware Requirements

Mac OS X Tiger runs on many kinds of Macintosh computers, but naturally, you'll have faster response and better graphics if you use a recent Macintosh system with lots of memory. For the processor, you can use a PowerPC G5, G4, or G3. In terms of RAM, you need 256 MB or more (more is better). You'll also need a CD/DVD drive and pointing device.

 When you upgrade to Mac OS X Tiger, you receive an installation DVD.

NOTE

Dashboard

Dashboard can turn your desktop into an array of software applications to meet everyday personal and business needs. Just as the dashboard in your car provides displays and controls in front of you for driving down the road, the Tiger Dashboard offers software in a dashboard-like display for driving your work or play (see Figure D-1).

Your Mac OS X Tiger Dashboard can be customized to display any combination of handy applications called widgets. For example, if you have investments, you can use the Stocks widget to monitor specific stocks and mutual funds. If there is a family member who is on a flight, you can monitor the progress of that flight to its destination through Flight Tracker. If you have an import business that requires working with suppliers in different countries, the World Clock enables you to quickly see what time it is in another country. Also, if you have a relative in another state, such as Alaska, use World Clock before placing a long-distance call so you don't get them out of bed. Table D-1 lists the Dashboard widgets with an explanation of what they do.

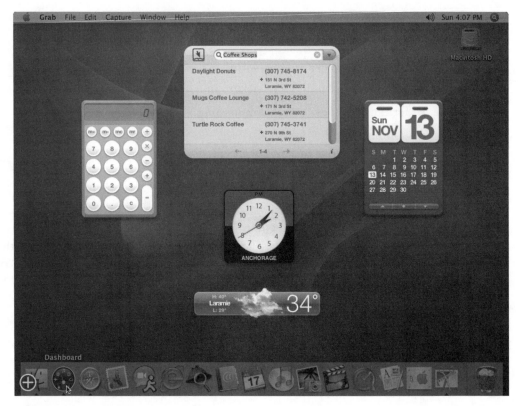

Figure D-1 Mac OS X Tiger Dashboard

Table D-1 Mac OS X Tiger Widgets

Widget	Purpose
Address Book	Stores and quickly retrieves information about contacts, such as family, personal, or business contacts
Calculator	Provides a calculator for everyday math functions, such as addition, subtraction, division, and multiplication
Calendar	Shows today's date and with one click changes to the calendar for the current month
Dictionary	Offers a desktop dictionary and thesaurus for finding definitions, synonyms, and antonyms
Flight Tracker	Displays the flight information and progress of airline flights
iTunes	Plays music from a collection of iTunes songs, with controls similar to a CD/DVD player
Phone Book	Provides the equivalent of Yellow Pages to find telephone numbers and addresses of businesses
Stickies	Sets up electronic "Post-it" notes on your screen, so you don't have to attach paper notes to your monitor or your desk
Stocks	Tracks the performance of specific stocks and stock/bond funds

Table D-1 Mac OS X Tiger Widgets (continued)

Widget	Purpose
Tile Game	Converts a photo you provide into puzzle pieces for you to put together
Translation	Takes a word or phrase in one language and provides a translation in a different language
Unit Converter	Converts common units such as weight, length, and money, from one kind of unit to another, such as feet to meters
Weather	Provides weather forecasts in the U.S. and internationally using AccuWeather as the source
World Clock	Gives the current time where you live and in other cities around the world, with daytime in white and nighttime in black

If these widgets aren't enough for your needs, you can download more from: *www.apple.com/downloads/dashboard*. At this writing there are over 1,880 widgets you can download in the following categories:

- Just Added
- Top 50
- Blogs & Forums
- Business
- Calculate and Convert
- Developer
- Email & Messaging
- Food
- Games
- Information
- International
- Movies & TV
- Music
- Networking & Security
- News
- Radio & Podcasts
- Reference
- Search
- Shopping
- Sports

- Status

- Transportation

- Travel

- Webcams

Besides Apple's Web site, you can download still more widgets from *www.widgettracker.com* and from *www.macupdate.com/dashboard.php?sub=6*. Also, you can program your own widgets in HTML, JavaScript, and CSS (cascading style sheets). Tiger's Xcode 2.0 provides tools for developing widgets. Check out *developer.apple.com/macosx/dashboard.html* for information about how to get started and for coding examples.

The commonly used ways to view Dashboard widgets in Tiger are to: (1) Click Dashboard in the Dock or (2) press F12 or Fn-F12 (for iBook or PowerBook). To clear your desktop of the Dashboard display, click anywhere in an open portion of the desktop (or click Dashboard or press F12/Fn-F12) and the widgets will disappear. Try Hands-on Project D-1 to use Dashboard.

Spotlight

Mac OS X users have always faced the same problems as Windows-based users when it comes to organizing and finding files. Nothing is more frustrating than to know you have created and saved a document, spreadsheet, song, or photo, but now you can't find it. Mac OS X Tiger offers Spotlight which does the following for you:

- Indexes files so you can find them faster

- Enables you to search for something by just typing a few letters of the name

- Quickly searches the computer's nooks and crannies for what you want, even if you're not sure how to spell it exactly

- Works in conjunction with the smart folders capability (see the next section) so you can organize files you've found according to different characteristics you choose

One reason why Spotlight is fast is that it not only indexes by file names, but by metadata associated with documents, such as the author, creation date, and lots of other information. Beyond this, it also indexes based on individual words inside a file. This includes regular text files, word processed files, and even PDF files used by Abode. But Spotlight does not work on files in the UNIX system and kernel. You have to use UNIX commands, such as *find* (see Chapter 10, Standard Operating and Maintenance Procedures and also Appendix A) or *locate*.

Spotlight is started by clicking the small blue magnifying glass to the right of the clock on the menu bar at the top of the desktop. You can enter one or more words on which to search, or even just one or two letters. As soon as you start typing Spotlight starts to display what it has found, updating the display with each letter you type. When you start typing you'll notice the speed of this tool. Figure D-2 shows a search on the word "account."

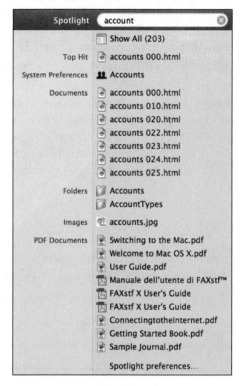

Figure D-2 A Spotlight search in Mac OS X Tiger

Hands-on Project D-2 enables you to explore the capabilities of Spotlight.

Folder Types

Folders are a handy way to organize what you want to do on a computer. Mac OS X Tiger offers three folder types that reflect the actions you want to take to organize the folder contents: regular, smart, and burn. A *regular folder* is simply the kind of folder you typically create for storing files. If you are a Mac OS X user, you have probably created lots of regular folders, which rely on your own sense of manual organization.

To help you organize your files on specific criteria—regardless of the files' locations—create smart folders. A *smart folder* is one you define on the basis of specific characteristics, such as all files created on the same date or all presentation files or all document files created by a certain person. Another use might be to organize music into smart folders that represent the type of music, such as creating different smart folders for popular, classical, and alternative music. The files in a smart folder may be physically in different regular folder locations on the hard drive or on another computer or server on the network. The files are not actually moved into a smart folder, but instead, the smart folder creates pointers to the actual locations. However, to the user, the files look and feel like they are in the smart folder. When you view it on the desktop, a smart folder appears as a folder icon with a gear inside. Smart folders work with Spotlight, because you can run a Spotlight search as you create a smart folder and then populate the folder with items the search has found—so you have those items instantly organized the next time you access them. Another option is to choose organizational criteria offered through the smart folder creation process—or you can specify your own criteria.

A *burn folder* is used to organize all of the folders and files you want to burn onto a CD or DVD. After you create the smart folder and drag other folders and files into it, you simply press a button to burn them all onto a CD or DVD. Visually, a burn folder is represented by a folder icon with a circle inside that has yellow and black pie-shaped slices, which is a radiation warning symbol. The general instructions for creating the three types of folders are presented next.

To create a regular folder:

1. Double-click Macintosh HD.

2. Navigate to the parent folder in which to place the new regular folder, such as in your account's home folder within the Users folder (e.g., /Users/mpalmer).

3. In the Finder, click File.

4. Click New Folder.

5. Type a name for the folder and press return.

To create a smart folder:

1. In the Finder, click File.

2. Click New Smart Folder.

3. In the New Smart Folder window you can specify where to look, such as Servers, Computer, Home, and Others. For example, to search on your computer (which is the default), select Computer.

4. Below the Servers, Computer, Home, and Others options, you can select the attributes for the folder's organization via four broad categories: Kind, Last Opened, Any, or Any Date (click the arrows in the appropriate box to see the organizational options within it). For example, you might click Any and select Presentations. Or click Any Date and select Within Last 2 weeks. Or use the Spotlight box in the upper-right corner for your own selection criteria.

5. After you make a selection, the files and items that match are instantly displayed through a Spotlight search.

6. Click Save to save your smart folder.

7. Enter the name of the saved smart folder in the Save As box.

8. Select where to save the smart folder, such as in your home folder or to the desktop.

9. Close any open windows.

TIP

Smart folders are a great device for backing up or archiving files. For example, you may want to save your spreadsheets every two weeks. You can create a smart folder containing all spreadsheets created within the last two weeks and then copy them to a CD (after you create the smart folder, create a burn folder and drag the contents into it to save time). Or create a smart folder of all family photos taken in the last year and save them to a CD, in case you lose a hard drive later.

To create a burn folder and write its contents to a CD:

1. Double-click Macintosh HD.

2. Navigate to the folder in which to place the new burn folder (or you can place the burn folder on the desktop and discard it later).

3. In the Finder, click File.

4. Click New Burn Folder.

5. Type the name for the burn folder and press return.

6. Find the files and folders you want to burn. Drag each into the burn folder you created.

7. Open (double-click) the burn folder.

8. Click the Burn button.

9. When asked, insert the CD or DVD into the CD/DVD drive.

10. Assign a name to the disc that reflects its contents.

11. Click the Burn button.

Automator

Computers are supposed to help users with repetitive tasks and Mac OS X Tiger offers a new tool called Automator for this purpose (see Figure D-3). For example, consider a situation in which you have 20 spreadsheets that are numbered in a specific order, such as budget01, budget02, to budget20. You've created a new spreadsheet that should be named budget07 for the proper sequence, which means you have to rename all of the old files beginning at budget07. In another situation, you are preparing documents for multiple clients and need to automate printing so the process goes faster without your intervention for each one. Tiger's Automator enables you to automate these and many other types of repetitive tasks.

To start Automator:

1. Click Go.

2. Click Applications.

3. Double-click Automator.

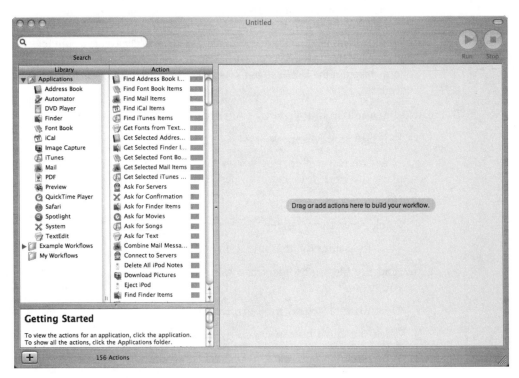

Figure D-3 Using Automator in Mac OS X Tiger

Tiger comes with a library of many types of Automator actions. Often actions can be linked to a specific application, such as using Address Book to update addresses or working with iCal for calendar activities. You can find more about Automator and download examples from the Automator Web site at *www.apple.com/macosx/features/automator*.

Built-in Dictionary

Mac OS X Tiger has a built-in dictionary you can access whenever you are in a document or are reading an e-mail and come across a word you don't know, or you want to check different meanings for that word. The steps for using the built-in dictionary are to:

1. Open the document.

2. Highlight the word.

3. Press Control-Apple key (⌘)-D

You can use the built-in dictionary in applications such as TextEdit, Mail, and others.

Universal Access and VoiceOver

Universal Access and VoiceOver offer ways to customize use of Mac OS X Tiger for better accessibility. For example, you can choose to enlarge text, have the computer read text aloud, and customize use of the keyboard and mouse.

VoiceOver is configured from the new Universal Access configuration option in System Preferences. To open the Universal Access tool:

1. Click System Preferences in the Dock; or click Go, click Applications, and double-click System Preferences.

2. Click Universal Access.

There are four panels of options that can be configured:

- *Seeing*—Turns on VoiceOver, zooms the display, and changes the white, black, and contrast elements of the display.

- *Hearing*—Flashes the screen for an alert and controls the volume level.

- *Keyboard*—Sets up keyboard characteristics such as sticky keys and slow keys.

- *Mouse*—Turns on or off the mouse keys, controls the movement of the mouse, and configures the cursor size.

.Mac Sync

.Mac Sync enables you to synchronize preferred settings in applications, preferences for multiple accounts and Mac computers, and data. For users of applications such as Mail and Safari, you can set up the system to synchronize settings. For networks containing multiple Macs, the settings on all of the computers can be synchronized—a concept similar to using group policy on Windows-based computers (see Appendix C). You can specify to synchronize the computers each hour, once a day, or once a week.

You can purchase a .Mac account membership through Apple, which lets you publish information via the Internet, such as mail account information or a calendar, so that associates or family members can access the information. If one person edits the information, the changes are automatically synchronized for all. To establish an account and manage .Mac Sync, click System Preferences in the Dock and double-click .Mac under Internet and Network. Click the Sync button and select the elements you want to synchronize, which include the following:

- Bookmarks
- Calendars
- Contacts
- Keychains

- Mail Accounts
- Mail Rules, Signatures, and Smart Mailboxes

After you make your selections, click Sync Now to start the synchronization process.

Xcode 2.0

For programmers, Xcode 2.0 offers a comprehensive application development environment for Mac OS X Tiger applications. Xcode 2.0 uses the UNIX/Linux GNU Compiler Collection (GCC) 4.0 compiler software for compiling C and C++ programs. A compiler is a program that reads lines of program code in a source file and coverts that code into machine language instructions so the code can be executed. By using GCC 4.0, when you develop programs in Xcode 2.0 you also have the ability to port C and C++ code to other UNIX/Linux operating systems.

NOTE Xcode 2.2 is available as of this writing. Go to Apple's Web site at *www.apple. com* to obtain the installation package. Also, if you want to use Xcode 2.0 and it has not been loaded from your Mac OS X Tiger Install DVD, you can install it by loading the DVD, displaying the files on the DVD, finding Developer.mpkg, and double-clicking Developer.mpkg.

Besides the GCC 4.0 compiler, Xcode 2.0 offers a multi-window tool from which to build application projects. From this window the developer can track code versions so there is no confusion over what versions exist and which version is the latest. As the lines of code grow and it becomes harder to see the bigger picture, the developer can construct GUI views consisting of overall models of the code, so the large-scale coding architecture is consistent and efficient.

To spot program code problems (or strengths) the Xcode 2.0 environment includes a sophisticated GUI debugger. Developers can set breakpoints so the code stops at specific places. Watchpoints can also be set to watch what happens when the values of program variables change. Further, Xcode 2.0 has a remote debugging capability so problems in the code can be determined from a different computer than the one used to run the code.

Other tools included with Xcode 2.0 include PackageMaker that enables the developer to package the code into a format that can be installed on the user's computer. There is also Icon Composer for designing new icons (icon files) by using properties of icons that already exist. After Xcode 2.0 is loaded look in /Developer/Documentation for documentation about the Xcode 2.0 tools.

Safari Enhancements

Safari is the default Web browser designed by Apple for Mac OS X. Safari is built as a Cocoa object-oriented application, which gives it complete compatibility with the Mac OS X Tiger Aqua desktop interface. Cocoa is one of the tools included in the Xcode 2.0 toolset. You can start Safari from the Dock by double-clicking the icon that looks like a compass.

Mac OS X Tiger also comes with Microsoft Internet Explorer and can support other Web browsers, such as Mozilla Firefox and Netscape Browser 8.0.

NOTE

Safari isn't new to Mac OS X operating systems, but Safari has a new *Really Simple Syndication (RSS)* feature for news feed and blog enthusiasts. When there is an RSS feed available from a Web site, a blue RSS icon appears on the address bar in Safari (see Figure D-4). Click the icon to see a list of articles via the RSS feed.

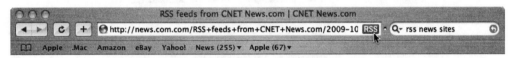

Figure D-4   Using Safari with the RSS icon in Mac OS X Tiger

RSS is a set of XML conventions for enabling Web feeds or syndication of articles through news sites and Web blog sites. Many of the feeds are from "weblog" sites that offer options such as podcasting (audio and video programs), vodcasting (video on demand), broadcatching (media file sharing), and others.

Beyond the RSS feature, Safari 2.0 in Mac OS X Tiger runs faster than other Web browsers on this operating system. It also runs faster than Safari 1.2 which is packaged with Mac OS X Panther. Of course the actual speed you'll experience is related to the speed of your Mac and Internet connection.

Try Hands-on Project D-3 to use the RSS feature in Safari.

Screen Savers and Desktop Backgrounds

UNIX/Linux-based systems have always sported a large variety of screen savers and desktop backgrounds. Consistent with the UNIX/Linux tradition, Mac OS X Tiger offers many new screen savers and desktop backgrounds. You can select these from the System Preferences option, Desktop & Screen Saver. Desktop backgrounds are stored in a series of folders as shown on the left pane in Figure D-5. When you click the Screen Saver button on the screen in Figure D-5 you see other options for screen saver pictures. Besides the ones shown, you can add your own.

Hands-on Project D-4 enables you to configure the desktop background.

Figure D-5 Desktop background configuration options in Mac OS X Tiger

Terminal Window Configuration Options

If you plan to use the terminal window to access the UNIX command-line features of your computer, consider customizing the terminal window display to meet your needs. The following characteristics of the display can be configured:

- *Shell*—Default shell
- *Processes*—Default processes and prompting for an open process before closing the window
- *Emulation*—Characteristics of the terminal emulation mode, such as escape characters, line wrap features, and audible and visual bells
- *Buffer*—Buffer size and scrollback (scrolling the screen presentation) characteristics
- *Display*—Cursor style, text style, and character set
- *Color*—Background and foreground colors and use of transparency
- *Window*—Window dimensions and title
- *Keyboard*—Key mappings

For example, you might prefer to have a terminal window in which the background is purple with the text shown in white. Or, if you use long command lines that frequently wrap around, you can increase the size of the terminal window for easier viewing. To remind you which shell you are using, you can have the title of the terminal window include the name of the shell. Another option is to change the title of the terminal window to your company's name, such as "McGregor Consulting" instead of "Terminal."

Here are the steps to use for accessing the terminal configuration options:

1. Click Go.
2. Click Utilities.
3. Double-click Terminal.
4. On the Terminal menu bar at the top of the screen, click File.
5. Click Show Info.
6. Click the up/down arrows in the box near the top of the window.
7. Select the characteristic you want to configure, such as Display.
8. Close the Terminal Inspector window when you are finished configuring the Terminal characteristics.

New Command-Line Commands

Mac OS X Tiger adds several new commands you can use in the terminal window's command line: *open*, *defaults*, *mdfind*, *mdimport*, and *mdls*.

The *open* command is used to start an application from the command line. For example, consider the file research.txt that is normally edited by using the TextEdit program in Mac OS X Tiger. You can open research.txt into the TextEdit GUI text editor application by entering the following command:

> *open research.txt*

If you are not sure that a text file is already associated with TextEdit, use the *-e* option with the *open* command to ensure TextEdit is used to edit the file:

> *open -e work.txt*

To specify an application to start, enter the *open* command, the *-a* option, and the name of the application:

> *open -a application*

You can learn more about the *open* command and its options by entering *man open* at the command line. Type *q* to return to the command prompt display when you are finished reading the documentation.

The *defaults* command is used to configure system preferences information from the command line by accessing the database of information used to manage the system preferences in Mac OS X Tiger. To learn more about this command, enter *man defaults*.

Use *defaults* with great care so that you don't make unanticipated changes. This command requires some research before you start, so not only should you understand the command, but also the nature of the system preferences information.

Three other new commands make use of metadata associated with Spotlight. These commands are: *mdfind*, *mdimport*, and *mdls*.

mdfind enables you to query the "metadata store" (the storehouse of metadata available to Spotlight) so you can find specific files—similar to using Spotlight, but in the command line. For example, you might be interested in finding the file, flower.jpg, because you are looking for a flower picture for a Web site. When you enter the command, *mdfind flower*, you'll see a listing of elements related to flower, including the full paths to flower.jpg (/Applications/ AppleWorks 6/Clippings/Photos/flower.jpg), and flower and butterfly (/Applications/ AppleWorks 6/Clippings/Plants/flower and butterfly) and several other query listings with paths. Enter *man mdfind* at the command line to learn more about how to use the *mdfind* command.

The *mdimport* command is used to import metadata from a file, folder, or disk into the metadata store on your computer. For example, you might obtain a folder from a colleague and copy it to your hard drive. You can use the *mdimport* command to import metadata elements from that folder. Use *man mdimport* to find out more about this command.

mdls enables you to view the metadata elements for a file. For example, prior to using the *mdimport* command, you can use *mdls* on a file to view its metadata elements. Or, if you want to view the metadata elements to use for an *mdfind* query, you might use *mdls*. For example, if you have a file called studynotes.txt in the Documents folder under your home directory, you can view its metadata elements by using the command:

> *mdls /Users/myfolder/Documents/studynotes.txt*

To learn more about *mdls*, enter *man mdls* at the command line.

UPGRADING TO MAC OS X TIGER

You can purchase the upgrade kit for Mac OS X Tiger from a software store or directly from Apple (*www.apple.com*). The upgrade kit contains the Mac OS X Tiger Install DVD. When you are ready to perform the installation, follow these steps:

Back up your important files before you upgrade. Also, consider upgrading at a time when you do not have important work that needs to be done immediately, in case there is a problem with the upgrade. For example, once in a while a vendor inadvertently sends a damaged DVD or CD and you may have to wait until you receive a replacement. This can happen with any operating system upgrade.

1. Start your current version of Mac OS.

2. Insert the Mac OS X Tiger Install DVD.

3. In the Mac OS X Install DVD window, double-click the Install Mac OS X icon (see Figure D-6).

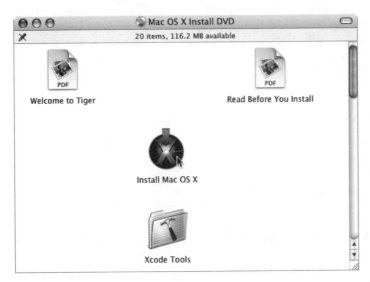

Figure D-6   Starting the Mac OS X installation

4. In the Install Mac OS X window, click the Restart button.

5. You may see a window asking you to provide the username and password for an Admin account. Enter the username (or use the default name provided) and the password and click OK.

6. Mac OS X will reboot.

7. Select the language you want to use, such as by clicking, Use English as the main language.

8. Click the right-pointing arrow in the bottom of the window.

9. On the Welcome to the Mac OS X Installer window you'll see the stages of the installation listed in the left pane of the window. These include:

    - Introduction
    - License
    - Select Destination
    - Installation Type
    - Install
    - Finish Up

10. Click Continue.

11. Read the Software License Agreement for Mac OS X and click Continue.

12. Click Agree to show you agree to the terms of the license.

13. Select the destination volume for the operating system, such as Macintosh HD (which is followed by the size of the volume, for example 55.9GB and the free space, for instance 50.1GB). The installation of the software requires 2.5 GB of disk space. When upgrading to Tiger on a volume with a previous version of Mac OS X, you'll see a statement that says, "You have selected to upgrade Mac OS X on this volume."

14. Click Continue.

15. Click Upgrade to perform a basic installation of Tiger.

16. A bar shows the progress while the system checks the installation DVD (do not skip this step) to ensure it is fully usable. If a problem is found, click Cancel, click Restart, eject the DVD, examine it for smudges or scratches, clean it, and start over at Step 7. (If the problem persists—unlikely, but possible—you'll need to contact Apple's customer support to obtain a new DVD. Do not go ahead with the installation because it is likely the installation will fail and you won't be able to use your computer until you obtain a new installation DVD.)

TIP   If you have trouble removing the DVD on a computer that does not have an external button to open the CD/DVD drive, try turning the computer off. Turn it on and immediately press the keyboard key to open the drive (keep pressing the key until the drive opens). Quickly remove the DVD before the drive automatically closes. Note that when the computer tries to reboot, you may go into a UNIX screen in panic mode. Don't panic, though, just turn off the computer (your old files are still there). When you get the replacement DVD, use this tip to open the CD/DVD drive and insert the DVD. Wait for the screen in Step 7 and go on with the upgrade.

17. The install process prepares the hard disk and continues to install files. At the end of this process you'll see a notice that the software was successfully installed.

18. Click Restart.

19. After the system reboots, you're done. Remove the Mac OS X Install DVD.

20. The Mac OS X Setup Assistant starts automatically.

21. If you have an Apple ID and password enter it now and click Continue. If you don't have an Apple ID, leave that information blank and click Continue.

22. If you see the Registration Information screen, update the information or complete the information if it is not automatically displayed. Click Continue.

23. Answer the information screen that asks where you will use the computer and what you do. Click Continue.

24. Click Continue on the Now You're Ready to Connect window. If you are not connected to the Internet you can send this information later.

25. If you are connected to the Internet, you can select different options to have a .Mac membership for access to special features on the Apple Web site, including .Mac Sync. There is a fee for the membership. There is also an option (No, thanks) to not enroll in a membership. Make your selection and click Continue.

26. Click Go on the Thank You window. You're done and ready to use the computer.

HANDS-ON PROJECTS

These Hands-on Projects enable you to learn about Mac OS X Tiger. You'll need an account to complete the projects. Use a personal account or one assigned by your instructor. Also, for Hands-on Project D-3, you need access to the Internet through your account.

HANDS-ON PROJECTS

Project D-1

This project enables you to learn about Dashboard in Mac OS X Tiger.

To use Dashboard:

1. Click the **Dashboard** icon in the Dock. (If there is no icon press F12 or Fn-F12 if you are using a laptop.)

2. What widgets are displayed?

3. Click the **plus sign** superimposed on the Dock on the left side.

4. Notice that the widgets you can place on the Dashboard are displayed under the Dock at the bottom of the screen.

5. Click the **arrow** at the right of the last widget displayed to see more widgets. Now click the **arrow** on the left side to see the first set of widgets.

6. Click **Dictionary** and notice that this widget is now shown on the Dashboard.

7. Notice that you can click Dictionary to look up a word or click Thesaurus to find a synonym.

8. Leave Dictionary as the default selection and enter the word **excellent** to see its definition.

9. Click **Thesaurus**. What are some words (or synonyms) you could use instead of excellent? What are two words that mean the opposite of excellent (antonyms)?

10. Click the **x** in the circle in the upper left of the Dictionary widget to close it.

11. Click the **Stickies** widget at the bottom of the screen.

12. Type **Meeting at 2 pm in room B15**, to practice posting a note.

13. Drag the sticky note to the upper right portion of the Dashboard.

14. Ensure that the World Clock is already on the Dashboard, and if not, click it at the bottom of the screen.

15. Move the cursor inside the World Clock. Notice that an i appears in the bottom right corner. Click the **i**.

16. In the Continent box, select **Pacific**.

17. In the City box, choose **Honolulu**.

18. Click **Done** and notice the time is now displayed for Honolulu.

19. Reconfigure the World Clock to show the time in your area.

20. Click the **X sign** in the Dock to clear the bottom of the screen of the widgets options.

21. Click the **Dashboard** icon (or press **F12** or **Fn-F12**) to close the Dashboard.

22. Click the **Dashboard** icon again (or press **F12** or **Fn-F12**). Notice the changes you made previously are still intact.

23. Close the Dashboard.

HANDS-ON PROJECTS

Project D-2

In this project, you try out the new Spotlight feature in Mac OS X Tiger.

To use Spotlight:

1. Click the **small magnifying glass** on the right side in the menu bar at the top of the desktop.

2. Type a **d**. Notice that Spotlight starts an instant search.

3. Slowly type the remaining letters, **ashboard** to see how Spotlight changes its display.

4. To the right of the Applications category, click **Dashboard**. Notice that Dashboard opens. Close Dashboard.

5. Open **Spotlight** again by clicking the magnifying glass.

6. If dashboard is still in the entry box, delete the word.

7. Type **itunes**. The item to the right of Top Hit is Spotlight's best guess about which item is most likely the one you want.

8. How many listings are there for itunes (see the number for Show All at the top of the window)? Notice that not all of the items are listed in the window.

9. Click **Show All (#)**. (The # represents the number of listings, which may vary from computer to computer, depending on the specific files on a computer.) Now you see a larger window with all of the listings.

10. What are the categories of listings for itunes (shown in the left column)? In the right pane notice that the categories are those represented by "kind" which is the selection under Group by, which is highlighted by default. Click **Date** under Group by to see how the categories change.

11. Close the Spotlight window.

12. Click the magnifying glass again. Type **jpg**.

13. Click one of the images listed (with a .jpg extension), such as **canyon.jpg**. Notice that the Preview application opens to show a .jpg picture.

14. Click **Preview** in the menu bar and click **Quit Preview**.

15. Open **Spotlight** one more time. Leave jpg as the default entry, or type **jpg** if the box is blank.

16. Click **Spotlight Preferences** at the bottom of the window. You can use this window to specify the order of categories and keyboard shortcuts for Spotlight.

17. Close the Spotlight window.

HANDS-ON PROJECTS

Project D-3

This project enables you to quickly explore the RSS feature in Safari. You'll need access to the Internet to complete the project.

To use the RSS feature in Safari:

1. Click the **Safari** icon in the Dock.

2. In the address bar enter, **news.com.com/RSS+feeds+from+CNET+News.com/2009-1090_3-980549.html** (or if you want to read Apple-related feeds go to **www.apple.com/startpage**).

3. Click the **blue RSS icon** in the address bar.

4. Notice the list of articles you can select to read. Also, notice that the address bar now shows "feed" instead of "http."

5. Select an article to read.

6. When you are finished reading, click the white back arrow in the amber-colored circle in the address bar.

7. Click the **blue RSS icon** in the address bar once again.

8. To hide the list, click **RSS** (now in blue letters) in the address bar.

9. Close Safari.

D

Another interesting RSS site is *www.nytimes.com*.

Project D-4

For this project you configure a desktop background in Mac OS X Tiger.

To configure the desktop background:

1. Click the **System Preferences** icon in the Dock; or click **Go**, click **Applications**, and double-click **System Preferences**.

2. Click **Desktop & Screen Saver**.

3. Notice the folders that contain pictures (or you can put in your own pictures via the Pictures Folder). Also, notice that you can select to change the background at a regular interval, such as every 30 minutes, and when you choose this option you can display the pictures in random order.

4. Click the **Nature** folder.

5. Click a picture.

6. Click the **Screen Saver** button and notice the options for screen savers. Also, notice you can select how long to wait until the screen saver starts, and you can set up hot corners.

7. Click a folder of screen savers, such as **Forest** and watch while several different pictures are shown every few seconds.

8. Close the Desktop & Screen Saver window.

9. Close the Applications window, if you opened it.

E

SUSE LINUX

SUSE Linux is a popular alternative to Red Hat Enterprise Linux and Fedora, particularly in Europe and more recently in North America. SUSE Linux is based on the standard Linux kernel, and can be run on 32-bit and 64-bit computers, as well as some mainframes. There are over 4,000 software packages available for SUSE Linux. Because it is well accepted in the Linux world, Novell purchased SUSE Linux in 2004 and has incorporated it with the NetWare operating system to provide Novell Open Enterprise Server. Novell Open Enterprise Server combines the traditional NetWare approach with the open systems approach used by UNIX and Linux development organizations, with the goal of broader appeal.

Novell also offers Novell Linux Desktop, which is a commercial version of SUSE Linux that works well with Novell Open Enterprise Server, so that Novell server clients can have Linux coupled with open systems software, such as OpenOffice.org. OpenOffice.org is a suite of office software that is available as open-source software. Open-source means that software is created as a collaborative project through one or more developers, and the source code is in the public domain at no charge. You can learn more about open-source on the Web site: *www.opensource.org/docs/definition.php*. OpenOffice.org offers word processing, spreadsheet, presentation, drawing, database, and other software. You can also purchase a commercial version from Novell called the Novell edition of OpenOffice.org, which offers additional features such as enhanced file conversion utilities for compatibility with Microsoft Office.

To learn more about the free version of OpenOffice.org, go to *www.openoffice. org*. To learn about the Novell edition of OpenOffice.org, visit *www.novell.com/products/desktop/features/ooo.html*.

TIP

You can obtain a free version of SUSE Linux from the Novell-sponsored openSUSE project. Novell calls its version SUSE Linux Personal (SUSE Linux 10.0 at this writing). Novell began the openSUSE project in August 2005 with a similar goal to the Fedora project sponsored by Red Hat—to make versions freely available to the public to promote greater use of Linux and for feedback on development initiatives. SUSE Linux Personal works well on the desktop in any environment, including in an office or organization. To learn more about the openSUSE project go to *www.openSUSE.org*.

SUSE Linux Features

SUSE Linux offers many features that are appealing to server and desktop users. Among these features are the following:

- Linux kernel
- Xen
- X Window interface with the GNOME and KDE desktops
- YaST
- Terminal window for commands
- Firefox Web browser
- OpenOffice.org software suite
- Apache Web server software
- Voice over IP (VoIP)
- Wireless capabilities
- Security features
- Development tools

Each of these features is discussed in the next sections.

Linux Kernel

In Chapter 1, Operating System Theory, you learned about the operating system kernel. At this writing, SUSE Linux contains the version 2.6 Linux kernel, which is the same kernel used by the following sampling of mainstream Linux distributions (those listed without parentheses are commonly used in North America and Europe):

- Best Linux (Sweden and Finland)
- Caldera OpenLinux
- Conectiva (Brazil)
- Debian
- EASYLinux-kr (Korea)
- eIT easyLinux
- Esware Linux (Spanish-speaking countries)
- eXecutive Linux (France)
- Fedora
- KSI-Linux (Russia)
- Linux Antarctica
- Linux Kheops (France)
- Linux by LibraNet
- Linux Edu PingOO (France)
- Linux MX (Mexico)
- Linux YeS (Russia)
- Mandrake
- MNIS (France)
- PHT TurboLinux
- Project Independence
- Red Hat Enterprise Linux
- Redmond Linux
- Skygate Technology EasyLinux
- Slackware
- Stampede
- SUSE Linux
- Turkuaz (Turkey)

E

- Xi Graphics mXimum cde/OS

- XTeam Linux (China)

Some of the new features in the Linux 2.6 kernel include:

- Can be scaled to 16 CPUs and higher

- Ability to handle hundreds of thousands of threads

- More advanced USB support for external devices

- Better support for high-bandwidth networking

- Improved asynchronous I/O

- Support for more types of CPUs and other hardware

- Supports up to four billion users and groups

- Supports up to 4095 device types

- Supports more types of modern storage devices

- Better "responsiveness"

At this writing the most recent release is Linux Kernel 2.6.14.

Xen

SUSE Linux 10.0 incorporates the Xen virtual machine monitor. A virtual machine (VM) is software that makes it appear as though several operating systems are running at the same time. For example, the virtual DOS machine is the technology that has enabled old-time DOS users to continue to run DOS programs in modern Windows-based operating systems.

Xen is a relatively new approach used in UNIX/Linux systems and enables you to run multiple operating systems, or multiple instances of the same operating system, on one computer. Xen is designed to accomplish this without degrading the performance of the computer. This capability can be important on computers that have multiple CPUs that need to be managed, such as a server that has four CPUs. It is also useful for running different operating systems on the same computer, for example SUSE 10.0 Linux and a Windows operating system.

SUSE 10.0 offers Xen 3. You can learn more about Xen, including the latest versions, by visiting the Web page *www.cl.cam.ac.uk/Research/SRG/netos/ xen/index.html*.

X Window Interface

As you learned in Chapter 2, UNIX/Linux systems enable the popular X Window interface for a GUI presentation that uses a pointing device. X Window enables the use of windows, dialog boxes, pull-down menus, and more. Currently, X Window is in the 11th version called X11. SUSE Linux uses XFree86, a free version of X11 for PCs.

NOTE

Besides SUSE Linux, XFree86 is used in Red Hat Enterprise Linux, Fedora, and in many BSD UNIX distributions, including Darwin (for Mac OS X). The advantage of using XFree86 is that you can port GUI applications from one UNIX or Linux distribution to another. To learn more about X Window and XFree86 visit the Web sites, *wiki.x.org/wiki* and *www.xfree86.org*.

The advantage of X Window is that you can use a desktop with a specific GUI appearance that provides a workspace for windows, icons, and other elements. SUSE Linux (as well as Red Hat Enterprise Linux and Fedora) comes with two desktop environments from which to choose, GNOME and KDE.

The GNU Network Object Model Environment (GNOME) is provided through the GNU Project (*www.gnu.org*), which is open source. If you choose to use it, you'll most likely find GNOME is very user friendly. Another advantage of GNOME is that there are many applications written for it, such as file-access applications, office suites, and utilities. The GNOME desktop has been particularly popular in North America, including the United States and Canada. Figure E-1 shows the GNOME desktop in SUSE Linux 10.0.

Figure E-1   GNOME desktop in SUSE Linux 10.0

KDE is also a popular desktop, especially outside of North America, but it has strong proponents all over the world. KDE is user friendly and offers more drag-and-drop capabilities than GNOME. Much UNIX/Linux software is also written for KDE. You can learn more about KDE at *www.kde.org*.

One difference between SUSE Linux 10.0 and Red Hat Enterprise Linux/Fedora is the selection of the desktop when you install the operating system. SUSE Linux 10.0 forces you to choose between GNOME and KDE during the installation. Red Hat Enterprise Linux and Fedora enable you to install one of these desktops, but also to include software, applications, and some features of the other desktop.

Because the GNOME desktop is already used in the examples for Red Hat Enterprise Linux and Fedora provided in this book, let's spend a few minutes examining the GNOME desktop in SUSE Linux 10.0. The first thing you'll notice in Figure E-1 is that there is a Panel at the top of the screen and there are new menu buttons (see Figure E-2) in this Panel. This is actually a characteristic of changes made to the newest version of GNOME (version 2.12.0 at this writing) since the previous edition of this book was written. There is also a Panel at the bottom of the screen (Figure E-3).

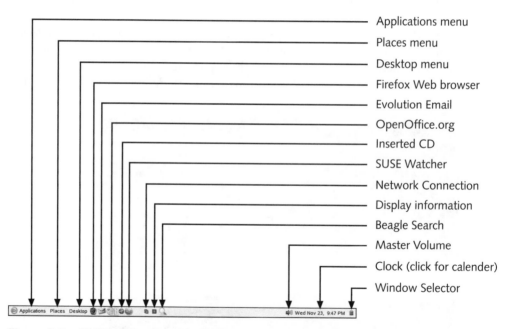

Applications menu
Places menu
Desktop menu
Firefox Web browser
Evolution Email
OpenOffice.org
Inserted CD
SUSE Watcher
Network Connection
Display information
Beagle Search
Master Volume
Clock (click for calender)
Window Selector

Figure E-2   GNOME top Panel in SUSE Linux 10.0

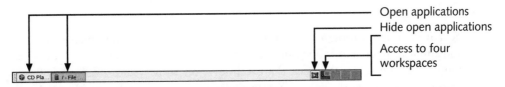

Figure E-3 GNOME bottom Panel in SUSE Linux 10.0

TIP If you prefer having a Panel at the bottom or on one side of the screen, you can drag it there. To change the location of a Panel, right click it, and click Allow Panel to be Moved. Then drag the Panel to the new location you prefer. Right-click the Panel again and click Lock Panel Position.

The new menu selections in the top Panel are:

- *Applications*—includes games, graphics, Internet, multimedia, Office (OpenOffice. org), System, Utilities, and SUSE Help Center applications, plus the Run Application option that enables you to run an application from the command line.

- *Places*—displays the File Browser for your home folder, the desktop, the computer, the floppy drive (if connected), the CD drive (if connected), plus options to connect to servers on your network, to search for specific files, and to view recently opened documents.

- *Desktop*—offers miscellaneous options including the GNOME Control Center to manage the desktop preferences, YaST (described in the next section), screen capture software, SUSE Help Center, information about the GNOME desktop, and options to lock the screen for security when you leave your desk, and to log out.

In addition to the menu buttons there are icons on the top Panel for Firefox Web Browser, Evolution Email, OpenOffice.org Writer, SUSE Watcher (part of YaST to track system updates), network status information, Display information (for the screen resolution configuration), Beagle Search, and others depending on how you have configured your system. The right side of the Panel contains a sound control icon, the clock (including the date), and an icon to select any of the open windows on the desktop.

On the desktop below the top Panel there are icons similar to those you have seen in Red Hat Enterprise Linux for Computer (to access files), for access to your home directory, and for Trash (to delete files). You may also see icons to access the contents of the floppy or CD drive.

At the bottom of the screen there is another Panel that contains buttons for your open applications (similar to the taskbar in Windows), a button to clear the desktop, and buttons to use any of four desktop workspaces. In GNOME you can have up to four desktop workspaces at the same time, so that when you have applications filling one desktop you can open another desktop workspace that is not cluttered. This is like having four desks in your office. When one desk is cluttered, you can move to another desk that is clean or at least less cluttered (until you run out of desks).

Try Hands-on Project E-1 to explore the GNOME desktop in SUSE Linux 10.0.

YaST

Yet Another Setup Tool (YaST) is used to install applications and to manage operating system and application elements on your computer. With YaST, you can check for updates to SUSE Linux over the Internet, check the patch level on your system (SUSE Watcher), configure hardware and network devices, set up network services, configure Novell AppArmor, and configure security, a firewall, and user accounts. Figure E-4 shows the YaST window.

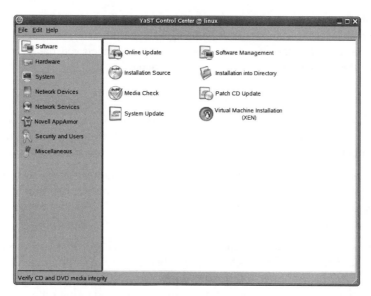

Figure E-4   Using YaST in SUSE Linux 10.0

Novell AppArmor is a security system for the SUSE Linux operating system and the applications that run on it. AppArmor protects against viruses and other malicious attacks and is important for security on both server and client systems. You can find out more about AppArmor at *www.novell.com/products/apparmor/overview.html*.

In Hands-on Project E-2 you open and use YaST.

Terminal Window

SUSE Linux 10.0 offers a terminal window that enables you to use the same Linux commands you have learned throughout this book and that are listed in Appendix A. In fact, once you open it, you'll notice the GNOME terminal window looks nearly identical to the one in Red Hat Enterprise Linux and Fedora. Most importantly, because Linux distributions are based on the same Linux kernel (although the versions might be different) you can use virtually the same commands. For example, the *ls* and *mkdir* commands you learned in Chapter 3 work the same way in the GNOME terminal window in SUSE Linux 10.0. The same is true of the *useradd*, *groupadd*, and *chmod* commands you learned in Chapter 9. Figure E-5 shows the GNOME terminal window in SUSE Linux 10.0.

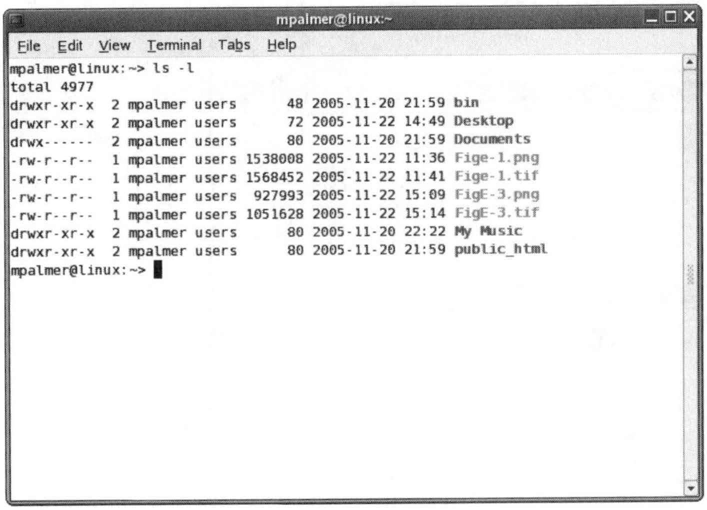

Figure E-5   GNOME terminal window in SUSE Linux 10.0

Besides the basic GNOME terminal window, SUSE Linux 10.0 offers three other choices for executing commands:

- *Konsole*—KDE's terminal editor with shell information.

- *Terminal Program – Super User Mode*—a great tool for employing root privileges (you need to log in using the root password) from any computer, which comes with features such as the ability to set bookmarks and a session menu to manage all kinds of functions, including the shell.

- *X Terminal*—enables you to run commands on one computer from another, similar to telneting into a computer, as in a client and server environment.

Try Hands-on Project E-3 to use the GNOME terminal window in SUSE Linux 10.0.

Firefox Web Browser

Firefox Web Browser has already made its mark among Web enthusiasts, garnering many positive reviews. SUSE Linux 10.0 and modern versions of Red Hat Enterprise Linux and Fedora use Firefox. This browser is basically a slimmed down and more efficient version of the Mozilla browser. Mozilla project is an open-source undertaking to help advance use of the Internet. Figure E-6 shows Firefox in SUSE Linux 10.0.

Features of Firefox include:

- Does not load ActiveX controls—a security feature to protect against malicious software

- Contains privacy tools to secure online activity

- Has built-in popup blocking

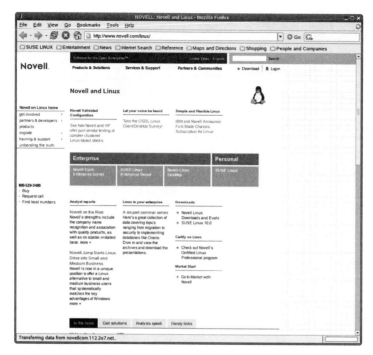

Figure E-6   Firefox Web Browser in SUSE Linux 10.0

- Enables multiple Web pages in one window through tab browsing
- Has an RSS feature for viewing RSS feeds
- Can be customized in many ways to fit a user's preferences
- Downloads quickly because the code base is slimmed down
- Includes developer tools, such as JavaScript

Because it's relatively new, Firefox is not without problems. For example there are some users who have encountered bugs in the software. Also, some users have reported problems created by the extra security in this browser, such as problems viewing certain popups they need to see or problems with certain RSS feeds. You can find out more about features and known issues for your version of Firefox at *www.mozilla.com/firefox/releases*.

TIP   In addition to Firefox, SUSE Linux 10.0 with the GNOME desktop comes with two RSS readers for feeds: Blam Feed Reader and Liferea Feed Reader. To access these, click Applications, point to Internet, point to RSS Reader, and select the reader you want to use.

Firefox is also available for Windows-based systems. Some users prefer it for the strong security features to foil spyware and malicious software. The tab browsing feature is another option popular with users. Plan to give it a try in SUSE Linux 10.0 or in new versions of Red Hat Enterprise Linux or Fedora to see what you think.

SUSE Linux 10.0 enables you to use three other Web browsers: Epiphany Web Browser, Konqueror, and the full version of Mozilla. To access any of these click Applications, point to Internet, point to Web Browser, and make your selection.

OpenOffice.org Software Suite

OpenOffice.org is a suite of office productivity software with applications similar to those in Microsoft Office. An important difference is that OpenOffice.org is open source, which means it's free to the user—and any user can join the project to work on new features. Users can download the latest versions from *www.openoffice.org*. They can also make copies and give them to others at no charge.

The suite of applications in OpenOffice.org is developed by hundreds of project members all over the world. Members of the OpenOffice.org project contribute in all kinds of ways from making code more efficient, to adding new features, to creating patches, to marketing the end product. As a grassroots project, this office suite is continuously evolving through the efforts of users to meet the needs of users.

SUSE Linux 10.0 comes with the Novell edition of OpenOffice.org. The Novell edition adds more capabilities for compatible file formatting—including fonts—with Microsoft Office products, so it is easier to port files back and forth. The Novell edition of OpenOffice.org includes the following elements:

- *Writer*—a complete word processor for writing short or book-length documents. Writer comes with style and formatting options and has unique features, such as AutoComplete to suggest how to complete words or phrases, AutoCorrect to catch spelling mistakes, and AutoFormat to format a document as you progress. It also comes with wizards to help format typical documents such as meeting minutes, letters, faxes, and others. Text created in Writer can be converted to HTML for use on the Web or to Microsoft Word for sharing with Microsoft Word users.

- *Calc*—a spreadsheet program for managing numbers and data. Calc enables the user to create formulas using "natural language," which is based on using familiar words instead of math formulas for calculations and statistics. Similar to Writer, Calc offers wizards to help with common actions. And similar to other spreadsheets, calc enables "what if" projections on data. Figure E-7 shows the Calc program.

SUSE Linux 10.0 also comes with Gnumeric Spreadsheet, which is part of the GNOME desktop project and is an alternative to Calc. Visit *www.gnome.org/projects/gnumeric* for more information about Gnumeric.

Figure E-7 Calc program in the Novell edition of OpenOffice.org

- *Impress*—a program for creating presentations including slide shows, drawings, outlines, handouts, and others. Impress comes with diagramming tools, animation capabilities, and 3D effects. You can convert Impress slides into Microsoft Power-Point format for users who do not have Impress for viewing slide presentations.

- *Draw*—a drawing package for creating graphics and diagrams. You might use draw to create a new icon, a drawing for a paper, an organizational chart, or a network diagram. Draw also supports 3D graphics and multiple formatting techniques. You can group individual elements into one object for easier arrangement and duplication.

- *Math*—a mathematical equation tool. Math can be used to set up and solve mathematical equations. You can use it as a standalone tool or from inside Writer, Calc, or Impress to set up and solve a math problem.

- *Base*—a tool for creating and maintaining databases. Base enables you to set up tables, indexes, queries, reports, and other functions typically available in robust database software. Wizards and SQL views can be used to help simplify work in Base. You can export Base data to Calc or vice versa.

In Hands-on Project E-4 you have an opportunity to use Impress to create and run a slide show.

Apache Web Server Software

Apache Web Server is the result of the open-source Apache Software Foundation project to provide Web server services. At this writing, over 70 percent of HTTP Web servers on the Internet are Apache Web Servers. Apache Web Server works on UNIX, Linux, NetWare, and Windows operating systems, but is particularly prevalent on UNIX/Linux and NetWare systems.

Apache Web Server is available in SUSE Linux 10.0 as well as in Red Hat Enterprise Linux and Fedora. Apache Web Server is a powerful Web server system that has many popular Web development language interfaces, such as Perl and others. It also provides security options, including logs of activity. Other features include:

- Handles thousands of simultaneous connections
- Support for multiple protocols, including IP version 6
- UNIX threading so systems can be scaled upward
- Filtering for better handling of scripts
- Shared object support to reduce memory use
- Organization of source code to make it easier for users to add their own modules

Voice over IP

Voice over IP (VoIP) is a technology that enables telephony connections over an IP network, such as a local area network or the Internet. VoIP offers the ability to place a local or long distance call for no cost other than the cost of your computer and Internet connection. Organizations are adopting VoIP as a way to cut their communications costs.

SUSE Linux 10.0 has built-in support for VoIP. Two commonly used VoIP telephone software applications are Linphone (with the GNOME desktop) and KPhone (with the KDE desktop). For example, to use Linphone from the GNOME desktop in SUSE Linux 10.0, click Applications, point to Internet, point to Telephone, and click Linphone.

Wireless Capabilities

SUSE Linux 10.0 supports 802.11a/b/g connectivity (often called WiFi) as well as Bluetooth. 802.11/a/b/g (the latest devices use 802.11g) is used to provide network connectivity, such as in a home, small office, or larger organization. Bluetooth also enables network connectivity, but is now more frequently used for wireless peripheral devices, such as a wireless keyboard or mouse.

If you plan to use a wireless Bluetooth device, you'll need to enable Bluetooth services via the YaST tool. The general steps for enabling Bluetooth in YaST are:

1. Click Desktop.
2. Click YaST. (If you are not logged into the root account, enter the root password and click Continue in the Password needed box.)

   3. Click Hardware in the left pane.

   4. Click Bluetooth.

   5. Click Enable Bluetooth Services.

   6. Click Finish.

   7. Close YaST.

Security Features

Because security is a great concern when you are connected to a network or the Internet, SUSE Linux 10.0 comes with several security features. One of the most important is the SUSE firewall. As is true for Windows XP with Service Pack 2, the SUSE firewall is automatically configured for security when you install the operating system. Besides blocking services that intruders might access, the SUSE firewall also uses Network Address Translation (NAT) to help disguise your IP address to outsiders. You can ensure your firewall is started by following these general steps in GNOME:

   1. Click Desktop.

   2. Click YaST. (If requested, enter the root password and click Continue.)

   3. Click Security and Users in the left pane.

   4. Click Firewall.

   5. Ensure the Start Firewall Now button is deactivated (which means the firewall is turned on). If it isn't deactivated, click the button to start the firewall.

   6. Click Next.

   7. Review the Firewall Configuration: Summary window.

   8. Click Accept.

   9. Close YaST.

Another security feature is AntiVir. AntiVir is virus protection software for your computer. AntiVir scans ongoing data activities for viruses and can be manually run to scan your files.

Novell AppArmor is still another security feature that was discussed earlier and that can be managed from YaST.

Development Tools

As is true for Red Hat Enterprise Linux, Fedora, Tiger, and most other distributions of UNIX/Linux, SUSE Linux 10.0 supports the creation of shell scripts, Perl scripts, and CGI scripts. It also comes with the GNU Compiler Collection (GCC) 4.0. In SUSE Linux 10.0 the implementation of GCC 4.0 includes the following programming languages:

- Java
- C

- C++

- ObjC

- Fortran

- Ada

Using SUSE Linux in the Novell Environment

E

When working in the Novell environment there are four choices for SUSE Linux operating systems. The choices range from server operating systems to operating systems for personal desktop use, as follows:

- Novell Open Enterprise Server

- SUSE Enterprise Server

- Novell Linux Desktop

- SUSE Linux

These choices are explained in the next sections.

Novell Open Enterprise Server

Novell Open Enterpriser Server enables an organization to use both Novell NetWare and SUSE Enterprise Linux Server. The advantage of this approach is that you can use two time-tested operating systems and the applications written for both. For example, your organization might be using a human resources and payroll application written to run in a NetWare environment. However, your organization may also want to run Linux-based software, such as specialized software for customer service needs and other software to track inventory. Novell Open Enterprise Server enables your organization to operate in both worlds.

In another scenario, your organization may be working to migrate from NetWare to Linux. Novell Open Enterprise Server enables you to proceed with the migration at a deliberate pace, without having to do an overnight switchover from one server system to the other.

Novell Open Enterprise Server offers management tools that can be integrated for use on both operating systems, so that server managers are more productive. It also takes advantage of the native security built into SUSE Linux systems.

The recommended hardware requirements for Novell Open Enterprise Server are:

- Multi-processor Pentium III, Xeon computer, or faster server-class computer

- 1 GB to 3 GB RAM

- 4 GB or more disk space

- Network interface

- Bootable CD or CD/DVD drive
- Mouse or other pointing device

SUSE Enterprise Server

SUSE Enterprise Server is for businesses and organizations that do not need compatibility with NetWare. SUSE Enterprise Server gives you access to thousands of open-source applications for all types of businesses and organizations. Also, SUSE Enterprise Server is a natural for businesses and organizations that develop their own applications, such as by using scripts, C, and C++.

One advantage of SUSE Enterprise Server is that it can scale from smaller x86 servers to mainframes, such as the IBM zSeries and S/390. Besides tools like YaST, server managers can use Novell ZENWorks Linux Management to manage software applications and server security.

The recommended hardware requirements for an x86 type of server running SUSE Enterprise Server include the following:

- Multi-processor Pentium III, Xeon computer, or faster server-class computer
- 1 GB to 3 GB RAM
- 4 GB disk space or more
- Network interface
- Bootable CD or CD/DVD drive
- Mouse or other pointing device

Novell Linux Desktop

Novell Linux Desktop is for users in a professional environment who connect to servers and who need productivity software. For example, one software package included is Novell Evolution. Novell Evolution provides e-mail, calendar, contact, and task management using an integrated format. Also, it is compatible with Microsoft Exchange for e-mail services in a network environment. Novell Evolution can also synchronize with Palm handheld devices.

Novell Linux Desktop has Citrix ICA client for users who need to remotely run applications on a Windows-based server. It also includes the Red Carpet Daemon for coordinated management from a server via ZENWorks, so that server managers can manage client desktops. Also, Novell Linux Desktop provides instant messaging for those who need this capability.

The recommended hardware for SUSE Linux Personal is:

- Pentium 3, AMD64, or Intel EM64T processor or faster CPU
- 512 MB RAM or higher

- 2 GB or more disk storage
- CD or CD/DVD drive
- Pointing device
- Network interface

SUSE Linux Personal

From the standpoint of Novell, SUSE Linux Personal is targeted for home use, including on a home or small office network. It also provides an excellent platform for developing applications. It has all of the features discussed in this appendix, but without some software, such as Novell Evolution and Citrix ICA.

SUSE Linux also can be effectively used in any organization for desktop computing. This is a robust, stable Linux operating system that can strongly compete with any others, including Red Hat Enterprise Linux and Fedora. And like Fedora, SUSE Linux 10.0 Personal is free. For UNIX/Linux enthusiasts it has much to offer. If you learn SUSE Linux with either the GNOME or KDE desktop, you will be able to find your way around virtually any Linux distribution for a desktop or server computer.

The recommended hardware for SUSE Linux Personal is:

- Pentium 3, Duron, Athlon, Athlon XP, Athlon MP, Athlon 64, Sempron, or Opteron or faster CPU
- 512 MB RAM or higher
- 2 GB or more disk storage
- CD or CD/DVD drive
- Pointing device
- Network interface (if you use it on a network)
- Sound and graphics cards for personal enjoyment

INSTALLING SUSE LINUX

A good place to begin learning about SUSE Linux 10.0 is by obtaining SUSE Linux Personal, which at this writing is SUSE Linux 10.0. You can download a free copy from *www.opensuse.org/Download*. Also, for a small fee, you can purchase it already burned onto a CD from *www.linuxcdshop.ca*.

The following are the steps for a clean installation of the free version of SUSE Linux 10.0 (Personal) using the GNOME desktop:

1. Turn on the computer so that you can insert the SUSE Linux version 10.0 CD 1 you've obtained or prepared for the installation.

2. On the first menu screen, use the arrow keys to select Installation.

3. You'll see a progress bar as the kernel is loaded (or you may see a black screen as the load progresses).

4. After the kernel is loaded, a GUI screen is displayed and you can make selections using the mouse. The left side of the screen shows the steps involved in the installation which are in three general stages—Preparation, Installation, and Configuration:

Preparation

Language

License Agreement

System Analysis

Time Zone

Desktop Selection

Installation

Installation Summary

Perform installation

Configuration

Root Password

Network

Users

Clean up

Release Notes

Hardware Configuration

5. Select the language you want to use, such as English (US) and click Next.

6. Read the license agreement. Click Yes, I Agree to the License Agreement and click Next.

7. The installation will probe devices on the computer to perform a system analysis.

8. Click New installation (because SUSE is new to this book, these instructions are for a new installation. If you already have an earlier version of SUSE Linux, you can also select Update at this point.). Click Next.

9. Select the Region and Time Zone parameters, such as USA and Central. Click Next.

10. Select the desktop you prefer to use. The selections are KDE (which is version 3.4) or GNOME (which is version 2.12). For this installation, select GNOME, which is consistent with the desktop used in the text of the book for Red Hat Enterprise Linux or Fedora. Click Next.

11. On the Installation Settings screen, you can configure Partitioning, Software, and Language. For this installation example, use the default selections. (If you need to use a partitioning method that is different than what is proposed, click Partitioning and select options to match your needs.) Click Accept.

12. If you change the proposed partitioning method, the installation will come back to the Installation Settings screen to show how the disk will be partitioned, including for the swap, root, and mount points. Click Accept to confirm the partitioning.

13. If you see the box, Confirm Package License: flash-player, click I Agree.

14. In the Confirm Installation box, click Install.

15. The computer will reboot. Wait until you see the Package Installation screen and a request to insert SUSE LINUX version 10.0 CD 2. Insert the disc and click OK.

16. During the installation of files and packages you'll be asked to insert SUSE LINUX version 10.0 CD 3. Insert the disc and click OK.

17. When prompted insert the SUSE LINUX version 10.0 CD 4. Click OK. If requested, insert the SUSE LINUX version 10.0 CD 5 and click OK.

18. On the screen entitled Password for the System Administrator "root" enter a password, confirm it, and click Next. (Note that if you enter a password with only lowercase letters, you'll see a warning that this is not a good security practice. If you see this warning, click No and use a different password or click Yes to proceed.)

19. On the Network Configuration screen you'll see the current configurations for the following elements:

   - Firewall
   - Network Interfaces
   - DSL Connections
   - ISDN Adapters
   - Modems
   - VCN Remote Administration
   - Proxy

   You can reconfigure any of these elements by clicking it. For this installation, leave the current configuration and click Next (you can change these configuration options later).

20. If you are connected to the Internet, click Yes, Test Connection to the Internet (and click Yes, then click Next, then click OK, and then click Next again). If not, then select No, Skip This Test.

21. On the User Authentication Method screen leave the default selection, which is Local (/etc/passwd). Note that the other options are:

   - LDAP
   - NIS
   - Samba

   Click Next.

22. On the New Local User screen, create a personal account for you to use. Enter your full name in the User's Full Name box. Enter your username in the Username box. Provide a password and confirm it (note that you should use a password with over five characters and with upper and lowercase letters). Leave Automatic Logon selected. Also, note that you can select to Receive System Mail on this account (but leave this box blank for now). Click Next.

23. The installation program will take a few minutes to write the system configuration.

24. Read the SUSE Linux 10.0 Release Notes. Click Next.

25. Review the selections on the Hardware Configuration screen. The elements on the screen include:

   - Graphics Cards
   - Printers
   - Sound
   - TV Cards
   - Bluetooth

   Click Next.

26. Click Finish.

27. The operating system will boot and you can log on to SUSE Linux.

HANDS-ON PROJECTS

SUSE Linux 10.0 can provide a satisfying experience with Linux, both from the desktop and from the terminal window. These Hands-on Projects enable you to learn about SUSE Linux 10.0. All of the projects are based on having the GNOME desktop installed.

Project E-1

In this project you explore the options on the SUSE Linux 10.0 GNOME desktop. Log on using your personal account, or you can use the root account if you do not have a personal account.

To explore the GNOME desktop:

1. Click the **Applications** menu in the Panel. What options do you see? Notice that some options have a right-pointing arrow to show there are menus associated with them.

2. One at a time, point to each of the options with the right-pointing arrow to view the associated menu for each option

3. Point to **Office** on the Applications menu, point to **Word Processor**, and click **OpenOffice.org Writer**. You can create and format documents using this free software.

4. Close the OpenOffice.org Writer window.

5. Click the **Places** menu in the Panel.

6. Click **Home Folder**. This action opens the File Browser into your home folder (with your account name) so you can manage files and folders.

7. Close the File Browser.

8. On the desktop, double-click the file icon with your account name plus the word Home, such as mpalmer's Home. Notice that the same window opens as in Step 6, providing File Browser access to the files and folders in your home folder. Close the File Browser window.

9. Click **Desktop** to view its menu options.

10. Click **GNOME Control Center**. The Desktop Preferences window opens with options to configure elements in GNOME. What options do you see?

11. Close the Desktop Preferences window.

12. Point to each icon in the Panel that is just to the right of the Desktop menu and view the label of the icon.

13. Click the icon for **OpenOffice.org Writer**. Notice this action opens the same application window as in Step 3.

14. Close the OpenOffice.org Writer window.

15. Right-click any open spot on the desktop. What options are on the shortcut menu?

16. Click **Create Folder**. Enter a name for the folder consisting of your first two initials and last name. Press **Enter**. Now you have a new folder on the desktop.

17. Right-click the folder you created and notice the selections on the shortcut menu.

18. Click **Properties** to view the folder's properties.

19. Close the folder's Properties window.

20. Click the folder you created on the desktop.

21. Drag the folder you created into the Trash icon to delete it.

Project E-2

For this project, you learn about the options in the YaST management tool in SUSE Linux 10.0.

To use YaST:

1. Click the **Desktop** menu in the Panel.

2. Click **YaST**. If requested, enter the root password and click **Continue**.

3. The left pane shows elements you can configure in YaST (refer to Figure E-3). Also, the right pane shows what can be configured for each element.

4. Click each selection in the left pane and notice the options that are displayed in the right pane.

5. Click **Hardware** in the left pane and click **Sound** in the right pane.

6. Your sound card should automatically be selected, but if it is not select it.

7. Click **Edit** to view the configuration options and information.

8. Close the Sound Card Advanced Options window.

9. Click **Network Services** to view the services you can manage or configure. What are some of the services you see?

10. Click **Security and Users**.

11. Click **Firewall.** Notice that you can use this tool to configure your firewall (similar to using a wizard in a Windows system).

12. Close the Firewall Configuration: Startup window.

13. Click **User Management** in the YaST Control Center @ linux window. You can use this tool to add, delete, and manage user accounts.

14. Close the User and Group Administration window and click **Yes** to abort.

15. Close the YaST Control Center @ linux window.

Project E-3

As mentioned earlier in this appendix, commands work the same in the SUSE Linux 10.0 GNOME terminal window as in the Red Hat Enterprise Linux and Fedora GNOME terminal windows. This project uses the same commands as Hands-on Project 3-5, following Steps 9 through 13 of that project. Only the steps to access the terminal window are slightly changed. In this project you open a terminal window and use the *mkdir* command to create a directory and the *ls* command to view the contents of a directory. Log onto your personal account, or you can use the root account.

To make a directory and view its contents using the terminal window:

1. Click **Applications**, point to **System**, point to **Terminal**, and click **Gnome Terminal**. (An even faster way to open the terminal window is to right-click an open area on the desktop and click Open Terminal.)

2. Type **ls** and press **Enter** to view the contents of your home directory. (Note that you can get a more detailed listing by using the **ls -l** command.)

3. Type **mkdir** plus a space, then your initials and the word Folder, such as MPFolder. Press **Enter**.

4. Type **ls** and press **Enter** to verify that you successfully created the new folder (or directory).

5. Type **exit** and press **Enter** to close the terminal window.

NOTE

Try other Hands-on Projects from any chapter in the book that involve using the terminal window and you'll find the commands work the same way in SUSE Linux 10.0. Also, remember that you can read the online documentation for a command by typing *man* a space and then the command—next press Enter. To exit the man page you are reading, type *q*.

HANDS-ON PROJECTS

Project E-4

In this project you learn how to create a simple slide show in OpenOffice.org Impress. Log onto your personal account, or you can use the root account. Check with your instructor about saving your work on the PC you use. If you do not save your work, omit Steps 23 and 24.

To create slides using Impress:

1. Click **Applications**, point to **Office**, point to **Presentation**, and click **OpenOffice.org Impress**.

2. After the Presentation Wizard starts, click **From template**. Select **Introducing a New Product**, if it is not already selected. Ensure that **Preview** is selected. Click **Next**.

3. Select **Dark Blue with Orange** for the presentation background. Click **Slide**. Click **Next**.

4. For Effect, select **Wheel Clockwise, 1 Spoke**. Click **Next**.

5. For the name of your company type your full name plus Associates, such as Michael Palmer Associates. For the subject of the presentation enter **New Mountain Bike Model**. Click **Next**.

6. Notice the default slide topics on the left in the wizard and the sample slide on the right. Click **Create**.

7. You should see a screen similar to the one in Figure E-8.

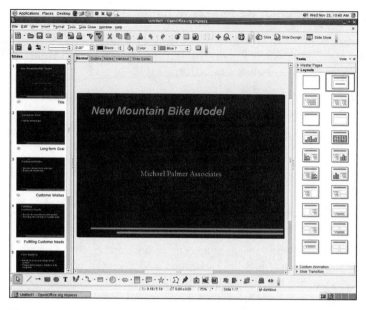

Figure E-8   Creating a slide show in OpenOffice.org Impress

8. Click slide number **2** on the left side of the screen.

9. Click behind the word "goal" and press the Back Space key to delete the text up to the bullet, but don't delete the bullet. Type **Create a new mountain bike to revolutionize the current market**.

10. Click slide number **3** on the left side of the screen.

11. Remove the default text and enter the following two bullets:

   ❏ **Customers want a new mountain bike design.**

   ❏ **The design will focus on a new frame and wheel approach.**

12. Click slide number **4** on the left side of the screen.

13. Remove the default text and enter the following two bullets:

   ❏ **The bike will be strong and fast.**

   ❏ **The bike will be light weight.**

14. Click slide number **5**.

15. Remove the default text and enter:

   ❏ **The bike will cost less than others.**

   ❏ **The bike will set new quality standards for its price range.**

16. Click slide number **6**.

17. Remove the default text and enter:

    ❑ **The bike will use a reinforced light–weight titanium frame and bend-proof wheels.**

18. Click slide number **7**.

19. Remove the default text and enter:

    ❑ **The next step is to outline tasks for engineering and marketing to launch the project.**

20. Click slide number **1** in the left pane. Click the **Slide Show** button in the top right portion of the screen to view your slide show.

21. Press **Enter** to advance from slide to slide.

22. Click **Click to exit presentation…**.

23. Click the **Save** icon (a floppy disk icon) in the top left portion of the screen.

24. Name the file with your initials plus Presentation, such as MPPresentation and click **Save** (by default the presentation will be saved in the Documents folder under your home folder).

25. Close OpenOffice.org Impress.

E

F

WINDOWS SERVER 2003 R2

Windows Server 2003 Release 2 (R2) is an interim version of Windows Server. It is an upgrade to Windows Server 2003 with many new features that will be in the Windows Server version currently code named Longhorn (see Appendix C for information about Microsoft operating system code names). Longhorn is scheduled for release some time in 2006. Windows Server 2003 R2 enables organizations to take advantage of important new server features now, without waiting for the release of Longhorn.

Most of the new features built into Windows Server 2003 R2 are targeted for medium- to large-sized organizations. Small office and home office users of Windows Server 2003 won't find as many advantages in this new release. However, there are some advantages for small offices. These advantages include a new version of the Microsoft Management Console, faster code execution (depending on the server hardware), a new Print Management Console, strong integration with .NET Framework, and improved security.

Medium- and large-sized organizations that use Active Directory, Distributed File System (DFS), clustered servers, and group policies will find valuable new features for managing their enterprise networks. Also, many of the same organizations who want to automate their server operations and use fewer support people will find advantages to using Windows Server 2003 R2.

Microsoft continues to stress improvements in security for all of its operating systems and Windows Server 2003 R2 is no exception. From the security standpoint, the R2 version comes with the new Windows Firewall first introduced in Windows XP Service Pack 2. The R2 version also integrates new security patches into the operating system code. It adds a new feature, called Post-Setup Security Updates, to guide server managers through new configuration activities related to patches and updates.

One element that has stayed the same in Windows Server 2003 R2 is the desktop appearance. You don't need to learn a new GUI interface. Using this desktop is as familiar as walking down a path you've walked many times before.

COMPARATIVE CHANGES

Windows Server 2003 R2 is another step forward in recognizing the central role servers play in an organization. Servers make a huge range of activities possible in an enterprise including network access and verification, file access, software access, resource sharing, network security, e-mail communications, and more. In many ways servers are joining together to take on many more activities than mainframes and other large computer systems that ruled in the past. Servers combined with a network are the mainframes of the present. In many locations, they must work 24 hours a day, seven days a week, without interruptions or slowdowns.

Windows Server 2003 R2 offers new features that medium- and large-sized organizations want for even more reliable, heavy-duty, and uninterrupted computing. The features in Windows Server 2003 R2 include:

- Integration with Service Pack 1
- Better performance
- Improved group policy management
- MMC 3.0 and the Print Management Console
- New server clustering capabilities
- Virtual server options
- Dynamic Systems Initiative
- Better identity and access management
- Better options for branch office servers
- Distributed File System enhancements
- Subsystem for UNIX-based applications
- Improved storage management

These features are discussed in the next sections, but we begin with a section that presents the hardware requirements for Windows Server 2003 R2.

Hardware Requirements

The hardware you need for the R2 version depends on the edition of Windows Server 2003: Standard, Enterprise, or Data Center. As you've learned in Appendices C, D, and E, when you size a server, plan to go beyond the bare minimum specifications for the operating system. Your server will run faster when you use a modern CPU and have plenty of memory. Also, adequate disk space is important for current resource use and anticipated growth.

Windows Server 2003 R2, Standard Edition

Windows Server 2003 R2, Standard Edition is the generic version of this server system and is used in small businesses. It's also used for general file, print, and Web server services in any organization. Microsoft's hardware requirements for Windows Server 2003 R2, Standard Edition are as follows:

- 550 MHz CPU or faster
- 256 MB RAM (512 MB or more is better)
- 1.5 GB of disk storage for the operating system (but you'll need much more for application, data, and user files)

Besides these specifications, Windows Server 2003 R2, Standard Edition also can support up to 4 GB of RAM for 32-bit servers (sometimes called x86 servers) and up to 32 GB for 64-bit (x64) servers. The operating system also supports up to four processors (two more than Windows Server 2003).

Windows Server 2003 R2, Enterprise Edition

Windows Server 2003 R2, Enterprise Edition is designed to meet the needs of networks with applications and Web services requiring high-end servers and a high level of productivity. This version supports clustering up to eight servers. *Clustering* is the ability to increase the access to server resources and provide fail-safe services by linking two or more discrete computer systems so they appear to function as one system. This operating system also supports hot-add memory, in which RAM is added without stopping the operating system or computer.

For Windows Server 2003 R2, Enterprise Edition the Microsoft hardware requirements are:

- 733 MHz CPU or faster
- 256 MB RAM (512 MB or more is better)
- 1.5 GB of disk storage for the operating system for 32-bit servers and 2 GB for 64-bit servers

Windows Server 2003 R2, Enterprise Edition supports up to 64 GB of RAM for 32-bit servers and 1 TB for 64-bit computers. The maximum number of processors supported is eight.

Windows Server 2003 R2, Datacenter Edition

Windows Server 2003 R2, Datacenter Edition is designed for environments with mission critical applications, very large databases, and information access requiring high availability. Like the Enterprise Edition, the Datacenter Edition enables hot-add memory for increased server availability. Windows Server 2003 R2, Datacenter Edition is the most industrial-strength platform designed for large database applications in any organization, such as a customer service database of thousands of customers (like the database of your favorite Internet store).

The Microsoft recommended hardware requirements for Windows Server 2003 R2, Datacenter Edition include:

- 733 MHz CPUs or faster (minimum of eight CPUs)
- 1 GB RAM or more
- 1.5 GB of disk storage for 32-bit servers and 2 GB for 64-bit servers

Windows Server 2003 R2, Datacenter Edition supports up to 128 GB RAM for 32-bit servers and up to 1 TB for 64-bit computers. This operating system requires a minimum of an 8-processor (8-way) computer and supports up to 64 processors.

There likely will be other R2 versions, such as for Small Business server and for Virtual Server (discussed later in this appendix), but the versions covered here are the core versions on which the others will be built.

Integration with Service Pack 1

Windows Server 2003 R2 is built upon features of Service Pack 1 for Windows Server 2003. Service Pack 1 includes many security updates related to network connectivity and to components used by Windows Server 2003. For server administrators, this means if you want to upgrade a currently running version of Windows Server 2003, you must first install Service Pack 1.

If your current Windows Server 2003 server does not have Service Pack 1, you'll receive an error message when you attempt to load Windows Server 2003 R2. The installation process will force you to stop and load Service Pack 1 first. Go to *www.microsoft.com/downloads/search.aspx?displaylang=en* to obtain Service Pack 1.

Key new features emphasized by Microsoft in Service Pack 1 (issued in March 2005) are:

- Addition of the same firewall made available to Windows XP in the Windows XP Service Pack 2. An important advantage of the new firewall is that it monitors traffic into and out of the computer (see Appendix C for more information about this new firewall).
- The new Security Administration Wizard to help guide you through the process of defining the role of your server and to block services you don't need, so attackers and malicious software can't get through.

- A new service, called Post-Setup Security Updates (PSSU) that prevents new incoming connections until the latest security patches are added to a server.

Hands-on Project F-1 shows you how to determine whether Service Pack 1 is installed in your version of Windows Server 2003. Also, Hands-on Project F-2 enables you to use the Security Administration Wizard.

Better Performance

Windows Server 2003 R2 offers better performance in areas that affect enterprise networks. For example, if a company has branch offices that are connected by wide area networks (WANs), Active Directory (see Chapters 2 and 9) is able to communicate faster over the WAN links. This enables users to log on faster to branch office servers and it enables branch office servers to devote more CPU resources to handling user requests. The performance enhancement is part of the Microsoft initiative to improve branch office server functions and Distributed File System (DFS) capabilities (discussed in more detail later in this appendix).

Microsoft also has rewritten some components in Service Pack 1 and in the R2 version so these components work faster. For example, performance enhancements have been made to SharePoint Services, which are services that enable users to collaborate on Word documents through a server. Another example is enhancements for faster Web-based functions.

Improved Group Policy Management

The group policy capabilities of Windows Server 2003 R2 enable organizations to manage how users employ Windows-based computers on their desktops. An organization can standardize how applications are accessed by users, including both specialized applications and those native to Windows, such as Control Panel elements. Through group policy implementation, both employee productivity and network security can be increased.

Windows Vista provides many additional group policies for added user productivity. Windows Server 2003 R2 adds the same group policies so a server manager can configure them from the server for use in an office or organization. If your organization anticipates using Windows Vista and also uses group policy management, plan to upgrade to Windows Server 2003 R2 to take advantage of the new group policy features.

MMC 3.0 and the Print Management Console

Windows Server 2003 R2 includes the newest version of the Microsoft Management Console, which is MMC 3.0. MMC 3.0 has expanded services to enable a network administrator to manage server functions across an enterprise of Windows servers. The goal of expanded enterprise management is to reduce the number of on-site (or third-party) server managers in different geographical locations that house servers. This is important to businesses that have branch offices and to universities in which servers are spread throughout different departments or colleges.

F

Besides a new version of the MMC, Windows Server 2003 R2 offers a new Print Management Console (see Figure F-1) for enterprise-wide control of network printers for one location. The new features of the Print Management Console are:

- Installation of network printers remotely from the computer running Print Management Console. For example, this feature provides the ability to install and set up a printer in a branch (off-site) office.

- Instantaneous views of printers that are not ready and of print jobs so you can manage printer resources and troubleshoot problems.

- Ability to view printer driver information, forms, printer ports use, and other general printer information.

- Option to create customized printer filters, such as to constantly monitor one or more printers subject to intermittent errors or errors associated with a specific user.

- Ability to set up Web features to remotely diagnose a printer problem, such as a jammed printer or one with an empty toner cartridge.

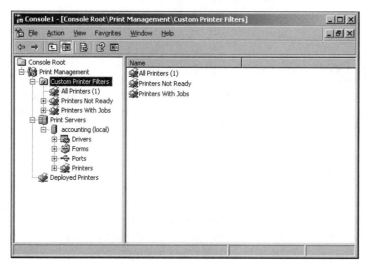

Figure F-1   Print Management Console in Windows Server 2003 R2

At this writing, the new Print Management Component is not installed by default when you update Windows Server 2003 to the R2 version. Hands-on Project F-3 shows you how to install the Print Management Component and then access the Print Management Console in the MMC.

New Server Clustering Capabilities

One way to scale a server system when you need more CPU power and flexibility is through clustering. For example, consider a company that rapidly grows from a few hundred customers to many thousands. The rapid growth requires larger customer service and human resources applications and large databases on the company's server running Windows Server 2003. One solution is to scale up to Windows Server 2003 R2, Enterprise Edition and cluster two or more servers to appear to work as one large server. This approach has several advantages. One advantage is that the company immediately has more CPU power. Another advantage is that if one server fails, operations fall over to the remaining servers so operations can continue.

Only two versions of Windows Server 2003 R2 enable clustering: Enterprise Edition and Datacenter Edition. Both of these editions offer the Cluster Service (CS). The new CS offered in the R2 versions of Enterprise and Datacenter includes easier setup for clustered servers and easier removal of one or more servers from a cluster. Also, in the Windows Server 2003 R2, Enterprise Edition up to eight computers can be clustered, which is six more than in the non-R2 Enterprise version.

In the Windows Server 2003 R2, Enterprise and Datacenter Editions, clustered computers are better integrated with Active Directory and with the servers' disks. Also, a disk on a clustered server can be expanded without removing a computer from the cluster. Another improvement involves failover services, which in the R2 version extend to computers that are geographically separated. Finally, there are improvements in how the *chkdsk* utility (see Chapter 3) gathers data about disks on clustered computers and how it logs its analysis.

Virtual Server Options

Virtual Server is a capability that enables you to run more than one operating system on your server. For example, consider a company that has a legacy mail-merge program designed for an older version of a UNIX operating system for a 32-bit computer. The company wants to continue using this program, but also uses Windows Server 2003 R2 for all other applications. Virtual Server enables that company to load the older UNIX operating system and Windows Server 2003 R2 on the same computer.

Another use of Virtual Server is when you want to have both a live environment and one for testing—but don't have the resources to purchase two computers. You can load two licensed versions of Windows Server 2003 R2 to accomplish both on the same computer. This is a practice that has often been used on mainframe computers in the past, because of the expense of purchasing two mainframes.

You'll need a computer that has two or more processors to use Virtual Server, so there is one processor for each operating system you load.

F

Dynamic Systems Initiative

One goal of Microsoft has been to make computer systems simpler to use and more self-managing. Beginning in 2003, Microsoft has worked with other vendors to help make this goal a reality through the *Dynamic Systems Initiative (DSI)*. DSI is a joint venture with Hewlett-Packard, Dell, IBM, Fujitsu Limited, and Fujitsu Siemens. One of the hallmarks for DSI is to embed knowledge in applications to define how an application behaves in different situations.

In Windows Server 2003 R2, Microsoft is beginning to implement DSI technology through enhancements to Microsoft Operations Manager (MOM) 2005. MOM is an application to help manage server operations in an organization, including monitoring servers, reporting on events, and providing alerts about problems.

Windows Server 2003 R2 is an ideal platform for MOM because Microsoft reports that the two combined environments can result in using 40 percent fewer people to manage servers. The version of MOM available for Windows Server 2003 R2 has the following new features:

- Can automatically take action on an alert, such as to restart a server or service

- Enables dynamic software patching while a server is running, without interruption

- Automates the process of distributing software to clients

- Can inventory systems on a network for pre-deployment patch planning, so administrators can determine which systems need patches and which ones should be patched first

- Uses SQL Server for database management of information about alerts, security, and other information

NOTE

To learn more about MOM visit *www.microsoft.com/technet/prodtechnol/ mom/mom2005/Library/f51a38d9-b44f-42c9-815a-d3494ae29b94.mspx*

Identity and Access Management

Windows Server 2003 R2 introduces new features for easier identification of authorized users and to ensure users access the right resources. One of the problems in the past has been to provide unified access to applications and data to both internal network users and users through the Internet. Active Directory provides access management through elements such as domains, trees, and forests (see Chapter 9), however these elements can prove hard to manage when Web services are introduced to the mix of user access needs. To fill the need, Microsoft introduces *Active Directory Federation Services (ADFS)*.

ADFS enables one sign-on for both network and Web-based resources. In one sense, ADFS is like a middleman integrated into Active Directory—handling security and authentication for different applications. Consider, for example, a bank that uses network applications to track user's bank account information. The same bank uses a newer Web-based service to enable users to complete loan applications over the Internet; and the bank loan officers use Web-based software to review those applications. In the past, a loan officer might have to use one network password to access information about the loan applicant's account and another to access the Web-based loan application software. This is because the two user validation processes (network and Web-based) have been kept distinct for the two types of access. ADFS integrates the access management in Active Directory so the loan officer only has to sign on once to access both types of applications—a process that Microsoft calls *single-sign-on (SSO)*. ADFS with SSO is an appealing addition for organizations that use multiple applications technologies in their network enterprise. Service to the users is simplified and security is strengthened at the same time.

Another innovation for Active Directory is the use of *Active Directory Application Mode (ADAM)*. ADAM enables Active Directory and software applications to communicate. ADAM provides coordination and authentication of users and user information through the Active Directory database. You might think of ADAM as a directory service for software applications, so that users can be authorized to use applications, or specific portions of applications. The advantage of ADAM is that it uses the same data (and database) about users as exists in Active Directory.

Windows Server 2003 R2 contains several enhancements to ADAM. For example, if a user changes her account password in ADAM, it is also changed in Active Directory for authentication to the network. Consider a payroll supervisor who uses a password to the payroll program used by a company. When the payroll supervisor changes her password used to access the payroll program, ADAM shares that password change with Active Directory, so the same password is used to log onto the network.

A third feature to make life easier for server administrators is *UNIX Identity Management*. On many combined Windows-based and UNIX/Linux networks there is no reason to have different user authorization information in servers running different operating systems. UNIX Identity Management enables information about users to be shared between UNIX/Linux and Windows Server 2003 R2. Information about users in Active Directory can be synchronized with UNIX and information in the UNIX *passwd* and *group* files (see Chapter 9) can be synchronized with Active Directory. In this way, the concept of SSO is shared among UNIX/Linux and Windows servers. Also, server managers do less work in maintaining user information. Figure F-2 shows the Microsoft Identity Management Tool for UNIX in Windows Server 2003 R2 (with Password Synchronization selected). You can access this tool from the Administrative Tools menu in Windows Server 2003 R2.

In short, the reach and value of Active Directory is enhanced by implementing ADFS (for application and Web service coordination), ADAM (for coordination between applications and Active Directory), and UNIX Identity Management. These are also examples of Dynamic Systems Initiative to make administration simpler and more automated by enabling server administrators to do less work. For example, consider a user who has just changed his password to access the network through Active Directory, but no longer

F

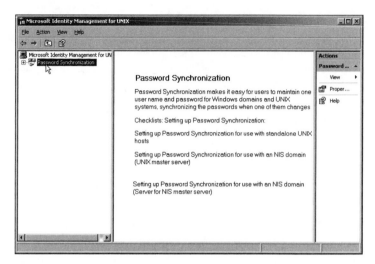

Figure F-2   Microsoft Identity Management Tool for UNIX

remembers it. He uses the same password for Web services, applications, and on a UNIX computer. When the user calls an administrator to change his password on all of these systems, the administrator only has to change it in one place, not in several different places.

Better Options for Branch Office Users

Since the introduction of Active Directory, Windows Server systems have included mechanisms to take into account branch offices or sites in a network enterprise. For example, consider a retail store that has centralized computing at its headquarters office and a server at each retail outlet store. In this case the retail outlet stores are like branch offices in the network enterprise. Another example is a corporation that is headquartered in Chicago, but has smaller manufacturing sites in Toronto, Des Moines, and St. Louis. Each manufacturing site has one or more servers that coordinate data access with servers at the headquarters site. The manufacturing sites are branches of the headquarters. A third example is a community college located in a metropolitan area that has small branch campuses in four neighboring cities. The community college has a main IT center and each branch campus has a single server that communicates with master servers at the main campus.

Active Directory offers ways to coordinate computing between main sites and branch offices. This enables users to go through the same validation process whether they access information on the branch office server or on a server at the main site. Servers in both locations can have the same Active Directory information to apply the same rules in allowing users to access information.

One of the problems with branch office computing is that Active Directory information must be consistently updated between the branch office server(s) and the headquarters servers. The trading of Active Directory information back and forth can create extra traffic on WAN links used to connect branch offices to main sites.

Windows Server 2003 R2 offers several enhancements for communications between branch offices and main sites. One enhancement is the use of Remote Differential Compression (RDC), which is designed to optimize transfers over data networks, so that significantly less bandwidth is used for Active Directory (and other) information exchange over WAN links. This means more bandwidth is available for users to do their work.

Another enhancement for branch office computing is in file replication. Windows Server 2003 R2 offers improved file replication so that it is easier to back up files from one location to another—for fault tolerance and disaster recovery. Another enhancement is the ability to make files published at one location available in another location.

The main purpose of improvements to branch office computing is to make it more reliable and easier to manage than in previous versions of Windows Server.

Distributed File System Enhancements

The *Distributed File System (DFS)* enables you to simplify access to shared folders on a network by setting up folders to appear as though they are accessed from only one place. If the network, for example, has eight Windows servers that make a variety of shared folders available to network users, DFS can be set up so that users do not have to know what server offers which shared folder. All of the folders can be set up to appear as though they are on one server and under one broad folder structure. DFS also makes managing folder access easier for server administrators and it can be used for constant backups of important files. DFS is configured using (1) the Distributed File System tool in the Administrative Tools menu (click Start, point to All Programs, and point to Administrative Tools) or (2) through the Distributed File System MMC snap-in.

DFS can be used between branch office and main office servers, which means it takes advantage of the new implementation of RDC for faster replication over WAN links. Also, DFS replication of files between servers on the same LAN is redesigned to be faster and more reliable.

Windows Server 2003 R2 offers a new DFS "failback" capability, which means that if one server fails, such as at a branch office, users' access to DFS folders and files is immediately redirected to the nearest working site—another branch office or the main office.

Many enterprise networks use DFS replication to increase user productivity and as a disaster recovery technique. On these networks, the enhancements to DFS make upgrading to Windows Server 2003 R2 very attractive.

Subsystem for UNIX-based Applications

Many organizations have a network enterprise that includes both Windows and UNIX/Linux servers. One difficulty with this approach is that some applications only run in Windows or in UNIX/Linux—but operations would be easier if they ran in either operating system. For this situation, Windows Server 2003 R2 has the new Subsystem for

UNIX-based Applications. This means you can compile and run UNIX/Linux applications on a Windows server.

For organizations that use SQL Server or Oracle databases, the Subsystem for UNIX-based Applications also offers better options for connecting applications to databases. This is especially important for organizations that use client/server and data warehouse systems, both of which can have very large databases connected with the applications they employ.

Improved Storage Management

Servers are vital for providing data storage options. One server may have any combination of storage devices including hard disks, disk arrays, CD/DVD drives, floppy disks, Zip drives, tape drives, optical discs, flash memory, and others. With all of these choices, tracking storage can be complex. For this reason Windows Server 2003 R2 offers new tools to help manage data storage: File Server Resource Manager and Storage Manager for SANs.

File Server Resource Manager (see Figure F-3) is designed to help server managers determine how storage is used on a server and to better manage storage. There are three important options within File Server Resource Manager:

- *Quota Management*—for setting quotas on volumes. With this option you can limit the size of selected folders and automatically send a notice when the size limit is about to be reached. Also, you can have automatic size quotas for all folders on a volume, including new folders as they are created. For multi-volume systems you can create a template to apply quotas to all or only certain volumes.

- *File Screening Management*—for screening files that users can save to a particular folder or storage medium. For example, your organization may have a problem conserving disk space because users store many audio files on a particular volume. You can create a filter to block audio files from being saved to that volume. You can also create a template so the same block is used for all volumes.

- *Storage Reports Management*—for creating reports about storage use, such as attempts to write blocked files and the status of quotas. With this tool you can view the most used files and the least used files to determine file use trends. There are many options for generating reports, which can be useful for projecting disk storage needs.

Try Hands-on Project F-4 to use the File Server Resource Manager.

The Storage Manager for SANs is a tool for managing storage area networks. A *storage area network (SAN)* is a fast network that contains components that can be shared for storage and for access to the storage. Files and folders are on storage elements that can include: (1) shared storage on servers or on clustered servers, (2) storage silos/arrays of multiple disks, and (3) other storage media. A SAN is actually like a subnetwork with high-speed connections and network devices to storage elements.

The Storage Manager for SANs is used to set up access to and manage a SAN. It can handle SANs that use either Fibre Channel or Internet SCSI technologies. Because Fibre Channel and Internet SCSI use logical unit numbers (LUNs), the Storage Manager for SANs enables

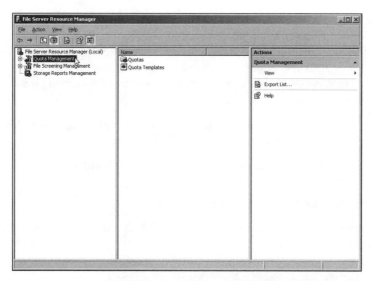

Figure F-3   File Server Resource Manager in Windows Server 2003 R2

you to set up and configure LUNs. A LUN is used to create a reference to a specific portion of a SAN, such as a disk array or only one disk in an array. By creating a LUN, you have a way to manage the storage it references.

The File Server Resource Manager and the Storage Manager for SANs must be installed as Windows components (Hands-on Project F-3 shows you how to install a component). Both are part of the Management and Monitoring Tools category in the Windows components listing. You can access these tools either from the Administrative Tools menu or as MMC snap-ins.

TIP

When you don't see a tool you want to use on the Administrative Tools menu or as an MMC snap-in, check to see if it has been installed as a Windows component. Click Start, point to Control Panel, click Add or Remove Programs, and click Add/Remove Windows Components.

UPGRADING TO WINDOWS SERVER 2003 R2

Upgrading from Windows Server 2003 to Windows Server 2003 R2 is a little more involved than some other operating system upgrades because you need to make certain that Service Pack 1 is already installed before you begin (see Hands-on Project F-1). If the service pack is not installed, you'll need to obtain it and install it first.

NOTE There are two discs available for installing Windows Server 2003 R2. Disc 1 contains files for installing Windows Server 2003 with Service Pack 1. Disc 2 contains files for installing the Windows Server 2003 components. If your Windows Server 2003 system already has Service Pack 1 installed, use only Disc 2 to upgrade to Windows Server 2003 R2, which is the installation method used in this section.

With Service Pack 1 already installed, use the following steps to upgrade to Windows Server 2003 R2 (ensure you have obtained a Product Key before you start):

1. Boot your current version of Windows Server 2003 and log onto the Administrator account.

2. Insert the Windows Server 2003 R2 Disc 2.

3. Wait until you see the Welcome to Microsoft® Windows® Server 2003 R2 screen (see Figure F-4).

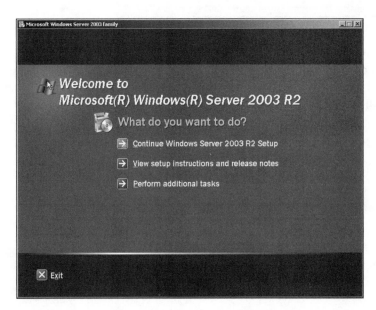

Figure F-4   Installing Windows Server 2003 R2

4. Click Continue Windows Server 2003 R2 Setup. You'll see a message that if you continue, you will not be able to uninstall service packs currently installed on the computer. Click Yes.

5. You'll see the Welcome to the Windows Server 2003 R2 Setup Wizard start. If you want to later access a shortcut on the desktop for documentation about new components in Windows Server 2003 R2, select this option. Click Next.

6. Enter the Product Key and click Next.

7. Click the option button for I accept the items in the license agreement (see Figure F-5). Click Next.

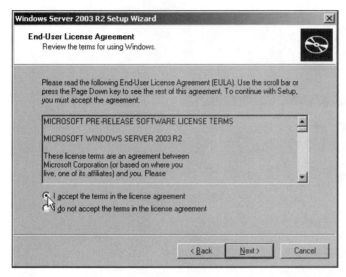

Figure F-5 Accepting the Windows Server 2003 R2 license agreement

8. On the Setup Summary screen, click Next.

9. Setup copies files to the computer.

10. Click Finish.

11. Exit or close all windows. Insert Windows Server 2003 R2 Disc 1 and wait until you see the Welcome to Microsoft® Windows® Server 2003 R2 screen. Click Install optional Windows components.

12. On the Windows Components screen, you can install or remove any of a wide range of components (see Figure F-6). For example, in Windows Server 2003 R2, Enterprise Edition, the components you can install are listed in Table F-1.

13. Some components have subcomponents and you can select some or all of the subcomponents. To view the subcomponents associated with one of the listed components, double-click it. Select the subcomponents you want and click OK (or click Cancel if you do not want to make changes).

14. After you have selected the components, click Next.

15. If requested, insert your disc labeled Service Pack 1 CD-ROM and click OK. If you are asked for the path to the CD, enter it (or accept the default or use the Browse button) and click OK. Similarly, if requested insert the Windows Server (your version) 2003 Installation CD and click OK. Next, if requested, insert the Windows Server 2003 R2 Disc 2 and click OK. Last, if requested, insert the Windows Server 2003 R2 Disc 1 and click OK.

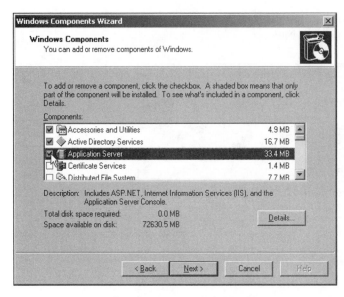

Figure F-6   Installing components in Windows Server 2003 R2

16. Click Finish.

17. Click Exit to close the Welcome to Microsoft® Windows® Server 2003 R2 screen (this is an optional step).

18. Click Yes to restart the computer.

Table F-1   Windows Server 2003 R2, Enterprise Edition components

Component	Description
Accessories and Utilities	Installs components that include a wizard to configure accessibility options, accessories such as Notepad, communications tools, games, and multimedia tools
Active Directory Services	Installs new R2 Active Directory Services, such as Active Directory Application Mode (ADAM), Active Directory Federation Services (ADFS), and Identity Management for UNIX
Application Server	Installs application services such as ASP.NET, COM+, DTC, Internet Information Services (IIS), and Message Queuing
Certificate Services	Manages certification authority for security through certificates
Distributed File System	Installs a system that enables folders to be shared from multiple servers as though they are in one place
E-mail Services	Installs POP3 e-mail capabilities along with the e-mail protocol of the Internet, which is Simple Mail Transfer Protocol (SMTP)
Fax Services	Enables fax capabilities

Table F-1   Windows Server 2003 R2, Enterprise Edition components (continued)

Component	Description
Indexing Service	Quickly searches file contents for specific words or strings of words
Internet Explorer Enhanced Security Configuration	Manages how users access Web sites
Management and Monitoring Tools	Installs tools to manage and monitor the server and the network
Microsoft .NET Framework 2.0	Enables the use of Microsoft .NET Framework 2.0 applications
Networking Services	Installs protocols and services for DNS, DHCP, WINS, and other network services
Other Network File and Print Services	Enables print services for UNIX and file and print services for Macintosh computers
Remote Installation Services	Enables the installation of Windows 2000, Windows XP, Windows Server 2003, and Windows Server 2003 R2 on remote computers that also can be booted remotely
Remote Storage	Enables Windows Server 2003 R2 to write files to remote devices, such as tape drives
Security Configuration Server	Limits the options for attackers and malicious software to access to a server
Subsystem for UNIX-based Applications	Supports a subsystem for UNIX-based software applications; a new R2 option
Terminal Server	Enables clients to run programs located on the server, as though they were terminals
Terminal Server Licensing	Controls licensing for terminal services
UDDI Services	Provides Universal Description, Discovery, and Integration (UDDI) capabilities within an enterprise or between business partners for Web services
Update Root Certificates	Enables automatic downloads of the most recent root certificates from Windows Update, as necessary
Windows Media Services	"Streams" multimedia from the server to the clients, so that an audio/video file starts playing before it is fully received
Windows Sharepoint Services	Installs a document management service to enable users to collaborate on projects through a server (.NET Framework and IIS cannot be installed when you install this component)

F

HANDS-ON PROJECTS

The Hands-on Projects in this section enable you to prepare for installing Windows Server 2003 R2 and then to experience new features in the operating system.

Project F-1

Before you upgrade Windows Server 2003 to Windows Server 2003 R2, ensure your version of Windows Server 2003 has Service Pack 1. In this project, you learn how to check for the service pack. You need to log on using an account that has Administrator privileges. Note that if you only have access to a computer running Windows Server 2003 R2, you can still use these steps to practice.

To determine if your system contains Service Pack 1:

1. Click **Start**, point to **Control Panel**, and click **System**.

2. Ensure that the **General** tab is displayed.

3. Look for Service Pack 1 (you may also see the version number) under the System section. If you don't see Service Pack 1, this means it isn't installed.

4. Click **Cancel**.

Project F-2

The Security Administration Wizard is an important addition to Service Pack 1. Use this project to open the wizard and learn about some of the security settings you can configure. Because there are many settings involved, you'll exit the wizard before finishing in Step 23. The Security Administration Wizard Windows component should already be installed before you start (if it is not, see the beginning steps in Hands-on Project F-3 to learn how to install a Windows component). You need to log on using an account that has Administrator privileges.

To use the Security Administration Wizard:

1. Click **Start**, point to **All Programs**, point to **Administrative Tools**, and click **Security Administration Wizard**.

2. After the wizard starts, click **Next**.

3. Ensure that **Create a new security policy** is selected and click **Next**.

4. Use the default server selection and click **Next**.

5. After the security configuration database is processed, click **Next**.

6. Click **Next** on the Role Based Service Configuration screen.

7. What server roles can be defined?

8. Leave the default roles selected and click **Next**.

9. Use the default client features that are selected and click **Next**.

10. Use the default options to administrate the server and click **Next**.

11. Use the default selections for additional services and click **Next**.

12. Leave the default for handling unspecified services and click **Next**.

13. Review the service changes and click **Next**.

14. Click **Next** on the Network Security screen.

15. If you see a review screen displayed, review the service changes and click **Next**.

16. Scroll through the list of ports that are selected to be left open. This is an important screen because it enables you to lock down services that are not needed for the role of the server. Note that the service going through each port, such as HTTP, is shown next to the port. On this screen you would leave unchecked each service that is not needed for the server's role. HTTP is left open (is checked), for example, because Web server was chosen earlier (see Steps 7 and 8) for one of the roles of this server. Click **Next**.

17. Confirm the port configuration and click **Next**.

18. Click **Next** on the Registry settings screen.

19. Click **Next** on the screen to set SMB security setting signatures (for network file sharing).

20. At this point you are getting an idea of the comprehensive security features that can be configured for a security policy. This is a good stopping point, because continuing goes beyond the scope of this book and this project is mainly intended to make you aware of the thoroughness of the Security Administration Wizard.

21. Click **Cancel** and click **Yes** to exit the Security Administration Wizard.

HANDS-ON PROJECTS

Project F-3

In this project you install the Windows Print Management Component that enables you to use the Print Management Console. Next, you configure the MMC to open the Print Management Console. Log on using an account that has Administrator privileges. Also, Step 26 will be more useful if there is at least one printer already connected to the computer you are using.

To install and use the Print Management Console:

1. Click **Start**, point to **Control Panel**, and click **Add or Remove Programs**.

2. Click **Add/Remove Windows Components**.

3. Scroll to find **Management and Monitoring Tools** and then double-click this option.

4. Select the box for **Print Management Component** (if it is not selected). What other management and monitoring tools can you choose to install?

5. Click **OK**.

6. Note that at this point you can make selections to install (or remove) any Windows component.

7. Click **Next**.

8. If requested, insert the disc labeled Windows Server 2003 R2 CD and click **OK**.

9. Click **Finish**

10. Close the Add or Remove Programs window.

11. To start the MMC, click **Start** and click **Run**.

12. Type **mmc** in the Open box and click **OK**.

13. Maximize the two console windows.

14. Click **File** and click **Add/Remove Snap-in**.

15. Click **Add**.

16. Scroll to notice the snap-ins that can be used in the MMC.

17. Click **Print Management** (see Figure F-7).

Figure F-7   Selecting the Print Management option for the MMC

18. Click **Add**.

19. Click **Add the Local Server**

20. Click **Finish**.

21. Click **Close**.

22. Click **OK**.

23. Click **Print Management** in the left pane to view the options under it.

24. In the left pane, click each of **Custom Printer Filters**, **Print Servers**, and **Deployed Printers** to view the elements under them.

25. In the left pane, click the name of the local server under Print Servers to view the elements under this. What elements are displayed under the server name?

26. Click **Drivers** to view the printer driver information for any printers connected to the local server.

27. Before you close the MMC determine the MMC version you are using. Click the **Help** menu at the top of the window and click **About Microsoft Management Console**. You should see Microsoft® Management Console 3.0, which is the new version.

28. Close the About Microsoft Management Console window.

29. Close the MMC.

30. Click **No** so your console settings are not saved.

HANDS-ON PROJECTS

Project F-4

This project enables you to use the File Server Resource Manager in Windows Server 2003 R2. The File Server Resource Manager must already be installed as a Windows Component (you'll find it under Management and Monitoring Tools when you use the Add/Remove Windows Components tool in Control Panel). Log on using an account that has Administrator privileges.

To use the File Server Resource Manager:

1. Click **Start**, point to **All Programs**, point to **Administrative Tools**, and click **File Server Resource Manager**. (You can also access this tool as an MMC snap-in.)

2. In the left pane click **Quota Management**.

3. Double-click **Quotas** in the middle pane. Are any quotas already set? What would you click next to create a quota?

4. Click **File Screen Management** in the left pane. What options appear in the middle pane under Name?

5. Double-click **File Screens** in the middle pane.

6. Click **Create File Screen**.

7. Click **Browse** and then click a volume, such as **Local Disk (C:)**.

8. Click the **Program Files** folder and click **OK**.

9. Click the option button for **Derive properties from this file screen template (recommended)**.

10. Click the **list arrow** in the box under Derive properties from this file screen template (recommend). What options do you see?

11. Click **Cancel** (you may have to click it twice) in the Create File Screen dialog box to close it.

12. Click **Storage Reports Management** in the left pane.

13. If necessary, resize the right pane so you can view its contents. What options are listed in the right pane?

14. Click **Generate Reports Now...**.

15. Click **Add**.

16. Click **Local Volume (C:)** (or another volume specified by your instructor).

17. Select a folder, such as **Program Files**. Click **OK**.

18. Click the box for **Large Files**.

19. Ensure **DHTML** is selected for the report format at the bottom of the dialog box.

20. Click **OK**.

21. Leave **Wait for reports to be generated and then display them** as the default. Click **OK**.

22. Wait for your report to be prepared.

23. If you see an Information Bar box, click **OK**.

24. If necessary, maximize the window containing the report. Use the scroll bar to review the contents of the report.

25. Close the report window.

26. Close the File Server Resource Manager window.

Glossary

8.3 filenames — Older-style file name format in which the name of the file can be up to eight characters long, followed by a period and an extension of three characters. See *extension*.

Accelerated Graphics Port (AGP) — A bus standard that has enabled adapter manufacturers to supply one hardware product to a variety of hardware platforms. Display adapters are typically plugged into the AGP slot on a motherboard.

account lockout — A security measure that prohibits logging on to a user account, such as one on a server, after a specified number of unsuccessful attempts.

activate — A procedure to register your copy of Windows operating systems starting with the Windows XP version. Without this activation, you will not be able to run your operating system for more than a small amount of time.

Active Directory — A Windows 2000/XP/Server 2003 database of computers, users, shared printers, shared folders, and other network resources and resource groupings that is used to manage a network and enable users to quickly find a particular resource.

active partition — The logical portion of a hard disk drive that is currently being used to store data. In a PC system, usually the partition that contains the bootable operating system.

ActiveX — An internal programming standard that allows various software that runs under the Windows operating system to communicate with the operating system and other programs.

address bus — An internal communications pathway inside a computer that specifies the source and target address for memory reads and writes. The address bus is measured by the number of bits of information it can carry. The wider the address bus (the more bits it moves at a time), the more memory available to the computer that uses it.

advanced intelligent tape (AIT) — A tape drive that has an erasable memory chip and has a capacity between 35 and 90 GB.

alias — In the Macintosh file system, a feature that presents an icon that represents an executable file. Equivalent to the UNIX/Linux link and the Windows shortcut.

allocation block — In the Macintosh file system, a division of hard disk data. Equivalent to the Windows disk cluster. Each Macintosh volume is divided into 216 (65,535) individual units.

alpha software — An early development version of software in which there are likely to be bugs, and not all of the anticipated software functionality is present. Alpha software is usually tested only by a select few users to identify major problems and the need for new or different features before the software is tested by a broader audience in the beta stage.

Apple Desktop Bus (ADB) — A serial bus common on older Apple Macintosh computers. ADB is used to connect the Macintosh keyboard, mouse, and other external I/O devices.

AppleTalk — Used for communications with Macintosh computers, this protocol is designed for peer-to-peer networking.

application programming interface (API) —
Functions or programming features in an operating
system that programmers can use for network links,
links to messaging services, or interfaces to other
systems.

application software — A word processor, spreadsheet,
database, computer game, or other type of application
that a user runs on a computer. Application software
consists of computer code that is formatted so that the
computer or its operating system can translate that
code into a specific task, such as writing a document.

assigning applications — A feature in
Windows 2000, Windows XP, and Windows
Server 2003 that enables an Active Directory group
policy to be set up so that a particular version of software is automatically started on a client (Windows
2000 or XP) through a desktop shortcut, via a menu
selection, or by clicking a file with a specific file
extension.

Asymmetric Digital Subscriber Line (ADSL) — A
high-speed digial subscriber line technology that can
use ordinary telephone lines for downstream data
transmission of up to 6 Mpbs and 576–640 Kbps for
upstream transmission.

asynchronous communication — Communications
that occur in discrete units in which the start of a unit
is signaled by a start bit at the front, and a stop bit at
the back signals the end of the unit.

Attention (AT) commands — A modem control command set designed by the Hayes company. This standard modem command set begins each command with
AT (for Attention) and allows communications software or users to directly control many modem
functions.

authentication — A scheme to identify and validate the
client to the server.

backbone — A main connecting link or highway
between networks, such as between floors in a building
or between buildings. Main internetworking devices,
such as routers and switches, are often connected via
the network backbone.

backup — A process of copying files from a computer
system to another medium, such as a tape, Zip disk,
another hard drive, or a removable drive.

Backup Domain Controller (BDC) — A Windows
NT server in a domain that has a copy of the domain's
directory database, which is updated periodically by
the PDC. The BDC also can authenticate logons to
the domain.

backward-compatibility — Hardware or software
designed to be compatible with many or all features of
earlier versions.

bad clusters — On a hard disk drive, areas of the surface
that cannot be used to safely store data. Bad clusters
are usually identified by the *format* command or one of
the hard drive utilities, such as *chkdsk.*

balanced-tree (b-tree) — A way of structuring a file
system that enables fast file access through creating an
internal file system tree structure off of the root that is
more horizontally oriented than vertically oriented.

basic disk — A physical hard drive. It contains primary
partitions, extended partitions, or logical drives which
are known as basic volumes.

basic input/output system (BIOS) — Low-level program code that conducts basic hardware and software
communications inside the computer. A computer's
BIOS basically resides between computer hardware
and the higher-level operating system, such as UNIX/
Linux or Windows.

Basic Rate Interface (BRI) — An ISDN interface that
consists of three channels. Two are 64 Kbps channels
for data, voice, video, and graphics transmissions. The
third is a 16 Kbps channel used for communications
signaling.

batch processing — A computing style frequently
employed by large systems. A request for a series of
processes is submitted to the computer; information is
displayed or printed when the batch is complete.
Batches might include processing all of the checks submitted to a bank for a day, or all of the purchases in a
wholesale inventory system, for example. Compare to
sequential processing.

Beginner's All-purpose Symbolic Instruction Code (BASIC) — An English-like computer programming language originally designed as a teaching tool, but which evolved into a useful and relatively powerful development language.

Berkeley Software Distribution (BSD) — A variant of the UNIX operating system upon which a large proportion of today's UNIX software is based.

beta software — During software development, software that has successfully passed the alpha test stage. Beta testing may involve dozens, hundreds, or even thousands of people, and may be conducted in multiple stages: beta 1, beta 2, beta 3, and so on.

binary backup — A technique that backs up the entire contents of one or more disk drives in a binary or image format.

binding — Associating or linking one or more protocols to be used by a network interface for data transmissions over a network.

BinHex — In the Macintosh file system, a seven-bit file format used to transmit data across network links that do not support native Macintosh file formats.

block allocation — A hard disk configuration scheme in which the disk is divided into logical blocks, which in turn are mapped to sectors, heads, and tracks. Whenever the operating system needs to allocate some disk space, it allocates it based on a block address.

block device — In the UNIX/Linux file system, a device that is divided or configured into logical blocks. See also *raw device*.

block special file — In UNIX/Linux, a file used to manage random access devices that involves handling blocks of data, including CD-ROM drives, hard disk drives, tape drives, and other storage devices.

boot block — The UNIX/Linux and Mac OS X equivalent of the DOS/Windows Master Boot Record (MBR), the area of the hard disk that stores partition information for the disk. For example, on a Mac-formatted disk, the first two sectors are boot blocks that identify the filing system, the names of important system files, and other important information. See also *volume information block*.

bridge — A network device that connects two or more segments into one, or extends an existing segment.

bus — A path or channel between a computer's CPU and the devices it manages, such as memory and disk storage.

bus topology — A network that is designed with a single central cable, to which all computers and other network devices attach. A bus topology has two end points. Each end point has a terminator to keep the electronic data signal from reflecting back along the path it just traveled.

cable modem — A digital modem device designed for use with the cable TV system providing high-speed data transfer. It may include an analog modem component that is used with a conventional telephone line connection for information sent from the user to the ISP.

cache controller — Internal computer hardware that manages the data going into and loaded from the computer's cache memory.

cache memory — Special computer memory that temporarily stores data used by the CPU. Cache memory is physically close to the CPU, and is faster than standard system memory, enabling faster retrieval and processing time.

carrier sense multiple access with collision avoidance (CSMA/CA) — A variation of CSMA/CD and the most prevalent protocol used in a wireless LAN.

carrier sense multiple access with collision detection (CSMA/CD) — A transmission control method used by Ethernet.

catalog b-tree — In the Macintosh file system, a list of all files on a given volume. Similar to a directory in the Windows file system.

CD-ROM File System (CDFS) — A 32-bit file system used on CD-ROMs.

cell — Format for a unit of data that is transported over a high-speed network, usually at speeds of 155 Mbps to more than 1 Gbps.

Centronics interface — An industry standard printer interface popularized by printer manufacturer Centronics. The interface definition includes 36 wires that connect the printer with the computer I/O port, though all of these pins aren't always used, particularly in modern desktop computers, which usually use a DB-25 connector.

Certified Cable Modem Project — Also called *Data Over Cable Service Interface Specification (DOCSIS)*. A project sponsored by the cable modem industry to provide a set of standards and equipment certification to pro vide stability to cable modem communications.

character special file — A UNIX/Linux I/O management file used to handle byte-by-byte streams of data, such as through a serial or USB connection, including terminals, printers, and network communications.

classless interdomain routing (CIDR) — A way to ignore IP address class designation by using addressing that puts a slash (/) after the dotted decimal notation.

clean computer — A computer from which all unnecessary software and hardware have been removed. A clean computer is useful during software upgrade testing because a minimum number of other software and hardware elements are in place, making it easier to track down problems with new software.

client — In a networking environment, a computer that handles certain user-side software operations. For example, a network client may run software that captures user data input and presents output to the user from a network server.

client operating system — Operating system on a computer, such as a PC, that enables the computer to process information and run applications locally, as well as communicate with other computers on a network.

client/server systems — A computer hardware and software design in which different portions of an application execute on different computers, or on different components of a single computer. Typically, client software supports user I/O, and server software conducts database searches, manages printer output, and the like.

cluster — In Windows-based file systems, a logical block of information on a disk containing one or more sectors. Also called an allocation unit.

clustering — The ability to share the computing load and resources by linking two or more discrete computer systems (servers) to function as though they are one.

coaxial cable (coax) — Copper wire surrounded by several layers: a layer of insulating material, a layer of woven or braided metal, and a plastic outer coating.

code — Instructions written in a computer programming language.

common language runtime (CLR) — Verifies code before it is run and monitors memory to clean up any leakage before it becomes a problem.

compact disc read-only memory (CD-ROM) — A non-volatile, digital data storage medium used for operating system and other software distribution.

Complex Instruction Set Computer (CISC) — A computer CPU architecture in which processor components are reconfigured to conduct different operations as required. Such computer designs require many instructions and more complex instructions than other designs.

Component Object Model (COM) — Standards that enable a software object, such as a graphic, to be linked from one software component into another one. COM is the foundation that makes object linking and embedding (OLE) possible.

container object — An entity that is used to group together resources, such as an organizational unit, an organization, or a country, as specified in the directory services of NetWare; or an organizational unit, domain, tree, or forest in Microsoft Active Directory.

control bus — An internal communications pathway that keeps the CPU informed of the status of particular computer resources and devices, such as memory and disk drives.

controller — A hardware or software component of a modem that defines an individual modem's capabilities. The controller interprets AT commands and handles communications protocols, for example.

cookie — A text-based file used by Web sites to obtain customized information about a user, such as the user's name, the user's password to access the site, and information about how to customize Web page display.

cooperative multitasking — A computer hardware and software design in which the operating system temporarily hands off control to an application and waits for the application to return control to the operating system. Compare to *preemptive multitasking*.

creator code — Hidden file characteristic in the Macintosh file system that indicates the program (software application) that created the file. See *type code*.

cyclical redundancy check (CRC) — An error-correction protocol that determines the validity of data written to and read from a floppy disk, hard disk, CD-ROM, or DVD.

cylinder — Tracks that line up from top to bottom on the platters in a hard disk drive (like a stack of disk tracks).

daemon — An internal, automatically running program, usually in UNIX/Linux, that serves a particular function such as routing e-mail to recipients or supporting dial-up networking connectivity.

data bus — An internal communications pathway that allows computer components, such as the CPU, display adapter, and main memory, to share information. Early personal computers used an 8-bit data bus. More modern computers use 32- or 64-bit data buses.

Data Communications Equipment (DCE) — A device, such as a modem, that converts data from a DTE, such as a computer, for transmission over a telecommunications line. The DCE normally provides the clock rate/clocking mechanism necessary for communications.

data fork — That portion of a file in the Macintosh file system that stores the variable data associated with the file. Data fork information might include word-processing data, spreadsheet information, and so on.

Data Over Cable Service Interface Specification (DOCSIS) — See *Certified Cable Modem Project*.

data pump — The hardware or software portion of a modem that is responsible for converting digital data into analog signals for transmission over a telephone line and for converting analog signals into digital data for transmission to the computer.

Data Terminal Equipment (DTE) — A computer or computing device that prepares data to be transmitted over a telecommunications line to which it attaches by using a DCE, such as a modem.

DB-25 — A 25-pin D-shaped connector commonly used on desktop computers, terminals, printers, modems, and other devices.

defragmentation — The process of removing empty pockets between files and other information on a hard disk drive.

defragmenter — A tool that rearranges data on a disk in a continuous fashion, ridding the disk of scattered open clusters.

desktop operating system — A computer operating system that typically is installed on a PC type of computer, used by one person at a time, that may or may not be connected to a network.

device driver — Computer software designed to provide the operating system and application software access to specific computer hardware.

device special file — File used in UNIX/Linux for managing I/O devices. Can be one of two types: *block special file* or *character special file*.

dial-up networking (DUN) — A utility built into Windows 95 and later versions to permit operation of a hardware modem to dial a telephone number for the purpose of logging on to a remote computer system via standard telephone lines.

differential backup — Backs up all files with an archive attribute, but does not remove that attribute after backup.

digital audio tape (DAT) — A tape drive that uses 4-mm tape and has a capacity of up to 72 GB.

digital linear tape (DLT) — A tape drive that uses half-inch magnetic tapes and has a capacity of up to 80 GB.

digital modem — A modem-like device that transfers data via digital lines instead of analog lines.

digital pad or **digital tablet** — An alternative input device frequently used by graphic artists and others who need accurate control over drawing and other data input.

Digital Signal Processor (DSP) — A software data pump used in software-driven modems such as the 3Com Winmodem.

Digital Subscriber Line (DSL) — A technology that uses advanced modulation technologies on existing telecommunications networks for high-speed networking between a subscriber and a telco and that offers communication speeds up to 60 Mbps.

digital video disc (DVD) — A high-capacity CD-ROM-like hardware device used for high-quality audio, motion video, and computer data storage. This is also referred to as digital versatile disc.

directory — Also called a folder in many file systems, an organizational structure that contains files and may additionally contain subdirectories (or folders) under it. In UNIX/Linux, a directory is simply a special file on a disk drive that is used to house information about other data stored on the disk. In other systems, a directory or folder is a "container object" that houses files and subdirectories or subfolders. A directory or folder contains information about files, such as filenames, file sizes, date of creation, and file type.

directory service — A large container of network data and resources, such as computers, printers, user accounts, and user groups, that (1) provides a central listing of resources and ways to quickly find specific resources, and (2) provides ways to access and manage network resources.

disk geometry — Critical information about a hard drive's hardware configuration. This information is often stored in an area of non-volatile memory in the computer.

disk label — The UNIX/Linux equivalent of a partition table in MS-DOS or Windows-based systems. The disk label is a table containing information about each partition on a disk, such as the type of partition, size, and location. Also, the disk label provides information to the computer about how to access the disk.

disk quota — Allocating a specific amount of disk space to a user or application with the ability to ensure that the user or application cannot use more disk space than is specified in the allocation.

disk striping — A disk storage technique that divides portions of each file over all volumes in a set as a way to minimize wear on individual disks.

Distributed Link Tracking — A technique new to NTFS 5 that ensures that shortcuts, such as those on the desktop, are not lost when files are moved to another volume.

distribution group — A list of Windows 2000 Server or Windows Server 2003 users that enables one e-mail message to be sent to all users on the list. A distribution group is not used for security.

domain — (1) A logical grouping of computers and computer resources that helps manage these resources and user access to them. (2) In Active Directory, a grouping of resources into a functional unit for management. The resources can be servers, workstations, shared disks and directories, and shared printers.

Domain Name Service (DNS) — A TCP/IP application protocol that resolves domain and computer names to IP addresses, or IP addresses to domain and computer names.

dot-matrix printer — An impact character printer that produces characters by arranging a matrix of dots.

dots per inch (dpi) — Used to measure the resolution of a printer or a video screen, the number of dots contained in an inch.

driver signing — A digital signature that Microsoft incorporates into driver and system files as a way to verify the files and to ensure that they are not inappropriately overwritten.

DUN server — In Windows 95 and later versions, a software utility that permits a desktop computer to answer incoming calls, log on a user, and, with other software, permits the user access to the computer's resources.

dye sublimation — A printer technology that produces high-quality, color output by creating "sublimated" color mists that penetrate paper to form characters or graphic output.

dynamic disk — In Windows 2000 Server and Windows Server 2003, a disk that does not use traditional partitioning. With dynamic disks you can create volumes that span multiple disks.

Dynamic Host Configuration Protocol (DHCP) — A network protocol that provides a way for a host to automatically assign an IP address to a workstation on its network.

emergency repair disk (ERD) — A startup disk in Windows 2000 for emergency repairs.

encryption — The encoding of data between the client and the server so that only the client or server can decode the information.

Enhanced IDE (EIDE) — A more modern, faster version of IDE used on most current computers.

Ethernet — A network transport protocol that uses CSMA/CD communications to coordinate frame and packet transmissions on a network.

execution-based cache — First-level cache in a Xeon CPU that stores decoded instructions and delivers them to the processor at high speed.

Explicitly Parallel Instruction Computing (EPIC) — A computer CPU architecture that grew out of the RISC-based architecture, and enables the processor to work faster by performing several operations at once, predicting and speculating about operations that will come next (so that they are even completed before requested). EPIC uses larger and more work area registers than CISC or traditional RISC-based CPU architectures.

Extended Capabilities Port (ECP) — Also called Enhanced Capabilities Port, a form of communication that allows for higher speed bidirectional communication between the computer and a printer, and a printer and the computer.

extended file system (ext or ext fs) — The file system designed for Linux that is installed, by default, in Linux operating systems. ext enables the use of the full range of built-in Linux commands, file manipulation, and security. Released in 1992, ext had some bugs and supported only files up to 2 GB. In 1993, the second extended file system (ext2 or ext2 fs) was designed to fix the bugs in ext and support files of up to 4 TB in size. In 2001, ext3 (or ext fs) was introduced to enable journaling for file and data recovery. ext, ext2, and ext3 support filenames of up to 255 characters.

extension — In MS-DOS and Windows-based systems, that part of a filename that typically identifies the type of file associated with the name. File extensions traditionally are three characters long and include standard notations such as .sys, .exe, .bat, and so on.

extents b-tree — Keeps track of the location of the file fragments or extents in the Mac OS HFS file system.

external clock speed — The speed at which the processor communicates with the memory and other devices in the computer; usually one-fourth to one-half the internal clock speed.

external commands — Operating system commands that are stored in separate program files on disk. When these commands are required, they must be loaded from disk storage into memory before they are executed.

fiber-optic cable — Consists of dozens or hundreds of thin strands of glass or plastic that transmit signals using light.

Fibre Channel — A means of transferring data between servers, mass storage devices, workstations, and peripherals at very high speeds.

file allocation table (FAT) — A file management system that defines the way data is stored on a disk drive. The FAT stores information about file size and physical location on the disk.

file attributes — File characteristics stored with the filename in the disk directory, which specify certain storage and operational parameters associated with the file. Attributes are noted by the value of specific data bits associated with the filename. File attributes include Hidden, Read-only, Archive, and so on.

file system — A design for storing and managing files on a disk drive. File systems are associated with operating systems such as UNIX/Linux, Mac OS X, and Windows.

firmware — Software logic that consists of one or more programs, which reside in a programmable chip on a card.

flow control — A hardware or software feature in modems that lets a receiving modem communicate to the sending modem that it needs more time to process previously sent data. When the current data is processed successfully, the receiving modem notifies the sending modem that it can resume data transmission.

folder — See *directory*.

forest — An Active Directory container that holds one or more trees.

fragmentation — Developing more and more empty pockets of space between files on the disk due to frequent writing, deleting, and modifying files and file contents.

frame — A data unit sent over a network that contains source and destination, control, and error-detection information, as well as the data.

full file-by-file backup — A technique that backs up the entire contents of one or more disk drives on the basis of directories, subdirectories, and files so that it is possible to restore a combination of any of these.

game pad — An input device primarily designed for interaction with games. Includes multiple buttons, wheels, or balls to effect movement of a variety of on-screen objects.

G.lite Asymmetric Digital Subscriber Line (G.lite ADSL) — A Plug and Play compatible version of ADSL that transmits at 500 Kbps upstream and 1.5 Mbps downstream.

graphical user interface (GUI) — An interface between the user and an operating system, which presents information in an intuitive graphical format that employs multiple colors, figures, icons, windows, toolbars, and other features. A GUI is usually deployed with a pointing device, such as a mouse, to make the user more productive.

group identification number (GID) — A unique number assigned to a UNIX/Linux group that distinguishes that group from all other groups on the same system.

hard link — In Windows 2000/XP/Server 2003 and UNIX/Linux, a file management technique that permits multiple directory entries to point to the same physical file.

hardware — The physical devices in a computer that you can touch (if you have the cover off), such as the CPU, circuit boards (cards), disk drives, monitor, and modem.

hardware abstraction layer (HAL) — Code in a Windows operating system that talks directly to the computer's hardware.

hardware compatibility list (HCL) — A list of brand names and models for all hardware supported by an operating system. Adherence to the HCL ensures a more successful operating system install. HCLs can often be found on operating system vendors' Web sites.

Hayes command set — See *Attention (AT) commands*.

Hierarchical Filing System (HFS) — An early Apple Macintosh file system storage method that uses a hierarchical directory structure. Developed in 1986 to improve file support for large storage devices. Mac OS Extended (HFS+) file system was released in 1998 with Mac OS 8.1 and is the file system used in Mac OS X.

High Bit-Rate Digital Subscriber Line (HDSL) — A form of high-speed digital subscriber line technology that has upstream and downstream transmission rates of up to 1.544 Mbps.

high-level formatting — A process that prepares a disk partition (or removable media) for a specific file system.

home directory — A user work area in which the user stores data on a server and typically has control over whether to enable other server users to access his or her data. This is a term that can be applied to the Windows 2000/XP/Server 2003, NetWare, Linux/UNIX, and Mac OS X operating systems. Also called a home folder.

Host Signal Processor (HSP) — A software approach to handling data pump duties in software-based modems such as the 3Com Winmodem.

hot fix — A procedure used by a file system that can detect a damaged disk area and then automatically copy information from that area to another disk area that is not damaged.

hub — A device often used in bus and star LANs to connect computers or devices to a local network.

hyper-threading (HT) — An Intel multithreading technology that enables a single processor to appear to the operating system as two separate processors, in which multiple threads of software applications are run simultaneously on one processor.

imagesetter — A high-end printer frequently used for publishing. Capable of producing film output.

incremental backup — A technique that backs up all files with an archive attribute, and then removes the attribute after backup.

Infrared Data Association (IrDA) — A group of peripheral manufacturers that developed a set of standards for transmitting data using infrared light. Printers were some of the first devices to support the IrDA specifications.

ink-jet printer — A character printer that forms characters by spraying droplets of ink from a nozzle print head onto the paper.

inode — Short for "information node." In UNIX/Linux, a system for storing key information about files. Inode information includes: the inode number, the owner of the file, the file group, the file size, the file creation date, the date the file was last modified and read, the number of links to this inode, and information regarding the location of the blocks in the file system in which the file is stored.

input/output (I/O) — Input is information taken in by a computer device to handle or process, such as characters typed at a keyboard. Output is information sent out by a computer device after that information is handled or processed, such as displaying the characters typed at the keyboard on the monitor.

Institute of Electrical and Electronics Engineers (IEEE) — An international organization of scientists, engineers, technicians, and educators that plays a leading role in developing standards for computers, network cabling, and data transmissionsas well as other electronics areas, such as consumer electronics and electrical power.

instruction set — In a computer CPU, the group of commands (instructions) the processor recognizes. These instructions are used to conduct the operations required of the CPU by the operating system and application software.

Integrated Drive Electronics (IDE) — A storage protocol in some desktop computer systems. IDE is significant because it simplifies the hardware required inside the computer, placing more of the disk intelligence at the hard drive itself.

Integrated Services Digital Network (ISDN) — A digital telephone line used for high-speed digital computer communications, videoconferencing, Internet connections, and telecommuting.

Integrated Services Digital Network Digital Subscriber Line (IDSL) — A DSL version that is compatible with a Digital Loop Carrier device that may be used on some telephone networks. IDSL provides upstream and downstream communications at 144 Kbps.

internal clock speed — The speed at which the CPU executes internal commands, measured in megahertz (millions of clock ticks per second) or gigahertz (billions of clock ticks per second). Internal clock speeds can be as low as 1 MHz and as high as more than 2 GHz.

International Telecommunications Union (ITU) — An international organization that sets telecommunications standards for modem and WAN communications, for example.

Internet Packet Exchange (IPX) — Developed by Novell, this protocol is used on networks that connect servers running NetWare.

Internet Protocol (IP) — Used in combination with TCP, this protocol handles addressing and routing for transport of packets.

interrupt request (IRQ) — A request to the processor so that a currently operating process, such as a read from a disk drive, can be interrupted by another process, such as a write into memory.

interrupt request (IRQ) line — A channel within the computer that is used for communications with the CPU. Intel-type computers have 16 IRQ lines, with 15 of those available to be used by devices, such as the keyboard.

I/O address range — A range of memory addresses that is used to temporarily store data that is transferred between a computer device or component and the CPU.

IP address — Used to identify a computer or network device and the network it is on.

journaling — The ability of a file system or software (such as database software) to track file changes so that if a system crashes unexpectedly, it is possible to reconstruct files or to roll back changes for minimum or no damage.

joystick — An input device shaped like a stick that allows for three-dimensional movement of an on-screen cursor or other object, such as a car, airplane, or cartoon character.

Kerberos — A security system developed by the Massachusetts Institute of Technology to enable two parties on an open network to communicate without interception by an intruder, creating a unique encryption key per each communication session.

kernel — An essential set of programs and computer code built into a computer operating system to control processor, disk, memory, and other functions central to the basic operation of a computer. The kernel communicates with the BIOS, device drivers, and the API to perform these functions. It also interfaces with the resource managers.

laser printer — A high-quality page printer design popular in office and other professional applications.

leaf object — An object, such as an account, that is stored in an organization or organizational unit container in the NetWare NDS.

level 1 (L1) cache — Cache memory that is part of the CPU hardware. See *cache memory*.

level 2 (L2) cache — Cache memory that, in most computer CPU designs, is located on hardware separate from, but close to, the CPU.

level 3 (L3) cache — Cache memory that is located on a chip or daughterboard, which is separate from, but close to the CPU, when L1 and L2 cache are both already built into the CPU.

line editor — An editor that is used to create text a line at a time.

line noise — Communications interference from any source, such as from electromagnetic interference (EMI) from electric motors or radio frequency interference (RFI) from radio-wave communications.

line printer — A printer design that prints a full line of character output at a time. Used for high-speed output requirements.

linear tape open (LTO) — A tape drive used in the high-end server market with a capacity between 100 GB and 1.6 TB.

Link Access Protocol for Modems (LAPM) — An error-checking protocol used in the V.42 standard that constructs data into discrete frame-like units for transmission over communications lines. Error checking is made possible because each unit is given a sequence number and a checksum. If a received unit is out of sequence or has the wrong checksum, this signals an error in the transmission.

linked list — Used in FAT file systems so that when a file is written to disk, each cluster containing that file's data has a pointer to the location of the next cluster of data. For example, the first cluster has a pointer to the second cluster's location, the second cluster contains a pointer to the third cluster, and so on.

local area network (LAN) — A series of interconnected computers, printing devices, and other computer equipment in a service area that is usually limited to a given office area, floor, or building.

logical drive — A software definition that divides a physical hard drive into multiple drives for file storage.

login script — In NetWare, a file of commands that is stored on a NetWare server and is associated with an account or a group of accounts. The login script runs automatically each time a user logs on to the account.

logon script — In Windows 2000 Server and Windows Server 2003, a file that contains commands that are run each time a user account logs on.

long filename (LFN) — A name for a file, folder, or directory in a file system in which the name can be up to 255 characters in length. Long filenames in Windows-based, UNIX/Linux, and Mac OS systems are also POSIX compliant in that they honor uppercase and lowercase characters.

low-level format — A software process that marks tracks and sectors on a disk. A low-level format is necessary before a disk can be partitioned and formatted.

LPT1 — The primary printer port designation on many desktop computers. Also designated line print terminal 1.

MacBinary — A format for Mac OS files that joins type and creator codes so that Mac files can be transferred over the Internet, or used via online services.

Macintosh Filing System (MFS) — The original Macintosh filing system, introduced in 1984. MFS was limited to keeping track of 128 documents, applications, or folders.

mapping — The process of attaching to a shared resource, such as a shared drive, and using it as though it is a local resource. For example, when a workstation operating system maps to the drive of another workstation, it can assign a drive letter to that drive and access it as though it is a local drive instead of a remote one.

master — In an EIDE drive chain, the main or first drive. Most EIDE interfaces can support two drives. One is the master (Drive 0) and the second drive is the slave. See *slave*.

Master Boot Record (MBR) — An area of a hard disk in MS-DOS and Windows that stores partition information about that disk. MBRs are not found on disks that do not support multiple partitions.

Master File Table (MFT) — In Windows NT, 2000, XP, and Server 2003, a file management system similar to the FAT and directories used in MS-DOS and earlier

versions of Windows. This table is located at the beginning of the partition. The boot sector is located ahead of the MFT, just as it is in the FAT system.

math coprocessor — A module optimized to perform complex math calculations. Early system architectures have a processor and an optional slot for a math coprocessor. Modern system architectures have a CPU with one or more built-in math coprocessors.

Media Access Control (MAC) address — A unique hexadecimal address assigned by the manufacturer, called a device or physical address, which identifies a NIC to the network.

medium filenames — In the Macintosh file system, the 31-character filename length that Macintosh OS has supported from the beginning.

Microsoft Disk Operating System (MS-DOS) — The first widely distributed operating system for microcomputers, created by Tim Patterson and a team, including Bill Gates, at Microsoft. This is generic computer code used to control many basic computer hardware and software functions. MS-DOS is sometimes referred to as DOS.

modem — A hardware device that permits a computer to exchange digital data with another computer via an analog telephone line or dedicated connection.

mounted volume — A shared drive in UNIX/Linux and Mac OS. See *mapping*.

multicast — A transmission method in which a server divides recipients of an application, such as a multimedia application, into groups. Each data stream is a one-time transmission that goes to one group of multiple addresses, instead of sending a separate transmission to each address for every data stream. The result is less network traffic.

Multimedia Extension (MMX) — A CPU design that permits the processor to manage certain multimedia operations—graphics, for example—faster and more directly. MMX technology improves computer performance when running software that requires multimedia operations.

multiprocessor computer — A computer that uses more than one CPU.

multitasking — A technique that allows a computer to run two or more programs at the same time.

multithreading — Running several program processes or parts (threads) at the same time.

multiuser system — A computer hardware and software system designed to service multiple users who access the computer's hardware and software applications simultaneously.

named pipe — In UNIX/Linux, a device special file for handling internal communications, such as redirecting file output to a monitor.

NetBIOS Extended User Interface (NetBEUI) — A protocol used on Microsoft networks that was developed from NetBIOS and is designed for small networks.

NetWare Loadable Module (NLM) — Program code that is loaded in NetWare to extend the capabilities of the operating system, such as for configuring a hard drive, managing the mouse connection, or setting up a USB port.

network — A system of computing devices, computing resources, information resources, and communications devices that are linked together by communications cable or radio waves.

network attached storage (NAS) — A way to directly attach storage to a network.

network bindings — Part of an operating system that coordinates software communications among the NIC, network protocols, and network services.

Network Device Interface Specification (NDIS) — Special elements, which programmers call "hooks" in the operating system kernel (program code), that enable the operating system to interface with a network. NDIS is from Microsoft.

Network File System (NFS) — Enables file transfer and other shared services that involve computers running UNIX/Linux.

network interface card (NIC) — A device used by computers and internetworking devices to connect to a network.

network operating system (NOS) — An operating system that enables a computer to communicate with other computers through network cable or wireless transmissions. A NOS enables the coordination of network communications, from sharing files and printers to sending e-mail.

New Technology File System (NTFS) — The 32-bit file storage system that is the native system in Windows NT, 2000, XP, and Server 2003.

Novell Directory Services (NDS) — A comprehensive database of shared resources and information known to the NetWare operating system.

Novell Distributed Print Services (NDPS) — Services used in NetWare version 5 and later that enable printers to attach to the network as agents, to be managed through a NetWare server, and to be accessed by NetWare and Windows-based clients.

Novell Storage Services (NSS) — The NetWare file system fully implemented in NetWare 6.0 and above that uses disk partitions, storage pools, and volumes.

object — An entity, such as a user account, group, directory, or printer, that is known to a network operating system's database, and that the operating system manages in terms of sharing or controlling access to that object.

Open Database Connectivity (ODBC) — A set of rules developed by Microsoft for accessing databases and providing a standard doorway to database data.

Open Datalink Interface (ODI) — An interface developed by Novell that allows the same NIC to carry data for different protocols.

open-source — Source code for software that is available to the general public free of charge.

operating system (OS) — Computer software code that interfaces with user application software and the computer's BIOS to allow the applications to interact with the computer hardware.

optical character recognition (OCR) — Imaging software that scans each character on the page as a distinct image and is able to recognize the character.

packet — A data unit sent over a network that contains source and destination, routing, control, and error-detection information, as well as data (related to the network layer of network data communications between two stations).

page file — Also called the paging file or *swap file*, an allocated portion of disk storage reserved for use to supplement RAM when the available RAM is exceeded.

parallel port — A computer I/O port used primarily for printer connections. A parallel port transmits data eight bits or more at a time, using at least eight parallel wires. A parallel port potentially can transmit data faster than a serial port.

parity checking — A data communications process that ensures data integrity through a system of data bit comparisons between the sending and receiving computer.

partition table — Table containing information about each partition on a disk, such as the type of partition, size, and location. Also, the partition table provides information to the computer about how to access the disk.

partitioning — Blocking a group of tracks and sectors to be used by a particular file system, such as FAT or NTFS. Partitioning is a hard disk management technique that permits the installation of multiple file systems on a single disk. Or, the configuration of multiple logical hard drives that use the same file system on a single physical hard drive.

payload — That portion of a frame, packet, or cell that contains the actual data, which might be a portion of an e-mail message or word-processing file.

peer-to-peer network operating system — A network operating system through which any computer can communicate with other networked computers on an equal or peer-like basis without going through an intermediary, such as a server or network host computer.

per-seat licensing — A software licensing scheme that prices software according to the number of individual users who install and use the software.

per-server licensing — A software licensing scheme that prices software according to a server configuration that permits multiple users to access the software from a central server.

personal digital assistant (PDA) — Handheld device, which, because of its size, is easily transported wherever you go. It includes features to assist you in organizing your time, such as a calendar, to-do lists, contacts, etc.

physical drive — Hard drive in a computer that you can physically touch and that can be divided into one or more logical drives.

pipelining — A CPU design that permits the processor to operate on one instruction at the same time it is fetching one or more subsequent instructions from the operating system or application.

pixel — Short for picture element. The small dots that make up a computer screen display.

Plain Old Telephone Service (POTS) — Regular voice-grade telephone service (the old terminology).

plotter — Computer hardware that produces high-quality printed output, often in color, by moving ink pens over the surface of paper. Plotters are often used with computer-aided design (CAD) and other graphics applications.

Plug and Play (PnP) — Software utilities that operate with compatible hardware to facilitate automatic hardware configuration. Windows versions starting with Windows 95 recognize PnP hardware when it is installed, and, in many cases, can configure the hardware and install required software without significant user intervention.

Point-to-Point Protocol (PPP) — Enables a computer to remotely access a network through a dial-up modem connection.

Point-to-Point Tunneling Protocol (PPTP) — Used to make a remote connection to a LAN over the Internet.

Portable Operating System Interface (POSIX) — A UNIX standard designed to ensure portability of applications among various versions of UNIX and other operating systems.

power management — A hardware facility in modern computers that permits certain hardware to shut down automatically after a specified period of inactivity. Proper use of power management facilities reduces hardware wear and tear, as well as energy usage.

preemptive multitasking — A computer hardware and software design for multitasking of applications in which the operating system retains control of the computer at all times. See *cooperative multitasking* for comparison.

Primary Domain Controller (PDC) — A server in a domain that authenticates logons, and keeps track of all changes made to accounts in the domain.

Primary Rate Interface (PRI) — An ISDN interface that consists of switched communications in multiples of 1.544 Mbps.

print queue or **print spooler** — A section of computer memory and hard disk storage set aside to hold information sent by an application to a printer attached to the local computer or to another computer or print server on a network. Operating system or printer drivers and control software manage the information sent to the queue, responding to printer start/stop commands.

privileged mode — The opposite of real mode and where you only use segment registers rather that real mode addressing.

production computer — Any computer used to perform real work, which should be protected from problems that might cause an interruption in workflow or loss of data.

protocol — An established guideline that specifies how networked data, including data sent over a telephone network, is formatted into a transmission unit, how it is transmitted, and how it is interpreted at the receiving end.

Public Switched Telephone Network (PSTN) — Regular voice-grade telephone service (the modern terminology).

publishing an application — Available in Windows 2000 Server and Windows Server 2003, setting an Active Directory group policy so that Windows 2000 and Windows XP Professional clients can install preconfigured software from a central server by using Add/Remove Programs (or Add or Remove in Windows XP) via Control Panel.

Rate Adaptive (Asymmetric) Digital Subscriber Line (RADSL) — A high-speed data transmission technology that offers upstream speeds of up to 1 Mbps and downstream speeds of up to 7 Mbps. RADSL uses ADSL technology (see *Asymmetric Digital Subscriber Line*), but enables the transmission rate to vary for different types of communications, such as data, multimedia, and voice.

raw device — In the UNIX/Linux file system, a device that has not been divided into logical blocks.

read-only memory (ROM) — Memory that contains information that is not erased when the power is removed from the memory hardware. ROM is used to store computer instructions that must be available at all times, such as the BIOS code.

real mode — A limited, 16-bit operating mode in PCs running early versions of Windows.

real-time system — An operating system that interacts directly with the user and responds in real time with required information.

Reduced Instruction Set Computer (RISC) — A computer CPU design that dedicates processor hardware components to certain functions. This design reduces the number and complexity of required instructions and, in many cases, results in faster performance than CISC CPUs.

redundant array of inexpensive disks (RAID) — A relatively inexpensive, redundant storage design that uses multiple disks and logic to reduce the chance of information being lost in the event of hardware failure. RAID uses various designs, termed Level 0 through Level 5.

registry — A Windows database that stores information about a computer's hardware and software configuration.

release candidate (RC) — The final stage of software testing by vendors before cutting an official release that is sold commercially. A release candidate is usually tested by a very large audience of customers. Some vendors may issue more than one release candidate if problems are discovered in the first RC.

Remote Access Services (RAS) — (1) A computer operating system subsystem that manages user access to a computer from a remote location, including security access. (2) A set of network services that can be installed on any Windows NT/2000/Server 2003 server connected to one or more modems.

Remote Installation Services (RIS) — Services in Windows 2000 Server and Windows Server 2003 that enable clients to download an operating system over the network, such as downloading and installing Windows 2000 Professional on a client computer via RIS on a Windows 2000 Server.

remote procedure calls (RPCs) — Enables services and software on one computer to use services and software on a different computer.

removable disks — A class of relatively high-capacity storage devices that use removable cartridges. These devices are used for data backup, long-term offline storage, and data portability among multiple computer systems.

resource fork — In the Macintosh file system, that portion of a file that contains fixed information, such as a program's icons, menu resources, and splash screens.

resource managers — Programs that manage computer memory and CPU use.

Rights Management Services (RMS) — Allows you to secure documents from copying, forwarding, and printing.

ring topology — One in which the data-carrying signal goes from station to station around the ring until it reaches the target destination. There is no beginning or end point, so there are no terminators.

root directory — The highest-level directory (or folder), with no directories above it in the structure of files and directories in a file system.

router — A device that joins networks and can route packets to a specific network on the basis of a routing table it creates for this purpose.

Samba — Used by UNIX/Linux and Mac OS X systems, a utility that employs the Server Message Block (SMB) protocol, which is also used by Windows systems for sharing folders and printers. Samba enables UNIX/Linux and Mac OS X systems to access shared Windows resources.

scanner — Creates a digital image from a hard copy that is then transmitted to the computer.

search drive — A mapped NetWare drive that enables the operating system to search a specified directory and its subdirectories for an executable (program) file.

sector — A portion of a disk track. Disk tracks are divided into equal segments or sectors.

security group — A group of Windows 2000 Server or Windows Server 2003 users that is used to assign access privileges, such as permissions, to objects and services.

Sequence Packet Exchange (SPX) — A protocol used on Novell networks that provides reliable transmission of application software data, usually in combination with IPX.

sequential processing — A computer processing style in which each operation is submitted, acted upon, and the results displayed before the next process is started. Compare to *batch processing*.

Serial Line Internet Protocol (SLIP) — A protocol sometimes used in UNIX/Linux for remote communications that transport TCP/IP.

serial port — A computer I/O port used for modem, printer, and other connections. A serial port transmits data one bit after another in serial fashion, as compared to a parallel port, which transmits data eight bits or more at a time.

server — A computer on a network that performs a function such as a file server that serves files to clients, or a print server that prints information for clients, or a database server that passes data from the server to the client.

server operating system — A network operating system that enables client workstations to access shared network resources such as printers, files, software applications, or CD-ROM drives, and allows administrators to manage the network.

service packs — Software "fixes" issued by the vendor to repair software problems, address compatibility issues, and add enhancements.

shadow file — With access limited to the root user, a file in UNIX/Linux that contains critical information about user accounts, including the encrypted password for each account.

share — An object, such as a folder, drive, or printer that an operating system or a directory service, such as Active Directory, makes visible to other network users for access over a network.

share points — Shared resources on a Mac OS X server.

Sherlock — In the Macintosh file system, a file search utility that can find filenames or text within files.

single-processor computer — A computer capable of supporting only a single CPU.

single-tasking — A computer hardware and software design that can manage only a single task at a time.

single-user system — A computer hardware and software system that enables only one user to access its resources at a particular time.

slave — In an EIDE drive chain, the secondary storage device. See *master*.

Small Computer System Interface (SCSI) — A computer I/O bus standard and the hardware that uses this standard. There are many types of SCSI in use today, providing data transfer rates from 5 Mbps to 320 Mbps.

star topology — A network arrangement in which all of the computers or devices (nodes) on the network connect to a central device such as a hub or switch. The hub sends the signal onto each segment, which has a computer at the end. Every segment is terminated inside the hub at one end and inside the computer at the other end.

start bit — In data communication, an extra bit inserted by the sending modem at the beginning of a data byte to help ensure that the received data is correct.

status bits — Bits used as part of a directory entry to identify the type of filename contained in each entry. The status bits in use are Volume, Directory, System, Hidden, Read-only, and Archive.

stop bit — In data communication, an extra bit inserted by the sending modem at the end of a data byte to help ensure that the received data is correct.

storage area network (SAN) — Technology that provides for interconnection between servers and storage systems without sending data over the corporate network.

storage pool — In the NetWare file system, a way to divide the use of a disk that can be a superset of disk partitions because one storage pool can house one or more disk partitions.

subnet mask — A designated portion of an IP address that is used to divide a network into smaller subnetworks as a way to manage traffic patterns, enable security, and relieve congestion.

super advanced intelligent tape (S-AIT) — A tape drive that has an erasable memory chip in the tape and a capacity between 500 GB and 1.3 TB.

super digital linear tape (SDLT) — A tape drive that uses both magnetic and optical recording and has a capacity between 1.2 and 2.4 TB.

Super VGA (SVGA) — Sometimes called **Ultra VGA (UVGA)**, a display technology based on VGA that provides a 1600 × 1200 or higher resolution and up to 16.5 million colors. See *Video Graphics Array*.

superblock — In the UNIX/Linux file system, a special data block that contains information about the layout of blocks, sectors, and cylinder groups on the file system. This information is the key to finding anything on the file system, and it should never change.

surface analysis — A disk diagnostic technique that locates damaged disk areas and marks them as bad. Some surface analysis tools are destructive to data because they also format a disk. Others can run without altering data, except to move data from a damaged location to one that is not.

swap file — Also called the *page file* or paging file, an allocated portion of disk storage reserved for use to supplement RAM when the available RAM is exceeded.

switch — (1) A network device that connects LAN segments and forwards frames to the appropriate segment or segments. A switch works in promiscuous mode, similar to a bridge. (2) An operating system command option that changes the way certain commands function. Command options, or switches, are usually entered as one or more letters, separated from the main command by a forward slash (/).

symbolic link — A special file in the UNIX/Linux file system that permits a directory link to a file that is on a different partition. This is a special file, which has a flag set in the inode to identify it as a symbolic link. The content of the file is a path that, when followed, leads to another file.

Symmetric Digital Subscriber Line (SDSL) — A form of digital subscriber line technology that is often used for videoconferencing or online learning. It offers a transmission speed of 384 Kbps for upstream and downstream communications.

Symmetric High Bit-Rate Digital Subscriber Line (SHDSL) — Also called G.shdsl, a DSL technology that can be transmitted over one or two wires and that can reach up to about 4 miles (over two wires). The upstream and downstream rates can vary in the range of 192 Kbps to 2.3 Mbps.

symmetric multiprocessing (SMP) — A computer design that supports multiple, internal CPUs that can be configured to work simultaneously on the same set of instructions.

synchronous communication — Communications of continuous bursts or blocks of data controlled by a clock signal that starts each burst or block of data.

system architecture — The computer hardware design that includes the processor (CPU), and communication routes between the CPU and the hardware it manages, such as memory and disk storage.

System V Release 4 (SVR4) — A variation of the UNIX operating system. It is very popular today along with the Berkeley Software Distribution (BSD).

tablet PC — A complete notebook-sized computer within a touch screen enabling the user to enter hand-written text via a digital pen device.

tar — A UNIX/Linux file archive utility.

task supervisor — A process in the operating system that keeps track of the applications that are running on the computer and the resources they use.

task switching — A single-tasking computer hardware and software design that permits the user or application software to switch among multiple single-tasking operations.

terminal — A device that has a keyboard but no CPU or storage and is used to access and run programs on a mainframe or minicomputer.

terminal adapter (TA) — A digital modem that permits computer-to-computer data transfer over a digital line, such as ISDN.

thermal-wax transfer — A printer technology that creates high-quality color printed output by melting colored wax elements and transferring them to the printed page.

time-sharing system — A central computer system, such as a mainframe, that is used by multiple users and applications simultaneously.

token — A specialized frame that is transmitted without data around the network until it is captured by a station that wants to transmit.

token ring — A network that uses a ring topology and token passing as a way to coordinate network transport.

topology — The physical design of a network and the way in which a data-carrying signal travels from point to point along the network.

total cost of ownership (TCO) — The cost of installing and maintaining computers and equipment on a network, which includes hardware, software, maintenance, and support costs.

track — Concentric rings that cover an entire disk like grooves on a phonograph record. Each ring is divided into sectors in which to store data.

Transmission Control Protocol (TCP) — A communications protocol that is used with IP; it facilitates reliable communications between two stations by establishing a window tailored to the characteristics of the connection.

tree — An Active Directory container that houses one or more domains.

trusted domain — A domain granted security access to resources in another domain.

trusting domain — A domain that allows another domain security access to its resources, such as servers.

twisted-pair cable — Consists of one or more pairs of twisted copper wires bundled together within a plastic outer coating. The wires are twisted to reduce electromagnetic interference or noise.

type code — In the Macintosh file system, embedded file information that denotes what applications were used to create the files. Mac OS type codes are used in much the same way as Windows file extensions that identify file types with .txt, .doc and other extensions. See *creator code*.

Ultra Extended Graphics Array (UXGA) — A display technology based on IBM's older eXtended Graphics Array (XGA) technology that provides a 1600 × 1200 or higher resolution and up to 16.5 million colors.

unicast — A transmission method in which one copy of each packet is sent to every target destination, which can generate considerable network traffic compared to multicasting, when the transmission is a multimedia application.

Unicode — A 16-bit character code that allows for the definition of up to 65,536 characters.

universal asynchronous receiver-transmitter (UART) — An electronic chip that handles data flow through a serial port or modem.

Universal Disk Format (UDF) — A removable disk formatting standard used for large-capacity CD-ROMs and DVD-ROMs.

Universal Plug and Play (UPnP) — An initiative of more than 80 companies to develop products that can be quickly added to a computer or network. These include intelligent appliances for the home. More information can be found at the Web site, *www.upnp.org*.

Universal Serial Bus (USB) — A relatively recent serial bus designed to support up to 127 discrete devices with data transfer speeds up to 12 Mbps (megabits per second). USB 2.0 supports a transfer speed of 480 Mbps. It is fully compatible with the original USB specifications. USB 2.0 is also referred to as Hi-Speed USB.

UNIX file system (ufs) — A file system supported in most versions of UNIX/Linux that is a hierarchical (tree structure) file system which is expandable, supports large storage, provides excellent security, and is reliable. ufs employs information nodes (inodes).

UNIX to UNIX Copy Protocol (UUCP) — A protocol used by UNIX/Linux computers for communicating through modems. UUCP can also be used on networks, but for these applications, it is usually replaced by the faster TCP/IP technology.

Upgrade Advisor — A tool available on the Windows operating system CD or via the Internet to check if your system hardware and software are ready for upgrade.

user identification number (UID) — A number that is assigned to a UNIX/Linux user account as a way to distinguish that account from all others on the same system.

Very High Bit-Rate Digital Subscriber Line (VDSL) — A digital subscriber line technology that works over coaxial and fiber-optic cables, yielding 51–55 Mbps downstream and 1.6–2.3 Mbps upstream communications.

Video Graphics Array (VGA) — A video graphics display system introduced by IBM in 1987.

virtual memory — Disk storage that is used when there is not enough RAM for a particular operation, or for all processes currently in use.

virtual private network (VPN) — A private network that is like a tunnel through a larger network—such as the Internet, an enterprise network, or both—and restricted to designated member clients.

volume information block — On a Mac-formatted disk, the sector after the boot blocks. See also *boot block*. The volume information block points to other important areas of information, such as the location of the system files and the catalog and extents trees.

volume label — A series of characters that identifies a disk drive or the file system it is using.

Web browser — Software to facilitate individual computer access to graphical data presented over the Internet on the World Wide Web, or over a local area network in a compatible format.

wide area network (WAN) — A system of networks that can extend across cities, states, and continents.

Windows Catalog — A list that contains brand names and models for all hardware and software supported by the Windows XP operating system. The Windows Server 2003 Catalog lists compatible hardware and software for Windows Server 2003.

Windows NT LAN Manager (NTLM) — An authentication protocol used in Windows NT Server 3.5, 3.51, and 4.0 that is retained in Windows 2000 Server and Windows Server 2003 for backward-compatibility for clients that cannot support Kerberos, such as MS-DOS and Windows 3.1x.

Windows Update — A Web-based function that allows you to download and install product updates for your Windows operating system.

Winmodem — A software-driven modem from 3Com Corporation that uses minimal hardware and the computer's CPU with software to conduct data communications.

wireless access point — A connection point between a wired network and a wireless one.

wireless media — Any form of communication that works where it is inconvenient, impractical, or impossible to install wires or cables.

word — Used to hold data or programming code in a computer. The size of a word varies among computers. 16-bit computers have a word size of 16 bits and 64-bit computers have a word size of 64 bits.

workgroup — A predefined group of member computers, which provides the ability to limit resource sharing on the basis of group membership.

workstation — A computer that has a CPU and usually storage to enable the user to run programs and access files locally.

X Window — A windowed user interface for UNIX/Linux and other operating systems.

Xon-Xoff — A software flow control protocol that permits a receiving modem to notify the sending modem that its data buffers are full, and it needs more time to process previously received data.

Zip® disk — A removable high-capacity floppy disk design from Iomega. Zip disks store a nominal 100 to 750 MB of data.

Index